THE RETURN OF CHRIST

BOOKS BY G. C. BERKOUWER

MODERN UNCERTAINTY AND CHRISTIAN FAITH

RECENT DEVELOPMENTS IN ROMAN CATHOLIC THOUGHT

THE TRIUMPH OF GRACE IN THE THEOLOGY OF KARL BARTH

THE SECOND VATICAN COUNCIL AND THE NEW CATHOLICISM

STUDIES IN DOGMATICS SERIES —

THE PROVIDENCE OF GOD

FAITH AND SANCTIFICATION

FAITH AND JUSTIFICATION

FAITH AND PERSEVERANCE

THE PERSON OF CHRIST

GENERAL REVELATION

DIVINE ELECTION

MAN: THE IMAGE OF GOD

THE WORK OF CHRIST

THE SACRAMENTS

SIN

THE RETURN OF CHRIST

Studies in Dogmatics

The Return of Christ

BY

G. C. BERKOUWER

PROFESSOR OF SYSTEMATIC THEOLOGY

FREE UNIVERSITY OF AMSTERDAM

WILLIAM B. EERDMANS PUBLISHING COMPANY
GRAND RAPIDS, MICHIGAN

Translated by James Van Oosterom
Edited by Marlin J. Van Elderen
from
the Dutch edition, *De Wederkomst van Christus*, I and II
published by J. H. Kok N.V., Kampen, The Netherlands,
1961 and 1963

72-178664

ABBREVIATIONS

AT	— Altes Testament, alttestamentliche, etc.
CD	— Barth, *Church Dogmatics*
CMH	— H. Berkhof, *Christ the Meaning of History*
Denz.	— Denzinger, *Enchiridion Symbolorum*
GD	— Bavinck, *Gereformeerde Dogmatiek*
Heid. Cat.	— Heidelberg Catechism
Inst.	— Calvin, *Institutes of the Christian Religion*
KV	— *Korte Verklaring*
OT	— Old Testament
NT	— New Testament, etc.
TDNT	— Kittel-Friedrich (ed.), *Theological Dictionary of the New Testament*

12183

CONTENTS

CHAPTER ONE

EXPECTATION OF THE FUTURE

WHENEVER ONE studies what the Bible says about the last things and how the Christian church reflects an *expectation* of these things, he is confronted by a seemingly overwhelming variety of themes. The coming of God's Kingdom, the present dispensation, the resurrection of the body, eternal life, parousia, signs of the times, the millennium, and the future of Israel — all these topics are part and parcel of this study.

It is readily apparent that these subjects are not merely a number of unrelated topics. Rather, each represents one aspect of a single expectation. All these aspects function within this expectation, and, moreover, have a definite bearing upon one another. Their major concern is often called *eschatology*, from the Greek word *eschatos*.[1] Their central focus is the anticipation of the future. To study them is to be concerned with the hereafter, with what we may expect from it, and with the grounds of our certainty about it.

Eschatology deals with God's final, definitive acts toward His creation, the last days, the promise of the future, and the expectation and hope occasioned by this promise. It does not deal with unrelated, independent events that are yet to take place; instead, it focuses on the concentration of all these events in the promise of Him who is the Last.[2] Scripture depicts Christ's coming as the consummation of the last things, and it is in connection with His coming that we encounter the many questions that believers, past and present, have discussed.

1. The word "eschatology" is now generally used to refer to the doctrine of the last things. Other words that have been used by systematic theologians to describe this locus of dogmatics include *de glorificatione* (à Marck), *de novissimis* (Turretinus) *de consummatione saeculi* (A. Kuyper).
2. Rev. 22:13: "I am the Alpha and the Omega, the first and the last (*ho éschatos*), the beginning and the end"; cf. Rev. 1:8; Isa. 44:6; 48:12; Kittel, in *TDNT*, s.v. *Alpha-Omega*, I, 1-3.

Promise and expectation

Because these last things center about the future return of
Christ, which is decisive for the whole of man's life and all of
creation, preoccupation with eschatology has always been a
matter of profound existential concern. Eschatology is not —
and may not be — a human construction of the future with a
more or less complete prediction of what is actually going to
happen. Rather, it points to a voice that calls to us in the history
of human events and speaks reliably about the future. This
is no human fabrication: it is in a real sense the voice of God,
even though it comes to us through the human voice of prophets
and apostles. Man is intimately bound up in this prophecy
of the future. He can never disengage himself from this involve-
ment; he can never be a disinterested spectator whiling away
his time on the sidelines. The apocalypse of the future touches
his very life.

So this expectation of the future is unlike expectations that
are grounded in either empirical historical events or relative
and uncertain speculations. This expectation does not permit
itself to become a mere hypothesis, a postulate, or the projection of human guesswork. It is and remains a response based
on the Word and the sure promises of God. "According to his
promise we wait for new heavens and a new earth in which
righteousness dwells" (2 Pet. 3:13).[3]

This relationship between promise and expectation automatically brings us into contact with all the burning issues of
eschatology. What is at stake here is the certainty as well as
the content of the promise. Our own human expectations and
hopes often lack real dependability. Ultimately they fail us
because we cannot control future events. Our most ardent hopes
are not always fulfilled, and there is a certain insecurity about
them latent within us. They are always qualified by a *maybe*.[4]
We cannot ultimately control future events, nor can we conclude definitively about the unknown. So we are constantly
faced with possibilities or probabilities, but never with cer-
tainties. We cannot avoid realizing that the process of history

3. Cf. Isa. 65:17; 66:22. NT words for "expect" include *prosdéchomai;
   apekdéchomai* (e.g. *hyiothesía* — Rom. 8:23); and *ekdéchomai*. Cf. Grundmann, in *TDNT*, s.v. *déchomai*, II, 50-59.
4. As was David's hope when, confronted with death, he fasted and wept,
   explaining, "*Who knows* whether the LORD will be gracious to me, that
   the child may live?" (2 Sam. 12:22).

is too complicated, too forbidding, too incalculable, and subject to too many varied factors to allow us confidence in what we may deduce about it.[5]

Already in the Old Testament we find pointed warnings against trying to penetrate the secret of the future. Significantly, these warnings are not based primarily on the impossibility and uncertainty of such speculation; they are rather admonitions not to become engrossed in such activity or to place trust in its findings. "Do not turn to mediums or wizards; do not seek them out, to be defiled by them; I am the LORD your God" (Lev. 19:31). Isaiah refers to the foolishness and futility of this activity (44:25). Israel's concern for the future was to be motivated by something other than mere human curiosity. The only legitimate expectation is the one oriented to Israel's God. This expectation alone transcends every condition and every doubt, because it is grounded in the immovable Rock and in His promises. Only of Yahweh can it be said that He "let none of his words fall to the ground" (1 Sam. 3:19; cf. Isa. 44:26; Josh. 21:45).

The content of the promise

Once this correlation between promise and expectation has been established, it becomes clear not only that the certainty of the expectation is dependent upon this mutual relationship, but also that the structure of the expectation is wholly determined by the *content* of the promise. This is made clear by the fact that God does not present man with a complete and detailed revelation in His promises. God does not replace man's concept of future events with a scheme of His own, tailored with all the facts and figures, an authorized blueprint of His plan for the coming age. If we expect our curiosity to be satisfied in this way we have misunderstood the essential promises of God.

The promise of the future does not permit us to see beyond the shrouds of time; it has not conferred upon us a special gnosis. When Christ promises to send the Comforter (John 16:13), who will declare the things that are to come (*ta*

5. The various aspects of this problem, including the psychological side of disappointment, are brought out well in an intriguing book by Leon Festinger, H. W. Riecken, and S. Schachter, *When Prophecy Fails* (1956), particularly ch. I, "Unfulfilled Prophecies and Disappointed Messiahs." Cf. also H. Focillon, *The Year One Thousand* (Eng. tr., 1968).

erchómena), he is in fact pledging to reveal the proper way
men will take to the truth *(eis tḗn alḗtheian pásan).* But this
proclamation of the Comforter will not in any way remove
the limitations of human experience or replace all secrets with
an exhaustive revelation. The sure expectation of the fulfilment of the promises still leaves room for the message: "It does
not yet appear what we shall be" (1 John 3:2; cf. Mark 13:32;
Matt. 24:26; Acts 1:7; 1 Thess. 5:1). Although we live within
the promises of the future, our knowledge, like prophecy, is
limited and imperfect *(ek mérous* — 1 Cor. 13:9). If our expectation is to remain legitimate and certain, we must respect
and honor the correlation between it and promise, always guard-
ing in humility against any intrusion of human fantasy that
would distort the real content of the promise. If there is anywhere in theology that a warning against excesses and a command to watchfulness are pertinent, it is here. How easily the
real promise can be transformed by man's subjectivity into a
purely human projection, invariably ending in disillusionment.
How often wish gives birth to a conviction that can result only
in disappointment.

The promise of the future is not the religious counterpart
of secular fortune-telling. God's promise does not offer a mystique to satisfy all curiosity. It is always characterized by a message, a proclamation that penetrates to the root of man's existence. It compels man to decide with respect to what is coming,
because the one who is coming enters his very life. The proclamation of the future is always existential: it calls forth from
within the structure of the coming Kingdom. Sometimes this
call or appeal can bear the force of threat. Preaching to Felix,
Paul spoke of justice and self-control and future judgment
(kríma toú méllontos — Acts 24:45). Earlier John the Baptist
had called the Pharisees to repentance with a warning of the
wrath to come (Matt. 3:7). The whole structure of eschatological preaching is determined in threats and comforts by
the gravity of what is to come.

We may never lapse into a futurist orientation to and a
correspondingly futurist expectation of what is to come, for
the promise of the future is inextricably connected with events
of the past. The Christian's expectation is a far different thing
from a generalization like "the seeds of the future lie in the
present." It is something completely determined by the unique
relation between what is to come and what has already occurred

in the past. The whole certainty of our expectation is grounded in this peculiar relationship. Because the expectation is directed to Christ, who has come and will come again at the end of time, it lacks a futurist character. Because the mention of Christ calls to our minds a familiarity — something and someone who has already been revealed — the future can never be labeled *terra incognita,* "the realm of the unknown."

True eschatology, therefore, is always concerned with the expectation of the Christ who has already been revealed and who will "appear a second time . . . to save those who are eagerly waiting for him" (Heb. 9:28). This double advent is the keystone of eschatology, distinguishing it from mere futurism. It is not the unknown of the future but the known in the future that is decisive for eschatological reflection. If this distinction between eschatology and futurism is not observed, the expectation loses its certainty and begins to show evidences of human projection. To avoid this pitfall we must acknowledge that the truly unpredictable aspects of the parousia do not constitute some strange futurism, concerning which we may at best give some unintelligible utterances, but constitute recognizable reality, the reality of the revealed Lord.[6]

So we have seen that the Christian expectation is not directed at abstract, unrelated events in the future, but at Jesus Christ Himself in His parousia, and that true eschatology may never lack this personal character. On this account, some have objected that the expression "the last *things*" depersonalizes the eschaton. Nonetheless, the use of this term has merits, particularly as a contrast to what has come to be known as personalism, or the personalistic view of the eschaton.[7]

Personalism concentrates the eschaton in the person of Jesus Christ in such a way that the emphasis on Christ's coming and our encounter with Him leaves little room for the last *things.* On the basis of the false antithesis between person and thing that characterizes all personalistic eschatology, there is no con-

---

6. Cf. Jude 21: "Wait for the mercy of our Lord Jesus Christ unto eternal life." Cf. also Titus 2:13. The relationship between past and future comes out clearly in Q. 51, Heid. Cat.: ". . . I may *await* with head held high the very Judge from heaven who has *already* submitted himself to the judgment of God for me and has removed all the curse from me."
7. Althaus, who strongly emphasizes the personal aspect, nonetheless entitles his study of eschatology *Die letzten Dinge* — "the last things" (7th ed., 1957).

sideration of the electrifying expectation of a new earth and the resurrection of the body. "Personal encounter" absorbs all "things" and results in a reduction and impoverishment of the expectation that leaves unanswered the question of who and what is really expected. It is one thing to depersonalize the eschaton, quite another to expect those *things* accompanying the coming of the Lord, who, after all, is "the first-born of all creation" (Col. 1:15), without whom "was not anything made that was made" (John 1:3), and in whom "all things in the heavens and things on earth" are united (Eph. 1:10). There is no better argument against this personalism than that confessed by the early church: "I believe in the resurrection of the body."

The emphasis that the only legitimate eschatology is that which is centered in the coming of Christ reminds us that this concentration includes awareness of those renewed things to which the Lord opens our eyes. The "things" do not cast a shadow on His actual coming unless the attempt is made to divorce them from their unbreakable connection with the person of Christ in order to posit them as the focal point of the expectation. Inevitably, personalizing of the eschatological expectation leads to the exclusion, not only of the last things but of Christ Himself.[8]

Reduction and concentration

In connection with the nature of the expectation, let us consider for a moment an important topic of eschatology, namely the problem of "reduction." Reduction involves the attempt to assimilate all the separate ideas that are of an eschatological nature and then to eliminate critically everything not directly related to the central religious expectation. Its motivation is a reaction to the numerous detailed and often fantastic notions and speculations that have arisen concerning the coming of Christ. The contention is that the contrast between these excessive schemes and the central message and sobriety of the gospel demands this sort of reduction. Often this problem is construed in terms of a distinction between apocalyptic and

---

8. Further comment on personalism can be found in G. Gloege, "Der theologische Personalismus als dogmatisches Problem," *Kerygma und Dogma*, I (1955), 23-41. A contrasting viewpoint is set forth by W. Joest in his critique of Gogarten's book, *Verhängnis und Hoffnung der Neuzeit; ibid.*, 77-83.

eschatology. On the one hand is apocalyptic, with its detailed images of the future events and its prophecies concerning what is to come; on the other is eschatology, which, compared to apocalyptic, constitutes a reduction in the direction of the central, focal point of the expectation. As an illustration, late-Jewish apocalyptic is contrasted with Christian expectation, not only as regards its content but also its formal structure. The apocalyptic is allegedly the area of configuration, fantasy and mystique, intensely preoccupied with scrutinizing what is actually going to happen in the latter days. But things are not all that simple. In late-Jewish apocalyptic, as well as in the Old and New Testaments, we encounter a sense of God's purposeful acts, in which different images and concepts play a definite role. In the Old Testament, there is Daniel and the so-called Isaiah Apocalypse (Isa. 24-27); in the New, the Synoptic Apocalypse (Mark 13) and the Revelation of John. These examples are sufficient to warn against making an oversimplified distinction between apocalyptic and eschatology.[9]

C. H. Dodd has remarked that the Book of Revelation is a "relapse into a pre-Christian eschatology" and for that reason is inferior to the teaching of Jesus.[10] H. H. Rowley suggests, however, that although there is a "common stock of apocalyptic" in Revelation, these elements "were worked into a design that is *sui generis.*" He does not consider it at all unusual that Daniel and Revelation are included in the canon.[11] The intention of these different apocalyptic presentations is what is important. It is simply not possible to place apocalyptic — as strange, confusing, and primitive — over against eschatology — as pure expectation free from strange and extraordinary presentation. Without denying that there are differences between apocalyptic and eschatological expectation, we conclude that the actual difference between late-Jewish apocalyptic and New Testament eschatology is the orientation of the latter to God's acting through Jesus Christ. Many apocalyptic presentations point to Christ's coming again at the end of time. The difference lies

9. In this connection, see P. Volz, *Die Eschatologie der jüdischen Gemeinde im NT Zeitalter* (1934), pp. 5ff.; H. H. Rowley, *The Relevance of Apocalyptic. A Study of Jewish and Christian Apocalyptic from Daniel to the Revelation* (1955), p. 165; O. Plöger, *Theokratie und Eschatologie* (1959), esp. Ch. III.

10. C. H. Dodd, *The Apostolic Preaching and Its Developments* (1936), pp. 40f.

11. *Op. cit.,* p. 134.

more in the particular orientation of the New Testament than in the formal structure. Reflecting on eschatological expectation is a matter of discovering the meaning of its apocalyptic structurization, the central point in which all the images and concepts cohere, and from which they obtain their meaning and direction.[12]

It is clear that in coming to an understanding of this apocalyptic structurization one cannot speak of "reduction." Comprehension and penetration — not reduction — are the goals of exegeting the biblical thought-world. Not only does the word reduction suggest a quantitative lessening of content, but it also raises the crucial problem of sorting out what is of central and what of peripheral importance, what is essential and what nonessential. To be sure, one might use the word reduction in a good sense to refer to the effort to get at the root and meaning of the words in which the eschatological message and expectation are couched, but it would probably be more precise and helpful to call this "concentration" rather than reduction, since it does not involve sorting out but comprehending.

Concentration in this sense does not amount to "de-eschatologizing" as some literalists have charged. Its aim is not to weaken the eschatological expectation but to get at the meaning of the eschatological promise, which has come to us couched in images and concepts whose understanding requires a patient effort.[13] Admittedly, in such a search for meaning the danger is always imminent that one's subjectivism will lead him to relativize the reality of the promise and expectation. One might make a distinction between the form and the content of this apocalyptic structurization, and then represent this content as a personalized, idealized eschaton, in which every temporal and teleological element is elbowed out to make room for an ex-

---

12. Cf. Lindblom's attempt to distinguish clearly between apocalyptic and eschatology, "Gibt es eine Eschatologie bei den AT Propheten?", *Studia Theologica*, VI (1953), 79-114. According to him, the essential difference is not in the particular concepts or motifs, but in the manner of representation: "Apocalyptic is revealed mystery doctrine of eschatological content" (p. 113). Cf. also H. van Oyen, *Eschatologie in de theologie van onze tijd* (1940), p. 209; J. Behm, *Die Offenbarung des Johannes* (1949), pp. 2f.

13. There is something obvious in this task — consider, for example, Rev. 11:8: "And their dead bodies will lie in the street of the great city which is allegorically called *(kaleitai pneumatikôs)* Sodom and Egypt, where their Lord was crucified."

istential relation between eternity and time in the "now" of every believer. But this danger can never cancel out the need for a careful interpretation of these apocalyptic concepts and images, because it is in such concepts and images that the consummation and the end of time are presented to us.

The problem of concentration and reduction in connection with the real nature of the Christian's expectation of the future has attracted considerable attention in our time. For the purposes of interpreting the Bible, we have seen, the method of concentration is the only permissible one. We then use the word reduction with an eye to the many accretions to the biblical expectation of the future that have accumulated during the course of history. Fantasy on the one side and rationalistic systematics on the other have menaced the purity and integrity of the expectation, and, as a result, even in dogmatics, the theologian who faces the problems of eschatology must begin with a critical reduction, that is, a simplification on the basis of the meaning of the biblical expectation itself.

Hans Urs von Balthasar, for example, talks about reduction in this sense.[14] Balthasar has no intention of demythologizing eschatology, a process that leaves the real problems of eschatology unsolved. In fact, it is perhaps more correct to speak of concentration — rather than reduction — here; for what Balthasar has in mind is the concentration of the eschatological expectation in Jesus Christ as the Last. The last things are then "elucidated as aspects of an event which is christological and ecclesiological in character." Balthasar feels that a general revision of eschatology is necessary, especially of the eschatological preaching of judgment, the christological connections of which must be developed.

Discussing the attitudes and approaches of theologians, Balthasar notes that "once theologians ... consider that they have 'certainty of faith' about the outcome of judgment, they decide in advance, unknowingly, a whole range of questions, and the consequences necessarily reach into what would seem the most remote parts of theology. These unavoidable conclusions ... are clearly inconsistent with what the Bible teaches on salvation, and so reveal their questionable character." Balthasar then brings

---

14. "Some Points of Eschatology," in *Word and Redemption* (Eng. tr., 1965), pp. 147-75. See also his "Christian Universalism" in the same volume, pp. 127-45; and *A Theology of History* (Eng. tr., 1963), pp. 111ff.

up the case of the French author Charles Péguy, who left the
Roman Catholic Church for a time because he could not tolerate the absolute eschatological presentations of heaven and
hell, salvation and judgment. The point here is not to argue
these much-discussed eschatological questions, but to examine
the method of understanding that comes into play. (We shall
return to Péguy and the question of universal reconciliation or
apocatastasis in Chapter XIII.) According to Balthasar, the
issue is one of how the testimony of Scripture is dealt with
by systematic theology. For example, whence does the impression arise that the preaching of Christ regarding judgment
enables us to derive a certain, unchangeable *knowledge* of future
facts and events? Without derogation to the doctrine of the
church, Balthasar pleads for an eschatology like Péguy's that
leaves open the outcome of the judgment and renounces any
final systematization in favor of a "theology of hope," founded
in personal obedience to Jesus Christ. Such a goal requires that
the whole of theology be remolded in view of the last things,
and a bringing out "how the eschata are present in all the
other tracts of theology."

Like Balthasar, Heinrich Ott sees eschatology not as a matter
of the last locus of dogmatics or the last chapter of a textbook
on systematic theology, but as a matter of the Kyrios — the Lord
— as *the* Eschatos. From this vantage point, Ott says, our entire
eschatological method must be structured; the eschaton cannot
be understood except as structuring our present reality. "The
message of Jesus' resurrection is the foundation and source of
all Christian eschatology."[15] Conquering death, it is itself the
breakthrough of the eschaton. What comes under discussion in
eschatology is not a knowledge of the future, but first of all
an acknowledgment of God as the one who is coming. All
eschatological questions are concentrated in Jesus Christ the
Lord. Concerning eschatological expectation, Ott says, "Faith is
directed at its object Jesus Christ. So the train of thought on
this question leads back from eschatology through pisteology
to Christology, until it terminates in the rest and unrest of
prayer."[16]

The eschatological promise and expectation as portrayed in
the Bible is not something essentially independent, neutral,

15. *Eschatologie. Versuch eines dogmatischen Grundrisses* (1958), p. 15.
16. *Ibid.*, p. 73.

or supernatural imparting a special knowledge to the believer and endowing him with insight into future events. We can speak of the actuality of eschatological preaching precisely because its message lacks this sort of supernatural characteristic. Eschatology is not a projection into the distant future: it bursts forth into our present existence, and structures life today in the light of the last things. This actuality is not, however, to be confused with actualism, an ever-present danger in eschatological reflection, which suggests a denial of the future and reduces the eschatological promise and expectation to a mere existential encounter in the present. Yet to oppose actualism by neglecting the actuality and relevance of the eschatological message as presented in the New Testament is certainly not the answer. The uniqueness of the New Testament proclamation is not only due to the absence of the speculative, but also to its lack of any neutral, abstract, or remote elements and its thoroughgoing emphasis on the expectation of Him who shall come to judge the living and the dead.

The characteristics of a Christian expectation

This actuality — the relevance and relation of the future to the present — makes it impossible to consider the Christian expectation of the future as of one piece with the general human inclination to a future of bliss. Eschatological expectation is not just ordinary longing fortified by some kind of self-evidence. It is rather the response to a promise, an aroused response triggered by the living promise of which Peter speaks (1 Pet. 1:3) : "Blessed be the God and Father of our Lord Jesus Christ! By his great mercy we have been born anew to a living hope *(anagennēsas hēmás eis elpída zōsan)*." It is clearly impossible to place this Christian expectation on the same level with other human expectations, as if there were only a difference in content and not in structure. The Christian expectation differs profoundly from ordinary longing or hoping precisely because it obtains its certainty from the promised — therefore assured — future. This promised future envelops the present and forms the touchstone of the veracity of the expectation. This spirit can also be detected in the apostolic exhortation to the faithful: "Let us hold fast the confession of our hope without wavering, for he who promised is faithful" (Heb. 10:23) .[17]

17. In connection with hope as a human phenomenon, see O. F. Bollnow,

Once we note that the Christian's expectation of the future bears an indelible stamp of certainty grounded in a steadfast trust in God's promise and is free from all guesswork and hypothetical encumbrances, we must remember that the expectation still is and will remain expectation, a faithful anticipation of what is to come. The Christian's present situation can be summed up in two words as "not yet." This unfulfilled condition plays a very significant role in eschatology, as we shall see throughout this study. It comes to the fore in passages that contrast hoping and seeing, for example, in Romans 8:24f.: ". . . hope that is seen is not hope: For who hopes for what he sees? But if we hope for what we do not see, we wait for it with patience" (cf. Heb. 11:1; 1 Pet. 1:8). Similarly, faith is often opposed to sight.[18] The sight will of course eventually come, but it has *not yet* been granted to the believer (1 Cor. 13).

This emphasis on the "not yet" in the Christian's expectation should not be construed as a devaluation of the promise. Quite the contrary, it stimulates and accents the expectation. The Christian finds his expectations sharpened in anticipation of what is to come. Peter ties it in with an "unutterable and exalted joy" (1 Pet. 1:8). Indeed, this "not yet" forges into the expectation the two essential qualities of patience and endurance (cf. Rom. 5:4). Exhorting the churches, the apostles sought to sustain their hope in the coming Lord by admonishing them to remain steadfast and patient (Rom. 15:4; cf. 1 Thess. 1:3). Their hope, with its certainty and joy, aimed straight at the future, described by Peter as the imperishable and undefiled inheritance, the outcome of faith (1 Pet. 1:4, 9; cf. vs. 13).

As presented in the New Testament, this hope for the future is never its own goal. It dominates and directs life in the present, and important consequences are inseparably integrated with it. In a real sense the future, with the order and integrity of the coming Kingdom, steps into man's existence in the form of this hope. The Christian community is addressed from out of the future, because it cannot and may not remain unaffected by its message. The community must live in patience and establish

Nieuwe Geborgenheid (1958), esp. pp. 79ff.; and G. Marcel, *Homo Viator: Introduction to a Metaphysic of Hope* (Eng. tr., 1960).
18. As in 2 Cor. 5:7. Kittel's critique of the translation "not by sight" does not change the essential meaning of the passage (in *TDNT*, s.v. *eídos*, II, 374).

the hearts of its members, "for the coming of the Lord is at hand" (James 5:8).

It is striking to note the call for sobriety addressed to the Christian community with regard to the future. The end must never produce nervousness or anxiety, nor induce passivity or anxious preoccupation. "Keep sane and sober" *(sōphronēsate kaí nēpsate)* (1 Pet. 4:7). In his commentary on this passage, E. Selwyn describes this composure as "a cool head and a balanced mind . . . the opposite of all *mania* or individual excitement."[19] The proclamation to which the expectation corresponds must lead to clarity of insight, introducing peace, not moments of anxiety and unrest, as Paul warns the Thessalonians (2 Thess. 2:2). The believer must gird up his mind (1 Pet. 1:13) and be prepared for activity and service with lamps burning (Luke 12:35). This sobriety is described as the exact opposite to the beclouding influence of strong drink, which distorts trustworthiness and clarity of vision. "Do not get drunk with wine, for that is debauchery," Paul says, "but be filled with the Spirit" (Eph. 5:18).[20] The expectation requires presence of mind, constant concern, and a sharp spiritual eye able to discern the present and the future. It requires untiring watchfulness: "So then let us not sleep, as others do, but let us keep awake and be sober" (1 Thess. 5:6; cf. 1 Pet. 5:8). "Since we belong to the day, let us be sober, and put on the breastplate of faith and love, and for a helmet, the hope of salvation" (1 Thess. 5:8; cf. Eph. 6:17). This watchfulness contrasts with living in the darkness, where all distinctions are blurred. It is true that in the last days, when the Spirit of the Lord is poured out, men will see visions and dream dreams (Acts 2:17), but these dreams will be radically different from the hallucinations and deceptive products of human imagination. The visions and dreams will be products of the Spirit of God, fulfilments of the prophecy of Joel that life in its entirety will be a concentrated hallowing the name of the Lord coming in His Kingdom (Acts 2:21; cf. Joel 2:32).

The distinctiveness of the Christian expectation of the future should now be a bit more evident. We have noted that this

19. *The First Epistle of St. Peter* (1949), *ad loc.*
20. Bauernfeind, in *TDNT*, s.v. *néphō*, IV, 936: ". . . the verb . . . is the opposite of intoxication, both 1. in the literal sense of intoxication with wine, and 2. in the figurative sense of spiritual intoxication attributable to other causes."

expectation is characterized by joy, certainty, patience, and sobriety. One might object at this point that these characteristics really only represent an ideal to which the Christian can never attain. Is not the "unutterable and exalted joy" of 1 Peter 1:8 a very remote thing? Theological reflection cannot be a mere analysis of the community's religious experience, but the forceful language that the New Testament uses to describe the Christian expectation demands a critical evaluation of the concrete reality of this expectation in the life of the community. This crucial question concerning the reality of the expectation has often been raised in sharp criticism of a church that has forgotten what it is to live out of the expectation of the future, a church that has not understood the meaning of the "not yet," a church that, assuming itself to live in the fulfilment already, full of perfect insight, dismisses the warning that the Christian can know only in part. The unfulfilled condition (the "not yet") and the expectation of what is to come are so correlatively joined that a denial or distortion of the one will naturally have an adverse effect on the other. Those of mystical leanings who pretend to experience the presence of God in all its perfection, claiming to have life in all its fulness and glory, and dismissing life on earth as "the lust of the flesh and the lust of the eyes and the pride of life" (1 John 2:16), leave no room for an expectation. For them the challenges to climb the watchtower (Hab. 2:1) or to ask, "Watchman, what of the night?" (Isa. 21:11) become wholly superfluous. There can be a real expectation only when one does not get all wrapped up in the events preceding the last things and remembers that he is still only on the road to the future. Only in the realization that "here we have no lasting city, but we seek the city which is to come" (allá tēn méllousan epizētoúmen — Heb. 13:14) can there be a real expectation. The idea of a fulfilled present makes of the expectation an illusion or, in terms of the dogma of the church, an ossified tradition.

So we see that the nature and intensity of the expectation are closely connected to the perspective on, and engagement in, the present life. The church has been accused throughout its history of gross distortion in its search for the meaning of the eschaton. In the light of the eschatological expectation, is it still a constantly searching church? Has it fallen prey to a thoroughgoing secularization of the eschaton? Does it remain true to the biblical expectation, or does it presume itself already to have entered a lasting city, forgetting the abiding city "whose builder and maker is God" (Heb. 11:10)? Has it lost the mark of the pilgrim and the joyous expectation, claiming instead with the Laodicean church "I am rich, I have prospered, I need nothing" (Rev. 3:17), symbolizing self-satisfaction and self-sufficiency without awareness of the "not yet," hence, without real, biblical expectation? Has it given itself over to smug complacency, drifting aimlessly because it has lost its goal of hope in the things that are not seen?

These pointed questions — really *one* question in several forms — are not refuted, of course, by a simple appeal to the considerable attention that the confessions of the church pay to the expectation. Such an appeal begs the question of whether or not these confessional statements play any significant role in the life of the people of God. The church must face squarely the question whether or not it really believes what it says about the comfort of the return of Christ (Q. 52, Heidelberg Catechism),[21] about "a most ardent desire" (Art. 37, Belgic Confession), about Him "who shall come again, with glory, to judge the living and the dead" (Nicene Creed), about "the resurrection of the dead and the life of the world to come" (Nicene Creed). Unfortunately, the history of the church proves that words and confessions, however lofty and theoretically sound, often signify nothing.

What of the reality of the church's confession regarding the expectation? F. L. Polak takes up the question of this expectation in connection with the doctrine of the providence of God, concluding correctly that the confession of the former is jeopardized if faith in the latter and its proclamation of God's sovereignty over all things is corrupted. Polak detects such a corruption and distortion at present, and he fears an imminent crisis in the doctrine of the expectation. Polak points to terminology and concepts that are on the tongue of every theologian — demythologizing, de-eschatologizing, de-Judaizing, in short, a general "debunking" of Scripture. His analysis is not meant to be pessimistic; he merely says that de-eschatologizing is a current, widespread fad and that people have begun to lose faith in the historic confession "that God's Providence

21. In addition, the Catechism discusses the assurance of eternal life (Q. 1, 32, 58); the benefits of the resurrection (Q. 45, 57); reward in the future (Q. 63); judgment (Q. 84); the coming Kingdom (Q. 123); and the final complete victory over sin (Q. 127).

is definitely directed to a soon-to-be-realized end of times, the consummation of His exalting plan of salvation for fallen man."[22]

As such, Polak's analysis begs the question whether one can really speak of a Christian expectation of the future. For the community of believers, this is a matter of life and death. The question is not whether such things as expectation, hope, and longing exist: obviously they do. As long as there is dismay and disillusionment, there will be hope for a better future, peace and justice. The real question is whether the biblical expectation is dubious or sure, uncertain or immovable. The critical meaning of this will become evident time and again as we see how crucial the eschatological expectation is in the New Testament proclamation.[23]

Contemporary interest in eschatology

From an analysis such as Polak's, which detects "defuturizing" and de-eschatologizing trends everywhere in contemporary eschatological studies, one can at least conclude that there is a renewed interest in eschatological problems. And much of the emphasis in this renewed interest has been placed on what we have called the actuality of the eschatological message. There seems to be a general protest against any futuristic interpretation of the eschaton, and an equally widespread rejection of simplistic tendencies to treat the study of the last things as an afterthought of dogmatics, a final — often unrelated — locus of systematics. Instead there is a desire to explain the eschaton as an approaching reality and the message of the coming Lord as not concerning a remote and irrelevant future, but an imminent reality. Over against futurism stands the concrete future penetrating and decisively determining the present. In the twentieth-century revival of eschatological studies there has been an attempt to shy away from projected constructs and postulates and to recapture the true relationship between the present and the city "whose builder and maker is God" (Heb. 11:10).

What is the source of this renewed interest? Some have suggested that it is largely the catastrophic and apocalyptic events of the twentieth century that have disclosed the relativity of meaning of those things preceding the eschaton. The

22. Polak, *Hoopvolle toekomstperspectieven* (1957), p. 40.
23. For Polak's analysis, see further his two-volume *De toekomst is ver-leden tijd. Cultuur-futuristische verkenningen* (1955).

nineteenth century has often been described as the heyday of evolutionism. In his *Evolutie* (1899) Abraham Kuyper wrote that the nineteenth century was expiring under the hypnotic influence of the dogma of evolution. In contrast, the twentieth century is seen as a time of the eschatological, otherworldly, transcendent acts of God. Such a radical division between the two centuries is indeed too superficial, but one cannot deny that a shift has taken place. The once evolutionistic, thisworldly view of the Kingdom of God has been set aside in favor of a much more dramatic view, in which the Kingdom is represented as a transcendent, triumphant reality.

It is tempting to draw the dividing line between these two in terms of the cataclysmic events of two world wars. But even before World War I a strong reaction against the evolutionistic, immanent interpretation of the Kingdom had already appeared. This reaction was first apparent among some New Testament theologians who developed a radical opposition to the views of Ritschl.[24] There must come an end, these theologians said, to this view of the Kingdom as one of ethical values and goals in which man must realize his own end, this notion that the Kingdom is a duty rather than a gift. The Kingdom must be recognized as the gift of God, something wholly other, and not in terms of a gradual process of evolution patterned after the course of human history.

The beginnings of this shift are fairly evident. Contrary to the nineteenth-century liberal concept of Jesus, Johannes Weiss and Albert Schweitzer held that Jesus was filled with prophetic certainty that the time was ripe for the establishment of God's Kingdom.[25] The New Testament image of the eschaton is completely shaped by this expectation. God's hour has come! There remains only a short time between expectation and fulfilment. Weiss was primarily interested in the *eschatological* accent of Jesus' preaching,[26] to which liberal theology, with its concentration on the cultural-ethical nature of the Kingdom, had given

24. For the concept of the Kingdom of God during this period see C. Walther, "Der Reich-Gottes-Begriff in der Theologie R. Rothes und A. Ritschls," *Kerygma und Dogma*, II (1956), 115-38; H. Frick, *Das Reich Gottes in amerikanischer und in deutscher Theologie der Gegenwart* (1926); F. Holmström, *Das eschatologische Denken des 20. Jahrhunderts* (1936); Karl Barth, *Die protestantische Theologie im 19. Jahrhundert* (1947), pp. 552f. (on Rothe).
25. Weiss, *Die Idee des Reiches Gottes in der Theologie* (1901), p. 4.
26. *Ibid.*, p. 6.

no consideration. The Kingdom of God, Weiss stressed, was not the product of human accomplishment, but a transcendent magnitude. Ritschl's idea that it could be achieved through human action was exegetically unjustifiable.[27]

This novel interpretation of the Kingdom, stressing its eschatological and transcendent nature, has exercised a profound influence on subsequent generations of theologians. It was carefully and extensively worked out by Albert Schweitzer in an attempt to indicate the character of the whole New Testament message in terms of "consistent eschatology."[28] Curiously, Schweitzer did not conclude from his analysis that this eschatological expectation was something essentially Christian. The Kingdom of God remained an immanent magnitude; the New Testament expectation that the transcendent acts of God were close at hand was for him a temporal limit that, in the course of history, was ultimately outdated. As a matter of academic honesty, however, Schweitzer did admit that the whole New Testament message — in particular the preaching of Jesus and Paul — was filled with this eschatological tension and expectation.[29] Furthermore, he admitted that it was not possible to present the Kingdom of God in terms of immanent, thisworldly categories.

Many of the advocates of consistent eschatology have devoted extensive study to the idea of expectation of the future in the New Testament, evaluating the history of Christendom in the light of the fact that this expectation has not materialized. This leads directly to the much-discussed problem of the so-called delay of the parousia, with which we shall be concerned in Chapter III. Our primary concern here is the theological shift itself, important because it has called attention to the eschatological structure of the New Testament proclamation.

The rise of dialectical theology has called eschatological inquiry back from excessive emphasis on the future to a study of the present relevance of the future. What had been for Schweitzer the direct result of exegesis without immediate consequences for faith now becomes the burning, existential, radical proclamation for all time — the present included. The subject

27. *Ibid.*, pp. 111f.
28. Schweitzer, *The Quest of the Historical Jesus* (Eng. tr., 1910), esp. in the chapter "Thoroughgoing Scepticism and Thoroughgoing Eschatology," pp. 348-95.
29. For Schweitzer on Paul, see his *The Mysticism of Paul the Apostle* (Eng. tr., 1931), and *Paul and His Interpreters* (Eng. tr., 1912).

matter of eschatology was liberated from the limitations of the so-called objective exegesis of the New Testament and placed in the center of dogmatics, the heart of the kerygma. Instead of speculating about an actual state of affairs, complicated by the apparent delay of the parousia, the call came to listen to the heartbeat of eternity in our temporal life, with all the day-to-day implications of this for our responsibility.

This turn of events came about in a vehement reaction — though different from that of Weiss and Schweitzer — against the evolutionistic, optimistic theologies of the nineteenth century, notably those of Schleiermacher and Ritschl. The vehemence of this reaction is illustrated by Emil Brunner's charge that Schleiermacher had created a vacuum, an eschatological gap, through blindness to the eschatological character of the New Testament message. This blind distortion led to an idea of progress that ignored the destructive and demonic tendencies in history. Brunner admits the insights of consistent eschatology, but wants to take them all completely seriously.[30]

Even before Brunner, Karl Barth, in his *Epistle to the Romans,* had pointed to the eschaton and called attention to the transcendent sovereignty of God over all that is temporal and human in morality, culture, and religion, stressing particularly that eschatology is not mainly concerned with futuristic conditions, but with complete actuality of the eschatological proclamation in the present. Barth reacted sharply against the older eschatology as a "short and perfectly harmless chapter" at the end of dogmatics.[31] Instead, he saw the eschaton — God as the Last — in the existential crisis of man living constantly at the brink of God's eternity. This eternity was not temporally remote but was intimately connected with and relevant for everyday life. Barth's thought in this period is sometimes characterized as "timeless" eschatology, which sees the parousia as nothing but a timeless symbol of the endless seriousness of eternity in every existential situation.[32] There was no end of history in terms of time on a horizontal plane, but only a vertical eschaton marked by the permanent crisis in life and the actual gravity of the nearness of God.

Thus the temporal future is transposed to the present and the actualized eschaton is no longer spoken of in temporal cate-

30. Brunner, *Die Mystik und das Wort* (1924), pp. 268f., 288ff.
31. Barth, *Epistle to the Romans* (Eng. tr., 1933), p. 500.
32. Holmström, *op. cit.,* p. 241.

gories but in spatial terms: the future is like the sword of Damocles. The "post" is replaced by "trans,"[33] and, against all futurism, the emphasis is on the ever-present heartbeat of eternity.

It was during this same period (1928) that Bultmann, writing in *Zwischen den Zeiten* ("Between the Times"!) discussed the eschatology of the Gospel of John. Bultmann too denied that eschatology was a matter of horizontal future, or of a final drama at the end of history.[34] The dimension of the eschatological relation of God's revelation to man in his moment of crisis was vertical and existential.

The tendency toward existential actualization in eschatology was found not only among the champions of dialectical theology.[35] Paul Althaus also leaned in this direction. In *Die letzten Dinge* (first edition, 1922), he too radically rejected so-called "end-historical eschatology." Eschatology was to be reconstructed not as the length-dimension but as the depth-dimension of salvation. Eschatology does not have to do with the history of the end or with the end of history, but with the "other side" of history. It is not apocalyptic.[36]

We can readily detect a serious attempt here to see eschatology as something other than a preoccupation with future events that has no bearing on the present. At the same time we should caution against the dangers of "detemporalization," because any such attempts will inevitably threaten the disintegration of the eschatological vision. Is it not possible that emphasizing the permanent limitation of the eschaton in the present blurs the reality of history? Does the tendency to replace the "post" by the "trans" not involve a weakening of the awareness of the real goal to which the New Testament points? Given this substitution, can one still speak of a return of the Lord? Is es-

---

33. Frick, *op. cit.*, p. 14.
34. "Die Eschatologie des Johannes-evangeliums." This article is included in English translation in *Faith and Understanding*, I (1969), 165-83.
35. See E. Thurneysen, "Christus und seine Zukunft. Ein Beitrag zur Eschatologie," *Zwischen den Zeiten*, IX (1931), 186-211.
36. On the method of eschatology, cf. Althaus, *Die letzten Dinge*, pp. 63-82. It is not our intent to identify Althaus with the dialectical theologians; for differences, see Thurneysen, *loc. cit.* Thurneysen himself saw no objection to speaking of an "end-historical" eschatology (p. 198). The similarity between Althaus and the dialectical school lies in the problem of the "actuality of the eschaton."

chatology merely to be concerned with the existential relationship in the present?

All these questions are raised in one form or another by critics of what is sometimes called "unhistorical eschatology." H. Frick warns that arbitrarily exchanging the temporal aspect for the spatial can lead to mysticism and deprive the gospel of its gravity; for mysticism is at home in spatial concepts, whereas revelation pertains to the temporal.[37] In "actualizing" eschatology is it necessary for the vertical dimension to absorb or completely relativize the horizontal?

The history of eschatology that reacts against futurism reveals that only Bultmann maintained his original position here. The thought of Barth and Althaus in this area underwent a noticeable evolution and correction, particularly in further consideration of the meaning of the horizontal dimension. Both begin to take greater note of the problems of history. Writing about the eternity of God in *Church Dogmatics* Barth recalls dialectical theology's emphasis on the No of divine judgment. He admits that this emphasis had been one-sided. He writes: "In the critical form in which it was presented, this could not unjustly be connected with the spiritual shaking experienced by European man through the world war. It was violently welcomed by some as an expression of the spirit of this time, and no less forcibly rejected by others, less receptive to this spirit, as a 'post-war phenomenon.' "[38] It was not made clear that it was not a general understanding of *limit* and *crisis* that was at stake, but the living God and His judgment and grace. Barth admits to an exclusive stress on God's "far-sidedness" without giving proper attention to His coming as such.[39] The eschatological reaction had been too strong, and had lost sight of the *telos,* the goal and end of history.

Reconsidering his exegesis of Romans 13:11 — "for salvation is nearer to us now than when we first believed" — Barth openly confesses: "But it is also clear that with all this art and eloquence I missed the distinctive feature of the passage, the teleology which it ascribes to time as it moves towards a real end."[40] Time is not empty, but full of meaning through "the

37. Frick, *op. cit.,* p. 14.
38. *CD,* II/1, 634.
39. *Ibid.,* p. 635.
40. *Ibid.;* cf. *Epistle to the Romans,* p. 500: "Will there never be an end of all our ceaseless talk about the *delay* of the Parousia? How can the

real and therefore the comforting and commanding presence of God."[41] Actuality no longer absorbs teleology but assigns it an important place.[42]

A similar correction is found in the thought of Paul Althaus. At first, closing ranks with those who distinguished between axiological and teleological eschatology, Althaus had constructed a vertical or axiological eschatology by way of the experience of eternal norms and values. Like Barth he later came to pay more serious attention to the horizontal dimension. Although he still maintained that the eschaton was a matter of actuality, of complete seriousness in the present, his later view of this actuality allowed room for the meaning of time, in which human life is oriented to a goal.[43]

This means that eschatology, besides being "actual," also becomes teleological. No longer is it a matter of a vertical validity of eternal values and norms, an actual timeless eschaton of permanent, immediate relationship to God; instead, the actuality of God as the Lord of history, who in history reveals perspectives of a real consummation, is once again recognized. There is much that is commendable in this shift from one-sided, exclusively actual eschatology to what we might call an *actual-teleology*. But this "actualizing" must never be done out of the framework of modern idealist or existentialist categories, but should proceed from an increasing recognition of the gravity of the biblical proclamation of the future. When this is recognized, it is again possible to see the contours that outline the New Testament message of the future: the contours of calling and admonition, comfort and salvation, struggle and victory.

This concept of actualization can in fact be interpreted

coming of that which doth not *enter in* ever be *delayed?* The End of which the New Testament speaks is no temporal event, no legendary 'destruction' of the world; it has nothing to do with any historical, or 'telluric' or cosmic catastrophe. The end of which the New Testament speaks is really the End; so utterly the End, that in the measuring of nearness or distance our nineteen hundred years are not merely of little, but of no importance."

41. *CD*, II/1, 638.
42. The consequences of this are far-reaching and of practical significance. See G. C. Berkouwer, *Wereldoorlog en theologie* (1945), p. 36; and Barth's concession that his own views concerning the parousia were inadequate, *CD*, II/1, 634ff.
43. Already in his earlier period Althaus had warned Barth against "skeptical devaluation of history." Cf. Berkouwer, *Wereldoorlog en theologie*, p. 15.

in a number of ways and can assume various concrete shapes. By itself, of course, the word "actualization" says little.[44] One word of caution is in order. The compelling appeal of actuality must not result in the absorption and disintegration of the reality of the future; nor does it mean that the eschaton begins to function as a timeless "encounter" or a vertical phenomenon lacking horizontal direction. It is exactly the reality of the future that makes the actuality conceivable. And on the basis of the biblical evidence, our question must be "how does this proclaimed future intervene in our existence today and determine our life?"

It is not the future, only the futuristic, that conflicts with the meaning of eschatology.

44. For example, when Althaus writes, in reference to the antichrist, that "the idea of the antichrist must be translated out of the theoretical realm into the actual," one would have to admit that this actuality has always been an unmistakable theme of the NT. An eschaton that can even momentarily be divorced from relevance to the present is unthinkable. *Die letzten Dinge*, p. 295. With respect to this actuality, see also F. W. Grosheide, *De verwachting der toekomst van Jezus Christus* (1907), pp. 74ff. Many who are antagonists of a particular *mode* of actuality readily accept the meaning of the motif of actuality. See e.g. E. Masselink, *Eschatologische motieven in de nieuwe theologie* (1946), and R. J. van der Meulen, *De Antichrist*. We shall consider the biblical proclamation of the antichrist in Chapter IX.

CHAPTER TWO

TWOFOLD EXPECTATION?

IN THE PREVIOUS chapter our discussion of the expectation of the future had specific reference to the parousia of Jesus Christ at the end of time. Throughout the history of the church and theology a second question, closely related to this one, has been discussed. Is there in addition to this expectation a more limited, *individual* expectation focusing on the salvation of the believer coming to the end of his own life? Does the teleology we talked about in Chapter I include not only the general kind of eschatology discussed there but also the *telos* of the individual believer? Is it legitimate, in other words, to speak of a "twofold expectation?"

The distinction sometimes made in this context between *individual* and *cosmic* eschatology is not an altogether happy one, since even the so-called cosmic eschatology does not in any way exclude the individual. Still, the intent of the distinction is quite clear: that it is permissible to speak of *telos* both with respect to the individual's end here on earth and with respect to the end of all things.[1] On this view, cosmic (or universal) eschatology deals with the parousia, the resurrection of the body, the new earth, in short, with the eschaton of total reality in which the whole of mankind is caught up. Alongside this is a more limited horizon of eschatological meaning — eschatology in its personal rather than universal aspects. The concern of individual eschatology is encapsulated in a question with which B. Telder entitled his book: "Death ... and then what?"[2]

---

1. Compare the prayer of Ps. 39:4: "LORD, let me know my end, and what is the measure of my days," and 1 Pet. 4:7: "The end of all things is at hand" *(pántōn dé tó télos)*. Among systematic theologians, Althaus, e.g., distinguishes between "personal fulfilment" and "fulfilment of the world," *Die Christliche Wahrheit*, II (1948), 475ff.
2. The complete title of Telder's book is *Sterven ... en dan? Gaan de kinderen Gods, wanneer zij sterven, naar de hemel?* (1960): "Do God's children, when they die, go to heaven?"

Obviously, there is something of a "last things" in the life of every individual; consequently, is it not proper to speak of expectation with respect to this individually limited horizon? After all, did not John hear the voice from heaven: " 'Blessed are the dead who die in the Lord *henceforth.*' 'Blessed indeed,' says the Spirit, 'that they may rest from their labors; for their deeds follow them!' " (Rev. 14:13) ?

The testimony of the church's confessions

This is not merely a subtle question for theologians. We are confronted by it in the confessions of the church. The Heidelberg Catechism affirms: "After this life my soul shall immediately be taken up to Christ, its Head" (Q. 57). So the subject of the duality of the expectation is introduced into the church. Is there room for a twofold orientation toward the end, one that includes both the individual and the universal aspects?

In discussions of the twofold expectation, the fear is often expressed that the unity of the expectation is destroyed by such a notion and that a dualism of expectation is the inevitable result. Many theologians, therefore, refuse to make such a division between the two. To divorce the two entirely would not be correct, of course. In no case can the individual expectation be an isolated entity, independent of the expectation of the eschaton. Significantly, the Catechism's mention of the immediacy of the believer's bliss arises in the context of a discussion of the resurrection of the body.[3] The Catechism presents the individual expectation and the eschatological expectation of conformity to the glorious body of Christ together. There is no warrant for an isolation or a dualism in which attempts would have to be made to establish the relationship and the unity.

But locating the unity and defining the relationship of the two aspects of the expectation is what has presented repeated problems. The problem comes to the fore in the church's preaching of the individual's end as salvation. The word "salvation" conjures up associations of peace and rest, of the end of the pilgrimage. Is this salvation the sole end, the fulfilment of the

3. The integral unity of the expectation is obvious from the correlative structure of the answer in the German: "nicht allein ... sondern auch. ..." The correlation is not maintained in all translations. Abraham Kuyper stressed the fact that the *resurrectio carnis* is intended here; *E Voto Dordraceno*, II, 196ff.

expectation, the promotion from faith to sight? If not — if indeed the expectation extends beyond the grave and ultimately points to the parousia itself — then the tension between the "already" and the "not yet" must remain even for those who, in death, await the coming of the Lord.

The church's stake in the problem of the duality of expectation is obvious. Can unity of expectation be maintained in the face of this supposed duality? Then there is a further danger that this individual aspect — including individual salvation — will begin to dominate the perspective and experience of the believer, leaving no room at all for the universal aspect of the future, regardless of what the official dogmas and confessions of the church say. So, it is argued, we end up with an individualizing of the expectation of the future, oriented to the individual's end, emphasizing exclusively the "henceforth" of Revelation 14:13, and determined only by one's particular interpretation of Hebrews 9:27, ". . . it is appointed for men to die once, and after that comes judgment."

Some have argued that this kind of eschatological individualism, this egoistical depreciation of the expectation,[4] is bound to result from any doctrine of a twofold expectation. They maintain it is inevitable, if a narrow perspective on individual "salvation" is allowed, that the broader, supra-individual aspects of the parousia would be pushed into the background and the confession of the early church, "I believe in the resurrection of the body," reduced to a formal dogma with no room for the real expectation concerning the future. How could the expectation of the parousia *not* get lost in this rank individualism and egoism?[5]

Given the renewed interest in recent years in the biblical teaching about the Kingdom of God, it is understandable that questions like these have once again come to the fore. These questions intimately concern the very life of the church and we cannot ignore them. They are not speculative curiosities; this quest for the true nature of the expectation is a matter of life and death for the church of Jesus Christ. How does the

4. Kuyper comments that "by far the majority of Christians do not think much beyond their own death"; *ibid.*, p. 201.
5. Kuyper urged the priority of the expectation of the Lord's coming and warned against spiritual selfishness and egoism, noting that the Bible says very little about the salvation of the soul immediately after death, but a great deal about the eschaton; *ibid.*, p. 202.

expectation of every believer relate to the universal expectation of the church? There are two possibilities: (1) that there is an irreconcilable duality leading inevitably to a dualism that extinguishes the spark of biblical expectation and Calvin's outlook on the ultimate manifestation of God's glory in His Kingdom,[6] or (2) that the church's language of faith concerning the expectation does essentially reflect biblical truth. All these questions cohere in what has historically been called the doctrine of the "intermediate state."

The confessions of the church present a duality in expectation of the future, but without a radical dualistic conflict between the two. Nor do they indicate a primacy of the one or the other. The Heidelberg Catechism refers to both the personal or individual and the universal. Question and Answer 52 point to the certain expectation ("I may await with head held high . . .") of the return of Christ, an expectation that is not antagonistic to the believer but a comfort to him — a personal comfort. But the Catechism speaks of the widest of possible horizons, a comprehensive and universal perspective. It does not speak of different, individual incidences of "hereafter"; rather, it anticipates the final Day, the Day of the Lord, the Judge from heaven (Q. 52). Above all, there is a confession of the resurrection, of which the resurrection of Christ is a sure pledge (Q. 45), and the hope of the coming Kingdom, in which God will be all in all (Q. 123).

There are numerous references in the Catechism to personal, individual life and its end, as well as to the hereafter. The Christian prays for grace in this life "so that we may be renewed in the image of God, until we attain the goal of full perfection *after this life*" (Q. 115). Death is spoken of as "an entering into eternal life" (Q. 57).[7] But it is especially the statement that one's soul is taken up to Christ *immediately* (Q. 57) that displays a strongly individual color and calls attention — in the

---

6. For this idea of Calvin, cf. K. Fröhlich, *Die Reichgottesidee Calvins* (1922), pp. 20f.

7. The English, following the German "Eingang zum ewigen Leben," has "entering into eternal life"; the Dutch, however, reads "*doorgang* [passage] tot het eeuwige leven." The possible difference of meaning has raised problems of interpretation with reference to the intermediate state. The scriptural references adduced (Phil. 1:23; John 5:24; Rom. 7:24) are not particularly helpful in this connection (tr. note).

context of the general eschatological expectation — to the "limited horizon" of individual expectation.[8]

The twofold expectation that unambiguously confronts us here lacks any hint of a destructive dualistic nature. The one expectation is not played off against the other. There is no talk of an isolated, independent intermediate state. For one thing, the notion of "immediacy" (Q. 57) is placed in an integral relationship to the expectation of the resurrection of the body. Again, the idea of "hereafter" is placed in an unmistakably universal perspective: "and hereafter rule with him in eternity over all creatures" (Q. 32; cf. Lord's Day 21).

The Belgic Confession emphasizes the universal eschatological perspective (Art. 37). The expectation focuses on the parousia of the Lord, in which all men will appear before the Judge of heaven and earth. After mention of judgment and comfort, the article concludes by confessing: "Therefore we expect that great day with a most ardent desire, to the end that we may fully enjoy the promises of God in Christ Jesus our Lord." Yet this broad perspective does not exclude the individual expectation: "... a sense of corruption should make believers often to sigh, desiring to be delivered from this body of death" (Art. 15). Again it is important to note that there is obviously no competition in the eschatological expectation between the "universal" and "individual." The church's confessions have historically maintained the duality of expectations, yet always as a duality within the great unity of eschatological expectation.[9]

This absence of a real problem is itself a problem for many people, who object that the confessions do not really answer any questions about the unity of the expectation but merely

8. Telder is, understandably, primarily concerned with Q. 57. He complains that the Catechism should have formulated its stand on the intermediate state more in line with the Scriptures; *op. cit.*, pp. 154, 163f.

9. Other expressions of this duality within unity are found in the Canons of Dort: "... having faithfully preserved them even to the end, should *at last* bring them, free from every spot and blemish, to the enjoyment of glory in His own presence forever" (II, 8; cf. III-IV, 17; V, 2); Westminster Shorter Catechism: "the souls of believers ... do *immediately* pass into glory ..." (Q. 37); Westminster Confession of Faith: "the souls of the righteous ... are received into the highest heavens, where they behold the face of God in light and glory, *waiting* for the *full* redemption of their bodies *(corporum suorum redemtionem expectantes)* (XXXII, 1); the Second Helvetic Confession: "the faithful, after bodily death, do go directly unto Christ ..." (XXVI, 3).

cover up the problems. Is it possible, they ask, to conceive of an expectation other than that of the return of Christ and His Kingdom? Should the individual expectation not be directly linked with the parousia? Individual eschatology deals with salvation "after this life, perfect blessedness" (Heid. Cat., Q. 58). What is the connection between this already perfect blessedness and the promises of a future yet to come? The vision of the parousia threatens to dissolve in the face of the seemingly all-absorbing importance of this perfect blessedness. What does one do, then, with the message of Paul about the ultimate future: "When Christ, who is our life, appears, then you also will appear with him in glory" (Col. 3:4)? Is there an essential difference between blessedness and glory? Is it possible that in the state of blessedness in the hereafter, one continues to have an expectant longing for an ultimate blessedness or glory?[10]

Since what is at stake in questions like these is the issue of what is properly the object of the Christian's expectation — not in an individualistic eudaemonism, but according to the real promises of God — there is a strong existential note in these discussions. How can I relate the fulfilment of the eschatological expectation to my own death? Does my own expectation have its own character that places a peculiar stamp on the whole expectation? The answers to these questions will determine to what extent our expectations are governed by the ultimate eschaton, and to what extent they are influenced by our consciousness of the concrete nearness and reality of our own personal end, as summed up by David: "But truly, as the LORD lives . . . there is but a step between me and death" (1 Sam. 20:3; cf. Pss. 39:6; 119:84).

Can we consider the question of the interim period of the intermediate state as a side-issue of the broader perspective regarding the eschaton? In other words, does the expectation relate concretely to the "time" between the death of the individual and the parousia of the Lord?

10. The Scotch Confession of Faith (1560) speaks of death in terms of the believers "departed in peace and rest from their labors" (Art. XVIII). Cf. the Westminster Confession on the *visio Dei (loc. cit.)*; Article 16 of the Irish Articles of Religion (1615) on the "sweet, pleasant, and unspeakable comfort" of contemplating election in Christ. Compare also Q. 58, Heid. Cat. ("perfect blessedness") with Art. XXXVII of the Belgic Confession ("that we may fully enjoy the promises of God in Christ Jesus our Lord").

Objections to the doctrine of the intermediate state

Let us consider first of all some of the criticisms to which the doctrine of the intermediate state has been subjected. This critique has taken a variety of forms, but by and large it is motivated either by anthropological or eschatological considerations. Anthropologically, the doctrine has been attacked because it allegedly posits a dichotomy of substance between "soul" and "body," leading to the assumption that there is an incorruptible *anima separata* that continues to exist in some special way in the intermediate state. This view of man, it is said, is essentially scholastic and distorts the biblical view of man as a unity.[11]

The eschatologically motivated criticism of the doctrine is closely related to the anthropological. This critique is twofold: first, that the doctrine denies God's judgment over the whole man, both body and soul;[12] and second, that it waters down and impoverishes the coming Kingdom of God and reduces the living hope to a narrow, individualized anticipation. The goal of the expectation is seen as having shifted from the eschaton to the limited and narrow horizons of individual existing and dying, thus gradually ushering out of the expectation the theme of the last judgment so strongly emphasized by the New Testament. Exclusive and exaggerated importance is given to one's individual lot in life and death and to the judgment of God and the appearance before His face at the time of death. Moreover, the doctrine of the resurrection is taken up in this same narrow, highly individualized process. It is true, these objectors admit, that the resurrection of the body is still formally confessed, but it no longer functions as a living hope and is instead down-

11. C. Stange points out further that this anthropological dualism goes against experience; *Das Ende aller Dinge* (1930), p. 202. For further comment on this same issue, see Berkouwer, *Man: the Image of God* (Eng. tr., 1962), pp. 252-65.
12. Both Althaus and Helmut Thielicke see the doctrine of the intermediate state as an attempt to escape the radical nature of death. In opposition to this is the thesis of the resurrection of the dead. There is also a very close connection with the doctrine of immortality. Thielicke writes: "Resurrection: that is the grave burst open; immortality: that is the grave renounced." *Tod und Leben*, p. 100. On the views of G. van der Leeuw, see Berkouwer, *Man: the Image of God*, pp. 251ff. Telder's critique in *Sterven ... en dan?* is couched in anthropological motifs. Unfortunately, he almost completely ignores present-day theology and philosophy.

graded to the level of an appendix to the eschatological expectation. In short, "the doctrine of the intermediate state is thoroughly individualistic."[13]

How can justice be done to the broader future — to the parousia — if such things as perfect blessedness, the *visio Dei,* and peace and rest are attributed to the intermediate state? Does the doctrine of the intermediate state not suggest that there can be a perfect blessedness that has not shared in the ultimate victory of Christ, the last and decisive triumph over the last enemy death, and the revelation of the fulness of the Kingdom of God or the new heaven and the new earth? Althaus goes on to talk about the spiritualistic and acosmic tendencies of the doctrine of the intermediate state and its concomitant reduction of the expectation.[14] What difference, he asks, is there between the orthodox doctrine of the intermediate state and the eschatology of the Enlightenment, which thought only of individual immortality?[15] May Christian thought have anything to do with this "private blessedness, without communion with the people of God, without considering the victory of Christ and the Kingdom?"[16]

After criticizing the doctrine of the intermediate state, Althaus asks what might take the place of this teaching, for he recognizes an individual hope besides the one of the eschaton.[17] So he tries to arrive at a solution that avoids the element of "competition" between the two hopes. At this point the concept of time comes into play. How can one apply the time that we experience to the hereafter? This becomes crucial for the dispute about the intermediate state. According to Althaus, our time is thrown up each moment on the beaches of eternity, the last day. "Does not the last day lie round about us, so that our death places us in simultaneity with the end of history, the coming of the Kingdom, the judgment?"[18]

13. Althaus, *Die letzten Dinge,* p. 156.
14. *Ibid.,* p. 157.
15. J. Pieper vigorously contests the identification of immortality as seen by the Enlightenment with Plato's concept. "Tod und Unsterblichkeit. Philosophische Bemerkungen zu einem kontroverstheologischen Thema," *Catholica,* XIII (1959), 84ff.
16. *Op. cit.,* p. 157.
17. *Ibid.,* p. 158.
18. *Ibid.,* p. 159; cf. also his *Die Christliche Wahrheit,* II, 509; and his *Unsterblichkeit und ewiges Leben bei Luther* (1930); also H. Vogel, *Gott in Christo* (1952), pp. 1043, 1045.

A. A. Leenhouts, claiming that the intermediate state is a fantasy, an age-old speculation in which the church has indulged,[19] agrees that the church's error here is based on a misunderstanding of time. The church failed to comprehend that "on the other side" of the grave time and the sense of time cease to be, so that an immediate connection in consciousness with the last day is created.[20] The last day borders immediately on our brief lifetime.[21] Leenhouts is not trying to renew the doctrine of soul-sleep, but he does retain the metaphor of sleep to indicate that there may be a time to which our consciousness has no access. Through this neutralization of time, he hopes to bridge the gap between dying and the parousia.[22] The deceased are "out of time"; therefore, one cannot project our concepts of time into their hereafter with a doctrine of an intermediate state.

Clearly Leenhout's remarks are based on a particular understanding of time, according to which one cannot and may not speak of "time" when referring to the situation beyond death. It is improper to force human concepts of time on situations that are not similar to our own experiences. Leenhouts uses the case of a passenger who has fallen asleep on a train trip to clarify his point. When he wakes up, the traveler has no notion of having taken a long trip. At first glance this comparison appears to suggest some validity to his argument, but in reality it illustrates nothing, because instead of having to do with the absence of time, it merely refers (Leenhouts admits as much) to the absence of a conscious, subjective experiencing of time.

This critique of the doctrine is based, it seems to me, on an a priori notion of a hereafter that allows for creatureliness but rejects time. Here one encounters the widespread opinion that time is opposite to eternity and that it is neutralized or abolished by eternity in the dissolution of the time-structure of our experience. Some have connected time with the fall of

---

19. Leenhouts, *In een punt des tijds* (1945), p. 7; cf. K. Schilder, "Is er een 'tussentoestand'?", *De Reformatie*, XXI (1947), 18-45. W. Koepp also uses the word "fantasy" in *Die Welt der Ewigkeit* (1921), p. 122.
20. *Op. cit.*, p. 4.
21. *Ibid.*, p. 5.
22. *Ibid.*, p. 25.

man, seeing salvation, then, to be a release from time, a transcending of all time-structure.[23]

Curiously, this view is often taken for a self-evident truth. It originates with a definition of time that shapes an outlook on the eschaton in terms of a dualism of time and eternity. Life "in time" passes away, ebbs out. Temporality is identical with perishability, with the limited character of life on the basis of the coming end. This notion lies behind Heim's claim that it is not just what we encounter in time, but the very form of time itself, that is at the bottom of all earthly sorrow. He sees time as something in itself incomplete and restless. If there is consummation, it can only consist in the overcoming of this form itself, in the coming to rest of the stream of time in the sea of eternity.[24]

In many theological circles there is considerable sympathy for this notion of the "abolition" of time. Some appeal for support of their view to the psalmist's phrase "we fly away" (Ps. 90:10). But this idea is not really self-evident at all. The psalmist is not addressing himself to an antithesis between time and eternity. He is concerned with the transitoriness of life, man's return to the dust, and man's encounter with the eternal, living God who consumes man in His anger (vs. 7) and makes him pass his days under His wrath (vs. 9).[25] It is something quite different to disqualify time as structure on the basis of a faulty identification of it with the transitoriness of man. Such an identification lacks credibility because it ascribes to time the condition brought about by sin *in* time. Eternity is then some kind of a supratemporal suspension, whereas the temporality of man the creature becomes a deficiency of his fall into sin. Carried to its logical conclusion, this would mean that ideal creatureliness, the ultimate good, would be for man to see a

---

23. K. Heim writes: "Time is the existence of the fallen, that is, of the creation fallen out of its immediacy to God." "Zeit und Ewigkeit. Die Hauptfrage der heutigen Eschatologie," in *Glauben und Leben* (1928), p. 553; on this tendency in eschatology, cf. G. Hoffmann, *Das Problem der letzten Dinge in der neueren evangelischen Theologie* (1929).

24. Heim, *op. cit.,* p. 555. Brunner also follows this line of thinking. He speaks of the linearity of time in opposition to the spatial, which is open for us "to all dimensions."

25. C. H. Ratschow notes correctly that basically the Psalmist does not see transitoriness as a problem of time but as one of guilt. "Anmerkungen zur theologischen Auffassung des Zeitproblems," *Zeitschrift für Theologie und Kirche,* LI (1954), 360ff.

thousand years as one day (Ps. 90:4; 2 Pet. 3:8). The Bible is clearly not talking about any ideal creatureliness here, but is addressing itself to the living, eternal God who transcends time, for whom the distinctions and differences of time make no difference. This does not mean, however, that man's temporality is an insufficiency from which he must escape in order to gain access to eternity, as though the key to the eschatological expectation can only be found in eternity. Nowhere does the biblical testimony about salvation proceed from this kind of antithesis between time and eternity.

In present-day theology this depreciation of time and the whole time-eternity dualism have come under fire from all directions.[26] The biblical view of time is altogether different. In fact, it does not proceed from a theoretical reflection on "time" as such. There is one passage in the Bible that has sometimes been thought to suggest that there is no time in the future — Revelation 10:5-6: "the angel . . . swore by him who lives for ever and ever . . . *that there should be no more delay.*"[27] Some have suggested that this statement parallels the eschatological perspectives of no more mourning or crying, pain or death, temple, night, or sea (Rev. 21:1, 4, 22, 25). One of the hallmarks of salvation, on this view, would be the conspicuous absence of time. But it is now generally accepted that this passage refers to no more *delay* rather than to no more time, and that it cannot be used in support of the idea that the Scriptures suddenly confront us with a change in time-structure indicating a transition from time into eternity.[28]

26. O. Cullmann reacted strongly against tying in time with fallen creation, asserting that time and eternity have temporality in common. Cullmann says that God's eternity must be expressed in terms of "endless time." *Christ and Time*, p. 63. Compare Berkhof's *Christ, the Meaning of History* (Eng. tr., 1966), pp. 186f.; and K. J. Popma's critique of Cullmann; *Levensbeschouwing*, II (1959), 332.

27. *hóti chrónos oukéti éstai.* The Dutch reads "dat er geen tijd meer zal zijn." Among English translations, only the KJV translates *chrónos* as "time." The Dutch Nieuwe Vertaling translates "er zal geen uitstel meer zijn" (tr. note).

28. According to Barth (*CD*, III/2, 624; cf. I/2, 49f.), the point of this text is that time is no more in the eschaton. Bavinck refers to Rev. 10:6 in connection with the cessation of time and makes a distinction between "extrinsic" and "intrinsic" time; *GD*, II, 132f. (Eng. tr., *The Doctrine of God*, 1951, p. 155). Bavinck's exegesis of the passage presents a theoretical view of "time." In contrast to this, see K. J. Popma, *Levensbeschouwing*, II, 326, and *Inleiding in de Wijsbegeerte* (1956),

In the whole array of time-eternity theories, then, it is impossible to find any meaningful interpretation valid for a critique on the intermediate state. Nowhere does Scripture disqualify time; rather, we detect a religious protest against what man as sinner has done in and with the time allotted to him. The believer is called to find out how he can make the most of the brief succession of moments in his lifetime,[29] how he can orient his life in time — still in the flesh — according to the will of the Lord.[30]

It is precisely within time that man's life can obtain profound meaning in the service of the living God. To see time as the essential structure of the fallen cosmos or the essential characteristic of man's depravity, and so to conclude that this structure must be abolished, can only threaten the meaning of our earthly existence.

The disqualifying view of time has often been deduced from the apparent disharmony between the past, present, and future. Man is seen as being at the mercy of his lot — his temporality — always searching for but never finding rest. Eternity is then seen as being freed from this lot. It is undeniable that sin and estrangement from God always tend to tear man away from the harmonious relationship of past, present, and future. The irresponsible man can become absorbed in the present and forget the past completely or he can lose himself in the present and forget the expectation of the fulfilment of God's promise.

p. 88: "Scripture does not offer us a doctrine of time." He dismisses such attempts as biblicism. See also commentaries *ad loc.* by Greijdanus and Behm. Greijdanus explains *oukéti éstin* and *ouk éstai* as referring to the cessation of time, the timeless existence of eternity. This exegesis has a long history. Cullmann cites Bede: "mutabilis saecularium temporum varietas cessabit." He rejects the interpretation of "time as structure" (*op. cit.*, pp. 49, 62), as does Berkhof, *CMH*, p. 186.

29. Eph. 5:6 (*exagorazómenoi tón kairón*); see also Col. 4:5. Büchsel writes: "*kairós* here stands for the opportunities offered by time"; *TDNT*, s.v. *exagorázō*, I, 128. Cf. Rev. 2:21: "I gave her time to repent." Also, G. Delling, *Das Zeitverständnis des NT* (1940), p. 154; T. von Zahn, *Die Offenbarung des Johannes* (1924), p. 549.

30. 1 Peter 4:2: *allá thelémati theoú tón epíloipon en sarkí biósai.* Such a life is to be contrasted with misuse of time: it has nothing to do with a depreciation or devaluation of time. Popma, in his otherwise valuable exposition, unjustly criticizes Berkhof for his supposed depreciation of time (despite Berkhof's own critique on depreciation), *Levensbeschouwing*, II, 309ff. When Popma remarks that Berkhof has capitulated to Barthian time-theology, he is referring to the very depreciation of time that Berkhof himself denied.

But the good news of God's acts in time, in human life, does not break through the time-barrier; rather, it restores the harmony and interrelatedness of these phases of time. The Old Testament believers are cautioned not to forget God's benefits (Ps. 103:2); the New Testament congregation is instructed to partake of the Supper in remembrance of Christ (Luke 22:19) and to commemorate the resurrection of the Lord (2 Tim. 2:8).[31] The gospel strikes the further comforting note that from past to present and from present to future Christ is always the same, "yesterday and today and forever" (Heb. 13:8). This certainly does not imply a dissolution of our temporality, but a reordering of the confused state of affairs in mankind. There is clarity and coordination, perspective on and insight into the direction of all our days.

In view of all this, it is difficult to see why a timeless eschatology has been so attractive to many, as if the solution to all the pressing problems that face us could be timelessness. What is actually meant by these many and varied formulations of timelessness? What is the real meaning of such difficult to conceive eschatological perspectives as "duration without succession" or the abolition and destruction of our time-structure?[32]

The contrast of past, present, and future with eternity, seen as an "eternal present," seems to require using these words ambiguously. Berkhof, opposing the depreciation of time, speaks of time as the "mould of our created human existence.... Consummation [means]... that time as the form of our glorified existence will also be fulfilled and glorified.... [It] means to live again in the succession of past and future in such a way that the past moves along with us as blessing and the future radiates through the present."[33] Confronted here with something that

---

31. One need only look in any concordance under "forget" and "remember" to see the biblical emphasis on the relatedness of past and present.
32. On the relation of duration and succession, see Popma, *Levensbeschouwing*, II, 329, and Kuyper, *Dictaten Dogmatiek*, I *(Locus de Deo)*, 300. Various scholars have called temporality into question. Cullmann conceived of time as linear and chronological; others have seen it as more psychological than chronological; still others favor a realistic view. For the psychological, see T. Boman, *Das Hebräische Denken im Vergleich mit dem Griechischen* (2d ed., 1954), esp. pp. 188-232; for the realistic, J. Marsh, *The Fulness of Time* (1952), pp. 19ff. See also Bultmann's discussion of Boman, *Gnomon* (1955), pp. 551ff.; and W. Eichrodt, "Heilserfahrung und Zeitverständnis im AT," *Theologische Zeitschrift*, XII (1956), 104ff.
33. Berkhof, *CMH*, p. 188.

transcends our experience, we can only stammer about it. Even the "foretaste" of this unity far transcends man's experience.[34] Just as even the holiest of men makes only a small beginning in obedience in this life (Heid. Cat., Q. 114), so none of us can make more than a small beginning of understanding his days, time, and prospects of eternity.

This point of view does not involve the abolition of time by eternity. The orientation of all our days to the service of God — without confusion, forgetting, or secularization — will be fulfilled in the "consummation." Even in this earthly life, the "filling" of life in time is not to be contrasted with the chronological succession of hours, days, months, years, because this succession is unmistakably tied up with the demand to make the most of the time.[35]

From all this it is obvious that any criticism of the doctrine of the intermediate state that presupposes an antithesis between time and eternity must be rejected. Even though these critics may dispute the rebuttal that their way of thinking tends toward pantheism and a notion of participation in the eternity of God,[36] they can no longer speak of life and death in a meaningful biblical way. On the basis of the destruction of the bond between creatureliness and time, some have even ventured to say that the deceased believer can immediately see Christ coming on the clouds of heaven.[37] The biblical perspective is entirely different. Scripture does not concern itself with an antithesis between time and eternity, but with the connection of temporality with the

---

34. *Ibid.*; cf. Popma, *Levensbeschouwing*, II, 320.

35. In this connection, compare the interpretation of the continuity of time as proof of God's slowness about his promise versus the interpretation of this continuity as indicative of God's forbearance (2 Pet. 3:9). It is striking that the NT gives no theory of time as such; nonetheless, time is by no means disqualified, since history — God's acts and man's responses — is inextricably connected with time. The NT also speaks of "the fulness of time" (Gal. 4:4) and the "acceptable time" (2 Cor. 6:2 — *kairō dektō*), as well as the abuse of time (cf. Luke 22:53 — "this is your hour, and the power of darkness"). See also R. Bijlsma, A. D. R. Polman, and J. N. Sevenster, *Chronos en Kairos. Het tijdsprobleem in het NT*, pp. 41, 49, 51; and Popma, *Inleiding in de wijsbegeerte*, p. 75.

36. Often the formulations of these theories overlap each other. Althaus, for example, does not believe that the laws of our temporality are valid "in God's eternity"; *Die Christliche Wahrheit*, II, 509. See also the distinction between *aeternitatis* and *aevum*: Popma, "De eeuwigheid Gods volgens Boethius," *Philosophia Reformata* (1957), pp. 28ff.

37. Leenhouts, *In een punt des tijds* (1945), p. 5.

ongoing course of history before the return of the Lord. The church's reflections on the intermediate state have always been predicated on the continuing absence of the day of the Lord.

A much more radical critique of the doctrine of the intermediate state is that which dismisses it as individualistic egoism that has lost all perspective on God's Kingdom. This critique has undergone some qualifications during the years: the idea that accepting the doctrine of the intermediate state *entailed* a dualistic view of the expectation has given way to the realization that, although this danger is indeed present, dualism is not strictly a necessary result of the doctrine. Thus Althaus, in his eschatological "retractions," sets forth two differing motifs: an eschatology of heaven and an eschatology of the judgment day. A complete harmonization of these two is impossible. The doctrine of the intermediate state he sees as an attempt to objectify these two in one unified concept, which detracts from the real meaning of eternity. Nevertheless, he says, the New Testament requires us to give both their due; thus, he can appreciate the songs of death and eternity, expectation of the final resurrection and the hope of heaven that are found in our hymnals.[38]

Only when justice is done to the scriptural message of communion with Christ, even through death, can the dangers that the doctrine of the intermediate state undoubtedly presents be avoided. One thing is certain: we must do away with a dualistic distinction between the two expectations, because it is precisely this dualism that has led to individualism and religious egocentrism. But it must also be understood that this phenomenon is not the necessary result of the doctrine of the intermediate state, but a result of the misunderstanding of this confession. Important, then, is the attempt to discover the harmony between these two aspects. Throughout history this attempt has always centered around the notion of a precursory aspect of the salvation in the intermediate state.

Foretaste and fulfilment

Mention of this precursory aspect of salvation in the intermediate state calls to mind the precursory aspect of blessedness in the present, earthly dispensation. The precursory nature of

38. P. Althaus, "Retraktationen zur Eschatologie," *Theologische Literaturzeitung,* LXXV (1950), 257ff. Cf. with his *Die letzten Dinge,* p. 157.

this blessedness is summed up in the biblical expression "the first-fruits of the Spirit" (cf. Rom. 8:23). The believer anticipates the fulfilment on the basis of this humble beginning. The beginning of the fulfilment is made here, in the here-and-now of this earthly existence. As we shall see, the "not yet" of the New Testament forms the background of our eschatological expectation. Apparently, there is also a kind of precursoriness in the doctrine of the intermediate state. As in life, so in death, there is tension between the "already" and the "not yet." At the same time we must recognize that the precursory element of the intermediate state differs from that of earthly life, since with respect to the intermediate state, we explicitly speak of "salvation," which will be obtained only in the hereafter. In what sense, then, can one speak of "precursoriness" in the intermediate state?

This question came to the fore in the 1300s during a controversy about the *visio Dei*, the beatific vision.[39] The teaching of Pope John XXII that the *anima separata* did not have a vision of God, that this vision would only occur after the resurrection of the body, set forth an emphasis on precursoriness that contrasted directly with the understanding of the church's tradition on the matter. The Dominicans and Pope Benedict XII understood the matter differently. In the encyclical *Benedictus Deus* the latter condemned and reversed John's ideas. Benedict held that the souls of departed believers immediately behold the divine essence. He did admit that the expectation, which still lacked its full, eschatological consummation, was incomplete, but he reacted vehemently against the interpretation of John XXII, which he felt relativized salvation too much. Over against this, the notion of a *gloria animae,* in which the vision of God was inherent, was posited.[40]

Pope John supported his interpretation by reference to Revelation 6:9: "I saw under the altar the souls of those who had been slain for the word of God." Though they received a white robe, they were told to rest a little longer (vs. 11). John

39. Relevant passages from the documents of this important controversy (Denz. 530) are cited in Berkouwer, *Sin* (Eng. tr., 1971), p. 556. A history of the controversy is provided in G. Hoffmann, *Der Streit über die selige Schau Gottes, 1331-1338* (1917). On the beatific vision see further Chapter XII below.

40. After Pope John's death, William of Occam wrote *Contra Johannem XXII,* in which he denied that the pope later did penance and recanted his views. Cf. Hoffmann, *op. cit.,* pp. 93ff.

argued that the souls cannot enter into joy without the body. His intent was to stress the unique and surprising elements of the eschatological event, but his opponents concluded that he had cast a shadow on the meaning of salvation. Durandus suggested that the white robe of the vision in Revelation was the *gloria animae* and that the period of rest mentioned in verse 11 did not detract from nor exclude the beatific vision. A comparison was drawn between the reward and the wages of a hired servant (Lev. 19:13) : it would not be withheld even for a time, but would be presented immediately to the deceased believer.[41]

Pope John's opinions were thought to be dangerous heresies. It was argued — curiously enough — that if the souls were indeed not yet saved, as John seemed to imply, they would still be susceptible to the deception of the antichrist. Clearly, the nature of the expectation was at stake here. Do the parousia and the resurrection of the body constitute the sole content of the expectation, and is all the rest a temporary "foretaste?" Or does the expectation of the intermediate state include a possibility of seeing God face to face? Historically, the Roman Catholic Church has turned its back on the ideas of John XXII, not to reject all precursoriness in the intermediate state, but to deny that salvation bears this radically relative stamp.

Nor did the Reformation escape this problem of fulfilment and precursoriness. For Protestant theology the question arose in connection with the teaching of the Catechism about "blessedness after this life" and with the interpretation of the resurrection of the body as the restoration and renewal of the whole man. Although Calvin differed sharply with Pope John, he is said to have come close to sharing the pope's views on the intermediate state.[42] In discussing John XXII and Calvin, Hoffmann cites the following remark of Calvin in the *Institutes:* "Meanwhile, since Scripture everywhere bids us wait in expectation for Christ's coming, and defers until then the crown of glory, let us be content with the limits divinely set for us: namely, that

41. Hoffmann, *op. cit.,* pp. 34f.
42. Calvin supposed that Pope John "openly asserted that souls are mortal and die along with bodies until the day of resurrection." He recommended that Rome remove John's name from the annals of "apostolic succession." Not one cardinal had taken issue with the pope, but the King of France was persuaded by the School of Paris to urge the pope to recall his proclamations (*Inst.,* IV.vii.28).

the souls of the pious, having ended the toil of their warfare, enter into blessed rest, where in glad expectation they await the enjoyment of promised glory, and so all things are held in suspense until Christ the Redeemer appear" (III.xxv.6). In his *Psychopannychia,* written during the struggle with the Anabaptists, Calvin dealt extensively with the intermediate state.[43]

Calvin disputed the doctrine of soul-sleep on the basis of the definite, unbreakable continuity that he detected in the scriptural presentation of God's work, which He will complete on the Day of Jesus Christ (Phil. 1:6; cf. Prov. 4:18). Maintaining this continuity, Calvin was confronted immediately with the problem of the nature of the intermediate state. He cautions against treating this as a matter of curiosity: "Many torment themselves overmuch with disputing as to what place the souls occupy and whether or not they already enjoy heavenly glory" (*Inst.,* III.xxv.6). For Calvin the parable of Lazarus, who was taken up into Abraham's bosom, was sufficient indication of assurance.

But there is also a specific duality of the expectation in Calvin's writings. On the one hand, Calvin spoke of the blessed assurance, the joy and peace of conscience. In death, the struggle against sin comes to an end. In death, there is a "vision of peace," but also a vision of God, when faith becomes sight. On the other hand, he maintains that this blessedness is still of a precursory nature. Within the intermediate state, the expectation still plays a significant role. The blessedness is indeed there, but the *crown* has not yet been attained. The endowment of the crown will be postponed until later, until the return of the Lord.

Thus for Calvin the whole intermediate state is focused on the expectation of what is to come — Christ's coming. His position on the intermediate state may be summed up as being concentrated in blessedness and expectation. There is no irreconcilable tension or dualism in Calvin's presentation. He speaks of blessedness, salvation, and peace, but only in dependence upon the final resurrection of the dead, in anticipation of "the happiest thing of all" (*Inst.,* III.ix.5). Ultimately, the intermediate state anticipates the day when all believers will

---

43. See also Calvin, *Brieve instruction contre les erreurs de la secte commune Anabaptistes;* T. F. Torrance, "The Eschatology of the Reformation," *Eschatology (Scottish Journal of Theology Occasional Papers),* No. 2, pp. 54ff.; *Kingdom and Church* (1956), pp. 90ff.

be called to possess the Kingdom. At that stage the fulfilment will be ushered in.[44] Calvin's stress on the bliss and salvation does not contradict his description of what was lacking. He prefers to connect these two themes of salvation and expectation. After death one sees the goal one expects, though this has not yet been achieved.

Calvin denies the identification of the expectation in the intermediate state with that of the believer on earth. On earth the believer hopes but does not see, whereas in death, the believer witnesses what he has long expected. Rest and salvation are not qualities in isolation, but are indissolubly connected to the resurrection. The patriarchs, he notes, did not receive the promise, but nevertheless saw from afar off. To detect in Calvin's position a relativization or denial of salvation — the accusation leveled against Pope John — is to miss the point that for Calvin bliss and expectation were not paradoxical but almost identical. For Calvin the bliss is made visible in the expectation of the return of Christ.

Throughout all of orthodox eschatology this matter has drawn considerable attention. Either the relationship or the difference between the intermediate state and the parousia has been emphasized. Bavinck faulted later Lutheran theology for what he thought was a tendency to erase the difference completely by speaking of full and essential beatitude in the hereafter.[45] He also detected this tendency among most theologians of the Reformed tradition, although he granted that the latter maintained the difference somewhat more effectively. In any case, much time and effort has been devoted by theologians to establishing the relationship between the "immediate" and "later" hereafter, and key words like beatitude, glory, expectation, fruition, and felicity have been used to mean very different things.

Communion with the Lord

Some have wondered whether the tensions that arise in the doctrine of the intermediate state and manifest themselves in the variety of definitions of it are not to be explained in terms of the inherent impossibility of deriving such a doctrine from the biblical expectation of the future. Is it not perhaps this

44. Cf. his commentary *ad* 1 Cor. 15:18, 19.
45. Bavinck, *GD,* IV, 587f.

inner contradiction that makes it impossible ever to clarify the connection between bliss and expectation? In any case, it is incorrect to judge that this doctrine is merely religious egocentrism and individualism that leaves no room for Christ's coming again in glory. The criticism of the doctrine itself is marked by a note of hesitancy, which can be readily explained from the nature of the New Testament teaching on this matter. Sometimes the notion of an intermediate state seems to suggest itself; other times an immediate entrance of the dead into eschatological communion with the Lord seems to be indicated. True, the intermediate state is never spoken of as an abstract, isolated eschatological theme,[46] but the New Testament makes clear that there is a limited *telos*, the horizon of the intermediate, during which the expected Lord has not yet come.

The overriding emphasis of the New Testament expectation is undoubtedly the parousia of the Lord. Yet this does not in any way detract from the attention given to the death of the individual believer. Rather, the continuation of the present dispensation and the delay of the coming of the Lord draw close attention to it. The personal horizon of one's individual lifetime comes into focus. Because this is always in the context of the broader expectation of the future, the doctrine of the intermediate state is not self-sufficient or autonomous. The intermediate state, rather than being an isolated area of strictly speculative interest, is introduced by the reality of the "time between."[47]

It should not surprise us that Scripture nowhere gives us a theoretical explication of the intermediate state. The anthropological critique of this doctrine, we noted, holds it to be beleaguered by contradictions and based on a false dichotomy of man that involves a conscious *anima separata* capable of enjoyment and anticipation. But to look for scriptural proof of the anthropological possibility of this doctrine is a vain effort.

Apparently, there is only one decisive — and for us, satisfac-

---

46. This is supported by Heb. 9:27: "it is appointed unto men once to die, and after that comes judgment." The theme here is the once-ness of the death of Christ, which is compared to man's death as unrepeatable. The phrase *metá dé toutó krisis* says nothing about the *time* of judgment. Cf. commentaries *ad loc.* by Zahn, Grosheide, Michel, and Spicq.

47. Cf. O. Cullmann's Ingersoll lecture (1954-55), "Immortality or Resurrection?", reprinted in *Christianity Today*, II (July 21 and August 18, 1958), part IV.

tory — answer to all the questions that arise: "... neither death, nor life ... nor things present, nor things to come *(oúte méllonta)* ... will be able to separate us from the love of God in Christ Jesus our Lord" (Rom. 8:38f.). This is no denial of the destructive power of death, which Paul designates elsewhere as the last enemy (1 Cor. 15:26), but an expression of trust in the continuity of our communion with the Lord, a communion of uninterrupted and unassailable power, effective also beyond death. Nowhere does Paul offer a justification of the anthropological possibility of the intermediate state. How this ongoing communion is possible in the face of death's ravages and destruction will have to remain part of God's secret counsel. But this mystery does not relativize the reality of this communion; it would be more correct to say that this reality becomes a meaningful force only if considered on the basis of the power and love of God.

What is pertinent here is our outlook on communion with the Lord, which, in the sphere of promise and expectation, counters all fears of the present time and the hereafter. In a view that is concentrated in Jesus Christ it is impossible to see the intermediate state as a shadow cast on the expectation of the parousia and the Kingdom. The New Testament does not present a "philosophy" of death, but it does speak very clearly of the promise of continuous communion. Throughout history, however, the pendulum has repeatedly swung from sharp reaction against individualism to blatant denial of the universal. Such polarizing tendencies are not to be found in Scripture. Neither the individual nor the universal suffers, because the former is always presented within the broader outlines of the latter. This can only be explained by the Lord's presence with those who pass away before His return. Cullmann is correct in observing that all the biblical images dealing with those who die before the parousia reveal that they are indeed with Christ.[48]

Christ's words to the malefactor on the cross have often been quoted in this connection: "Truly, I say to you, today you will be with me in Paradise" (Luke 23:43). In the lostness and destruction that mark our frail humanity, this promise of Christ is of profound comfort. A brilliant light is thrown into the unimaginable darkness. Face to face with the spectre of death,

48. *Ibid.* (Aug. 18, 1958), p. 15.

man is given, in simple but unmistakable terms, a perspective dispelling all doubts and removing all loneliness. Presented in these words, the promise of Paradise immediately introduces light, peace and joy. It is true, this reality is not closely defined or fully revealed, but this does not take away its reality. As Calvin suggests, speculation or curiosity about this completely misses the point, and fails to understand that in being *with Christ* this reality is completely described.[49]

There is only one eschatological expectation. Whenever the limited horizon of one's personal expectation commands exclusive attention and is removed from its context, the inevitable result is the de-eschatologizing that characterizes religious individualism. Calvin's description of the expectation as waiting for the ultimate crown is lost and the comfort relativized. De-eschatologizing obscures the biblical view of the resurrection of the body and the new earth.

Of course, such an individualistic impoverishment is not the intent of the New Testament. Even when attention is focused on the limited horizon of one's personal end, there is no trace of such individualism. We see this in the Second Letter of Peter, where the author, though he knows that "the putting off of my body *(hē apóthesis toú skēnōmatós mou)* will be soon" (1:14), still speaks of himself in the "we" of the congregation (3:13). In this connection let us look closely at the comment of Paul that is so frequently cited in discussions of the intermediate state: "My desire is to depart *and be with Christ"* (Phil. 1:23).

Inevitably Paul reflected from time to time on the historical situations in which he was carrying out his mission work. There were situations so difficult and demanding that he "despaired of life itself" and thought of himself as sentenced to death (2 Cor. 1:8f.). Again later, while in prison in Rome and sorely threatened by dangerous circumstances, he was led to reflect on matters concerning his own death, which seemed imminent. But Paul was not preoccupied with these prospects. He did not in any way individualize his expectation. Instead he called attention to the day of the Lord, writing to the congregation at Philippi that the Lord was at hand (1:6, 10; 4:5).

But the force of his circumstances was not to be denied. Paul also turned his attention to the limited horizon. In prison

49. Cf. Jeremias in *TDNT*, s.v. *parádeisos*, V, 765ff. See also Rev. 2:7.

he yearned for the congregation (1:8). He carefully considered the two possibilities: to be with Christ or to remain in the flesh serving the congregation. The former is "far better" (*pollố gár mállon kreisson*), whereas the latter is "more necessary" (*anankaióteron*). Both are conditioned by the consideration as to how Christ should be magnified, "whether by life or by death" (1:20). And Paul did not know which to choose (1:22). On the one hand was the road of martyrdom, on the other the road of working and caring for others. He was personally inclined to the gain of being with Christ.

Small wonder that this passage has played an important role in the various views of the intermediate state.[50] Telder's interpretation of the "gain" of which Paul speaks as a gain for Christ, His name, His work, and His church[51] is contradicted by the fact that Paul says precisely that it is more necessary for the sake of the church for him to remain. And his manner of speaking about the gain is intensely personal: "For to me to live is Christ, and to die is gain" (1:21). Certainly Paul was here confronted with a very difficult situation. He carefully weighed both possibilities and still could not decide. But the unity of his expectation is not destroyed. It is not easy to get a precise impression of Paul's view on these two prospects. He continues: "I know that I shall remain and continue with you all ..." (1:25). The people will glory "because of my coming to you again" (1:26). That he did not know exactly what would happen to him is illustrated by the fact that he intended to send Timothy as soon as he discovered what would become of him (2:23). Whatever his considerations may have been — and, as we have said, that is not at all clear — his reflections on his own end did not threaten to reduce the ultimate glory. Facing his own death, he nevertheless retained his vision of the crown that he and all the faithful would receive (2 Tim. 4:8).

Nowhere does the New Testament divorce the view of the limited horizon from the return of Christ, nor is there any hint of competition between the two. The view of the limited horizon arises in connection with the fact that Christ has not yet returned, a topic that we shall deal with more completely in the next chapter. Whether one speaks of this delay as post-

---

50. In addition to Cullmann's lectures cited above, see J. N. Sevenster, "Einige Bemerkungen über den 'Zwischenzustand' bei Paulus," *NT Studies,* I (1955), 294ff.; H. Thielicke, *Tod und Leben,* p. 208.
51. Cf. Telder, *op. cit.,* pp. 93f.

ponement or simply as a staying away until the appointed time has been reached, it has bearing on our discussion on the intermediate state of one's "limited horizon." Because the Lord has not yet come and the last enemy, death, still faces us, we are confronted by this whole matter of an individual outlook. The circumstances of our life and death make this a very crucial issue. Bavinck alludes to this when he notes that the apostolic fathers had no doctrine of an intermediate state at all. According to him, this matter was not raised until the church discovered that Christ would not come as soon as they had originally thought.[52] Yet the continuity of life during the time until the return of Christ is a very important consideration. It could be maintained that this concern was found in the New Testament church already. Despite their intense longing for the day of the Lord, which was thought to be very near indeed, the believers realized that their death might be nearer yet. However, this problem must be considered in relation to the broad perspective of the return of Christ. Neither the limited horizon nor the universal expectation is given exclusive attention in the New Testament.[53]

Treasure in earthen vessels

Does the New Testament say anything specific about the intermediate state? Paul's remarks in 2 Corinthians 5 about treasure in earthen vessels are often cited in this connection. Can this passage provide any light for a successful study of this state? Let us consider this passage briefly.

There are ominous dangers and hazards connected with the service one gives in the Kingdom of God. Persecution and imprisonment, bodily harm and even death are never far removed from man in this life. "For while we live we are always being given up to death for Jesus' sake" (2 Cor. 4:11). Yet in this peril lies the key. The radiance of God's promise bursts through: God "will raise us also with Jesus" (4:14). This word of courage dwarfs any danger confronting the believer (4:16-18).

---

52. *GD*, IV, 583f.
53. H. N. Ridderbos remarks that the NT "in its prophetic utterances places us much closer to the return of Christ than can be grasped by our awareness of time; which is why the New Testament does not devote nearly as much attention to the intermediate state as is currently given by the Christian community in its expectation of the future"; *Gereformeerde Weekblad*, Nov. 25, 1960.

After this broad eschatological perspective comes the more limited horizon. We are presented with the dissolution of the tabernacle and the subsequent construction of the building from God (5:1). Everything bears an expectant note: "we ... long to put on our heavenly dwelling" (vs. 2). The important question is this: what did Paul mean by his imagery of "buildings," "houses," "clothes?" Was Paul speaking of the ultimate eschatological fulfilment, the incorruptible, spiritual body of 1 Corinthians 15, or was he referring to a more limited horizon, a more personal and individual goal, which we would designate as the intermediate state?

The question becomes the more urgent when Paul adds: "So that by putting it [our heavenly dwelling] on we may not be found naked" (5:3). There is in this a longing to be clothed, as opposed to being unclothed. Because of this, many interpreters see this as a reference to the resurrection and a parallel to 1 Corinthians 15, where Paul speaks of "putting on" the imperishable and the immortal (1 Cor. 15:54). According to H. D. Wendland, Paul's words refer to the change from one mode of existence to another, from the mortality of earthly existence to life, the glory of the future in the Kingdom. The longing is to be with Christ, which will become reality only in the parousia.[54]

Contrary to this exegesis is one that maintains that Paul is referring here to a personal reunion with Christ after death. According to Cullmann, "these dead are kept with Christ even before their body is raised." This exegesis leaves room for an intermediate state, although closely related to the final resurrection.[55] It stresses the important fact that the Lord does not leave the departed to themselves, either at death or in the period before His return. The basis for all certainty and trust is Paul's confession: "whether we live or whether we die, we are the Lord's" (Rom. 14:8).

F. W. Grosheide feels that 2 Corinthians 5 makes no mention of an intermediate state.[56] Nor does he accept Wendland's idea that Paul is writing here about the fulfilment and the glorified, imperishable body. He will go no further than to say that 2 Corinthians 5 refers to the contrast between the mode

54. Wendland, *Die Briefe an die Korinther* (1954), pp. 170ff.; cf. 1 Thess. 4:17.
55. Cullmann, *Christ and Time*, p. 239.
56. Grosheide, *Comm.*, pp. 140, 144; see also *KV*, p. 70.

of earthly existence and "entering into the state of life in heaven," the change from "being away from home" to "coming home," the transition from "being in the body" to "being at home with the Lord."[57]

Why does Grosheide insist that there is no intermediate state? He speaks of "being clothed" in the sense of existence in heaven.[58] His probable meaning is that Paul does not picture an intermediate state because he presents only *one* horizon separating earthly existence from the one and only future. So, he says, for Paul judgment and salvation come immediately upon death. Thus, Grosheide sees the expectation as emphatically indivisible.

Since there is no division in the *one* expectation, we cannot find the intermediate state as an independent theme in Paul. Similarly Paul did not fix the time of the parousia, but encouraged believers to live *as if* Christ were coming immediately. This *as if* is no fiction, but a preparation for a single expectation of the future. In this single expectation the believer receives his unassailable courage (2 Cor. 4:16; 5:6).

We may speak of an intermediate state only if we guard against fantasy and objectification beyond the realm of the expectation. Surely there can be no division in this single expectation. However, it is possible, on the basis of the reality of ongoing time, the present dispensation, also to turn our attention to the limited horizon, remembering always that this attention must remain within the broader context of a single, indivisible expectation of the future.

Thus when Paul writes to the Thessalonian Christians about those who had died in the Lord, he continues to admonish the people to live in full expectation and to present the integral relatedness of all of life to communion with the coming Lord. He could reflect on the dissolution of the earthly tabernacle and the "coming home" to the Lord, and also remind the congregation of the perspective on the ultimate future: "For we must all appear before the judgment seat of Christ..." (2 Cor. 5:10).

We should consider further the much-discussed words of verse 3 — "so that by putting it on we may not be found naked." Some have interpreted this as an expression of a longing to

57. *Comm.*, pp. 145, 157.
58. *Ibid.*, p. 152; he asserts that Paul never wrote about an intermediate state.

be clothed with the new body without passing through death — that Paul did not want to die before the parousia.[59] This exegesis is not supported by the text, which does not suggest a preference as to time or situation of death.[60] It is more likely that Paul is simply making an aside here to the effect that the comfort and encouragement of the eschatological perspective would vanish if the believer were to be found naked by God. Grosheide feels that this is a passing reference to the unrenewed man who has lived his life without Christ.

In any case, this should not be interpreted as a defense of the separation of body and soul (nakedness as the bodiless existence of the *anima separata*). Paul would undoubtedly have recoiled from any arguments sustaining an anthropological dualism. Apparently, the thrust of his message is a warning to believers not to be found wanting in the day of the Lord. E. E. Ellis has seriously disputed the anthropological view, and instead compares this passage with Hebraic eschatology, in which "nakedness" refers not to a division between body and soul, but to shame and guilt: "the guilty under the glaring light of God's judgment."[61] As parallels, he adduces the account of the man who attended the wedding feast without a wedding garment (Matt. 22:11) and John's exhortation to abide in the Lord, so as not to "shrink from him in shame at his coming" (1 John 2:28; cf. Rev. 3:17). In addition to being a warning, Paul's words constitute a great comfort. Considering the journey from here to being with the Lord, Paul discounts the danger that the faith and trust of the believer will turn out to be an illusion and that he will be confronted with the sudden terror of being found naked before the face of the Lord. Paul had no doubts about his faith in the eschatological expectation, but he feared false glorying that would not correspond to the demands of God. Paul indeed wanted to be "clothed" rather than "unclothed," but this does not mean that, terror-stricken and faced with death, he feared the destruction of his body.[62]

59. So Bachmann, *Komm., ad loc.* (Zahn, *Komm.,* p. 221); cf. Wendland, *op. cit.,* p. 170; and Cullmann, "Immortality or Resurrection?" (*loc. cit.,* Aug. 18, 1958), p. 15: "He would like to be still alive at the time of Christ's return."

60. Cf. A. Oepke, in *TDNT,* s.v. *dýō,* II, 319.

61. Ellis, "II Corinthians V, 1-10 in Pauline Eschatology," *NT Studies,* VI (1960), 220ff.

62. Compare 2 Cor. 5:3 (*ou gymnoí heurethēsómetha*) with 1 Pet. 1:7 (*hína tó dokímion hymôn tês písteōs...heurethê eis épainon kai dóxan kai*

Throughout this all, we can clearly perceive a unity in the eschatological expectation. As time moves toward the parousia and the Lord has not yet come, there are numerous possibilities.[63] The expectation of the coming Lord does not exclude the more limited horizon with its "passing through," its being absent from the body (2 Cor. 5:8). Yet within these possibilities there is still only one expectation which is well-pleasing to the Lord (2 Cor. 5:9). The historical continuity in the intermediate time does not break the expectation up into two separate expectations; at least, this is not the intent of the doctrine of the intermediate state. This doctrine was primarily concerned with the reality of the promise that not even death could separate the believers from the communion with Christ, not, as sometimes has been charged, with positing an isolated fulfilment, independent of the eschaton. This is why the duality of broad and limited horizons need not lead to insoluble incongruities in the expectation of Christ's return.

Soul-sleep

So it is extremely difficult to determine whether a specific New Testament passage about the expectation relates to the broad or limited horizon. This is not surprising, for it only indicates that the one horizon is not overshadowed by the other — that in life's journey to the grave the perspective on the ultimate future does not diminish.[64]

This is the primary reason for Calvin's strong opposition to the doctrine of soul-sleep.[65] His resistance to the doctrine was not the conclusion of a carefully developed anthropological

timḗn). Neither passage deals with a crisis of certainty, but with testing as a way to freedom. See also Oepke, in *TDNT*, s.v. *gymnós*, II, 774. "It is hardly conceivable that Paul should have thought of the intervening state as one of dreadful nakedness. Cf. Phil. 1:23 *(sýn Christṓ einai)*."

63. Karl Prümm, *Diakonia pneumatos. Der 2. Korintherbrief als Zugang zur apostolischen Botschaft* (1960), p. 170.

64. When Barth says that "the NT Christians never asked independently concerning the being or state of men in death, or tried to find an answer in the postulate of an intermediate state," but simply accepted Jesus' message that He was the resurrection of the body (*CD*, III/2, 639), he is opposing the doctrine of the intermediate state (as independent) that we also reject.

65. Calvin's rejection parallels the strong words of the Scotch Confession, Art. XXII: "not that they sleep, and come to a certain oblivion, as some fantastics do affirm. . . ."

argument about the possibility of the existence of an *anima separata* as a way in which God sustained the believer after the dissolution of the earthly tabernacle.[66] Nor was it a reflection of an antithesis between ontology and personalism, in which the personalistic is seen as casting a shadow over the reality of continuous communion with the Lord in the hereafter. One must resist coming to a merely theoretical understanding of God's preserving work in the life of the departed, and thus obliterating the New Testament message of the comfort of being with Christ.[67] Calvin emphasized — correctly — that the Scriptures do not tell us any more. The doctrine of soul-sleep, with all its theoretical speculation, cannot be based on what Scripture has to say about "falling asleep."[68]

Bavinck points out that, on the surface, the testimony of Scripture appears to favor a doctrine of soul-sleep in the way it talks about dying.[69] Nevertheless, he contends, any attempt to claim scriptural support for this doctrine is illegitimate. Scripture, he feels, focuses on the *change* from life into death, and does not deal with an analysis of the condition of death. There is nothing particularly Christian about the notion of "soul-sleep"; it is found outside the Bible,[70] and even in Scripture,

66. An example of such an anthropological view is found in Thomas Aquinas, who defended the possibility of *anima separata;* cf. *Summa contra Gentiles,* II, 81. Bavinck also speaks of the possibility that the soul "can if necessary continue activity without the body" (*GD,* IV, 594).

67. In my conclusions on the intermediate state as God's secret (*Man: the Image of God,* p. 265), it was not my intention to explain this state in terms of a distinction between "heart" and "functional aspects." Cf. J. A. Heyns, *Die onsterflikheit van die siel* (1959), p. 53.

68. For Luther's views on the intermediate state and soul-sleep, see Althaus, *Die letzten Dinge,* pp. 146ff.; and *Unsterblichkeit und ewige Sterben nach Luther. Zur Auseinandersetzung mit Carl Stange* (1930); C. Stange, *Das Ende aller Dinge,* pp. 180ff. The difficulty in Luther is his constant use of the analogy of natural sleep to the "sleep of death." (Many Roman Catholic theologians thought that Luther supported soul-sleep.) But Luther was primarily concerned with *peace* and *rest,* not with *unconsciousness.* See Calvin's discussion of "falling asleep" in *Psychopannychia,* especially regarding Acts 7:60; John 11:11; 1 Thess. 4:13; and Job 14:7-12.

69. *GD,* IV, 539ff.; cf. 594.

70. See Oepke in *TDNT,* s.v. *katheúdō,* III, 431-37; Bultmann in *TDNT,* s.v. *thánatos,* II, 14n.: "*Koimásthai* is used for the sleep of death from the time of Homer."

it appears in various contexts.[71] Only in the Gospels is a special meaning attached to "falling asleep." Even there, the important thing is not the word "sleep" as such, but rather the way in which Christ uses it in an environment of death. Where death has obviously come, Christ speaks of "sleeping."[72] But precisely because the use of the word "sleep" presents the believer with the power of the Lord, which itself "relativizes" death, we can see that Scripture is dealing with death on an entirely different level from the doctrine of soul-sleep. This level takes the believer facing death to the promise of dying *in the Lord* (cf. Rev. 14:13 — *hoi en kyriō apothnēskontes*). Death is seen in the context of the Lord of life.

What meaning, then, should be given to the phrase "falling asleep?" It might be used as an analogy to death to portray the cessation of strife and all other activities of life. But there is a deeper, New Testament usage of the word to refer to dying *in the Lord*. And in this case, these words assume a meaning that is the exact opposite of the doctrine of soul-sleep. In this insight into the victory of the Lord over death, man is directed, not to a study of death, but to an understanding of life.

Accordingly, the doctrine of soul-sleep has become an anthropological argument in direct opposition to the confession of the victory of the Lord over death. It should be dismissed by the church as a distortion of the secret of God.

Legitimate twofold expectation

Again we must emphasize the dangers of individualism and egocentrism. Even if one feels that Kuyper was generalizing when he contended that the majority of Christians do not think beyond their own grave (see above, note 4), the dangers involved here must be recognized. One can become so absorbed in his own existence that the great expectation of the future is obscured or completely erased. This sort of individualism not only affects the expectation of the future, but seizes the whole of life as its prey, throwing man back into the restrictive bonds of sin, which inevitably stifle the newness of life. The perspective

71. Paul speaks of "falling asleep" *(koimāsthai)* in a general sense; e.g., 1 Cor. 7:39; 11:30; also of "falling asleep in Christ" (1 Cor. 15:18; 1 Thess. 4:13-15). The word is also used by blasphemers: 2 Pet. 3:4.
72. Cf. Matt. 9:24: "the girl is not dead, but sleeping." Also John 11:11, 13: "...Lazarus has fallen asleep.... Now Jesus had spoken of his death." On this passage see also Berkouwer, *Man: The Image of God*, pp. 245ff.

is reduced to the narrow "ego," the stress falls on the self, and there is barely any time or interest or attention for the coming Kingdom and the resurrection of the body. There is then no further awareness of Paul's warning: "Let each of you look not only to his own interests, but also to the interests of others" (Phil. 2:4). The prayer to *our* Father that His Kingdom come becomes a strange and foreign incantation.

One might investigate to what extent criticism of the doctrine of the intermediate state has been motivated and strengthened by the symptoms of individualism that have always been present among Christians. But it is more useful to examine how strenuously the biblical proclamation resists such individualistic perversions and shows that the various aspects of the single expectation are and will remain indissoluble and irreducible.

First of all, it is impossible to dismiss the salvation of the individual in the name of the community and the coming Kingdom. Nowhere does the New Testament criticize or relativize concern for the individual's existence and future, and any critique of individualism that ignores this will be a meaningless protest. Yet within the personal perspective, the universal goal of the Kingdom remains. To oppose the "personal" or "individual" to the "universal" or "cosmic" is to create a false dichotomy. The universal encapsulates the personal; and during the time when the Lord has not yet returned, attention must also be focused on the life and death of the individual.[73] In death, as well as in life, the individual's expectation is still typified by the "not yet" of the unfulfilled condition. But these two unfulfilled conditions are not identical: the earthly one is filled with sorrow and struggle, guilt, and the threats characteristic of life on earth. It should not surprise anyone that attempts to elucidate all these things leave much to be desired. Yet this is not due to the problematics of time, its present reality and its supposed nonexistence in the future, but to the incomprehensibility of God's providence.

The New Testament describes the glory of those who have died in the Lord in the same way as it describes that of those who remain behind, that is, as being with Christ. These words of encouragement do not in any way endanger the outlook on the future. They are founded in Him who is, was, and is yet

---

73. Cullmann is to the point here: "The dead in Christ share in the tension of the interim time"; "Immortality or Resurrection?", *loc. cit.* (Aug. 18, 1958), p. 15.

to come, without denying the individual his proper place. The limited horizon is perhaps best illustrated in the case of individual martyrdom, but it requires only a reading of the Book of Revelation to realize that martyrdom is a far cry from individualism. Even these incidents of personal suffering are always oriented to the broad horizon of the rule of Jesus Christ.

To conclude: the legitimacy of the concept of a twofold expectation depends entirely on how one looks at it. One can speculate about it and, on the basis of an anthropological analysis, offer a more or less detailed concept of an intermediate state. But this leads to a number of problems that are of no concern to the New Testament. One is not justified, it would seem, in formulating theoretical constructs about the way God permanently sustains the lasting communion and calls to rest the deceased believers. Who would pretend to be able to add anything to the proclamation of the New Testament? How could one offer greater comfort than that given by Romans 8? What could surpass the brilliant light of the Word casting its ray into the frightful total darkness in which man finds himself? Whoever deems this insufficient, preferring to step outside the real meaning of expectation and construct an elaborate (and necessarily mystical) concept of the state of the deceased, finds himself on shaky ground.[74]

These conclusions are not tantamount to skepticism. We must always recognize the unity of expectation. By the very fact of this unity all religious individualism and depersonalization is excluded. This unity is always concentrated in Christ Himself. Christ, as the object of the expectation, is the sole guarantee that the expectation does not degenerate into religious egocentrism. The reality and presence of the Lord, who has triumphed over the demonic forces, reveals the inadequacy of certain theories and practices developed by man in his excessive concern about the intermediate state. One thing is certain: the condition of "being with Christ" does not relativize the expectation, but reinforces it. A legitimate doctrine of the intermediate state, despite what some have thought, need not shut the door to true perspectives on the coming Kingdom of the Lord, just as it need not blur the reality of the new earth in which there is righteousness in the presence of Christ. In view

74. K. J. Popma, *Levensbeschouwing*, II, 258ff., contends that every anthropologically oriented problematics of death must end in dualism.

of all this, the age-old dilemma concerning individual and universal horizons recedes into oblivion and is replaced by the more sure and lasting confession: I believe in the resurrection of the body.

CHAPTER THREE

CRISIS OF DELAY?

W E HAVE SEEN that our reflection on the intermediate
state must take into account the fact that Christ has not
yet come. As long as human history continues, we are confronted
by the problem of individual dying — "falling asleep" in the
Lord — before the parousia. We concluded in the last chapter
that our attention to this may not absorb our broader expectation of the coming Lord; in other words, none of us must
become preoccupied with his own death. Individual eschatology must always remain in a direct line with general eschatology to prevent us from falling into an individualistic depreciation of the broad goal of the future.

Recent theology has featured renewed discussion of this problem of individual eschatology in the continuity of time. It is
argued that the New Testament had no need for attention
to this horizon, since its constant emphasis is the *nearness* of the
Lord's Kingdom. So we are brought face-to-face with the theme
of the *delay* of the parousia, a theme that has been the concern of many twentieth-century scholars. Whereas the previous
chapter dealt with what has been called the intermediate *state,*
this chapter is concerned with the intermediate *time* — the present dispensation — and the seemingly long duration before the
return of the Lord. Does this extended period of time contradict the New Testament message of the *nearness* of the parousia?
Ought we not, in all honesty, speak of an eschatological perplexity or embarrassment here? We referred earlier to Bavinck's
statement that the early fathers taught no doctrine of an intermediate state because they thought of the parousia as close
at hand. Whether or not Bavinck's specific historical analysis
here is correct, we must look closely at what follows from it:
that at first the object of eschatology was only the parousia —
seen as close at hand — but that later this attention to the par-

ousia could not help being influenced by the fact that the Lord had not yet, in fact, returned.

Consistent eschatology: the delay of the parousia

Ever since Albert Schweitzer gave currency to the expression *Parusieverzögerung* — delay of the parousia — this issue has come to play an important role in eschatological thought. The meaning of Schweitzer's expression is clear: in the mind of the expectant New Testament community the coming of Jesus Christ on the clouds was delayed. Those who see this delay as the central problem of the New Testament proclamation judge it to be something more than a mere process of delay. They think of it rather as a not-coming-to-pass or a not-being-fulfilled of Christ's return. They do continue to speak of "delay" in order to remain faithful to the expectations and experiences of the early church. Such conclusions, of course, have a great bearing on the whole nature of the eschatological expectation. Schweitzer wrote that "the whole history of 'Christianity' down to the present day, that is to say, the real inner history of it, is based on the delay of the Parousia, the non-occurrence of the Parousia, the abandonment of eschatology, the progress and completion of the 'de-eschatologising' of religion which has been connected therewith."[1]

Obviously, Schweitzer was talking about something more than a mere delay. "Delay" does not mean cancellation, but simply implies that what is expected has been postponed until some future date. Still, a delay, particularly a long one, can raise serious doubts about the actual fulfilment. Jewish wisdom literature realized that "hope deferred makes the heart sick" (Prov. 13:12). If the delay of the parousia is interpreted as a cancellation of the promise, the hearts of the believers are indeed made sick and their expectation seriously jeopardized. This makes the whole discussion crucial. The New Testament did not look on expectation as a projection into the future, but as a response to God's promise. The correlation between this promise and its fulfilment is indestructible. The whole direction of the Christian community has always been toward the future, based, not on some futuristic fantasy, but on the promise of the living God. Were, now, the return of Christ to be cancelled, the result would not merely be disappointment or

---

1. *The Quest of the Historical Jesus*, p. 358.

disillusionment but a crisis of faith in the veracity and dependability of God. The Scriptures rule out this possibility in the strongest of terms (Num. 23:19; cf. 1 Sam. 15:29; Ps. 89:35; Josh. 21:45; 23:14). The word of God remains the truth against all lies on into the future. The relationship between Yahweh and Samuel — "He let none of his words .fall to the ground" (1 Sam. 3:19) — is typical of all of God's dealings with man. Faith rests on the irreversible dependability of God, and the Bible resists any attempt to cast shadows of doubt on this (cf. Jer. 28:9, 15, 17; Rom. 9:6; Titus 1:2; Heb. 6:15, 18).

So if delay were to mean cancellation, eschatology would be in grievous difficulty. Such an interpretation of delay is precisely the theme of so-called consistent eschatology. Noting that the entire New Testament points consistently to the immediate coming of the Kingdom, the champions of this view call attention to the impasse brought about by the delay and the crisis resulting from the failure to realize what had been awaited with such certainty. The whole history of Christianity is then seen in the light of this delay and the various efforts that have been made to explain it.[2]

According to consistent eschatology, the New Testament expectation is, under the influence of Jesus' preaching, radically eschatological. The Kingdom is seen as very close at hand. Through the transcendent working of God, the present dispensation will soon be ended, replaced by the glorious mani-

---

2. A great deal — both pro and con — has been written about consistent eschatology. Besides Schweitzer, *op. cit.*, are F. Buri, *Die Bedeutung der NT Eschatologie für die neuere protestantische Theologie* (1935); and "Das Problem der ausgebliebenen Parusie," *Vox theologica*, XVIII (1948), 104-26; M. Werner, *The Formation of Christian Dogma* (Eng. tr., 1957); and *Der protestantische Weg des Glaubens*, I (1955), pp. 97ff.; E. Grässer, *Das Problem der Parusie-verzögerung in den synoptischen Evangelien und in der Apostelgeschichte* (1957). Among critical evaluations of consistent eschatology are O. Cullmann, *Christ and Time* (Eng. tr., 1950); "Das wahre durch die ausgebliebene Parusie gestellte NT Problem," *Theologische Zeitschrift*, III (1947), 177ff.; and a review of Grässer, *op. cit.*, entitled "Parusie-verzögerung und Urchristentum," *Theologische Litteraturzeitung*, LXXXIII (1958); W. Michaelis, *Der Herr verzieht nicht die Verheissung* (1942); F. Flückiger, *Der Ursprung des christlichen Dogmas. Eine Auseinandersetzung mit A. Schweitzer und M. Werner* (1955); H. Schuster, "Die konsequente Eschatologie in der Interpretation des NT, kritisch betrachtet," *Zeitschrift für die NT Wissenschaft*, XLVII (1956), 1-25; Barth, *CD*, III/2, 468, 485f., 497, 509; J. Gnilka, "Parusie-verzögerung und Naherwartung in den synoptischen Evangelien und in der Apostelgeschichte," *Catholica*, XIII (1959), 277-90.

festation of the Kingdom of God. So there can be no such thing as a peaceful development of history, an opportunity and time for the Christian life, a history of the Christian church, or a development of a policy for Christian mission. There can only be a view of the immediate time. The words of Christ were not intended to order life on earth but to be an interim ethic for the brief time before the realization of the coming Kingdom, requiring radical and uncompromising decisions.

In the light of this imminent expectation — or *Naherwartung* — the problem of the *delay* becomes painfully evident. The first delay was when Christ's own expectations were not fulfilled.[3] After Jesus' death, the delay became the problem of the whole Christian community. That the parousia did not come was the key that consistent eschatology used to unlock the secrets of the history of the church and Christianity. The phenomenon of Christianity, its history and dogma, had to be explained in terms of this central and disillusioning problem of the delay, and this led to the de-eschatologizing of religion.[4]

It is interesting to note how absolutely the proponents of consistent eschatology are convinced of the self-evidence of their fundamental thesis. Schweitzer wanted to take seriously everything in the New Testament, and he took Matthew and Mark to be far more reliable than the champions of historical criticism had thought. He pointed out that Mark 13 clearly taught that the Kingdom of God was to be expected within the lifetime of the first generation of believers. Jesus Himself referred to the brevity of this interim period, and the apostolic witness was to the same effect (Matt. 10:23; Mark 9:1; 13:30; Phil. 4:5; James 5:8; 1 Cor. 7:29, 31). The end of all ages was thought to be at hand.

These passages cannot reckon with a long duration and

3. Schweitzer considered the first "postponement of the Parousia" to be found in Matt. 10:23; *op. cit.*, p. 358. After that, Christ supposedly shifted His emphasis to the coming of the Kingdom through His death. On this, see H. B. Knossen, *Op zoek naar de historische Jezus. Een studie over Albert Schweitzers visie op Jezus' leven* (1960), ch. I; and H. A. Babel, *La pensée d'Albert Schweitzer. Sa signification pour la theologie et la philosophie contemporaine* (1954), ch. I.

4. It is important for Schweitzer's personal view of the gospel as actual proclamation that he did not lose the essence with the temporal form (*Naherwartung*, late-Jewish eschatological concepts from Daniel and Enoch). Cf. Schuster's comments (*op. cit.*, p. 22) about Schweitzer's statement that "the late-Jewish Messianic world-view is only the crater out of which the flame of the eternal religion of love blazes forth."

continuity of history as we know it. They are loaded with a compelling and appealing dynamic and actuality without which the New Testament is meaningless. From such an exegetical conclusion one can understand the impasse in which Christian faith was caught as history continued. Every passing day contradicted the expectation; faith in a future coming of Christ slid into the abyss.[5]

So it is not surprising that the theme of the delay of the parousia enjoys so much attention in our time. It arose in reaction to the oversimplifications of evolutionistic eschatology, with the discovery that what New Testament eschatology is all about is the coming Kingdom and the somber warnings of fire to be cast on the earth (Luke 12:49). The consequences of this discovery were drawn, and the more seriously the *Naherwartung* of the New Testament was taken, the more emphasis fell on the depth of the impasse. From the combination of these two basic motifs — the radical expectation of the nearness of the parousia and the evidently contradictory continuity of history — the proponents of consistent eschatology derive the irrefutability of their view.

It is understandable that from this point of view one can detect tendencies to de-eschatologize the expectation. At the same time one might also speak of "historicizing," not in the sense of abandoning the expectation because of the crisis of delay, but in the sense of developing a completely new concept of history, which originally had been conceived of as nothing more than an abbreviated pause until the reappearance of the Lord. Attention was directed to the real space and time in which life had its being. This new interpretation did not take the form of resignation or submission to the factual course of history, but the form of a new view of duration.

The vacuum that was created by the delay was filled up by a process of historicizing. According to consistent eschatology, this filling-up process has its origins already in the New Testament and comes to the fore in the early church. It is in the Gospel records of Jesus' death: the curtain of the temple was torn, the earth shook, rocks were split, tombs were opened, and the bodies of the saints were raised (Matt. 27:51-53). This,

---

5. H. Joachim Schoeps concludes: "There can be no question that the objective course of world history has belied New Testament eschatology"; · *Paul: The Theology of the Apostle in the Light of Jewish Religious History* (Eng. tr., 1961), p. 123.

according to Werner, was the end, the breakthrough of the Kingdom of God, a completely eschatological event, portrayed in
terms of the end of the world in Jewish apocalyptic. Later, the
Christians did not know what to make of all this. When it became apparent that the end had not come after all, these events
came to be interpreted as signs that pointed to the real end.
Thus, these gripping events were de-eschatologized. Their burning eschatological witness lost all interest and meaning, and they
were ignored as an incomprehensible riddle.[6]

This was only the beginning. Werner goes on to explain all
Christian dogma as merely a "filling up" of this vacuum. The
crisis of this unfulfilled expectation is accompanied by a completely different understanding of the gospel. The striking Pauline view — "the old has passed away; behold, the new has come"
(2 Cor. 5:17) — is gone, replaced by history operating on a horizontal plane. The church is no longer the community of the
end-time in the last generation; instead, under constraint of the
continuing delay of the parousia, it resumes historical continuity.[7] Thus, eschatological concern is replaced by a new interest in what will happen in the "intermediate time." The "two
ages" scheme, involving the relationship between present dispensation and parousia, can no longer function as it was intended, and de-eschatologizing goes on in the time line of history.

It was not only in this one New Testament passage that the
symptoms of the delay of the parousia were thought to be
found. Consistent eschatology discovered symptoms of the delay of the Kingdom in all kinds of Scripture passages. Grässer,
commenting on the Synoptic Gospels, remarked that "the fact
of the delay of the parousia is actually everywhere presupposed."[8]
Numerous scriptural references were claimed to support — directly or indirectly — the view of consistent eschatology.[9] Of particular significance for consistent eschatology is Christ's correction to those who supposed that the Kingdom would immediately *(parachrēma)* appear, in the parable of the nobleman
going to a far country to receive kingly power for himself (Luke
19:11f.). In all these references the New Testament supposedly

6. Werner, *op. cit.*, p. 98.
7. *Ibid.*, pp. 636-40.
8. *Op. cit.*, pp. 2, 77.
9. Among them, Matt. 25:5 *(chronizontos dé toú nymphíou)*; Luke 12:45
(chronizei ho kýriós mou érchesthai); Luke 20:49 *(apedémēsen chrónous
hikanoús)*.

attests to the impasse of the delay that was present in the early church (cf. Luke 21:9 — "the end will not be at once"). The church settled down to a long wait after its original expectation of the nearness and immediacy of the parousia had been revised to allow for a distant future.

Some recent theologians consider the impasse caused by the delay to be particularly evident in the peculiar structure of Luke and Acts, finding in Luke's "theology" a dramatic shift from Matthew's and Mark's, inasmuch as Luke clearly gives attention to the delay of the parousia.[10] His theology shows signs of historicizing, of allowing for a "history of salvation" on a horizontal plane, by elbowing the original expectation out of the foreground and calling attention to the church's role in and mission message to the world.

Grässer speaks of Luke's "uneschatological way of thinking," whereby Christendom becomes incorporated into world history.[11] The Kingdom of God is no longer a transcendent, apocalyptic act of God, close at hand. It becomes a realm of peace and rest, instead of a divine spectacular full of surprises. Discounting the delay, Luke begins to think in terms of the "spatial" linearity of time. The apocalyptic expectation gives way to the theme of the history of salvation — promise-fulfilment. The eschaton still has a place in this theme, but its place is now on the periphery.[12] A new time — *post Christum* — has been ushered in. What started out as a short interim period has become an entirely new age in which the Word and the extended tasks of the church begin to function between the two advents.[13] Moreover, what was allegedly begun in the Gospel of Luke reaches its climax in the Acts of the Apostles. The very name of this book indicates a new period of historicizing. "Acts": there is history in all its ups and downs. Only a person who reckons with the continuing of the world could undertake such a book.[14] After

---

10. This particular interpretation is found in H. Conzelmann, *The Theology of St. Luke* (Eng. tr., 1960), pp. 95-136; and "Zur Lukasanalyse," *Zeitschrift für Theologie und Kirche*, XLIX (1952), 16-33; E. Lohse, "Lukas als Theologe der Heilsgeschichte," *Evangelische Theologie*, XIV (1954); P. Vielhauer, "Zum 'Paulinismus' der Apostelgeschichte," *Evangelische Theologie*, X (1950); and Grässer, *op. cit.*, pp. 210ff.
11. *Op. cit.*, p. 211.
12. E. Haenchen writes: "Although the apocalyptic tradition still exists, Luke no longer looks out on the world with the eyes of an apocalypticist"; *Die Apostelgeschichte* (1956), p. 89.
13. Grässer, *op. cit.*, pp. 199f.
14. Vielhauer, *op. cit.*, p. 13.

Acts 1, the author does not deal with the eschaton any more. Grässer points out that the Kingdom is mentioned seven times in Acts, but there is no mention of the coming of the Kingdom, because that has lost its *actuality*. What is central is the mission of the church: the parousia is on the outer fringes. Luke has already thought in terms of "all that are far off" (Acts 2:39) ; consequently, he becomes the theologian of the history of salvation.[15] Pentecost "is regarded by Luke as the birthday of the Church."[16]

In this special attention to Luke and the shift in the view of the eschaton we encounter one of the most important problems of eschatology: is it proper to speak of "historicizing" as de-eschatologizing?[17] Attention to the church in history is undeniably one of Luke's themes. But is this attention a revision of the original expectation of the first generation of Christians? Some think so. The *kairos,* they claim, is not at hand in the writings of Luke: when Luke speaks of the time as "at hand," it is the deceiver speaking (Luke 21:8; cf. Matt. 24:23-26).[18] This is another Gospel with its own peculiar message. The end is divorced from the historical events, which demand all the attention. Therefore, it is concluded, de-eschatologizing always goes hand in glove with historicizing.[19]

It is not only consistent eschatology that has pointed to a difference in the theology of the Gospel of Luke and Acts. Whereas consistent eschatology stresses the spiritual crisis brought on by the delay of the parousia, Sevenster, for example, argues that the really significant thing in the Lukan writings is the out-

15. Grässer, *op. cit.,* pp. 210-15.
16. E. Lohse, in *TDNT,* s.v. *pentēkostē̂,* VI, 50; cf. Vielhauer, *op. cit.,* p. 12: "Eschatology has moved from the center of the Pauline faith to the end and become a *locus de novissimis.*" Conzelmann claims that for Luke the length of the present dispensation is in principle a matter of indifference; "Zur Lukasanalyse," *loc. cit.,* p. 31.
17. In this connection see Haenchen's discussion of the end of Acts; *op. cit.,* p. 664. Haenchen feels that Luke's failure to report the death of Paul is related to his desire to demonstrate the benevolence of the Roman Empire in allowing the proclamation of the gospel.
18. Marxsen comments: "He can scarcely express more pointedly the degree to which he knows he is removed from the *kairós*"; *Mark the Evangelist. Studies on the Redaction History of the Gospel* (Eng. tr., 1969), p. 191.
19. According to Conzelmann, Luke accepted much of Mark, but was original in that his basic motif is the delay of the parousia; "Zur Lukasanalyse," p. 19.

pouring of the Holy Spirit.[20] Acts deals with the consolidation
of the church, with the creation of structures "that may have
to serve for a long time." But then Sevenster comes to a conclusion wholly different from that of consistent eschatology. He
does not see Luke's attention to the historical perspective as
symptomatic of a crisis of delay. After all, he argues, nowhere
does Acts allude to an existing or forthcoming spiritual crisis.
So Luke should not be placed in opposition to any original
expectation of an imminent return, since in the New Testament the notion that the parousia was at hand "certainly did
not play the dominant role attributed to it by consistent eschatology." The difference thus lies in the question whether
the attention to history and the church can be called a symptom
of de-eschatologizing and historicizing that downgrades the eschaton to an irrelevant concluding chapter.

For consistent eschatology the latter is the case. It proceeds
from a tension between a vertical miracle of God and the horizontal course of history in human events. These two are mutually
exclusive. The former represents the eschaton; the latter, seen
as unalterably opposed to the former, represents de-eschatologizing. Man and the church, being in history, were forced to de-
eschatologize. This constituted the crisis of the delay, which was
also the crisis of man.[21]

But does the New Testament really present a crisis or impasse or disappointment? Undoubtedly the fact that the Lord
has not yet come plays a considerable role, and there are surely
traces in the New Testament that indicate that His coming
had been expected sooner. But it does not necessarily follow from
this that a crisis is inevitable. A crisis will arise only if faith
in God's promises about the parousia is lost.[22] Understandably,
the critics of consistent eschatology have often used this as their
point of departure. According to Cullmann, the problem of the

20. Sevenster, "Handelingen en het probleem der nabije parousie," in
Arcana Revelata (1951), pp. 19, 121ff.
21. Cf. Conzelmann, *The Theology of St. Luke*, p. 14: "Luke is confronted
by the situation in which the Church finds herself by the delay of
the Parousia and her existence in secular history, and he tries to come
to terms with the situation by his account of historical events." See
further on Luke and eschatology, H. J. Cadbury, *The Making of Luke-
Acts* (1926; repr. 1958), pp. 282-96.
22. See Bornkamm, "Die Verzögerung der Parusie," in *In Memoriam Ernst
Lohmeyer* (1951), pp. 116, 125f.

New Testament expectation is not the delay as such, but the fact that in spite of this delay — which was apparent to the earliest Christians — the specific original Christian hope was not shaken.[23] Cullmann speaks of delay, but not in the sense that it obscures the expectation. He does not see de-eschatologizing in the New Testament, because the moment of time that was most important for the New Testament was the resurrection of Jesus Christ from the grave. Because salvation has already come through the death and resurrection of Christ, the problem of the date of the parousia can no longer be of decisive importance.

The New Testament does present a pronounced expectation of the future. It is in no way a futuristic expectation, but is founded squarely on the reality that has already come.[24] As long as one remains faithful to this fundamental truth, delay cannot possibly lead to a crisis. The portals to the future, in a historical sense, remain open. The faith of the church was reconciled to the "delay" because the church was acquainted with the events of cross and resurrection that had ushered in a new time.[25]

Cullmann illustrates his criticism of consistent eschatology with an oft-quoted example from World War II. The Allied victory was already implicit in the invasion of Normandy heralding the beginning of the decisive battle; the end had only to be *realized*.[26] Similarly, the community of believers, living out of faith in the accomplished work of Jesus Christ, could no longer lapse into a crisis of delay, as was believed by consistent eschatology. This comparison is central in Cullmann's thinking, and he sees it as sounding the death-knell for consistent eschatology. The proponents of consistent eschatology, naturally, think otherwise. Cullmann's illustration has strengthened, not lessened, the intensity of the dispute. F. Buri argues that Cullmann's analogy breaks down at the crucial point, for as time passes and a victory-day does not come after a battle that is thought decisive, the

23. Cf. "Das wahre NT Problem," *loc. cit.,* p. 177.
24. Cf. Cullmann, "The Return of Christ," in *The Early Church* (Eng. tr., 1956); also *Christ and Time.* On Cullmann, cf. Jean Frisque, *Oscar Cullmann. Une théologie de l'histoire du salut* (1960), esp. pp. 85ff.
25. Cf. also W. G. Kümmel, *Promise and Fulfilment* (Eng. tr., 1957), pp. 64ff.; Schuster, *op. cit.,* pp. 8ff.; Flückiger, *op. cit., passim.*
26. "The decisive battle in a war may already have occurred in a relatively early stage of the war, and yet the war still continues." *Christ and Time,* p. 84.

decisiveness of the battle begins to be called more and more into question.[27]

It is incorrect to attribute Buri's reluctance to accept Cullmann's illustration to the difference between his understanding of time and Cullmann's. In fact, the longer one reflects on Cullmann's analogy, the less convincing it becomes. On D-Day the strength of the Allied military position was apparent to all. It was from this strength that the people took courage. But the certainty of ultimate victory, which is the focal point of the analogy, was still very much in question. Marsh correctly criticizes Cullmann's illustration for its failure to account for "the position of men in an occupied territory, who in spite of its having been liberated, still live, for lack of news or lack of conviction about the news, as if their country were under the dominion of the occupying power."[28] In Paul's eyes the powers were dethroned, and the victory obtained on the cross was not a "decisive" but a "final" victory — not D-Day, but V-Day. Admittedly, Cullmann's analogy breaks down at these points. Yet one must honor his intention to emphasize that the promise is not nebulous, but founded concretely in God's work *in history*. From this historical perspective, the promise has obtained its certainty and has become the stimulant for the Christian community. The central problem in the discussion of consistent eschatology is the question of the relationship between the "already" — the *fait accompli* of Christ's death and resurrection — and the "not yet" — the unfulfilled condition. Consistent eschatology doubts that the "deferred hope" that makes the heart sick can still be significant for the life and practice of the Christian community. It doubts that this hope and expectation is possible at all in the continuity of history, thinking it would instead degenerate into the plaintive cry of the servant: "My master is delayed in coming" (Luke 12:45).

This, of course, does not solve the problems of consistent eschatology. We must pay close attention to its preponderant stress on what it calls the *Naherwartung* of the Kingdom in the New Testament. It is not only in the Synoptic Gospels that this expectation of imminence is found, but also in the apostle Paul. According to Schoeps, the epistles of Paul and the central consciousness out of which they are written are mis-

27. "Das Problem der ausgebliebenen Parusie," *loc cit.*, p. 117.
28. *The Fulness of Time*, p. 178.

understood unless one recognizes "that Paul only lives, writes, and preaches, in the unshakeable conviction that his generation represents the last generation of mankind."[29] Others detect a certain development in Paul's thinking with regard to the time of the parousia as it became evident to him that the Lord would not come again within his generation. In other words, when it appeared that death had not yet been defeated, Paul became preoccupied with a possible delay and the meaning of intermediate time. Cullmann states that Paul "in his later letters altered his original opinion, expressed in 1 Thess. 4:15, that he would still be living at the Parousia,"[30] citing in this connection 2 Corinthians 5:1ff. and Philippians 1:23. But where consistent eschatology finds a "crisis of delay," Cullmann maintains that *in principle* nothing has changed in Paul's teachings. The Archimedean point in Paul's thinking is not, according to Cullmann, a futuristic one, but one founded squarely on what has already occurred.[31]

So even this broad outline of the discussion of the delay makes it evident that we must examine closely the relationship between the expectation of faith and the fact that the Lord has not yet returned.

Delay in the Old and New Testaments

A word of caution is in order here. To speak of a "delay" presupposes the background of a completely fixed period of time. Delay then consists in crossing the boundaries of this fixed period of time. Consistent eschatology maintains that the original New Testament expectation proceeded from such a concept of a fixed period of time, deriving this original expectation from Jesus' preaching. But it must be kept in mind that the concept of delay can also result from an incorrect interpretation of God's dealings in history.

Already in the Old Testament we encounter the idea that the fulfilment of God's promises had been delayed, if not altogether cancelled. When Israel, faced with ominous threats and utter despair, begged for the fulfilment of God's promises

---

29. Schoeps, *Paul,* p. 102, where he refers, among other things, to Paul's recommendation of celibacy in 1 Cor. 7:24ff.
30. *Christ and Time,* p. 88.
31. On Pauline eschatology, see also G. Vos, *The Pauline Eschatology* (1930; repr. 1961); M. Werner, *The Formation of Christian Dogma* (Eng. tr., 1957), esp. pp. 183ff.; Schweitzer, *The Mysticism of Paul the Apostle.*

and fulfilment did not come, even when the eleventh hour appeared, it was faced with some seemingly serious inconsistencies. Against the superior might of its enemies, it became uncertain and tended to doubt that God had remembered His people. "I say to God my rock: 'Why hast thou forgotten me? Why go I mourning because of the oppression of the enemy?'" (Ps. 42:9). A crisis in the expectation threatened, though trust and hope in God finally surmounted the doubt (vs. 11). Learning that God would not manifest Himself, Israel was driven to ask: "We do not see our signs; there is no longer any prophet, and there is none among us who knows how long. How long, O God, is the foe to scoff? Is the enemy to revile thy name forever? Why dost thou hold back thy hand, why dost thou keep thy right hand in thy bosom?" (Ps. 74:9-11). The "how long?" presupposes the continuity of a period of time that is no longer comprehended by the people and suggests a delay in the saving work of Yahweh (cf. Ps. 89:46, 49). There appears to be a waiting and watching but no fulfilment: "'Watchman, what of the night?' The watchman says: 'Morning comes and also the night'" (Isa. 21:11f.). For Israel, the plea "how long?" implied that God had forgotten it and did not hear its cry (Hab. 1:2).

The grave doubts that arose under these circumstances were dispelled by the words of the promise. There is indeed a call to watchfulness, but this is not without its rewards. "For still the vision awaits its time; it hastens to the end — it will not lie. If it seem slow, wait for it; it will surely come, it will not delay" (Hab. 2:3). Here we encounter again the correlation we mentioned earlier between delay and expectation. This delay may not be interpreted as nonfulfilment, but must be seen as subject to the renewed admonition to expectation.

During the time of Ezekiel the problem of "delay" reached critical dimensions: "Son of man, what is this proverb that you have about in the land of Israel, saying, 'The days grow long, and every vision comes to nought'? Tell them therefore, 'Thus says the LORD God: I will put an end to this proverb, and they shall no more use it as a proverb in Israel.' But say to them, The days are at hand, and the fulfilment of every vision" (Ezek. 12:22f.). Israel's use of this forbidden proverb illustrated its disbelief in prophecy. It was easy for the prophets to speak, promise, and admonish on the basis of their divine mandate, but there had to be truth and credibility in it. And, the critics hastened to add, this was the element their promises lacked. Day followed upon day, but things did not improve. This led first to a "philosophy of delay" and later to doubts that the promises would come true at all. What is remarkable about the Lord's response to this attitude is that the expectation is not put off to a remote and distant future, but is rather redefined: "The days are at hand, and the fulfilment of every vision." There must be no more mention of delay (vs. 25). When the critics complain that the fulfilment is somewhere in the distant future, the Lord replies that "none of my words will be delayed any longer" (vs. 28).

Undoubtedly there was a delay or "sojourn" in God's dealings with Israel, a time in which the fulfilment of His promises had not yet appeared. But in spite of the critics, who saw in this delay an indefinite postponement or cancellation of the promise, Yahweh has sworn that His words will not fall to the ground. The promise of today may be the reality of tomorrow, and the continuity of time does not serve to disqualify the reliability of the Lord or of His words. The Lord promised that in the days of the rebellious house of Israel He would speak the word and perform the deed (vs. 25).

The New Testament, too, mentions those who have come to incorrect conclusions about the problem of delay. Here it is the "delay" of the parousia that is scorned by the "scoffers" (2 Pet. 3:3; Jude 17). " 'Where is the promise of his coming? For ever since the fathers fell asleep, all things have continued as they were from the beginning of the creation.' "[32] These scoffers drew their negative conclusions about the parousia from their disbelief in the promise of God. They no longer believed in or expected the promise of the parousia. They followed their own passions, making it impossible for them to consider the "eschaton" without falling into an abyss of unbelief characterized by mockery, presumptuousness, and the haughty pomp of pretended certainty in allegedly irrefutable arguments. The believer must beware of such conceit (2 Pet. 3:1, 8, 14, 17).

The author of the epistle reminds his readers that the "unchangeableness" the scoffers find in history from the beginning of creation is a fiction. Such a philosophy of history denies the significance of the flood, which was a *pronounced* judgment,

---

32. 2 Pet. 3:4: *"poú estin hē epaggelía tḗs parousías autoú"*; Bertram feels that these scoffers may have been Gnostic Libertines; *TDNT*, s.v. *empaigmonḗ*, V, 636.

beginning inconspicuously as an ordinary shower and growing and growing into an apocalyptic happening of catastrophic proportions. The rain became a flood in a precisely fixed time-period: "in the six hundredth year of Noah's life, in the second month, on the seventeenth day of the month..." (Gen. 7:11). At once, everyone knew that there was only one means of salvation — the ark. Thus God's divine judgment "concerning events as yet unseen" (Heb. 11:7) was fulfilled. The skeptics "deliberately ignore" (2 Pet. 3:5 — *lanthánei gár autoús toúto thélontas*) the fact that their arguments about the unchangeableness of history lose all credence in the face of the accomplished promises and judgments of God.

Of course, the cataclysmic event of the flood does not constitute the sole argument against such skeptics. Nor are the lacunae in the skeptics' arguments the only thing in which the believer can take comfort. The biblical promise concerning the expectation is clear: "But do not ignore this one fact, beloved, that with the Lord one day is as a thousand years, and a thousand years as one day. The Lord is not slow about his promise as some count slowness, but is forbearing toward you, not wishing that any should perish, but that all should reach repentance" (2 Pet. 3:8f.). We shall discuss in Chapter IV how this passage bears on the meaning of the prolonging of time. Here our interest is in how the author conspicuously denies any notion that God is stalling His return. To interpret the slowness as a deliberate attempt by God to stall the coming of His Kingdom is to misunderstand seriously God's intention.

This rebuttal is significant because the author does not substitute *Fernerwartung* for *Naherwartung*. "The day of the Lord will come like a thief," and the believer is called to anticipate this day with all earnestness and diligence (vv. 10, 12, 14, 18). But the continuity of time is not evidence of a slack, indecisive God. And to prevent all kinds of pretensions and skepticism, Scripture reminds us of the glory and eternity of God in contrast to men. For Him a thousand years are as one day.

Obviously this reference to Psalm 90 does not solve all the problems connected with the delay either. The problem that we face here is that the promise of the future presented to us in the New Testament is characterized in terms of the human understanding of time: *nearness*. (This, incidentally, is also maintained by consistent eschatology.) According to Käsemann, Peter's reference to Psalm 90 makes every apocalyptic expectation completely meaningless. Indeed, "if we ascribe to God a time-scale different from our own, we are no longer in a position to maintain seriously the 'soon' of the apocalyptic believer, but are compelled to refrain from any utterance about the time of the Parousia."[33] Käsemann's meaning is clear: if we attempt to explain the continuity of history by positing a different *divine* time-concept, all references to the future in the *human* time-concept lose their meaning, as do all references to "nearness" and "imminence." Thus it may appear that Peter devaluates the meaning of the continuity of time on the basis of the divine "time-concept."[34]

In this reflection on the continuity of time are we not being given a perspective on the eternity of God — that He no longer measures with our time-standards and that things appear differently to Him from how they do to us? We see man as no more than a frail creature carrying with him the seeds of death, whose life is spent in the twinkling of an eye. Over against that mortal weakness is the Lord of "endless times,"[35] who transcends all time, so that man cannot measure or evaluate His work.

But if one now raises the question whether this profound contrast between God and man does not exclude all perspective on nearness, he is forgetting that Peter was merely addressing himself to the skeptics, attempting to destroy their simplistic rationale of history. He was not explaining the human concept and experience of time as a meaningless accommodation, and it is incorrect to say that he postponed the fulfilment of the Christian hope to an undetermined time.[36] He is rejecting no more than the mockery made by the men in his day. To this extent his citation of Psalm 90 is meaningful, sufficient, and effective.[37] Behind his remarks is neither an irrational view of

33. E. Käsemann, "An Apologia for Primitive Christian Eschatology," in *Essays on NT Themes* (Eng. tr., 1964), p. 194; cf. H. Windisch, *Der Hebräerbrief*, p. 102.

34. Cf. F. Hauck, *Die Kirchenbriefe* (1953), p. 100.

35. J. Ridderbos, *De Psalmen*, II, 398; cf. Zahn, *Komm.*, p. 256.

36. A. Weiser, *The Psalms* (Eng. tr., 1962), pp. 597f.: "In the sight of God vast spaces of time such as a thousand years, the detailed events of which man cannot even take in at a glance, are as yesterday when it is past, or as a watch in the night, which was the smallest unit of time for man in those days."

37. G. Delling, *Das Zeitverständnis des NT* (1940), p. 116. Delling completely misses the point when he writes: "Even their refutation does not show the actual NT understanding of time." Cf. Cullmann, *Christ and Time*, p. 69.

time nor a concept of eternity that obscures attention to time,[38] but the rejection of a pretentious and illegitimate interpretation of history. The continuous duration of time — the "length" of time — must be interpreted in terms other than on the basis of the "slowness" of God. It points instead to the patience of the Lord.

The protagonists of consistent eschatology know, of course, that Peter is not talking about a deliberate slowness on God's part, but they do not see that this takes anything away from their case. In fact, they often quote 2 Peter to support their fundamental view of New Testament eschatology. They reason that the believers to whom the epistle was addressed found it necessary to begin reflecting on the continuity of time, in view of the fact that there was evidently a delay in the coming of the Kingdom. By pointing to the meaning of intermediate time, it is felt that the author is trying to turn the distress of the delay into a virtue. Werner feels that the awareness of the delay had become so acute at this time that it threatened the faith of the Christian community. What 2 Peter 3:8ff. is trying to do is to make an apologia of sorts, in which the delay of the parousia is interpreted as nothing more than a misunderstanding.[39]

It is not difficult to find the fallacy in this line of reasoning. In the first place, the epistle does not give one the impression of trying to find a makeshift solution for the crisis of the delay. We emphasize again that Peter is reacting strongly to the skeptics who were making the delay their central thesis and who showed no sign of sincere concern for, or belief in, the promises of God. The skeptics were playing with words and using the Scripture to their own advantage. In the second place, there is no trace of de-eschatologizing in 2 Peter. The community is warned not to be misled by the mockery of unbelievers or their incorrect interpretations of history, backed up only by apparent evidence. The believers are admonished to be busy in the expectation of the promise: "But, according to his promise, we wait for new heavens and a new earth in which righteousness dwells" (2 Pet. 3:13).[40]

---

38. Cf. G. von Rad's strange interpretation of eternity in Psalm 90, *OT Theology* (Eng. tr., 1962), I, 453f. Von Rad reads only of resignation in the Psalm, without any confidence.

39. *The Formation of Christian Dogma*, p. 43.

40. On this, see further Michaelis' criticism of the way consistent escha-

Naherwartung *in the New Testament*

All this has been preparatory to our discussion of what consistent eschatology calls the *Naherwartung* — the expectation of the nearness of the Kingdom — in the New Testament. Consistent eschatology sees the expectation of the coming of the Kingdom within the first generation of believers as the heart and soul of the early church. Clearly we cannot simply ignore this view of eschatology, even if its interpretation of history as the "slowness of God" is to be rejected. Even though we recognize that every attempt to find a crisis of delay permeating the New Testament depends on interpretations, we are obligated to deal with the accents of the nearness of the Kingdom found in the New Testament. We read there that the end of all things is at hand; that the believer is to be sane and sober (1 Pet. 4:7); that the Lord is at hand (Phil. 4:5); that the judge is standing at the door (James 5:8, 9); that the time is near (Rev. 1:3). These passages have constantly presented problems for New Testament preaching. What does the New Testament mean by the last days, the last hour? What does it mean when it says that "the night is far gone, the day is at hand" (Rom. 13:12)? In what sense has the end of ages come upon the community of believers (2 Cor. 10:11)? How are Paul's words to be explained when he says that God will soon *(en táchei)* crush Satan (Rom. 16:20)?

In view of these passages, it is understandable that the subject of a crisis of delay has been raised, all the more so because all of these passages clearly apply and appeal to our experience and concept of time. Even though one finds himself in agreement with the emphasis of Kümmel, Cullmann, and others on the present-ness of salvation, he must account for the theme of "nearness" in the New Testament. Is it just coincidence that the intermediate time is said to have grown very short (1 Cor. 7:29 — *ho kairós synestalménos estín*), and is subject to definite limitations? Is this present time not a compressed, "shortened" time, which by virtue of its shortness causes great intensity and expectation? Within that *short* time, the attention of the community is focused on what is fast approaching; life on earth is determined by the ethos of a brief time period.

tology has dealt with 2 Peter; *op. cit.* Käsemann is incorrect in his comment (*op. cit.*, p. 170) that "the whole community is embarrassed and disturbed by the fact of the delay of the Parousia." Cullmann is right in speaking of the correction of an "error in perspective"; *Christ and Time*, p. 87. See also Barth, *CD*, III/2, 509f.

Nowhere does the New Testament speak of an unappointed, unlimited time period that will always remain. "The form of this world is passing away" (1 Cor. 7:31 — *parágei gár tó schêma toú kósmou toútou*). "For a little while *(olígon)*," says Peter, "you may have to suffer various trials" (1 Pet. 1:6; cf. 5:10).

Concerning the gift of the promise, the letter to the Hebrews is unmistakably clear: "For yet a little while, and the coming one shall come and shall not tarry" (Heb. 10:37).[41] This note of promise is the opposite of delay. But is this in fact not an affirmation of the thesis of consistent eschatology, which sees this brief time period — in terms of the first generation — as the central motif of the New Testament expectation?

So much is clear: in all these passages (and others, such as Matt. 24:22; Mark 13:20; Luke 18:8; Rev. 1:1, 3; 22:20) there is no trace of a vertically suspended eternity-concept that absorbs the eschaton in permanent, timeless relation and leaves no room or meaning for the continuity of history as such. On the contrary, the New Testament message is directed to a goal in history, a coming reality. Once this is accepted, we can deal meaningfully with the questions raised by the term "nearness."

Since the actual course of history did not correspond to these repeated references to the nearness of the parousia, some have interpreted these expressions of imminence as the form — fragile and perishable — of the expectation, in distinction from its content.[42] Such a simplified separation of form from content in eschatological preaching and expectation, labeling the form (nearness) as an error, would seem incorrect, since all the references to nearness are not merely neutral time-fixations, but existentially laden warnings connected with the shortness of time.

The conclusion is inescapable that "nearness" is an absolute-

---

41. Heb. 10:37 cites two OT passages: "yet a little while" is from Isa. 26:20 (LXX: *mikrón hóson hóson*); "and the coming one shall come and shall not tarry" from Hab. 2:3 (LXX: *hóti erchómenos héxei kaí oú mé chronísē*). Cf. C. Spicq, *L'épitre aux Hébreux*, II (1953), 331ff.

42. Althaus, *Die letzten Dinge,* discusses this in chapter VII. He writes: "The expectation of the temporal nearness of the end, as it prevails in the NT, was not fulfilled through the course of history, but proved to be a temporal historical boundary." But the expectation that the end is near "signifies not only a boundary of the view. Much more it is at the same time the perishable and fragile form in which the eschatological judgment of the world, essential to the faith at all times, and its knowledge of the ever real possibility of the last day expresses itself" (p. 273). Note the difference between Althaus and consistent eschatology.

ly essential component of the eschatological proclamation of the New Testament. Cullmann argues that the "unshakably firm conviction that the battle that decides the victory has already taken place" means that the expectation of nearness does not have to do "with the determination or limitation of a date. . . . The error is explained on a psychological basis in the same way that we explain the hasty determinations of the date of the end of the war when once the conviction is present that the decisive battle has already taken place."[43] Understandably consistent eschatology remains unconvinced by the analogy. These "hasty determinations," they argue, are not based on a "promise," as was the New Testament expectation that the last things were near and the Lord was coming quickly.

In order to comprehend the meaning of the nearness concept, we should make it clear that again and again the New Testament stresses the fact that the time of the Lord's return remains unknown to us. This unknown aspect is not introduced in a context of secrecy, but in order to extend an urgent call to watchfulness. "Watch therefore, for you know neither the day nor the hour" (Matt. 25:13; cf. Mark 13:32f.). The New Testament emphasizes this watchfulness because man does not know when the Lord shall return, whether in the evening, at midnight, at cockcrow, or in the morning (Mark 13:35). The servant is warned not to be found asleep when the Lord returns. This unknown quality demands watchfulness throughout the four watches of the night.

The believer is called to an attitude that does not *reckon* but constantly *reckons with* the coming of the Lord. If the Lord comes in the third or fourth watch of the night, there must be no talk of mistakes in the first or second watch. Such an error is precluded by the very nature of the expectation. "Let your loins be girded and your lamps burning, and be like men who are waiting for their master to come home from the marriage feast, so that they may open to him at once when he comes and knocks. Blessed are those servants whom the master finds awake when he comes" (Luke 12:35-37). Contrasted to this watchfulness is the attitude of the servant who said to himself, "My master is delayed in coming," and so did not bother to put his affairs in order. His lot is to be "put with the unfaithful" (vs. 46 — *metá tōn apistōn*). Although he knew the will of his

43. *Christ and Time*, pp. 87f.

master, he had no arrangements (Luke 12:47),[44] so he was unprepared for his arrival.

The Lord's coming will be unexpected, but it will not be un-expected. This seeming equivocation really gets at the heart of the Christian expectation. In this context arises the familiar image of the thief in the night. "If you will not awake, I will come like a thief, and you will not know at what hour I will come upon you" (Rev. 3:3; cf. 1 Thess. 5:1). This suddenness will not present a danger for those who have expected the Lord's return. Paul wrote to the Thessalonians: "But you are not in darkness, brethren, for that day to surprise you like a thief" (1 Thess. 5:4). The suddenness and incalculability demand constant vigilance and preparation. But the destructiveness in the analogy of the thief in the night disappears for the "sons of the day" (1 Thess. 5:5). The danger lies in being unprepared for the coming of the Lord.[45]

At one time the New Testament presents the urgent nearness of the Kingdom and the fact that it must remain unknown. Some have found in this a contradiction, claiming that once one speaks of the Kingdom as "nearby," it is no longer possible to maintain the "unknown" dimension. Grässer claims that this unknown is a formulation by the early Christians to account for the delay of the parousia, that the original expectation contained no such unknown since the believers knew the day and the time: the Lord would reappear within that generation.[46]

44. *mē hetoimásas.* In the OT the concept of being ready is expressed in terms of a firm heart, trusting in the Lord (Ps. 112:7; LXX 111:7 — *hetoimē hē kardia*). Cf. Amos 4:12 — "Prepare to meet your God, O Israel"; LXX — *hetoimázou*).

45. The indeterminate quality of the great day is found in Jesus' words to the Pharisees who asked *when* the Kingdom would appear. "The kingdom of God is not coming with signs to be observed" (Luke 17:20f. — *metá paratērếseōs*). Compare the situation in the days of Noah (eating, drinking, marrying) and Lot (drinking, buying and selling, planting and building) with the days in which the Son of Man will be revealed (Luke 17:26-30). The times of Noah and Lot were without watchfulness; cf. Matt. 24:39: "and they did not know *(ouk égnōsan)* until the flood came...." On the image of the thief, W. Straub writes: "The *tertium comparationis* is the suddenness and the unforeseenness of the event"; *Die Bildersprache des Apostels Paulus* (1937), pp. 50f.; see also P. S. Minear, *Christian Hope and the Second Coming* (1954), chapter 9: "The Thief."

46. Grässer, *op. cit.,* pp. 77, 82, 84ff., 95: "it is most improbable that Jesus, who proclaimed the immediate nearness of the end, motivated his call to watchfulness with an appeal to uncertainty and not to certainty."

It takes a good deal of arbitrary bending and twisting of the New Testament evidence to arrive at such a conclusion. On this view, everything connected with the continuity of history must simply be dismissed as theology concocted by the church, a "problematics of delay."[47] The notion of nearness is interpreted as a precise time-fixation of the original expectation; and no mind is paid to the fact that the unknowable aspect and the "watchfulness" proclaimed by the New Testament are directly related to each other and furthermore to the nearness. The New Testament leaves a veil over the mysteries of the coming day, but this does not permit us to act as if the Lord were not to be expected for a long time *(Fernerwartung)*. This would certainly deprive the eschaton of its actuality. The time, the actual moment of Christ's return, is known only to the Father — "It is not for you to know times or seasons which the Father has fixed by his own authority" (Acts 1:7) — and this hiddenness determines the total direction of the Christian community.

Some have claimed that the New Testament does not merely affirm the possibility of this "nearness" (Christ's return during the first watch of the night) but that it confirms it as certainty. Three particular passages in the New Testament are cited as positing an undeniable time-fixation — passages in which Jesus places the fulfilment of the eschaton within the first generation of believers. First is His charge to the apostles: "When they persecute you in one town, flee to the next; for truly, I say to you, you will not have gone through the towns of Israel, before the Son of man comes" (Matt. 10:23). Second is a word about the coming Kingdom: "Truly, I say to you, there are some standing here who will not taste death before they see the kingdom of God come with power" (Mark 9:1). Finally is His warning: "Truly, I say to you, this generation will not pass away before all these things take place" (Mark 13:30).

Consistent eschatology sees these three prophecies concerning the immediate generation, which have not come true, as errors and miscalculations. Even Kümmel, who generally disagrees

---

47. On the distinction between Jesus and the church, see H. W. Bartsch, "Zum Problem der Parusieverzögerung bei den Synoptikern," *Evangelische Theologie*, XIX (1959), 116-31. For Grässer's method, see his judgment on "Our Father" *(op. cit.,* pp. 95ff.). Cf. also Schweitzer's rejection of the authenticity of 2 Thess. 2 on the grounds that it must have been written after Paul's death when "Christian teachers found themselves obliged to find such means of reconciling believers to the delay [of the parousia]"; *The Mysticism of Paul the Apostle,* p. 42.

with consistent eschatology, concludes from these passages that "Jesus reckoned on the coming of the Kingdom of God and of the Son of Man in glory within the lifetime of the generation of his hearers." "This prediction of Jesus was not realized and it is therefore impossible to assert that Jesus was not mistaken about this."[48] Kümmel cautions, however, against overestimating the significance of this "error," since the number of texts "that place a definite limit to the imminent expectation is extraordinarily small and it is correct to conclude from this fact that this idea did not receive much emphasis in Jesus' message."[49]

Understandably, these three prophecies of Christ are often cited by consistent eschatology, since they are of decisive importance for this view. It is safe to say that consistent eschatology stands or falls with these words.

The most discussed of the three passages is undoubtedly Mark 9:1. Among the explanations of this passage are suggestions that it applies to the resurrection of Christ, to Pentecost, or to the destruction of Jerusalem as manifestation of the power of the Messiah. Romans 1:4 is used for further support of this interpretation: "[Christ] who was designated Son of God *(tou horisthéntos hyioú theoú)* in power . . . by his resurrection from the dead." The effect of the cross is the power evident in the resurrection of the Lord.[50]

In contrast to interpretations of this passage that relate it to the future — and thus find error and miscalculation in it — C. H. Dodd sees here an illustration of realized eschatology. For Dodd, Mark 9:1 is not so much a reference to the *coming* of the Kingdom as to the fact that its having come needs to be *seen* or recognized. The Kingdom has already come; and the believers must see, discover, and recognize that. They must

48. *Promise and Fulfilment,* pp. 64, 149; and his *Das NT: Geschichte der Erforschung seiner Probleme* (1958), p. 288, with reference to Luke 17:20.

49. *Promise and Fulfilment,* p. 149. Kümmel goes on to say that "there is no doubt a contradiction between the prediction of a concrete date for the coming of the Kingdom of God and the emphatic statement that this date could not be known. . . . But in reality the solution of this problem is of very subordinate importance because the question of the appointed date of the Kingdom of God was for Jesus in no way a vital concern" (pp. 150f.). According to Kümmel, Jesus uses contemporary imagery of an imminent expectation, which can be detached from his message, to clothe the certainty of God's redemptive action in living words (p. 152).

50. On Rom. 1:4, see O. Michel, *Der Römerbrief, ad loc.* He relates the "in power" to Mark 9:1. On *horízō,* see Schmidt, in *TDNT,* s.v., V, 452f.

"awake before their death to the fact, that the kingdom of God had come."[51]

The untenability of Dodd's exegesis has been pointed out by a number of scholars. This "seeing" is not a matter of gaining awareness of something that is already present, but of seeing through an eschatological manifestation, a coming of the Kingdom. It is hardly possible to dismiss the problems that these three passages raise in this way.[52] Whether Christ's words relate to the parousia or to the coming of the Kingdom in crucifixion and resurrection has always been a question of considerable importance, and to dismiss the latter suggestion out of hand is certainly incorrect. Berkhof believes that "the Gospel writers considered this expression fulfilled in Jesus' transfiguration on the mountain. 'Some' were allowed to be witnesses of this. The word 'some,' however, could also have another nuance and mean that the eyewitnesses, as opposed to the world, could view and understand the signs of the arrival of the Day of the Lord."[53]

In any case, a close connection is apparent between present revelation and the future. This is clear from Christ's reply to the high priest: "Hereafter (ap' árti) you will see the Son of man seated at the right hand of Power ..." (Matt. 26:64). This "hereafter" indicates a fixed period of time. It speaks of the present revelation in this decisive time. But this does not force one to choose between an exclusively present orientation and a futuristic one.[54] Such an antithesis could not explain the problems of these three passages, because in terms of the character of Jesus' preaching it is a false antithesis. The prophetic words of Christ pertain both to the present *and* the future. Error in Jesus' thinking is in fact excluded, because the coming of the Kingdom can only be described in a way that recognizes the chronological reference in its unique relationship to both the present and the future.

The same thing applies to what Jesus says about the passing away of "this generation." Ridderbos, among others, sees this as a reference to the *evil* generation, rather than to a definite

51. C. H. Dodd, *The Parables of the Kingdom* (1935), p. 54.
52. For criticism of Dodd's interpretation, see Kümmel, *Promise and Fulfilment*, pp. 23-26; and Bornkamm, "Die Verzögerung der Parusie," in *In Memoriam Ernst Lohmeyer*, p. 117.
53. *CMH*, p. 75; cf. Barth, *CD*, III/2, 499: "it is best to see the fulfilment of Mk. 9:1 in all three events, transfiguration, resurrection, *and* Parousia."
54. Cf. Ridderbos, *The Coming of the Kingdom* (Eng. tr., 1962), p. 503.

time.[55] In any case, even after saying this, Jesus added that no one knows of that day or hour when heaven and earth shall pass away (Mark 10:32).[56] Finally, whereas many understand Matthew 10:23 as a direct reference to time, Christ is actually talking about the hate and persecution to be faced by believers. The thrust of Christ's words is to give a perspective on the events of the future that will bring comfort to the believers.[57] Consistent eschatology interprets all of these passages as providing a definite time limitation, ignoring the fact that all proclamations about the parousia are concretely structured by the mystery of the Kingdom, which is coming and has already come.

The nature of the divine revelation in Jesus Christ makes it apparent that the New Testament "nearby" can be properly understood only on the basis of this mystery of the Kingdom. What may at first glance appear to be contradiction and error is clarified by this framework with its peculiar present and future aspects. Despite all the biblical references to the unknowable, the "nearby" remains; the proclamation about the Kingdom is expressed in terms of the present also. This does not amount to a denial of the chronological continuity of history and its replacement by an eternity concept. The "nearby" is on a level with the New Testament message that the time had fully come (Gal. 4:4).

We are often at a loss to explain much of the scriptural language about the reality of the Kingdom. We frequently think of it as an enigma, if not a contradiction. This is a problem that evidently did not bother the apostles. When we hear the expression "the end of the age" (Heb. 9:26), we hardly think of Bethlehem, but instead only of the Day of Judgment. Our notion of "the last hour" is different from John's (1 John 2:18). This is probably why we no longer fully understand the call to watchfulness that is so closely connected with the proclamation of the "nearby."

The message of what has already come, together with what is to come, concerns the reality of the Kingdom. It warns the believers against living in expectation of a far-off reality

---

55. *Ibid.*, p. 502.
56. *Ibid.*, pp. 499f.
57. Ridderbos places the emphasis in this passage on the flight rather than on the mission of the disciples; *ibid.*, p. 509. Cf. Schnackenburg, *God's Rule and Kingdom* (Eng. tr., 1963), pp. 204f. Barth, *CD*, III/2, 499f.

(Fernerwartung). According to Paul, the Lord is now nearby, now is the time, now He is standing in front of the door. Now is the time to wake from sleep. "Nearby" is not an error, not the fragile form of the eschatological expectation, but a word that expresses "the characteristic aspect of the early Christian situation, being used of the eschatological fulfilment, of the great turning point in world history, of the coming of the kingdom of God directly into the present as the miracle of God."[58] The message of the "nearby" dramatically underscores the inescapability and gravity of the biblical proclamation (cf. Luke 21:32). It is not a method of calculating the date of the parousia, but, in connection with the incalculability of that date, it forms our perspective on the nature of the *Naherwartung*. It is not a matter of a play on words, but the *only* expression that can give meaning to the present in terms of the last days.[59]

So, it is not our intention to "abandon our empirical notions of time, which envisage time in our Western thinking as a continuously moving line, divisible into measurable sections."[60] For what might such an "abandonment" really mean? Does it imply that "nearby" as an expression of the gravity and the actuality has nothing to do with "time?" Rather, the "nearby" precludes a flight into the superficiality of *Fernerwartung* in which the eschaton loses its meaning at the expense of the present. The actuality of the eschatological message must always be stressed. Althaus, who speaks of the "nearby" as a "fragile form," nonetheless finds a profound meaning in this form, that is, that *all* eschatological expressions derive their decisive and actual seriousness from the "nearby." The "nearby" indicates that the eschaton is not a futuristic entity beyond our horizons. To this extent Althaus is on the track of the nature of eschatological expectation. Watchfulness and actuality are two sides of the same coin. The true congregation may never be like the servant whose affairs were in chaos because he did not expect the coming of his master. The eschatological "nearby" can only be understood in terms of a radical event in time. The primary error of consistent eschatology is not that it "overestimates" the

58. Preisker, in *TDNT*, s.v. *engýs*, II, 331.
59. In this connection, consider the references to "nearness" in OT prophecy. Cf. Isa. 13:6; 51:5; 56:1; Joel 1:15; 2:1; Hab. 2:3, *et al*. See also Ridderbos, *The Coming of the Kingdom*, pp. 523ff.
60. Schnackenburg, *op. cit.*, p. 213.

New Testament eschaton, but that it misrepresents the *nature* of this eschatological "nearby."

The lasting value of the so-called realized eschatology (which we shall consider further in Chapter IV) and of Cullmann's critique of consistent eschatology is that they have broken with a futuristic scheme of the eschaton,[61] and called attention to the fact that what has already come in the present time of salvation has brought about a change in the relation between the promise and the fulfilment.[62] This is the primary reason why the Lord's not yet having come has not caused any crisis or impasse of delay. This is not to say that the meaning of the Lord's "sojourn" has not been an important consideration in eschatological reflection. Nor does it imply that the New Testament has nothing to say about it. After all, watchfulness implies delay. And it is the experiencing of this particular "not yet" — most acute, it appears, in times of persecution — that has given rise to the agonizing cry, "how long?"

Nevertheless, the experience of this "not yet" must not lead to conclusions about the "slowness" of the Lord. That is contradicted by the very words of Scripture. The very use of the word "delay" by Cullmann and Cadbury is probably at the root of much of the difficulty here, for this word is ambiguous, suggesting on the one hand a subjective impression of a process that — to our minds — has been delayed, and on the other hand the idea that the original plans of God have, for one reason or another, been changed and subsequently delayed. Perhaps it would be more meaningful to speak of "sojourn" than "delay," suggesting anticipation of an appointed time and presenting no crisis of doubt concerning the meaning of the period of waiting.

During the period of this waiting there is no change in the expectation itself, but new opportunities continually present themselves. Within this experience there is a new call and specific mandate. To say this is not de-eschatologizing, which would sidetrack our attention to the problems of this

---

61. On this, see also Kümmel, *Promise and Fulfilment, passim;* and four essays in Davies and Daube (eds.), *The Background of the NT and Its Eschatology: Studies in Honour of C. H. Dodd* (1954): H. J. Cadbury, "Acts and Eschatology," pp. 300ff.; C. K. Barrett, "The Eschatology of the Epistle to the Hebrews," pp. 363ff.; E. G. Selwyn, "Eschatology in I Peter," pp. 394ff.; and E. Schweitzer, "Gegenwart des Geistes und eschatologische Hoffnung," pp. 482ff.
62. On this new relation cf. Gnilka, *op. cit.,* pp. 281f.

period of the present dispensation. De-eschatologizing is possible only in a futuristic expectation. Only in a futuristic interpretation is there a possibility of disappointment and loss of faith. The "not yet" of the New Testament can only strengthen the expectation. The conclusion that the eschaton becomes only a peripheral concern fails to recognize the fact that the New Testament places the present in the context of the future and the "delay" can only result in estrangement if the reality of what has already come is no longer recognized and understood.

In conclusion, let us examine some of those Pauline passages from which it has been concluded that the apostle spoke of a definite, fixed period of time. The important question is what Paul meant by his use of the pronoun "we." "Lo! I tell you a mystery. We shall not all sleep, but we shall all be changed, in a moment, in the twinkling of an eye, at the last trumpet" (1 Cor. 15:51f.). "We who are alive, who are left until the coming of the Lord, shall not precede those who have fallen asleep. For ... the dead in Christ will rise first; then we who are alive, who are left, shall be caught up together with them in the clouds" (1 Thess. 4:15-17). Is Paul speaking of a certain knowledge when he talks thus about the "living" on the occasion of the Lord's return?

We can begin by stating that in the first instance (1 Cor. 15) Paul was surely not primarily interested in fixing a definite time. Other questions occupied his mind. He was addressing himself to the "newness" of the eschatological moment: the perishable must put on the imperishable; the mortal immortality (1 Cor. 15:53). In this connection he mentions a secret, a mystery that will be revealed. A change is coming that will affect everyone, but within the eschatological horizon of this change there is a difference. Both the living *and the dead* will be included in the change, but those who are still living at the time of the parousia will not die, even though they will also be changed. Since Paul then writes to the Thessalonians, "we who are alive ...," some have concluded that he considered himself to be among those who would not taste death, and that accordingly, he fixed a definite period of time for the parousia.

There is every reason to believe that Paul lived in the expectation of a soon-to-be-realized parousia. He did not live in a *Fernerwartung*. Yet his message applies to two groups of believers: the living and the dead. His concern is not to fix the time. Later in the same letter to the Thessalonians he warns them to expect the day of the Lord to come as a thief in the night (5:2). But in and on the basis of this expectation, he speaks of the living, of which he was one, and takes into account the *possibility* that the Lord will come again within his lifetime. Who, after all, could reasonably expect Paul to portray his eschatological message in terms of *Fernerwartung?* Finally, Paul did not care to have certain knowledge concerning his own life; indeed, he really minimized the difference between those living and dead at the parousia, because both would participate in the ultimate change.

Paul's line of reasoning in 1 Corinthians 15 is not precisely the same as that in 1 Thessalonians 4. The former passage is oriented to those who will be alive at the parousia, whereas the latter speaks of the dead in the Lord, indicating that the living will have no priority over the dead at the time of the resurrection.

Clearly, Paul did not present a "nearby" expectation in the sense of definitely fixing the time as one might do with ordinary schedules.[63] The horizon of the expectation is entirely different from a prognosis of time or periods of time. Consequently, it is foolish to talk about an error in judgment among New Testament writers, and equally fruitless to speak of a crisis of delay resulting from such an error. Continuous expectation of and watchfulness for the coming of the Lord, who will appear as a thief in the night, exclude the possibility of such a crisis.[64]

The call to watchfulness

Consistent eschatology, with its view of the New Testament and the history of the church, is a purely human construction. It speaks of the delay of the parousia and really means that the promise of the future is not going to be fulfilled. Even in the confusion of delay and nonfulfilment it is evident that the principle of consistent eschatology is the latter, and that the whole cumbersome structure, including its eschatological problematics and view of the Christian faith, proceeds from it. The fact that the "sojourn" of the Lord did not lead to a crisis

63. Compare Schweitzer's unacceptable explanation of 1 Thess. 4:17; *The Mysticism of Paul the Apostle,* p. 137.
64. It is evident that the Thessalonian congregation had not lapsed into such a crisis: they were concerned about those of their number who had already died, an entirely different problem from that of the so-called delay.

in the early church nor to de-eschatologizing indicates that consistent eschatology has completely missed the point. It has not taken into consideration the fact that, because the Lord did not return in the first watch of the night, the expectation became the more acute in the second watch. That is the direction Paul took when he wrote: "For salvation is nearer *(engýteron)* to us now than when we first believed" (Rom. 13:11).

To this "nearer," Paul adds the admonition that "it is full time now for you to wake from sleep" (vs. 11). The comparative difference between "near" and "nearer" does not obscure the eschaton. The theme of this time is not an increasing crisis in the expectation of faith, but an urgent call to watchfulness.[65]

Yet, is it not reasonable to wonder whether consistent eschatology may not have had a point after all? Years, decades, and centuries have passed since the New Testament was written. Despite the stern reprimands addressed to skeptics in 2 Peter, is there not some basis to their mockery? Are there not reasons, if not to doubt, at least to raise serious questions? Although slowness on the Lord's part is explicitly denied, is it not understandable that many have mistaken and misinterpreted the words of promise written long ago: "The night is far gone, the day is at hand. Let us then cast off the works of darkness and put on the armor of light" (Rom. 13:12)?[66] All these hesitations can be summed up in the recurring question of the meaning of the present dispensation, the time between the Lord's ascension and return.

How is this "time between" to be understood in the light of the words of our Lord: "Surely I am coming soon. Amen" (Rev. 22:20)? This "Amen" dispels all doubts. It focuses attention, through all the watches of the night, on the future and on Him who is and was and is to come. It presents a different nearness from that encountered in the Old Testament. The Psalmist writes that "the LORD is near to all who call upon him."[67] Israel was without comparison among all the nations because of this nearness of God (Deut. 4:7). We must

---

65. Consistent eschatology sees the distinction between *engýs* and *engýteron* as symptomatic of the impasse. On the meaning of the introductory *"kaí toúto"* of Rom. 13:11, see commentaries *ad loc.* by Ridderbos and Michel.

66. Cf. the comments by Stählin, in *TDNT*, s.v. *prokópē*, VI, 716.

67. Ps. 145:18 (LXX 144:18 — *engýs*). See also Pss. 34:18; 119:151; Isa. 55:6; Jer. 23:23.

not slight this nearness, which is manifested throughout all of Israel's history. It was the key of God's revelation in the Old Covenant.[68] But this Old Testament nearness is not the end of the ways of the Lord. In the New Testament the theme occurs again: "The Lord is at hand" (Phil. 4:5). But it is clear that the intent in the New Testament is more than a spatial analogy, more than a mere coming in the continuous line of history.

There is a nearness that reminds us immediately of the future. In belief, not in skepticism, we begin to look for the meaning of what seems to us like a very long time indeed. This search is not an attempt to discover the inscrutable ways of God, but a reverent effort to determine the meaning of the present dispensation, now that the night is far gone and the day at hand.

68. See Martin Schmidt's excellent *Prophet und Tempel. Eine Studie zum Problem der Gottesnähe im AT* (1948).

CHAPTER FOUR

THE MEANING OF THE "TIME BETWEEN"

W E CONCLUDED the preceding chapter by saying that
we should undertake our search for the meaning of
the "time between" Christ's ascension and His return in belief. The meaning of this time has often been the object
of skeptical and unbelieving, even mocking, inquiry. At the
outset, we should make it clear that our intent in this chapter
is not to deal with the more general question of whether or
not history has any meaning at all and, if so, what. This inquiry
has occupied the attention of many scholars throughout the
centuries. Such an analysis of history usually includes questions
about the unity, origin, and goal of history: is history an enigmatic, meaningless, chaotic series of events, or is there in this
undeterminable process a central direction toward a specified
goal according to some meaningful plan? Even among those
who do find meaning and direction in history, there are many
variations; and emphases and nuances differ surprisingly.

The differences between various philosophies of life can
often be described as differences in their concepts of the meaning of history. Believer and unbeliever, optimist and pessimist,
Christian and skeptic — all have explored the central meaning
of history. The defeatist simply allows the tidal wave of events
to swamp him, because there is nothing he can do about it;
the activist constantly wants to plunge into the affairs, because
he is confident he has discovered the meaning of history and
wants to make himself of maximum service. Humanism, socialism
and communism all claim to have found the directedness that
influences life from day to day and gives rise to human responsibility.[1] Because each man looks at events with his own
eyes, different and conflicting theories of history continue to

1. Pieter Geyl traces this phenomenon in Soviet historians, noting their
emphasis on "the beneficial motive power of history"; cf. *Debates with
Historians* (1958).

96

crop up. Behind these different theories are all sorts of different a priori's, which directly structure the resultant theory — whether optimistic, negative, or defeatist.[2]

The fulness of time

But as we said, our concern in this chapter is not with the meaning of history as such or with questions of its origin, unity, and goal, but with the meaning of what is called the present dispensation, the interim, the "in-between time" until the return of the Lord. Not that the meaning of the present dispensation can be divorced from the meaning of "history"; in fact, the two are very closely related. But our attention here will focus on what the New Testament proclaims about the fulfilment of time in the divine revelation in Jesus Christ. We are not going to search out the meaning of concrete events in general, but rather consider the development of time after *the* event that is proclaimed as God's decisive and reconciling act in history: this dispensation as the time-period between *that* fulfilment and the end of the ages.[3]

To deny the importance of this specific inquiry would yield an interpretation that held to the automatic continuity of history in its broken and incomplete form and disregarded the New Testament proclamation of the time of salvation, with its themes of reconciliation, the end of the ages, and the disappear-

2. Geyl challenges Toynbee's claim that his history is the result of "strictly empirical investigation" (*ibid.*, p. 164); cf. also his critique of Sorokin (*ibid.*, pp. 151-56); and his further comments in *Use and Abuse of History* (1955). Illustrative of a positive appreciation of the meaning of history is Hegel, who detected the "cunning of reason" in history, from which the entire course of history can be explained. See also Karl Löwith, *Weltgeschichte und Heilsgeschehen* (1952), pp. 55ff.

3. With reference to the meaning of history, Herman Dooyeweerd makes a sharp distinction between the historical aspect of cosmic reality and "history in the sense of concrete events"; J. D. Bierens de Haan, Dooyeweerd, et al., *De zin der geschiedenis* (1942), p. 6. Compare also the distinction between the "modal nucleus of the historical mode of experience" and "what has happened in the past"; *Maatstaven ter onderkenning van progressieve en reactionnaire bewegingen in de historische ontwikkeling. Verslag Koninklijke Nederlandse Akademie van Wetenschap, 1808-1858*, p. 63. The distinction takes note of the fact that no historian considers every event, but must — theoretically and practically — maintain certain selective criteria. Clearly the primary objective of our inquiry into the meaning of the "time between" is the fulness of the concrete event in this dispensation, since the inquiry concerns the *continuing* of history as such.

ance of the mortal, the dark, and even death itself. In the light of the New Testament it becomes clear that the question whether or not the history in which we are living has meaning, whether or not life is worth living, can never be a skeptical one. Our reflection on the meaning of the present dispensation can only be founded on a firm conviction about the *fulfilment of meaning* accomplished in the revelation of Jesus Christ. What is the meaning of these many days and times that — to our understanding at least — have gone on for so long since the time has *fully* come?[4]

One cannot escape the urgency of the New Testament about this question. The New Testament does not exclude reflection about the entire course of history in its relation to God, including both the relationship between Yahweh and Israel, and that between God and the nations of the world. Such reflection, which turns on the relationship between world history and redemptive history, is characterized by a search for unity and interaction, and is important with respect to the question of the role of the "world" — the non-Jewish nations — in Yahweh's dealings with Israel.[5] The present dispensation, however, with its own peculiar character and content, is, as it were, thrust on us by the New Testament, with its pervasive talk of events during the time of salvation. There is in all this a reference to a goal, an ultimate, and a fulfilment, summed up in the words "In many and various ways God spoke of old *(pálai)* to our fathers by the prophets; but in these last days *(ep' eschátou tõn hēmerõn)* he has spoken to us by a Son" (Heb. 1:1f.).

The time of the Old Covenant is portrayed as the time of expectation and anticipation of what the God of Israel would do in the future. This expectation climaxes in Simeon, who was "looking for the consolation of Israel" (Luke 2:25 — *prosdechómenos paráklēsin toú Israél*) and who was permitted the

4. John Marsh asks, "If history has been fulfilled, but still continues, how and when will it end? And since it must continue, what is its significance until it ends?"; *The Fulness of Time* (1952), p. 121. Berkhof uses this quotation as the epigraph for *Christ the Meaning of History*. Although Berkhof is concerned with the general problem of the meaning of history, the meaning of the present dispensation occupies a considerable part of his thinking too (cf. chapter III).

5. In this connection is raised the often-discussed problem of the relation between history and the providence of God. Cf. Berkouwer, *The Providence of God* (Eng. tr., 1952), chapter VI: "Providence and History"; and Herbert Butterfield, *Christianity and History* (1949).

vision of this salvation (vs. 29).[6] The time of a gulf between promise and fulfilment appeared to have passed to make room for the present fulfilment, a theme sounded in Jesus' words after John's arrest: "The time is fulfilled, and the kingdom of God is at hand: repent, and believe in the gospel" (Mark 1:15; cf. Matt. 3:2).

Evidently, a very decisive moment in history had come, a turning point that demanded a radical and immediate decision, a conversion, in order for man to enter into the Kingdom. There can be no doubt that the fulfilment of this time of salvation is indissolubly connected to the coming of Jesus Christ into the world. He is the subject of the angels' hymns on Christmas night; He is the horn of salvation come to set His people free. Now there is liberation, light in darkness, redemption from the enemy through the grace of God (Luke 1:68f., 78f.; cf. vs. 54). This is the realization of the promise given (cf. vv. 55, 70). Christ has come to fulfil the law and the prophets (Matt. 5:17; cf. 3:3f.; 4:14). The road has been traveled; the goal attained; and an endpoint seems to come in view. After Christ read from Isaiah 61, He closed the scroll and added: "Today this scripture has been fulfilled in your hearing" (Luke 4:21).

The fulfilment about which Christ spoke was not merely a formal coming-true of earlier prophecies; it signaled the appearance of the reality of salvation,[7] the fulfilment, the *now*, the today of the time of salvation, the Messianic season of the acceptable year of the Lord.[8] This is what Paul meant when he wrote that God had sent His Son "when the time had fully come" (Gal. 4:4).[9] This is not just a highly significant phase that turns out to be relative after all, or a subdivision of the total time-continuum with the character of eternity. No, it is the "hour of all hours,"[10] because it has the weight of eternity. Here if anywhere all notions of futurism are strikingly absent.

6. Cf. Anna's witness to all who awaited the redemption (*lýtrōsis*) of Jerusalem (vs. 38); and Matt. 11:3.
7. On the fulfilment of the law and the prophets, see H. N. Ridderbos, *The Coming of the Kingdom*, pp. 292ff.; A. A. van Ruler, *De vervulling der wet* (1947), pp. 301ff.
8. Luke 4:19 — *kērýxai eniautón kyríou dektón;* cf. Isa. 61:1 — to "proclaim" (Heb. *liqrō'*; LXX *kálesai*).
9. *tó plērōma toú chrónou.* Cf. F. W. Grosheide, *De volheid des tijds;* and C. F. D. Moule, " 'Fulness' and 'Fill' in the NT," *Scottish Journal of Theology*, IV (1951), 79ff.
10. Delling, in *TDNT*, s.v. *nýn*, IV, 1113.

Throughout, attention is focused on the present: "Behold, now is the acceptable time *(kairós euprósdektos); now* is the day of salvation" (2 Cor. 6:2). This time — which is history nonetheless — is so special and unique that it can be said about those living then, "blessed are your eyes, for they see, and your ears, for they hear. Truly, men longed to see what you see, and did not see it, and to hear what you hear, and did not hear it" (Matt. 13:16f.).[11] The unseen and unheard is now a present reality, and what had been hidden from the foundation of the world is proclaimed (cf. Ps. 78:2; Matt. 13:35). In comparison with its former hiddenness, its uniqueness now comes into sharp focus. Paul too speaks of this reality as "the revelation of the mystery which was kept secret for long ages but is now disclosed and through the prophetic writings is made known to all nations according to the command of the eternal God, to bring about the obedience of faith" (Rom. 16:25f.).

Does Paul's expression "kept secret" in Romans 16:25 allow us to speak of God's *silence* in the period preceding the eschatological time of salvation?[12] Clearly not. This new revelation of Jesus Christ is the fulfilment of a promise spoken by God. But its reality is so complete as to make Paul speak of God's keeping it secret in former times. Hidden for generations, it was now made manifest (Col. 1:26).

This is the profound difference between the "former" and the "present." We have been shown God's time, which, in a very special sense, has now come. This does not negate the consideration that *all* time is His and that He is King of the ages (1 Tim. 1:17). But this Messianic time of salvation is of special and decisive importance in the continuity of time. It is described in Christ's words: "from the days of John the Baptist until now the kingdom of heaven has suffered violence, and men of violence take it by force" (Matt. 11:12). Whatever this difficult saying may mean,[13] the decisiveness of this time is

11. See commentaries *ad loc.* by Grosheide and Zahn; also H. N. Ridderbos, *op. cit.,* p. 73.
12. Cf. O. Michel, *Der Römerbrief,* pp. 352f.; cf. Odo Casel, *The Mystery of Christian Worship* (Eng. tr., 1962), pp. 9ff., 97ff., on Paul's idea of mystery.
13. Much has been written about the meaning of "men of violence take it by force" *(biastai harpázousin autēn).* Grosheide, in his commentary *ad loc.,* refers it to the publicans' and sinners' drawing of the Kingdom to themselves. Ridderbos points to the parallel passage in Luke 16:16: "The law and the prophets were until John; since then the good news

indicated by its having come after the days of John the Baptist. This fixes the Baptist's place in terms of the history of salvation, and, therefore, the least in the Kingdom of Heaven is greater than John (Matt. 11:11).[14] Law and prophecy applied until John the Baptist: then the new time entered (Luke 16:16; cf. Matt. 11:13). Now the injunction, "He who has ears to hear, let him hear" (Matt. 11:15), takes on new meaning.

The New Testament portrays this new and unique time of salvation, which began with the coming of Christ, in a variety of ways. It is expressed particularly in the distinction between "former" and "now." This distinction is not meant to devaluate God's dealings with the world in times past. Rather, the past obtains its meaning in its orientation to what comes later. In the "now" of the time of salvation, the veil has been removed, and the reality of Him who was "manifested in the flesh" (1 Tim. 3:16), is with us. This manifestation is of a decisive and, therefore, singular character because of the unity of the event. Christ appeared once at the end of ages, "to put away sin by the sacrifice of himself" (Heb. 9:26). He has accomplished this once and for all in an unrepeatable event. Repetition of this event would be superfluous and is, in fact, impossible: "there is no longer any offering for sin" (Heb. 10:18).

Does this not clearly indicate the end, fulfilment, and goal of God's plans on earth? Has the promise not been unmistakably fulfilled in this event? Has the dynamic of the expectation not finally been consummated in this new condition of life in which the appearance of the Lord is seen? Has the time of grace not now come; have the goodness and loving kindness of God, our Savior, not now appeared (epephánē — Titus 3:4)? Is sin not put away (Heb. 9:26) and death abolished (2 Tim. 1:10)? Is the true light not already shining (1 John 2:8 — édē phaínei)? Is it not true that we are *now* saved by baptism, *now* adopted as children of the Most High, *now* (nýn) justified through the blood of the Lamb (1 Pet. 3:21; 1 John 3:2; Rom. 5:9)?

The undeniable uniqueness of this fulfilled time has frequently been designated as "kairos," as distinct from the more

of the kingdom of God is preached and everyone enters it violently" (pás eis autēn biázetai; KV, I, 219. See also Foerster, in *TDNT*, s.v. harpázō, I, 472f., and Schrenk, s.v. biázomai, ibid., 609-14).
14. Cf. Ridderbos, *KV* on Matthew, I, 218.

general "chronos." However, such a precise distinction has little support in the New Testament itself. The New Testament does not seem to contrast kairos to chronos, especially not in the sense of underscoring the significance of kairos at the expense of chronos. Often, the two are juxtaposed with respect to the eschatological expectation, as, for example, in Acts 1:7: "it is not for you to know times *(chrónoi)* or seasons *(kairoí)* which the Father has fixed by his own authority" (Acts 1:7; cf. 1 Thess. 5:1). It appears that kairos often conveys more the sense of "moment," in distinction from "period" or "season." Still there is no total division between the two. Sevenster sees the kairoi as "pivotal points in God's plan of salvation."[15]

The kairos was fulfilled in the coming of Jesus Christ (Mark 1:15). Amid the continuity of chronoi, the kairos demands of man a decision of faith. When judgment came on Israel in the form of its enemies, it was because they did not know the time (kairos) when God would visit them (Luke 19:44). Thus attention to the kairos does not depreciate the chronoi.[16]

If all this is so, a new question arises. What does it mean in terms of the ultimate end and culmination of history? Is the meaning of the expressions cited above really as important and radical as it first appears to be? The church has often reflected an understanding of these passages that relates them to the future: *in the last days* there will be difficult times; or the consummation of the world is a *future* reality.[17]

New things are revealed in an old world, like the spring flowers that appear on the earth and the time for singing that comes (S. of Sol. 2:12). More than that, we have it on apostolic authority that "if any one is in Christ, he is a new creation; the old has passed away, behold, the new has come" (2 Cor. 5:17).[18] Is this not a radical transformation? Can there be any

---

15. "Chronos en Kairos in het NT," in *Chronos en Kairos. Het tijds-probleem in het NT* (1952), p. 10; cf. A. D. R. Polman's remarks; *ibid.*, p. 26.
16. Cf. Delling in *TDNT*, s.v. *kairós*, III, 455-64: Kairos as "the decisive point of time," "the (divinely given) opportunity," and "the main points in the history of salvation." Delling's discussion of "Erfüllung der Zeit," "Überwindung der Zeit," "Aufhebung der Zeitlichkeit," and "Zeitenthobenheit" (*Das Zeitverständnis des NT*, pp. 91, 110ff.) imposes foreign categories on the NT message.
17. Cf. 2 Tim. 3:1 *(enstésontai)*; 2 Pet. 3:3 *(eleúsontai)*; Jude 18 *(ésontai)*.
18. *tá archaía parélthen, idoú gégonen kainá.*

objection to the paraphrase that Seesemann suggests: "The new sets the old wholly to one side. They are incompatible"?[19]

When God proclaims the days of the new covenant and the author of the Epistle to the Hebrews, speaking from the point of view of the time of salvation and the end of all ages, announces that the old covenant "is ready to vanish away" (Heb. 8:13), does this not indicate a transformation of everything in the time of salvation, a renewal of everything, now that "the form of this world is passing away" (1 Cor. 7:31)? Are we not confronted in this biblical terminology with an entirely different reality from what we often suppose and accept it to be? Is the believer frequently not more concerned with and frightened by the old than exhilarated by the new about which the New Testament testifies in undeniable terms?

We need not digress at this point about the future newness of the new heavens and the new earth (Rev. 21:1). We have not forgotten this perspective, but our concern here has been to point to the uniqueness and singleness of the time of salvation, presented in the New Testament as the fulfilment and the culmination.[20]

Realized eschatology

Not surprisingly, many theologians have stressed what is called the *Gegenwart*-character of salvation, claiming that in New Testament eschatology the accent falls on the reality in the present time, rather than on a remote future. The term used to describe this particular view is *realized eschatology*.[21] The meaning of the term is that the Kingdom of God *has come*. It is no longer a matter of expectation, but of fulfilment and realization. C. H. Dodd defines its difference from Jewish expectation thus: "the eschaton has moved from the sphere of

19. In *TDNT*, s.v. *palaiós*, V, 719f.
20. Behm writes, "thus *kainós* becomes a slogan of the reality of salvation which we know already in Christ"; in *TDNT*, s.v. *kainós*, III, 449.
21. The term "realized eschatology" is C. H. Dodd's. In this connection, compare his interpretation of the gospel: "It represents the ministry of Jesus as realised eschatology"; *The Parables of the Kingdom* (1946), p. 49. Dodd is aware of the inadequacies of the term "realized eschatology," and cites amendments suggested by G. Florowsky ("inaugurated eschatology") and J. Jeremias ("sich realisierende Eschatologie"), adding "which I like, but cannot translate into English." *The Interpretation of the Fourth Gospel* (1953), p. 447.

expectation into that of realized experience."[22] This theory of a present eschaton is substantiated by reference to the early church, which lived in the belief that a new age had come, as was abundantly clear from the presence of the Holy Spirit.[23] The old apocalyptic scheme of things had been nullified through the coming of the Messiah and the revelation of the Kingdom.[24] According to Dodd, Paul preached this realized eschatology; and in the Gospel of John the future element of eschatology was completely subordinated to the idea of a *present* eschaton.[25] This present eschaton concerns eternal life, which is already *here and now* a realized fact because of the constant presence of Christ in His Holy Spirit.[26] Therefore, Dodd concludes, the testimony of Paul and John constitutes the most important and most progressive development in all apostolic preaching.[27]

To accept "realized eschatology" as the correct interpretation of the New Testament has, of course, important bearing on one's quest for the meaning of the present dispensation. Does realized eschatology not deprive this quest of some of its urgency? This can be seen in discussions of the Gospel of John by various scholars. This Gospel places a great deal of emphasis on the presence of salvation in the present time. Although Dodd and Bultmann, for example, differ in their views of this Gospel,[28] they do agree on one central point, namely in accenting the *present* eschaton. As a result, no importance is attached, in principle, to the future perspective.[29]

Of course, no one would deny that John does indeed emphasize the presence of salvation. The important thing for this Gospel is what is happening presently through Christ, what is now already of decisive importance. "Truly, truly I say to you, he who hears my word and believes him who sent me, has eternal life; he does not come into judgment, but has passed from death

22. *Ibid.*, p. 50.
23. Dodd, *The Apostolic Preaching and Its Developments*, pp. 22, 32, 33.
24. *Ibid.*, p. 36.
25. *Ibid.*, pp. 42f.
26. *Ibid.*, p. 43; cf. also Dodd, *The Interpretation of the Fourth Gospel.*
27. *The Apostolic Preaching*, p. 54.
28. With respect to the nature of the presence, there is an essential difference between Dodd and Bultmann, which one might call a difference between a Platonic and an existential view.
29. W. G. Kümmel writes that "the prophecies of Jesus offer no broad historical outlook"; *Das NT. Geschichte und Erforschung seiner Probleme* (1958), p. 495.

to life" (John 5:24). Then in the next verse we read about the dead hearing the voice of the Son of God in terms of a peculiar time-fixation: "the hour is coming, *and now is*" (vs. 25). Whoever believes has passed the judgment; whoever does not believe presently experiences the judgment.

The events of salvation are so drastic in this present time of grace that even the estimation of death undergoes a characteristic change: whoever keeps the Lord's word will never see death (John 8:51). Because Christ is the resurrection and the life, whoever believes in Him, "though he die, yet shall he live" (John 11:25f.).

Jesus' statement in John 11 that whoever believes in Him will never die is set against the background of Martha's reference to the future. Martha understood Christ's words about the resurrection of Lazarus to apply only to an event of the last day. And after this word about the future Christ points to the present, to what presently — in Him, who is the Resurrection — is already reality (vs. 24).[30]

Bultmann concludes from all this that there is no mention of any future or dramatic element in John's eschatological perspective, because for John "the eschatological event is already being consummated."[31] He admits that there are indeed some hints about the future in the book, among them Jesus' statements that "the hour is coming when all who are in the tombs will hear his voice and come forth" (John 5:28f.), and that "he that eats my flesh and drinks my blood has eternal life, and I will raise him up at the last day" (6:54; cf. vs. 39; 12:48). These he judges to be in conflict with the present eschatology, and concludes that they must not have been original. So, on this view, in the real message of the Gospel the decisiveness of the present elbows any "problem" of an interim time out of the picture.

---

30. Bultmann speaks of an impure element here, that the conversation about the resurrection is linked with the raising of Lazarus. According to him, Jesus' words do not aim at correcting Martha's understanding through the raising of Lazarus, but at indicating that "the idea of the eschatological *anástasis* is so transformed that the future resurrection of Martha's belief becomes irrelevant in the face of the present resurrection that faith grasps"; *The Gospel of John: A Commentary* (Eng. tr., 1971), p. 402. Cf. Dodd, *The Interpretation of the Fourth Gospel*, pp. 364f.
31. "The Eschatology of the Gospel of John," in *Faith and Understanding*, I, 165.

The way Bultmann dismisses the future aspects of the eschaton from the Gospel of John has been subjected to heavy criticism, much of it justifiable. But the fact that Bultmann's interpretation is incorrect does not allow us to ignore the fact that this particular Gospel talks extensively about the decisive present-ness of salvation, not excluding the future as such, but all *futuristic* eschatology. The New Testament constantly stresses the future aspect of the expectation, especially in its metaphorical language of the "harvest." In John (e.g. 4:35f.), as well as in the other Gospels, the harvest is portrayed as something future. In the parable of the weeds in the wheat, the servants are as yet forbidden to root out the weeds, because the harvest has not yet come (Matt. 13:24-30, 39).

In the Gospel of John, Christ depicts the harvest as appearing to be much closer. He speaks of those who, at the time of sowing, say: "There are yet four months, then comes the harvest" (John 4:35). This serves as an excellent illustration of time and duration. Christ then calls on His hearers to observe what is going on in the field right now — "I tell you, lift up your eyes, and see how the fields are already white for harvest." The harvest is apparently not a matter of a more or less distant future, but of the present. This comes to characteristic expression when He adds that the reaper already receives his wages and "gathers fruit for eternal life, so that sower and reaper may rejoice together" (John 4:36). According to Grosheide, this close connection of sower and reaper is not to be interpreted to mean that sowing and reaping in eschatological time are, as Bultmann claimed, contemporaneous, because "together" *(homoú)* may have a "numerical" as well as a "temporal" meaning.[32] But it is difficult to deny that in John 4 sowing and reaping are also closely related in a temporal sense. In contrast to a long duration ("yet four months..."), Jesus points to the whiteness of the fields and the fact that the reaper, wages in hand, is gathering the fruit. The harvest is not something in the future to be awaited patiently; the white fields can already be seen. "The time of the harvest has already come."[33] Bultmann sees this as a paradoxical picture of the time of salvation, and he notes correctly the similarity here with Amos: "Behold, the days are coming, says the Lord, when the plowman shall overtake

---

32. *Komm.*, I, 313.
33. Bultmann adds, "[the harvest] does not belong to some future time, but always to the present"; *The Gospel of John*, p. 197.

the reaper and the treader of grapes him who sows the seed" (Amos 9:13).

"The plowing is barely completed and the harvest has already ripened."[34] That is how it will be in the Kingdom. Sower and reaper will rejoice together. The ripeness of the fields determines the entire passage. Here is where the accent of the presence of salvation in the present time must undoubtedly fall.[35]

Throughout this Gospel there is something of the simplicity and radicalness of the ultimate decisions of believing, seeing, and hearing the acts of salvation that God has accomplished through Christ. Christ is the light of the world, the living water, the bread from heaven. So decisive is His coming that the judgment of the whole world is consummated in Him. When the hour of the glorification of the Son of man comes, the prayer for the glorification of His Father's name is answered by a voice from Heaven: "I have glorified it, and I will glorify it again" (John 12:28). "Now is the judgment of this world; now shall the ruler of this world be cast out" (John 12:31). From this Bultmann concludes that the future will bring nothing new and that all apocalyptic visions of the future are idle dreams.[36] Thus he discards all "end-historical" eschatology, which he considers to be foreign to the emphasis on the present. The expectation of the coming of Christ in glory at the end of time he sees as the product of the mythical world-view of the New Testament. The "eschaton" in the decisive sense — God's acts through the man Jesus of Nazareth — leaves no room for such a coming in glory.[37] Nor can we speak of a second "eschaton," or of a fulfilling, supernatural intervention by God.[38] Since this is the case, the "problem" of "intermediate time" — the question

34. C. van Gelderen, *Amos,* p. 297; cf. A. Weiser, *Die Propheten,* I (1949), 179.
35. Zahn claims that it is not a matter of simultaneity, which would be without interest in this connection; *Comm.,* p. 259. This is surely no argument: simultaneity accents the togetherness of sowing and harvest in the time of salvation. Bouma writes that sowing precedes reaping by a short time, but incorrectly concludes that in the Kingdom, the actual growing requires years, even centuries; *KV,* I, 432. This is precisely the opposite of what the passage says, and certainly does not follow from the fact that the one sows and another reaps, which does not mean to introduce a prolonged period of time, but merely to illustrate the lowliness of the workers in the harvest.
36. *The Gospel of John,* p. 431.
37. Cf. "History and Eschatology in the NT," *NT Studies,* I (1954), 5-16.
38. *Glauben und Verstehen,* III, 84.

of the meaning of the present dispensation — simply falls away for Bultmann. The eschatological event has nothing whatever to do with a *futurum*. Naturally, his view allows for the continuity of time, but this continuity creates no problems with respect to the future and its relation to the present. The eschatological event has been completed and completes itself time and again in the proclamation of the Word. Christ is not a figure of the past; He is *Christus praesens*. "Eschatology ... is not the future end of history, but history is swallowed up by eschatology."[39]

Buri argues that "dekerygmatizing" should follow closely upon demythologizing, because what Bultmann proclaims as the content of the kerygma — a new understanding of the self — does not require the preaching of Christ. On such a view salvation does not hinge upon one single moment in history.[40] Although Bultmann has categorically denied this conclusion, he maintains persistently that the presently decisive "eschaton" precludes any future eschatology. He supports this by constant reference to the passages we discussed above, which speak of the presence of salvation. In addition to these Johannine passages, he cites the epistles of Paul.[41] Although the future and dramatic aspects are not lacking in Paul, as they are in John,[42] he argues that there is really no difference in principle between the two; in fact, Paul also believed that the eschatological judgment was a thing of the past by virtue of the present righteousness and reconciliation with God.

Now the element of the future in the Pauline expectation cannot be denied. Bultmann describes Paul's view of what has occurred and what is yet to come as the paradox of this life of hope.[43] But the meaning of the word "paradox," with its nonnegotiable implications of tension, quickly disappears when Bultmann adds that, whereas John consistently followed this present nature of salvation through to its radical conclusion, Paul still continued to cling to the old mythological view of

39. "History and Eschatology in the NT," *loc. cit.*, pp. 15f.
40. F. Buri, "Entmythologisierung oder Entkerugmatisierung der Theologie," in *Kerygma und Mythos*, II (1952), 85.
41. See D. E. Holwerda, *The Holy Spirit and Eschatology in the Gospel of John* (1959), pp. 103ff.
42. Cf. "The Eschatology of the Gospel of John," *Faith and Understanding*, I, 176n.
43. "Man in God's Design," *Studiorum NT Societas* (1952), p. 56.

the future.[44] One can hardly speak of a paradox any more! Then he goes on to place John and Paul in one line by claiming that in Pauline eschatology too the role of history has been eclipsed.[45]

It seems clear to me that there is a much more profound relationship between the present and future in Paul than Bultmann gives credit for. Paul's view of the future is not a foreign idea borrowed from traditional apocalyptic, but something essentially connected with his faith in Christ. Bultmann relativizes Paul's expectation by saying that for Paul the future is "only . . . the completion and confirmation of the eschatological occurrence that has now already begun."[46] Clearly, the word "only" is the key to Bultmann's interpretation. It is impossible to reconcile this "only" with the brilliant glow of Paul's expectation evident from his epistles.

"Completion" and "confirmation" — without the "only" — would be a more accurate approximation of Paul's expectation. "Completion" does play a decisive role in Paul's thinking and hoping. He does not think of a destruction of history in eschatology. The future is in no way threatened or deprived of meaning by what has already been granted and received in the present. Paul was impressed by both the reality of the time of salvation in Christ and the uniqueness of the return of Christ. There is no paradox here. On the basis of the presence of salvation the windows to the future are opened. Expectation, with its kerygmatic and pastoral concern, is not an alien body in one's reflection on present salvation. It is the very source of such reflection. Consequently, neither exclusively "realized eschatology" nor "futurism," which dissociates the future from the present, will serve as a characterization of Pauline eschatology.

We should let Paul speak for himself. In all of his admonitions and consolations to the churches, he transcends any conflict between the present and the future. Throughout, it is not a paradox, but a dynamic relationship — and with it, as we shall see, the tensions — that is evident in Paul's writings. "For since we believe that Jesus died and rose again, even so, through

44. *Glauben und Verstehen*, III, 89f.
45. "History and Eschatology in the NT," *loc. cit.*, p. 13: "Thereby eschatology has wholly lost its sense as goal of history and is in fact understood as the goal of the individual human being."
46. *Theology of the NT* (Eng. tr., 1951), p. 306.

Jesus, God will bring with him those who have fallen asleep" (1 Thess. 4:14). The believers wait for the coming from heaven of the Son of God whom God has raised from the dead (1 Thess. 1:10). There is no evidence of conflict between attention for the present and future. Paul constantly emphasized the relevance of the present, the new time of salvation, for the future. This is the fundamental difference between Bultmann, who wants to rid eschatological existentiality of any future orientation, and Paul, who, in the present reality of the time of salvation, anticipates the coming of the Lord and glorification (Rom. 8:18).

Hence we are confronted by the dominant eschatological theme of the New Testament, one which negates all dilemmas resulting from human configurations such as realized or futuristic eschatology. The terms "realized" and "futuristic" may warn us against placing disproportionate emphasis on the future and the present respectively; they never in themselves constitute an adequate and satisfactory interpretation of the genuine New Testament promise and expectation.[47]

"Already" and "not yet"

Another way of phrasing the question of what the "time between" means is to ask if it is possible on the basis of the New Testament to explain why the divine plan of salvation in this time bears the characteristic "already" and "not yet" aspects. How can one explain it that, while we have continually fixed our attention on the accomplished — the "already" — history still continues? Why is this present dispensation a time of walking by faith, not sight (2 Cor. 5:7)? Is the continuity of life in this form not an enigma difficult to reconcile with the triumphant proclamations about what has already occurred in the *fulness* of time? Again, we must caution against skepticism; we must seek out the answers on the basis of our faith in the "kairos" of God's acts and of the biblical message testifying to these acts.

---

47. W. C. van Unnik writes: "Since the death and resurrection of Jesus the Messiah, the new covenant has been realized. But this is not yet the definitive time, it is only the beginning." Concerning the tensions of the present dispensation he writes that "all these tensions cannot diminish the intense joys that excited Paul"; "La conception de la nouvelle alliance," in *Littérature et théologie pauliniennes (Recherches bibliques V)* (1960), p. 124. See also T. F. Torrance, "The Modern Eschatological Debate," *Evangelical Quarterly*, XXV (1953), 45ff., 94ff., 167ff., 224ff.

Does this continuity of history not undeniably call to mind that which was thought to be passé: sinfulness, guilt, and corruption? The present dispensation is concerned with the concrete world, in which our entire life is spent. Thus, to ask what the present dispensation means is to ask whether, on the grounds of what has been accomplished (the "already"), an unfulfilled condition (the "not yet") can be possible and real.

There is a variety of ways in which the New Testament speaks of this unfulfilled condition. The eschatological reality of the future does not consist of tying together the loose ends of what can already be seen in broad outline. No, it is a powerful and novel perspective on the works of God. Not only has Christ appeared at the end of the age (Heb. 9:26), but there is also a future "close *(syntéleia)* of the age" (cf. Matt. 13:39f., 49; 24:3; 28:30). Along with the perspective on Christ's coming in the fulness of time, we read of God's intention, "as a plan for the fulness of time, to unite all things in Christ, things in heaven, and things on earth" (Eph. 1:10).

Here is an ultimate goal to which the dealings of God are directed. Through the riches of salvation already given it is possible to speak of fulness; yet in this fulness there is room for a broad future-perspective. According to God's plan *(oikonomía* — Eph. 1:10), there is a final fulfilment, a completion of salvation.[48] At first glance this fulness that is given might seem to exclude any possibility for a new perspective, because it fills the gap in our present condition, and therefore renders a new fulfilment superfluous.[49] On closer examination, this interpretation appears erroneous, inasmuch as both the fulness and the prospect of eschatological fulfilment are held out to the believers of apostolic days. The perspective is of the fulfilment in which all things will be united under one Head, Christ.

The importance of the "not yet" in the New Testament discussion of the present state of salvation can only be explained from this perspective. Paul, convinced of what already is, speaks urgently of what is to come. He speaks of this "not yet" in a variety of ways: the eager longing *(apokaradokía)* of the waiting creation (Rom. 8:19), the subjection of the creation to futility *(mataiótēs)* (vs. 20), its bondage to decay (vs. 21), and its groan-

---

48. Cf. Delling, in *TDNT*, s.v. *plērōma*, VI, 305.
49. Cf. Paul's prayer that the Ephesians might "be filled with all the fulness of God" *(eis pán tó plērōma toú theoú* — 3:19; cf. 1:23). See also the commentaries by Grosheide *(ad loc.)* and Ridderbos *(ad* Col. 2:10).

ing in travail (vs. 22). At the same time, he speaks of believers groaning inwardly as they await the adoption (vs. 23). This is not to question or deny the salvation already received, but to indicate what is yet lacking. When Paul contrasts hoping with seeing, he adds nevertheless that "in this hope we were saved" (vs. 24 — *tḗ gár elpídi esṓthēmen*). This hope is the central theme of the present dispensation, in which faith and sight are contrasted.[50]

Life in the present dispensation can be described as being "away from the Lord" (2 Cor. 5:6). Life is full of "good courage" and at the same time is fulfilled by the perspective on the manifestation of glory (vs. 10; cf. vs. 8). The tension between the "already" and the "not yet" continues to present itself, most evidently in the triumphant words used to describe the victory of Christ followed by the expectation of the eschatological dethroning of death as the last enemy. Paul is radically clear and definitive on this point: "He disarmed *(apekdysámenos)* the principalities and the powers and made a public example of them *(edeigmátisen en parrēsía),* triumphing over them *(thriambeúsas)"* (Col. 2:15). Paul's words here, like what he says about the abolition of death (2 Tim. 1:10 —*katargeín;* cf. Heb. 2:14), are so complete and final that it is difficult to miss their intent. This word *katargein,* which Paul uses in 1 Corinthians 1:28 to mean "render insignificant, set aside,"[51] is also used to indicate the eschatological dethroning of death as the final enemy. Here again the tensions between the "already" and the "not yet" are terminologically visible: the accomplished fact does not exclude the eschatological perspective on the actual reality. From the one dethronement, there is a perspective on *the* dethronement. Emphatically, the dethronement is already a fact: the enemy has been disarmed (which Ridderbos suggests is the best trans-

50. In his commentary on Rom. 8:24, Ridderbos does not accept the parallelism between hoping/seeing and faith/sight on the ground that Rom. 8 is not talking about glorified sight but about building on visible things. It seems to me that the "who hopes for what he sees?" of Rom. 8:24 is in fact connected with the tensions that come to the fore in 2 Cor. 5:7. Greijdanus, in his commentary on Romans (I, 382), speaks of hoping as applying to the absent and the future. See also van Leeuwen and Jacob, *KV* on Romans, p. 180. One is reminded of the classic definition of faith in Heb. 11:1 — "the assurance of things hoped for, the conviction of things not seen"; and the reference, later in the same chapter, to Moses, who "endured as seeing him who is invisible."

51. Delling, in *TDNT,* s.v. *katargéō,* I, 453.

lation). How could this image of the victor who has successfully overcome his foe be improved upon or supplemented?[52] At the same time that we become aware of this triumph, a window opens to the future.

The prominent tension in the New Testament between the "already" and the "not yet" is recognizable not only in the groaning, corruptibility, and subjection of the creation and in the power of death, but also in the life of every believer. Life in the "time between" is characterized by temptations and conflict, crises and fear, alienation and sin. The community of believers is in a constant state of activity, a proceeding toward a goal, a pilgrimage full of tension and imperfection, all of which is summed up by the phrase "not yet." To be sure, the community is graced by the presence of the Holy Spirit (1 Cor. 6:19), who has brought renewal (Titus 3:5), freedom (2 Cor. 3:17), and sonship (Rom. 8:14). But this fulfilment is not a conclusion in itself; it is a perspective on the future, a house with open windows.[53] When the Spirit was poured out upon the congregation, His power was revealed in the form of the church in the last days: through persistence, prayer, and the breaking of bread in communion. As a result of what had been accomplished, the battle with the powers of evil was joined, a race in which the believers look "to Jesus the pioneer and perfecter *(archēgós kai teleiotés)* of our faith," laying aside "sin which clings so closely *(euperístatos)*" (Heb. 12:1f.).[54] The outcome of this race is surely not in question. Yet it is a conflict that requires persistence and steadfastness.[55]

There is no hint of either an exclusively futuristic or an exclusively present eschaton. Indeed, the relationship between the "already" and the "not yet" constitutes the hallmark of the life of the community of believers. This connection is most vividly illustrated by Paul when he dismisses one "already" to posit another: "Not that I have already *(édē)* obtained this or am already *(édē)* perfect; but I press on *(diōkō)* to make it my own *(katalábō)*, because Christ Jesus has made me his own"

52. Delling speaks of "the divine triumphant march through the world," in *TDNT*, s.v. *thriambeúō*, III, 160.
53. Cf. H. Berkhof, *De mens onderweg. Een christelijke mensbeschouwing* (1960), p. 100.
54. Cf. O. Michel, *Der Herbräerbrief*, p. 289.
55. Stauffer distinguishes five motifs of thought expressed by *agōn*, etc., in primitive Christianity; in *TDNT*, s.v., I, 136ff.

(Phil. 3:12).[56] Here we see a healthy motion, a unique striving, a forgetting of what is behind and a pursuing of what is ahead. There is nothing morose, pessimistic, or defeatist in this; instead, there is a strong inclination and motivation to be active in the light of what has been already received in prayer and steadfastness, faith, hope and love, and watchfulness and expectation.

The unfulfilled condition — the "not yet" — can also be approached on the basis of what is written about the gift of the Spirit. The believers received the Spirit as "firstfruits" (Rom. 8:23). This gift is at once a possession, a rich, blessed, and unquestionable reality, and an *initial* endowment. As an initial gift, it stands in direct line with the *expectation*. Furthermore, the Spirit is called the "guarantee" (2 Cor. 1:22; 5:5 — *arrabōn*), a word that clearly conveys the eschatological nature of both "already" and "not yet." There is no cause for skepticism about the reality of this gift. The very awareness of its reality is "the guarantee of ... full future possession of salvation."[57] The Holy Spirit is the guarantee of our inheritance (Eph. 1:14). God has prepared us for the transition from the mortal to the immortal through His gift of the Spirit as pledge. Thus, "already" and "not yet" are not contrasted in an irreconcilable antithesis.[58] Through what has been given, the believer obtains a perspective on a *new* fulness, namely, the reality of the inheritance. The designation *"first* fruits" indicates the beginning-character of the gift of the Spirit;[59] the designation "pledge" indicates the veracity of the promise and validity of the expectation. Both designations firmly establish the correlation between present and future.

In this connection, we are also reminded of the place occupied by these two aspects — present and future — in the son-

---

56. Cf. the "not yet" in vs. 13: "I do not consider that I have made it my own" *(egō emautón oúpō logízomai kateilēphénai);* and in 1 Tim. 6:12 — "take hold of the eternal life *to which you were called."*
57. Behm, in *TDNT,* s.v. *arrabōn,* I, 475.
58. Cf. Barth's denial of "contradiction"; *CD,* IV/3/2, 910: "To be sure there is a plain and irremovable distinction; but there is no flat contradiction." See also the examples he gives (p. 911), and his conclusion: "... the lines between the Then, the Now, and the One Day everywhere intersect."
59. "In the LXX *aparchē* is first used in the original sense ... of the 'firstfruits' of the field or flocks which is offered to God"; Delling, in *TDNT,* s.v. *aparchē,* I, 484. Cf. Deut. 18:4. Phil. 1:6 speaks of God's beginning *(enarxámenos)* a good work that He will bring to completion at the day of Jesus Christ *(epitelései áchri hēméras Christoú Iēsoú).*

ship of God. In Romans 8, Paul stresses the present reality of the sonship thus: "For all who are led by the Spirit of God are sons of God" (vs. 14). The Spirit is the Spirit of sonship; hence the cry: "Abba! Father!" (vs. 15). This Spirit bears witness with our spirit that we are children of God.[60] This sonship provides a perspective on the future, which includes not only mention of the inheritance and ultimate glory ("if children, then heirs..."— vs. 17), but also of expectation ("we wait for adoption as sons"— vs. 23).

Hence there is both a real sonship and an expectation of the future: "full *hyiothesia* is still an object of hope."[61] The difference has been interpreted in a variety of ways, with the result that the whole matter has been more obscured rather than clarified. Weiss's definition of sonship in the present time as "an inner relationship only and a divine privilege, to which the real and objective situation, however, does not yet correspond,"[62] gives one the distinct impression that what is being given with the right hand is being taken away with the left. To understand the sonship and the eschatological reality — including John's remarks that it does not yet appear what we shall be (1 John 3:2) — we must relate these to the fulness and perfection,[63] and remain convinced of the reality and correlation of the "already" and the "not yet."

Suffering and martyrdom

Finally, we should give some attention to the clear indications of the "not yet" in the New Testament references to the suffering of believers. There is surely good reason to speak with Paul of "the sufferings of this present time" (Rom. 8:18) — *tá pathémata toú nýn kairoú*). This suffering is not worth comparing with the glory that will be ours; but this does not in any way deny or even lessen the reality of this suffering. And the eschatological perspective of the future is often described

---

60. On the distinction between slaves and sons, cf. Gal. 4:6f.
61. Oepke, in *TDNT*, s.v. *pais*, V, 653; cf. 1 John 3:1f.
62. As quoted by J. L. de Villiers, *Die betekenis van 'hyiothesia' in die briewe van Paulus* (1950), p. 126. The word is used five times in Paul's letters: Rom. 8:15, 23; 9:4; Gal. 4:5; Eph. 1:5.
63. On the fulfilment of our sonship, see De Villiers (*ibid.*, pp. 188ff.). In his commentary on Romans, H. N. Ridderbos sees *hyiothesia* as the *apokálypsis* of the sons of God (8:19). This is no doubt true, but the secret of 1 John 3:2, to which Ridderbos also refers, remains just that (pp. 186, 188).

negatively in terms of this suffering, as, for example, when we read that "God will wipe away every tear . . . and death shall be no more, neither shall there be mourning nor crying nor pain any more, for the former things have passed away" (Rev. 21:4; cf. Isa. 25:8).

We must see the reality of this suffering as a concrete manifestation of the "not yet." Obviously, all suffering was not done away with by the triumph of Jesus. In Gethsemane Christ told the officers from the chief priests and Pharisees "if you seek me, let these men go their way" (John 18:8). But those words did not establish a universal rule. The disciples would suffer. The singularity of the Lord's suffering is apparent,[64] but later the suffering of His followers would also become visible. They were not exempt from suffering; quite the contrary, through the suffering of the Lord they were being prepared for their own times of trial. The world would hate them (John 15:18), and even as the Lord Himself was persecuted, so they would also be persecuted (John 15:20). They would be sent as sheep in the midst of wolves (Matt. 19:29; Mark 10:28). Throughout this all runs the promise of the reward and the blessing of the "now in this time" (Mark 10:30); yet this does not eliminate the gravity and terror of the suffering.

During the "time between," the consequence of following the Lord is bearing the cross. The connection between these two is so close that whoever is not prepared for this cannot be His disciple (Luke 14:27, 33). Here is contained a mysterious relationship between the Lord and His disciples; their lives are characterized by the principle that a servant is not greater than his master (John 15:20). Although this does not constitute a theodicy of suffering, a way is shown upon which they can walk, not as rebels or insurrectionists, but in patience and longsuffering. This is clearly expressed in the thought that "it is enough for the disciple to be like his teacher, and the servant like his master" (Matt. 10:25).[65] So it may be said that to suffer

---

64. Michaelis writes: "The uniqueness of the passion of Jesus is reflected in the fact that *pathein* occurs only in sayings of Jesus relating to His own person"; in *TDNT*, s.v. *páschō*, V, 916. Cf., however, the use of *páschein* in 1 Peter.

65. *arketón tō mathētē*. Cf. the persecution (vs. 23) and the comment in vs. 25: "If they have called the master of the house Beelzebul how much more will they malign those of his household." In this connection see Kittel, in *TDNT*, s.v. *arkéō*, I, 464ff.; and 2 Cor. 12:9, with reference to Paul's thorn in the flesh: "My grace is sufficient for you" (*Arkei soi hē cháris mou*).

with the Lord is essential for the Christian community. The New Testament does not describe the reality of suffering as being coincidental or neutral; it cuts straight to the heart or meaning of this suffering and portrays it in many profoundly significant ways.

When Paul linked the sonship and the inheritance with each other, he added: "provided we suffer with him in order that we may also be glorified with him" (Rom. 8:17 — *eiper sympáschomen hina kai syndoxasthṓmen*). Again, the apostle is not giving a simplistic teleological theodicy, minimizing and eclipsing the purpose of suffering in the world. Instead, Paul is demonstrating that the full reality of suffering is part and parcel of the eschatological perspective. In a surprising way, suffering is meaningfully connected with joy, as when Paul rejoices in the suffering he experienced on behalf of the congregations (Col. 1:24).[66] In his suffering, and in the experiences of all the apostles, who were "always being given up to death for Jesus' sake" (2 Cor. 4:11), lies a meaningful and purposeful goal. When death, or the threat of it, was at work in the apostles, life was in full bloom in the community (vs. 12). In this way they carried the death of Jesus in their own bodies (vs. 10). This life is at once feeble and strong: feeble because of the element of persecution; strong, because it receives direction in the midst of discontinuity and despair (vs. 8). It is the reality of the efficacy of Christ's death that is manifested in concrete terms in the believer's life and sheds light on his suffering. This light on the eschatological expectation is the meaning of the current bitterness. This same reality will also reveal how meaningful the present dispensation will have been.

The suffering endured by the faithful is not something fateful or an irrational fact against which they are unequally matched. A case of suffering is an event that is meaningful only because of communion with Christ and God's providence. This is why suffering is not foreign to the follower of Christ. The New Testament cautions the believers against being overawed by this suffering: "Beloved, do not be surprised *(mḕ xenizesthe)* at the fiery ordeal which comes upon you to prove you, as though something strange *(hōs xénou)* were happening to you" (1 Pet. 4:12). It is through tribulation that they must enter

66. On Paul's expression in Col. 1:24, "I complete what is lacking in Christ's afflictions...," see Berkouwer, *Faith and Sanctification* (Eng. tr., 1952), pp. 153ff.

the Kingdom of God (Acts 14:22 — *dei hēmás eiselthein*). This necessity is not a blind and uncontrollable fate, but the stamp of discipleship in the communion of the Lord.[67] It has been prophesied that suffering and persecution will increase as the day of the Lord approaches. Pain will begin, and as it continues there will come persecution, death, and hate, all for the sake of the Lord's name (Matt. 24:8f.).

It has been suggested that behind this exhortation lies the incomprehensibility of suffering for believers, "having been newly converted and made heirs of the messianic kingdom."[68] Possibly a whole new problematic of the present dispensation had arisen, which had failed to understand the meaning of suffering. The point in question is itself not irrelevant, but the New Testament response is unmistakably clear when the connection is drawn between disgrace suffered for Christ's sake and salvation. The New Testament opens our eyes to the meaning of suffering (1 Pet. 4:14; cf. 2:19; 3:14; 4:16).

All this by no means underestimates the reality of suffering. Quite the contrary, it is a matter of grave concern. True, it is always spoken of in connection with grace and salvation from the divine perspective, but it is and will remain an *unjust* suffering (1 Pet. 2:19 — *páschōn adikōs*). Moreover, it leaves the impression that injustice continues to thrive in the world. If one has to suffer for the cause of the Lord, it indicates how disjointed things are in this present dispensation. It proves that there is no *apokálypsis* yet, no revelation of the *true* state of affairs as known only to God.

The most impressive illustration of this confused state of affairs in the present world is not merely the disgrace and threats — though admittedly grievous — that are suffered by the believer as the price for the injustices committed by the world, but death itself. We are reminded of the tragedy of the martyrs, whose stories demonstrate dramatically the reality of the "not yet." In the face of the terrible frightening darkness of inestimable suffering, Mary's *Magnificat* (Luke 1:46-55) appears to have no meaning for the present dispensation. Even the New Testament reflects some of the human incredulity in the apparent triumph of evil. No less than the Lord Himself, informed of John the Baptist's death, felt the compulsion to withdraw

---

67. On tribulation in the NT, see Schlier in *TDNT,* s.v. *thlíbō,* III, 143-48.
68. E. Selwyn, *The First Epistle of St. Peter,* p. 220.

to a lonely place (Matt. 14:13; cf. Mark 6:31). This experience continued in the early church, as witnesses to the gospel became martyrs for it in the new dispensation. Yet this dispensation had nevertheless been stamped by what had been accomplished ("already") and the true light had already penetrated through the blackness of unbelief and injustice (cf. Acts 7:59-8:3; 12:2; Rev. 2:13).

But this continuous, unjust suffering — this relentless persecution of the Lord's own — did not bring about a crisis in the community. In fact, precisely in those times when injustice seemed to run rampant, joy reached its greatest heights. For example, earnest prayer was made by the church when Peter was imprisoned (Acts 12:5), everyone fulfilled his mission (vs. 25), and all were filled with joy and with the Holy Spirit (13:52). All this in a time of persecution! The unceasing confusion remained; there was no easing of conditions but an intensification of distress, such as Israel had experienced under the old covenant.

In the context of salvation and victory and sonship and the presence of the Spirit, it is possible for questions to arise, easily leading to a crisis as imminent threats of martyrdom become temptations to leave the faith. Something of this appeared in the early centuries of the Christian church on occasions of persecution when there was witness and readiness, but also signs that some no longer felt able to bear *this* particular challenge. When the crisis passed, there was much soul-searching in the church. This was particularly true during the judgments on the *lapsi* in the days of the Novatian controversy and on the *traditores* at the time of the Donatist controversy. Such judgments reflected a crisis of the meaning of the present dispensation. Lapsing from the faith had assumed frightening proportions. Though none of us would care to sit in judgment over the *lapsi,* it is nevertheless very clear from the New Testament that this massive lapse indicated a loss of awareness of the meaning of the present dispensation. The challenges these people confronted were, without a doubt, second to none in intensity. The threat to life was as grievous as it had been during the days of John the Baptist, who had to die because of the dismal, amoral "triumph" of demonic powers (Mark 6:21-29).

The figure of the martyr has always attracted a great deal of attention in Christian thought. There seems to be a halo cast over the martyrs; and many have pointed to this light and their almost unendurable suffering, suggesting that this not only proves the steadfastness of the martyr, but also that this type of dying is special and qualitatively different from other death. This raises the question of the so-called martyriological interpretation of the New Testament word *mártys*, which sees the witness as a martyr, and martyrdom as essential to the witnessing activity. Accordingly, the kind of witnessing that led to martyrdom is seen as the most significant kind. In the course of history, this special quality of martyrdom has often been united with a meritorial element.[69] The *light* in this present darkness is stressed. The problem is not whether there is a connection between witnessing to the gospel and martyrdom, but whether the two are necessarily and essentially connected. Now the New Testament understanding of witness does not necessarily include martyrdom. Witness is invariably directed to the Lord and His resurrection (Acts 1:8, 22). This orientation is important. All too often the witness himself has been placed in the center of the stage, and the testimony is seen as the result of the witness's death, rather than the other way around.[70]

The New Testament does not draw isolated attention to the martyr himself.[71] Rather, it calls attention to the distress and terror of dying for the witness.[72] The passage that supposedly shifts the emphasis from "witness" to "martyr"—Acts 22:20—points in precisely the other direction. Paul is here confessing the guilt of his persecution of the church by imprisonments,

69. Cf. Erik Esking, "Das Martyrium als theologisch-exegetisches Problem," in *In Memoriam Ernst Lohmeyer* (1951), p. 227.
70. In the first thesis of his *Getuigen van Jezus Christus in het NT* (1933) R. Schippers suggests that "witness" nowhere carries the meaning of martyr in the NT (as against Karl Holl); see also pp. 124ff., and 195ff. (on Antipas). Cf. further H. F. von Campenhausen, *Die Idee des Martyriums in der alten Kirche* (1936), chap. II; Strathmann, in *TDNT*, s.v. *mártys*, IV, 495: "Antipas in [Rev.] 2:13 is not a witness because he is put to death; he is put to death because he is a witness, i.e., in the sense of proclamation of the Gospel."
71. Cf. Von Campenhausen's discussion of "heroicizing martyrology" (*op. cit.*, p. 119); and K. Rahner's excursus "On Martyrdom," in *On the Theology of Death* (Eng. tr., 1961), pp. 89-127.
72. Note the description of the woman in Rev. 17:1-6: "drunk with the blood of the saints and the blood of the martyrs of Jesus." This image with all of its terror is quite compatible with the Old and New Testament portrayals of resistance even to the point of death. This does not relativize steadfastness and loyalty, but it makes no distinction between those witnesses who are killed and those who are not. The witness unites them. Cf. also Rom. 8:36 (Ps. 44:22).

torture, and consent "when the blood of Stephen thy witness was shed." Doubtless, Stephen's death stands in direct relation to his witness to Jesus, but "there is nothing to suggest that the death was an essential part of his testimony."[73]

It is instructive to note how the Book of Revelation speaks about martyrdom, namely, as distress and terror "permitted" by God. We read about those souls who had been killed for the Word, and the witness they bore. They cry out: "O Sovereign Lord, holy and true, how long before thou wilt judge and avenge our blood on those who dwell upon the earth?" (Rev. 6:9-10). There is no trace of skepticism in this plea. The clear implication is that God is able to triumph over apparently triumphant injustice.[74]

The question does however illustrate the tensions that are integral to the cross-bearing church.[75] It is a legitimate question — how the slaying of the pious by the godless can be reconciled with the unlimited dominion of the holy and faithful God that is to have dawned.[76] The meaning of the continuity of time is what is asked for in the question "how long?" The question does not imply doubt about the "already"; it is asked on the basis of the "already."[77] And the answer that is given is surprising. First of all, each receives a white robe, the unmistakable sign of victory; but in addition to this, each is told "to rest a little longer, until the number of their fellow-servants and their brethren should be complete, who were to be killed as they themselves had been" (Rev. 6:11). The significance of this is that, while the light of the future beams its rays into the situation, history still continues in the paths of this present injustice, albeit within the imminent and actual boundary fixed by the word "until."

The words of Scripture about the souls under the altar reflect the unfulfilled condition and the divine response in times

73. Casey, as quoted by Schippers, op. cit., p. 126; cf. Von Campenhausen, op. cit., pp. 31ff.
74. S. Greijdanus, Comm., p. 155.
75. Similar urgent questions can be found in the OT in connection with Israel's distress. Cf. Ps. 44:22 (sheep for the slaughter); vs. 23 ("Rouse thyself! Why sleepest thou, O Lord? Awake!"); vs. 24 (God's hiding His face and forgetting Israel's oppression); vs. 26 (the appeal to God's steadfast love); 74:10 ("How long?"). In the NT this "how long?" receives a deeper and stronger accent from the notion of fulfilment.
76. Cf. J. Behm, Die Offenbarung des Johannes, p. 41.
77. Cf. H. Schlier, "Zum Verständnis der Geschichte nach der Offenbarung des Johannes," in Die Zeit der Kirche (1956), pp. 271ff.

of threats and persecution. They do not describe or define the present dispensation, but they do reply clearly to the cries against injustice. The present time is preeminently a time of waiting. The "not yet" can only be understood and its threats sustained in terms of the "already" and the unfailing promise of God.[78]

There is little in Scripture to commend the embarrassment the church has often shown about the future, when it is attacked by unbelievers who charge that the promise of the future is nothing but a bill that comes due in eternity, which one can use to shut out sensitivity to current distress and injustices. The church, it is true, has categorically rejected such views, but its witness concerning the future has occasionally sounded very strange and remote when compared to the great voice from the throne describing the New Jerusalem (Rev. 21:3). Yet the reality of the darkness and the dread cannot be relativized; it remains a darkness, real and unalterable, vividly characterizing the "not yet" of the present dispensation.

God's intention in history

Reflecting on the meaning of the present dispensation soon leads one to the discovery that it cannot be treated as a special theme or problem. It can only be dealt with indirectly, and then only in the framework of consolation, admonition, and mandate. The most emphatic and explicit reference to it is found in 2 Peter 3, in connection with the alleged "slowness" of God. We discussed this passage in our previous chapter in connection with the problem of "delay." Now we should examine what Peter added to his rebuttal of the skeptics: "[He] is for-

---

78. There is a remarkable parallel with the "souls under the altar" in the parable of the unjust judge in Luke 18:1-8. Christ concludes this parable by asking "Will not God vindicate his elect, who cry to him day and night?" (vs. 7a). Then follows the difficult clause *kai makro-thymeí ep' autoís* (vs. 7b). The RSV translates this as "Will he delay long over them?" Greijdanus interprets the *kai* as concessive ("even though he delay . . ."); *Komm.*, II, 849. Nor does Zahn *(Comm.,* p. 609) think that these words form a continuation of the question. In my opinion the concessive interpretation is improbable since immediately thereafter mention is made of God's *speedy* vindication of the elect (vs. 8). In any case, the keynote here of time — filled with injustice — is the future, from which the meaning of the present dispensation can only be understood as the time between the triumph of the Lord and His second coming. On the interpretation of Luke 18:7b, see also Horst, in *TDNT,* s.v. *makrothymía,* IV, 380f.

bearing toward you, not wishing that any should perish, but that all should reach repentance" (2 Pet. 3:9).

Peter sees an extremely close connection between duration — the continuing of history — and the patience and forbearance of God. Not only must we observe and believe that for God a thousand years count as one day; we are also called to recognize another fact — misinterpreted by many as "slowness"— namely, the revelation and manifestation of God's compassion.[79] In the continuity of time, God creates room and opportunity for repentance and conversion. How sharply this is contrasted to neutral and unbelieving attempts to analyze and interpret the course of history!

Hauck writes of 2 Peter that it fixes a significant point of departure, but that the author was unable to solve the "problem" of the present dispensation.[80] Indeed, in 2 Peter 3, the author does not develop an "ethic" of the present dispensation at all; but the religious aspect in his view of the continuity of history, together with the fact that the Lord has not yet returned, is of decisive importance. History is not merely a matter of the proverbial stream of time, carrying all life wherever it wishes; what is important *in* this continuity is the abiding presence of the living God and His favors, which are oriented to, and climax in, His call to repentance.

According to Hauck, the writings of John present a fundamental solution to the difficulty which surpasses that of 2 Peter.[81] This solution is said to be the idea of the present nature of salvation, on account of which the delay of the fulfilment becomes religiously tolerable. However, it is difficult to see how one can speak of a more "profound" solution in John than in Peter. After all, Peter too knew of the salvation that had already been given (2 Pet. 1:1, 3, 4), and it is exactly because of this reality that he urged on the believers on their way to the future (1:3-11). He underscored the importance of the for-

79. Cf. Hauck: "It corresponds not only to God's greatness — that His measure of time is different — but primarily to His love that He defers the return"; *Die Kirchenbriefe,* p. 99.
80. "He defers the fulfilment of the Christian hope for a definite time and can give a religious ground for this delay, but for the resultant 'between-time' he can point to no fully religious blessing and no comprehensive religious duty (responsibility for the world)"; *ibid.,* p. 100.
81. *Ibid.*

bearance of God, which is immediately connected with the ongoing duration of history.[82]

This thought of God's proclaimed intention with time is
not an isolated fact in the New Testament. When Paul urges
believers to pray "for kings and all who are in high places,"
he intends to hold before his readers the quiet and peaceable
life, as opposed to undisciplined and rebellious living (1 Tim.
2:2f.). This is the life pleasing to God. Paul adds that it is
God's will that all men come to knowledge of the truth (vs. 4).
In the peace and quiet of life there is opportunity for the
proclamation and dissemination of the gospel. The continuity
of this life is directly related to God's plan (vs. 3). Both 2 Peter
3:9, dealing with the forbearance of God, and 1 Timothy 2,
dealing with earthly powers and their function of preserving and
protecting,[83] refer directly to God's plan in the ongoing process
of time.

If this is a time of waiting, it is a period of divine waiting,[84]
to which human waiting must correspond. The theme that characterizes the entire present dispensation is "Be patient *(makro-
thymḗsate)*, therefore, brethren, until the coming of the Lord"
(James 5:7). James uses the analogy of the farmer waiting for
the coming of the harvest "until it receives the early and the
late rains."[85] Thus the bond that links the waiting of Him who
is the Lord of all history and the waiting of the community in
faith and prayer is indivisible.

The problem of history in its continuity has often been related to Paul's discussion of the "restraining" and the "restrainer"
in 2 Thessalonians 2. There is a clear time-aspect in this. Paul
warns the Thessalonians against being "quickly shaken in mind"
by any claims "to the effect that the day of the Lord has come"
(vs. 2). By contrast he tells them what must come to pass first
(vs. 3 — *prṓton*). He points to the coming revelation of the

---

82. "In the *makrothymía toú kyríou* the epistle finds the solution to the
difficult problem which the community then had to face, namely, that
the promise of the *parousia* had not yet been fulfilled." Horst, in
TDNT, s.v. *makrothymía*, IV, 386.

83. Cf. Barth, *CD*, III/2, 510.

84. Cf. 1 Pet. 3:20: "when God's patience waited in the days of Noah";
Selwyn speaks of "God's longsuffering patience, the purpose of which
was to give man time for repentance" *(op. cit.,* p. 201); see also the
ultimatum in Luke 13:6-9.

85. "The saying is an urging to patient waiting for the parousia"; Dibelius,
Der Brief des Jakobus, p. 223.

man of lawlessness, who is presently being restrained. "Do you not remember that when I was still with you I told you this? And you know what is restraining him now *(tó katéchon)* so that he may be revealed in his time. For the mystery of lawlessness is already at work; only he who now restrains *(ho katéchōn)* it will do so until he is out of the way" (vv. 5-7) .

The "not yet" and the continuity of time are here mentioned in one breath. On the surface this appears to refer only to the coming of the man of sin, but this cannot be dissociated from the appearance of the Lord in His parousia (vs. 8 — *tē epiphaneia*) . Alongside this "not yet" is an "already," but this "already" is not that of the given salvation, but of the presently active *(ēdē energeitai)* evil in the world (vs. 7) .

From this tension of "not yet — already," attention shifts to the restrainer. It is difficult to get at Paul's meaning here, because he was addressing the believers in Thessalonica on an issue that was familiar to them. Consequently, he did not elaborate on the issue. Many exegetes have attempted to reconstruct the circumstances surrounding this particular message, but with little success. Some exegetes are certain that, for Paul, the restrainer was the Roman state in general and the emperor in particular. They argue that the purpose of the Roman state was to maintain justice in order to restrain the power of evil. Roman justice compelled unrighteousness to await its day, that is, until the restrainer — the Roman state — would be taken away. Using this argument they come to speak of divine restraining through the authority of government in its preserving function. In other words, the state becomes the protector of the church in times of exceptional difficulty and provides *Lebensraum* for it.[86] A bearable situation is created; there is a relative degree of order; and the chaotic and catastrophic destruction accompanying the revelation of the demonic powers is stayed.

It is not difficult to see how this idea has arisen, since government is often mentioned in terms of the preservation of orderly life in the New Testament. This government, as min-

---

86. Van Leeuwen, *Komm.*, p. 432. He goes on to speak of the operation of common grace in this connection. Cf. also Stauffer's remark in his *NT Theology*, p. 85: "The civil power is set up as a bulwark against the powers of chaos, but it can only keep these powers in check, never really subdue them. The fight against them will never come to an end, and in the end it must succumb to their final onslaught." See G. Kittel, *Christus und Imperator*, p. 23.

ister of God (Rom. 13:4 — *diákonos theoú*), does not bear the sword in vain, and executes God's wrath on the wrongdoer. By virtue of such passages, many tended to equate the government with the restraining force that impeded and postponed the coming of the man of lawlessness.

Others disagree. Cullmann, for example, calls the reference of restrainer to the state the least probable hypothesis of all, because throughout late-Jewish and early Christian apocalyptic the state is portrayed as a satanic embodiment.[87] It would be curious indeed, he reasons, if what had been the right arm of Satan would suddenly come to be seen as the instrument for his frustration. The obvious question that Cullmann's remarks raise is whether this is really the way the New Testament looks on the state. Cullmann himself agrees that it conforms to God's plan that there should be a state for the duration of this era.[88]

For Paul too the state did not have final control or unbridled authority, but "it maintains a certain dignity in that it stands in an order which is still willed by God."[89] This, however, tends to vitiate Cullmann's rather outspoken views about the state as a satanic power. Cullmann's defense is weak; yet it can be said that the restrainer-state exegesis is not necessarily excluded from his view. This should be kept in mind when we consider Cullmann's views on the nature of the restrainer. He discusses this "mysterious apocalyptic passage"[90] and seeks an understanding of it that is in harmony with John Calvin's thesis that the restraining power is the missionary preaching of the end. Whereas Cullmann sees no point of contact between restrainer and state in the New Testament, he maintains that the real point of contact is between restrainer and missionary preaching, since the eschatological passages make it clear that before the end comes the gospel must have been proclaimed in

---

87. *The State in the NT* (Eng. tr., 1957), p. 64n.; cf. *Christ and Time*, pp. 164ff. See also Kittel, *Christus und Imperator*, p. 23, who calls it the "best-grounded" interpretation; Schnackenburg, *Die sittliche Botschaft des NT* (1954), p. 168, who finds the "political" interpretation "of little probability"; W. Stählin, "Die Gestalt des Antichristen und das Katechon," in *Festgabe Joseph Lortz*, II (1958), p. 10, who refers to it as a "widespread and well-grounded exegetical tradition," which is still not self-evident. Also cf. the remarks by Hanse in *TDNT*, s.v. *katéchō*, II, 829f.; and Berkhof, *CMH*, pp. 128-31.

88. *The State in the NT*, p. 62.

89. *Ibid.*, p. 64.

90. Hanse, in *TDNT*, s.v. *katéchō*, II, 829.

all the world (Matt. 24:14; Mark 13:10). This proclamation precedes the appearance of the antichrist, and fills the time of the present dispensation. Cullmann understands "what is restraining" as the mission-message, and "he who restrains" as Paul's designation of himself in his apostolic mission-consciousness during the last time.[91]

So there are two distinct interpretations of the passage: the political and missionary. Both have something appealing, and yet both leave something to be desired. Because both of them seem to be somewhat arbitrary and projectional, there are a host of different variations on these themes. This in itself is largely explained by the fact that Paul in no way concretized his own views about restrainer/restrained. It is probably better to acknowledge this and admit to a degree of uncertainty in these passages, rather than attempt to speculate about them.[92]

A case can undoubtedly be made for a retardation of the coming of the man of lawlessness through the activity of some temporary force in history, even though we do not know the nature of this force. There is definitely a restraining of the manifestation of lawlessness. Some have objected to the localization of the political and missionary interpretations on the ground that the universality of evil demands a more extensively applied power. Stählin feels that against the molestation of order and law (anomia) there is a conserving force, which cannot be concretely defined, whose time and place of operation cannot be determined exactly.[93] The notion of a conserving force requires acceptance of a boundary that God has placed to delimit the effects of chaos, similar to the boundary created to conserve life and protect it from chaos at the time of creation. Against the chaotic forces attempting to destroy the ordered boundaries is this conserving force, which will continue to be effective until the full revelation of the mysterium iniquitatis.[94]

91. Cf. Calvin on 2 Thess. 2:6: "I think that at least I hear Paul speaking of the universal call of the Gentiles."

92. Hanse says (loc. cit., 830): "A more exact interpretation is hardly possible." G. Kittel (op. cit., p. 23) expresses the same hesitation when he writes of the political interpretation that it is "not completely unequivocal." Augustine admitted that he did not know "quid sit in mora, quae causa sit dilationis eius." The tenuousness of this whole matter is demonstrated by the number of other identifications that have been suggested: "The Council of God," "legions of angels," and the like.

93. Loc. cit., p. 12.

94. Ibid. Cf. Abraham Kuyper, De Gemeene Gratie, I, 444f.; Dictaten Dogmatiek, V (Locus de Consummatione Saeculi), sec. 4, p. 212.

Thus, there has been a great deal written about the restraining of evil. But what does Paul mean by the *removal* of this restraining force (2 Thess. 2:7) ?[95] In all the uncertainty shrouding Paul's discussion about the restrainer, there is no trace of arbitrariness with respect to the present dispensation. This is not to say that people do not act arbitrarily, but their arbitrariness cannot negate the meaning and direction of history that has been fixed for all time by God. Indeed, even here, where evil is seen as evolving toward some consummation, this time period is portrayed as remaining firmly in the grasp of the hands of God. This should also be sufficient to warn us not to construct a *problematic* about the meaning of the present dispensation. Admittedly, if we consider the triumph of Jesus Christ and the continuity of history with its confusion and the nature of the "not yet," many questions arise.[96] These questions appear in the gospel too, but the gospel provides answers to these questions, not in the form of rationalistic constructs, but in the form of admonitions and consolations pointing to a future when the meaning of history, present dispensation included, will be made clear. "And before the throne, there is as it were a sea of glass, like crystal" (Rev. 4:6).

If we reflect on the meaning of the present dispensation from the point of view of the good news, realizing that life in its length and breadth is under the providence of a compassionate God, it is clear that the future in no way devalues life in this present dispensation. The corruptibility of things indeed urges us on to righteousness, faith, and expectation, but this is entirely different from saying that life in the present loses its value and significance. Amid all the limitations of the "not yet," the New Testament quite clearly underlines this value. Yet in church history we see evidence of excessive emphasis placed on either the present or the future. A strong emphasis on the future has often relativized the present, and vice versa. This was not so with Paul. Concluding his important eschatological message in 1 Corinthians 15, he urged the believers

---

95. With reference to the political interpretation, cf. F. K. Schumann, "Geschichtstheologische Fragen um den ludus de Antichristo," in *Gedenkschrift für W. Elert* (1955), pp. 62ff.

96. The problem of evil in the present dispensation already appears in Gregory of Nyssa. Cf. J. Daniélou, "Comble du mal et eschatologie chez Grégoire de Nysse," in *Festschrift J. Lortz*, II, 40ff.

to be steadfast, "knowing that in the Lord your labor is not in vain" (vs. 58).

Meaninglessness — "labor . . . in vain" — can only result from an "eschaton" of death, the unfulfilled "eschaton" of estrangement from God, who is the Lord of the ages. Then one says "let us eat and drink, for tomorrow we die" (1 Cor. 15:32). But the real eschaton stimulates new interest and concern for existence in the here and now. The call to make the most of the time (Eph. 5:16) comes into this present situation, not *despite* the fact that the days are evil, but *because* of it. This perspective of actively making the most of the time is not a modification of the eschatological expectation, but its consequence. In this connection we recall Martin Buber's oft-quoted remark that we are obviously still living in an unredeemed world. He concluded this from his thesis that there is no midway point in history, only a goal. World history, according to Buber, has not yet been decisively breached.[97] This "not yet," obviously, is quite different from the New Testament "not yet." The latter creates room and opportunity for work while it is day (John 9:4)[98] and adequately prepares man for his work (2 Tim. 3:17; cf. 4:1, 5). Through this, life is truly saved and preserved for the future. To gain some understanding of how this works is not to attempt a neutral analysis of the present dispensation, but is a consequence of the salvation granted by Christ to those who — in the mystery of the present dispensation — take no offense at Him (Matt. 11:6).

Calling and mission

How is the meaning of the present dispensation revealed in the calling of the believer? The New Testament makes it clear that the answer to this is found in the direction of the proclamation of the Word throughout the whole world, in witnessing to the end of the earth (Matt. 25:19; Acts 1:8). This is not merely a theoretical answer, but an actual and existential one. After all, the proclamation and dissemination of the gospel to all men is directly related to the "already" condition, to that which has already occurred in unalterable reality and fills history to the end of the earth with the proclamation of salvation. This

97. Cf. W. Aalders, *M. Buber*, pp. 39f. See also the splendid study by Hans Urs von Balthasar, *Martin Buber and Christianity* (Eng. tr., 1961).
98. Christ's comment here about His own life finds its analogy in human existence.

spatial end *(éschatos)* corresponds to the eschatological dealings of God in and on the basis of the Messianic fulfilment. Manson has correctly written that New Testament eschatology "holds open the door to a large hope for history. . . . Here is the clearest evidence, that the world-mission of the church has stepped into the interval dividing the incarnation of the Lord from the age of glory."[99]

There has been a great deal of discussion about this calling to proclamation during the entire present dispensation. Some have claimed that Christ's understanding of the Kingdom left no room for a lengthy dispensation in which a *universal* mission would take place. This universal message has been contrasted to the particular element in Jesus' preaching — His concentration on the lost sheep of the house of Israel (Matt. 10:5f.; 15:24). In response, it has been contended that this particularism of Jesus was of a very special nature, and that it is incorrect to set up a particularism/universalism dualism and classify Christ's preaching as particularistic. Not only did Christ's messages apply to others outside the house of Israel (cf. Matt. 8:5-13; Mark 7:24-30; Luke 13:28f.), but the whole relationship between particular and universal appears to become caught up in the continuity and dynamic of redemptive history.

Besides, the "everywhere" of the preaching of the gospel (cf. Mark 14:9) is not to be denied. First *(próton)*, the Word must be preached to *all* peoples (Mark 13:10).[100] In the profundity of God's plan, what may be called the particular (Israel) moves into the universal (all nations). This particular/universal relationship is not a contradiction, but a progressive continuation of the history of salvation. This continuity does not indicate a "development" or "shift" in Jesus' thinking: earlier particularistic and later universalistic. The fact that "salvation is from the Jews" (John 4:22) does not support particularism at all. The progressive continuation that unfolds through, with, and in Israel does not exclude a perspective on the whole world, but rather includes it.[101] At the breaking point of Israel's rejection

---

99. "Eschatology in the NT," *Scottish Journal of Theology Occasional Papers,* No. 2, pp. 15ff.

100. The parallel passage in Matt. 24:14 lacks the *próton,* but adds "then the end will come."

101. Insightful in this connection is D. Bosch, *Die Heidenmission in der Zukunftsschau Jesu. Eine Untersuchung zur Eschatologie der synoptischen Evangelien* (1959), pp. 111-15, 193ff.

of the Messiah, there came an abrupt historical change in the continuity of history from particularity to universality. In the way of the gospel confronting the world, there came a filling of the entire present dispensation through universal proclamation.

This universality, dimly reflected in Christ's remark to the Syrophoenician woman, "Let the children first be fed" (Mark 7:27; cf. Matt. 10:6), comes to full expression in the missionary outreach of the church.[102] In this change from particularity to universality, we find the great secret of the history of salvation. As early as the fulfilment of time — in Christ — it was indisputably clear that Christ was indeed the Light of the world (John 8:12) and that salvation had been prepared in the presence of all peoples (Luke 2:31).[103] The broad, universal perspective was not lacking during the time of concentration on Israel, even though it became visible only through Israel's rejection. There is resistance to this continuity and change in the New Testament. One of the most prominent examples is Peter, who had to learn that he was not to judge common or unclean anyone whom God has cleansed (Acts 10:15; 11:1, 18), since the Holy Spirit had now been poured out on the Gentiles too. The breakdown of the church's resistance to this and the irresistible continuity of history are obvious. No one could deny the water of baptism to anyone who had received the Holy Spirit. Peter asks the circumcision party in Jerusalem, "If then God gave the same gift [of the Spirit] to them as he gave to us when we believed in the Lord Jesus Christ, who was I that I could withstand God?" (Acts 11:17). This inability to with-

102. J. Jeremias writes: "The Gentile mission is the beginning of God's final act in the gathering of the Gentiles. The Gentile mission is God's own activity. As God's eschatological activity, it is an anticipation of the visible enthronement of the Son of Man, and as such it is the 'actual sign' of the period between Easter and the Parousia"; *Jesus' Promise to the Nations* (Eng. tr., 1958), p. 74. Cf. Bosch, *op. cit.*, p. 193; H. J. Margull, *Theologie der missionarischen Verkündigung. Evangelisation als oekumenisches Problem* (1959), pp. 77ff.

103. As the community of believers itself became the "light of the world" (Matt. 5:14) and the apostolate went forth into the world, the prophecy about the Servant of the Lord was fulfilled (Isa. 49:6). In Acts 13:47 Paul quotes another prophecy about the Servant (Isa. 42:6) in terms of his own apostolic calling as "a light for the Gentiles." Cf. Acts 9:15; Eph. 3:3f., 6.

stand God parallels God's eschatological deed, revealing and realizing His salvation for the *world*, despite human resistance.[104]

If missions is in fact closely connected with the eschatological expectation,[105] it is important to note that the community of believers on its way to the future assumes a very central and meaningful place. The church receives a mandate in this darkness, a mandate that will be fulfilled by the Lord Himself. It might even be said that the meaning of the present dispensation becomes visible in the church. Needless to say, such an explanation is fraught with possibilities of misinterpretation. But it is not only possible, it is necessary to speak of the community that expects and proclaims the Lord in this way. In missions, the relationship between the "already" and the "not yet" assumes a specific mode. This relationship is not only relative to the community's own existence and imperfection, but to the whole world, which must be apprised of the mystery of the ways of God. It is not surprising, then, that the proclamation is a necessity *(anángkē)*, a requirement placed on the community on its way to eschatological fulfilment (1 Cor. 9:16). This necessity is a tempestuous impulse arising from the "already" of the present salvation. Paul admitted to being under obligation *(opheilétēs)* to Greeks and barbarians, to the wise and the foolish (Rom. 1:14).

So one cannot comprehend the "eschaton" or live in anticipation of it if he ignores this necessity, this obligation. There can be no distinction in this area between the "being" and the "well-being" of the church. It is a matter of the church's very being to turn towards the world, to give without pay, having received without pay (Matt. 10:8). The tie between eschatological expectation and mission call is essential and indissoluble.[106] The church that fails to understand its mandate in

104. Obviously there is a close relation between this discussion of God's acts and the matter of the future of Israel. We shall consider the latter subject in detail in Chapter XI.

105. Cullmann calls Matt. 28:20 "a clear reference to the eschatological character of the mission, which must take place precisely in the intermediate period and which *gives to this period its meaning"; Christ and Time*, pp. 162f.

106. On the self-evidence of this relationship see D. van Swigchem, *Het missionair karakter van de christelijke gemeente volgens de brieven van Paulus en Petrus* (1955); Harry R. Boer, *Pentecost and Missions* (1961); J. van den Berg, *Waarom zending?* (1959), esp. pp. 18ff. (the motif of expectation).

this area inevitably becomes entangled in its own outlook on the meaning of the present dispensation. It is in imminent danger of wrapping itself up in an introverted, internal problematics that forfeits the meaning of the present dispensation. The expectation cannot remain vibrant and operative if the overwhelming richness of Christ's grace in the coming age is not shown and if the peace to which we have access in the Father is not proclaimed (Eph. 2:7, 17f.; cf. Isa. 57:19).

Considering the message of the gospel and the route prescribed for the church, there can be no doubt about the meaning of the present dispensation. Doubt can arise only if this route is not faithfully followed. Only then will the continuity of history become an inexplicable riddle. The quest for the meaning of the "time between" is never treated as an isolated, theoretical question by the New Testament. The way-is lighted by the accomplished, historical fact ("already") and the unfulfilled condition ("not yet"). The church is not offered a complete insight into the ways of God, which are inscrutable (Rom. 11:33), but it must steadily go on its way having shod its feet "with the equipment of the gospel of peace" (Eph. 6:15; cf. Rom. 10:14f.). In the light of this mandate, doubt about the present dispensation recedes into oblivion. Real doubt can result only from an estrangement from the reality of reconciliation. How could this time, filled as it is with God's reconciliation and its attendant ministry, not have the most profound meaning?

Time and again the church has asked whether this profound meaning can actually be detected in the course of this dispensation. This is the question of the "signs of the times," which we shall consider in Chapter VIII. In order to get the proper perspective on such questions, one must first of all come to an understanding of the meaning of the present dispensation and of Christ's words: "I came to cast fire upon the earth; and would that it were already kindled" (Luke 12:49). Christ says this in the context of a discussion of discerning the times. There is a limit to the ability to discern the times in which everything will be accomplished. Thus, a neutral analysis of history will never do; the signs of the times are explicable only on the basis of discernment of this meaningful present time.

The reason for eschatological tensions

We have considered the fact that the search for the meaning of this dispensation is grounded in the message of recon-

ciliation, the new, immortal life that has been brought to light
(2 Tim. 1:10). Why, now that salvation has come at the end
of the age (Heb. 9:26), is there still the eschatological tension
of the unfulfilled condition? Why does the fulness of salvation
not penetrate beyond all the boundaries of relativity? Since all
the powers have been disarmed (Col. 2:15), why does the fulfilment not obliterate all attempts at resistance? Karl Barth has
given a great deal of attention to questions like these. He
explains them in terms of the incontrovertible "not yet" as "the
most striking determination of the time" since the resurrection
of Jesus Christ from the dead.[107] To be sure, the "not yet" is
not primary or decisive in this dispensation: only what Christ
has done and what — through Him — the power of the Spirit
means in the end of time are primary and decisive. Only in and
through this confession can the "not yet" be satisfactorily dealt
with.[108]

Barth maintains that one must consider the "not yet" from
out of the framework presented by the reality of the victory
and of Easter as the main festival of the Christian church.[109]
In the resurrection of Christ in our world — "in the days of
Tiberius Caesar before the gates of Jerusalem and therefore in
the place and time which are also ours, in our sphere" — was
revealed what Christ's death really meant.[110] What is at stake
is the irreversible, unassailable salvation that was now revealed.
In the light of this decisive act of salvation, the question arises
why the total, universal, and definitive power of Easter is not
yet unambiguously and incontrovertibly knowable.[111] Why is the
present not yet completely fulfilled?[112] How is it that this in-
comparably powerful event "should not yet have by a long way
the corresponding total, universal and definitive effect," and that
the world should merely continue "as if nothing had happened,
as if the last and first hour had not struck, as if Christ were not
risen?"[113]

The answers proposed to this question are numerous. Some
talk about a *concealment* of Christ's victory. This is not a sat-

107. *CD,* IV/3/2, 903.
108. This is a clear point of contact between Barth and Cullmann, both of
them sharp critics of consistent eschatology.
109. *CD,* IV/3/1, 284.
110. *Ibid.,* p. 298.
111. *Ibid.,* p. 306.
112. *Ibid.,* p. 316.
113. *Ibid.,* p. 317.

isfactory answer, because "why may it be known only under that veil when the Easter event means the removal of the veil which covers the reconciliation accomplished in Jesus Christ and its fruit?"[114] Others say that we are only at the *beginning* of the manifestation of the power of reconciliation; but this answer, however correct in itself, does not really answer the question.

So why are we still living in the "not yet," why do "we still have a long way to go ... to the investing of our corruptibility with incorruption?"[115] Barth denies, and rightly so, that this question is unjustifiable and unbiblical, because "this question does not originate in man's sombre and skeptical assessment of himself and the world, but at the point where he is summoned to be confident and comforted in relation to himself and the world."[116] The question does not arise from unbelief, but from faith. Why do we yet live in the period of faith, and not of sight?[117]

After rejecting several possible answers, Barth cautiously moves toward his own explanation. It cannot be that this dispensation is simply an accidental and arbitrary phenomenon. To prove this he repeatedly refers to the "already" and "not yet," the beginning and the fulfilment.[118] He speaks of Jesus Christ Himself on His own way. "As the Revealer of His work He has not yet reached His goal. He is still moving towards it."[119] Anticipating His coming, the eternal light has already burst forth in the world. Jesus *is* the Victor; but His battle is not yet completed, and the unfulfilled condition of the present is grounded in this fact.

Why is there a "not yet" instead of a radical, triumphant consummation? Because Christ gives the reconciled creature *time* and *space* in order that he may participate in the harvest, not only as mere spectator, but as co-worker.[120]

Reconciliation for Barth is not an act in which man has no specific place; on the contrary, its purpose is to create joy, thankfulness, and praise, as well as the true discipleship to which

114. *Ibid.,* p. 318.
115. *Ibid.,* p. 320.
116. *Ibid.,* p. 324.
117. *Ibid.*
118. *Ibid.,* p. 326.
119. *Ibid.,* p. 327.
120. *Ibid.,* p. 329; cf. pp. 327f.

man is now called.[121] In between the "then of the Easter event"
and the "one day of the final appearance of Jesus Christ" comes
the clear sound of a voice calling man to service. True, within
time, evil, imperfection, and trials still abound,[122] but all this
has a radical opposite.[123] Man now lives in the regnum of the
change — in the period of the "already" but also of the "not
yet" — and life is not merely a negative spectre, but "a specific
form of greatness of the pitying love of God, a specific demonstration of the reconciliation of the world, as it is accomplished
in Jesus Christ."[124] In this time, Jesus Christ is "here and now
the hope of us all, and is thus present in the promise of the
Holy Spirit."[125]

But does Christ's glory not shine through all this? Is there
after all only a *last* promise, and not a preceding one? Is God
righteous and true only at the eschaton? Is not Christ already
our Leader, Intercessor, and Lord? "What basis is there for the
speculative wish or postulate that the first form of the Parousia,
presence and revelation of Jesus Christ should also have been
its last?"[126] No, the history of salvation also has *this* form. Although the "not yet" is undoubtedly a very present reality, it
is nevertheless true that "to Him there is really to be ascribed
praise and thanksgiving even *e profundis* and in and under
all the sighing for the progress and conclusion of His work."[127]
The present dispensation is equally under the seal of thankfulness and joy; Barth appropriately concludes his reflections
with a reference to Isaiah's striking image of eagles, who though
continuously in flight seldom tire.[128]

Throughout Barth's discussion of this subject the places of
both the "already" and the "not yet" are given their due. Has
he explained the "not yet" in the light of the primary and
decisive "already"? He repeatedly comes back to a stress on the
importance of the comfort and the task in the "not yet." This is
the central theme of the expectation in the New Testament:
the meaning of the present dispensation can only be fruitfully
discussed in terms of its relation to mandate and exhortation.

121. *Ibid.*, p. 332.
122. *Ibid.*, p. 334.
123. *Ibid.*, p. 360.
124. *Ibid.*, p. 361.
125. *Ibid.*
126. *Ibid.*
127. *Ibid.*, p. 362.
128. *Ibid.*, p. 367; cf. Isa. 40:31.

In this dispensation Christ is indeed seen through the eyes of faith as the sympathetic High Priest mentioned in Hebrews 4:15. But at the same time this reference to the Lord, who Himself has not yet come to the end of His road, may never be construed as a solution to the question of the meaning of the continuity of time in this dispensation. Barth's views are very effective against theories of pan-eschatologism, which relativizes or denies the meaning of salvation in the present,[129] but his reference to the *e profundis*, however meaningful for this entire dispensation, does not explain the present dispensation. When the goal of Christ's supreme act of love is attained, according to the promises of the Spirit, there will come a time in which everything will be "without spot or blemish." Then our perspective on the merciful acts of Christ will no longer be shrouded from sight. When He appears a second time, without sin (Heb. 9:28),[130] He will be known as the true Lord, who will live and reign forever. Although the fact that this merciful Lord is the focal point of all man's imperfections and sufferings is indeed a comforting testimony, it can never explain why the triumph of the Lord has not yet penetrated into all corners of human existence and why it has not yet been manifested to all.

Thus it is not surprising that Barth, although he first rules out the "not yet" as a possible explanation of this time, later returns to this "beginning" and "not yet." *Within* this "time between," the calling and meaning of the Christian community lie. Precisely because the church has been called out of darkness and now may be known as the light of the world, a conspicuous relativity is manifest in it, just as the case was with chosen Israel, whose status as God's people, distinct from other nations, gave no cause for self-elevation but only for deep humility (Amos 3:2). In the light of the "already," that is, in the light of the Lord Himself, sin is revealed. This is the time when the judgment begins with the household of God (1 Pet. 4:17), and when believers are called to conduct themselves with fear, know-

---

129. Cf. *ibid.*, IV/3/2, 912, where Barth rejects the "broadening of the concept of the eschatological," according to which everything becomes eschatological. This is a protest against timeless eschatology (see above, Chap. I). "The time has surely come when we should awaken from this pan-eschatological dream."

130. Cf. Berkouwer, *Sin* (Eng. tr., 1971), pp. 566f.

ing that they were ransomed with Christ's precious blood (1 Pet. 1:17-19).

Should the church take this stand, all misunderstanding of the meaning of the "time between" vanishes. It must be careful not to draw a direct conclusion from the triumph of Christ to its own perfection, possible or real. On the other hand, it must not, in an effort to ward off any tendencies to perfectionism, elevate the "not yet" to the status of norm in its own existence, at the expense of restricting the triumph of Christ. At the entrance to the present dispensation the church is greeted by words of triumph and reconciliation, of consolation and promise of plenty, of the breakthrough from death to life, in Jesus Christ. When the dispensation begun in this way is also seen as the time of many setbacks, its meaning can only be grasped by reflection on the victory of Jesus Christ.[131] It is no coincidence that what Paul writes about the victory is without a trace of false glory; the victory is, after all, visible only "through him who loved us" (Rom. 8:37). The meaning of the present dispensation can be discovered only in the unity of this love and the victory. Time will go on until the end. It is not ours to scrutinize thoroughly the nature and structure of the "time between." Our concern must rather be with the mandate that comes into the present and alone can explain the meaning of this age.

Whoever would know more is seeking for something that is not available. Only in the forward movement towards the complete revelation does this meaning become apparent, as well, incidentally, as the meaninglessness of sin. For this reason the undeniable "not yet" can never serve as an alibi for our defeats. The road of "not yet" can only be a road to glory if constructed with the permanent perspective supplied by the "already." The

131. In connection with the judgment of the household of God (1 Pet. 4:17) we read that "the righteous man is scarcely *(mólis)* saved" (vs. 18), a statement that has been much discussed in terms of assurance of salvation. The LXX of Prov. 11:31, which is quoted in this verse, gives an incorrect rendering of the Hebrew text, which deals with recompense in this life. Selwyn's gloss — "But Christians can commit themselves into God's hands in perfect serenity" *(op. cit.,* p. 226) — can hardly be correct, in this context at least. Rather this word *mólis* focuses, in the full tension of the gospel, on the path in the movement of faith from the "not yet" to the "already." Perseverance on this path can be attained only with the deepest humility, and then in fact *is* attained.

secret of the eschatological expectation is not locked in what is enigmatic about the present dispensation, but in what is understandable.

CHAPTER FIVE

THE REALITY OF THE PAROUSIA

LET US NOW turn our attention to what the Bible says about the return — the coming again — of the Lord. The expressions "coming *again*" and "return" have a prominent place in the language of the church and the creeds with reference to Christ's coming at the end of the world. These expressions have been criticized on the grounds that they do not give a pure translation of the Greek *parousia* and that they might create an erroneous impression of a parallel with Christ's first coming in the flesh. Albrecht Oepke writes that "a basic prerequisite for understanding the world of thought of primitive Christians is that we should fully free ourselves from this notion [of more than one parousia]."[1] The parousia is, after all, an entirely different event from the incarnation. It was only later in church history that people began to speak of more than one parousia.

This objection does not, it seems to me, disqualify the use of the expression "return" or "coming again," which is not intended to place Christ's appearing in the flesh and His reappearance in glory on the same level, or to describe the difference between the two in terms of *first* and *second* coming. Granted that "parousia" does not mean "coming again" or "return," and that one must pay special attention to the uniqueness of this coming of the Lord.[2] At the same time we must remember that when the early church spoke about Christ's

---

1. In *TDNT*, s.v. *parousia*, V, 865.
2. "The noun [*parousia*] means 'arrival,' not 'return.'...The Christians... were, of course, aware and mindful that the event spoken of was in point of fact a second arrival, duplicating in a certain respect that of the incarnation." G. Vos, *The Pauline Eschatology* (1930; repr. 1966), p. 75. Vos's choice of the word "duplicating" here is less than felicitous. He goes on to explain that the fact that the phrase "second parousia" did not develop "is only explainable from the intensively prospective outlook of the early Church." Cf. J. A. T. Robinson, *Jesus and His Coming* (1957), pp. 16ff.

coming again, it harked back to His original coming and going. It is incorrect to conclude from this that both events, past and future, were put on the same level by the early community. This is evident from the fact that Hebrews 9:28 explicitly states that Christ "will appear a second time *(ek deutérou)*, not to deal with sin but to save those who are eagerly waiting for him."[3] This clearly indicates the uniqueness of the event.[4]

There is a direct point of contact here with the message of the angels on the mount of ascension, who prophesied that Jesus "will come in the same way *(hoútōs eleúsetai)* as you saw him go into heaven" (Acts 1:11; cf. John 14:3). This is not a levelling off of the two appearances, but a reference to a clear and meaningful connection between them. What is crucial here is a proper understanding of His coming. At the outset, then, we should examine the New Testament use of the word *parousia*. The word is not limited to Christ's coming in glory: it can also be used in connection with the "coming" of a person (Stephanas in 1 Cor. 16:17; Titus in 2 Cor. 7:6), and even with the "coming" of the man of sin (2 Thess. 2:9). But it obtains a special significance when used for the coming of the Lord: *the* parousia. In contrast to the parousia of the man of sin is His coming, His manifestation, which is the heart of the believer's expectation. Parousia refers, as do certain other New Testament words,[5] to His coming in glory (Mark 8:38), to His manifestation at the close of the age (Matt. 24:3), to the day when the Son of man is revealed (Luke 17:30).

The presence and absence of Christ

The reason for the church's speaking of the return or second coming of Christ is not to blur the difference of meaning be-

---

3. Oepke asserts that "the *ek deutérou* of [Heb.] 9:28 is not Pauline"; *loc. cit.*, 868. Cullmann, however, places strong emphasis on this word, as shown from the title of his *The Return of Christ*. On Heb. 9:28, see his *The Christology of the NT* (Eng. tr., 1964), p. 103.

4. Especially in connection with the *chōris hamartias*. On this, see Berkouwer, *Sin*, pp. 565f., and C. Spicq, *L'épître aux Hébreux*, II, 270.

5. Among these other words are *epiphaneía* (linked with *parousia* in 2 Thess. 2:8; cf. also 1 Tim. 6:14; Titus 2:13); *phaneroûn* (1 Pet. 5:4); and *éleusis* (Luke 21:7 in Codex Bezae; *tês sês eleuséōs* instead of *hotan méllē taúta ginesthai*). Cf. P. L. Schoonheim, *Een semasiologisch onderzoek van parousia met betrekking tot het gebruik in Mattheüs 24* (1953), pp. 16ff.

tween the first and second comings; but to stress that it is He who has come who will come again at the end of time. In other words, attention is focused on the relationship between these two, without ignoring the novel and unique character of the parousia. This consideration of its uniqueness does not reflect a compulsion to speculate about future glory or to probe into inscrutable mysteries. What lies behind it is the realization that, on the basis of the New Testament, one cannot look on His coming in glory as on a coming into a dispensation that was void. The church knew of His coming in the flesh and His promise for the present dispensation, even after His departure. It was precisely this promise that made a simplistic antithesis between His coming anew and His *absence* in the present dispensation impossible. Concerning the present dispensation Christ had spoken of His actual presence *with us:* "Lo, I am with you always, to the close of the age" (Matt. 28:20). This — eschatological — message is a promise of comfort and encouragement until the end. The church was constantly reminded of the word of its Lord: "For where two or three are gathered in my name, there *am I* in the midst of them" (Matt. 18:20). This is an important aspect for our reflection on the parousia — the presence of Christ in the future. It is true that Paul considered death as being "with Christ," but it does not follow from this that the present dispensation can be considered an empty period of time without Christ. Paul himself writes about Christ's living in the hearts of believers (Eph. 3:17). Throughout the entire history of the church runs the confession of the present reality of the *Christus praesens*.[6]

In discussing the biblical proclamation of the parousia it is necessary to keep this in mind. What is really the point of contact between Christ's presence as experienced in this dispensation — His living in the hearts of believers — and the expected parousia? Clearly, the answer to this is decisively determined by how one understands Christ's presence in the church. The perspective on the parousia originates with the community of

6. This receives a more specialized emphasis in the doctrine of the *praesentia realis* in the elements of the Lord's Supper. This is a Reformed — as well as Roman Catholic and Lutheran — emphasis. Cf. Berkouwer, *The Sacraments* (Eng. tr., 1969), ch. XI, "The Real Presence," pp. 219-43; G. P. Hartvelt, *Verum Corpus* (1960); and L. Stählin, *Christus praesens. Vorerwägungen zu einer Grundfrage der Kirchen- und Dogmengeschichte,* p. 5. According to Stählin, the church holds fast to the presence of Christ as the "midpoint of its life, which cannot be given up."

believers, who have constant communion with their Lord. Needless to say, the answer to this question will involve making distinctions, the kind of distinctions that have sometimes unfairly been dismissed as scholastic. Consider the Heidelberg Catechism. After its explanation of Christ's ascension and His return (Q. 46), the question is asked: "Then, is not Christ with us unto the end of the world, as he has promised us?" The answer makes a distinction: "As a man, he is no longer on earth, but in his divinity, majesty, grace, and Spirit, he is never absent from us" (Q. 47).

Regardless of whether or not this distinction is clear or expedient,[7] it is apparent that it points to a particular *mode* of Christ's presence. His presence is confessed to be real, a communion that keeps and preserves. The confession of the ascension therefore does not have to do with a distance, abstracted from our lives, but with an imminence that is proclaimed as a comfort. At the same time, we are impressed that Christ's presence is not such as to diminish or exclude the complete and profound meaning of the parousia.

Lutheran doctrine holds not merely to a presence as portrayed in the Heidelberg Catechism, but to a physical presence. It confesses that in the sacrament Christ's body and blood are truly present.[8] From Paul's words in 1 Corinthians 10:16, the Lutherans conclude that communion would not be possible if Christ were not bodily present. The Roman Catholic Church also emphasizes the presence of Christ unlocked in the miracle of transubstantiation, through which the *totus Christus* becomes an actual, physical reality. Finally, the Belgic Confession says that "what is eaten and drunk by us is the proper and natural body and the proper blood of Christ" (Art. XXXV).[9]

Because of these emphases, the question has often been raised: what then is the meaning of the parousia? The Catechism asks whether Christ is really with the believer now.[10] But the question could also be turned around. Are the meaning and reality of the parousia not sacrificed through excessive stress on the confessed presence of Christ in this dispensation, concretized

---

7. Cf. Berkouwer, *The Person of Christ* (Eng. tr., 1954), p. 76.
8. Art. X, Augsburg Confession: "quod corpus et sanguis Christi vere adsint."
9. Cf. Hartvelt, *op. cit.,* p. 183.
10. Popma sees this question not as speculative, but a simple, childlike appeal to what is promised in Matt. 28:20. *Levensbeschouwing*, II, 280.

in the sacrament of the Lord's Supper? Does this leave any room for a burning and living expectation? Is the present dispensation so inhabited by the Lord as to justify speaking of a *realized* eschaton? But realized eschatology, we have seen, leaves little or no room for serious consideration of the future.

The importance of these questions lies in the meaning of the church's confession of the presence of Christ. That meaning was *not*, as has sometimes been thought, a representation that arises from psychological reminiscence, or an impression that proceeds from the historical Jesus. Nineteenth-century liberal theology sometimes talked about the presence of Christ and saw the present dispensation as filled with the real presence of Christ's impressive personality.[11] This is something entirely different from what the early church understood by Christ's promise in Matthew 28:20. The church wanted to take seriously the consolation "Lo, I am with you always." It saw this as a promise of real and personal communion.[12] Given this concern, its questions arose not from curiosity but from reflection on the nature of this presence in the light of the indisputable historical event of His departure.

The importance of these questions is illustrated by the fact that the Roman Catholic "fulfilment" theory of the present dispensation has frequently been styled as a form of realized eschatology. Those who have said this have questioned whether Roman Catholic theology, with its concept of "church" as *corpus Christi* and its attendant doctrine of the eucharist, leaves any room for a burning eschatological expectation. Harnack saw the Roman Catholic replacement of the presence of Christ with papal vicarage as a kind of de-eschatologizing.[13]

11. Cf. H. C. von Hase, *Die Gegenwart Christi in der Kirche* (1934), pp. 15ff.
12. Against "idealizing" and "irrealizing," Anders Nygren writes that the presence is a matter of a here and now that may not be minimized. Also, *anámnēsis* is not a matter of "remembrance of something only historically past." Nygren rejects any notion of "representation" in the sense that the life of Christ is before us — for example, in preaching — *as if* it were a reality. This *as if* cancels out the presence. "Die Gegenwart Jesu Christi in Wort und Sakrament," in *Bekenntnis zur Kirche. Festgabe für Ernst Sommerlath* (1961), pp. 294-98. Cf. the discussion of Elert's interpretation of the Reformed doctrine of the Lord's Supper in Berkouwer, *The Sacraments*, ch. XI.
13. Harnack, "Christus praesens — vicarius Christi," in *Sitzungsberichte der preussischen Akademie der Wissenschaften, 1927*, pp. 415-46. Taking Matt. 28:20 as his point of departure, Harnack discusses the sacramental

Clearly, this touches a very sensitive spot in ecclesiastical controversies. It is not only Protestant scholars who have called attention to this problem. The Catholic theologian P. Schoonenberg has written that Roman Catholic spiritual life, preaching, and theology do not appear to be very eschatological. The Counter-Reformation concentrated on the *visible* church and often placed near-exclusive stress on the mass as representing the supreme sacrifice, although Schoonenberg feels that this was not intended as "a denial of what had been submerged" (i.e., the future), and supports this with reference to the strong emphasis on the qualifier "until He comes."[14]

The charge that Roman Catholic doctrine obscures the expectation of the parousia is closely related to another charge: that Catholic doctrine does not do justice to the meaning of Christ's ascension.[15] From the Catholic side it is vigorously denied that this is the case, that there is any notion of Christ's leaving heaven again and again to be present in the eucharist. Fortmann writes: "Christ remains, body and blood, in heaven." It is true that there is an actual presence in the eucharist, but this presence is a *presentia invisibilis,* which escapes detection in the elements, which at once show and conceal. Because of the concealment, the presence of the Lord does not make the parousia superfluous. There is no "unwarranted anticipating of future glory at Jesus' return." Fortmann calls the presence of Christ a *pledge* of future glory, a "beginning realization." To support this he cites the scriptural passages dealing with the

Gegenwart (in transubstantiation), the succession and the vicarage. Harnack sees the complications as being in the (antithetical) relation between presence and replacement. He spends little time on what the Roman Catholic Church confesses to be the real presence in the full sense of the word, namely, the sacramental presence, through which the passage from Matt. 28:20 is seen as superabundantly fulfilled.

14. Schoonenberg, "Een katholieke visie op het parousie-probleem," *Vox Theologica,* XVIII (1947), 102. On the mass as representing the supreme sacrifice, see also Odo Casel, *The Mystery of Christian Worship,* pp. 40f.; re Casel's teaching see Berkouwer, *The Sacraments,* ch. XIII. Cf. also Yves de Montcheuil, "Signification eschatologique du repas eucharistique," *Mélanges théologiques* (1946), pp. 24ff.

15. This charge is not entirely without foundation: Erich Przywara wrote concerning the mass: "The great mystery of the holy mass, almost as the revocation of His ascension — the holy mass, the ever new return to earth of Him who has gone to heaven"; *Gott* (1926), p. 134.

first fruits of the Spirit.[16] On the one side, there is an accentu-
ating of the presence of Christ; on the other side there is a limit-
ing of it, or, better, a reference to a specific *mode* of this presence, which does not endanger the validity of the parousia-
expectation.

The tendency towards realized eschatology and de-eschatologizing in Catholic theology has also been found in the Roman
Catholic concept of the church as the body of Christ. Everything
seems to be fulfilled in the church. Does this leave room for
expectation of the coming Kingdom? Cullmann talks about
"the Catholic absolutizing of the period of the Church." He
alludes to "the reference of the thousand year Kingdom (Rev.
20:4) to the Church, a view that goes back to Tyconius," as
inevitably leading to the fading away of the expectation. He
notes the "decision of the Congregation of the Holy Office,
according to which faith in the visible return of Christ no
longer is regarded as obligatory (it can 'not be taught as
certain') ."[17]

However, we are not primarily concerned here with Roman
Catholic views of eschatology. Our primary concern is the problematics of the relationship between the presence of Christ
in this dispensation and in His parousia. In view of the *presentia
realis,* how can there yet be a strong expectation? This may
well be called an "ecumenical" question. It may be asked as a
child would ask it, or it may be just another source of speculation, in which case one runs the risk of throwing into confusion the whole relationship between ascension and presence,
and of both to the parousia.

The danger of filling the present dispensation with things
that are in flagrant conflict with any expectation is obvious.
This was the case in the degenerate "Christian" attitude of the
Láodiceans: "I am rich, I have prospered and I need nothing"
(Rev. 3:17). They thought that the lasting city had already
come (Heb. 13:14). Only when we have become aware of the
hazards of a fictitious and illegitimate fulfilment can we begin
to understand how Christ is actually present without doing

16. H. J. H. M. Fortmann, "Bijdrage tot het gesprek over de tegenwoordig-
heid van Christus in de eucharistie," in *Jubileum-bundel voor Prof. G.
Kreling* (1953), pp. 104f.
17. *Christ and Time,* p. 147.

harm to the eschatological expectation and the *new presence*
of Christ in His parousia.[18]

So it is because of the presence of Christ, which we confess,
and our communion with Him that questions about the reality
of the parousia arise. In considering this matter, the obvious
New Testament witness about the *absence* of Christ cannot be
ignored if one wishes to maintain the real character of Christ's
coming. Nor can one escape the question à la Fortmann and
Casel by positing a distinction between His presence in the
present dispensation as an "invisible presence," and that in
the parousia as a "visible presence," and then arguing that the
"visible presence" in the parousia makes the presence in this
dispensation visible by unveiling what is real, where the real
could not previously be seen. In this case, the presence itself
would not in fact be the difference between present and parousia;
the difference would be the *mode* or *form* of the presence: now
concealed, later revealed.

This word "unveiling" clearly points to a central category
of eschatology. It has the same force as the word *apokálypsis,*

18. Some light is shed on this question in the revised form for the celebration of the Lord's Supper of the Gereformeerde Kerk. The form speaks
of Christ, who acquired for us the life-giving Spirit, who lives in us and
through whom we have true communion with Christ. In this context
the form then refers to a strong, eager looking out "for the hour when
He shall celebrate the marriage supper of the Lamb with us." The
prayer before the celebration of the Supper asks for grace to await
with uplifted head the Lord Jesus from heaven, who "will celebrate
the supper of the wedding of the Lamb with us in Thy kingdom."
This addition to the original formulary accentuates the connection between the earthly Lord's Supper and the marriage supper of the Lamb.
This harks back to Christ's institution of the Supper, when he said: "I
tell you I shall not drink again of this fruit of the vine until that day
when I drink it new with you in my Father's kingdom" (Matt. 26:29;
cf. Mark 14:25; Luke 22:18). These words refer to the entire present
dispensation, filled with the reality of the gift of the Lord's Supper
and directed at the same time to a *new* communion. The call to the
celebration goes out "until he comes" (1 Cor. 11:26). And as real as
this gift of the Lord's Supper is, these words give us at the same time
an impression of distance, of a radical difference between *now* and
later. The congregation, as it celebrates the Lord's Supper, is led to the
window through which they look out on the marriage of the Lamb,
hearing the promise: "Blessed are those who are invited to the mar-
riright supper of the Lamb" (Rev. 19:9: *eis tó deipnon toú gámou toú
arníou;* cf. Behm, in *TDNT,* s.v. *deipnon,* II, 34: "the images of the
eschatological banquet and the marriage-feast...merge into one another").

the removal of the *kálymma,* the cover under which something was hidden (cf. Exod. 34:34f.; Isa. 25:7; 2 Cor. 3:15). But does this unveiling, particularly the distinction between visible and invisible, cast any light on the reality of the parousia? The difficulty is that the opposite of "unveiling" is "concealment," not "absence" or "sojourn." On the basis of this "unveiling," then, one might expect the parousia to be described not as a matter of *coming,* but merely of *seeing.* The motif of *seeing* is of course found in the New Testament (cf. Heb. 9:28 — *ophthêsetai;* 1 John 3:2), but only in connection with *seeing His coming,* His appearing. In Jesus' confrontations with men, this matter of seeing with the eyes was of some concern. His glory can be seen but only with the eyes of faith.[19] Peter discovered that Jesus was the Christ, a discovery he made not through flesh and blood, but through the revelation of God *(apekálypsen ... ho patêr mou),* who Himself had removed the cover (Matt. 16:17).

Although "revelation" is not a "fixed historical or eschatological objectivism,"[20] there is at the same time a condition of "not-seeing," which is not the result of the eyes' being closed. John speaks of having seen (1:14); but he also maintains the eschatological expectation that has not yet been fulfilled — "we shall see ..." (1 John 3:2 — *opsómetha).* And Peter writes: "Without having seen *(ouk idóntes)* him, you love him; though you do not now see *(árti mê horôntes)* him, you believe in him" (1 Pet. 1:8). This does not have to do with the blindness that is brought about by the "god of this world ... to keep [unbelievers] from seeing the light of the gospel of the glory of Christ" (2 Cor. 4:4; cf. vs. 3); rather, Peter is referring to a condition of not seeing *even though* the eyes are opened in faith and love. When Christ called Thomas not to be unbelieving, he added that "those who have not seen and yet believe" shall see salvation (John 20:29). It is this condition of not seeing that is related in the New Testament to His departure. We may not distinguish here between objective and subjective, and explain the condition of not seeing as a result of defective eyes. The inability to see is related to God's dealings through Christ in the history of salvation, and indelibly stamps the entire period of the present dispensation.[21]

19. John 1:14 — *etheasámetha tên dóxan autoú;* cf. 1 John 1:1 — *etheasáme-tha.*
20. Oepke, in *TDNT,* s.v. *apokalýptō,* III, 581.
21. The subject of the *visio Dei* is discussed in Chapter XII, below.

Christ prepared His disciples for His departure. He told them
that He would go to the Father, and they would no longer see
Him (John 16:7, 10, 16). A very noticeable change then occurred in the relationship and communication between the
Lord and His followers. But this change is not a devaluation
or impoverishment of their communion. His departure would
be to their advantage (vs. 7) and He would not leave them
desolate (14:18).[22] There has been a great deal of discussion
about whether the words that immediately follow — "I will come
unto you"[23] — apply to Christ's return from the dead or to
His parousia. Whatever the case, it is clear that Christ's departure would not mark the beginning of a sad and empty era.
This is precluded not only by the arrival of the Paraclete, but
by the fact that the coming of the Spirit is not a substitute for
Christ's presence, as if the Spirit were a replacement for a
totally absent Christ.[24]

This leads us to the mystery of the relation between Christ
and the Holy Spirit. The change in the relationship between
Christ and the disciples cannot be portrayed as simply a change
from the presence of Christ to that of the Holy Spirit. Yet,
a definite distance is implied. "You will seek me and you will
not find me; where I am you cannot go" (John 7:34; cf. 8:21f.).
This distance cannot be equated with the word "absence." There
is a change from seeing to no-longer-seeing, from Christ's being
with them to His not being with them; there is a departure from
out of their circle.

22. Cf. Berkouwer, *The Work of Christ* (Eng. tr., 1965), ch. VIII, "Christ's
    Ascension," pp. 202-22. Bultmann writes that the sorrow "in which the
    disciples are plunged by the departure of Jesus is not to be misunder-
    stood along the lines of psychology or fiction. On the contrary, it char-
    acterises the situation of loneliness which is the lot of those whom
    Jesus has called out of the world ... and who are yet in the world ...
    and against whom the hatred of the world is directed. ..." In *TDNT*,
    s.v. *lýpē*, IV, 321. Cf. also Bultmann's commentary on John, *ad loc.*
23. John 14:18 — *érchomai prós hymás*. On the theological content of the
    érchesthai sayings in the Gospel of John, see Schneider, in *TDNT*, s.v.
    érchomai, II, 671-73; see also Seesemann, *ibid.*, s.v. *orphanós*, V, 488.
    Cf. John 14:3 *(pálin érchomai)*; 21:22 *(héōs érchomai)*. On *orphanós*
    see Holwerda, *The Holy Spirit and Eschatology in the Gospel of John*,
    pp. 38-48.
24. Schneider says concerning the coming of the Paraclete: "The form of
    coming has changed, the personal coming being replaced by a pneu-
    matic"; *TDNT*, s.v. *érchomai*, II, 673. I do not find this terminology
    too enlightening: the opposite of "personal" is "impersonal," not
    "pneumatic."

In his discussion of fasting, Christ asks, "Can the wedding guests mourn as long as the bridegroom is with them?" (Matt. 9:15). "Seen from the standpoint of the Messianic eschatological center of the message of Jesus, fasting is transcended."[25] Otherwise, the time of salvation would merely be a time of filling old skins with new wine. But Christ goes on: "The days will come, when the bridegroom is taken away from them and then they will fast."[26] This signals a change in the situation, heralding the coming suffering. The road the disciples must go passes through Christ's separation from them. Yet, the meaning of the time of salvation is not relativized by their separation. Earthly analogies cannot capture the mystery of the time of salvation completely.[27] In these analogies the focus is always on the transition. But it is not just a matter of "one" change from joy to sadness. The present dispensation cannot be characterized merely as a time of weeping and lamenting: Christ promises that sorrow will turn into joy (John 16:20). The meaning and joy of the time of salvation will be made manifest, even after the ascension, through the power of the Spirit.

The time of waiting characterizes both the time of salvation and the future. The church's mandate is to live on its way to the future out of this salvation and the constant consciousness of it. It is the time of thankfulness and insight. The "absence" of the Lord is at the same time the preparation of a new way that was cleared in His going away. What we say about the presence and departure of the Lord, however much we may try to compare it to human coming and going, becomes comprehensible only on the basis of the unique mystery of Christ's appearance and His work. In ordinary human existence, "presence" and "absence" are mutually exclusive. In the case

25. Behm, in *TDNT*, s.v. *nēstis*, IV, 932; cf. also J. Jeremias, *ibid.*, s.v. *nýmphē*, IV, 1103; Grosheide, *Comm., ad loc.*

26. The introduction of fasting into the church has often been defended by reference to this text. The NT epistles do not mention fasting at all. On the Koine textual variant of 1 Cor. 7:5 (*nēsteia kai tē proseuchē* for *tē proseuchē*), which is reflected in the King James translation ("prayer and fasting"), see Grosheide, *Comm., ad loc.*; P. G. Kunst, "Bidden en vasten," in *Arcana Revelata* (1951), p. 55.

27. The meaning of the analogy of the woman in travail (John 16:21), whose sorrow in anguish changes to joy at the birth of a child, does not explain the mystery of Christ, but points, analogically, to that mystery. The analogy includes both a reference to the meaning of the sorrow and a counterpart to the proclaimed experiencing of Christ's going away.

of Jesus Christ, the mystery renders this analogy unintelligible. "In the language of the Bible . . . this neat distinction of things breaks down." The question "Is the Lord absent or present?" cannot be asked.[28] It all comes down to the mode of His presence in His departure. We are not dealing here with some irrational formulation that has abandoned all hope for clarity, but with the actuality of His person, manifested in a multiplicity of ways. To do justice to this actuality both the promise of His presence and the reality of His departure must be fully acknowledged.

It is no enigmatic paradox that it is better for the Lord to go away than to stay. It is rather a brilliant light, reflected in all the New Testament. The focal point of Christ's ascension is not the cloud that took the risen Lord out of the sight of His disciples (Acts 1:9); Christ Himself had told Mary not to hold Him, for He was going up to the Father (John 20:17). All of time until the parousia will be characterized by this departure. After Pentecost Peter preached not only about the need for Christ to suffer but also about the sending anew of Jesus, "whom heaven must receive until the time for establishing all that God spoke" (Acts 3:18, 21).

But then what is the meaning of talk about Christ's presence in this dispensation? The gospel refers incontrovertibly to this presence, especially in Christ's own promise to be "with you to the close of the age." In this promise lies the reality of communion with Him. The Lord is not far off; He is nearby. This nearness can be confessed only in faith; this fact explains the historic difficulties about the meaning of the Lord's Supper. The church knew that it could only properly speak of the Lord's nearness on the basis of His departure. The danger was that the church would forsake this confession of His presence in this dispensation and slight His Lordship and presence in Word and Sacrament, thereby relativizing the promise of "with you."

This presence is not an image or an "as if." It is a reality; but it is a reality that cannot be grasped unless it is also kept in mind that the nearness involved is that of Christ who is not yet here, though He is coming. Many have considered this to be a self-contradiction; absence and presence are, after all, usually considered to be contraries. The church's confession of a real presence is judged to be a human projection into a vacuous and meaningless dispensation. One of the greatest

28. P. S. Minear, *Christian Hope and the Second Coming*, p. 98.

dangers for the church is our failure to see coming to us in Christ's presence that which is our portion in Him, and the consequent temptation to speak only of a nonactual presence of Christ in Word and Sacrament. This reflects a misunderstanding of the clear testimony of the gospel in Christ's promise to be with us till the close of the age. If one thinks there is a contradiction between the ascension of Christ and the actual nearness in which He lives in our hearts through His Holy Spirit, this contradiction must be traced to the gospel itself. Christ would then not be present in this dispensation: one could only speak of His presence in the parousia and during the short time He was on earth.

In the hymns of the church we certainly sing of Christ's presence in this dispensation. Still, we probably think about it less — rather than more — than we should. Consider Christ's prophecy of what will be revealed in the last judgment (Matt. 25:35ff.). He is speaking here eschatologically about our treatment of Him in the present dispensation. *He* is the one who is thirsty or hungry and is satisfied (or not); *He* is the one who is a stranger, and finds shelter (or not); *He* is the one who is naked, sick, and in prison, and is cared for (or not). This creates the impression that the Lord is really and actually present: any notion of pseudo-presence is unambiguously ruled out. The righteous will then ask Christ, astonished, "Lord, when...?" "Truly, I say to you, as you did it to one of the least of these my brethren, you did it to me" (Matt. 25:40). We must be careful not to interpret this as merely a manner of speaking, for in Christ's mysterious presence in one apparently simple deed of compassion, a radical decision is made: "inherit the Kingdom!" (vs. 34).

It is easy and dangerous to enmesh oneself in a theoretical, analogical analysis of the meaning of Christ's "presence," and promptly conclude that the gospel is shot through with contradictions. To do this is to misunderstand His real presence and to pass Him by unnoticed. There are the righteous who will ask "Lord, when?" but there are also those at his left hand with no notion of His presence. They also ask "Lord, when...?" Considering the Lord's presence, it is not surprising that after the eschatological insight into "the removal of what is shaken" (Heb. 12:27), the transition is made to brotherly love and hospitality, "for thereby some have entertained angels unawares. Remember those who are in prison..." (Heb. 13:1-3). And He who will

judge on His day, who freely informs us about His presence
in this dispensation, is greater than the angels.

Unveiling in the parousia

So we cannot consider Christ's promise to be with us and
His novel presence in the parousia as expressions of faith that
compete with and negate one another. On the basis of the
gospel one can say that the expression "the return of Christ"
denotes the central theme of the expectation of salvation, from
which it follows that the Lord who is coming is the same as
the Lord who has already come. At the same time the uniqueness of the parousia is maintained. Throughout the New Testament the parousia is referred to as a coming in glory. It is an
indubitable and manifest coming. Here is a profound difference
— of immense significance for the history of salvation — from His
original coming in the flesh. His first coming fulfilled the prophecy concerning the Servant of the Lord, who "will not cry or lift
up his voice, or make it heard in the street" (Isa. 42:1-4; Matt.
12:18-21). This fulfilment was verified by Christ's strict orders
not to make Him known.[29] Here there was still the concealment,
the mystery of the Messiah, the silence, the possibility of offense, and the opportunity to proclaim the gospel in parables
and miracles.

In the parousia this concealment is done away with. This
unveiling is different from the change that took place in the
manner of preaching after Pentecost, from concealment through
parables and the like to open proclamation (cf. Acts 26:26),
for even this latter proclamation is not the definitive, visible
manifestation of Christ in all His glory. To be sure, the proclamation goes forth to the end of the earth (Acts 1:8) and to all
nations (Mark 13:10); but in the parousia the manifestation
is irresistible, enveloping the entire world, when the Son of
man comes "as the lightning comes from the east and shines
as far as the west" and all the tribes of the earth stand before
the glorified and omnipotent Son of God (Matt. 24:27, 30).

The parousia, however, is not only described in terms of

---

29. Matt. 12:16 (phanerón). Cf. the question of the Jews: "How long will
you keep us in suspense? If you are the Christ, tell us plainly" (John
10:24). Christ's answer (vs. 25) does not eliminate this concealment;
only in faith can one see His glory through the humiliation. On the
notion of "concealment" in the Gospel of John, see the appendix to
H. N. Ridderbos, *Zelfopenbaring en zelfverberging* (1946), pp. 66-69.

this manifestation of glory. This coming, although individual, cannot be treated in isolation from its context. This was the error of the scoffers of 2 Peter 3. They isolated the promise of Christ's coming, distorting it grotesquely to fit their fancy, and made it an independent fact, which, quite understandably, had not come true. The answer to this mockery leads to the perspective, based on His coming, of new heavens and a new earth (vs. 13) .[30]

This is not a matter of a play on words that places Christ's coming, going, and coming again all on one level; on the contrary, the return of Christ will make it clear what His prior coming in the flesh and His departure really meant. The parousia, viewed according to the biblical perspective, transcends the problems of human seeing or not seeing what is already reality. To give exclusive emphasis to this seeing is to depreciate the actual event of the parousia at the expense of its noetic aspect. Oepke's definition of the parousia as "the definitive manifestation of what has been effected already as an eschatological reality"[31] gives its due to the connection of the parousia with what has already become reality in Christ. But the definition leaves one question unanswered. The parousia will definitely come as an unveiling, a revelation, a taking away of the cover, but what is meant by "revelation?" Elsewhere, Oepke defines revelation as "the actual unveiling of intrinsically hidden facts."[32] This is not very helpful. True, throughout the New Testament we encounter the contrast between concealment and revelation, but there is no indication here that only that which had previously been invisibly present will become visible. Rather, the revelation of the concealed things refers to a *novel* activity of God, in which His intentions are revealed, that is, become reality (Rom. 16:25). In this way the word "revelation" is used for Christ's coming (cf. 1 Cor. 1:7; 2 Thess. 1:7; 1 Pet. 1:7, 13; 4:13). We read that there will be a showing of "what must soon take place" (Rev. 1:1 — *deíxai ... há deí genésthai en táchei*) .

To compare revelation to pulling back a curtain or unveiling a statue is too noetic an analogy. It depends too much on the actual condition of "seeing." "Seeing" is involved here, but

30. Minear writes, "How broad and inclusive was the contour of promise"; *op. cit.,* p. 204.
31. In *TDNT,* s.v. *parousía,* V, 870.
32. *Ibid.,* s.v. *apokalýptō,* III, 591.

it is a seeing directed at what *happens* in the fulfilment, in a new reality. The analogy of unveiling fails to convey the mystery of the parousia if one sees the unveiling as that which fulfils and completes, for what fulfils and completes is Christ's coming in glory. To be sure, there is an intimate connection between His coming in glory and what He is now: "When Christ who is our life appears, then you also will appear with him in glory" (Col. 3:4). But the unveiling of the parousia coincides with *a new reality*. The coming of this new reality is what the parousia is all about. There is no need to relativize His presence in this dispensation — His living in the hearts of His followers — in order to recognize this new reality.

Calvin speaks of this reality as follows: "First, we must understand that as long as Christ remains outside of us, and we are separated from him, all that he has suffered and done for the salvation of the human race remains useless and of no value for us."[33] There is no talk here of a division between Christ Himself and the *power* proceeding from Him. Such a division is unthinkable on the basis of Paul's triumphant cry that nothing can separate him from the love of God in Christ Jesus (Rom. 8:35, 39). We should therefore be assured that the indubitable reality of communion with Christ in the New Testament cannot really weaken the eschatological expectation of His ultimate coming. On the contrary, the reality of this communion in the present dispensation is the indispensable stimulant of the expectation, because His ultimate coming will be a coming in all glory, fulfilling what presently is known as the firstfruits of the Spirit, the "not yet" reality of the present dispensation. As a "second coming," then, the parousia is not a mere repetition of His original coming, but the unchallenged revelation and irreversible fulfilment of the meaning and force of reconciliation. The meaning is revealed in the fulfilled reality.

The Christian church confesses not only Christ's return; both the Apostles' Creed and Nicene Creed clearly state that He will come to judge the living and the dead. This is a true reflection of what the New Testament itself says. Paul has written that Christ "is to judge the living and dead" (2 Tim. 4:1). He has been ordained by God to this task (Acts 10:42). God has fixed a day when the man whom He has appointed will judge the world in righteousness (Acts 17:31). It is the Son of man

33. *Inst.*, III.i.1; cf. III.xi.10 on the nature of our union with Christ.

who will be the judge, and all shall appear before His judgment seat (John 5:22, 27; 2 Cor. 5:10) .[34]

Mention of this judgment in the New Testament frequently refers to its righteousness (Acts 17:31; 2 Tim. 4:8; 1 Pet. 2:23; John 5:30). This righteousness is closely connected with the fact that everything will be revealed before the judgment seat: it is not only Christ who will be revealed, but also the living and the dead. This judgment is just; it corresponds to the way things are in this present reality. It will be a true unveiling, an unveiling of what was already seen by the eyes of God during the present, earthly existence.

The hour and day of the parousia is not an event unrelated to life on earth: it is the hour of giving account (1 Pet. 4:5). On that occasion what really happened on earth will become manifest. We might refer to it as an eschatological crisis, in which the deepest reality and ultimate direction of mankind will be revealed, for man, revealed before Christ's judgment seat, will "receive good or evil, according to what he has done in the body" (2 Cor. 5:10). It is the day that will disclose everything: "each man's work will become manifest" (1 Cor. 3:13) .[35] It is the Lord in His coming, "who will bring to light (phōtísei) the things now hidden in darkness and will disclose (phanerósei) the purposes of the heart" (1 Cor. 4:5).

Here the veil is removed and the hidden made plain. Paul speaks of the revealing (apokálypsis) of the sons of God (Rom. 8:19), and the light of the parousia, which makes everything plain. Clearly, this "unveiling" or revelation does not stand over against the reality of eternal life as the noetic over against

---

34. Cullmann speaks of judgment as "the primary eschatological function of the coming of the Son of Man"; *The Christology of the NT*, p. 157. 1 Pet. 4:5 speaks of *God* as ready to judge the living and the dead. This is not in conflict with the other NT authors: Paul speaks of both the judgment-seat *(bḗma)* of Christ (2 Cor. 5:10) and the judgment-seat *(bḗma)* of God (Rom. 14:10; cf. vs. 9: "to this end Christ died and lived again, that he might be Lord both of the dead and of the living").

35. *hē gàr hēméra dēlósei*. Cf. in this verse *apokalýptetai* and *phanerón*. Eph. 5:13 uses "exposing" as a parallel of revelation; cf. vs. 11 — exposing *(elénchete)* the "unfruitful works of darkness" is the mandate of believers. See also vs. 13b — "anything that becomes visible is light." Greijdanus paraphrases this as "divested of darkness, made free, withdrawn from its mystery and unknownness, so that it is seen in its nature"; *KV* on Ephesians, p. 114. Schlier's interpretation that this verse refers to the heathen who will come to the light in this way is difficult to defend; *Der Brief an die Epheser* (1958), p. 240.

the ontic. To pose such a dilemma is to deny the reality of the parousia, in which the reality of eternal life and this unveiling are inseparably united.[36]

Because of this unveiling the message of the parousia can never make one indifferent towards earthly existence, for it places a heavy responsibility on this life. The idea of a competition between attention to the present and attention to the future is precluded. In the light of the real parousia, the present cannot lose its meaning. The last judgment will not appear as *another*, a *second* judgment, but will reveal the reality of the crisis of this present existence — vis-à-vis Jesus Christ — and raise this reality above all ambiguity and doubt.[37] This future of the coming judgment penetrates, by way of the kerygma, into earthly existence, in order to preserve the church so that it may appear without blame before her Lord (1 Thess. 5:23).

John speaks of the love perfected in us, which is evidenced in confidence for the day of judgment (1 John 4:17). This love casts out fear (vs. 18). The believer knows of the ultimate revelation before the judgment seat, and he does not fear it. The wonderful message of the gospel of the parousia removes the possibility of sudden terror, and preaches instead a confidence for the last day. This is indeed a message of comfort, and it may be said to make the way to the future possible.[38]

Here we encounter one of the most profound truths about the eschaton and Christian life. Hand in hand with this confidence is *openness*, being unashamed; this attitude is "simply a reflection of the fulness of the love of God for us in which we abide."[39] This confidence results from the hope held fast to the end (Heb. 3:6; 10:19). The link between parousia and confidence in the New Testament is contrasted to that between parousia and unbelief and disobedience. For the disobedient unbelievers there can be no openness or confidence. Rather, they will cry to the

---

36. Cf. H. Ott, *Eschatologie*, pp. 41f.; and Berkouwer, *The Triumph of Grace in the Theology of Karl Barth* (Eng. tr., 1956), pp. 329ff., 344.
37. In John 12:47 we read that Jesus did not come into the world to judge *(krinein)*. John 3:17 states that "God sent the Son into the world, not to condemn *(krinein)* the world," but to save it. There is no real contradiction here. Jesus tells the Pharisees, "I judge no one. Yet even if I judge my judgment is true" (John 8:15f.). See further, C. H. Dodd, *The Interpretation of the Fourth Gospel* (1953), pp. 209ff.; and Büchsel, in *TDNT*, s.v. *krinō*, III, 938.
38. Cf. Schlier, in *TDNT*, s.v. *parrēsia*, V, 881f.
39. *Ibid.*, 882.

mountains, "Fall on us, and hide us from the face of him who is seated on the throne, and from the wrath of the Lamb" (Rev. 6:16), for they will be unable to cope with the prospects of the last day.

There can be no doubt as to the concreteness with which the New Testament speaks of this judgment. Although it concerns ordinary existence, there is nevertheless no hint of any moralism to it. The judgment is Christ's, who has come and will come again. In it, all of life is made manifest. The entire judgment has been given to Him (John 5:22). Clearly and simply it points to the depth of man's crisis: "Truly, truly, I say to you, he who hears my word and believes him who sent me, has eternal life; he does not come into judgment, but has passed from death to life" (John 5:24). The judgment — the crisis — is concentrated in Christ Himself: it is not an unveiling of all things in general, but of one's relationship to Christ in particular. For that reason He was ordained to judge (Acts 10:42) and in that way He will judge the living and the dead. Love sets the criteria for judgment, the love of God that appeared in Christ.[40]

This is why we read of the judgment seat of Christ (2 Cor. 5:10), of the wrath of the Lamb (Rev. 6:16); this is why it is said that everyone who pierced Him will see Him again (Rev. 1:7) and that all the tribes of the earth will mourn (Matt. 24:30; cf. Zech. 12:10). The unveiling is a revelation in and face to face with Christ and His revelation. Face to face with Him everything becomes visible. Previously, the life of man was visible only to the eyes of Him who sees the heart and the mind (Jer. 20:12), before whom no creature is hidden (Heb. 4:13); in the last day, every cover and veil hiding a man's motives, direction, and inclination will be removed. What was done in secret will be rewarded (Matt. 6:4, 6, 18); every careless word will be accounted for (Matt. 12:36; cf. Eccl. 12:14).

The New Testament presentation of Christ as the *kritēs* and the parousia as *His* revelation indicates a decisive aspect of the future. So it is understandable that the parousia is a matter of kerygmatic concern, which addresses the present concrete life, as when Paul spoke to Felix and "argued about justice and

---

40. M. Schmaus, *Von den letzten Dingen (Katholische Dogmatik, IV/2, 1959), p. 258. He continues: "The norm is not Good and Evil in general, nor the abstract idea of Good and Evil, nor an impersonal worth or worthlessness, but Christ."

self-control, and future judgment" (Acts 24:25). What is said about the future is no futuristic apocalypse, nor the announcement of an incredible and fantastic series of events, but the preaching of the final unveiling of earthly life. For this reason it cannot be maintained that the present and future are mutually exclusive and that John left no room for a future aspect because of the critical nature of the present. John's emphasis on the present and the present passing from death to life (5:24; 1 John 3:14) does not exclude the eschatological perspective. It is the internal historical decision that will be clearly and unmistakably revealed at the last judgment, and this decision points beyond the present in prayerful expectation of the day when all will be revealed.[41] The parousia can only be comprehended in terms of this intensely close connection between the present and future.[42]

From the spectacular apocalyptic images that the biblical writers use to portray the Day of the Lord, some have concluded that the great event of the parousia will be strange indeed. Let us turn our attention to this belief.

In the first place, the parousia cannot be thought of as strange in the sense of sudden or surprising, for the believers are specifically called out of darkness so that the day will not surprise them like a thief (1 Thess. 5:4) or a snare (Luke 21:34). But neither will the reality of the parousia be strange in comparison with life on earth. Rather, it will be a matter of life in all its complexity and variegation, the depths and heights for which psychology and psychoanalysis have groped. In the parousia life will lay aside its no less complex and variegated *kálymma*, when the very purposes of every heart will be disclosed (1 Cor. 4:5).[43]

41. Althaus, *Die letzten Dinge*, pp. 178f.
42. The connection between the now of judgment, as found in John 5, and the parousia enables the church to speak in its confessions of never coming into judgment (Heid. Cat., Q. 56) without ignoring passages like 2 Cor. 5:10. In this connection, see also Q. 52 and the theme of humility in Art. 23, Belgic Confession.
43. In Art. 37, Belgic Confession, the last judgment is clearly related to life on earth ("according to what they shall have done in this world, whether it be good or evil"). Reference is made to 2 Cor. 5:10 and Matt. 12:36. The Confession speaks of the "secrets and hypocrisy of men" which "shall be disclosed and laid open before all." Referring to Rev. 20:12, which speaks of books being opened and the dead being judged on the grounds of what is in these books, according to their works, the Confession adds "(that is to say, the consciences)," surely an

In the crisis of the parousia, everything is disrobed before the sight of God and before the throne of Christ the Lamb. No longer will evil be called good and good evil; no longer will darkness be turned into light and light into darkness; no longer will bitter be made sweet and sweet bitter (Isa. 5:20). This is the inevitable radical end of all human deceptions. The conflict between good and evil will come to an end, as will arguments about motives, intentions, and the nature of good. Everything will be analyzed. No longer will the problem of evil *sub specie boni* exist.[44] In the face of the coming of the Lord, life will become clear, not in a human judgment, but in the judgment of the Lord, who so frequently warned against human judgments with their lack of patience and righteousness and their failure to take into full account the hardness of man's heart (Matt. 7:1f.; John 7:24; James 4:11). Error will be exposed: real error, turning away from the Lord. This exposure will be clearer, fairer, truer, and more thorough than any *anathema sit, damnamus,* or *reiectio errorum* pronouncements in the annals of the church. And the church, the *ecclesia militans,* with all its dividedness, its discipline and insubordination, its preaching, its love, must remember that the judgment begins with the household of God (1 Pet. 4:17; cf. Jer. 25:29; Ezek. 9:5f.; Mal. 3:1-5), that its life too will be revealed *as it really is.*

In this revelation, all pretended motives will count for nothing, and the route of sophistry will be made impassable. It will be revealed who really believed that giving was more blessed than receiving (Acts 20:25) and who closed his heart to the needs of his brother (1 John 3:17).

Those who think of the parousia as an unimaginable event usually give too exclusive attention to it as a cosmic event, the moment when all things will dissolve (2 Pet. 3:11). Rather than thinking cosmically, one should first of all think apocalyptically (in the true sense of that word) about what is truly unimaginable, the *unveiling* of everything in an incontrovertible clarity and discernibility. This will be the moment of man's revelation.

incorrect exegesis. Although the unveiling is related to conscience, in the removal of secrecy, Rev. 20:12 is not talking about conscience but about what actually happened and has not slipped into oblivion (cf. Dan. 7:10). Greijdanus allies himself with Art. 37 (*Komm.,* p. 412); cf. Schilder, *Heidelbergse Catechismus,* I (1947), 87-89. On the relation between the "books" and the "book of life" in Rev. 20:12, see J. Behm, *Die Offenbarung des Johannes,* pp. 105ff.

44. See Berkouwer, *Sin,* ch. VIII, "The Question of Essence."

It will not be a relative and superficial judgment, like the verdicts of man (1 Cor. 4:5), but a judgment having a clarity that will dispel all hiddenness. There will be no "problem" of sin against the Holy Spirit, no justification of the terrible persecutions in the name of service to God (John 16:2), no rationalization of antisemitism, no justification of means by ends. All excuses will be scrutinized, all motives known. In this way the parousia will not be strange: life, as it actually happened in its hourly, daily, and yearly sequence, will be fully known.

It does not follow from all this that the parousia is merely a sort of moralistic climax to history. After all, the judgment before which life will be placed and under which it will come is the judgment of the crucified and risen Lord. Needless to say, His judgments on faith and unbelief will not ignore the concrete life and deeds of man. Judgment will be passed on all men's works.[45] From this it is evident that the central decision of life, namely for Christ or against Him, is the crucial factor and circumscribes life in its entirety. One's whole life and its central direction will be laid bare in the parousia.

Besides this unveiling of the intents of man's heart, there will come an exposure of the powers who made themselves great in the world.[46] Paul speaks of the powers that were disarmed through the victory of Christ (Col. 2:15). But faith in this victory does not permit the believer to abdicate his responsibility to battle against these forces, which continue to oppose Christ and deny and ignore His triumph. The parousia will unmask these too.

The proclamation of this present dispensation is that God made the wisdom of this world foolishness, that through the weakness of the Man of Sorrows, the weakness of God is shown to be stronger than men (1 Cor. 1:25). In the parousia the wisdom and power of God will be evident to all (cf. 1 Cor. 2:8), and the foolishness and futility of man will be revealed in a definitive unveiling of the mystery. The power of God was already apparent in the cross, yet man — the believer included — daily refuses to acknowledge this power. During this dispensation, it is still possible to debate these things, as some among the Areopagites did (Acts 17:32ff.), but the parousia is

---

45. On judgment according to works, see further Berkouwer, *Faith and Justification* (Eng. tr., 1954), pp. 103-12.
46. Cf. Popma, *Levensbeschouwing*, II, 413f.

the end of this debate. Then those who make themselves strong will be reduced to naught, just as Christ reduced the man of sin simply through His appearance (2 Thess. 2:8).

This will be the fulfilment of what Hannah saw from afar (1 Sam. 2:1-10) and what Mary saw in her vision of the time of salvation (Luke 1:46-55). It would not be incorrect to call this the most spectacular aspect of the parousia. It is anticipated in the account of the fall of Babylon (Rev. 18). The city is portrayed in its pride (vs. 7) as great (vv. 10, 16, 18, 21), but all this will be revealed for what it is in the light of the judgment of the mighty God (vs. 8).

Finally the parousia will reveal that the astonishing promise of eternal life for those who believe (John 6:40, 47, 58), coming to people surrounded by a world of death, was no exaggeration. If we can properly call the unveiling of the powers the most spectacular aspect of the parousia, this is certainly the most *lovely*. "Light is sweet, and it is pleasant for the eyes to behold the sun" (Eccl. 11:7). To His promise, "he who believes in me, though he die, yet shall he live" (John 11:25), Jesus adds, "Do you believe this?" Perhaps Martha's response is entirely appropriate: "Yes, Lord; I believe that you are the Christ, the Son of God, he who is coming into the world" (vs. 27). It is with this faith that we must look on Him who wept at the grave of Lazarus (vs. 35). Christ's words, "shall never die," bring us face to face with a great mystery. Our own perhaps wavering answer to questions about our faith seems to be more direct and realistic than Martha's.[47] But we must remember that Christ's words were spoken in the context of the death of Lazarus and its seeming finality. In the parousia everything will be made known: the meaning, depth, richness, and above all the reality of life in Him who is the Resurrection and the Life.

What will the parousia be like?

Christians have always wondered if it is possible, on the basis of what the Bible says, to get a concrete notion of what Christ's return will be like.[48] The New Testament does not only talk

---

47. Bultmann notes correctly that "the answer of Martha shows the genuine attitude of faith in that she avoids the statement about the *zōē*, drops the 'I,' and speaks only of 'Thou'"; *The Gospel of John*, p. 404.

about the suddenness and incalculability of the event, which might support the idea that it will be totally unknowable like the lightning, which "comes from the east and shines as far as the west" (Matt. 24:27) ; it also tells us, more descriptively, that He is "coming in clouds with great power and glory" (Mark 13:26). He will send out His angels with the sound of trumpets, and this will herald the coming of cosmic catastrophes, the darkening of sun and moon, the falling of the stars, and the shaking of the powers of heaven (Matt. 24:24; cf. 2 Pet. 3).

This return of Christ "on the clouds of heaven"[49] is a familiar image. This designation is not meant as a locating of the event or as a simple indication of an appearance in nature. As Minear notes, the clouds of heaven are more than a "mere terrestrial phenomenon."[50] To say this is not to "demythologize" the event of the parousia, but to follow the Bible's own usage of "clouds" in connection with the history of salvation. Sometimes, as in the account of Christ's ascension, the cloud is what covers and conceals (Acts 1:9). In John's vision the faithful are taken to heaven in a cloud in the sight of their enemies (Rev. 11:12; cf. 1 Thess. 4:17). On the other hand, in the Old Testament the cloud often signifies God's glory and presence among the people, His majesty in the theophany. It is impossible to sum up in one word exactly what these clouds mean. There is something ambivalent about speaking of clouds with respect to the majesty of God. The Psalmist sings of clouds and thick darkness surrounding God, hidden in an impenetrable mystery, with fire going before Him to burn up His adversaries (Ps. 97:2f.). But the cloud is also the symbol of God's blessed presence and providence in Israel's exodus from the land of Egypt (Ex. 13:21-22).[51] Later, the glory of the Lord appeared in the fire when Moses was called out of the midst of the people (Ex. 24:15-18). The elements of concealment are dispelled as God mercifully reveals Himself, still from a distance, in the cloud.

All of this considered, we can understand something of how

---

48. Schoonheim talks about the following elements: personal and direct, visible, public, sudden, majestic, surrounded by angels as judge and redeemer, and irresistible; *Een semasiologisch onderzoek van parousia*, p. 93.
49. Matt. 26:64 *(epí tōn nephelōn);* cf. Mark 14:62 *(metá tōn nephelōn);* the reference is lacking in Luke 22:69.
50. *Op. cit.,* p. 124.
51. Cf. W. H. Gispen, *KV* on Exodus, I, 150.

Christ's coming is pictured in the New Testament. The emphasis is on the actuality of Christ's coming in glory and splendor. Notice that in this appearance we encounter no longer the ambivalence of a cloud, but the complete manifestation of His coming. That He will appear on or with the clouds of heaven emphasizes His *being seen*. When Jesus tells the Jewish council "hereafter you will see the Son of man seated at the right hand of Power, and coming on the clouds of heaven" (Matt. 26:64), He is — as the Messiah in humiliation — referring back to the prophecy of Daniel: "and behold, with the clouds of heaven there came one like a son of man.... And to him was given dominion and glory and kingdom, that all the peoples, nations and languages should serve him; his dominion is an everlasting dominion, which shall not pass away, and his kingdom one that shall not be destroyed" (7:13f.). In the context of Christ's humiliation, these words point to the future glory and power of the Son of man as Judge of the world.[52] These words convey the aspect of wrath in His future coming (cf. Rev. 1:7).

So the ambivalence is no longer in the simultaneous concealment and revelation — distance and nearness at the same time — but in the glory that is manifested in its relationship to those who await or do not await Him for their salvation, and face this judge who is the Crucified and Risen One.[53] Thus His coming on the clouds is not an entirely new and separate aspect of His coming, but an indication of His appearance in glory in *this* world. This introduces an element familiar to all men. It is similar to the use of the word "day" to designate the time of His return.[54] The intent here is to eliminate any imaginary projections about His return, in agreement with what the angels said to the disciples after the ascension: that Jesus would return

52. Cf. H. N. Ridderbos, *KV* on Matthew, II, 208ff.; and, in this connection, the reference in Rev. 14:14 to "one like a son of man" who is "seated on the cloud." Clearly this refers to the coming judgment, especially in line with the harvest metaphor in vv. 14 and 15.

53. This ambivalence through the correlation of the day with faith and unbelief is already clearly expressed in Amos' words against those who illegitimately desire the day: "Why would you have the day of the LORD? It is darkness and not light" (5:18; cf. also Joel 2:2; Zeph. 1:7-9, 14-16).

54. Among these temporal references are the day that God has fixed (Acts 17:31; cf. 2:20; Rom. 2:5, 16; 13:12); the day of Jesus Christ (1 Cor. 1:8; 2 Cor. 1:14; Phil. 1:10, etc.); "that day and hour" (Matt. 24:36); and "a moment" (1 Cor. 15:52). Cf. K. Dijk, *Over de laatste dingen. De toekomst van Christus* (1953), pp. 51ff.

in the same way as they saw Him go into heaven (Acts 1:11). In Minear's words, we conclude "that the return of Christ with the clouds will be an event that belongs to the same order of reality as all early visitations of God that have been accompanied by the cloud."[55]

This coming manifest nearness is the content of all preaching. The heavens received Him "until the time for establishing all things" (Acts 3:21). At that time, the present dispensation will draw to a close. This message is preached in order that men may look for Him and find Him, and not "shrink from him in shame at his coming" (1 John 2:28).

There has been some question about the meaning of "the sign of the Son of man in heaven" (Matt. 24:30). Because nothing is said about the nature of this sign, it is generally assumed that this refers to Christ's appearance itself.[56] Zahn sees it as implying the perspicuity of His coming, the clarity and visibility of His appearance. Throughout the centuries many questions have arisen about this appearance, some bordering on doubt, others on open denial. Some have seen this appearance as a mythical expression of the meaning of the salvation of the cross, in which God deals in mysteries. Formulated differently, this question — which is really a question of the legitimacy of the church's expectation — can still be raised.[57]

For Bultmann, this can no longer be a theological conclusion. Everything about the coming of the Lord is incredible for the man of today, who is convinced that the primitive worldview is obsolete. The problem thus becomes one of discovering whether the New Testament embodies "a truth which is quite independent of its mythical setting."[58] Bultmann maintains that "the *mythical eschatology* is untenable for the simple reason that the parousia of Christ never took place as the New Testament expected. History did not come to an end . . . and it will continue to run its course."[59]

55. *Op. cit.*, p. 127.
56. Cf. Grosheide, *Comm., ad loc.;* Ridderbos, *KV* on Matthew, *ad loc.* Zahn *(Komm., ad loc.)* distinguishes the sign from the visible coming, without, it seems to me, adequate grounds.
57. Cf. Bultmann, "NT and Mythology," in *Kerygma and Myth* (Eng. tr. rev., 1961), p. 3: "All this is the language of mythology, and the origin of the various themes can be easily traced in the contemporary mythology of Jewish Apocalyptic and in the redemption myths of Gnosticism."
58. *Ibid.*
59. *Ibid.*, p. 5.

The form that demythologizing takes here is extremely sharp, and it disavows the actual expectation of the church to the point of ridicule. This sharpness is reminiscent of the mockery and scorn occasioned by the fact that the Lord had not yet returned during the time of the New Testament. We do not intend to make a simplistic identification of the skepticism confronting the author of 2 Peter with Bultmann's critique. Each has its own peculiar motives. But the two are equal in the sharpness with which they dismiss the return of the Lord. Therefore, some decision has to be made about this criticism. This decision cannot be a scientific one, leading to pronouncements on the future that can then be measured off against Bultmann's concept of the end as the outcome of natural development. The decision must be an expression of faith in the coming Lord, taking full account of the fact that Christ's parousia — with all of its implications — is always presented to us in prophetic-apocalyptic language, which in the nature of the case must be inadequate.[60] Some have tried to formulate a concept of the future along biblicistic lines, understanding apocalyptic language as a literal, chronological description of future events. Such attempts invariably end in confusion and contradictions that cannot be harmonized.[61]

But precisely for this reason the message of the parousia is not dependent on one or another more or less radical change in the concept of the world.[62] The important question involved in all this is whether the meaning of the cross (according to Bultmann *the* eschatological event) by its very nature excludes Christ's coming again, not only because, according to our modern concept of the world, it must be seen as impossible, but also because it is superfluous. Once again, we are thrown back on the notion of unveiling; and everything depends on the content we give to this unveiling. What is the meaning of the "revelation?" For Bultmann this question is decisive for the relation

60. Cf. H. N. Ridderbos' reference to Matt. 24:29 as a figurative description which is, however, not purely figurative since the description refers to a real end; *KV* on Matthew, II, 153f.
61. Regin Prenter correctly places biblicistic eschatology over against the existential eschatology of Bultmann; *Schöpfung und Erlösung*, II (1960), 512. Related issues here include the millennium (see Chapter X below), the signs of the times (see Chapter VIII below), and the interpretation of Mark 13, which is examined by G. R. Beasley-Murray, *Jesus and the Future* (1954).
62. Cf. H. de Vos, *NT en mythe* (1953), pp. 80ff.

between cross and resurrection. Here too Bultmann follows the same line of thought. The resurrection of Christ as an historical event is unbelievable and unacceptable for one who thinks biologically. It cannot be seen as the act of God. It is nothing more than "an attempt to convey the meaning of the cross."[63] One could say that the meaning of the cross was not revealed in the resurrection, but in the Easter-faith of the disciples. Bultmann does not mean that this is the view of the New Testament itself. The New Testament looked variously at the resurrection as a *new reality*, as much in the stories of the empty tomb and the appearances of the Lord as in Paul's "dangerous procedure in 1 Corinthians 15, where he adduces the witnesses of the fact of the resurrection."[64] But in reality it is a matter of an "understanding" faith, in which the meaning of the cross is revealed and unveiled.[65]

In contrast, the faith of the church testifies to an entirely different revelation, one whose character is not exclusively noetic. The antithesis between unveiling and new reality is rejected. On the basis of the preaching of the coming Lord, the church has lived in another expectation of the unveiling, a very concrete unveiling, to be manifested in a new act of God with man. There is, therefore, an essential connection between the eyewitnesses of the resurrection and the reality of Christ's appearance on the one hand, and the return of Christ on the other. According to Bultmann no expectation of His coming can ever be "existential," because it can never be more than a faith-acceptance of certain "announcements" concerning a future event. Such a faith can never be part of one's own life and cannot possibly have any meaning for that life.

Only by retaining Gnostic mythology could one come to an eschatological perspective in which one would speak of a future event, deeming the eschatological event of the cross, which directs itself to us, insufficient. Indeed, the church's confessions do speak expectantly of a future. But this expectation lacks the *impersonal* characteristics that Bultmann said it must have. If one does not obscure the difference between the *personal* and the *individualistic*, he must admit that the expectation of the future bears a preeminently *personal* stamp. It is not a blind

63. "NT and Mythology," *loc. cit.*, p. 38.
64. *Ibid.*, p. 39.
65. *Ibid.*, p. 41; cf. *Theology of the NT*, pp. 305f.

faith in future events, but a concentration of everything "that must soon take place" (Rev. 1:1) in Christ. The prayers of the church are turned to Him: "Come, Lord Jesus!" (22:20).

This prayer is no postulate or construction of the human heart. It is not a projection on the future. It is a response to Christ's promise: "Surely I am coming soon. Amen" (vs. 20). There is no arbitrariness here, for we read that both the Spirit and the bride plead for the coming of the Lord (vs. 17). This anticipates a revelational coming, but the unveiling will not be one that can be contrasted to the new reality, the reality of His coming. The prayer belongs to the "time between," as is confirmed by the benediction: "The grace of the Lord Jesus be with all the saints" (vs. 21). In distress and persecution, confusion and terror, amid the public exhibition of the powers of darkness, in short, in the "not yet," the church goes on as the *ecclesia militans.* The present dispensation in which it lives is not an empty, idle vacuum. The reality of grace — the *presentia realis* — is undeniable, and it is evidenced in the faith and militance of the community. This grace does not shut the eyes of the church to the "not yet" but stimulates its expectation. It does not isolate the church from the world, but arouses its interest in the world, not in spite of, but *because* of, the expectation of the Lord.

We should bear in mind that Bultmann's exceptionally sharp attack on "mythical eschatology"[66] is not the only form of de-eschatologizing. There are nontheoretical attempts to understand the reality of the parousia that fall into the same error. We saw, after all, that the Christian expectation of the future, according to Bultmann, is "incredible not only for the scientist, but for *every modern* man." There is also a danger of de-

---

66. On the "myth" of the parousia, see also J. A. T. Robinson, *Jesus and His Coming* (1957). Robinson claims that this myth is necessary in order to understand that "we *live* in the day of the Son of man" (p. 181). He also speaks of the "distortion" of this myth in the Pauline and Synoptic writings. The attack on "mythical eschatology" has itself been subjected to pointed criticism. Regin Prenter writes: "There is more radical proclamation of Christ in the clumsiest apocalyptic notion of holocaust and the return on the clouds of heaven than there is in a demythologizing that believes that it can dispense with any idea of the end of history and Jesus' return at the last day, because *the new life that we have to await is completely developed in the moment of existence* when faith lays hold of actual existence in its being-given-over to the future, over which we have no control"; *op. cit.,* p. 15.

eschatologizing from arguments other than those derived from the so-called "mythical" structure of the New Testament and the alleged need for positing a new world-view. In this kind of de-eschatologizing, the present as well as the future is challenged. The witness of the New Testament and the prayer for the coming of the Lord become a matter of profound embarrassment for the church. Its expectation of the future and hence its mandate for the present fall away. The future becomes a futuristic matter unrelated to the present. The present hope of that which can not yet be seen is jettisoned. But this obscurantism backfires because the structure of the eschaton cannot be broken. Such de-eschatologizing does not only deprive us of a perspective on the end, but also negates the meaning of the present life and its responsibility in the light of the final unveiling.

When the Apostle's Creed confesses that Christ will come again, it also speaks of the resurrection of the body. In the creed the confession of the resurrection does not immediately follow the confession of the return. The return is presented in connection with Christ; the resurrection with the Holy Spirit. To interpret this as division or dualism would be a mistake that would not only reflect a basic misunderstanding of the confession of the Triune God, but would introduce a fundamental dualism in the single unified expectation. There is therefore an indissoluble tie between the expectation of the coming of the Lord and the resurrection. To seek to dissociate them is to deprive the eschaton of its meaning. We shall see how complete the connection between these two is in the next chapter, as we turn our attention to what the Bible says about the future resurrection.

CHAPTER SIX

RESURRECTION

W E ARGUED in Chapter II that the only legitimate doctrine of the intermediate state is one that maintains the unity of the eschatological expectation and keeps this expectation free from egocentric individualism, which precludes an expectation of Kingdom, of the new heaven and the new earth, and of the resurrection of the body. Already in the early church this great perspective on the resurrection of the body was incorporated into the confession. Later this confession was the subject of numerous ecclesiastical controversies, which often threatened to submerge this belief in spiritualism or individualism. In the early creeds the resurrection was already confessed: it was only later supplemented by the confession "and the life everlasting."[1]

The reason that the confession of the resurrection of the body found a place in the creeds of the church so early is that this doctrine receives clear and emphatic attention in the New Testament. In its arguments against spiritualism and the spiritualistic view of salvation as the departure of the soul from the body, the church repeatedly appealed to the witness of the Word. In New Testament times, the resurrection of the body was expressly denied by the Sadducees (Matt. 22:23; Luke 20:7), a denial that led to the rift between them and the Pharisees, "for the Sadducees say that there is no resurrection, nor angel, nor spirit; but the Pharisees acknowledge them all" (Acts 23:8). But the denial of the resurrection was not just an incidental teaching that found its only adherents outside of the community of believers, such as Paul encountered in Athens (Acts 17:18, 32). The church itself faced a denial of the resurrection. Paul writes to Corinth: "how can some of you say that there is no resurrection of the dead?" (1 Cor. 15:12; cf. vs. 35). He also

1. For the history of this see J. N. D. Kelly, *Early Christian Creeds* (1960).

warns against the teaching of Hymenaeus and Philetus, "who have swerved from the truth by holding that the resurrection is past already. They are upsetting the faith of some" (2 Tim. 2:17f.) .

Against the background of these tensions the expectation of the resurrection in the New Testament is clear and imposing. This expectation is not a futuristic one, unrelated to the present. It rests in a promise inseparable from the salvation already granted. It is depicted as being rooted in an immovable foundation. Does this mean that we are to think in terms of an entirely new expectation, an entirely new hope resulting from the encounter with Christ and His resurrection from the dead?[2] Is not this resurrection contained in Peter's doxology: "we have been born anew to a living hope *through* the resurrection of Jesus Christ from the dead" (1 Pet. 1:3) ? Does this expectation pertain only to an unexpected and surprising New Testament event, an expectation precisely dated as an event of the history of salvation, with no antecedent or precedent in earlier times? In other words, do the connections between the resurrection of Christ and the resurrection of the dead suggest that there was not — nor could there have been — such an expectation under the old covenant?

Death and resurrection in the Old Testament

Thus, the first subject we shall consider in this chapter is whether Israel had an "eschatology," especially in connection with the resurrection of the dead. The question does not concern the expectation in Israelite religion in general, but the particular expectation of the resurrection.[3]

2. According to Acts 4:1f., the Sadducees were "annoyed" because the apostles were "proclaiming in Jesus *(en tō Iēsoú)* the resurrection from the dead." On this passage see Grosheide, *Comm.*, I, 125; and *KV* on Acts, I, 62.
3. What should one understand by "eschatology" in connection with Israel's expectation of the future? Several who have denied that there was an eschatology in Israel (particularly in the Former Prophets) do not intend to rule out all expectation of the future. By "eschatology" these scholars understand a dualistic view involving a sudden end to this world-order and its replacement by a new one that is entirely different. With respect to the Former Prophets, Mowinckel does not speak of "eschatology" but of "the future hope"; *He That Cometh* (1956), pp. 125ff. J. Lindblom sees eschatology as thoughts pointed to a future in which the circumstances of history and the world are so changed that one can really speak of a new state of affairs, of something completely different; "Gibt

We can begin with the general observation that the Old Testament describes death as an inevitable, all-powerful, and irreversible reality. Death is called "the way of all the earth" (Josh. 23:14; 1 Kings 2:2).[4] The Old Testament is not concerned with a mere certification of the phenomenon of death and the limitations of human existence, but with a break that becomes apparent with the good earthly life in all its relationships.[5] This break becomes apparent in the inevitability of death. The grave is an insurmountable and difficult reality. Death and the grave are used as similes for the strength of love and the cruelty of jealousy (Song of Sol. 8:6). "Truly no man can ransom himself, or give to God the price of his life, for the ransom of his life is costly, and can never suffice, that he should continue to live on for ever, and never see the Pit" (Ps. 49:7-9). Throughout Israel's religion runs the terror of death and what it may contain. When distress and danger mount for the Israelite, it is as if death were being perceived: "I am reckoned among those who go down to the pit.... Thy wrath lies heavy upon me, and thou dost overwhelm me with all thy waves" (Ps. 88:4, 7).

Above all, the finality of death comes to the fore: to die is to be cut off from the land of the living, without the possibility of return. In death the antithesis to life is clear. Where there is life, there is hope, "but the dead know nothing, and they have no more reward; but the memory of them is lost" (Eccl. 9:5). They can no longer participate in what goes on under the sun;

es eine Eschatologie bei den AT Propheten?" *Studia Theologica*, VI (1953), 82. See also T. C. Vriezen, "Prophecy and Eschatology," *Supplementum ad VT*, II (1957), 200ff., 223. Among the wealth of literature on the question of Israel's eschatology, some valuable studies are A. T. Nikolainen, *Der Auferstehungsglaube in der Bibel und ihrer Umwelt*, I (1944), ch. V; H. Birkeland, "The Belief in the Resurrection of the Dead in the OT," *Studia Theologica*, III (1950-51); R. Martin-Achard, *From Death to Life* (Eng. tr., 1960); Strack-Billerbeck, *Exkurs:* "Allgemeine oder teilweise Auferstehung der Toten?" *Komm. zum NT aus Talmud und Midrasch*, IV (1928), 1167ff.; W. Eichrodt, *Theology of the OT* (Eng. tr., 1958), pp. 299ff.; H. Molitor, *Die Auferstehung der Christen und nicht-Christen nach dem Apostel Paulus* (1936), pp. 91ff.

4. *derekh kol-hā'āretz.*

5. The Psalmist's questions, "What man can live and never see death? Who can deliver his soul from the power of Sheol?" (Ps. 89:49), touch on something more than the mere establishment of the phenomenon of death. Compare the Psalmist's reflection on the loving God who turns man back to the dust (Ps. 90:3).

and so the call comes to the living: "Go, eat your bread with enjoyment, and drink your wine with a merry heart" (vs. 7). Now — in life — is the time to work, "for there is no work or thought or knowledge or wisdom in Sheol, to which you are going" (vs. 10). Terror at the thought of death is most gripping for the Israelite when he thinks of the possibility of life's being removed in the flower of youth (cf. Isa. 38:10; Ps. 102: 23f.). The days of the godless will be shortened (Prov. 10:27); on the other hand, the lengthening of days is seen as a divine blessing (Exod. 20:12; Deut. 5:16; cf. Eph. 6:3). The promise of Yahweh to Zechariah was that "old men and old women shall again sit in the streets of Jerusalem, each with staff in hand for very age" (8:4). Thus the glory of life is opposed to the bitterness of the soul (Isa. 38:15), in which man, fearful of what is to come when he will no longer see Yahweh in the land of the living, is indeed faced with a terrible prospect (vs. 11).

The strong emphasis on this death as severance from life, as the enemy of earthly existence, as the counterpart to the joy of life (in spite of everything!), as a one-way street[6] — "water spilt on the ground which cannot be gathered up again" (1 Sam. 14:14; cf. Job 16:22; Ps. 19:13) — has led many to the conclusion that Israel knew of no real hope or expectation for the life to come, that death, the end of one's human lifetime, the ominous border separating man from Sheol, was thought to be the individual's horizon. Is Israel not proof of the unchangeableness, gravity, and finality of death, which defies any attempt to find some meaning in it? Moreover, does this not represent the unique meaning of Israel's witness concerning life and the earth, namely to remain true to the earth and anticipate its salvation?[7]

Clearly, this is all closely related to questions about the possibility and meaning of eschatology in Israel. The familiar words *diesseits* (here and now) and *jenseits* (hereafter) come into consideration here, especially in connection with the prevalent characterization of the religion of Israel and the central structure of the Old Testament as *diesseitig*, thisworldly. It is important to understand the precise meaning of *diesseitig* here, for it is

6. Barth, *CD*, III/2, 593.
7. A. A. van Ruler emphasizes this point when he remarks that Buber was correct in faulting the Christian church of the ages for forsaking the visionary OT faith in the possibility of the sanctification of the earth; *The Christian Church and the Old Testament* (Eng. tr., 1971), p. 91.

surely not a matter of an *antithesis* between *diesseits* and *jenseits*.[8] Once again we are back to the question concerning Israel's eschatology.

Although it cannot be denied that in the Israelite view of death a great deal of emphasis was placed on the meaning of this present life on earth, it does not follow that there was no real eschatological expectation.[9] Recently, this expectation has been given renewed attention, without thereby ignoring Israel's conscious awareness of the finality and inevitability of death.[10] In this darkness did Israel have no light? Some have answered this question by noting that the human limits of existence did not, for the Israelite, correspond to the divine limits. For him, death was not a "fatality" that neither man nor Yahweh could alter. The omnipotence of God surpassed the power of death. He is the living God (Josh. 3:10; Pss. 18:46; 84:3; Jer. 23:36). For Him death is no unalterable, irreversible horizon, no insurmountable barrier. "The Lord kills and brings to life; he brings down to Sheol and raises up" (1 Sam. 2:6). Responding to man's impotence in the face of death and his lack of perspective on it, God says, "See now that I, even I, am he, and there is no god beside me; I kill and I make alive; I wound and I heal" (Deut. 32:39). He is Lord over death as well. There is no escaping Him in Sheol, the realm of the dead (Amos 9:2; Ps. 139:7). He has the power to reverse the irreversible in a new *creatio ex nihilo*. We see this in times of serious illness, when death appears to be inevitable and only God can save

8. While rejecting this dilemma between *diesseits* and *jenseits*, N. H. Ridderbos maintains that the OT teaches us to take earthly life seriously; "Het OT en de geschiedenis," *Gereformeerde theologisch tijdschrift*, LVIII (1958), 8f.; cf. his earlier article, "Het OT in de prediking," *ibid.*, LVI (1956), 146f.; and Leo Baeck, *Aus drei Jahrtausenden* (1958), esp. pp. 28-41.

9. "Yahweh's grace *('emeth)* has no further relevance to the dead. They are cut off from His hand. And this is for centuries the real sting of death in OT religion.... The lack of a point of theological orientation for views as to the state of death means that in Yahweh religion these are held without the definition and integration otherwise characteristic of the OT"; G. von Rad, in *TDNT*, s.v. záō, II, 847. Cf. H. Birkeland, *op. cit.*, 61.

10. Cf. Nathaniel Schmidt, "The Origins of Jewish Eschatology," in "A Symposium on Eschatology," *Journal of Biblical Literature*, XLI (1922), 102ff.

(Job 33:19-26). But it applies equally to the case of death itself, where the boundary has already been crossed.[11]

The Israelite who commits himself to Yahweh in light of the divine promise of the future attests to this. Those who have studied the Israelite expectation of the future generally recognize that for the Old Testament believer the prospects of a life after this life were in many respects concealed in a thick cloud.[12] Many have argued that this does not imply a denial of an expectation, and they concentrate their attention particularly on several psalms in which a strong expectation for the future seems to surface: Psalms 16, 49, and 73. Mentioning those who see in these psalms reference only to a temporary salvation from death, Bavinck notes that even if this were so, the Old Testament nevertheless points to God's dominion over death.[13]

Others have in recent times formulated much more positive statements about these psalms. For Von Rad, Psalm 16 speaks of "holding fast to the grace of Yahweh" (vv. 9f.); Psalm 49 speaks boldly and clearly about the redemption of the soul from Sheol (vs. 16); while Psalm 73 speaks of the certainty of fellowship with God (vv. 23ff.). "One may say that here the Old Testament belief in the hereafter finds its purest formulation."[14]

Does this harmonize with the nature of Sheol, the realm of the dead?[15] Is the gravity of Sheol as the place of oblivion, the place of no return, not negated by this faith in a fellowship with the Lord that transcends death? We should bear in mind that it is not easy to arrange all the facets of the Old Testament idea of the future in some logical synthesis. God's being hidden is presented neither in the Old Testament nor the New as something transparent from the standpoint of present reality with its prospects of the final break. But saying this does not

---

11. C. Barth attempts to show that the entire Psalter deals exclusively with salvation from — not out of — death; *Die Errettung vom Tode in den individuellen Klage- und Dankliedern des AT* (1947); cf. P. J. van Leeuwen, *Het Christelijk onsterfelijkheidsgeloof*, pp. 30ff.
12. N. H. Ridderbos, "Het OT en de geschiedenis," p. 9.
13. *GD*, IV, 578.
14. In *TDNT*, II, 848.
15. On this see J. Coppens, "Het onsterfelijkheidsgeloof in het psalmboek," *Mededelingen van de Koninklijke Vlaamse Academie voor Wetenschap*, 1957. Coppens deals with these three psalms, rejecting the interpretation of C. Barth on the grounds that it is impossible to understand deliverance from Sheol metaphorically (p. 21).

deprive the expectation of its actuality. How is this harmony between Sheol and the expectation to be explained? Nothing of the radical gravity of death is discounted; at the same time the believer continually retains his faith in the God of life. The latter perspective presupposes the radicality and horizon-lessness of what is possible from the human side. On the basis of his own existence man is unable to determine the meaning of death or to reduce its ultimate seriousness. But this seriousness of death remains subject to divine possibilities, which come into play at the point where man encounters the irreversibility of death. At this moment, on the border between life and death, Yahweh's power of life becomes operative in Israel's religion. Sheol does not have the last word.[16]

This power of life of Yahweh is related to resurrection, a theme that comes up in Ezekiel's visions of the light of divine revelation falling on the demise of the people of God. Israel is described in the contours of death: the valley filled with dry bones. With an eye to the utter despair of the people, Yahweh asks Ezekiel, "Son of man, can these bones live?" (37:3); and then, in the face of the unalterability of death, He replies with these liberating words: "Behold, I will open your graves, and raise you from your graves, O my people" (vs. 12).

Obviously this prophecy refers to the revival of Israel's existence as a nation, not to the "resurrection of the dead." The images of death as final (cf. vs. 11) do give an insight into the almighty power of God, and for this reason some have interpreted Ezekiel 37 as a prophecy of the resurrection of the dead.[17] It is difficult to defend this interpretation. To be sure, the people are called to an awareness of the living God,

16. Coppens speaks of a gradual supersession of the traditional concept of Sheol which he feels was not given in the revelation to Israel; *ibid.*, p. 19. Bavinck speaks of a moral-spiritual antithesis woven into the antith-esis between life and death; *GD*, IV, 577f. Historically, he says, the question about the future of individual persons stayed entirely in the background; not until after the Exile, when religion became individ-ualized, did this question become prominent, even though the data for it were present in earlier revelation. See also, in J. Ridderbos's com-mentary on the Psalms, his remarks *ad* Pss. 6:5; 49; 88:10-12.

17. On Ezek. 37 see Birkeland, *op. cit.*, 73ff.; Nikolainen, *op. cit.*, 130, 138. Concerning it as a prophecy of the resurrection, see, among others, Martin-Achard, *op. cit.*, pp. 93ff.; Jacob, *op. cit.*, p. 310; Noordtzij, *KV* on Ezekiel, p. 372; and G. C. Aalders, *Ezechiël, ad loc.* Aalders finds here no revelation concerning the resurrection, but a connection with this doctrine.

for whom there are no limits. In His infinite power, He places limits on the power of death and removes it from its position of power. The triumph of Yahweh becomes evident at the precise point where death appears to be at the peak of its power. Thus this prophecy does not deal with an abstract possibility, but with a divine act in restoring His people Israel. This proclamation of God's merciful power of life does not relativize the power of death, but makes it subservient to and contrasts it with God's power, as the light of resurrection shines into the utter and despairing darkness.[18]

We encounter not only Yahweh's power of life in the Old Testament, full of wonderful perspectives for Israel's national existence that defy imagination. We also read of the *destruction of death* as the great manifestation of Yahweh's power of life, glory, and mercy. This comes to the fore in the so-called Isaiah Apocalypse (ch. 24-27), later cited by Paul in his discussion of the resurrection of the dead (1 Cor. 15:54).[19]

The focal point of this prophecy is the mountain of God, which will be the place of the coming festivities and great joy. There Yahweh will destroy the veil presently covering all nations and peoples (25:7). "He will swallow up death forever; and the Lord God will wipe away tears from all faces" (vs. 8). Nowhere in the Old Testament do we find more profound perspectives than these, not even in Isaiah 65, where the prophet speaks of the creation of the new heaven and the new earth (vs. 17; cf. 2 Pet. 3:13). For when salvation is described in Isaiah 65 it is in terms of the child who "shall die a hundred years old, and the sinner a hundred years old [who] shall be accursed" (vs. 20; cf. Zech. 8:4);[20] in other words, it amounts to the lengthening of life, after which death will still follow. Isaiah 25, however, has a much more definitive character: the destruction of death for all time forms the content of the pro-

---

18. On the alleged parallel between Ezek. 37 and Hos. 6:2 ("After two days he will revive us; on the third day he will raise us up, that we may live before him"), cf. Martin-Achard, *op. cit.*, pp. 81ff.; C. van Gelderen, *Hosea*, p. 204.

19. Among the discussions of these chapters are E. S. Mulder, *Die teologie van die Jesaja-Apokalypse, Jesaja 24-27* (1954), particularly pp. 105ff.; O. Plöger, *Theokratie und Eschatologie* (1959), pp. 69-97. On the authenticity of the Isaiah Apocalypse, see M. A. Beek, *Inleiding tot de Joodse apocalyptiek* (1950), pp. 11ff.

20. Cf. K. Elliger, *Die Kleine Propheten* (1951), p. 130; Martin-Achard, *op. cit.*, p. 129.

claimed joy.[21] This is a prelude to the future reality: "Thy dead shall live, their bodies shall rise" (26:19), according to Mulder a straightforward expression of belief in the resurrection.[22] To this is added the challenge: "O dwellers in the dust, awake and sing for joy!" Along with Daniel 12:2, this verse is often cited as giving an explicit Old Testament perspective on the resurrection of the dead, because this verse addresses itself to more than the revival of Israel's nationhood.

Some have concluded that this notion of an individual resurrection is a radical revision of Israel's expectation, due to exposure to Persian religion, under whose influence a corporative, national expectation was replaced by an individual one. Originally, the restoration of the entire nation was expected; the individualistic belief "came in when the Israelite eschatology was strongly influenced by the Iranian."[23] So, despite many obstacles, this dogma came to be dominant in rabbinic literature, "because it corresponded to vital religious interests, above all the belief in a retaliation after death."[24]

Given the background of Israel's concrete belief in Yahweh's power of life, it is evident that the expectation of the resurrection is more than a foreign influence, although it must be granted at the same time that the Old Testament says very little about the resurrection. Vriezen disregards the theory of Persian influence as unnecessary for explaining what was already implicit in Israel's expectation.[25] He sees the resurrection-expectation as a result of faith in God's power of life, which also rules Sheol (cf. Hos. 13:14), and of the fact that the resurrection of the unified person, body and soul, in his concrete earthly existence is the only way in which the Israelite expectation of eternal salvation can be expressed. There is no reason to isolate the reference to awakening in Daniel 12:2 as a foreign element in Israel's expectation. What Daniel 12:2 says is closely related to "a time of trouble" (vs. 1) and in this trouble there is a perspective not only on the deliverance of the nation, but

21. J. Ridderbos sees the destruction of the veil as the removal of sorrow; *KV* on Isaiah, I, 178; cf. Mulder, *op. cit.*, p. 31.
22. *Op. cit.*, p. 50. Cf. Nikolainen, *op. cit.*, 131; Martin-Achard, *op. cit.*, p. 130ff.
23. Birkeland, *op. cit.*, 77.
24. *Ibid.*, 78.
25. *Op. cit.*, 216.

also on the awakening of "those who sleep in the dust of the earth."[26]

Von Rad sees Isaiah 26:19 and Daniel 12:2 as belonging to "a different religious stream" from the Psalms. The Psalms concern faith; Isaiah and Daniel the objective nature of the expectation of the end.[27] But there is no reason to make such a distinction on the basis of these passages. Both thoughts are united by their perspective on the saving acts of God in the awakening and the ending of threats to His people. Both posit the redeeming power of God against what seems to be a hopeless and inescapable situation from a human point of view.[28]

What seems definitive for man in its inevitability is neither inevitable nor definitive for God. He provides a return from the land from which there was no return. Even if one is ill-disposed to "systematize" Israelite eschatology,[29] he must acknowledge the impressive force of this message. The raising of the dead is mentioned only very incidentally and enigmatically in the Old Testament (cf. 1 Kings 17:17-24; 2 Kings 4:18-37; 13:20f.), unlike the New Testament, where such signs are central. But in these incidental and fragmentary accounts, as in the translation of Enoch (Gen. 5:24) and the ascension of Elijah (2 Kings 2:1-12) there is an unambiguous testimony to the power of the *living* God.[30]

26. Cf. G. C. Aalders, *KV* on Daniel, p. 268. According to Aalders the intent of this passage is not to give an argument about the resurrection, but to comfort martyrs. On the notion of a general resurrection, see Strack-Billerbeck, *loc. cit.*, who refer to the ambiguity of Dan. 12:2. It is clear that in general the outlook here is directed on the righteous, and that the unrighteous come up for discussion in connection with the twofold judgment of mankind. The Strack-Billerbeck *excursus*, incidentally, is given in explanation of John 5:28.

27. *TDNT*, II, 848.

28. On Dan. 12:2, see H. B. Knossen, "De oorsprong van de voorstelling der opstanding uit de doden," *Nederlands theologisch tijdschrift*, X (1955-56), 296ff. Knossen does not accept the interpretation that Dan. 12:2 constitutes an *objectification* compared to the *faith* of the Psalms.

29. Cf. Eichrodt, *op. cit.*, p. 515: "As one surveys the picture of the eschatological resurrection hope, in so far as this is developed within the OT, one receives the impression of a concept of faith which has not yet been elaborated or fixed in a dogmatic form, but is still elastic and bound up with the actual struggle for assurance of God."

30. On Enoch and Elijah, see E. Jacob, *op. cit.*, pp. 307f.; Martin-Achard, *op. cit.*, pp. 65-72. Karl Barth, *CD*, III/2, 635ff., speaks of "an extraordinary intervention of God"; cf. Berkouwer, *The Triumph of Grace*, pp. 161ff.

The resurrection of Christ and the resurrection of the dead

The danger is that this testimony to the power of the living God will lead men to take death less seriously than it should be, as if this ultimate lack of a problem were man's doing rather than God's. Furthermore, on the basis of this power — not an unknown *potentia absoluta,* but the power of the God of Israel, who alone does wondrous things (Ps. 72:18) and for whom nothing is too hard (Gen. 18:14) — it is understandable why the testimony of the Old Testament resounds throughout the New Testament. Some Old Testament passages become, in fact, chief witnesses for the New Testament testimony to the resurrection of the dead. Surprisingly this happens precisely where the resurrection of Jesus Christ forms the fundamental basis of the doctrine of the resurrection of the dead.[31]

The difference between the Old and New Testaments is not that the one lacks and the other has an eschatology. Rather it is that only in the New Testament is the meaning of the reality of Yahweh's power of life fully revealed. The focus is no longer on what God *can do,* but on what He *has done.* All the earlier incidental and fragmented references to resurrection center in the fact of salvation through the actual resurrection of Jesus Christ, the first-born from the dead. In the proclamation of the gospel to the world, it is revealed that God's power of life is not just a "possibility," but an act of the living God, whose power extends beyond the limits of death and supersedes the reach of Sheol.

It would be unbelieving bravura to say that the New Testament believer can now do without the Old Testament.[32] For to say this not only reflects an extreme form of biblical criticism, but also peculiar eschatology, which has not paid very close attention to Israel's testimony about death and life. Christ's conquest of death does not support this point of view. This tri-

---

31. Cf G. J. Streeder, *De prediking van de opstanding der doden in het NT,* pp. 34ff.

32. One is reminded of Harnack's comment that the rejection of the OT was an error that the church of the 2nd century avoided; that the retention of the OT was a destiny that the Reformation of the 16th century could not avoid; but that the conservation of it as a canonical document by Protestantism since the 19th century is the result of religious and ecclesiastical paralysis; *Marcion* (1924), p. 127. One might rather say that this rejection is an indication of *eschatological* paralysis.

umphant message is indeed the central thrust of the New Testament, but Christ's victory can be fully grasped only by those who have fully understood the profundity and seriousness of what the Old Testament says about the utter depths of despair in which God's power is revealed. This is the implicit (and occasionally explicit) greatness of Old Testament eschatology, which is only fully understood when life is revealed (John 11:25; 1 John 1:2).[33]

The New Testament expectation is not just a carry-over from the Old Testament with nothing added. Something much more profound is operative, as is shown by the concentration of the expectation in the fulfilment of the time of salvation ushered in with the coming of Jesus Christ.[34] There is a sense in which one may speak of a continuation of the Old Testament promise, but only if one understands that this promise is *now* made visible in its new actuality. *Now* Christ has "abolished death and brought life and immortality to light *through the gospel*" (2 Tim. 1:10) — through what is proclaimed. *Now* there is fulfilment of the expectation. On the boundary between the old and new dispensations stood Simeon, "looking for the consolation of Israel" (Luke 2:25). He saw the salvation of God, and then he could depart in peace (vv. 29f.). But this fulfilment at the same time is not the *end* of the expectation, but the beginning of a new era, in which windows to the future are opened anew. What happens *now*, in the time of salvation, is at once fulfilment and new foundation, a new reality breaking through in this world and offering a guarantee of future salvation.

Throughout its history, the Christian church has always held to the unity of the two Testaments and the continuity of God's dealings with man. Thus it is no devaluation of the

---

33. On the difference between the OT and NT, see further F. Baumgärtel, *Verheissung. Zur Frage des evangelischen Verständnisses des AT* (1952), p. 50.
34. Coppens notes correctly that the triumph over death in the NT is connected with redemptive history, but then adds, incorrectly I think, that Pss. 16, 49, and 73 are unrelated to any event in the history of salvation or eschatology; *op. cit.*, p. 19. This fails to take full note of the relation between Yahweh's power of life in the OT and the grounding of life in the resurrection of Christ.

Old Testament to say that the expectation of the resurrection is squarely founded on the resurrection of Jesus Christ.[35]

It is evident that the believers are also included in His resurrection: "God raised the Lord, and will also raise us up by his power" (1 Cor. 6:14). From this connection between the resurrection of Christ and that of the believers, we *know* "that he who raised the Lord Jesus will raise us also with Jesus" (2 Cor. 4:14). The resurrection of believers is the outcome and an indication of the power of Christ's resurrection. The link between the two is most clearly expressed in the phrase "the first-born from the dead." The "priority" that Christ has implies a sequel.[36] He is "the resurrection and the life" (John 11:25), the "Author of life" (Acts 3:15), who "gives life to whom he will" (John 5:21). "This is the true God and eternal life" (1 John 5:20).

As we shall see, this is not merely a causal relationship, in which the resurrection of Christ *in the past* is the cause, and the resurrection in the future the effect. It is clear that the resurrection from the dead is immediately connected with what has already become reality in the life of the believer. But in the biblical promise of the resurrection of the dead, its connection with the resurrection of Jesus Christ is central and dominant.[37]

This relationship is attested to by Paul's sharp rebuttal to "some" in the Corinthian church who said that there is no

35. Karl Barth is correct in speaking of "the radical change of view brought about with the giving of a solid basis to the OT hope"; *CD*, III/2, 620. Cf. also what he says about what the OT did not and could not explicitly say before Christ's birth; p. 624. One should remember that "not explicit" or "not concrete" does not necessarily mean "vague."

36. On the connection between Christ's resurrection and that of believers, cf. also 1 Thess. 4:14 ("... even so ..."); Eph. 2:5 ("... alive together with Christ ..."); Col. 3:4 ("... Christ who is our life ..."); Acts 4:2 (see above, note 2). See also Oepke in *TDNT*, s.v. *egeirō*, II, 336f. In addition to the expression "the first-born from the dead" (Col. 1:18; Rev. 1:5), cf. 1 Cor. 15:20, 23 ("first fruits" — *aparchḗ*); Rom. 8:29 ("the first-born among many brethren"); Acts 16:23 ("the first to rise from the dead").

37. Cf. Heidelberg Catechism, Q. 45: "The resurrection of Christ is a sure pledge to us of our blessed resurrection"; cf. Q. 57: "... this flesh of mine, raised by the power of Christ...." See also Art. 20, Belgic Confession: "... that through Him we might obtain immortality and life eternal." The same relationship is pointed out by H. Rendtorff, "Auferstehung des Fleisches, Bekenntnis zur Kirche," in *Festgabe für E. Sommerlath*, pp. 307-12.

resurrection of the dead (1 Cor. 15:12). Paul's question —
how could they deny the resurrection of the dead? — reflects
apostolic astonishment. Notice that Paul does not choose as the
point of departure for his reply the omnipotence of God, which
would in itself be sufficient explanation for the miracle of the
resurrection.[38] No, Paul considered these Corinthians' opinions
strange for another reason. How could they come to such a
conclusion "if Christ is preached as raised from the dead?" For
Paul, one cannot believe in the resurrection of Christ and still
doubt the resurrection from the dead. The preaching of the
risen Lord closes the discussion on the possibility of resurrection from the dead. It erases any doubt about it. The connection is, in fact, so close that "if there is no resurrection of the
dead, then Christ has not been raised" (vs. 13). To deny the
resurrection of the dead does not just do away with the eschatological perspective, but with the *foundation* upon which
the community was built as well. Consequently, what Paul
had proclaimed is robbed of its content; it becomes vain (vs.
14). Paul and the other apostles turn out to be false witnesses,
misrepresenting God, because they had preached the resurrection of Christ, "whom he did not raise if it is true that
the dead are not raised" (vs. 15). Moreover, those who have
already died are caught up in a "crisis"— a wholly imaginary
one! — "those who have fallen asleep in Christ have perished"
(vs. 18).

Finally the light of direct statement shines through this
indirect train of thought: "But in fact Christ *has been* raised
from the dead, the first fruits of those who have fallen asleep"
(vs. 20). He is the first, and He is not to be isolated from
those who follow Him in that miraculous sequence: "Christ the
first fruits, then at his coming those who belong to Christ"
(vs. 23). Because of Christ's resurrection, the eschatological
perspective is unassailable. With the denial of the resurrection
from the dead, *everything* is denied; life sinks into the abyss
and its meaning becomes illusory: "If the dead are not raised,
'Let us eat and drink, for tomorrow we die'" (vs. 32).

It is not enough to speak only of the results and conse-

---

38. Paul is not relativizing the aspect of power that the resurrection from
the dead bears: 2 Cor. 1:9 and Acts 26:8 clearly indicate the apostle's
emphasis on this aspect. But Paul never sees it as a case of *potentia
absoluta;* rather, it is a witness to what God does and has done (cf. 2
Cor. 1:10).

quences of Christ's resurrection. There is a far deeper meaning implicit in the relationship between the resurrection of the dead and the resurrection of Jesus Christ. This meaning is locked in the resurrection of Christ, as He Himself is "designated *(horisthéntos)* Son of God in power" (Rom. 1:4).[39] According to Paul, one cannot consider Christ's resurrection *by itself,* only to draw the theme of the resurrection of the dead into this perspective *later.*

Bultmann, who is critical of the "dramatic" element that remains in Pauline eschatology, admits that the apostle "defines the life of the believer as life characterized by faith in Christ's resurrection and hope for his own resurrection."[40] Attention is drawn to the reality of salvation, which came to light in Christ's resurrection, but at the same time it is focused on the future reality of the resurrection.

Here we are once again confronted with an unmistakable "not yet." This resurrection is a reality of the future, and to claim with Hymenaeus and Philetus "that the resurrection is past already" would be to swerve from the truth (2 Tim. 2:18). According to Paul, this is a serious error, for it has upset the faith of some. Some scholars see a connection between this form of "realized eschatology" and the denial of the resurrection that was found in Corinth about the same time. At first glance there appears to be no similarity between admitting a resurrection that supposedly had already taken place and denying outright any resurrection at all. But the two are not as different as they may appear to be. The heresy referred to in 2 Timothy 2:18 should be understood as a form of spiritualism, which believed that the transition from death to life and to the resurrection from the dead had already been completed through regeneration.[41] In this spiritualism there is no future resurrection, nor a truly eschatological perspective. Some have suggested that reference may have been made to Paul's own writings (for example, Romans 6) to support this teaching, since there apparently did exist in the early church the belief that the believer need not die in view of the present salvation.[42]

---

39. *horízein* here should not be understood in an adoptionist sense, but as indicating the reality of the *now* of revealed power; cf. Acts 10:42; 17:31.
40. Bultmann, re Barth's *The Resurrection of the Dead,* in *Faith and Understanding,* I, 67.
41. C. Bouma, *Komm.,* p. 29; Zahn, *Komm.,* p. 303.
42. Cf. Joachim Jeremias, *Die Briefe an Timotheus und Titus* (1953), p. 49.

In any case, the result of both the heresy about the resurrection of the body and the denial of it is identical: a future resurrection is rejected. This leaves us with the question of what grounds were adduced for the denial by those in Corinth. The conjecture that the resurrection had already occurred was probably spiritualistic, but an outright denial may have any number of motives.

In all probability the motive of those in Corinth was similar to that of Hymenaeus and Philetus. These Corinthians most likely did not intend a brute, rationalistic denial of the resurrection. It could well be that in this denial Paul was confronted by the logical conclusion of the "gnostic" heresy of 2 Timothy 2:18.[43] In that case, we might ask whether Paul was addressing himself to the background (the resurrection has already taken place) or to the specific results. Judging from the way he formulates his response, the latter is his intent, as well as to deal with the denial of the *future* resurrection. For Paul there were more far-reaching consequences than these doubters themselves imagined when they said, "Let us eat and drink, for tomorrow we die" (1 Cor. 15:32; cf. Isa. 22:13). There is a sort of nihilism, which Paul counters with a warning: "Come to your right mind, and sin no more" (1 Cor. 15:34). It is probable that Paul is not here giving their philosophy of life, but his opinion of what the inevitable consequences of the denial of the future resurrection are.

The extent to which Paul expected and proclaimed the future resurrection is apparent here. The "already" element is present in his eschatology, but he never applies this "already" to the resurrection of the dead. For Paul that "already" is an illusion that completely misses the reality of true salvation and underestimates the gravity of death. Paul's "already" does not relativize the eschatological expectation.[44] Faced with the denial of the future resurrection, he points out the results: the proclamation would become futility and falsehood, and life would

---

43. According to Zahn, the conjectures of 2 Tim. 2:18 are not specifically gnostic; *Komm.*, p. 303. W. Schmithals maintains that denial of the resurrection is a fundamental dogma of gnosticism; *Die Gnosis in Korinth* (1956), p. 72. J. Schniewind writes that time and again since the days of Chrysostom these words of 2 Tim. 2:18 have been seen as the "Corinthian" thesis; "Die Leugner der Auferstehung in Korinth," *Nachgelassene Reden und Aufsätze* (1952), p. 114.
44. Cf. Schniewind, *op. cit.*, p. 117.

completely lose its meaning. The fulfilment is coming in the future, in the final triumph when the last enemy death will be dethroned (1 Cor. 15:26), when the mortal will become immortal, the perishable imperishable (vs. 53). Then — and only then — the promise "death is swallowed up in victory" will become actuality.[45] Paul concludes here with the blessing from the Isaiah Apocalypse. This promise has not yet become reality, but that will happen. Old Testament prophecy already spoke of the swallowing up of death, but now that Paul has seen the foundation upon which this reality will be built, the full and profound meaning of this prophecy can be properly understood.

Paul combines this quotation from the Isaiah Apocalypse with a quotation from Hosea: "O death, where is thy victory? O death, where is thy sting?"[46] The Old Testament outlook on

45. *katepóthē ho thánatos eis níkos.* The relation of this to Isa. 25:8 has always been the subject of much discussion, because Paul does not quote here from the LXX, which reads *katépien ho thánatos ischýsas* — "death, having become strong, swallowed [them] up." The Massoretic Text reads *billa' hammāweth lānetzach* — "He has swallowed up death for ever." Zahn considers the LXX here incomprehensible, since it makes "death" the subject, in distinction from the Hebrew, in which God is the subject, which essentially corresponds with 1 Cor. 15:54. The addition of *eis níkos* in the Pauline quotation is usually related to the root *nātzach* ("victory"). See further the commentaries by Zahn and Grosheide, *ad loc.*

46. Hos. 13:14 reads: "Shall I ransom them from the power of Sheol? Shall I redeem them from death? O Death, where are your plagues? O Death, where is your destruction? Compassion is hid from my eyes." The question has been raised whether Paul uses what is a prophecy of damnation in Hosea as a prophecy of salvation. There are two small differences between Paul and the LXX in the portion quoted. Paul's citation replaces the LXX *hē díkē* with *tó níkos* (vs. 55a) and *hádē* with *thánate* (vs. 55b). There is considerable disagreement about the interpretation of Hos. 13:14 itself. Weiser found in this verse the first foundations of the religious hope for resurrection; *Das AT Deutsch* (1949), p. 84. To support this interpretation he is forced to translate *nōcham* as "vengeance": "vengeance [die Rache] is hid from my eyes." Over against this interpretation is that found in Gispen's commentary on Hosea (1949), which translates *nōcham* as "compassion." Gispen admits that there is a subjective element in the choice between a prophecy of salvation or damnation: he makes his choice on the basis of the context — cf. the coming of the east wind (Assyria) in vs. 15 and 14:1-3 (Weiser dissociates 13:14 from 14:1). The LXX translates *nōcham* as *paráklēsis;* the Vulgate as *consolatio.* See also A. de Bondt, *Wat leert het OT aangaande het leven na de dood?* (1938), pp. 87ff., who defends the interpretation of the passages as a prophecy of salvation. This interpretation is unmistakably in accord with the

the power of Yahweh — His unlimited power over Sheol — receives concrete confirmation according to Paul in the resurrection of Christ. In triumphant words he indicates the resurrection of Christ as the basis upon which reconciliation is obtained and the sting of death forever removed (vv. 56f.). He concludes with a prayer of thanksgiving: "Thanks be to God, who gives us the victory through our Lord Jesus Christ."

In Paul's discussion of this indissoluble relationship between the resurrection of Christ and the resurrection of the body,[47] between the salvation that has appeared and the eschatological triumph over death, he does not only confirm the future resurrection as such, but also reflects on questions that seem to have been used as counter-arguments to it. Consider the passage (1 Cor. 15:35-44) where he talks about the resurrected body. What Paul says here has been the subject of considerable exegetical criticism.

Bultmann sees this as nothing more than a "misleading, polemical section."[48] Admittedly, Paul's train of thought has a polemical point of departure. He begins with a number of questions that "some one will ask": "How are the dead raised? With what kind of body do they come?" (vs. 35). Perhaps these questions had been raised by those who denied the resurrection, in an effort to demonstrate its impossibility and absurdity. One is reminded of the Sadducees' question to Jesus about marriage in the resurrection (Matt. 22:23-33).[49] In any

OT teaching of Yahweh's power of life; Martin-Achard, *op. cit.*, pp. 92f., observes that Paul is subscribing here to "Yahweh's crushing superiority over the infernal powers." The problem of Paul's citation of Hos. 13:14 is important for the study of Pauline hermeneutics; for our purposes, however, it is sufficient to observe the triumphant word about the power of God over death that is expressed here in connection with Isa. 25.

47. From Paul's description of the future as "being with Christ," Bultmann concludes that "Christ is not the cosmic ground of a future condition of existence, but the historical foundation of our present life"; *Faith and Understanding*, I, 93. However, no such dilemma existed for Paul, because the reality of salvation implies the future resurrection. Schniewind correctly notes that the perspective of 1 Cor. 15 is presented against the background of Christ's *bodily* resurrection; *op. cit.*, pp. 121ff.

48. *Faith and Understanding*, I, 93.

49. Cf. Wendland, in *Das NT Deutsch, ad loc.* Grosheide argues that Paul's exclamation "You foolish man!" only makes sense if there really were people asking such questions.

case, they called into question the *imaginability* and *thinkability* of the resurrection.[50]

Paul's answer is sharp and without hesitation: "You foolish man!" The perspective of faith is not in the least bit of danger. This counterargumentation can only yield to a reference to renewed reliance on God's dealings in the future. Paul turns to nature for an example. The mysterious process of sowing and reaping is not an automatic process that does not arouse any amazement. What is sown is not the body-to-be, but the kernel of it, which does not grow by its own strength but is given a body by God, an individual body for each seed. All the emphasis in this passage falls on the act of God, which certainly does not follow as a matter of course from the human act of sowing as such. There is a *miracle* in the seed's transition from kernel to body.

The questions that Paul is dealing with here — and the background against which they are to be understood — concern the perspicuity of the resurrection of the body. Paul's goal is to bring the perspective that he preached within the realm of human experience. The reality of this perspective must be considered dependent on the fact that the resurrection can be perceived. When questions such as Paul seems to be confronting here are raised in an effort to prove the meaninglessness of the resurrection, Paul reminds his readers by analogy of grain in its transformation from kernel to "body."

Obviously, Paul did not intend to *prove* the resurrection of the body by this line of thought and make it acceptable to human understanding through "natural theology" or "natural cosmology."[51] He is careful to guard against his readers' forming conclusions based solely on human reasoning. For that reason, in his analogy of the seed he points out the miraculous power of God, which gives the body to the kernel. From the seed itself nothing can be expected unless one keeps his

---

50. Cf. P. A. van Stempvoort, "De opstanding dezes vleses in 1 Kor. 15," *Vox Theologica*, X (1939), 179; Streeder, *op. cit.*, p. 102.

51. When Calvin writes about "proving" the resurrection (*Inst.*, III.xxv.4), he is definitely not thinking of rational proof. "This fact [the resurrection] would not be so hard to believe if we paid proper attention to the miracles thrust before our eyes throughout all the regions of the world. But let us remember that no one is truly persuaded of the coming resurrection unless he is seized with wonder, and ascribes to the power of God its due glory."

eyes open to the miracles of God. So it goes with the sowing of this earthly body. The reference to nature (for the analogy from creation also presupposes faith in the living God) is intended to break down all pretentious rationalistic questions. He intends to expose this seemingly real and meaningful problem for what it is.

Some have seen Paul's argument here as reflecting the idea that there is a *praeludium* of the resurrection in creation.[52] In other words, just as there is in nature a way to life through death, so also there is a way to the resurrection from the dead through death. It is not clear exactly what content the word *praeludium* has here; but it is clear that the reference to the "bare kernel" and to what God does, while directed against questions about the perspicuity and conceivability of the resurrection, clears the way for what Paul elsewhere calls the destruction of "arguments and every proud obstacle to the knowledge of God" (2 Cor. 10:5). Paul does not want to make the leap from a phenomenon in nature to the resurrection of the dead, but in this polemical situation and on the basis of his unshakable certainty, he rejects all pride with reference to the mystery of God's future act.[53]

That Paul was not driving at proving the identity of the resurrected body to the earthly body that is sown[54] is evident from his mention of the great variety of "flesh" and the difference

52. According to Wendland, Luther and Calvin, like Paul, conceived of the life of creation as an indication and prelude to the coming life of resurrection; *Komm.*, p. 132. Cf. Calvin's commentary *ad* 1 Cor. 15:39: "...a sort of foreshadowing *(praeludium)* of the resurrection ..."; vs. 36: "...a kind of representation *(imago)* of the resurrection ..."; *Inst.*, III.xxv.4.

53. Zahn refers incidentally to John 12:24, where Jesus talks about the grain of wheat that falls into the earth and dies and bears fruit, an indication of the fruit of Christ's death by an image from nature; *Komm.*, p. 458. In his commentary on John, Grosheide speaks of "the law of life of the kernel of grain"; II, 217.

54. Often this passage is exegeted as if it were such a proof, in terms of the divine consolation of the *totalitas materiae*, an argument rejected by Bavinck on physiological grounds; *GD*, IV, 677. When Bavinck himself says that the church has always held fast to this identity over against dualism (the body as prison house of the soul) and tries to state wherein this identity consists, he confesses that we do not know what it is that remains the same through all metamorphoses. As a result, the identity is negatively expressed as being independent of raw material, its changes and quantity. It seems clear to me that one can draw no conclusions on the basis of Paul's remarks here.

in glory between celestial and terrestrial bodies (vv. 39ff.) . The one flesh or body can become visible reality in many different forms. Paul judges this too to be God's work. He is not concerned with an hypothetical difference in glory among those resurrected from the dead,[55] but with God's manifold and mighty work of creation in its essence, which, while it receives a multiplicity of forms, cannot be exhaustively analyzed and comprehended by man. Just as Paul detected the living God at work in all of creation, so also he sees the miraculous power of God at work in connection with the future.

Spiritualism and dualism

Such was Paul's polemical method in calling attention to the miracle that he knew from the promise and preached. The analogies he used were not intended to be the foundation of his proclamation about the future. They function only within the framework of what is believed and known in Jesus Christ.[56] It is clear to what extent Paul sees the future work of God as connected with the bodily resurrection, and how far he is from any spiritualistic notion that a spiritual resurrection is sufficient and from any abolition of the larger expectation in a belief in regeneration as "realized eschatology." The expectation of the resurrection of the dead was not, for Paul, of secondary

55. Cf. Grosheide, *Comm.*, p. 419; *KV* on 1 Corinthians, p. 201. Grosheide does not deny that one might speak of a difference among the resurrected on the basis of what Paul says in vv. 40f., but calls such an interpretation application in place of exegesis. (But then how should one "apply" the text?) Cf. Calvin, *ad* 1 Cor. 15:41: "An error is usually made in the application of this, for people think that Paul meant to say that after the resurrection there will be different degrees of honour and glory for the saints. That is, of course, perfectly true, and other passages of Scripture bear witness to it; but it has nothing to do with what Paul has in mind here." The *hoútōs kaí hē anástasis tṓn nekrṓn* (vs. 42) refers to what follows: the perishability of what is sown and the imperishability of what is raised.

56. Barth writes, "The bringing forward of analogies, and the conclusion drawn from them, point not to something sought, but to something already found"; *The Resurrection of the Dead* (Eng. tr., 1933), p. 186. The contrast made by Fuchs between *hope* (cf. Rom. 4:18) and Paul's "arbitrary" comparison with natural phenomena in 1 Cor. 15 misses the polemical function of the latter passage and Paul's right to speak analogically on account of his certainty. See Fuchs's chapter, "Die Auferstehungsgewissheit nach 1 Kor. 15" in *Zum hermeneutischen Problem in der Theologie* (1959), pp. 205ff.

importance, but is incorporated in the salvation extended by the Resurrected One, who is Himself the Resurrection.

The church has always been beleaguered by the forces of spiritualism. Early in its history it began to confess the resurrection of the dead — the whole man — in its creeds. Nowhere in the gospel of Christ is salvation portrayed as the soul's liberation from the body. When Paul says, "We wait for adoption as sons" (Rom. 8:23), he adds, "the redemption *of* our bodies," not "the redemption from our bodies."[57]

But what are we to make of the peculiar expression in 1 Corinthians 15:44 — "a *spiritual body?*" Are we to deduce from this that Paul was not, after all, primarily concerned with an actual corporeality, but with something "spiritual?" Does this not inevitably lead to a dualism between body and soul? Can speaking of a "spiritual body" accomplish anything but throwing us into confusion? If the resurrection is a matter of a spiritual body, how much meaning is there to confessing a "resurrection of the body?" Paul's expression has nothing to do with spiritualism. In speaking about what God would send in the future through the miracle of His grace, Paul adds that the body to be raised would be a spiritual body. For him, this falls in line with the distinction between the first and second Adams. The spiritual body is contrasted to the physical, but Paul's use of "spiritual" and "physical" conveys a specific meaning. The Greek word translated here as "physical" is *psychikós.* This word is also found in 1 Corinthians 2 to describe the spirit of this world as against the Spirit of God (vv. 12, 14). "The unspiritual *(psychikós)* man does not receive the gifts of the Spirit of God . . . and he is not able to understand them because they are spiritually *(pneumatikós)* discerned." This is not an anthropological dualism between "psyche" and "pneuma," but an illustration of the difference between human wisdom and that taught by the Spirit (vs. 13). *Pneumatikós* means here "that which is characteristic of the Holy Spirit."[58] Over against this is the natural, unspiritual man, who, as being, has life and nothing more.[59]

Now the distinction between "unspiritual" and "spiritual"

57. Cf. O. Michel, *Komm., ad loc.*
58. Grosheide, *Comm.,* p. 88.
59. *Ibid.,* p. 91.

in 1 Corinthians 2 is clearly and closely circumscribed. But in chapter 15 both words are applied to the body. This is significant for understanding the eschatological "spiritual body." This spiritual body of the future is a matter of the gift and power of the resurrection of Christ. It involves a perspective concerning reality that is wholly dominated by the Spirit — the *Pneuma.* In Romans 8:11 Paul makes a direct parallel between the resurrection of the mortal body and the Spirit who dwells in the believers. The expectation is directed to glorification through the Spirit of Christ. The "spiritual body" does not have to do with what we sometimes call "spiritualizing." "Spiritualizing" always presupposes a dualism, which in turn carries with it a devaluation of the body, which is nowhere to be found in Paul's teachings. He speaks of the body as "controlled by the *pneuma.*"[60] This Spirit is already at work within man's body, but only in the resurrection will it completely rule man's life. This is not a gradual process of evolution, but an entirely novel divine act in which the Spirit will be manifested. It is the transition from mortality to immortality, from perishability to imperishability. This transition does not disqualify the body, but it does indicate a break. This break is not between the lostness of the body and the soul's liberation from it, for the Spirit of God already lives within man's concrete earthly existence. At present, however, there remain perishability *(phthorá)*, weakness *(astheneía)*, dishonor *(atimía)*, and humiliation (vv. 42f., 50; cf. Phil. 3:21). Then there will be imperishability as the body is raised through the power of Christ. The spiritual body stands in the full light of the destruction of death.[61]

Is there a difference between the expressions "resurrection of the flesh" and "resurrection of the body?" W. Bieder has

60. Schweizer, in *TDNT*, s.v. *pneúma*, VI, 421. Cf. also E. Käsemann's remarks on 1 Cor. 6:19f., in *Exegetische Versuche und Besinnungen*, I, 286ff.

61. The meaning of vs. 46: *all' ou próton tó pneumatikón allá tó psychikón* ("But it is not the spiritual which is first but the physical") is not really difficult. In the context of Paul's antispiritualistic polemic, it is directed against those who thought that the "pneumatic" was primary (in a special sense and over against the corporeal), all the more so because the contention that the "pneumatic" was older than the "psychic" was the most pregnant expression of the whole Gnostic understanding of existence. Cf. W. Schmithals, *Die Gnosis in Korinth* (1965), p. 136. The passage has nothing to do with a "priority of the natural" as found in several earlier and later anthropological distinctions.

considered this point and answers affirmatively.[62] (Note that he is not asking whether modern man can accept the concept of the resurrection of the "flesh," and whether, in the light of this, the church should alter the expression *resurrectio carnis* in the creed.) Bieder examines the liturgies of various churches in Switzerland. Most of them confess to the resurrection of the *body*,[63] and Bieder concludes that their revision of the creed's *carnis* is due to the churches' "consciousness of a dilemma." Moreover, he sees this as a Paulinization of the creed, since Paul believed that *flesh* cannot inherit the Kingdom of God (1 Cor. 15:50), for which a different *pneumatic* body is promised. Bieder asks why the church in many places did not stay with the Nicene formulation, which is faithful to 1 Corinthians 15:13, in speaking of the resurrection of the *dead*. Does not the expression *resurrectio carnis* leave the impression of a magical event? Furthermore, does it not indicate a way of thinking that has preference for considerations of *substance*, a way of thinking that wants to see a continuity in the preservation and resurrection of the *substance* of our earthly flesh?[64] Did the church not go too far in its stand against docetism and spiritualism by positing a *resurrectio carnis*? Is not Paul's point precisely that there is a complete difference in kind between the "spiritual" body and the "physical" body?[65] Consequently, Bieder concludes, it would be better to speak of the resurrection of the *body*, although extreme caution must be taken not to consider this resurrection in isolation from Christ, the first fruits of the dead.[66]

It seems to me that this does not present a real dilemma for the creed. Bieder himself admits that even the word *body* does not in itself provide a guarantee that the great eschatological event will not be treated in isolation from the resurrection of

62. "Auferstehung des Fleisches oder des Leibes?" *Theologische Zeitschrift,* I (1945), 105-20.
63. *Ibid.,* 106. The Argovian liturgy reads "Auferstehung des Fleisches"; the others, respectively, "de la chair," "des Leibes," "du corps," "des corps."
64. According to Bieder, the effect here is to subsume under the categories of substance the wonderful act of the Redeemer God towards man who has fallen into sin, which disregards the fact that the only continuum between the present and the hereafter is God, who freely gives, not the substance of the flesh or the body. *Ibid.,* 107, 119.
65. *Ibid.,* 107.
66. *Ibid.,* 119.

Christ. The close connection of this resurrection with the resurrection of Christ is a pervasive Pauline theme, and there is no indication that the early church ever lost this perspective. Nor did the church judge the difference between the "resurrection of the body" (Apostles' Creed) and the "resurrection of the dead" (Nicene Creed) to have any significant consequence. The church was not interested in categories of substance or isolated metaphysical miracles, but in the reality of the miraculous power of God towards this our flesh, this weak, perishable, and mortal body; in short, towards the whole man in his earthly existence. Therefore, regardless of how much the eschaton was seen in relation to the indwelling of the Spirit, it was not yet realized, but remained the object of the expectation: God's act through the power of Christ.

Even though it may be argued that the expression "resurrection of the body" does not take anything essential away, that does not alter the fact that the other expression — *resurrectio carnis* — is intended to convey something of the miracle of "putting on" the imperishable and immortal (1 Cor. 15:53). Thus, the words of the creed should not be judged to be un-Pauline.[67] Nor can this be established by the appeal to Paul's remark that "flesh and blood cannot inherit the kingdom of God" (1 Cor. 15:50). Bieder's rejection of the expression *resurrectio carnis* suggests that, according to the creed, flesh and blood *can* inherit the Kingdom. This argument ignores the fact that Paul adds immediately, "nor does the perishable inherit the imperishable." Moreover, when Paul says that in the great transformation to come the perishable must *put on* the imperishable, the objections raised against the expression *resurrectio carnis* may also be leveled against the expression "resurrection of the body."

Every attempt to explain the great change of 1 Corinthians

67. Cullmann too feels that *resurrectio carnis* cannot be reconciled with Pauline teaching on the grounds that Paul saw the flesh as the power of death, which must be destroyed. Thus *resurrectio carnis* is, according to Cullmann, a misunderstanding of biblical terminology. "Immortality or Resurrection?", *Christianity Today*, August 18, 1958, p. 14. E. Brunner writes: "But the flesh will not rise again. The resurrection of the flesh stands of course in the creed but is excluded by what Paul says in 1 Cor. 15:35-53." *Eternal Hope* (Eng. tr., 1954), p. 149. Brunner appeals specifically to vs. 50 ("flesh and blood cannot inherit the kingdom of God, nor does the perishable inherit the imperishable") in this connection.

15:51 and to concretize the continuity on the basis of anthropological distinctions should be rejected. At the same time, every effort to detract from the reality of the miracle that comes — through Christ's power — over the whole man should be resisted. There is no room for a dualistic and spiritualistic interpretation that would exclude the body from the eschatological fulfilment.[68]

Obviously, no one is able to describe fully the great change of which Paul wrote. But this does not take anything away from the emphasis Paul placed on the reality of this eschatological event. This transition concerns the passage from perishability to imperishability, from mortality to immortality. If we try to investigate further the *mode* of this transformation, we learn nothing more than that it will take place in a moment *(en atómō)*, in the twinkling of an eye, at the last trumpet (vs. 32).

Paul also writes about a transformation in Philippians 3:21, where he says that Christ "will change *(metaschēmatísei)* our lowly body to be like his glorious body, by the power which enables him even to subject all things to himself."[69] It is not in the least surprising that all attempts to give a satisfactory exegetical explanation of this change from lowliness to glory give the impression of groping and stammering.[70] What does come across — even in Paul's frugality of words — is that he is talking about a reality through the act of God. This reality is assumed into the sphere of our expectation and consolation, without any effort to satisfy our desire for it to be "imaginable."[71]

68. Cf. Prenter, *Schöpfung und Erlösung*, II (1960), 541ff. Joachim Jeremias tries to show that 1 Cor. 15:50a "does not refer to the resurrection of the dead." He sees here an indication of the *living* in distinction from the dead (cf. *phthorá*, vs. 50b, in connection with the parousia). It seems to me that even with this exegesis, in which *phthorá* is seen as an *abstractum pro concreto*, the passage still has indirectly to do with the resurrection. Jeremias himself says that it has to do with the resurrection "by analogy." For the rest, it should be noted that Jeremias opposes throughout the notion that there is a "complete annihilation" in 1 Cor. 15:50 in consequence of Hellenistic influence ("a spiritualization of the Pauline conception of the resurrection"). "Flesh and Blood Cannot Inherit the Kingdom of God," *NT Studies*, II (1955-56), 151ff.
69. Cf. Lohmeyer, *Komm.*, p. 162.
70. Cf. Berkhof, *CMH*, p. 188: "This is a stammering attempt to express what is above our experience"; and Popma's critique of Berkhof, *Levensbeschouwing*, II, 320.
71. The same applies to Rom. 8:29, where Paul talks about the predestination of the elect, "to be conformed to the image of his Son" *(symmórphous tḗs eikónos toú hyioú autoú)*.

Paul is talking about the glorification of this humiliated, fragile, and inadequate human body. Now there is conformity to His death; then there will be conformity to His resurrection and glory (Phil. 3:10; Rom. 6:5). Characteristically lacking any futuristic orientation foreign to man's present experience, Paul directs his conformity with Christ's death towards the future conformity: "becoming like him in his death, that if possible I may attain the resurrection from the dead" (3:11).

Paul knew that he was on the way to the resurrection. This miracle cannot be divorced from what happens in this dispensation; being conformed to Christ's death is a prelude to and a sign of the future conformity.[72] Life in its entirety is caught up in this expectation and decisively determined by it. As a result, Paul nowhere excludes the body from this future perspective. Quite the contrary, it is always noteworthy how much emphasis Paul gives to man in all his concreteness and corporeality. "Your body is a temple of the Holy Spirit" (1 Cor. 6:19). "Glorify God in your body" (vs. 20).[73] "My little children," he exclaims, "with whom I am again in travail until Christ be formed in you!" (Gal. 4:19). "We are always carrying in the body the death of Jesus, so that the life of Jesus may be manifested in our bodies" (2 Cor. 4:10; cf. vs. 11).[74]

Paul speaks of a concrete human being, not just a soul or spiritual existence that has a body as a temporal burden foreign to it, but a being that is really human in its bodily existence according to God's purpose. Man's whole existence is affected by the revelation of Jesus Christ's resurrection. There is no trace of dualism here.

This is clear from Paul's observations on man's sexual life. The body is not devaluated as something ignoble, but when temptations present themselves the body's proper function is

---

72. Cf. Michel in *TDNT*, s.v. *katantáō*, III, 624: "By suffering Christ draws Paul into His death and fashions him in His own likeness with a view to resurrection from the dead."

73. Zahn sees this *en tō sōmati* as an expression of the locus of or means for God's glorification. The words "locus" and "means" are too mechanical and tend to separate what is inseparably connected. See also Grosheide's commentary, *ad loc.*, on whether "in your body" is meant locally or instrumentally; and Käsemann, *op. cit.*, p. 278.

74. The word used for "death" is *nékrōsis*. According to Bultmann, "the word is obviously chosen instead of *thánatos* because the reference is to dying with Christ, not as basically fulfilled in the act of baptism, but as continually actualised in the concrete life of the apostle"; in *TDNT*, s.v. *nékrōsis*, IV, 895. Cf. also Gal. 6:17.

indicated. "The body is not meant for immorality, but for the Lord, and the Lord for the body" (1 Cor. 6:13). A more pertinent admonition is hardly imaginable. And Paul goes on immediately to place the relation between the body and the Lord in an eschatological perspective: "God raised the Lord and will also raise us up by his power" (vs. 14). The resurrection of the body is as clearly professed here as in 1 Corinthians 15. It is precisely this future that is concretely experienced in everyday life, in the bodily aspect as well. Paul warns against prostitution by reminding them "your bodies are members of Christ." Because this relationship is so close and so intimate, it is impossible to take these members of Christ and make them members of a prostitute. Such a relationship would mark the whole life as illegitimate, for "he who joins himself to a prostitute becomes one body with her" (vs. 16).[75] There are profound consequences in such disqualified relationships, all of them entirely opposite to uniting oneself to the Lord and becoming one spirit with Him.[76]

These were Paul's warnings against depreciating the body and disregarding its eschatological purpose. The body is for the Lord, as He is for the body. Fornication leads only to a total lack of perspective, to an ominous "eschaton" in which the end is worse than the beginning. Man, in the totality of his existence, is summoned to the service of the Lord. Salvation makes demands on the whole man: he is not his own; he was bought with a price (1 Cor. 6:20). The great eschatological promise of verse 14 is important to the purpose of the body. The body cannot be considered abstractly as an independent substance, but only in the light of its destiny: resurrection from

75. Horst writes, "according to Scripture this [sexual] union is more than an incidental function of the members. It is a coming together as one *sōma*, and it is thus of far-reaching significance for the whole physico-spiritual personal life"; in *TDNT*, s.v. *mélos*, IV, 565. On this passage see also E. Best, *One Body in Christ* (1955), pp. 75ff.

76. Compare vs. 16 (*ho kollōmenos tē pórnē*), vs. 17 (*ho kollōmenos tō kyriō*), and Gen. 2:24 (LXX: *proskollēthēsetai*). What is notable about the quotation from Gen. 2 in this context is that in Genesis the expression refers to the unity of man and woman that is created in life by God. Paul cites the saying in order to indicate that the union of a man with a woman has special meaning. Cf. Eph. 5:31, a less complicated quotation of Gen. 2:24. On Paul's use of Gen. 2:24 see Schlier, *Der Brief an die Epheser* (1958), p. 262. There is a detailed examination of 1 Cor. 6:16 in D. Daube, *The NT and Rabbinic Judaism* (1956), pp. 80ff. Daube sees a clear indication of androgyny here.

the dead. Although the final glorification has not yet taken place, the signs of this transformation are already evident in the call to service and in the bonds of communion with the Lord (cf. 1 Thess. 4:3, 7f.). In this bodily existence the bell of the future sounds. In the fragility and weakness of bodily existence and the decay of the outward man there is not an escape from corporeality but a perspective on a new harmony.[77] Paul calls on the Christian community, with an appeal to the mercy of God, "to present your bodies as a living sacrifice, holy and acceptable to God" (Rom. 12:1; cf. 1 Pet. 2:5).[78] In the light of salvation the meaning of bodily existence is revealed and all dualistic tendencies are overcome completely. It is not a matter of two separate spheres — soul and body; for the living sacrifice of the body is inextricably connected with the renewal of the mind and the proving of the will of God (Rom. 12:2).

Paul sums up what is required of the Christian thus: "present your bodies as a living sacrifice, holy and acceptable to God." This is not stand-pat moralism: the believers are called to transformation and renewal.[79] They must not be conformed to this world but taken up with the process of transformation, a metamorphosis of their entire existence.[80] There is an essential relation between this initial transformation and the transformation to take place in the future. Cullmann correctly speaks of the "proleptic deliverance of the body."[81] Although the final transition is God's definitive miracle, it can never be conceived as an isolated cosmic problem or a question about substance. It frees the believer from death and frees him for a new life in the service of God, already beginning in this life.

Paul describes the transformation that begins in this life

---

77. Cf. Paul's own example in 1 Cor. 9:27: "I pommel my body and subdue it, lest after preaching to others I myself should be disqualified." According to Rengstorf, "his *sŏma*, with all that belongs to physical life, is fully and emphatically subordinated to his office, and has a right to existence only in so far as it at least does not hamper him in the discharge of this office"; in *TDNT*, s.v. *doulagōgéō*, II, 280.
78. Cf. Selwyn, *op. cit.*, p. 162; C. Pauwels, "God eren met het lichaam," in *Lichamelijkheid* (1951), pp. 189ff.
79. *metamorphoústhe tĕ anakainōsei toú noós*.
80. Cf. O. Michel, *Der Römerbrief*, p. 261. Behm defines this metamorphosis as "a process by which the transcendent eschatological reality of salvation works determinatively in the earthly lives of Christians"; in *TDNT*, s.v. *metamorphóō*, IV, 759.
81. The title of an essay by him in *The Early Church*, pp. 165-73. See also E. Brunner's treatment of 2 Cor. 3:18 in *Eternal Hope*, p. 146.

as the discontinuation of the dominion of sin in this mortal
body, and the yielding of one's members to God as instruments
of righteousness (Rom. 6:12f.). This new orientation of the
concrete, bodily man is the prelude to the resurrection.[82] Nowhere is it more apparent than here how unsatisfactory is the
dilemma between realized and futuristic eschatology, for this
dilemma is completely unable to get to the heart of the eschatological perspective. It might be argued that the term "prelude
to the resurrection" is equally unsatisfactory, but who can
formulate adequately the relation between the "already" and
the "not yet" with regard to the human body in its present
existence? At any rate, we are reminded of this relationship
and its concomitant responsibilities, which make it impossible
to play off the present against the future, since what God in
Christ has joined together, no man may put asunder.

Resurrection of the body and the gospel message

The spiritualistic denial or relativization of human corporeality smacks of unreality because it abstracts one element
from the living human being created by God. Consequently it
blurs the outlook on God's eschatological act. The gospel strongly opposes such unreal conceptualization, which does violence
to the joy of the Kingdom as it is reflected in this time of
salvation. The message of the gospel is not a "spiritual" thing,
but good tidings applied to man's entire existence, his total
experience. "The blind receive their sight and the lame walk,
lepers are cleansed and the deaf hear, and the dead are raised
up, and the poor have good news preached to them" (Matt.
11:5).

Here if anywhere it is clear that spiritualism preaches
another gospel (Gal. 1:7). As it is portrayed in the gospel, the
Lord saw the disruption of life by sickness and death as a
fearful destruction. He who is the Resurrection and the Life
(John 11:25) wept at the death of Lazarus (vs. 35). "He was
deeply moved in spirit and troubled" (vv. 33, 38). He did not
respond to His friend's death with pacifying words about the
security of the soul; He responded with intense prayer and
a call to faith in the glory of God: "Did I not tell you that if
you would believe you would see the glory of God?'" (vs. 40).
The Lord willed that the leper be cleansed and the demons

---

82. Cf. K. J. Popma, *Levensbeschouwing*, II, 265.

driven out (Mark 1:41, 34). Throughout His Messianic work shines the light of the resurrection.

Not incorrectly, these miracles of healing have been seen as "signs" of the Kingdom that has come. But they are not incidental or haphazard signs, eventually to be replaced by other signs. They occur precisely where the bodily existence of man is threatened or disrupted.[83]

The meaning of these miracles is revealed in a special way in Matthew's portrayal of them as the fulfilment of Isaiah's prophecy: "He took our infirmities, and bore our diseases" (8:17; cf. Isa. 53:4). This passage has always been the subject of considerable exegetical attention, since it does not relate the Old Testament prophecy to its fulfilment in the mission of the Messiah in general, but in a specific, concrete way to the healing miracles.[84] In what is now happening Matthew sees the fulfilment of the prophecy of the Man of Sorrows. The Gospel of Matthew has often been considered to provide a special interpretation of the miracles of Jesus that are given in the Gospel of Mark.[85] Matthew's point of departure is the healing of the sick, the miracles of restoration in the time of salvation, which he relates to the prophecy of the Man of Sorrows. Isaiah 53 speaks of the Man of Sorrows as "acquainted with grief" (vs. 2), and says of Him that "he has borne our griefs and carried our sorrows" (vs. 4). He was "smitten by God, and afflicted" (vs. 4). How shall we describe the relationship between this image of the Man of Sorrows and the Messianic time of salvation with

83. "Miracles in the NT are in their deepest essence signs accompanying the Gospel, a self-manifestation in the sphere of our corporeality of the God who addresses us"; Käsemann, "Is the Gospel Objective?", in *Essays on NT Themes,* p. 53. See also G. Ebeling's discussion of "Jesus and Faith" in *Word and Faith* (Eng. tr., 1963), pp. 201-46, in connection with Christ's words to the Samaritan leper, "Your faith has made you well" *(sésōken)* and to the blind man of Jericho (Luke 17:19; 18:42).

84. For the relationship between OT prophecy and the mission of the Messiah, compare Matt. 1:5 (Luke 7:22) and Isa. 35:5f.; Luke 4:18f. and Isa. 61:1f. Matthew's quotation of Isa. 53:4 in 8:17 follows directly the description of three miracles — the leper, the centurion's servant, and Peter's mother-in-law — and the indication that He did many other miracles "that evening" (vs. 16).

85. Heinz-Joachim Held, "Matthew as Interpreter of the Miracle Stories," in *Tradition and Interpretation in Matthew* (G. Bornkamm, G. Barth, and Held; Eng. tr., 1963), pp. 165-299; esp. pp. 246ff. Cf. also C. H. Lindyer, *Het lijden in het NT* (1956), pp. 57ff.

its healing of bodily afflictions?[86] How shall we sum up the connection between His bearing our ills and His removing them in the Messianic era?

Matthew saw in the words of the prophecy the reality that was visible to all — compassion in the midst of need.[87] This bodily need is inseparable from the totality of human existence that is healed. What is confronted by the might of the Messiah is actual bodily distress and destruction. The removal of guilt and punishment is never isolated from these bodily disruptions. The opposition of the Kingdom to this disruption — demon-possession (Matt. 8:28-34), paralysis (9:1-7), blindness (9:27-30), and death (9:18-26) — is one triumphant opposition, revealing itself in the Messiah and proceeding from His humiliation.

Later Matthew writes: "He healed them all" (12:15). The deeper meaning of this remains hidden (vs. 16), but even here prophecy — again from Isaiah — is fulfilled: that He would bring justice to victory even though no one would hear His voice in the streets (12:17, 19f.; Isa. 42:2, 4). Out of the depths of the humiliation of the Man of Sorrows the meaning of restoration is revealed. Held feels that the notion of bringing justice "to victory" is a Matthean addition, with no foundation in any of the sources.[88] But Matthew sees the establishment of justice on earth in these miracles of healing as victory. How much the gospel of reconciliation focuses on man in his bodily existence! At the precise point where the inevitability of distress as it confronts human powerlessness is evident to all, we see the Messiah coming and acting in answer to man's call for mercy (Matt. 9:27; 15:22; 20:30f.).

Even when Christ did not explicitly refer to His future work — the resurrection on the last day — there is evident in His Messianic work an overriding and unmistakable relationship

86. Held, *loc. cit.*, p. 260.
87. Cf. Matt. 15:30f.; 20:34 ("Jesus in pity"); 17:17. Held calls attention to the contrast between Isa. 53:4 (LXX) (which he calls "spiritualising"; p. 260): *hoútos tás hamartías hēmôn phérei kaí perí hēmôn odynátai* and Matt. 8:17: *autós tás astheneías hēmôn élaben kaí tás nósous ebástasen.* See further Oepke, in *TDNT*, s.v. *nósos*, IV, 1096f., who says that "Mt. 8:17 applies Is. 53:4 to the healing Christ in a version of its own."
88. *Op. cit.*, pp. 261f. Cf. Isa. 42:4: "till he has established justice in the earth" (LXX: *héōs án thê epí tês gês krísin*). Cf. H. N. Ridderbos, *KV* on Matthew, p. 235, on the bruised reed and the dimly burning wick as images of weakness, helplessness, and pitiableness.

to the future, as He approached man in his misery with these signs of healing. He stands among them with His healing power. There is no room for spiritualism here. Christ came to grips with all the problems that face man in his total creatureliness.

There are passages in the Gospels that speak more explicitly of the resurrection. This comes to the fore in Christ's dispute with the Sadducees, when He points up the flaws in their opposition to the doctrine of the resurrection. Their attempt at *reductio ad absurdum* with an appeal to the Old Testament law of levirate marriage ran up against Christ's wisdom. "You are wrong, because you know neither the scriptures nor the power of God" (Matt. 22:29). Christ reminds them of the words of the Lord, "I am the God of Abraham, and the God of Isaac, and the God of Jacob" (vs. 32; cf. Exod. 3:6). This had been spoken in a time when these patriarchs had already passed away. So the significance of what follows comes into focus: "He is not God of the dead, but of the living." Though he might have cited a more explicit word about the resurrection from either Isaiah or Daniel, Christ sees the mystery of the resurrection wrapped up in these words of the *living* God, who, in His faithfulness and mercy, enters into communion with man and preserves him in that communion.[89] Through this communion the resurrection becomes real. This contains no separate treatment of body and soul, but speaks of the whole man, on whom the living God bestows His mercy. In this joyful message, which touches the whole man, is the most profound argument against a spiritualistic misinterpretation of God's intent with respect to creation and fulfilment.[90]

In view of the strong connection between the eschatological perspective of the resurrection and the message of salvation, what are we to make of the passage in the Epistle to the Hebrews that seems to water down the central meaning of the resurrection? The author writes: "Let us leave the elementary doctrines

89. Additional details about this dispute are provided in the parallel account in Luke 20:27-40; especially in vv. 35 ("those that are accounted worthy"), 36 ("sons of the resurrection"), 37 ("even Moses showed"), 38 ("for all live to him"). Cf. further on this dispute, Nikolainen, *op. cit.*, II, 33ff.

90. Spiritualism cannot appeal to Luke 20:36 — "because they [those who attain the resurrection] are equal to angels" (*isángeloi;* Matt. 22:30; Mark 12:25 — *hōs ángeloi*). Any simplistic extension of the lines from this age (*aiōn hoútos*) to the coming age (*aiōn méllōn*), such as the Sadducees did in their reasoning, is contraindicated.

of Christ and go on to maturity" (Heb. 6:1). What precisely is meant by this "leaving the elementary doctrines of Christ?"[91] Does this mean that all these things mentioned here — repentance, ablutions, the laying on of hands, the resurrection of the dead, eternal judgment — are passé on the way to fulfilment, no more than a stage along life's way? How is this to be understood in terms of the central meaning of the eschatological expectation in the rest of the New Testament?

We should keep in mind that the author was expressing himself to a particular mentality here. The Hebrews had "become dull of hearing *(nōthroí)*" (5:11). Considering how long they had been Christians, they should have been teachers of the faith; instead they were like children *(nếpios)* who still needed milk (5:13). This is a critical estimate of a congregation that was not yet on the way, not yet in motion.[92] The Hebrews were urged on to progress, if God should allow the time for it (6:3).

The theme here is *periculum in mora.* Because the Hebrews are making no progress toward maturity, the danger of apostasy is a very real one. The "maturity" *(teleiótēs)* of which the author speaks is not a Gnostic intellectualism, but the wisdom of faith, buttressed by a steady diet of decision-making *(diákrisis)* about questions of good and evil (5:14).[93] The congregation is urged not to ossify in this initial stage as if they were always going to be involved in laying the foundation. The exhortation to leave the elementary doctrines is not a depreciation of these first principles, but a warning not to stand still as if they were at the end of a journey, which is what they were doing in their

91. *aphéntes tón tês archês toú Christoú lógon.*
92. The metaphor of milk *(gála)* and "solid food" *(stereá trophế)* is a familiar one used to indicate the process of maturation. Paul uses it in writing to the Corinthians (1 Cor. 3:1), who, he says, are *nếpioi en Christô* ("babes in Christ"), not *pneumátikoi* ("spiritual men"). Paul fed them with milk, not solid food *(brôma)*, because they were not ready for the latter. Another use of the milk-imagery is found in 1 Pet. 2:2: "Like newborn babes, long for the pure spiritual milk *(tó logikón ádolon gála)*, that by it you may grow up to salvation." Here the metaphor focuses on the new birth *(hōs artigénnēta bréphē)*. See further W. Grundmann, "Die *nếpioi* in der urchristlichen Paränese," *NT Studies,* VI (1959), 191.
93. On the use of *teleiótēs* in Hebrews, cf. P. J. du Plessis, *Teleios. The Idea of Perfection in the NT* (1959), pp. 206ff. Schlier speaks of "a kind of gnosis" and "profounder teaching" in connection with "solid food" in Heb. 5:12ff.; in *TDNT,* s.v. *gála,* I, 646. These expressions contribute little to the understanding of the passage.

dulness. In their preoccupation with the principle of the resurrection of the dead these believers had immobilized themselves. They failed to realize the task to which this principle committed them.

This is not a watering down of the eschatological perspective. The author sees "repentance from dead works and faith toward God" as the first beginnings of faith — not as something secondary or unimportant. The expectation is no less existential; the content of the faith is not diminished. There is no de-eschatologizing in Hebrews (cf. 4:1-10; 9:27; 10:27-31; ch. 11, 13), but a warning against misunderstanding the eschatological perspective.[94]

The assumption of Mary

There have been many recent attempts, both in Protestant and in Roman Catholic circles, to give the bodily aspect of man's existence its due in eschatology. Among all the variations in contemporary eschatological thought, there is a generally antispiritualistic and anti-idealistic tendency, as the realization grows that man's bodily existence cannot be excluded from his total creatureliness or ignored in discussions of it.[95] Often the eschatological perspective of the resurrection of the body is discussed in this connection. If one does not isolate in a futuristic way the eschaton from the salvation that is already given as the first fruits of the Spirit, who lives in the body as His temple (1 Cor. 6:19), a proper regard will follow for the points of contact evident in the biblical witness, where an immediate connection is made between the resurrection from the dead and the destiny of the body: the body for the Lord and the Lord for the body (1 Cor. 6:13f.).

There is an issue in Roman Catholic theology that has indirect bearing on the bodily aspect of eschatology, the doctrine of the assumption of Mary. On the surface, of course,

94. Cf. Bertram, in *TDNT*, s.v. *nēpios*, IV, 917-20.
95. Consider the symposium *Lichamelijkheid* (1951), a collection of essays by Roman Catholic scholars on the fiftieth anniversary of the Dominican monastery in Zwolle. Strong emphasis is placed on "the modern problem" with existential philosophy. Cf. R. W. Thuys, "De lichamelijkheid bij G. Marcel en J. P. Sartre," and his critique of idealism, p. 12. K. J. Popma feels that Sartre made a "significant contribution" in this area and had a "considerably more accurate view" than most of Protestant orthodoxy, which still swore by the scholastic anthropology; "Vrijheidsfatalisme," *Bezinning*, XV (1960), p. 171.

this has little direct relevance to the *resurrectio carnis* of the Apostles' Creed. But an essential connection between the two is expressed in the proclamation of the Apostolic Constitution *Munificentissimus Deus* (1950) that Mary was taken up bodily into heaven. Undoubtedly, there is an eschatological aspect to this; for it is possible, according to this doctrine, to speak of the anticipation of taking part with Mary in the resurrection: an "incidentally realized eschatology."

When this dogma was officially constituted,[96] Pope Pius XII expressly stated that it must be seen as an indication of the value of human life, which is dedicated in its entirety to carrying out the will of the Father. In a time when materialism and the consequent depravity threatened to extinguish any beacons of virtue, this dogma recalled the exalted calling to which body and soul are consecrated,[97] and reminded the believer that belief in Mary's bodily assumption to heaven can strengthen and fructify his faith in his own resurrection. Apparently, this is not a matter of adding one more dogma to a series of dogmas and indicating that there is no intention of denying the resurrection of the body. Instead, the new dogma is specifically directed to strengthening faith in the resurrection.

The two motifs apparent in this dogma — the external and the internal — come together in the consideration of the purpose of human life — particularly of bodily life. "In this magnificent way all may see clearly to what a lofty goal our bodies and souls are destined."[98] There is thus a clearly eschatological element in this dogma. One might say that there is an "ethos" that must follow from the establishment of this realized eschaton: there are elements of encouragement and warning in this dogma. It is a new guarantee, a confirmation of *our* resurrection. (This does not mean that the dogma is a *new* one in the fullest sense of that term: inherent in every constitution of dogma is the qualifier that what is being constituted really belonged to the original wealth of revelation all along, but is shedding its full light for the first time.)

96. Already in 1943, in the encyclical *Mystici Corporis Christi* Pius XII had spoken of Mary's glorification in heaven in terms of body and soul.
97. On the anthropological motif, cf. A. H. Maltha, *De tenhemelopneming van Maria* (1950), pp. 22ff.
98. *Munificentissimus Deus,* sec. 42, tr. J. C. Fenton, S.T.D. A partial text of the constitution appears in J. H. Leith, ed., *Creeds of the Churches* (1963), pp. 457-66.

It is certainly incorrect to say that the Roman Catholic Church intends in this new pronouncement to deny that the actual and deepest guarantee of the eschatological expectation is the resurrection of Jesus Christ from the dead. Nowhere in the Roman Catholic Church or its theology is the New Testament witness to the correlation of these denied or called into question. But against this background, this concrete, realized eschaton commands full attention: it becomes a meaningful sign of the certainty of the promise.[99]

It is not our intention to give a thorough explication of Roman Catholic Mariology or even of the dogma of the assumption.[100] Our discussion is limited to the relation between the assumption of Mary and the resurrection of the body, that is, to the directly eschatological aspect of this new dogma. It should be noted that in doing this we are not placing this teaching in a foreign context: Mariology has continued to play an important eschatological role since Pope Pius XII issued *Munificentissimus Deus* in 1950. Karl Rahner placed the dogma in an eschatological light by speaking of the "privilege of the 'anticipated' resurrection of Mary" and connected this privilege with the realized eschaton.[101] In Mary the fulfilment of redemption was already made visible to faith. We have frequently encountered the word "already" in discussing the salvation message of the New Testament. There is an "already" in what Rahner says also: the end of times has *already* begun in the resurrection of Jesus Christ from the dead and Mary's assumption is the manifestation of this "already."[102] In this assumption, this "already," he sees the *normal* — even if not the *general* — condition reflecting the victory over sin and death. "Even the salvation of the body has already begun in its completion."[103] We spoke earlier of Cullmann's "anticipated re-

---

99. Cf. M. Schmaus, *Mariologie* (1955), pp. 245ff.
100. See Berkouwer, *The Conflict with Rome* (Eng. tr., 1957), esp. the chapter "Ave Maria," pp. 152-78. *Verdienste of genade?* (1958), pp. 71ff.; *The Second Vatican Council and the New Catholicism* (Eng. tr., 1965), ch. 8, "Mary."
101. "Zum Sinn des Assumpta-dogmas," *Schriften zur Theologie*, I (1954), 245. See also Schillebeeckx in *Theologische Woordenboek*, II (1957), 3139, who discusses under the heading "the theological significance of the eschatological Mary-mystery" first of all the assumption.
102. Rahner, *op. cit.*, p. 245.
103. *Ibid.*, p. 251.

demption"—his analogy to World War II—but Cullmann interpreted this as the reality of service and the journey to the final transition in the parousia. For Rahner this anticipation is concrete and completely realized. He is talking about a new dimension that already belongs to our present reality.

Rahner suspects that Protestants reject the new dogma because they really know only a theology of the cross as formula of present reality, but not a theology of glory, which is for them in the last analysis only a promise, not something that already is.[104] He counters this by saying that it is not a matter of a word of promise that stays remote from our reality, that we must see the assumption of Mary as the elucidation of the situation of salvation as it already exists.

In this sense the dogma of the assumption has eschatological significance. It is a *partially* realized eschatology, different from C. H. Dodd's realized eschatology.[105]

Rahner is undoubtedly mistaken to interpret Protestant objections to the dogma of the assumption as resulting from a preference for the theology of the cross as the formula of present reality. Such an explanation reduces Reformation eschatology to a kind of futurism that stands over against the *theologia gloriae* as a theology of the "already." On the basis of the New Testament, one may certainly dispute a *theologia gloriae* in the way Luther did when he pointed out that man can come to the Father only through the crucified Lord. But to see the words "cross" and "glory" as reflecting "not yet" and "already" respectively is to ignore how important a role the "already" plays in Reformation eschatology. This "theology of the cross" does not lead to a futuristic eschaton without an "already" and with an external, *otherworldly* word of promise.[106] If that were the case, Reformation eschatology would indeed represent a break with the message of the New Testament. But when one develops his concept of the "already" and the "not yet" from the

104. *Ibid.*, p. 252.
105. Clearly this "anticipation" stands or falls with the dogma of the immaculate conception; cf. *Munificentissimus Deus*, sec. 4. Schillebeeckx, *loc. cit.*, 3139, points out that the church fathers saw Mary's virginity as an anticipation of the eschatological life. The general belief is that Mary actually died before her anticipated *resurrectio carnis. Munificentissimus Deus* says only that "having completed the course of her earthly life, [she] was assumed body and soul into heavenly glory"; sec. 4.
106. Rahner, *op. cit.*, p. 252.

incontrovertible message of the New Testament, he is by no means obligated to accept just any "already" that is posited.

The Roman Catholic Church itself rejects one definite "already" — that of a visible millennium before the return of Christ, even though this doctrine of the millennium is also a form of "realized eschatology." One could make a plea for the millennium by using the same reasoning as Rahner uses against the Protestants, and then criticizing those who disagree with this millennial doctrine as adherents of an inadequate "theology of the cross."

In short, what is decisive for the correctness of the doctrine of the assumption is whether or not it is a legitimate consequence of the New Testament "already" (cf. 2 Thess. 2:2; 2 Tim. 2:17). It must be concluded that the dogma of the assumption as expressed in *Munificentissimus Deus* does not meet this test: that it is rather the outcome of Roman Catholic Mariology as a whole.[107]

We have pointed out that the doctrine of the assumption does not intend to diminish the force of the confession of the *resurrectio carnis,* but to reinforce faith in it. Here we encounter the central point of the certainty of the future. It is clear in the New Testament that Christ is the sure foundation of this faith, and everything is dependent upon Him. It is hard to see how the notion that the assumption is the guarantee of the resurrection can avoid casting some doubt on this faith. Sometimes one can detect something of this doubt when the dogma of assumption is defended by a line of reasoning like the following: "Christ has risen, but He was God; so what does that do for us? True, we have learned that His destiny would be our destiny and we accept that; but how wonderful it is to see this personal hope increased and fulfilled and crowned with tenderness by the confession that..." and then follows the presentation of the assumption of the pure creature, Mary, who has bodily ascended into heaven.[108]

We must be careful not to impute such a curious reference to Christ's divinity in this connection to Catholics in general, but it does illustrate where one can end up if one effaces the

---

107. For Rahner's views, see also "Die unbefleckte Empfängnis," *Schriften zur Theologie,* I, 223ff.; "Virginitas in partu," *ibid.,* IV (Eng. tr., 1966), 134ff.; K. H. Schelkle, *De bijbel over Maria* (1960), pp. 79ff.

108. Maltha, *op. cit.,* p. 29; cf. p. 30: Mary as the "security" for the resurrection.

eschatological boundary (even if only partially) by talking about this particular *fait accompli, this* realized eschaton. The gospel itself says nothing about an eschaton realized in Mary: why would one want to supplement the biblical "already" of the first fruits of the Spirit poured out upon man at the time of Christ's departure, or go beyond the biblical "not yet" of the promised destruction of death, the last enemy, in the great transformation?

There has always been a good deal of dispute about the scriptural evidences for Mariology in general. With reference to the dogma of the assumption, however, there is hardly any mention of this dispute. Even in what Pope Pius XII said one encounters little if any scriptural support; it is treated as though this were self-evident in the Bible.[109] This is surely open to question, and the demand for explicit scriptural support is legitimate and is not just biblicism or fundamentalism. It is a question prompted by an "already" confessed by Protestants and Catholics alike as central to revelation and by the clarity with which faith about the future is established in connection with the crucified and risen Lord.

The present dispensation is characterized by both the "already" and the "not yet." If the promise bore a futuristic stamp, it would have little relevance in the here and now, where the last enemy is still about. But the mystery of the gospel is that we are reminded in the eschatological promise of Him through whom "we utter the Amen ... to the glory of God ... who establishes us with you in Christ, and has commissioned us; he has put his seal upon us and given us his Spirit in our hearts as a guarantee" (2 Cor. 1:20-22). In this seal and guarantee all other pledges, such as the partially realized eschatology we have been discussing, which lacks certainty and thus needs to be established by the authority of the church, fall away.

The eschatological expectation is always marked by struggle. "I believe, help my unbelief!" (Mark 9:24). This is not a dia-

---

109. Curiously, certain individual authors cited by the apostolic constitution refer to passages of Scripture, but these do not function in *Munificentissimus Deus* as proof texts. Cf. sec. 38: "All these proofs and considerations ... are based upon the Sacred Writings as their ultimate foundation. ... Consequently it seems impossible to think of her, the one who conceived Christ, brought Him forth, nursed Him with her milk, held Him in her arms, and clasped Him to her breast, as being apart from Him in body, even though not in soul, after this earthly life."

lectic between certainty and doubt or an attempt to balance opposing feelings. It is the linking of a creed and a prayer, a connection not at all foreign to the eschatological expectation. The individual is drawn into this expectation and places his stamp on it. The "already" of the transformation from death to life is always linked with brotherly love (1 John 3:14) and seeking the "holiness without which no one will see the Lord" (Heb. 12:14).

How then can the eschatological expectation be fulfilled without a struggle? The church is called to this struggle and thus also to expectation, called to "take hold of eternal life" (1 Tim. 6:12) and to "strive to enter by the narrow door" (Luke 13:24).

CHAPTER SEVEN

THE NEW EARTH

T HE DISCUSSION of the resurrection from the dead leads us directly to a consideration of the "new earth." The link between these two aspects of the eschatological promise is the fact that the *resurrectio carnis* talks about a future for the *body*. This body is not an abstract, spiritual existence having nothing to do with the earth, but something that has a place and a manifold function *in the earth*.

The scriptural testimony

The obvious danger in talking about the new earth is that of falling into all sorts of excesses and fantasies — constructs and postulates that go far beyond what the Bible says. Still, we cannot excuse ourselves from discussing this matter, for Old and New Testament alike deal explicitly with the new earth. Three texts in particular come readily to mind: "For, behold, I create new heavens and a new earth" (Isa. 65:17; cf. 66:22) ; "According to his promise we wait for new heavens and a new earth in which righteousness dwells" (2 Pet. 3:13) ; "Then I saw a new heaven and a new earth; for the first heaven and the first earth had passed away" (Rev. 21:1) .

All three of these passages reveal an eschatologically cosmic perspective, whose meaning is often ignored out of a kind of religious and soteriological self-centeredness, a parallel to the one-sided interest in "heaven" and in the intermediate state apart from the resurrection of the body.[1] Just as one runs the risk of separating body from soul in the eschatological expectation, so one can also speak of blessedness without this cosmic aspect to it. Such an approach does not repudiate what the

---

1. A. Köberle comments: "This cosmic aspect of redemption was increasingly lost to Western Christendom since the Age of Enlightenment, and to this day we have been unable to restore it to its strength and clarity"; *Der Herr über alles* (1957), p. 103.

Bible says about the new earth, it simply pays it no mind. The cosmic perspective is just not assimilated into the larger expectation. One accepts the fact that God created heaven and earth and that His power is manifested in the goodness of all things, but it is as if the creation-perspective is obliterated in eschatology and becomes superfluous on account of salvation. This leads directly to one of the many dichotomies in which man has tried to capture God's work: the dilemma of the cosmic versus the soteriological.

Scripture sees no such dilemma. From 2 Peter 3:3 we see that the believer's interest in the new earth is not something isolated and independent. The new earth (the cosmic) is marked in a particular way: it is where righteousness dwells. This description of it is not explicit in Isaiah 65:17, but it is certainly not foreign to it. Isaiah's reference to the creation of the new earth is in the context of the joy of the nation. He speaks of no more weeping and distress, of long life, of building houses and planting vineyards (65:18-21). These great blessings will extend even to the animal kingdom. The wolf and the lamb will feed together (vs. 25). Then comes the prophecy of the Messianic rule of peace: "They shall not hurt or destroy in all my holy mountain, says the LORD," a prophecy that recalls the Messianic perspective of Isaiah 11:9: ". . . for the earth shall be full of the knowledge of the LORD as the waters cover the sea."

Nor does the passage in Revelation portray an isolated cosmic perspective on the new earth. John sees the new Jerusalem coming down from heaven, and hears the great voice speak of God's dwelling with men and wiping away all tears and of the end of death and mourning (21:1-4). Any dilemma between soteriological and cosmic disappears completely in the richness of this perspective. The tree of life is there, but so are the throne of God and the Lamb and His servants (22:1-4). The new heaven and the new earth will be a realm of peace and harmony, in contrast to what presently exists on this earth and what presently disrupts life in this dispensation. Once again, it is a perspective of righteousness, unlike the forces and spiritual powers that now control and dominate affairs on earth.

Furthermore, all these passages are not mere predictions of the future, but prophecies that are wrapped up with calling and admonition. One of Jesus' beatitudes shows this: "Blessed are the meek *(hoi praeis),* for they shall inherit the earth" (Matt.

5:5). It is the only one of the beatitudes that is cited from the
Old Testament: "Those who wait for the LORD shall possess the
land.... The meek *(hoi praeis)* shall possess the land" (Ps.
37:9, 11). In Jesus' promise this passage assumes eschatological
import: the land that the meek shall possess is no longer Canaan,
but the new earth.

The beatitudes are sometimes said to be "paradoxical." The
accuracy of this characterization depends, of course, on the
meaning one attaches to the word "paradox." If it is used in the
same sense as in Luke 5:26 (after Jesus' healing of a leper) —
"We have seen some strange things *(parádoxa)* today"— to indicate something that runs counter to human thinking, one can
rightly call the beatitudes paradoxical. They are not logically
contradictory, but they convey an idea of something unexpected:
in this case, that the inheritance of the earth is not for the
brutal and hard of heart, but for the meek (cf. Isa. 29:19f.),
who learn from Christ in His gentle and lowly kingship (Matt.
11:29; 21:5). Their inheritance is the analogy of His dominion
over the whole earth (Matt. 28:19). This prospect is of a
piece with the other eschatological promises of the beatitudes:
comfort (vs. 4), satisfaction (vs. 6), seeing God (vs. 8), and
reward in heaven (vs. 12). The Old Testament Promised Land
takes on a broader horizon — the new earth.[2]

The title of this chapter is not intended to limit our attention
to the "new earth" and to ignore the "new heaven." In general
the Bible speaks of both of these together in the familiar phrase
"new heaven and new earth" (a notable exception is Matt. 5:5).
This expression harks back to the biblical witness to God as
Creator of heaven and earth. One must take care not to substitute a false and oversimplified notion for the scriptural testimony about heaven. For example, heaven should not merely

2. On the beatitudes in general, see H. N. Ridderbos, *De strekking der
bergrede naar Mattheüs* (1936), esp. pp. 236ff.; on the element of paradox in them, see H. Schröer, *Die Denkform der Paradoxalität als the-
ologisches Problem* (1960), pp. 110ff. Schröer denies that the beatitudes
are logical paradoxes, for they refer to changes in situations, and lack
the element of simultaneity. To explain the absence of "blessed are the
meek" among the Lucan beatitudes (6:20-23), some have surmised that
this beatitude is actually an expansion of "blessed are the poor." On this
view, then, the Matthean addition "in spirit" *(tō pneúmati)* is seen as
closely related to the blessing of the meek. Cf. Jacques Dupont, *Les
béatitudes* (1958), p. 256: "Matthew shows himself to be concerned to
make explicit the virtualities of this word ['*anāwîm* — Ps. 37:11]."

be considered, without further ado, as the place of salvation, in the sense of "going to heaven." After all, the Bible begins by telling us that both heaven and earth are the created work of God (Gen. 1:1; cf. vv. 8f.; 2:1, 4; Pss. 96:5; 121:2; Matt. 11:25; Acts 14:15; 17:24; Rom. 4:11).[3]

Of the "heavens" we read that they will pass away (2 Pet. 3:10) and be dissolved (vs. 12; cf. Rev. 6:14; 21:1). Both earth and heaven (RSV: sky) will flee from the presence of Him who is on the throne (Rev. 20:11). However, though both are often included in the same prophecy, they are also expressly distinguished. The heavens are higher than the earth (Isa. 55:9); God is in heaven, whereas we are on earth (Eccl. 5:2); heaven is God's throne, the earth His footstool (Isa. 66:1). Needless to say, these passages are not intended to provide some kind of cosmological map: the Bible makes it clear that "heaven and the highest heaven" cannot contain Him (1 Kings 8:27; cf. Heb. 4:14; 7:26; Eph. 4:10).[4]

Scripture maintains a distance between heaven and earth. While "heaven and earth" are spoken of as created by God, at the same time there is emphasis on the fact that God, in His majesty and mercy, acts from *above*. Christ is the living bread that came down from heaven (John 6:50f.; cf. 6:38; 3:13). His coming has a *direction* to it: from above (*ánōthen* — John 3:31). It proceeded from God (John 8:42).[5] The Kingdom of God is announced as the "kingdom of heaven" (Matt. 3:2; 2 Tim. 4:18). From this usage of the word it is obvious that Scripture is not primarily interested in satisfying the curiosity of our imaginations about what heaven is like. Much more important is the utter seriousness and evident power of the emphasis in the divine message on the coming and the acts of God.[6] The accent falls on the reality of the appearance and dealings of God, not on the formal idea of spatial direction.

---

3. Cf. K. Schilder, *Heaven — What Is It?* (Eng. tr., 1950), pp. 39ff.
4. It would be incorrect to accuse Schilder of violating Barth's warning against making an "ontology of heaven" (cf. *CD*, III/3, 442). In *Heaven — What Is It?*, Schilder places strong emphasis on both the creaturely aspect of heaven and on the point of departure of God's acts in His dwelling with men.
5. Cf. H. Bietenhard, *Die himmlische Welt im Urchristentum und Spätjudentum* (1951), pp. 82ff.
6. Cf. Schilder, *op. cit.*, p. 38; Barth, *CD*, III/3, 426f.; Traub, in *TDNT*, s.v. *ouranós*, V, 513-35; Bietenhard, *op. cit.*, pp. 77f.; J. G. Davies, *He Ascended into Heaven* (1958), *passim*.

Thus there is no contradiction in speaking of the passing away of heaven and earth and at the same time talking about the direct relation between God and "heaven" in the contrast between Him who comes from heaven and him who is of earth (John 3:31). In the eschatological vision of Revelation 21, John sees the new Jerusalem "coming down out of heaven from God," and at that moment "the dwelling of God is with men."[7] Without ignoring "heaven," even for a moment, one can at this point talk about the eschatological perspective of the new earth that God will give to the sons of men (cf. Ps. 115:16).[8]

The emphasis placed on the new earth in the expectation raises the question of how this new earth, in which righteousness dwells, will come forth from this present world. To ask this question is not to delve speculatively into what is hidden from us or to attempt to draw conclusions about the new earth from the phenomena of this one. Rather, it is a question that stems from the variety in the scriptural teaching about the future, the different images and apocalyptic forms. Clearly, the thrust of this teaching is never an isolated description of cosmic events, though there is frequent reference to cosmic catastrophes as signs of the judgment of all things. To human understanding these often appear to be of disproportionate and immensely appalling dimensions. We have mentioned a number of these above,[9] but we should note here that all of them are connected with the expectation of the new heavens and earth.

Christ's apocalyptic prophecies also indicate the cosmic aspect of the future: "the sun will be darkened, and the moon will not give its light, and the stars will be falling from heaven, and the powers in the heavens will be shaken" (Matt. 24:29; Mark 13:24f.; cf. Luke 21:25f.). These prophecies hark back to apoca-

---

7. Rev. 21:2f.: *ek toú ouranoú apó toú theoú...hē skēnē toú theoú metá tōn anthrōpōn.*
8. At the beginning of our discussion of what the Bible says about heaven, we might well have written, with Bietenhard (*op. cit.,* p. 257): "The Christian message is dependent on no particular picture of reality; by the same token it does not collapse when the prevailing picture of reality changes and is replaced."
9. Specifically the events mentioned in 2 Pet. 3:10-12: the passing away of the heavens *(hoi ouranoí pareleúsontai)* and the dissolution of the elements *(stoicheía lythēsetai).* Cf. also 1 John 2:17 — "the world passes away and the lust *(epithymía)* of it." On *parérchomai* as passing by in the sense of passing away, cf. Schneider, in *TDNT,* s.v., II, 682.

lyptic passages in the Old Testament (cf. Isa. 13:9-11; 34:4; 51:6; Ezek. 32:7f.; Amos 8:9; Micah 1:4). In all these judgments, God punishes the world for its evil (Isa. 13:11). Since there are always people in view, to whom these judgments are directed, people to whom the message and the admonitions to shun evil, unrighteousness, and unbelief come, it is obvious that this is not an *isolated* cosmic event. There will be an end to the pride of the arrogant. "Therefore I will make the heavens tremble, and the earth will be shaken out of its place, at the wrath of the LORD of hosts in the day of his fierce anger" (Isa. 13:13). In broad daylight the sun will vanish and darkness will fill the earth, and God will turn feasts into mourning and songs into lamentations (Amos 8:9f.).

The attempt is frequently made to come up with a systematic harmonization of all the scriptural images and concepts that bear on this transition from the present to the new earth. The object of this effort, of course, is to make obvious how everything is going to come about. Increasing opposition to this particular use of the Scripture has arisen, not out of an unwillingness to consult Scripture, but from the question whether the Bible intends at all to orient us to what might be called the "history" of the future with these images and concepts. How are the multiform scriptural passages about the future to be understood? Karl Rahner has written extensively about the "hermeneutics" of these eschatological pronouncements. He argues forcefully that these images and concepts are not the "anticipated report of a spectator of the future event," and that to contend that they are is false apocalyptic.[10] He strongly emphasizes that the eschaton is the fulfilment of what has already been obtained through Jesus Christ, and that Christ as "beginning" is "the sole and adequate law of the end, and hence the fulfilment bears in all things the traits of this beginning."[11] The eschaton is not merely an "addition" foreign to the reality of salvation in which we now live, but the as-yet-hidden fulfil-

---

10. Rahner, "The Hermeneutics of Eschatological Assertions," *Theological Investigations*, IV (Eng. tr., 1966), pp. 323ff.; cf. p. 330. Rahner's entire article actually centers on the distinction between eschatology and apocalyptic: eschatology is an extrapolation from the present into the future; apocalyptic an interpolation from the future into the present (p. 337). Thus he also distinguishes between "de-eschatologizing" and "de-apocalypticizing" (p. 337).
11. *Ibid.*, p. 333n.

ment, presented to us in apocalyptic images and concepts. Thus one must distinguish between the mode of expression and its content, and in structuring this one must always pay attention to what is intended in the passages (see Chapter I above).

Not only is it impossible to systematize these images and concepts (the coming on the clouds, the trumpet sound, the opening of the graves, the falling of the stars, etc.), but to do so violates the intent of these passages. These observations are not meant to deny the judgment and the parousia, but are a protest against a biblicistic eschatology and its efforts to describe the end, an enterprise particularly prominent in connection with the exegesis of the Book of Revelation.[12]

But then what is the intent and meaning of the eschatological perspective? Obviously, it is not a strange fantasy proclaimed as a future event apart from the "already" in Jesus Christ. The whole gospel points the way *from Christ* to the fulfilment. It is surely a false reaction to Bultmann's exegesis of Johannine eschatology to neglect the force of the eschaton in the "already" of the judgment and the transition from death to life. Rahner talks about a "christological" interpretation of these eschatological sayings—not an arbitrary selection according to personal theological preference, but an attempt to understand the role of the "already" on the way to the future.

Abraham Kuyper once wrote that in understanding the Revelation of John, one must make a connection between it and "what Christ Himself, in various ways, urged on the believers concerning His return."[13] Certainly, such a connection is necessary, but it must also be borne in mind that what is at stake is Christ's entire work and whatever is included in it according to the merciful purpose of God (Eph. 1:9f.).[14]

All these various images and apocalyptic concepts point up the gravity and radicalness of Christ's judgment and the fact

---

12. For the discussion of image-language and apocalyptic concepts, Abraham Kuyper's *Van de Voleinding* is of some interest. Kuyper believed that the passages we have been discussing were earlier interpreted as metaphorical, but that in the present — in the light of modern warfare (cf. Rev. 9:16f.) — it is apparent that these prophecies give surprisingly clear and distinct concepts of things that we see coming to pass. A closer study of this book shows that this basic hermeneutical principle is not generally applied: note his comments on Babylon, Armageddon, chiliasm, the symbolic in Rev. 20:1-10, and the singular character of the apocalypse.
13. *Ibid.*, p. 327.
14. Rahner, *loc. cit.*, p. 336.

that the whole man and the entire world are included in this judgment. Since what is central is not a reportorial eyewitness account, but the concepts of fulfilment, maturation, harvest, it is impossible to demythologize the New Testament message from the point of view of an altered world-view. If one casts aside the notion of Christ's coming "out of heaven," thus rejecting the reality of the parousia and at the same time the ascension, one automatically rules out the resurrection of the body and the new earth. Down this route lies the denial not only of the future perspective, but also of the "already" that gave rise to it, which demands full attention to the future, not as spectators who are gathering information, but as those who themselves must come out of Babylon, lest they take part in her sins (Rev. 18:4).

We should certainly recognize that it is not all that easy to separate "apocalyptic" from "eschatology" or "form" from "content" by drawing one sharp line.[15] The consequential distinction is that between the spectator and the person involved in the real future as a result of salvation in Christ. The actuality of the eschatological proclamation, its *telos*-character, structures the message itself.

We should be on guard for two dangers here: First of all, the danger of a depersonalized eschatology, which takes the stance of a spectator watching a series of very peculiar events, without understanding, for example, the meaning of the *Lamb* in Revelation or taking into account the great variety of the apocalyptic images in that book. One must remember that, in whatever forms the future is preached — always meaningful and applicable to us — it is always the future *of the Lord,* who once came and is coming again. Without Him there can be no talk of fulfilment. A second, equal danger is that of an eschatology that is personalized to the extent of completely disregarding the importance of "things"— the new earth — in its emphasis on the encounter with the Lord. Obviously such a view of the future also fails to recognize the coming Lord. For this Lord talked about His Father, heaven, the Kingdom, blessedness, and seeing God. But when He talked about these things He did not spiritualize man's relation to God. He knew better than anyone else that His Father was creator of heaven and earth; and when we recognize the connection between "seeing God" and "inheriting

15. Rahner seems to me sometimes to suggest that it is a fairly easy matter; however, he does recognize the difficulties involved; cf. *ibid.,* p. 336n.

the earth" in one single eschatological perspective, we also recognize that through Christ there is neither contradiction nor even tension in this outlook.

Annihilation?

Many people fail to see this relationship between seeing God and at the same time inheriting the earth. A closer examination shows that their idea of a tension or contradiction between the two arises from their interpretation of the last judgment as involving the total annihilation of the created world. The apocalyptic contours of the biblical proclamation of fulfilment include, it is believed, the teaching that this earth will come to an end in a catastrophic destruction. Since this earth has been in the service of the evil one, and since death and sin have inhabited it to the extent they have, it is concluded that no prospect of a future could possibly remain for this earth.[16] On this view, if there is any evolution, it is an evolution within the order of sin and death, and therefore also subject to utter destruction in the judgment. The confession of the expectation of a new heaven and a new earth can then be understood only in terms of this complete annihilation, which will be followed immediately by a *creatio ex nihilo* free from any continuity with the old world.[17]

16. Cf. E. Böhl, *Dogmatik* (1887), p. 610.
17. The most forthright contemporary opposition to this point of view is that of Pierre Teilhard de Chardin, *The Phenomenon of Man* (Eng. tr., 1959). However possible it is that some catastrophic disaster will end the world, Teilhard says, we have "higher reasons" for being sure that this will not happen (p. 275). This confidence is of a piece with his view of evolution in the past and the perspective of God as Omega, "the centre of centres" (pp. 289, 294). In this, according to Teilhard, is the reconciliation of the results of scientific investigation and the Christian faith. Destruction therefore plays no role in this, but rather personalization: "The end of the world: the overthrow of equilibrium, detaching the mind, fulfilled at last, from its material matrix, so that it will henceforth rest with all its weight on God-Omega" (pp. 287f.). This view of spiritualization also has an effect on the victory over "hatred and internecine struggles ... in the ever-warmer radiance of Omega." One can speak of the perspective of peace and justice in the way of evolution. The critical question, discussed by Roman Catholic scholars as well as others, is summed up by Hans Urs von Balthasar, who asks "whether Teilhard de Chardin, in his eschatological outlook, succeeds in avoiding a simple incorporation of the eschatological data of revelation into a system of universal cosmic evolution"; "Some Points of Eschatology," in *Word and Redemption*, p. 174.

Seventeenth-century Lutheran theologians accepted this position, with a curious conclusion. Quenstedt, for example, disputed the contention that the new earth involved a mere change in quality or a renewal of the old, arguing instead that the old would totally and finally disintegrate. Others, however, rejected this argument.[18] The question is whether there is a radical break and a complete discontinuity between the old earth and the new, so that the creation of the new earth could in truth be called a new *creatio ex nihilo;* or whether a continuity between old and new exists, thus making it a matter of change or renewal, an idea Althaus calls a "philosophical enervation of the destruction of the world."[19]

Althaus sees the idea of "change" as a long and persistent tradition, unanimously held by Irenaeus, Augustine, Gregory the Great, Thomas Aquinas, and all of medieval theology, on into present-day Catholic dogmatics.[20] This, he says, relativizes the Scripture and results in a devaluation of the seriousness and gravity of death. It is nothing more than a metaphysical continuity-concept that forcibly links the old and the new.

But why should we delve into this question? Is this complicated and subtle discussion anything more than a scholastic effort at theoretically clarifying the end with all kinds of not

18. For a survey of Lutheran thought on this matter cf. Althaus, *Die letzten Dinge*, pp. 353ff.; T. Kliefoth, *Christliche Eschatologie* (1886), p. 297; K. Hase, *Hutterus redivivus* (1883), pp. 286ff. Later, annihilation was denied by Beck, who contended that the *core* of earthly life would be preserved; cf. G. J. Lindyer, *Johann Tobias Beck* (1951), p. 122. A. F. C. Vilmar denies the annihilation of substance, saying of it that it was formerly held zealously to be a necessary part of orthodox doctrine; *Dogmatik*, II (1874), 331. On Quenstedt, cf. H. Schmid, *Die Dogmen der evangelischen-lutherischen Kirche*, p. 544. The idea of annihilation is worked out extensively in Gerhard's consideration of the *consummatio saeculi; Loci theologici*, IX (1895), 159. Gerhard holds that the annihilation is completely and essentially not *accidentaliter* but *substantialiter*. Present-day Lutheran dogmatics hardly pays any attention to the dilemma, but the old perspective remains. Prenter says that the nonhuman cosmos is not an indifferent appendage to human existence, and he speaks of the rebirth of the world; *Schöpfung und Erlösung*, II, 543. See also H. Vogel, *Gott in Christo* (1952), pp. 1058ff., against the false eschatological radicalism which denies that the world not only belongs to God but will belong to Him. This denial, according to Vogel, would also fail to recognize the intimate connection of the man of God with God's world, in token of which the creation of man stands.

19. *Die letzten Dinge*, p. 352. Cf. Berkhof, *CMH*, pp. 180ff.

20. *Die letzten Dinge*, p. 350.

particularly clear distinctions? One gets this impression particularly when it comes to arguing about what will and what will not be annihilated or renewed. Reformed theology has been particularly inclined to walk this road. Calvin, for example, in his commentary on 2 Peter 3:10, distinguishes between substance and quality. The cleansing of heaven and earth "so that they may be fit for the kingdom of Christ" is not a matter of annihilation, but a judgment in which something will remain. The things will be consumed "only in order to receive a new quality, while their substance remains the same." According to Bavinck, the annihilation of substance is an impossibility, but the world, her appearance laid waste by sin, will vanish. There will not be a new, second creation, but a re-creation of what exists, a renaissance. Substantially, nothing will be lost.[21] One is struck by the fact that the word "substance" is very crucial for this discussion. Sometimes *substance* is contrasted to *quality,* sometimes to *accident;* in other cases *being* is opposed to *form.*

The theological distinction between substance and accident is no doubt most prominent in connection with the Roman Catholic doctrine of transubstantiation, according to which the bread and wine of the sacrament are changed substantially into the body and blood of Christ, but their accidents remain. In the distinctions of eschatology in Reformed theology the reverse is the case: the accidents vanish, but substance remains.[22]

Even on a theoretical level, such distinctions leave much to be desired. They are theoretical attempts to capture "the end," but they remain unclear. Claiming to be scientific — or at least semi-scientific — they do not at all correspond to what the Bible says about the end. Like the doctrine of transubstantiation, they all depend on the supposition that substance and accident are separable; thus they contribute nothing to the expectation of faith.[23]

21. *GD,* IV, 699, 702.
22. Cf. A. Schweitzer, *Die Glaubenslehre der evangelischen reformierten Kirchen,* II, 727. Compare also what Calvin says in his discussion of 2 Pet. 3:10 ("their substance remains the same") with the Tridentine expression of transubstantiation: "the species only of the bread and wine remaining" (13th sess., Canon 2).
23. Cf. Greijdanus, *Komm., ad* 2 Pet. 3. He speaks of a complete consumption which does not, however, extend to the point of annihilation of matter in the fullest sense. *Things* may vanish; the elements themselves will not be taken away. K. Schilder agrees with Greijdanus, but places strong emphasis on the "wholly other" aspect: so completely

Nowhere does the Scripture attempt to clarify this transition. There is mention of "passing away," and "disappearing," but nothing is added to this by way of explanation. Scripture's purpose is to warn and admonish man about the coming judgment. Calvin certainly realized this. Commenting on 2 Peter 3:10, he writes that the author's purpose is not "to give a subtle disquisition about fire and storm and other things, but only to introduce the exhortation which immediately follows, that we too should strive to newness of life." Nor can one appeal to what Paul says in 1 Corinthians 7:31 — "for the form of this world is passing away"— in support of this distinction. Paul is not talking here about a distinction between the external ("the form") that will pass away and the internal that will remain. "The form of this world" could well be rendered "this world as we know it." It seems to me that the distinctions between being and form or substance and accident are not in the least necessary for understanding the eschatological admonitions of the Bible.

Nevertheless, we ought to try to find out the motives for the use of these distinctions in historically Reformed circles. However unsatisfactory the distinctions may be in themselves, they have been made. The theologians who did so did not mean to minimize the radicalness of the judgment. They felt that it was erroneous and arbitrary to fix one common denominator — destruction or annihilation — for all the Bible's eschatological pronouncements on judgment. They pointed out that what the Bible says about the new heaven and new earth is expressed in various ways. Although Peter spoke of the perishing of the world that then existed in the flood (2 Pet. 3:6 — *ho kósmos apóleto*), he apparently was not referring here to total destruction or annihilation. Similarly, Paul spoke of the setting free of creation from its bondage to decay (Rom. 8:21), not of its annihilation. Furthermore, the creation waits eagerly for this liberation. These passages probably do not furnish any foundation for making the kind of distinction we have been talking about, but they do present a perspective that includes the earth as we know it. Often, this distinction has been argued for by reference to Psalm 102:25-26, where the psalmist talks about heaven and earth wearing out like a garment and being

other, in fact, that one will not be able to speak of "recognition." There will be no finding back what now exists, yet it will be the same earth. *Heaven — What Is It?*, pp. 69ff.

changed like raiment. The notion of change (rather than annihilation) was squarely founded on this passage.

One may well dispute the contention that this psalm supports making substance/accident type distinctions,[24] but the motive for drawing these distinctions, namely, to reject the simplistic idea of "total annihilation," can surely be appreciated. Those who champion the view of total annihilation deny, of course, that Psalm 102 makes any mention of change in the sense intended by those who distinguish "substance" and "accidents." Gerhard, for example, writes that Psalm 102 speaks of *interitus* and *perditio* in contrast to God, who forever remains the same.[25] By the same token he disqualifies the use of Romans 8:21 in this connection, on the ground that Paul is not talking about the future of this earth, but about the liberation of it from the misuse to which it has been subjected by man. In other words, Romans 8:21 testifies to annihilation, not to renovation or renewal.[26]

Understandably, those who see the new earth as a *creatio ex nihilo* following a total annihilation are not impressed by distinctions between substance and accident. Unfortunately, they did not see beyond these fallible, inadequate, imprecise distinctions to the motive behind them: the desire to retain the principle of *liberation* essential to the biblical witness. This perspective (which is apparent in the phrase "the new *earth*") was completely ignored by those Lutherans who emphasized annihilation. Yet Scripture presents a duality concerning the new earth, which includes both the judgment and the continuity-perspective.

This is not to suggest that what the Bible says about the work of God can be captured in cosmological or scientific distinctions. All the same, both aspects — judgment and continuity — find scriptural support. Thus, "regeneration" (*palingenesia*) can be spoken of as an eschatological event (Matt. 19:28; RSV —

24. Cf. J. Ridderbos, *Comm., ad loc.*
25. *Op. cit.,* 160ff.
26. *Ibid.,* 173-75. Gerhard acknowledges that *bārā'* in the OT does not always mean *creatio ex nihilo;* nonetheless this word does convey a meaning, a *prima et propria significatio* that points to creation from nothing, e.g., in Gen. 1:1. Just as the sea shall be no more (Rev. 1:1), so the earth shall disappear. Also, "new" in the Bible certainly does not always refer to "renewal," but can also indicate something completely new and different.

"the new world"), as can the restitution *(apokatástasis)* of all that God has spoken (Acts 3:21; RSV — "establishing").[27]

Although these passages exclude the possibility of seeing annihilation as a fundamental concept of eschatology, they should not have the effect of diminishing the force of judgment. The New Testament does not exclude either the judgment or the perspective of continuity and restoration. This would be the case if "restoration" and "restitution" were to be judged according to human categories, on the analogy of human "restoration." But the New Testament talks about renewal and liberation through judgment. Behind the biblical witness lies no personalistic distinction between "man" and "cosmos." Rather, we read of their relatedness to each other. There is no dualism or personalism here: consider the curse of the ground "because of you" (Gen. 3:17),[28] the eager longing for the future of the creation in its subjection to futility (Rom. 8:19f.). The world is indisputably included in the eschatological judgment. God "has wrought desolations in the earth" (Ps. 46:8); He will "twist its surface and scatter its inhabitants" (Isa. 24:1); He will make it again "waste and void" (Jer. 4:23 — *tōhû wābhōhû;* cf. Gen. 1:2); the fruitful land will become a desert (Jer. 4:26). "The earth shall mourn, and the heavens above be black" (vs. 28). The perspective of restoration and renewal is evident here. Thus, the words of judgment are never isolated and cosmic, but part and parcel of the general eschatological admonitions. In this way the perspective of the new earth arises.

In its proclamation of the judgment on the earth, the Bible speaks of destruction and passing away, and also prophesies that God "once more . . . will shake not only the earth but also

---

27. On Matt. 19:28, cf. P. Gennrich, *Die Lehre von der Wiedergeburt* (1907), pp. 4ff.; Büchsel, in *TDNT*, s.v. *palingenesía*, I, 688: "The Jewish faith in the resurrection of the dead and the renewal of the world is clothed in this term." On Acts 3:21, cf. Grosheide, *Kommentar, ad loc.;* Oepke, in *TDNT*, s.v. *apokatástasis*, I, 391ff. We shall discuss this word further in Chapter XIII below.

28. Aalders sees no relationship between Gen. 3:17 and 8:21 ("'I will never again curse the ground because of man . . .'."); *KV* on Genesis (8:21). R. Rendtorf disagrees, holding (incorrectly, it seems to me) that 8:21 marks the end of the curse pronounced in 3:17, since the time of blessing has now arrived (cf. 8:22): "Genesis 8, 21 und die Urgeschichte des Jahvistes," *Kerygma und Dogma,* VII (1961), 69ff. The Hebrew words here are *'rr* (3:17) and *qll* (8:21), but both relate to the "ground." There is surely a connection between 3:17 and 8:21, but also a difference in the way the earth is involved; cf. 2 Pet. 3:6.

the heaven . . . in order that what cannot be shaken may remain"
(Heb. 12:26f.).[29] This passage is not a denial of the crisis of
the coming judgment, but it is still a note of gracious consolation
for the future. The author is not making cosmological distinctions between substance and accident, but is talking about
what remains, what is unshakable: "Let us be grateful for receiving a kingdom that cannot be shaken . . ." (vs. 28). From
this point of view we cannot forget the world nor isolate it
from God's ultimate purposes. The author moves from his
discussion of "the removal of what is shaken" to an admonition
to gratitude, reverence, and awe, "for our God is a consuming
fire" (vs. 29). This is not an ominous concept of God suddenly
dropped into the conversation: the author is describing the way
to the future. On the way to the new world, what is important
is not the length of time nor the prediction of the end of the
world, but gratitude, which knows of the continuity in the judgment of God.

The beatific vision and the new earth

All of this brings us back to the notion of the competitive
themes in eschatology: if we look forward to the fulfilment and
the beatific vision of God is there any room left for the expectation of the resurrection of the body and the new earth?

The Lutheran dogmaticians who adhered to the view of
total annihilation did so, according to Althaus, not only as
defense against any minimizing of the gravity of the judgment
(the dominant motive in Althaus' own protests against the
theory of "transition" and continuity of the earth), but also
because they believed that the redeemed no longer had need
of the earth in view of the immediate vision of God that marked
their presence with the Lord. Probably they did not formally
deny the reality of the new earth — after all, it is mentioned in
the Bible — but it remained something indeterminate and in
the dark. The concept came to be seen as merely a synonym
for heaven.[30]

Behind the alleged tension between seeing God and the new
earth lies a wholly unbiblical concept of God. Carried to its
logical outcome this conception would require a denial of

29. Bertram writes: "In the OT creation stands under the threat of divine
    shaking and the promise of divinely given unshakability"; in *TDNT*,
    s.v. *saleúō*, VII, 70. Cf. also Hagg. 2:6, 8, 22.
30. *Die letzten Dinge*, p. 354; cf. Böhl, *Dogmatik*, p. 611.

everything created and an evaluation of Genesis 1:1 as the least comprehensible verse in the whole Bible. Once on this route, it is obvious that the resurrection of the body could find a place in the creed only by an inconsistency. Thus arises a crass form of personalism and spiritualism which considers *things* to be of no importance in the coming glorification. Calvin's judgment on this position minces no words: he talks about "men hungry for empty learning" who ask "what purpose is to be served by a restoration of the world, since children of God will not be in need of any of this great and incomparable plenty but will be like the angels, whose abstinence from food is the symbol of eternal blessedness."[31] When the emphasis on seeing God undermines one's interest in this world — and his concern for mankind — the next step is for him to start looking for the vision of God already in this life. Hezekiah's lamentation on the death-bed from which he later recovered is then transmogrified into something illegitimate and foreign: "I shall not see the LORD in the land of the living; I shall look upon man no more among the inhabitants of the world" (Isa. 38:11).

If this view is followed, the existence of Israel as God's chosen people also becomes a riddle; for if one thing is certain, it is that Israel cannot be understood in terms of an abstract, mystical, and isolated relationship to God, it can only be understood in relation to the glory of its inheritance, the land of Canaan. This land, and Israel's intense attachment to it, did not threaten communion with Yahweh; it is precisely the visible manifestation of that communion. There was no element of "competition" in the religious consciousness of the Israelite as he reflected on the mighty act of God in delivering His chosen people from Egypt and leading them to the land of milk and honey.[32]

The land is the fulfilment of the promise. This is the essential meaning of the *land* for the Israelites in the light of God's glory. Israel's joy does not compete with its fellowship with God unless Israel distorts the meaning of the land.

31. *Inst.*, III.xxv.11.
32. The joy and blessing of the land are clearly expressed in Deut. 26:10f.; 28:8, 11f.; only if Israel ignores the voice of Yahweh will curses come (vv. 15f., 23, 63, 66f.). According to von Rad, in possessing the land, Israel had come to rest. "Not one of all the good promises which the LORD had made to the house of Israel had failed; all came to pass" (Josh. 21:45; cf. 23:14); *OT Theology*, I, 303ff.

Only if one misunderstands the coherence in the work of God can he find tension or contradiction in what is proclaimed about the eschaton. The opinion that the themes of the new earth and the vision of God are competitive can only stem from an unbiblical idea of God's glory that relativizes or even eliminates concern for *things* and *mankind*.[33] When the expectation of a new earth is denied or relativized, the meaning of life *on this earth* breaks down. The psalms that sing of the glories of nature can then only be seen as cultic expressions of a false nature-religion. Either the eschaton blesses this life or — as a fictitious eschaton — it tarnishes and decomposes it. What a joy it is, then, to read that in His promise of a new earth the God of the present and the future "did not leave himself without witness, for he did good and gave you from heaven rains and fruitful seasons, satisfying your hearts with food and gladness" (Acts 14:17). For this reason — because of *this* God — one is on the wrong track if out of his desire to see God he allows the vision of the new earth to fade away into an incomprehensible and superfluous eschatological mystery. If one follows this route, he must then also conclude that a rigorous asceticism is the only meaning left to religion in this life — an asceticism, free from the world and from his neighbor, that is directed to the greater glory of God and his own *individual* salvation.[34]

With that kind of eschatological "joy," the entire traditional notion of divine mercy and divine grace is dispensed with.

33. In connection with *diesseits* and *jenseits,* this "competition" problematics surfaces from time to time in the works of Dietrich Bonhoeffer, who noted particularly the significance of the OT for a clear insight into the profound "thisworldliness" of Christianity; *Letters and Papers from Prison* (Eng. tr., 1953, paperback, 1962), pp. 161ff., 225ff. "Thisworldly" here is not contrasted to "eschatological" but to "otherworldly" (in the sense of escapist). Illustrative of this is the short excerpt from Bonhoeffer's letter of June 2, 1944 on the Song of Solomon as "an ordinary love poem, which is probably the best Christological exposition too" (p. 192). Cf. further G. Ebeling, *Word and Faith* (Eng. tr., 1963), pp. 98ff.; and on the problem of "thisworldliness" R. G. Smith, "Diesseitige Transzendens," in *Die mündige Welt*, II (1956), 104ff.

34. Asceticism has historically been closely related to eschatological expectation: reorientation of eschatological thinking brings with it shifts in ascetic thinking. Cf. K. Rahner, "The Passion and Asceticism," *Theological Investigations*, III (Eng. tr., 1967), 58-85; "Reflections on the Theology of Renunciation," *ibid.,* 47-57; cf. also "The Resurrection of the Body," *ibid.,* II (Eng. tr., 1963), 203ff.; J. van den Berg, "Rondom het begrip ascese," *Bezinning*, XV (1960), pp. 154ff. (on Rahner, p. 165).

Such a view presents an outlook on a reality in which everything else is pushed aside while in the background arises the figure of a God who is not only jealous when man turns away from Him to idols, but who is also jealous when man delights in all the works of His hands.[35] No, there must be both vision of God and new earth.

This view cannot be disputed by appeal to Paul's statement that God will be "everything to every one" (1 Cor. 15:28).[36] Paul is undoubtedly referring to the final purpose of God's ways, when His presence will be known and experienced as an indubitable, blessed actuality. The subject of this universal statement is the no-longer-partial, the definitive and all-inclusive. But it is also a matter of the reality of Him who through His presence does not annihilate all things, but brings them to fulfilment.[37]

The Christian faith and its expectation have often been interpreted in terms of an irreconcilable opposition between heaven and earth, and thus seen as a flight from this God-given reality to a *jenseits* with all the characteristics of an unearthly unreality. Jewish scholars in particular have attacked the Christian faith on this basis, contrasting it with Israel and its love for the land and for this world where God in His covenant has continued His dialogue with man. Martin Buber passionately disputed the antithesis between heaven and earth, his major objection being directed against apocalyptic, beginning

35. Augustine's remarks about eschatological joy are often cited in this connection; cf. R. Lorenz, *"Fruitio Dei* bei Augustin," *Zeitschrift für Kirchengeschichte,* LXIX (1950), 75ff., which includes a rather complete bibliography; also Althaus, *Die letzten Dinge,* p. 357.

36. *hína é ho theós pánta en pásin.* A variety of forms of mysticism have appealed to this passage for support; cf. Althaus, *op. cit.,* p. 357. The passage also plays a role in Teilhard de Chardin's *The Phenomenon of Man,* p. 294. Teilhard refers to it as "a superior form of 'pantheism.'" J. Héring disputes the use of the word "pantheism," substituting instead "panentheism"; *Le royaume de Dieu et sa venue* (1959), p. 209. But the latter term is no more useful for understanding this text.

37. Paul clearly does not hold to the idea of annihilation or of absorption in God; rather it is a matter of the subjection of everything in the fulfilment. Cf. Rom. 11:36; 1 Cor. 8:6. 1 Cor. 15:28 is much discussed in connection with the concept of a "messianic interim"; cf. Berkouwer, *The Work of Christ,* pp. 220f. We shall deal with this topic further in Chapter XIV below.

with Ezekiel and Daniel (which he judged to be of Persian origin, not Jewish) and later Christianized.[38]

At some point, Buber believes, the prophetic was replaced by the apocalyptic. In the process, Israel's attachment to this world was lost, and with it the real secret of Jewish religion. Prophetic religion believes in the idea of the redemption of the earth; apocalyptic religion abandons the earth as hopelessly lost. For Buber this constitutes the radical difference between Judaism and Christianity, and makes them unintelligible to each other: "Now to the Christian, the Jew is the incomprehensibly obdurate man, who declines to see what has happened; and to the Jew, the Christian is the incomprehensibly daring man, who affirms in an unredeemed world that its redemption has been accomplished."[39] Without going into the problem of Jewish messianism, we should note that Buber feels that the Christian expectation of the future excludes an element that is one of the essential features of Jewish eschatology, the dialogue between God and man *on the earth.*[40]

Buber emphasizes the connection between creation and Creator. Redemption must come and men receive it *on the earth.* "So it is not only with his thought and his feelings, but with the sole of his foot and the tip of his finger as well, that he may receive the sign-language of the reality taking place. The redemption must take place in the whole corporeal life. God the Creator wills to consummate nothing less than the whole of his creation."[41]

In his critique of the Christian expectation, Buber seems to look on it as nothing more than a form of dualism, a visionary otherworldliness, a kind of Platonism, which makes God into nothing more than an "idea," with no real relevance for this world.[42] Is Buber attacking anything more than a caricature of Christianity when he criticizes this notion of heaven over against earth as a place to which one can flee? Why does he not look beyond these spiritualizing caricatures of Christianity to

---

38. On the distinction between prophetic and apocalyptic see Buber, "The Two Foci of the Jewish Soul," in *The Writings of Martin Buber* (ed. W. Herberg, 1956), pp. 272f. Apocalyptic eschatology, which looks for another world, stems from Iranian dualism, according to Buber.

39. *Ibid.,* p. 276.

40. *Ibid.,* p. 274; cf. "The Faith of Judaism," *ibid.,* p. 264.

41. *Ibid.,* p. 265.

42. Cf. Hans Urs von Balthasar, *Martin Buber and Christianity* (Eng. tr., 1961), p. 56.

the true meaning of the Christian expectation of the future, as it is evidenced in the New Testament references to the new heaven and the new earth? It is difficult to say. But as a critique of the true New Testament eschatology Buber's observations are inapplicable. The true New Testament expectation includes the new earth, and the present life is founded on and proceeds from this expectation. Only with an eye to God's future can one understand the richness of life in the present.[43]

We talk often about the concept "relation" which plays so prominent a role in our thinking about reality. We speak of man's relation to God, man's relation to the world, man's relation to his fellow man, the relation of the first commandment to the second. All these relations — which are not parallel — are not just concepts but a reality. In the fulfilment we shall see the full meaning of these relations revealed and unveiled. Not until then will the greatness of God's grace in all these relations be seen to the full extent. Then it will be disclosed to us how much the love of God *is* the first commandment and how strong the relationship is between that commandment and the second; how greatly the creation has longed for liberation; how exclusively the body is for the Lord and the Lord for the body; and how binding is the relation between devotion to the Lord and to the new world. For at that time the course of sin will have been run and the meaning of things will be revealed.

What will the new earth be like?

We saw that the judgment is not an isolated cosmic, macrocosmic aspect of the fulfilment, which one can treat separately from mankind as a microcosm. Without exception, whenever the Bible talks about the future — even in its cosmic aspects — that future is related to *man,* just as Peter did not treat the flood as an isolated cosmic event, but used it as a point of departure for his appeal to the believers (2 Pet. 3). Thus, when the Bible uses all kinds of apocalyptic imagery, the believer who is listening to it aright will not work himself into a frenzy over the apocalyptic trial of catastrophic events to come. No, the very meaning of the proclamation is this: that the believer is called

43. In addition to Buber on this issue, see Leo Baeck, *Aus drei Jahrtausen-den* (1958), particularly the chapters "Romantische Religion" (pp. 42ff.) and "Judentum in der Kirche" (pp. 121ff.; Eng. tr. in *The Pharisees and Other Essays,* 1947, pp. 71-90).

to salvation in a framework that includes the prospect of new heavens and a new earth (2 Pet. 3:14, 17f.). Only if that connection is made can he find a viable route to the future.

But what is the nature of the contrast between this age and the future age?[44] The present age approaches its end, but this will not be total dissolution or annihilation, for there is an age to come. Christ spoke of this new age as the age when those who have given up something for His sake will receive eternal life (Mark 10:29f.).[45]

Contrasted to the coming age is the present evil age (Gal. 1:4), which will be replaced (1 John 3:14). This transition will not be something gradual — like the transition from the 19th century to the 20th — but will be a transition through a crisis. There is a relation between life in the present world and in the coming world: the author of Hebrews speaks of tasting the heavenly gift in this life (6:4). Nevertheless, there is still a boundary separating the present from the future age, from the *coming, new* earth.[46]

Oetinger's remark that the end of the ways of God is corporeality is frequently quoted, not as an overestimation of corporeality but in order to point out the concreteness and actuality of human, creaturely existence, to which the God of life gives a future. This theme of concreteness recurs time and again in the expressions of those who have contested the spiritualizing of the expectation of the future. According to Eduard Thurneysen, the world into which we shall come in the future of Jesus Christ is not another world, but this world, this heaven and this earth, both having passed away and become new. These forests and fields, these cities and streets, these people will be there in the showplace of redemption.[47] Brunner considers this unbiblical on the ground that the appearance of this world will pass away.

---

44. Cf. Sasse, in *TDNT*, s.v. *gḗ*, I, 678, on the *aiṓn méllōn* as new heaven and earth.

45. For the contrast between the two ages see Matt. 12:32; Luke 20:34f.; Eph. 1:21; cf. also Heb. 2:5: "the world (*oikouménē*) to come." See also Sasse, in *TDNT*, s.v. *aiṓn*, I, 204ff.

46. Some have pointed to the parallel between the NT references to this age and the coming age and Jewish apocalyptic. The difference between the two is the relation of the coming age to the present evil age. In the NT this is already meaningful as a result of the mystery of Christ.

47. "Christus und seine Zukunft," *Zwischen den Zeiten*, IX (1931), 209, with reference to 1 Cor. 15:53.

He thus concludes that we have no idea what the new heaven and the new earth will be and no ground to speculate about it.[48]

On the surface Brunner's judgment certainly looks modest and commendably restrained. But if he is completely correct about this, why do the Old and New Testaments not talk about an "x" — an unknown quantity — instead of arousing these various concepts of what the new heaven and the new earth will be like and talking about the longing of the creation for freedom from its perishability? The need for sobriety in talking about these matters ought not to lead one to overlook the equal need for certainty. We may not leave that which is inextricably connected with the *resurrectio carnis* in the shadows, least of all in the shadows of spiritualization.[49] God is "not God of the dead, but of the living" (Matt. 22:32). Better the extreme concreteness of Thurneysen than dualistic spiritualizing of the expectation, which is foreign to the works of God and wraps the future in impenetrable darkness. Althaus's comment here is to the point: questions about the coming corporeality and about the coming world must be answered as a unity,[50] not out of a desire to systematize, but with an eye to the Lord, "who abolished death and brought life and immortality to light through the gospel" (2 Tim. 1:10).[51]

Thus the eschatological expectation cannot be isolated from the context of earthly life, any more than the *resurrectio carnis* can be dissociated from the glorification of God in the body in this present existence (1 Cor. 6:20). Seen this way, this life is not without mystery. To say this may lead to a kind of romanticized, simplistic theodicy which fails to take seriously the utter earnestness of death. If so, the eschatological expectation be-

48. *Eternal Hope*, p. 204.
49. Thurneysen, *loc. cit.*, p. 207.
50. *Die letzten Dinge*, p. 359.
51. Someone may ask whether this sort of eschatological perspective is not equivalent to the worst kind of religious egocentrism, which values personal beatitude above the *Soli deo gloria*. One could counter this by asking whether the other, spiritualizing perspective does not run the risk of ignoring the carol of the angels, in which God's glory is intimately connected with the well-being of man, and Paul's remark that "the Spirit searches everything, even the depths of God" (1 Cor. 2:10). The religious egocentric or individualist is only the demonic *Doppelgänger* of the person who listens with astonishment to the voice that John heard in his vision of the new earth: "God himself will be with them; he will wipe away every tear from their eyes" (Rev. 21:3f.). In this *Soli deo gloria* this *Doppelgänger* will be unmasked.

comes nothing but a flight from the hard realities that face us. This kind of flight from reality differs sharply from the flight to God (Heb. 6:18), which is not a false romanticism, but a believing realism that recognizes all aspects of the "not yet." This same letter that talks about the city to come, also says that "we do *not yet* see everything in subjection to him" (Heb. 2:8).[52]

We may not fantasize about the end and purpose of God's ways, but neither may we limit the immeasurable riches of God's miraculous eschatological act.[53] This is why the "not yet" in the New Testament never represents a threat to future perspective, but is a stimulant of the expectation. What Paul says about partial knowledge and seeing in a mirror dimly (1 Cor. 13:12) comes in the context of his hymn to *love*. The eschatological boundary is indicated through the use of the words "now" (*árti*) and "then" (*tóte*). This boundary also sets limits to human understanding, thus forbidding speculation and rashness. John reaffirms this boundary: "It does not yet appear (*oútō ephaneróthē*) what we shall be" (1 John 3:2). This eschatological boundary cannot be compared with any other, for it is the line that divides the present from the future age and yet does not separate what God through Christ has united.

The author of Hebrews speaks of seeing from afar (11:13). Without faith, prayer, and salvation, this seeing from afar becomes a crisis and an estrangement. But it is written of Abraham that although he did not receive the promises, he nevertheless saw the coming salvation and greeted it from afar. This eager joy in the anticipation of the apocalyptic land is probably the most compelling argument against obscuring the expectation. The joy of this pilgrimage is jeopardized if this "from afar" is abandoned in favor of the "nearby" of a city of human construction (13:14). It also disintegrates if the promises of the heavenly country and Kingdom (11:16; 2 Tim. 4:18) are considered as threats to this earthly existence. This has happened

52. This remark comes directly after a quotation from Ps. 8:4-6, a psalm that begins by saying "O LORD, our Lord, how majestic is thy name in all the earth" (vs. 1). It might be argued that the glory of God's name seems to be less "hidden" in Ps. 8 than in Heb. 2. The clue here is the "not yet." It is clear from the connection between seeing and not seeing ("... we do not yet see ... but we see Jesus ...") that the "not yet" does not apply to what the psalmist is talking about, but anticipates the final revelation of Christ.
53. Cf. Hauck, in *TDNT*, s.v. *perisseúō*, VI, 59-61; Eph. 2:7.

time and again as a result of a hermeneutics that allows the joy of seeing from afar to disappear completely in favor of concern for the earth, or to rigidify into an empty knowledge about the end that is enervatingly disconcerting in its inevitability.

The whole gospel militates against such hermeneutics, for it is precisely ordinary earthly existence that is redeemed. *Because the Lord is at hand,* the church is called to joy and forbearance without anxiety, knowing that the peace of God will keep their hearts and minds in Jesus Christ (Phil. 4:4-7). They are told to think about whatever is excellent and worthy of praise (vs. 8). Then life on this earth is not devaluated, but called. The expectation has consequences for this present existence. The new earth is never a strange and futuristic fantasy, but a mystery that penetrates into this existence and will make itself manifest there, where steadfast love and faithfulness meet, where righteousness and peace kiss each other (Ps. 85:10), and where the lines that seem blurred to us now will come clearly into focus.[54] This perspective includes a note of warning. It points to the hidden manna, the white stone with a new name written on it (Rev. 2:17). It will be *spiritual;* "the Spirit and the bride say, 'Come'" (Rev. 22:17). But at the same time it will be *earthly,* and it will be on earth that the voice will sound: "Let him who is thirsty come, let him who desires take the water of life without price."

54. The unity of this expectation has often been threatened in the Christian church by the constant arguments about pre-, post-, and a-millennialism, a subject that is treated in Chapter X below. The issue is not just one of how to interpret Rev. 20, but one that bears on the entire philosophy of history.

CHAPTER EIGHT

SIGNS OF THE TIMES

IN ITS EXPECTATION the church has always spent a great
deal of time considering what are usually called the signs
of the times, realizing that the parousia of the Lord — despite
the fact that no one knows its day nor hour — cannot be divorced from the time — the history — that precedes it. Christians have devoted close attention to those concrete historical
events that seemed to signal the approaching future with its comforting and alarming character, seeing these events as heralding
the impending parousia of Him "who is and who was and who
is to come" (Rev. 1:4). Momentous significance has always been
attached to these so-called *signa praecursoria,* not only because
they seemed to proclaim that the coming of the Lord was at
hand, but also because they revealed the nearness of this coming historically. This nearness could be seen and detected in the
course of a history filled with eschatological tensions that showed
themselves in very concrete, characteristic, and typical signs.

In Chapters III and IV we dealt with the question why time
still continues and why the "already" of God's Kingdom is still
offset by the "not yet." Our concern in this chapter is with a
different question: to what extent does the "time between" include signs of the nearness of the parousia? To what extent do
specific historical events signify the coming of the Kingdom?

That these signs have been much discussed is not surprising.
The church hears the Lord's promise "I come quickly" (Rev.
22:20) and inevitably wonders what role the things that are
happening in the world around it play in this expectation. Does
history itself testify that the "end of the ages" (Matt. 28:20) is
presently approaching? Basic to all reflection about the signs
of the times is the belief that the present dispensation is not a
void and meaningless epoch, not a confusion of unrelated and
incidental events, but a time that may well be described as the

235

way to a goal, and that in this time there are signs to indicate that this goal is near, that the end of the way is in sight.

The nature of the signs

Granted that there are signs, what is their nature? What aspect of an historical event qualifies it as a sign? A commonly agreed upon requirement is that the sign be a spectacular event, breaking into the normal course of history and irresistibly drawing attention to itself, something like the psalmist was talking about when he said: "those who dwell at earth's farthest bounds are afraid at thy signs" (Ps. 65:8). The peculiar and the convulsive become the object of the search for signs because the signs deal with *discerning* the times and interpreting the *special* significance of events. It did not seem possible that the signs of the times could have to do with history in general, with events in all their multiformity, but had rather to do with exceptional fragments of history. If this is so, however, the question immediately arises, how is it possible to assign a "margin" of noetic value to certain events? How can one detect in certain events this transparency with respect to the coming of the Lord?

The preceding questions are meaningful, because how one answers them will naturally affect the concreteness of his eschatological expectation. In one's attention to the signs of the times, his expectation touches life in the present, the course of current history in which daily life takes place. Not that it is a matter of computing the date of the parousia from the signs: for the most part, this attention to the signs has been given in full awareness of the New Testament message that the reign of Christ is still hidden, and that man does not know when that future day will be. Life is still lived in expectation waiting for the promise of the Father: "It is not for you to know times and seasons which the Father has fixed by his own authority" (Acts 1:7).

The New Testament places such strong emphasis on the Christian's being ready at all times for the return of the Lord that one might wonder whether the whole essence of faith is summed up in the word "watchfulness." And does preoccupation with the signs of the times not run the risk of trying to mark the time of the parousia in some sense, even if not attempting to fix the date exactly? Is this quest for visible, tangible signs in earthly life anything more than an attempt to lift the veil of secrecy? Does the church need to do anything more than watch for the Lord in all the watches of the night (Mark 13:33-37) ?

It is true that the New Testament often sets faith and the quest for signs over against one another. It is evident that concern for signs can often be an abdication of the responsibility of faith. The Pharisees, Mark reports, asked Jesus for a spectacular sign *from heaven* in an effort to test Him (8:11). After Christ drove money-changers from the temple He was asked for "a sign" (John 2:18), that is, for His credentials; significantly, He dismisses such questions as coming from an "evil and adulterous" generation (cf. Matt. 12:38f.; 16:4; Luke 11:29). In the face of the authority of Christ and the reality that came in Him, any demand for a sign as something extra and confirming is clearly superfluous and unbelieving, and, therefore, meaningless. When signs are requested so that "we may see, and believe you" (John 6:30), the demand for signs competes with faith, and they are absolutely denied: "Truly, I say to you, no sign shall be given to this generation" (Mark 8:12).[1]

But sign and faith are not always mutually exclusive. John writes of signs of the Kingdom that open the eyes to whatever the signs signify (cf. 2:11; 4:48). There *are* meaningful signs. After His resurrection Christ appeared to His disciples "by many proofs" (Acts 1:3). But these were not objective, rational proofs that would automatically convince even the most hardhearted (cf. John 12:37). Depending on the direction of the human heart a sign can be interpreted in any number of ways (cf. Matt. 28:13; Mark 3:22; John 12:40). The reactions to the raising of Lazarus (John 11:43f.) differed from the reactions to the raising of the widow of Nain's son (Luke 7:16). Only when signs are seen through the eyes of faith can they display their meaning and significance, because signs have their own significative language. There were signs of the time of salvation, and Christ reproached His contemporaries for not recognizing the uniqueness of that period. They knew how to interpret natural phenomena, but they could not interpret or discern the times (Matt. 16:4; Luke 12:56). In one of His parables He says, "Look at the fig tree, and all the trees; as soon as they

---

1. Cf. A. Vögtle, "Der Spruch vom Jonaszeichen," in *Synoptische Studien für A. Wikenhauser* (1953), pp. 230ff. The sign of Jonah, as reported in Matt. and Luke, is on an entirely different plane from the spectacular sign desired to put an end to uncertainty. Cf. also M. H. Bolkestein, *Het verborgen rijk* (1954), p. 157.

come out in leaf, the summer is already near" (Luke 2:29f.). *Seeing* and *knowing* are hardly distinguished: "when you see these things taking place, you know that the kingdom of God is near" (vs. 31). Through this analogy with natural phenomena, Christ emphasizes the seeing and knowing of the revelation of the time of salvation, which is manifested for all men to see.[2]

But when most people talk about signs of the times they are not thinking in terms of the present time of salvation and the discernment of it, but in terms of the moments preceding the coming of the parousia. Actually, of course, the two — the coming end and the present time of salvation — cannot be divorced. When Christ spoke of the destruction of the temple, the disciples asked for a sign about the manner of His coming: "When will this be, and what will be the sign of your coming and of the close of the age?" (Matt. 24:3). Christ does not dismiss this question as unbelieving, but gives it a serious and profound reply. He does not reveal in a neutral way a series of events to come in the distant future; the key word is "take heed" (Mark 13:23, 33). There is no mention of a future that is cut loose from the present. Those things that are already beginning to happen are closely related to the approaching redemption: "when these things begin to take place, look up and raise your heads, because your redemption is drawing near" (Luke 21:28). The whole point is that from now on they must be watchful, facing the future without fear, not being led astray (Matt. 24:5), but enduring (vs. 13) and taking heed to themselves (Mark 13:9). Supported by the Holy Spirit (Mark 13:11), they will have wisdom and soundness of speech, "which none of your adversaries will be able to withstand or contradict" (Luke 21:15).

Clearly, then, the signs are unalterably related to the present and to faith. The signs are not arbitrary, but they reflect the reality of the approaching Kingdom. They are not a neutral list of future events, but they point the way to the future and stimulate the direction of every activity to the triumphant and dynamic coming of God's Kingdom. There is no talk of a *timeless* existential relationship that has nothing to do with the concrete course of history. The signs involve seeing what takes place and being on the way to what is yet to come on the earth (Mark 13:29).

This has been the traditional position of the church. But

2. Cf. Jeremias, *The Parables of Jesus* (Eng. tr., 1955), p. 96.

there has been a repeated tendency to isolate the signs of the times from their context in the Gospels. Some interpreters have gone so far as to locate the signs of the times in a future end-time that they see as not yet having begun. Consequently, the sign-concept is divorced from the present. Signs are seen as an aggregate of events of significative character, but without realizing that summer is already near when leaves appear on the trees (Luke 21:30). Isolated and formalized, the signs come to be seen as an arbitrary conglomeration of events that can somehow or other function as signs.[3] Consequently, the proclamation of the signs becomes a mere description of events that are not yet actuality, but some day will come about.

The curious thing about this displacement is that the signs of the times are derived from the Gospels, where they always appear in a very real context. This is probably the real problem in the traditional understanding of the signs of the times, a problem that is of a piece with the problem of the continuity of history and the so-called delay of the parousia. However justifiable the arguments against consistent eschatology, one cannot use these arguments as a basis for transposing every sign found in the Gospels to a not-yet-begun end-time. Such a displacement can only lead to the kind of confusion that attends every effort to compute the date of Christ's return.

The dangers inherent in all of this become even more clear when we consider how the various New Testament data dealing with the coming of the Kingdom have been dealt with. We read in the New Testament of a religious antithesis that will be revealed in the deception of false christs, in the hate and persecution suffered for Jesus' name, in the multiplication of wickedness as love grows cold (Matt. 24:5, 8.12). In addition there will be wars and rumors of wars, famines and earthquakes (vv. 6f.). The final crisis is portrayed in terms of catastrophic natural events: the darkening of sun and moon and the falling of the stars (vs. 29). "Then will appear the sign of the Son of man in heaven" (vs. 30).

3. This critique of "formalization" is not meant to downgrade what Rengstorf says about the sign as formal concept (in *TDNT*, s.v. *sēmeion*, VII, 211ff.). Rengstorf is talking about the indication-character of signs (cf. the concept *'ôth* in the OT), from which it obviously does not follow that eschatological signs are to be isolated from what they are signs of. Cf. also T. van der Walt, *Die Koninkryk van God — naby* (1962), pp. 181-93.

This variety eventually led to the formation of a definite tradition concerning the signs of the times. The intent was to catalogue and systematize all of the New Testament data about the end. The data from the Gospels were supplemented by passages from the rest of the New Testament, particularly the "rebellion" (2 Thess. 2:3) and the revelation of the man of lawlessness (vv. 3, 7). Finally, the whole picture was rounded off with the apocalyptic images and concepts found in the Book of Revelation.[4]

In all such attempts at systematization the emphasis repeatedly seems to fall on the catastrophic aspects of the signs of the times, an accent that is also reflected in corresponding popular accounts. A. F. C. Vilmar writes of an ancient popular tradition — widespread throughout the East already in the twelfth century — that there were fifteen signs of the judgment day. In almost all of them the catastrophic element was distinctly dominant.[5] As time went on, wars and rumors of war, famines and earthquakes continued to play a pervasive role in the popular notion of the signs of the times. What people concentrated on was the dark side of the signs. This was especially true among people who no longer expected things to get better in this life. The basic motif was alarm. As a result, men no longer knew how to account for periods of relative peace and prosperity or the periodic "golden age."

Such an interpretation of the signs does not necessarily indicate pessimism. For prophecies of catastrophe are evident in the New Testament, particularly in Luke's Gospel, where the subjective experience of eschatological events is vividly described: "upon the earth distress of nations in perplexity at the roaring of the sea and the waves, men fainting with fear and with foreboding of what is coming on the world" (21:25f.). Not only will there be natural and national catastrophes, but "there will be great tribulation such as has not been from the beginning of the world" (Matt. 24:21), "and if the Lord had

4. This kind of systematizing is often encountered in dogmatics. More recent eschatology is characterized by a certain concentration here. Thus, under the category "indicators of the end" Althaus includes the completion of the preaching of the gospel, the antichrist, and the millennium; *Die letzten Dinge*, pp. 279ff. Similarly C. Stange, *Das Ende aller Dinge*, p. 226. Schmaus adds to these the afflictions of the church and chaos in creation, but does not mention the millennium, although he does list the conversion of the Jews; *Katholische Dogmatik*, IV/2 (1959), 165.
5. *Dogmatik*, II (1874), 310.

not shortened the days, no human being would be saved" (Mark 13:20). Consideration of the catastrophic aspect of the end is thus not illegitimate. Nevertheless, the one-sidedness that often attends this consideration raises several difficult problems. For example, what is to be made of the undeniably frequent repetition of some of these catastrophes in the course of history? If they happen again and again in completely different eras, how are we to evaluate their eschatological significance?

This question arises in an exchange of letters between Augustine and Hesychius. Hesychius believed that what he took to be signs of the times occurring around him indicated the nearness of the parousia. Augustine, on the other hand, felt that these wars (and eclipses of the sun) were characteristic of all of history and thus did not have any peculiarly eschatological significance. However, Augustine did not have much of a following among later theologians, who interpreted contemporary wars and rumors of wars as signs of the times, pointing specifically to their *proportion* and *modality*. The signs are subsumed under the category of the conspicuous.[6]

Abraham Kuyper argues that what is significant is the *abnormality* of a given event. This is what makes it incontrovertibly into a sign. Examples would be an earthquake that shook the entire world, a worldwide famine, a universal war. The eschatologically qualified war would be one *without apparent cause*.[7] A sign must be a "completely exceptional and abnormal phenomenon," which because of its conspicuousness is obviously a sign of the end of the times. The emphasis on abnormality corresponds closely to Kuyper's general view of signs as belonging to the "end-time." He believed that near the end of this dispensation there would be a return to the "economy of miracles," which, at the end of the apostolic age, had given way to an "economy of gradual process."[8] At that time the signs will appear with their astonishing and unusual character, and as a result they will be direct indications of the parousia

6. On Augustine and Hesychius, see Kliefoth, *Christliche Eschatologie* (1886), p. 127. K. Dijk speaks of miraculous signs and surprising events that relate in clear language that Christ is returning; *Het einde der eeuwen*, p. 115.

7. *Dictaten Dogmatiek*, V (*Locus de Consummatione Saeculi*), 136f.

8. *Ibid.*, p. 117, probably influenced by Kliefoth (*op. cit.*, p. 129), who also speaks of the disappearance of signs and wonders since the apostolic age and the return of these.

at hand. Kuyper sees these catastrophic events as divorced from any apparent cause, which thus indicates their sign-character.

As far as I know, this way of looking at it — considering causelessness as determinative for the sign-character of an event · — has had little influence. Kuyper's example of the French Revolution, for example, as a "causeless" war is hardly convincing to anyone who knows a little history. But even more telling is the consideration that the New Testament says nothing about the "modality" of wars. It does not provide any grounds for supposing that the signs belong to some supernatural realm: the signs are indicated as earthly. The only war that is descriptively qualified in the Bible is the *holy* war, the "war of the LORD" (Num. 21:14), which has to do with the antithesis between Israel and the surrounding nations.[9] In the New Testament the catastrophic element of the signs focuses on disruption and chaos in the life of man, which is never isolated or abstracted from the events themselves. Their meaning is much more extensive and profound. First of all, the context of all signs is the decision that must be made for or against Jesus Christ. The catastrophic aspects form, as it were, the dark accompanying contours of the religious decision that is at issue in the eschaton. In apocalyptic language they indicate the seriousness of faith and unbelief at the coming of the Kingdom. So, the point is not a "phenomenological" approach to war, for example, as such; rather, in complete agreement with the apocalyptic images of the Old Testament, the point is the totality and decisive seriousness of the eschaton.

The Old Testament portrays the day of the Lord in terms of the darkening of sun, moon, and stars (Isa. 13:10), the desolation of the earth (vs. 13), and the disruption of life (24:1, 3f., 18f.). These and prophecies like these are repeated in the New Testament, where they serve as the basis of urgent appeals to remain steadfast and watchful. This does not mean to put Jewish apocalyptic on a par with the eschatological proclamations of the New Testament. The two are profoundly different. Late-Jewish apocalyptic exhibits definitely pessimistic strains that are not to be found in the New Testament. Eschatology undergoes a tremendous change in the New Testament when the "apocalypse" is centered in Jesus Christ and His Kingdom.

9. Cf. G. von Rad, *OT Theology*, I, 17. Bauernfeind, in *TDNT*, s.v. *pólemos*, VI, 509, in connection with Amos 2:14-16.

"The Christian apocalyptist is distinguished from the Jewish by this wholly new, Christocentric understanding of the End time which exhibits the inner ground of all the occurrences of the End time. Because of this, the form of these events has lost its decisive worth and is no longer useful for the purposes of calculation."[10] Furthermore, the outlook on the future as it is portrayed in the New Testament rules out any human attempt at calculation. To be curious on this score merely proves that one does not really understand the events of history. The coming salvation can only be awaited in a state of complete preparedness, something entirely different from the brooding about the future characteristic of late-Jewish apocalyptic.[11]

In this perspective, calculation is not necessary, desirable, nor even possible.[12] Calculation of approximate temporal conclusions from certain selected phenomena cannot be the intention of the signs. The shift of emphasis from the signs themselves to calculation stems from the belief that the eschatological proclamation is intended to give a more or less exact narrative account of some events that are to be expected in the future. This idea, of course, is widespread with respect to the interpretation of the Book of Revelation. Numerous sects have elevated this alleged "narrative account" character of Revelation to a hermeneutical principle, and the narrative accounts they have come up with as a result have been immeasurably capricious and implausible, sometimes even contradictory.[13] It is impossi-

10. M. Rissi, *Time and History* (Eng. tr., 1966), pp. 74f.
11. It is true that Daniel refers to the hiddenness of these things (12:9); cf. J. T. Nelis, *Daniel* (1954), *ad loc.;* and Noth, "Die Geschichtsverständnis der AT Apokalyptik," in *Gesammelte Studien zum AT* (1957), p. 292.
12. According to Delling, "in spite of the attempts of OT prophets (1 Pt. 1:11), Christians cannot calculate these times"; in *TDNT*, s.v. *kairós*, III, 461. Peter says that the prophets "inquired *(ereunóntes)* what person or time was indicated by the Spirit of Christ within them," which Delling paraphrases as a "diligent search for the moment of the appearance of the Messiah"; *ibid.*, s.v. *ereunáō*, II, 657. Cf. however K. H. Schelkle, *Die Petrusbriefe* (1961), pp. 39ff., and Daniel's reaction to reading Jeremiah's prophecy of the length of "the desolations of Jerusalem" (Dan. 9:3ff.). This "inquiring" of the prophets is something other than "calculation." Furthermore, the situation is different as a result of the fulness of time (Gal. 4:4; Mark 1:15).
13. One of the many examples is the twelfth-century mystic Joachim of Fiore, who interpreted the one thousand two hundred and sixty days of Rev. 12:6 to mean that the third status of history, the *ordo monachorum* or the age of the Spirit, would be inaugurated in A.D. 1260. Cf. M. A. Beek, *Inleiding tot de Joodse apocalyptiek*, pp. 121ff.; K. Löwith,

ble to isolate the "hermeneutics" of Revelation from the total New Testament proclamation of the future.

Nor is there warrant for contrasting an apocalyptic element in Revelation with a narrative or reportorial element in the eschatological sayings of Jesus as found in the Gospels. Such a contrast is precluded by the Gospels themselves, which are incomprehensible without an apocalyptic background. For this reason systematization and chronologization are impossible.[14] To be sure, there is a unity in the whole proclamation, the unity of the call to preparedness, watchfulness, and steadfastness. But this unity can be understood only if one realizes the part that apocalyptic coloring plays in it.

For example, the Gospels underline the particularity of the great tribulation in no uncertain terms: "such as has not been from the beginning of the world until now, no, and never will be" (Matt. 24:21). Obviously this harks back to Daniel 12:1: "there shall be a time of trouble, such as never has been since there was a nation even till that time." According to G. C. Aalders, Daniel's reference is to the persecution of the Jews under Antiochus Epiphanes.[15] Now a strictly "reportorial" eschatology has difficulty understanding the meaning of this language, but the fact that Matthew harks back to Daniel points to an eschatological light that penetrates through all times and thus catches the attention of people in every era and circumstance. Even when the New Testament talks about the "tribulation," there is a clear connection with certain Old Testament passages (cf. Isa. 26:17; 66:8). From all this it is evident that the various eschatological passages in the New Testament are not "reportorial," not mere narrative accounts, especially not narrative accounts of events to take place in a localized "end-time," which is then to be considered as future. The Gospels are surely not talking about an "end-time" dissociated from our time — or that of the disciples — which has not yet begun. Now some might argue that such a notion of an "end-time" can help explain the length and duration of time since the Lord said "I come quickly," but it is impossible to dispose of consistent eschatology and the problem of the "delay of the parousia" by resorting to

Weltgeschichte und Heilsgeschehen (2d ed., 1953), pp. 136ff., 190ff.; and F. Sassen, "De opvatting van de geschiedenis bij de Scholastieken van de XIIe eeuw," in the collection *Geschiedenis* (1944), pp. 67ff.

14. Cf. W. Trillhaas, *Dogmatik* (1962), p. 449.
15. *KV, ad loc.; Daniel* (1962), p. 305.

an interpretation that sees Jesus' eschatological proclamations as
going over the heads of His disciples to the church of all ages.
These remarks of Jesus are directly and immediately addressed
to His disciples. "*You* will hear of wars and rumors of wars;
see that *you* are not alarmed" (Matt. 24:6) ; "They will deliver
you up to tribulation and put *you* to death" (vs. 9) ; "if any
one says to *you,* 'lo, here is the Christ' ... do not believe him"
(vs. 23) . Thus Luke talks about armies surrounding *Jerusalem*
and flight from *Judea* to the mountains (21:20f.) . "These are
the days of vengeance, to fulfil all that is written" (vs. 22) .[16]
Eschatological preaching cannot be divorced from this contemporaneity. The signs are too concrete to be interpreted as an
explanation of catastrophes to take place in some remote "end-
time": they appear on the horizon of the lives of the apostles.

It has been suggested that Luke's concretizing and localizing
depends on his peculiar theology, which is said to discount the
delay of the parousia. Presumably, his interest shifted from the
"nearness" of the Kingdom to history. Conzelmann feels that the
passage about Jerusalem is uneschatological and falls outside the
realm of "signs." It seems to me that this interpretation destroys
the eschatological perspective of the entire chapter, which speaks
not only of the desolation of Jerusalem but also of the great
eschatological distress of nations and signs in the sun, moon,
and stars (Luke 21:20-28) . In its eschatological unity, Luke's
Gospel reveals that it follows the structural law of all eschatological preaching: the imminent horizon is not to be excluded, but takes on a decisive meaning.[17]

The "signs" are treated within the context of the contemporary situation and contemporary attitudes; which is why Luke's
reference to Jerusalem is not a symptom of de-eschatologizing,
but a meaningful perspective that rids eschatology of any futurism. The concretization proves that the signs of the times cannot
be interpreted futuristically, that such an interpretation mistakes
the gravity of eschatological preaching, which is relevant for all
times, and that it is impossible to distinguish on the basis of
the New Testament between the last days and an end-time in
which the signs will take place.

16. In connection with the fulfilment of all that is written, cf. Mark 13:30
   and the remarks of H. N. Ridderbos, *The Coming of the Kingdom,*
   pp. 499f.
17. For Conzelmann's brief treatment of Luke 21:22 cf. *The Theology of
   St. Luke,* pp. 132-35.

Continuous reinterpretation

The apocalyptic perspective is always of *present* significance. It proclaims its message of comfort and admonition in terms of motifs and realities that are being revealed now and will be revealed shortly. So we cannot ignore this preaching by transferring its relevance to some unknown future date.[18] To give this decisive and actual aspect of the apocalyptic proclamation its due is not to demythologize it, for what is at issue here is not this or that world-view — as Bultmann supposed — but the understanding of the *intention* of the apocalyptic structurization from the point of view of the central message of God's salvation. Karl Rahner has, as we noted above, suggested the substitution of "de-apocalypticizing" for "demythologizing." This term, however, creates the impression that the biblical message must be divested of the "apocalyptic" by some mechanical process.

But how are we to understand the biblical message in this apocalyptic material? Rahner distinguishes between the form of the eschatological assertions of Scripture and their content, with the intent that nothing of the essential content of the apocalyptic message is lost.[19] *Everything* is important in this New Testament message, because every structuring is related to, and must be understood from, the central meaning. This apocalyptic proclamation is not intended as speculation from afar or an attempt through secret language to transcend the realm of contemporaneity, but it proceeds from the Spirit's revelation consonant with each particular period of time. The apocalyptic-eschatological presentations penetrate a particular time, and there find their *Sitz im Leben*. The actuality of the eschatological message consists in this fact: that it never loses its contem-

---

18. Consider the tribulations *(thlípsis)* in Rev. 1:9; 2:9f.; 3:10 (on the whole world); 1 Cor. 7:26. Consider further the concrete, actual and eschatological vision of Agabus, who "foretold by the Spirit that there would be a great famine *(megálē limós)* over all the world" (Acts 11:28). The dating of this is given: in the days of Claudius. On the relation of this text to the alleged Lucan tendency to de-eschatologize and historicize, cf. W. Bieder, "Die missionarische Bedeutung der Oekumene und die ihr drohende Verkirchlichung," *Evangelische Theologie*, XXII (1962), 180; and G. Friedrich, in *TDNT*, s.v. *prophḗtēs*, VI, 848n.

19. "The Hermeneutics of Eschatological Assertions," *Theological Investigations,* IV, 344ff.

poraneity.[20] This perpetual contemporaneity makes it impossible to consider it as a kind of advance eyewitness account. It must be seen as a reference to what is included in the salvation already obtained and to what some day will be reality in the mode of fulfilment.[21]

The person who interprets apocalyptic images and concepts literally and takes them for detailed narrative accounts of the end-time completely misconstrues the biblical witness, which "has no intention of describing the actual phenomena of the eschata themselves."[22] He is actually doing the same thing as those who try to calculate the future through events or signs. Both approaches forget that the structure of the eschatological promises is completely determined by the salvation that has already appeared. Sooner or later one must conclude, perhaps painfully, that a systematizing of the signs mentioned in the various books of the Bible just cannot be done.[23] For — in the New Testament particularly — we encounter variations of these signs. In the course of events, the eschatological light of the promise is reflected differently under different circumstances. We might say that there is *continuous reinterpretation,* in which nothing of the eschatological promise is sacrificed. But if one wants to calculate these things he cannot allow for reinterpre-

20. S. Herrmann points out this element of continuing relevance in the OT: "Because Israel forsook its God, the enemy would bring catastrophe on the people, whether that enemy was the Assyrians (for the eighth-century classical prophets) or later the Babylonians." "Das Prophetische," in *Probleme AT Hermeneutik* (1960), p. 358.

21. Rahner, *loc. cit.,* pp. 330, 336.

22. *Ibid.,* p. 336n. According to Oepke, although the "intricate visions" of Jewish apocalyptic "seem to have little to do with genuine prophecy," they have the same aim, "to strengthen the severely tried community in faith in the living God"; in *TDNT,* s.v. *apokalýptō,* III, 578. U. Wilckens correctly points out that the intention of the apocalyptic texts far surpasses mere calculation; "Das Offenbarungsverständnis in der Geschichte des Urchristentums," in *Offenbarung als Geschichte, Kerygma und Dogma,* Beiheft 1 (1961), p. 49.

23. Although Rahner has been particularly vocal in his opposition to reportorial eschatology, the fundamental difficulty with it was recognized already much earlier. Valuable insights into this are provided by Charles Hodge. In spite of his unsatisfactory distinction between "great truths" and "details," he writes, more clearly, that "prophecy...is not intended to give us a knowledge of the future analogous to that which history gives us of the past"; *Systematic Theology,* III (1872), 790f. K. Frör similarly rejects this type of project; *Biblische Hermeneutik* (1961), p. 80.

tation. Calculation fixes its concepts and makes no allowance for changing times. Reinterpretation, on the other hand, serves as the basis for the continuing actuality of the eschatological promise. Thus, the signs are not pertinent to only a remote end-time. No, for believers they are summons to constant watchfulness.[24]

So we cannot understand the signs by making a distinction between natural life and a number of "supernatural" acts of God, and considering the latter to be signs on the basis of their unusual and spectacular character as the "finger of God" in the natural course of events. But the meaning of the signs has often been circumscribed in this way, thus in effect canonizing an element of Jewish apocalyptic that accented the transcendent or supernatural in the divine acts at the expense of the human and natural. Such a view runs afoul of Christ's own careful warning against misunderstanding the mode of His appearance: "The kingdom of God is not coming with signs to be observed; nor will they say, 'Lo, here it is!' or, 'There!'" (Luke 17:20). The words Christ uses are obviously not directed against "seeing" the signs but against an expectation of the Kingdom oriented to the spectacular and unusual, and thus neglecting the element of personal decision.[25]

The Kingdom is much closer than is often supposed. Because it is not a supernatural structure, it can easily escape notice. But it is "in the midst of you" (Luke 17:21). This is important evidence against those who want to isolate the signs of the times as purely "supernatural" phenomena. Such isolating tendencies, moreover, subject one's view of the signs to the extent to which one's world-view has developed and to the ever-changing limits of what qualifies as human experience. A phenomenon that is considered abnormal or supernatural at one time may later come to be seen as purely natural due to developments in scientific knowledge. On this view, therefore, a sign may lose its significance as a sign. Numerous evidently erroneous eschatological predictions have fallen down at this point: the broadening of human experience has explained away an apparent paradox, and

24. Schmaus, *Katholische Dogmatik*, IV/2, 194; cf. R. Schippers, *Mythologie en Eschatologie in 2 Thess. 2* (1961), pp. 10, 13-15.
25. In this connection, cf. A. Rüstow, "*Entós hymōn estín.* Zur Deutung von Lukas 17, 20-21," *Zeitschrift für die NT Wissenschaft*, LI (1960), 197-224; and Bent Noack, "Das Gottesreich bei Lukas," *Symbolae Biblicae Uppsaliensis*, X (1948).

thus deprived the phenomenon of its power to shock and un-settle people.[26]

But eschatological preaching is independent of such changes in human understanding of the universe, for it does not proceed from acts of God that are significant because they are super-natural, nor is it a narrative account of the future. Rather it bears witness to the last days from the point of view of the sal-vation that has already come. In the last days, as it awaits the Kingdom, the Christian community is reminded of the necessity of continually rethinking its position *vis-à-vis* Jesus Christ. Such reminders do not allow for reportorial eschatology and the em-barrassing errors of calculation inevitably allied with it, which clearly violate the prohibition against trying to figure out the date of the parousia.[27] History itself has contradicted each of these calculations in turn, but no sooner does one prove to be false than the next one is proposed.

But what of the frequently encountered opinion that present-day events seem to be fulfilling scriptural prophecies in detail? Kuyper, for example, wrote (in 1935) "that in the last ten years, a whole series of phenomena have arisen that correspond di-rectly to what is predicted in Revelation."[28] He speaks of "defi-nite indications" that "in an astonishing way have so literally become reality that many have concluded that the fulfilment is most certainly rapidly approaching."[29] Discussing the trumpets of Revelation 9, he talks on the one hand about literal fulfil-ment, on the other about figurative language.[30] Kuyper was in-trigued mostly by "literal" fulfilment of prophecy, and he saw this in the ominous threats of modern warfare.

This is a prime example of reportorial eschatology. Behind it lies the assumption that the real intent of the Book of Reve-lation was to issue detailed statements about the future — in this case about the early twentieth century. Presumably, then, Scripture provides a special descriptive history of the signs as an outstanding part of history as a whole. This requires system-atization of the signs into a coherent whole, a kind of photo-

---

26. Cf. the discussion by W. Nigg, *Das ewige Reich,* p. 177, of the impres-sion made on the followers of Joachim of Fiore by the sudden death of Frederick II in 1250.

27. A good example is the Montanist expectation of the descent of the new Jerusalem into Pepuza; *ibid.,* p. 115.

28. *Van de Voleinding,* IV (2d ed., 1935), 159.

29. *Ibid.,* p. 160.

30. *Ibid.,* p. 158; cf. p. 141.

graphic image that can later be seen to correspond to the contemporaneous world of experience. But the Bible does not mention autonomous facts or events that can be readily and incontrovertibly recognized. If that were its intention, one could ask why the signs are not so precisely fixed that any discussion about whether or not a given event is a "sign" would be excluded.[31] The Bible witnesses to the eschatological proclamation of what became in Jesus Christ the reality of salvation and its future fulfilment. It does not allow us to interpret history from the abnormal and spectacular level.

It is well to remember the scriptural warning that there will arise false prophets and false christs with signs and wonders to try to lead believers astray (Mark 13:22). Similarly, the parousia of the lawless one will be with "pretended signs and wonders" (2 Thess. 2:9). Even the beast of Revelation 13 is capable of performing great signs, such as making fire come down from heaven (vv. 13f.). Thus the believer cannot merely be on the lookout for spectacular events: he must have his eyes open to the decisiveness of contemporary events for or against Christ. The biblical testimony about the signs must be continually recast on the basis of the true essence of the eschatological proclamation, the "already" that points to the fulfilment to come. The signs of the times remain centered around the message of the crucified and exalted Lord.

Because Jesus Christ is the first and the last (Rev. 22:13), the eschatological proclamation is strongly Christological. It is not "a supplementary piece of information added to dogmatic anthropology and Christology, but simply *their* transposition into the guise of the fulfilment."[32] The clarion call of New Testament eschatology is to steadfastness until the end within a deceptive and antagonistic environment. For this reason the call to heed the signs of the times applies even in a "golden age." Too often, reflection on the signs has been cut loose from the Kingdom, their concentration-point. The results are always disconcerting. All the strongly apocalyptic words mean nothing unless they are centered in and receive their meaning from the Messiah.

If we center these apocalyptic signs in Jesus Christ, we cannot pay attention only to the dark side of the eschatological

---

31. An objection raised by Rahner, *loc. cit.*, p. 336n.
32. *Ibid.*, p. 335; cf. the discussion of the *Sitz im Leben* of the eschatological sayings, p. 336.

events as proclaimed in the Old and New Testaments. Traditionally, this has been the case. Wars and rumors of wars are considered the important signs. But the primary concern is the universal spread of the gospel of Jesus Christ (Mark 13:10). This preaching stands in a clearly eschatological context: "this gospel of the kingdom will be preached throughout the whole world, as a testimony to all nations; and then the end will come" (Matt. 24:14).[33] Usually those who have catalogued the signs of the times have included this, but frequently it has been seen as just another element in the "narrative account." Some have tried to reckon the nearness of the parousia on the basis of how much of the world has been evangelized, a determination that Walter Kreck correctly dismisses as unverifiable.[34] At any rate, this is the focal point of the Kingdom. The dynamic of the proclamation of the gospel will dominate the last days. In place of the blinding of the minds of unbelievers, there will be eyes opened by "the light of the gospel of the glory of Christ" (2 Cor. 4:4), by the offense of the cross, "the power of God for salvation to every one who has faith" (Rom. 1:16). In the last days the preaching of the gospel is the focal point of *all* the signs. In it all the signs can and must be understood. From this perspective the signs are not isolated events with some formal character validating them as signs. The point is the *purpose* of Christ's coming: "God sent the Son into the world, not to condemn the world, but that the world might be saved through him" (John 3:17). When this is given its proper place, it is obvious how misdirected is the special attention given to the catastrophic aspect of the signs.

With this decisive gospel, a wholesome and critical regulation of insight comes into the world and illumines the way to the future. It is not an analysis of the bewildering complexities of history, but a pointer to the light that has already appeared ("the old has passed away; the new has come" — 2 Cor. 5:17). "The darkness," John writes, "is passing away and the true light is already shining" (1 John 2:8); thus, the eyes must remain open to all the signs of the coming Kingdom. But this preparedness does not take the form of seeing the signs as neutral formal proofs of the nearness of the parousia. It must take the form of faith wisely and perceptively conformed to the unanimous witness of the New Testament.

33. Cf. Chapter IV above, pp. 129ff.
34. Kreck, *Die Zukunft des Gekommenen* (1961), p. 163.

Because it is Christ who reveals what is great and small in the eyes of God, the community of believers may no longer be captivated by what may superficially appear to be important but has nothing to do with service (cf. Mark 10:43). Nor can it ignore what may seem to be small, trivial and inconspicuous. The mourning are comforted (Matt. 5:4), the persecuted blessed (vs. 10); the meek shall inherit the earth (vs. 5). The wisdom of the world has been made foolish (1 Cor. 1:20); the foolishness of God is wiser than men, His weakness stronger (vs. 25).

Arguments and proud obstacles to the knowledge of God are now being exposed (2 Cor. 10:5). These basic human motives are already being clarified in history, as the Lord approaches "soon" (Rev. 22:20). As we have emphasized, this implies neither a complete removal of the veil nor a gnosticism about the course of history, but as the church reads the Bible it is filled with the "enduring message of apocalyptic,"[35] and is thus freed from the shackles of trying to reckon the date of the parousia, and also from errors.

The day drawing near

The purpose of discerning the signs, then, is to gain an understanding of the times. "You know what hour it is *(eidótes tón kairón),*" Paul says (Rom. 13:11). He is not crediting his readers with a theoretical insight into the philosophy of history and all of its ramifications, nor is he suggesting that they preoccupy themselves with an "end-time" distinct from their own time. No, Paul's point is clear: "it is full time now for you to wake from sleep."

Such is the description of the kairos. How simply the New Testament talks about knowing and understanding time in the illumination of the eschatological expectation. In the light of the time that is coming it becomes possible to understand one's own contemporary situation. This understanding does not include an answer to Augustine's unanswerable *"quid est ergo tempus?"*[36] This is an understanding of time from the point of view of the salvation that has appeared and is being proclaimed. On the road to the fulfilment, the harvest, we have kairos, the opportunity to do what is good (Gal. 6:10). We must "make the most of the time" (Eph. 5:16; Col. 4:5). That

35. H. H. Rowley, *The Relevance of Apocalyptic* (1955), chapter IV.
36. *Confessions,* XI.xiv.

is possible only through the guidance of the Holy Spirit, who opens our eyes so that no mistake is possible.

Our knowledge of events is fraught with hesitation and uncertainty; explanations elude us. International tensions repeatedly bring to light our fallibility and finiteness. But what does the New Testament have to say about understanding time? A simple insight, a clear discernment into profound motives in the light of the Lord: "You have been anointed by the Holy One, and you all know" (1 John 2:20).[37] This was written during a perilous period in the history of the community, when the lie threatened to replace the truth of God. This "knowing" is not an esoteric secret, nor is the "anointing" something to be arrogant about. It is a knowledge from the Spirit, founded in Jesus Christ, who has not abandoned His elect, but guides them into all the truth (John 16:13). In this clarity and simplicity there is something that calls forth our endurance when the complexities of human existence threaten to engulf us and obscure our vision. This simplicity and consolation cannot be lost unless we see the signs of the times from the fulfilment of time in Christ's coming (Mark 1:15). The church must realize and understand that the night is far gone and the day at hand (Rom. 13:12). It is called to this insight in times of chaos and in times of prosperity and progress. The Kingdom of God is coming — in grace and judgment — and its compels us to make decisions with regard to everything that alienates man from salvation and everything that confirms him in it.

This is how *time* should be understood by the Christian community. The language of the last things is not the language of the spectacular or the supernatural; nor is it dependent on the evolution of one's world-view. It is too simple and childlike to satisfy scientific demands. But it was for this childlikeness (*apekálypsas autá nēpíois*) that Jesus thanked His Father (Matt. 11:26). Childlike, we understand the call to steadfastness "all the more as you see the Day drawing near" (Heb. 10:25).

"You see the Day drawing near . . ." — how ingenuous these words sound in our dark and disoriented age. What is the secret reality of this seeing? The time may have been fulfilled in

---

37. Cf. KJV, ASV, "ye know all things." According to Schnackenburg, *Die Johannesbriefe* (1953), p. 135, the considerations involved are manuscript testimony and grammatical questions (*pánta* as object of *oídate;* the lack of an object for *oídate* if one chooses *pántes*). Schnackenburg finally opts for *pántes* as the *lectio difficilior*.

Christ, but what of our times, when the psalmist's expression seems more appropriate: "We do not see our signs; there is no longer any prophet, and there is none among us who knows how long" (74:9)? What is the believer's seeing and understanding of the time? Psalm 74 is often said to be symptomatic of the religious vacuum in Israel that was filled by apocalyptic. But then, what is meant by this "seeing the day drawing near?" Is it not unreal to talk about this "seeing" when we know that we cannot distinguish a supernatural realm to which the signs belong? Does it make sense to look for signs in the immanent and determinate process of present history? Do signs still play a role in the life of the community?

It is not easy to answer these questions. There was a day when the signs were in the forefront of every sermon about time: anything unusual or catastrophic was claimed to be a sign of the times. Whether or not they were sensational, these sermons were always somewhat incredible, because of their onesided emphasis on the dark side of things. Gradually the frequency of such sermons abated. The ominous themes were too forced: people became used to hearing prophecies of doom and started taking them for granted. Furthermore, they became accustomed to seeing the kinds of events that reportorial eschatology called certain signs of the end. The very days of catastrophe — of wars, famines, and earthquakes — can draw attention away from the eschaton and plunge us deep into defeatism or perspectiveless determinism. Finally, a great uncertainty can overtake us when we consider that the worst terrors from our point of view are not supernatural at all, but natural, brought on by the power of man. And surely no one would care to maintain any longer that we need not be intimidated by certain somber possibilities on the basis of the contention that what we already know about future events from the New Testament does not mention this kind of calamities.

Lacking that kind of certainty, how should we face the future? How shall we see the day approaching? What is the content of the reassurance that God guides the course of history, and that Jesus Christ has been given all power in heaven and on earth? What shall we make of the hiddenness of Christ's regime, at the same time trying to discern the signs of the times? There is a close parallel here with John's vision recorded in Revelation 5: "no one was found worthy to open the scroll or to look into it" (vs. 4). Obviously the contents of the

scroll were important: John wept much over its apparent inaccessibility. But there was no reason to be dismayed because
Christ, who has conquered, is found worthy to open the book
(vv. 5, 9).

The Lamb and the scroll

Nowhere is Christ's central meaning for the future more clearly indicated. The future is not a dark, impenetrable mystery;
it is what Christ came to disclose. What are we to make of this
imagery? The Lamb, standing before the throne of God as one
slain, takes the scroll from the right hand of Him who is seated
on the throne (5:6f.). One by one He opens the seven seals
(6:1, 3, 5, 7, 9, 12; 8:1). In apocalyptic language, history under
His dominion is being unrolled. Does this mean that, armed
with this principle, we can survey and scrutinize and comprehend the broad contours of human history with this more profound insight? No, we know that this principle does not provide us with a special gnosis elevated beyond all other knowledge. But does this then not leave us with an inevitable, neutral
interpretation of history with its aspects of light and dark? Is
the slain Lamb anything more than an irrelevant abstraction?
Or is there a possibility for us to transcend "believing" by
"seeing," in order to see the day approaching? One thing is
certain: we cannot use this passage as mere predictions with
which to reckon the date of Christ's return. What is important
is the perspective of faith. This vision is not a list of sudden
miracles that will take place in an "end-time" and make everything clear. There are signs during every era in which Christ
reigns. This was true in the days of the letter to the Hebrews
when persecutions hounded the believers, and in the days of
John, when, in the face of the revelation of the "antichrist,"
the last hour was proclaimed (see Chapter IX below).

It is apparent from all this that the New Testament signs
do not pertain to an objective, chronological report or description, but to the deep dimensions that, in the light of the crucified Lord, determine the course of history. This realization is
as important in periods of prosperity and progress as in times
of dire need and universal upheaval. Like a tightly stretched
bow, the eschaton stands above times in which one talks about
the *corpus Christianum* and above times of apostasy, secularization, and persecution. It must be related as much to the "golden
ages" as to apocalyptic periods. To pay attention to the signs

of the times is to understand time. This understanding is free from arbitrary calculation, and it has nothing to do with an isolated "end-time."

Reportorial eschatology has always gone awry in its concretization of and emphasis on outstanding events. Despite the express warnings of the New Testament, there have always been those whose eschatology consisted largely of trying to calculate the date of the parousia and to interpret the signs of the times only in terms of some remote "end-time," rather than in terms of the last days.[38] The constructs of what we have called reportorial eschatology may seem to provide an adequate response to the theory of the delay of the parousia, but its negative effects are often not realized. In its preoccupation with war, with the chaotic phenomena of history, uncertainty enters in and the heart of the real eschatological proclamation is lost. But those who perceive in the apocalyptic pronouncements of the New Testament the utter seriousness of the fulfilment and the eschaton come to an increasing understanding of time. This understanding of time can face without wavering the proclamation of new christs and of an eschaton that the cross makes foolishness, denials that Jesus is the Christ, futile efforts at theodicy.

Our difficulties with the New Testament proclamation of the future are not because of its complexity but because of its simplicity. The true New Testament eschatology sees through every secularized eschaton as an impotent effort by man to open the scroll. It dismisses every pessimistic view of history as rash and groundless. On guard against such errors and more and more immune to them, the "sons of light and sons of the day" (1 Thess. 5:5) do not calculate, but understand in patience and faith and expectation, and in the certainty that it was not in vain that Christ died in loneliness beyond the gates of Jerusalem.

Reportorial eschatology, with its formalizing of the signs and isolating of them in an "end-time," has often been defended by the claim that, although man cannot himself unveil the mysteries of the future, Christ, in His omniscience, has revealed everything to His followers. Accordingly, the several stages of the end of times can be known by believers. But again, once one goes this far, it is extremely difficult to draw a line and

38. Cf. Schippers, *Mythologie en Eschatologie,* p. 13.

resist the urge to engage in the calculation that is forbidden. Furthermore, Christ Himself admitted that He did not know everything; for example, He did not know the day of the parousia (Matt. 24:36; Mark 13:32) . Does this have bearing on the nature of Christ's eschatological message? Obviously, this statement by Christ is a profound mystery; at the same time, the explicitness of it also makes for a certain clarity. Still, despite this clarity many interpreters hesitate to take these words literally, finding them difficult to reconcile with the divinity of Jesus Christ, which they feel implies His omniscience.[39] Now if we cannot accept that conclusion — which boils down to translating "not knowing" as "knowing" — we are bound to conclude that the very essence of Christ's message concerning the future ties in with this. Is the very point of Christ's eschatological preaching — its highest and most decisive value — perhaps not to orient us to historical events, but to point, in the images and concepts of apocalyptic, to the fulfilment of the eschaton in the last days? That He does not know the date does not detract from the importance and reliability of this message.[40] The clearly defined limit on Christ's knowledge teaches us to listen to His message. Though He knows no more of the date of the parousia than the angels do, He does know the present in all the depth out of which that day will arise. Thus *in* His not-knowing He speaks with complete certainty, pointing from the indubitable present to the future and calling for watchfulness and steadfastness.

So there is every reason to believe that the nature of Christ's eschatological preaching is related to the limitation of His knowledge that He Himself attests. It is not a limit on the reliability of what He says, but on the way in which He says it. If Mark 13:32 indeed belongs, as Rahner suggests, to the basic elements

39. The commentaries are very cautious in their treatment of this passage. H. N. Ridderbos talks about the limitation of Christ's office, which did not include omniscience; *KV* on Matthew, *ad loc.* J. A. C. van Leeuwen says that the Son "knows nothing of the day and hour" and mentions His human limitation; *KV* on Mark, *ad loc.* Grosheide refers to Acts 1:7; *Komm. ad loc.*

40. The earlier resort to a doctrine of accommodation in this connection, besides being essentially rationalistic, mistakes the profundity of Christ's preaching by explaining this statement as merely incorrect — in the name of science, of all things. Cf. Grosheide, *Hermeneutiek,* p. 130; *Christelijk Encyclopedie,* I, s.v. *accommodatie.*

of Jesus' teaching,[41] there is no reason to divorce Christ's not knowing the date of His parousia from the nature and intention of His eschatological preaching as a whole. Admittedly we are confronted here with a great mystery about the person of Christ. But we should never underestimate the significance of this clearly attested limitation of Christ's knowledge.[42]

So the church has always recognized its ignorance of the date of the parousia. Closely related to this unknown is the warning to be watchful (Mark 13:33). At the same time, however, more and more uncertainty has arisen in the Christian community over the signs of the times. We have seen how interpretation of the signs often spills over into an attempt to calculate the date of the parousia. As a result, tensions arise

41. *Loc. cit.*, p. 329n.; cf. also his "Dogmatic Reflections on the Knowledge and Self-Consciousness of Christ," *Theological Investigations*, V (Eng. tr., 1966), p. 195; and O. Cullmann, *The Christology of the NT*, p. 288, who suggests that "Mark 13:32 is much more difficult to explain as a later invention of the Church than as a genuine saying of Jesus."

42. The text in question does not appear in the parallel account in Luke 21; and the phrase "nor the Son" is lacking in several manuscripts of Matt. and Mark. Cf. T. van der Walt, *Die Koninkryk van God — naby*, pp. 244ff. Van der Walt speaks of a "bipolar Christology," with a reference to Mark 10:40 ("it is not mine to grant") that is not really too enlightening, inasmuch as 13:32 deals with Christ's knowledge. Roman Catholic theology has always been cool to the idea of Christ's not knowing, due to a general belief that Christ partook in a *visio beata et immediata* already during His earthly life. Recently, more attention has been given to the meaning of this not-knowing. Rahner in particular has broken with a long tradition in an interpretation of the *visio beata* which stresses Christ's not knowing, in order further to understand the eschatological preaching of Jesus "as a prediction about the completion of what Jesus proclaims about himself and his mission in the present. For the content of Jesus' eschatology surpasses the eschatology of his times in only one point, which is however decisive and transforms all the rest: namely, that he himself in person is salvation and judgment..."; *Theological Investigations*, IV, 338n. This is not a rejection of the uniqueness of the person of Christ nor of the *vere Deus:* it is merely the consequence of what Christ Himself says. This text has played a role in disputes over modernism in the Roman Catholic Church; cf. the correspondence between Blondel and Hügel, as recorded in R. Marlé, *Au coeur de la crise moderniste* (1960), pp. 114-38; and between Loisy and Blondel, *ibid.*, pp. 70ff. On the kenotic view of the *visio beata*, see also E. Gutwenger, *Bewusstsein und Wissen Christi* 1961), p. 154; and comments by E. Schillebeeckx, "Het bewustzijnsleven van Christus," *Tijdschrift voor theologie*, I, 227-51. See also Berkouwer, *De strijd om het Rooms-katholieke dogma* (1940); *The Person of Christ* (Eng. tr., 1954), pp. 211ff. On the *visio beata*, see further Chapter XII below.

with respect to constructs about the "end-time," which frequently disturb the faith-consciousness of the Christian community. These tensions are directly related to how one understands the Bible's witness about the eschaton, a relationship that is demonstrated by the confusion caused by various sects, who base their eschatology squarely on their own hermeneutics.

Holding to the clarity of Scripture, the church has usually resisted such confusions. Still, about the signs of the times, uncertainty remains. In the next three chapters, we shall discuss three of these eschatological themes or "signs" in greater detail: first, the negative sign of the antichrist; next, the positive sign of the millennium; and finally the theme that probably draws more attention than any other in contemporary eschatology, the future of Israel as a sign.

CHAPTER NINE

THE ANTICHRIST

P ROBABLY THE FIRST association that enters the mind of most people when they hear the term "antichrist" is a sense of great mysteriousness. To be sure, we hear a lot of talk about antichristian powers or movements, but there is a long-standing tradition that applies the term "antichrist" to a person of the future. Although this person will be known because of his intent, there is still a great deal of mystery about him. Although we may be acquainted with a few facts about him, it seems that all we really know is that he is not here.

Person or power?

It is not as if people have given a great deal of serious thought to this traditional figure of the future out of either apprehension or steadfast faith in the Almighty. Reflection on the antichrist fluctuates considerably. At present, there is nothing like the concentration on the approaching danger of the antichrist that led Hepp to his dire challenge of 1919: "To the tents, and mobilize for the conflict!"[1]

What about the antichrist? The urgent language of Hepp's appeal was intended to convey the *actuality* of the witness concerning the antichrist (although Hepp adds immediately that the antichrist might well not appear for another century or more). How is the church to react to what the New Testament clearly depicts as actuality when it talks about the antichrist? For in the deepest sense, the point of what the Bible has to say cannot be this characteristic "mysteriousness" of the antichrist, but a message that demands close attention.

The effort has often been made to do away with this mysteriousness by arriving at a set of descriptions that will make the antichrist easily recognizable when he comes. But this mys-

1. V. Hepp, *De Antichrist* (1919), p. 255.

teriousness will not be done away with so easily, for the passages in the Bible that talk about the antichrist do not readily lend themselves to this enterprise. This results in a curious situation. If ever certainty, clarity, and the possibility of recognition seem to be necessary, it is here. After all, Scripture is very real and serious in its treatment of the antichrist. It is as if we are armed against an imminent danger that approaches from among human existence. In the same way that the community must resist (antistête) the devil (James 4:7) who prowls around like a roaring lion (1 Pet. 5:8), it is called to arm itself against the final danger, the ultimate eschatological confrontation. Uncertainty here would surely be fatal.[2]

A survey of the historic teachings about the antichrist brings two main lines of thought to the fore: (1) that the antichrist is a power or movement; and (2) that the antichrist is a human person at the end of history. Naturally, the second line of thought does not exclude talk of antichristian tendencies and powers, but it sees all these as eventually being consummated in the figure of the antichrist. Those who take this expectation seriously have often been filled with anxiety about the prospect of his coming, unless they could defer the expectation of him to some remotely future generation.

The concreteness of their expectation of the antichrist has often led people to conclude on the basis of the existential situations in which they found themselves that the antichrist was presently in the midst of human life and that they faced an immediate eschatological confrontation with him. No longer was attention directed to the various unchristian or antichristian forces in human life; people thought of one human being, who, because of his completely antithetical actions, could be judged to be a "sign" of the end of time. This identification of the ultimate opposition is prevalent in times of crisis and exceptional danger. The person apparently responsible for the critical situation is considered to be the antichrist. Time and again, this shock of recognition, this identification of the antichrist bolstered by proof-texts, has been followed by a reaction when the measure of chaos introduced by the alleged antichrist turns out to have fallen short of being the ultimate conflict after all. With the return of relative stability, concern about the anti-

2. There is a parallel here with the mysteriousness of the sin against the Holy Spirit, which also requires the believer to be on his guard. Cf. Berkouwer, *Sin* (Eng. tr., 1971), pp. 323ff.

christ subsides. We see this, for example, in the disappearance of the identification of Nero as antichrist in the fourth century after the Edicts of Galerius and Constantine ended persecution of the church. Apocalyptic terror was replaced by feelings of security and peace.[3]

A radical and intriguing example of identification of the antichrist arose during the Reformation, when individual popes and the papacy itself were thought by many to be the antichrist. The gravity of this identification — surely one of the most painful aspects of the conflict between Roman Catholic and Protestant — is apparent when one considers the high place the Roman Catholic Church accords to the pope as vicar of Christ.[4]

The Reformers' attack on the papacy is easy to dismiss as "antipapism," but we ought to analyze the background and motives that led to this identification. Althaus gives Luther a great deal of credit for his position, not because Althaus would agree with Luther's particular identification of the antichrist as an objective fact, but because Luther's position was eschatologically actual — something to be watchful for — and not

3. Cf. Pauly, *Real-Encyclopädie der klassischen Altertumswissenschaft*, s.v. *Antichrist*, I, 583; Augustine, *De Civitate Dei*, XX.xiii. L. Müller, in his introduction to Vladimir Soloviev, *Übermensch und Antichrist. Über das Ende der Weltgeschichte* (1958), discusses the relevance of the year 1836 for J. H. Jung (pseud. Heinrich Stilling) and Bengel. When the year passed, apocalyptic disquiet also subsided (p. 7). Soloviev himself, under the influence of the teaching of Nietzsche (who wrote *Der Antichrist* in 1888), saw history as going *sub specie venturi Antichristi*. Soloviev's "short story of the Antichrist" (Eng. tr., 1915) is well known. Identifications of the antichrist have been frequent throughout history. At the time of the French Revolution and the Napoleonic wars, the identification of Napoleon with Apollyon (Rev. 9:11) was common. In 1799 Jung (Stilling) wrote his famous *Siegesgeschichte der Christlichen Religion in einer gemeinnutzigen Erklärung der Offenbarung Johannis*, discussed by H. Schlier, "Vom Antichrist," in *Theologische Aufsätze für Karl Barth* (1936), p. 119. Cf. also the comments on the German miracle play *Ludus de Antichristo* (ca. 1160) by F. Schumann, "Geschichtstheologische Fragen um den Ludus de Antichristo," in *Gedenkschriften für W. Elert* (1935), pp. 62-71.

4. Among the extensive literature on this struggle are H. Preuss, *Die Vorstellungen vom Antichrist im späteren Mittelalter bei Luther und in der konfessionallen Polemik* (1906); E. Bizer, *Luther und der Papst* (1958); Althaus, *Die letzten Dinge*, pp. 282-97. On Calvin's position cf. H. Berger, *Calvins Geschichtsauffassung* (1955), pp. 73ff. John Henry Newman was also concerned with this problem, stating in the *Apologia pro Vita Sua* that he himself had thought the pope was the antichrist (beginning with Gregory I) until 1843.

futuristic. Luther felt himself surrounded by great eschatological tensions, and part of this for him included the role played by the antichrist. For Luther the antichrist was not a remote figure of some future "end-time" but a threatening and dangerous possibility each and every day. Given this kind of expectation of the future (we might call it a *Naherwartung*) the contours of world and church history become extremely important. Luther concentrated his attention on *the last hour*. Besides 2 Thessalonians 2:4, he read Psalm 10.[5] This psalm had traditionally been related to the antichrist, and Luther felt that the unrestrained opposition to the believers recorded in it clearly anticipated the situation prevalent in his day. "Arise, O LORD" (vs. 12) undoubtedly referred to the last day. Luther believed that the fulfilment of this psalm was taking place in his day, and his suspicion became certainty when he related the identification to *the last hour*.[6]

Calvin was no less concerned with this problem than Luther, particularly in connection with the unyielding opposition of the Roman Catholic Church to evangelical doctrine. The difference between Luther and Calvin was that the latter tended to identify the antichrist not so much with an individual pope, but with the ecclesiastical kingdom that would allegedly be sustained through all the ages. In principle, however, there was a good deal of agreement between the two Reformers here.[7] Not that all this was original with the Reformers. When Luther first mentioned to Georg Spalatin his suspicions about the pope, this identification already had a long history, summed up in the medieval question *an papa sit antichristus?*[8] For Luther the problem became more eschatologically oriented.[9] In times that clearly reflected to him the last hour, he spoke angry and unambiguous words of warning and resistance. The pope was

5. Bizer, *op. cit.*, pp. 11ff.
6. Kliefoth proceeds from the argument that the antichrist is a figure of "the last of all times" to reject Luther's identification as unbiblical because "in accordance with the word of prophecy there would still be another age." *Christliche Eschatologie* (1886), pp. 218ff. But Luther's belief was precisely that his age was "the last of all times." On Luther cf. also W. Köhler, *Dogmengeschichte*, II, 486ff. Köhler points out that Luther found confirmation in the sun eclipses of 1514, 1518, and 1531.
7. Cf. Calvin's commentaries *ad* 2 Thess. 2:7; 1 John 2:18; *Inst.*, IV.ii.12; IV.vii.25.
8. Cf. F. Heiler, *Der Katholizismus. Seine Idee und Erscheinung* (1923).
9. Cf. T. F. Torrance, *Kingdom and Church* (1956), pp. 20ff.

considered to rank along with the Turks as the greatest danger to the Christian faith.[10] The main point was that the danger was *present,* not relegated to the future.[11]

So the problem of the antichrist should not be dismissed blithely. We may smile condescendingly and talk about their "obvious error" when we hear that the Reformers identified pope and antichrist. But if our condescension stems from the notion that the antichrist is some remote phenomenon to appear in an end-time long after us, we have forgotten that the Reformers' intuitive conception of an actual and active antichrist is a New Testament emphasis. Let us consider, then, this actuality of the New Testament antichrist in the remainder of this chapter.

The actuality of the antichrist is tied in with the divergence in the concepts of antichrist that we discussed earlier; that is, whether the antichrist is a movement or power, or whether he is a person. Those who see the antichrist in terms of antichristian power naturally admit to this actuality because every era is more or less confronted by the power and influence of antichristian movements. On the other hand, those who personify the antichrist may also consider him an actuality. Even though the time of his appearance is not known, it is inconceivable that his actuality will fade away because an early appearance is not expected. Traditionally there has been a strong preference for a personal concept of the antichrist, based in large measure on 2 Thessalonians 2:8, where Paul establishes a close connection between the coming of the lawless one and the parousia of the Lord. There seems to be a strongly personal aspect to Paul's description of the annihilation of the antichrist: "the Lord Jesus will slay him with the breath of his mouth and destroy him by his appearing and his coming."

10. In 1529 the Turks were threatening Vienna, which Luther interpreted as a sign of the imminence of the Kingdom. Most of all, however, he was attracted by the immediately ecclesiastical aspect of the antichrist. Cf. R. Pfister, "Reformation, Türken und Islam," *Zwingliana* (1956), 360-64. In the Articles of Smalcald, the Turks are mentioned specifically as *christianorum atroces hostes.*

11. It is interesting to note the gradual change of this identification as time passed. The simple equivalence of pope with antichrist faded away in pietism and during the Enlightenment. In the 19th century the pope was seen by some as the forerunner of the antichrist. Later the figure changed to the "anti-Christian" in Rome. Barth spoke of the doctrine of *analogia entis* as the invention of the antichrist. Cf. Preuss, *op. cit.,* pp. 266ff.

Antichrist and antichrists

The impression created by what is said in this letter to Thessalonica of a *personal* antichrist has strongly influenced later thought. On the basis of this passage, along with the principle of the unity and harmony of Scripture, some students of the subject have interpreted the other texts that refer to the antichrist, concluding that 2 Thessalonians 2:8 necessarily decided the issue. But we must remember that where the Bible uses the name "antichrist" itself — in the epistles of John — it speaks about this antichrist in a different way from Paul. Moreover, we ought not to read and interpret John on the basis of Paul. In the first place, the clear notion of *the* personal antichrist is not to be found in John. He says that the believers have heard that an antichrist will come, and adds, "so now many antichrists *(antichristoi polloi)* have come" (1 John 2:18). Suddenly we are confronted by a number of antichrists, not as something in a distant future, but as a present reality. The actuality — whether of "antichrist" or "antichrists" — looms large. All of it is summarized in one unmistakable characterization that would seem to rule out any possibility of doubt: "This is the antichrist, he who denies the Father and the Son" (2:22; cf. 2 John 7).

How is this to be reconciled? A common solution is to distinguish between "forerunners" (antichrists) and *the* antichrist.[12] The "antichrists" are presently with us; the "antichrist" will appear at the end of history. In this sense Bavinck referred to the antichristian powers throughout history, but believed that one day these powers would be embodied in one kingdom of the world, the apotheosis of apostasy.[13] At any rate, whether John is talking about antichrists or the antichrist, the crux of his message is a warning. The central meaning of the antichrist, according to John, is the great lie, the denial that Jesus is the Christ. The antichrist assumes the form of ultimate heresy, a false doctrine that will some day appear. This realization would seem to militate against the conclusion that the "antichrists" are merely forerunners of a final antichrist. There is no hint here of two concepts concerning present and future; it is *one* forceful message.

12. K. Dijk, *Het einde der eeuwen*, p. 156; Hepp, *op. cit.*, Chap. IV. Hepp names as forerunners Herod and Pilate among others.
13. *GD*, IV, 659.

The hour, which was announced in advance, has come. In the appearance of the many antichrists and the liar, John discerns the last hour (1 John 2:18; 4:3). According to Schnackenburg, "with the warning note that 'antichrists have come' John intends to characterize contemporary time as eschatologically meaningful and call his readers to watchfulness in the face of the danger threatening them."[14] Exceptional watchfulness is required, for the last and apparently decisive hour has come. The alarm sounds, the enemy is before the gates, or rather, he has already infiltrated into the city. John returns to this theme later in the epistle: "every spirit which does not confess Jesus is not of God. This is the spirit of antichrist of which you heard that it was coming, and now it is in the world *already*" (4:3). He is already operative through the infectious lie. This evident presence is the primary argument against the view that the many antichrists are merely "forerunners."[15] Rather, John identifies the antichrist in the unmistakably clear form in which the community of believers might recognize him. For John "the antichrist is 'coming' in the false teachers; that is, he is to be understood as a phenomenon of the 'last hour' realized in the false teachers."[16] Elsewhere he writes: "For many deceivers have gone out into the world, men who will not acknowledge the coming of Jesus Christ in the flesh; such a one is the deceiver *(ho plános)* and the antichrist" (2 John 7). Instead of an idea of "forerunners," the emphasis is on *the* antichrist, *the* deceiver, as herald of the last hour. What the believers had heard was now appearing before them in the reality of the great heresy.[17] For John, every-

14. Schnackenburg, *Die Johannesbriefe,* p. 125.
15. Calvin was particularly concerned with harmonizing 2 Thess. 2:8 and 1 John 2:18. "John only meant that certain sects had already arisen which were fore-runners of a future scattering.... Properly speaking, antichrist was not yet in existence. But the mystery of his ungodliness was working secretly." The way to learn to know antichrist is from Paul's description (that is, in 2 Thess. 2), and thus Calvin arrives at the notion of "fore-runner" as an interpretation of John. Cf. his commentary *ad* 1 John 2:18.
16. Schnackenburg, *loc. cit:*
17. For the idea of "forerunner" cf. Dijk, *op. cit.,* p. 149; H. Asmussen, *Wahrheit und Liebe* (1949), p. 64; Greijdanus, *Comm., ad loc.* Opposed to the idea are Pauly, *loc. cit.;* R. J. van der Meulen, "Veractualisering van de Antichrist," in *Arcana Revelata* (1951), p. 69. Van der Meulen says that the false teachers were not forerunners, but "in them the Antichrist of the end was present." It seems to me, then, that van der Meulen is inconsistent when he says that John divorces the *actual* antichrist from the present (p. 74).

thing depends on how one responds to this deception. The denial
of the Son entails that one does not have the Father (2:22; cf.
3:24; 4:3f.). The No of the false teachers stands in obvious
opposition to the Yes of God in Jesus Christ (cf. 2 Cor. 1:20).
It is John's intent to make this clear to the believers, to point
out a "unique front" — false prophecy (1 John 4:1).[18]

The false teachers have often been considered to be gnostics
of some form or other. For John the summa of the gospel is that
Jesus is the Christ (1 John 5:1, 5). Christ is not an apparition,
distinguishable from the historical Jesus, but one who came "by
water and blood . . . not with the water only but with the water
and the blood" (vs. 6), a polemical remark directed against
those who admitted the baptism of Jesus but denied the redemptive power of the blood of the cross. There are three witnesses, John says: Spirit, water, and blood (vs. 8). In this defense against deception, the community is equipped with sufficient insight to discern the antichrist.[19]

Understandably, the *actuality* of the biblical account of the
antichrist is the emphasis of much reflection on 1 John. This
actuality is apparent when we consider that the heresy to which
John was addressing himself was not something remotely abstract, but something that had been preached by false teachers
who had gone out from that community (2:19). Their departure had revealed what motivated them most deeply, but the
fact that they had risen from among the community urged
watchfulness and extreme caution. This should not be interpreted as an "actualizing" of the idea of antichrist. Wherever the
Bible uses the word "antichrist," it refers to something real
and actually present. Thus, John's intent was not to *actualize*
the antichrist, but to *activate* the congregation.

Clearly, the actuality of the antichrist as portrayed by John
accords with the entire eschatological proclamation of the New
Testament. Althaus correctly observed that the New Testament
proclamation of the antichrist is not an irrelevant prediction of
some remote future, but an alarm signal: "The church must
always look for the antichrist as a reality present among it or
as an immediately threatening future possibility. . . . The recog-

18. Schnackenburg, *op. cit.*, p. 14.
19. There is a noteworthy parallel between this polemic of John and that
of Paul against those who claimed spiritual gifts (1 Cor. 12). In the
latter passage the central issue is the confession that Jesus is *kýrios;*
the heresy expressed itself in the *anáthema 'Iēsoús* of some (vs. 3).

nition of the antichrist is a deadly serious matter; all other talk about antichrist is idle and irresponsible play."[20]

One wonders whether this Johannine perspective is not completely lost in circles where there is a belief in a personal antichrist projected into a more or less distant future. On such views, what one has is a kind of "knowledge" of an event that is coming sometime, but does not really affect the present. Compare this with the actuality of the antichrist as it was seen during the days of the Reformation. There was certainly more eschatological seriousness and expectation then than there is among those who hold to this idea of an essentially vague and undetermined personality of the future. Curiously, the Reformers — though they certainly gave due consideration to 1 John — generally relied on 2 Thessalonians, a passage that has customarily been used as support for the interpretation of the antichrist as person. The Reformers, however, focused on the idea that the antichrist, rather than being external, proceeded immediately from the church itself.

The religious cloak

This "religious" character of the opposition preoccupied the Reformers. Theirs was not just the bitter tone of antipapism. They were predominantly concerned and anxious about the well-being of the church. Calvin was not worried greatly that the name of Christ or of the church would be wiped out. He was concerned that the antichrist "misuses a semblance of Christ and lurks under the name of the church as under a mask."[21] Thus 2 Thessalonians 2:4 plays an important role in Reformational polemics, because, according to Paul, the man of lawlessness "takes his seat in the temple of God." The Articles of Smalcald, as well as Calvin, refer to this. It was clear to Calvin that this text "cannot be understood otherwise than of the papacy."[22] *In the temple of God:* this prophecy was being fulfilled right before his eyes. The temple was being profaned by "sacrileges beyond number."[23] This reference to Paul's words is not a reduction of the antithetical character of the antichrist, but an indication of a specific mode of his activity. For the Reformers the antichrist was all the more dangerous because he

20. *Die letzten Dinge,* pp. 283, 285.
21. *Inst.,* IV.vii.25.
22. *Ibid.,* IV.ii.12.
23. *Comm., ad* 2 Thess. 2:4.

donned this religious cloak. Similarly, Vladimir Soloviev, fascinated by the phenomenon that evil invariably manifests itself in the guise of the good — *sub specie boni* — interpreted 2 Thessalonians 2:4 in this light: because the danger comes from within, the church has added reason to beware in her own existence.

During the Reformation, this theme of the antichrist's taking his seat in the temple of God was taken very seriously. The temple of God was not that in Jerusalem, but the church, and the antichrist's strategy was primarily to drive the true God out of this temple and replace Him.[24] Prior to the fourth century, however, the church had supposed the word "temple" to refer to the real temple, and only later was this interpretation gradually replaced by that of "church." Zahn points out that at the time of Paul's second epistle to the Thessalonians the temple had not yet been destroyed and was still considered by Christians to be the house of God. Even so Zahn recognizes the element of profanation: "The temple at Jerusalem appears as the *form* of something far more comprehensive." In other words, whatever is meant by "temple," the horror is that which the Reformers experienced — *in the church*.[25]

All of this is closely related to the way Paul described the antagonist, the man of lawlessness. What is primarily important is that Paul was addressing himself to the believers in Thessalonica, who were on the verge of losing all perspective and living as if "the day of the Lord has come" (2 Thess. 2:2).[26] Whatever the precise background of this feeling was, what is at issue is the actuality of the day of the Lord in the highest sense. The concentrated expectation had been replaced by the experience of the present; the "not yet" had given way to an "already." Paul sees the acute hazards in this substitution, and objects to the Thessalonians' "already" as a perversion of the truly Pauline "already" (2:2f.). He returns to the theme of "not yet" in order to reintroduce the dynamic into the static

24. Cf. J. A. C. van Leeuwen, *Kommentar*, p. 427; R. Schippers, *op. cit.*, p. 13; M. J. Westhuizen, *De Antichrist in het NT* (1916), p. 59.
25. Cf. Zahn, *Komm.*, ad loc.
26. *hōs hóti enéstēken hē hēméra toú kyríou.* KJV: "as that the day of Christ is at hand"; ASV — "as that the day of the Lord is just at hand." G. Vos offers "has already arrived"; *The Pauline Eschatology*, p. 95. See also commentaries ad loc. by B. Rigeaux and J. A. C. van Leeuwen, and also ad 3:11 (concerning the relation of this to the parousia problematics of the Thessalonians).

life of the community. The day of the Lord must *first* be preceded by apostasy and the man of lawlessness (vv. 3f.).

It is these words in particular that have led to the assumption that the antichrist will be a concretely human person. It is important first of all to reject the proposition that Paul's thought here takes the form of a *Fernerwartung*, an expectation of a distant parousia. To say this misses the point: that Paul is talking about something that was very real for him too. Paul was certainly acquainted with this particular "already": "the mystery of lawlessness is already *(ḗdē)* at work" (2:7). This "already" is a radical and eschatologically decisive event, the parousia of the antichrist and the parousia of the Lord who will slay the man of lawlessness. In apocalyptic form, and with reference to the Old Testament, Paul delineates the ultimate conflict, which, though it is not yet a reality, is certainly at hand. The reference to Daniel is obvious in the salient points of the description of the man of lawlessness: setting himself up as a god, the apostate direction of those under his influence, self-exaltation, and blasphemy — all of these characterize Daniel's apocalyptic passages (cf. 7:20f., 25; 11:32). In one forceful event everything plays itself out: the "parousia" of the man of lawlessness is immediately his downfall, as prophesied in Isaiah 11:4. All of this apocalyptic imagery is intended to call the Thessalonians back to their senses, back to the expectation that was to determine the life of the community.[27] Paul was not dismissing the actuality of the expectation, but merely the static notion of an "already" that some had substituted for it. In view of all this Vos's remarks appear to be a bit hasty: "We may take it for granted, then, that the antichrist will be a human person."[28] That Paul speaks of the antichrist here in "personal" terms does not decide the issue; for this was also John's mode of presentation, yet John clearly spoke of an antichrist already present. This is too facile a way to deal with the elements of Old Testament apocalyptic present here. Furthermore, it allows for the notion of a long duration of time to be consummated in an "end-time" when the antichrist as person will finally appear.[29] This completely ignores the actuality that Paul is

27. Cf. Strobel, *Untersuchungen zum eschatologischen Verzögerungsproblem* (1961), p. 102: this was "an interpretation counseling caution."
28. *Op. cit.*, p. 113.
29. Cf. J. A. T. Robinson, *Jesus and His Coming* (1957), p. 106, on the "highly coloured apocalyptic passages of 2 Thessalonians." See also Schippers, *op. cit.*, pp. 10ff.

trying to preserve: the mystery is already at work! This actuality may not be threatened by a fantastic "already." Paul made room only for the final confrontation, which had to *remain* the object of the community's attention.

All of this argues against the effort to reconcile Paul and John by means of depicting John's "antichrists" as *forerunners.* Not only does this effort at harmonization fail to account for John's clear testimony to *the* antichrist in the last hour, but it also misinterprets the intention of the apocalyptic representations — that is, precisely to make possible a recognition of the "anti" as it manifests itself in the historical process. There is no reason to posit with certainty on the basis of the New Testament that the antichrist as portrayed there is a person of the end of history. Yet this has frequently been supposed, partly on the grounds of 2 Thessalonians 2 (with consequences for 1 John 2), partly because the personal aspect lends itself to being taken more seriously than "antichristian powers." Obviously this latter is erroneous reasoning, if only because "person" and "powers" are not all that easy to separate.

Extreme caution must be taken before one attempts any concretization of the "anti." Neither the personal aspect nor the power aspect may be excluded a priori. The "anti" can cling to the forms and dynamics of history in many different ways. What we are *not* given in the New Testament is a photograph-like representation of the antichrist. The heart of the message is the permanent state of watchfulness to which we are called. One signal recurs time and again. The antichrist, the many antichrists, the deceiver, the antagonist, the man of lawlessness: the "anti" assumes numerous shapes depending on times and circumstances. But it is always recognizable.

Before investigating further this problem of variety, we should pause to consider a theory in which the religious motif (the temple of 2 Thessalonians 2 in the polemic of the Reformers) assumes a special form in the so-called imitation-motif. What this means can best be illustrated by reference to the meaning of the prefix "anti." How correct is it to translate this preposition by the simple word "against?" Is there not an element of replacement involved here?[30] In other words, is the primary sense of "antichrist" not someone bent on usurping the place of God and Christ? It is important to note that the

30. Cf. Büchsel, in *TDNT*, s.v. *anti*, I, 372f. Cf. 1 Pet. 5:8 *(antidikos)*.

translation of "anti" as "in place of" does not necessarily imply a weakening of its other meaning — "against." "In place of" indicates a specific mode of being against.

Now this nuance of "in place of" has been developed by some theologians into the "imitation-motif" we mentioned above. In other words, the antichrist assumes the image of Christ with the intent of misleading.[31] Werner Foerster sees an "antithetic parallelism" between the slain Lamb and the antichrist as portrayed in Revelation 13. The horns of the beast are described as "like a lamb" in verse 11. This opponent of Christ is thought to take on the image of the Lamb in his attempt to mislead.[32] E. Stauffer is most emphatic on this score, stating that the antichrist's pet theme is "a perverted Good Friday, of antichrist's mortal wounds and their miraculous healing."[33]

Now what is at issue here is not just the specific tactics of the kingdom of darkness (which Paul talks about in 2 Cor. 11:14) or the interpretation of the "anti" as "in place of," but the motif of *imitation*. And it seems to me that the grounds adduced to prove the existence of this imitation-motif are too incidental and too weak to give it much credence. The phrase "like a lamb" in Revelation 13:11 is immediately followed by the words "it spoke like a dragon." It seems more logical to interpret this as a reference to the false prophets, who come in sheep's clothing, but inwardly are ravenous wolves (Matt. 7:15).[34] So also the alleged parallelism in the healing of the mortal wound of the first beast (Rev. 13:3) has to be treated with discretion. Some commentators see this as a prophecy of

31. Particularly with reference to the *pseudóchristoi* of Mark 13:22 and Satan's disguise as an angel of light (2 Cor. 11:14), analogous to the disguise of his servants, the false apostles. Cf. Berkouwer, *Sin*, pp. 237ff.
32. Foerster, in *TDNT*, s.v. *thērion*, III, 134f.; cf. also Zahn, *Komm.*, *ad loc.*; G. Stählin, "Die Feindschaft gegen Gott und ihre Stellung in seinem Heilsplan für die Welt," in *Der Leibhaftigkeit des Wortes* (1958). Stählin talks about the "devilish copy of Christ," "similarity to Christ," and "imitation" (pp. 55f.).
33. Stauffer, *NT Theology* (Eng. tr., 1955), p. 215. In the commentaries, examples of parallelism are numerous; cf. E. Lohmeyer, *ad* Rev. 17:8 ("the beast . . . was, and is not, and is to ascend . . ."): "like a demonic aping of the title of God 'who was and is and is to come.'" An analogy of the trinity is also found by some in Revelation: the dragon, the beast, and the false prophet. Cf. Berkhof, *CMH*, p. 115: "The Antichrist is the demonic reflection of the Son in the pattern of a trinity made up of the dragon and the two beasts." See also Kuyper, *Van de Voleinding*, IV, 242ff.
34. So Bousset, *Die Offenbarung des Johannes*, p. 424.

the destruction and subsequent revival of the Roman Empire; others relate it to the legend of the death of Nero and his subsequent return as the antichrist.[35] Undoubtedly, the wound represents the ability of the demonic power to hold its own and to manifest itself again in the face of opposition until it succumbs finally to the omnipotence of the Lamb.

What comes to the fore, then, is the element of the apocalyptic conflict of power, not the element of imitation.[36] Great power is at the disposal of a fierce "anti," just as the dragon wages war in anger on those who keep the commands of God (Rev. 12:17). The beast of the sea (13:1-10) is also controlled by the powerful "anti," who is portrayed in all his terror and godless blasphemy. One is reminded of the fourth beast of Daniel 7 challenging the Most High and His saints (vs. 25).[37] The "anti" evidences itself in contemptuousness, haughtiness, usurpation, radical opposition, and blasphemy (Dan. 11:36ff.). The Apocalypse is filled with rumors of war, as the nations gather from the four corners of the earth for conflict and besiege the encampment of the saints and the holy city (Rev. 20:7-10; cf. Luke 21:20).

In the exercise of this power, the two witnesses are killed (Rev. 11:7),[38] and authority is given to the beast "over every tribe and people and tongue and nation" (13:7). His jurisdiction seems unchallengeable: "if any one is to be taken captive, to captivity he goes" (13:10). The struggle is depicted in the strongest terms: everything is at stake. It is concentrated no longer in the four beasts of Daniel 7, but in the one beast as

35. For the former interpretation, cf. Greijdanus, *Comm., ad loc.* The historical background of the Nero-legend has been thoroughly investigated by various scholars. Cf. Paul S. Minear, "The Wounded Beast," *Journal of Biblical Literature,* LXXII (1953), 93-101. Minear understands the wound (*plēgē,* vv. 3, 14) as "a God-inflicted plague ... released through the Messiah in his crucifixion and exaltation" (p. 99). According to this exegesis the exercise of the beast's power is possible only by hiding "the fact that he has been killed." But Rev. 13 emphasizes the re-vivification and rejuvenation of the beast. The form of the worship, according to vs. 4, is "Who can fight against it?" The victory then comes up in 17:8: "The beast that you saw was, and is not, and is to ascend from the bottomless pit and go to perdition" (cf. vs. 11). Minear does not do justice to the depiction of the event.
36. Cf. V. Hepp, *De Antichrist,* pp. 176ff.
37. Cf. M. Noth, "Die Heiligen des Höchsten," in *Gesammelte Studien zum AT,* pp. 274ff.
38. Cf. D. Haugg, *Die zwei Zeugen* (1936), p. 21.

executioner of the dragon's power and deception, the counterpart of the fourth beast of Daniel, which is uniquely distinguishable from the other three (Rev. 12:9ff.; Dan. 7:7). And once
again the call sounds: persevere in the faith.

Confronting the power of the beast is the power of the Lamb,
whose victory has been assured and whose glory guaranteed
(Rev. 5:5f., 12). The conflict described here is unique, for it
leads to the victory of the slain Lamb: the blood of the Lamb
shall triumph and shall reveal His supremacy.[39] This supremacy
is the great mystery of the Apocalypse. The Lamb is worthy to
receive power, and the battle will be won in justice through
Him who is clad in a robe dipped in blood (Rev. 19:13).[40]
Thus the power of the "anti" is clearly qualified. It is a power
that looms up on the horizon of history, a universal power,
absolutizing itself and showing no respect for any boundaries.
Yet because of this contempt, the Lamb exposes its utter impotence.

Without really emphasizing the imitation-motif, it is clear
that the might of the "antichrist" is a "conditional" power. It
is an antithesis called forth by a thesis, as we can see in all
the variety of what the Bible says about antichrist. This variety
manifests itself to us as actuality. It would be meaningless to
try to systematize all these data and come up with something
like a photograph that could be used to identify the antichrist,
for the "anti" can, during the course of history, assume a multiformity of shapes and manifestations, not mere ideas but concrete realities. The systematizer is bound to run aground on
1 John 2 and 2 Thessalonians 2. Systematization here misses
the point of what is revealed about the antichrist. When the
light of the eschaton falls on time, it calls forth the "anti" —
the one "anti" — in its various forms. To say this is not to
dehistoricize the idea of the antichrist. Quite the contrary,
simply because the times and circumstances into which the "anti"
makes its inroads change, there must be continuous reinterpretation of the idea of the antichrist.[41] We might legitimately

39. W. Koester, "Kirche und Lamm in der Apokalyps," in *Vom Wort des
Lebens* (1951).
40. Cf. H. Schlier, "Zum Verständnis der Geschichte nach der Offenbarung
Johannes," in *Die Zeit der Kirche*, pp. 265ff.; and *Vom Antichrist. Zum
13. Kapitel der Offenbarung Johannes*, pp. 16ff.
41. R. Schippers, *op. cit.*, p. 10.

speak of a "pneumatic-historic" view of the antichrist.[42] Let us consider a couple of examples that bring out this idea of reinterpretation.

Reinterpretation

First of all, we can examine the "desolating sacrilege" (or "abomination of desolation") in Christ's eschatological sermon of Mark 13. What is noteworthy is that Christ does not speak about this horror as about an event in some ancient past. There is a particularly prominent actuality about what He says. A very relevant admonition is evident: "when *you* see the desolating sacrilege set up . . ." (Mark 13:14).[43] Christ is not referring back to the tribulations of Israel during the time of Antiochus Epiphanes, but to today and tomorrow. When the desolating sacrilege comes, Christ proclaims, "then let those who are in Judea flee to the mountains." Daniel's words are assumed into a relevant proclamation dealing with a grave crisis affecting Judea and putting its inhabitants to flight. There is widespread uncertainty as to the precise meaning of this "desolating sacrilege,"[44] but this much is clear: it constitutes an admonition reinterpreting Daniel's vision. What Daniel says is applied to the imminent

42. Consider the account of the death of the two witnesses in Rev. 11:8: "their dead bodies will lie in the street of the great city which is allegorically *(pneumatikōs)* called Sodom and Egypt, where their Lord was crucified." Lohmeyer writes, correctly, that the images of the Apocalypse are thus only to be understood "pneumatically" *(op. cit.,* p. 91). This is something other than what is understood in history as "spiritualizing," for it is not a fading of history, but a reference to the fact that its applicability and actuality are not captured in and limited to one particular time. Despite some valuable insights in his commentary, Lohmeyer's train of thought is too much determined by the notion of timelessness, as evidenced by what he says about John: "Thus time and history do not concern him, only the suprahistorical and subterranean powers" *(ibid.,* p. 190 and *passim).*
43. *hótan dé idéte.* Cf. Matt. 24:15. Matthew refers back to Daniel, and describes the desolating sacrilege as "standing in the holy place"; Mark refers to it as "set up where it ought not to be."
44. The masculine form of the participle in Mark 13:14 *(hestēkóta)* to modify the neuter *bdélygma* (the so-called *constructio ad sensum)* has led some to conclude that a person is meant, namely, Caligula. Rowley points out the parallel between Antiochus and Caligula, each of whom commissioned a statue of himself in the temple. Cf. also J. A. C. van Leeuwen, *Komm., ad loc.;* H. N. Ridderbos, *KV* on Matt. 24:15, and *The Coming of the Kingdom,* pp. 488ff.; Bolkestein, *Het verborgen rijk* (1954), p. 283.

destruction of the temple in Jerusalem. In this way the eschaton becomes transparent for contemporary life. This is no forced actualization, but an indication of what really is actual. En route to the future the warning against the abomination sounds. This abomination appears in forms that depend on the circumstances. Such a variety is evident among the Gospel writers themselves. For example, Luke, without mentioning Daniel, crystallizes the abomination in his own way: "when you see Jerusalem surrounded by armies, then know that its desolation *(erḗmōsis)* has come near" (21:20).[45]

The second example is the prophecy of Gog and Magog in Ezekiel 38-39, referred to in Revelation 20. Ezekiel describes a pitched battle: hostile forces from the north engage the people of Israel and go down to ignominious defeat. The meaning of Gog in Ezekiel has been the subject of considerable debate. Is this an historical or an eschatological figure? According to Aalders, the Gog of Revelation 20 cannot be identified with Gog of Ezekiel, because the Old Testament Gog was primarily a historical power and cannot be divorced from the account of Israel's exile.[46] J. Ridderbos, on the other hand, sees Gog as directly related to the final struggle in the end of time, so that it is one with the apocalyptic prophecy of Revelation 20. Rather than being a figure from the past, Gog is the enemy of the *time after*.[47] The northern powers — the north frequently having been the origin of Israel's woes (cf. Joel 2:20) — is an image that anticipates the eclipse of the antigodly powers of the world.[48]

Now it seems to me that the historical and eschatological interpretations of Gog are not mutually exclusive. In the apocalyptic depiction of the struggle against the powers of the world (cf. the earthquake of Ezek. 38:20, 22), there can be a per-

---

45. "Abomination that makes desolate" *(shiqqûtz)* in Dan. 12:11 "denotes the desecration of the temple by an image or altar of Zeus"; Foerster, in *TDNT*, s.v. *bdélygma*, I, 600. On all these passages — Luke 21:20; Mark 13:14; Dan. 9:27; 11:31; 12:11 — cf. G. C. Aalders, "De gruwel der verwoesting," *Gereformeerd theologisch tijdschrift*, LII (1960), 1-5. Cf. also Aalders, *Comm.*, pp. 229ff., the discussion of the difference in number between Dan. 9:27 ("abominations") and Mark 13:14 ("abomination"). Aalders relates the Marcan account only to Dan. 11:31 and 12:11.
46. Aalders, *Ezechiël*, II, 213.
47. *Het Godswoord der profeten*, IV, 155, 159.
48. *Ibid.*, p. 172.

spective — through the history of a definite period — that can be assumed into the eschatological proclamation of the New Testament. When Gog is thus mentioned in Revelation 20, one could say that "the mysterious darkness of evil is reiterated with a voice from the past."[49]

This is a perspective on the last abomination. Although the Gog of Ezekiel 38 and 39 is framed in historical terms, with names that seem to indicate local political relationships (38:2, 5; 39:1), all of these details have practically disappeared from Revelation 20. The localization of the account in Ezekiel is unimportant for the Apocalypse, where the foe comes from the four corners of the earth (20:8). No longer is the prophecy one of "Gog, of the land of Magog" (Ezek. 38:2), but "Gog and Magog," an indication that the details are no longer critical, another proof of the fact that the apocalyptic message is not reportorial but oriented to the proclamation. This is not intended to set prophecy over against apocalyptic, though in the New Testament apocalyptic we see the material concentrated in connection with the definitive conflict and victory expressed in such images.[50]

In this way Revelation portrays actual distress in terms of the end, projecting present time against the screen of the fulfilment. From this we may conclude that the Apocalypse does not issue prognostications about chronological events or the history of the church or of humanity. It is well to bear this in mind when discussing the figure of the antichrist, which cannot be isolated from the apocalyptic whole. Despite all this, however, the Revelation of John has been subjected to numerous literal interpretations — as though it were a narrative account of the future — based on illumination and inspiration, in order to indicate how and when these prophecies will be realized.[51]

---

49. Beek, *op. cit.*, p. 22.
50. Kuhn summarizes the "one characteristic difference" between Ezek. and Rev. in these terms: "Prophecy has become apocalyptic." In *TDNT*, s.v. *Gṓg kai Magṓg*, I, 791. Aalders acknowledges the relation between Ezek. and Rev. when he speaks of a "probable" further extension of the prophecy, and of Antiochus as a type of the antichrist; *Ezechiël*, II, 247.
51. Prominent among the many examples of this are the efforts to locate the final battle in Armageddon (Rev. 16:16). The connection of this with Megiddo is much disputed, and, as Joachim Jeremias points out, "the riddle of *Hár Magedṓn* still awaits solution"; in *TDNT*, s.v., I, 468. At any rate, it is surely arbitrary in the extreme to look for this Armageddon in the Near East somewhere. René Pache states that the

These interpreters assume that Revelation is talking about a particular person of later history (an "end-time") and that it provides us a clear concept, with the reliability of a photograph, with which we may easily recognize the antichrist when he appears.[52] On this view, the antichrist is still coming. But the epistles of John (the only place in the New Testament where the word "antichrist" is used) speak of him without placing him in some distant future: in fact, he was present in John's day. Surely this recommends caution. It is evident that the localizing in the New Testament is of a different sort, which cannot be divorced from the last days, but remains an intrinsic part of them.[53] What is clear in the New Testament references to "the antichrist" is that this is not a supernatural or super-human concept, but takes place and manifests itself on a human level. Behind the antichristian powers the shadow of the "demonic" may fall, but with the concept "the antichrist" we find ourselves not on some remote evil terrain, but on the well-known terrain of our daily human existence. Indeed, the human level of the antichrist is one of the most compelling messages of the New Testament. It is a human force — a human "anti" — that elevates itself and disintegrates through the victory of the Lamb.

For John and Paul the antichrist is seen as operating on human terrain — he is the deceiver, the man of lawlessness. He is at home there, and exhibits all kinds of human traits. It is this human aspect that is gripping in the enigmatic words of Revelation 13:18: "This calls for wisdom: let him who has understanding reckon the number of the beast, *for it is a human number*, its number is six hundred and sixty-six" (cf. 15:2).[54]

final war must take place in Palestine "for several reasons easy to understand"; *Le retour de Jésus-Christ* (1958), p. 225. Cf. on this problem A. Kuyper, *Van de Voleinding*, IV, 244.

52. Clear examples of this are found in V. Hepp, *op. cit.*, pp. 187ff., in a chapter entitled "A Biographical Sketch of the Antichrist." On the basis of Rev. 13:3, Hepp argues that the antichrist will be crushed only to rise again.

53. In the quest of this localizing the past has also played an important role. From the fact that the tribe of Dan is not included in the list of the 144,000 sealed (Rev. 7:5-8), it has been concluded that the antichrist would come from Dan, an interpretation dating back to Irenaeus (*Adv. haer.* V.xxx.2), who cites Jer. 8:16 and comments, "This, too, is the reason that this tribe is not reckoned in the Apocalypse along with those which are saved." Cf. Gen. 49:17; commentaries *ad loc.* by Zahn, Michel, and Greijdanus; Hepp, *op. cit.*, p. 133.

54. Cf. the summary by Rühle, in *TDNT*, s.v. *arithmós*, I, 462-64.

In general, more attention is given to the "riddle" of this number than to the fact that it is "a human number," in other words, that all the subhumanity of the beast is still human, proceeding from among men, and setting itself up over against God and men. Understanding the number of the beast is a matter of wisdom. The number must be "reckoned." Understandably, with all its mysteriousness, it has played an important role in reflections on the nature of the antichrist and how he is to be recognized. It is curious that this passage instructs the believer to "reckon" or calculate, whereas elsewhere the New Testament says that calculating the future is impossible. The words are so specific and clear as to exclude Greijdanus's contention that this "calculation" will occur only when the antichrist has personally come, and that we can now have no more than general insights.[55] This interpretation is even more unacceptable because this reckoning is so closely related to the great boycott of verses 15-17. Moreover, the reservedness of this interpretation results from a certain understanding of the antichrist that holds to a definite "end-time" (to come after us), rather than to "the last days" and the "imminent" end. It should be remembered that this number 666 suddenly comes up in the context of "the mark of the beast." If this number cannot be understood and reckoned, everything would be lost in the last hour.

Through the course of the centuries this number 666 has been shrouded in mystery. One cannot reassure himself with the thought that the number will remain mysterious for a longer or shorter time, to be revealed later.[56] The inclination to let it be mysterious can probably be traced to a reaction against the many fantastic calculations that have arisen in an effort to spot the antichrist. Yet we may not be tempted into concluding with Schmaus that "what the antichrist is, is a deep mystery."[57] Schmaus does not mean by this that there is something enigmatic about resistance to the blessed glory of the Lamb — "They hated me *without a cause*" (John 15:25) [58] — but that there are

---

55. *Komm.*, p. 284.
56. "The Apocalypse decisively expresses the opinion that the name submits itself to calculation by him who has understanding"; Bousset, *Die Offenbarung des Johannes* (1896), p. 429. Bousset adds, ironically, "Irenaeus, Luthardt, Hoffman, and Zahn know better than that."
57. *Katholische Dogmatik*, IV/2, 171.
58. On this verse cf. Berkouwer, *Sin*, pp. 136f.

gaps or lacunae in our knowledge of this mystery.[59] But the reckoning of Revelation 13:18 precisely refers to the removal of the mysterious, so that what is coming can be clearly assessed.

To attain this kind of clarity, some have chosen the route of symbolism. Greijdanus, for example, sees the number 6 as indicative of the fulness of the creaturely "without the holy stamp of the divinely instituted peace." The number 666 indicates dominion over nature and jurisdiction over all earthly powers, but a dominion and jurisdiction without — indeed, turned against — God.[60]

Considerable objections have been voiced against this particular explanation of the number 666 by analogy to other symbolic numbers in Revelation.[61] After all, the point is not just the interpretation of apocalyptic numbers in general. There is something specific and concrete about this number. In other words, by means of this number John meant to indicate a concrete antichristian power or person, so that the Christian community could mobilize for the conflict with this power or person. This "code" has not incorrectly been called the key to the identification of the beast. The name of the beast is thought to be hidden in the number 666. For example, the numerical values of the letters of the name "Nero Caesar" written in Hebrew characters add up to 666.[62] On this view, the Apocalypse is addressing itself here to the universal power of Rome under the Neronian persecutions. But there is nothing resembling unanimity

59. Westhuizen (op. cit., p. 113) says that the number guards the secret, and will not be fulfilled until the appearance of the antichrist.
60. Greijdanus, loc. cit. This explanation is frequently encountered; cf. Berkhof, CMH, p. 120: "a symbol of man's highest development of power outside the sabbath of God's work." K. Schilder, Woord en Kerk, I (1948), 257, sees 6 symbolically as the near-divine, whereas 666 indicates "that the antichrist will develop a power in all the relationships of life, which almost emulates the divine, but will be destroyed before having fully developed its evil power." Cf. also G. Menken, "Het getal 666," Gereformeerd theologisch tijdschrift, XXXVI (1935), 135ff.; Kuyper, Dictaten Dogmatiek, V (Locus de Consummatione Saeculi), sec. 5, pp. 221, 231; Hepp, op. cit., pp. 238ff.
61. Behm, op. cit., p. 79.
62. Nun (50) plus resh (200) plus waw (6) plus nun (50) plus qoph (100) plus samekh (60) plus resh (200) equals 666. Bousset called this "the solution to the apocalyptic riddle"; op. cit., p. 429. A. Sizoo, however, claims that it is very difficult to find a solution because there are many names that add up to 666; "Isopsepha en het getal 666," in De antieke wereld en het NT, pp. 164f. Examples of such calculations are given by Rühle (TDNT, loc. cit.).

about the interpretation of the number 666, and it appears extremely difficult to arrive at a conclusive answer. To admit this may leave the impression that the riddle remains and wisdom and understanding are lacking. But just because it is difficult for us to say with certainty what John was talking about 1900 years ago does not make this as yet undeterminable number a "mystery" for us. If it specified the number of an antichrist in the "end-time" (after us), our uncertainty about it would constitute a real danger. But because John points out the antichrist and admonishes the believers to exercise wisdom, we understand how actual is the confrontation between the community and the antichrist.[63]

Recognizing time and again the pervasive force of the "anti," the believer can understand the thrust of the eschatological admonition: "Here is a call for the endurance of the saints, those who keep the commandments of God and the faith of Jesus" (Rev. 14:12). In every transformation of the "anti," the call to endurance remains the constant. All forms of futurism are excluded. The eyes must be focused on the true future, the coming of God. The constant reinterpretation necessitated by the ongoing course of history is not evidence of contradiction, but is proof of the fact that no single moment of the "last days" is excluded from the eschatological proclamation. In the tensions of our expectation of the end, we must keep an open ear to the sounds produced by history. Wherever the traces of opposition occur, the antichrist can be found, its form differing from time to time, "but the outlines of the figures are fundamentally the same."[64]

Great care must be exercised in judging whether something is or is not a figure of the antichrist. Such care has not always been observed in the past. Of some rash interpretations, Rowley has written: "It is easy for us to see that they were mistaken and that their prophecies were unfulfilled."[65] Numerous controversial historical figures — the pope, Napoleon, Hitler, Stalin, to name a few — have been classified as manifestations of the antichrist. Can this all be dismissed as arbitrary? To respond

63. Wikenhauser points out that "the key to the solution [of this number] must have been lost early, for already Irenaeus no longer possessed it"; *Die Offenbarung des Johannes* (1949), p. 97. Cf. Irenaeus, *Adv. haer.* V.xxx.3.
64. Rowley, *op. cit.*, p. 156.
65. *Ibid.*, p. 157.

with that charge alone is not enough. When the dynamics of history and the avalanche of events reflect so profoundly and undeniably the motives of the "anti," it will not do simply to dismiss the problem with a condescending reference to past mistakes. Regin Prenter is correct in pointing out that none of these concrete identifications is absolutely incorrect *per se*.[66] There is more eschatological relevance to these identifications than to a view of the antichrist that relegates it to a distant future about which we need not be concerned.

Perhaps someone may suggest that this notion of continuous actuality and reinterpretation sells short the seriousness of the eschatological proclamation. Is this seriousness, they object, not intimately connected with the coming figure in the "end-time"? Such an objection misses one very important point: the profound seriousness reflected in every biblical reinterpretation, perhaps most of all in the passage where the name "antichrist" itself appears, where everything is at stake because there are those who deny that Jesus is the Christ (1 John 4:2ff.). The seriousness is not in the special aspect of what is yet to come, nor in the mysteriousness of the various descriptions of the antichrist, but in the reality of opposition and the perseverance it must arouse. Surely there is more danger that this will not be taken seriously if the antichrist is supposed to be a figure of the future and what we are presently confronted by are only forerunners.[67]

Apostasy and antithesis

The danger of weakening the seriousness of the eschatological proclamation is vividly illustrated by considering one of the concomitants of the appearance of the antichrist, namely, apostasy.

In 2 Thessalonians 2, Paul is not writing about two separate and independent signs. The rebellion is closely connected

---

66. *Schöpfung und Erlösung*, II, 521.
67. Some manuscripts of Rev. 13:18 read 616 for 666. There are some interpreters who account for this by the difference between the Greek and Latin forms of the name "Nero" (Greek *Neron;* Latin *Nero*); cf. footnote 62 above. However, the number 616 also gives rise to a different identification of the beast, namely, the emperor Caligula (in Greek *Gaios Kaisar; gamma* [3] plus *alpha* [1] plus *iota* [10] plus *omicron* [70] plus *sigma* [200] plus *kappa* [20] plus *alpha* [1] plus *iota* [10] plus *sigma* [200] plus *alpha* [1] plus *rho* [100] equals 616). Perhaps 616 raises anew this (meaningful!) problem of reinterpretation.

with apostasy, a direct reference to the Daniel Apocalypse (cf. Dan. 11:31f.). Paul is not alone in attaching great eschatological importance to apostasy. Christ Himself linked deception and apostasy with the appearance of false prophets. He urges His disciples: "Take heed that no one leads you astray" (Matt. 24:4). Love will grow cold as wickedness is multiplied (vs. 12). This apostasy is an eschatological omen, and Paul sets it against the background of "pretended signs and wonders" (2 Thess. 2:9). But it can be more than an omen; it can become reality through the relentless persecution that jeopardizes the power of perseverance. There is even mention of a threat so great that the days will have to be shortened (Matt. 24:22; Mark 13:20; cf. 2 Pet. 2:9; Rev. 2:10; 3:10). The whole New Testament resounds with warnings against being bewitched (Gal. 3:1), swerving from the truth (2 Tim. 2:18), religious shipwreck (1 Tim. 1:19), departing from the faith (1 Tim. 4:1). All of these expressions boil down to one warning, a warning against falling away after once having known the truth (cf. Heb. 6:5; 10:26; 2 Pet. 2:20). These are not warnings against remote possibilities, but against dangers and threats that arise *now,* within the life of the community, which is presently beset by persecutors and deceivers.

Apostasy, then, is described as an eschatological phenomenon "in time of temptation" (Luke 8:13) of the last days.[68] The Old Testament as well is filled with warnings against apostasy and estrangement from God (cf. Ps. 95), but apostasy attains its deepest seriousness and is represented in its darkest tones in the last hour. Apostasy is the falling away from supreme love, from faith, from the communion of the saints (cf. Eph. 4:13f.). It is a departing from the way of life. Despite the multiplicity of references, the warnings sound against this single, ominous apostasy, which can only be understood in terms of the salvation that has already come in Christ. As long as there is a way to be walked and people to walk it, there is the danger of straying from it. As long as there are heights of love to be ascended, there is the chance of falling back (cf. Rom. 11:11; 1 Cor. 10:12; Rev. 2:5). As long as there is light, there is the possibility of receding into the darkness (John 3:19). Notice that this apostasy always has a relational character. It cannot be depicted as an isolated moral phenomenon. Like the anti-

---

68. Cf. Schlier, in *TDNT*, s.v. *aphistēmi*, I, 513.

christ, it always stands in relation to Him who is the First and the Last. The horizon of His cross and resurrection forms the background of the eschatological apostasy. The New Testament concentrates apostasy in all its forms, including its last and clearest form, in its conflict with the light, now that the darkness is passing away (1 John 2:8).[69]

This apostasy requires careful and serious attention. Irresponsibility is a grave danger here, as is evident all too often in the history of the church. Traditionalism is particularly prone to a loose application of the term "apostate" and the temptation to see apostasy everywhere. Consider the sects, for example, who often consider the institutional church as nothing more than the incarnation of a continuous process of apostasy. It is essential for a proper understanding of apostasy to grasp the relational aspect of it, to take account of that from which man has fallen away. The rejection of human institutions has sometimes been construed as apostasy, and the New Testament makes clear how often Jesus and Paul were accused of apostasy from the law (cf. Acts 21:21). This accusation is a clear example of an erroneous concept of "apostasy." This kind of interpretation of apostasy, measuring according to its own standards and missing the convulsive power of the new in Christ (2 Cor. 5:17), obscures the real meaning of apostasy — of the falling away — in the last days.

In his study of the "mystery of evil," Antanas Maceina examines this eschatological apostasy further.[70] Apostasy, he contends, arises either through *denial* or *forgetfulness,* and he raises the question of which of these two is the more prominent element in the eschatological apostasy. Now it seems to me impossible to get very far with this kind of analysis. Maceina himself concludes that the element of forgetfulness is the more prominent. The element of denial is conflict with God, but forgetfulness is the further stage of apostasy, when God is no longer real to a person. Apostasy is manifested in the

---

69. None of this is intended to imply that apostasy could not or did not exist before the appearance of salvation in Christ. Pagan and pre-Christian apostasy are specifically indicated in Rom. 1:27; Titus 3:3-7; cf. also 2 Pet. 2:18; Rev. 20:3. But it is clear that for the New Testament the concentration of all apostasy comes *after* the revelation of grace. Cf. Michaelis, in *TDNT,* s.v. *piptō,* VI, 164ff.; Braun, *ibid.,* s.v. *planáō,* VI, 242ff.

70. Maceina, *Das Geheimnis der Bosheit* (1955), pp. 195ff.

general apathy of everyday existence, the absolute indifference
to God for which atheism is not even a viable alternative.

There is undeniably an element of truth to all this. Forgetting God is certainly to be included in any characterization
of the apostate heart. It is not for nothing that the New Testament calls the believers to *remembrance* of the death of Christ
and His resurrection (1 Cor. 11:25; 2 Tim. 2:8). Forgetfulness
was an important contributing factor in Israel's apostasy (cf.
Ps. 106:13, 21, 24f.; Ps. 103:2). But to concentrate eschatological
apostasy in forgetfulness is to go too far. Apostasy as described
by the New Testament manifests itself in various ways, including conflict, forgetfulness, denial, blasphemy, hypocrisy, and
heresy. The Bible gives us no psychological or sociological explanation of apostasy; instead it points out its deepest intention
and reality as the darkness, on which man must turn his back
and face the Light that has ascended.

Like the Bible's warnings against the antichrist, those against
apostasy are insistent admonitions. They point the believer to
one way, the Way of Life to be walked in the here and now.
This way is walked in the midst of other people. Naturally, the
believer is brought into contact with these people.

How does the reality of the "anti" and of apostasy function
in the midst of this existence? This question brings us to the
subject of another "anti" immediately related to the antichrist,
that is, the "anti" of the antithesis. Does the "anti" of the antichrist result immediately in an antithesis *among people?* Does
not the human aspect of the antichrist automatically reveal an
unbridgeable abyss, the opposition between faith and unbelief
that pervades human history?

Undeniably the Bible speaks with repeated warnings about
the opposition between men. It is an opposition that brings
far-reaching consequences. Probably this comes out most clearly
in the series of Pauline questions recorded in 2 Corinthians
6:14-16: what righteousness has to do with unrighteousness;
what fellowship light has with darkness; what accord there can
be between Christ and Belial; what a believer has in common
with an unbeliever; what agreement the temple of God has
with idols.[71] All these questions are introduced by the admonition: "Do not be mismated with unbelievers," placing us, in

71. All the words Paul uses in this parallel structure — *metoché, koinōnía.
symphōnēsis, merís, synkatáthesis* — set up antithetical pairs of concepts. Cf. the commentaries by Bachmann and Wendland, *ad loc.*

the midst of life, before the gravity of this "antithesis." Paul then goes on to quote loosely from Leviticus (26:11f.), Ezekiel (37:27), and Isaiah (52:11). The separation is necessary because God lives among His people. He is the Father; they are His sons and daughters. Unless they have received His grace in vain, they may not permit assimilation. The heart of the matter is the antithesis between Christ and Belial (vs. 15),[72] which becomes visible in all these other "antitheses."

The conclusion of these antithetical statements is expressed in verse 16: "For we are the temple of the living God." Paul's words are the more noteworthy because they recall a passage from Jeremiah's prophecy: "Do not trust in these deceptive words: 'This is the temple of the LORD, the temple of the LORD, the temple of the LORD'" (7:4). Jeremiah was talking about Israel's faithlessness (3:6, 8, 14) and "perpetual backsliding" (8:5); and Israel's antithesis was a false and irreligious one, summarized in its boast: "*We* are wise, and the law of the LORD is with *us*" (8:8). As a result, the unquenchable fire of God's wrath was poured out on Israel (7:20).

Later in Jewish history this "antithesis" was embodied in the isolation and self-elevation of the Pharisees over against the rest of the people, the accursed sinners and publicans. They too thought *koinōnia, symphōnēsis, meris* (1 Cor. 6:16) with "sinners" impossible. But the Pharisees' flagrant misuse of "we," their dark antithesis, does not deprive the Pauline "we" — "we are the temple of the living God" — of its meaning. This Pauline particularity can be maintained without lapsing into Pharisaism, only because of the radical nature of the reconciliation in which it is founded. Only against this background can the antithesis be maintained. It is not the smug "antithesis" of Israel in Jeremiah's day, nor the pretentiousness of the Pharisees centuries later. It is grounded in the reality of grace and is filled with the omnipresence of Christ. So there can be no arrogance about it. That this is so is apparent from the fact that reconciliation is perfected in sanctification (cf. 2 Cor. 7:1) and is indissolubly related to the sonship. The "deceptive words" of Jeremiah's time and Paul's words may bear some superficial resemblance to each other; it is their tone that differs. The "we" is no longer accented; all attempts at self-elevation and

---

72. Grosheide sees this as a name for the devil and the antichrist both; *Komm., ad loc.;* cf. Bachmann, *loc. cit.*

autarchy are renounced; and the direction is entirely different: "Open your hearts to us; we have wronged no one, we corrupted no one, we have taken advantage of no one" (2 Cor. 7:2).

Everything depends on the relationship, the content, the direction, and the clarity of this antithesis. This antithesis must never be called into question. It is held up against those Corinthian libertines who were jeopardizing the freedom obtained in Jesus Christ, with the message of grace, which is not futile. It is set against lawlessness, darkness, and false gods (cf. Rev. 18:4). All practical syncretism is ruled out, for the first commandment retains its force in the life of God's community. On the basis of the temple of God's presence in the community, the Pauline particularity can be clearly and comprehensively understood.

When the meaning and content of the antithesis are clear to us in this way, we can also understand the nature of the conflict against apostasy in the last days, and thus also against the antichrist. The weapons used are peculiar: truth, righteousness, the gospel of peace, faith, prayer, and the Word (cf. Eph. 6:13-18).

One of the consequences of this is that this antithesis can never be a smug isolationism. Not only is this impossible — "since then you would need to go out of the world" (1 Cor. 5:10) — but the break with sin has a positive goal as well. From the reality of our sonship we are called to walk as "children of God without blemish in the midst of a crooked and perverse generation" (Phil. 2:15). We are to be lights in the world, fulfilling the new commandment, so that the true light may shine, the evidence of a life lived in Christ (1 John 2:8; cf. Matt. 5:16). There is no greater responsibility possible than the one contained in this antithesis. The antithesis is not intended to curse, but to bless. It fills the road to the future with expectation and vocation. This is the biblical notion of the antithesis, one that makes Paul shed tears for the enemies of Christ's cross (Phil. 2:18). This is the meaning of the "we" of the antithesis. Paul's tears are not sentimental, nor do they weaken the antithesis. They stem from the misconstruing of Christ's salvation on the part of those who "live as enemies."

Those who ignore the relationship between the antithesis and sonship, and between the antithesis and proclamation, fall into a haughty concept of themselves that is nothing but apostasy and turning away because it fails to comprehend the gravity of the last days or the fulness and the mystery of the cross. The only way not to be ashamed in the face of the antithesis, the only way to understand the meaning of the last days and of the "anti" in "antichrist" is through a Christ-centered, cross-centered perspective.

So apostasy is not a matter of ideas or abstractions unrelated to daily life. The message of James' epistle is that true faith has to be lived. In a similar way apostasy is unbelief that is lived. It may be lived in the fierceness of the renegade or in the quiet alienation of the outsider; it may be exhibited in moral disintegration or in persecution of the saints. The warning against apostasy goes out to the community of believers: "what accord has Christ with Belial?" Against this apostasy stands the triumphant light.

It was said in the fourteenth century that when the antichrist came, everyone, including children, would immediately recognize him. One thing is clear: the recognition of apostasy and antichrist is indeed possible, for the character of the "anti" itself is clear: it is "anti" the Lord.

Still, it sometimes seems very difficult in everyday life to recognize the "anti" and apostasy. In addition, the fear of sounding Pharisaical often weakens the antithesis. An illustration of this problem is the discussion in German theology of Heinrich Vogel's notion of "solidarity with unbelievers."[73] Some saw in this an illegitimate and extremist elimination of the antithesis. Thus, Gloege, addressing himself to universality in Barth's grace-theology, argues that the New Testament calls for distance between believers and unbelievers. Vogel, on the other hand, argues that in relation to his own people, Israel, Paul was *for* them, not *against,* and in this way he maintained "solidarity" with unbelievers. Christ died for His enemies and for unbelievers. When he then goes on to discuss atheism, Vogel claims that contempt for atheistic errors is never called for; instead, we should make a "practical attack" on it.

Now it is clear that much of this dispute centers around the meaning of the word "solidarity." But it also serves to demonstrate how often the notion of the antithesis is approached

---

73. Cf, H. Vogel, *Wir Christen und die Atheisten* (1958); F. W. Marquardt, "Solidarität mit den Gottlosen? Zur Geschichte und Bedeutung eines Theologoumenon," *Evangelische Theologie,* XX (1960), 533-52; G. Gloege, "Zur Versöhnungslehre K. Barths," *Theologische Literaturzeitung,* LXXXV (1960).

on the basis of fear of the danger of Pharisaism. For the gospel there is no contrast between solidarity and antithesis. If Christ truly died for the unrighteous — "while we were enemies" (Rom. 5:10) — this reality must determine our attitude towards God's enemies. Recognition of this hostility is characteristic of the New Testament: it is never minimized (cf. Acts 13:10; Rom. 11:28; 1 Cor. 15:25f.; Col. 1:21; James 4:4). But it is precisely into these hostile surroundings that the message of peace comes. To be sure, the community in its turmoils is to "have nothing to do with" those who will not listen to the gospel, but at the same time comes the compassionate call: "Do not look on him as an enemy, but warn him as a brother" (2 Thess. 3:15). Because Christ's death was not a response to human love and sympathy, but to enmity and unrighteousness, the proclamation of the gospel of peace is the only answer to all animosity. This is the meaning of the antithesis in the last days. If anyone tries to look at the antithesis outside of the message of the gospel he has forgotten that he himself is one of those referred to when Paul says "Christ died for the ungodly" (Rom. 5:6).

In these last days, the choice is between illumination and blindness. On our way to the city, we have the promise of "the God who said, 'Let light shine out of darkness,' who has shone in our hearts" (2 Cor. 4:6). Where the light shines, the darkness is revealed as the misunderstanding of light. In the deepest sense, then, "the antichrist" is a phenomenon *after* Christ. If there are "forerunners" of the antichrist, it is not the many "antichrists" of 1 John 2, but the forms of the "anti" in the period of the old covenant. Now that "the darkness is passing away and the true light is already shining" (1 John 2:8), the "anti" reveals itself. It is here now, and we may not underestimate its power and danger. "Let anyone who thinks that he stands take heed lest he fall" (1 Cor. 10:12). But it is clear at the same time that this "anti" has no future, bound as it is to the darkness, which shall pass away. Its power is only the suggestive power of deception. From this deception the believer is called back to steadfast perseverance: "But as for you, man of God, shun all this" (1 Tim. 6:11). Considering the richness of God's grace, we may think it enigmatic that "all this" still has an allure, that it still threatens, and that the antichrist appears *after* Christ.[74] But the way is shown to us in the admonitions of

74. Cf. Berkouwer, *Sin*, chapter V.

the Word. It is not the way of rational theodicy; it is the way of struggle, the good fight, fought with clear recognition of the enemy and effective weapons. "Here is a call for the endurance of the saints, those who keep the commandments of God and the faith of Jesus" (Rev. 14:12).

And beyond this, a new blessing (Rev. 14:13), added to the many others, all of which have one common origin — the voice from heaven.

CHAPTER TEN

THE MILLENNIUM

CERTAINLY ONE OF the most controversial and intriguing questions of eschatology is that of the legitimacy of the expectation of a thousand-year reign — the millennium — before the return of Christ. This view is often called "chiliasm" (from the Greek word *chilia* — thousand — Rev. 20:2-6).

Obviously one's view of the thousand years of Revelation 20 is intimately connected with the rest of his eschatology. How he thinks of this passage gives a specific color and structure to his expectation. If you firmly expect an earthly reign of peace, your interpretation of the present state of affairs is naturally going to differ from that of someone who does not share such an expectation. There is more to this than a simple contrast between optimism and pessimism, because even among those who do not embrace chiliasm the expectation of a new earth plays a significant role. But chiliasm contains a passionate expectation with its own color and content, because it is oriented to what is to be realized in this present dispensation. This explains why the word "chiliasm" is often used to denote optimistic ideals and expectations outside the context of the Christian faith. In general, wherever there is longing for a better world and the certainty that this longing will somehow be fulfilled, the word chiliasm crops up. Clearly this gives the term a meaning entirely different from what it originally meant. We might call this a humanizing or secularizing of the concept, since in this form it bears no relation at all to God's reign of peace.[1]

1. For socialism and communism as the expectation of a "kingdom of peace" without social tensions, cf. F. Gerlach, *Der Kommunismus als Lehre vom tausendjährige Reich* (1920); J. Taubes, *Abendländische Eschatologie* (1947). W. Nigg, *Das ewige Reich* (1944), deals with all sorts of "chiliasm," many of which bear little or no relation to the Christian faith and are dominated by human activity; e.g., the philosophical chiliasm of Lessing and Kant, which had nothing to do with

291

Thisworldliness — the motive of chiliasm

Originally, however, chiliasm was of Christian roots and was in no sense a form of cultural optimism or humanistic activism. Just because of this claim to Christian origin, it has come up for discussion again and again. To be sure, chiliasm has often been dismissed as nothing more than fantasy or utopianism. But the fact that, despite this rejection of it by the church, chiliasm has continued to prosper and renew itself should make us wary of any attempt to dismiss it out of hand. Besides, chiliasts themselves maintain that their expectation is not the result of their own fantasy or projection, but is founded squarely on the biblical witness. There are not many references in the Scripture to support chiliasm, but what references there are surely attract attention.

The key passage is the twentieth chapter of Revelation, where the reign of peace is described as marked off by two decisive moments. It exists in the period between the binding of Satan and his release and consists of the thousand-year reign of the believers with Christ. It involves a spectacular event in history, introduced by the first resurrection, which is supposed to be a bodily resurrection (vv. 4-6). This reign of peace will interrupt the course of history in a very special, unsuspected way. In other words, on this view there is not only the ultimate biblical perspective on the new heaven and new earth in which righteousness dwells (2 Pet. 3:13), definitive and all-inclusive, but also a view of what might be called a *temporary* eschaton. It will be the unveiling of a mystery hitherto unknown. Christ's lordship will be made known *on the earth* to all the inhabitants of the earth in an intermezzo of history. There is no intention in this to deny the power of evil with its worldwide ramifications, but this power is not insuperable and permanent. The millennium is nothing but the reality of Christ's triumph on earth.

the person of Jesus (p. 312). Cf. also K. Dijk, *Het rijk der duizend jaren* (1933), pp. 149ff.; M. Schmaus, *Katholische Dogmatik*, IV/4/2, 440ff. For the 19th century, cf. C. Walther, *Typen des Reich-Gottesverständnïsses* (1961). Walther sees utopian chiliasm as the hallmark of 19th-century liberalism, idealism, and socialism. For the 20th century (particularly National Socialism and the Third Reich), cf. Norman Cohn, *The Pursuit of the Millennium. Revolutionary Messianism in the Middle Ages and Its Bearing on Modern Totalitarian Movements* (1962), pp. 310ff., on the "apocalyptic" language of Alfred Rosenberg and of Hitler in *Mein Kampf*.

Now there have been scores of exegetical battles waged over chiliasm, but because of chiliasm's concern with the present world and present dispensation, battles of another nature have been fought as well.[2] Indeed, the exegetical aspects of the discussion often take a back seat to more general arguments about the structure of the world. Thus there are those who reject chiliasm as a fantastic utopianism on the ground that what it expects is impossible within the boundaries of this dispensation. For example, Brunner rejects chiliasm because he feels that the Kingdom of God obviously cannot enter into this historical world. Sin will always continue to play a role in this world, and negative powers will always operate in this dispensation, precluding a radical and fundamental transition to the good, "in spite of all counter-action by the Holy Spirit." For Brunner, a Christian's hope is not for a reign of peace in this dispensation, but for the resurrection and life eternal. Brunner feels that chiliasm reflects a certain view of the *structure* of reality and is *a priori* determined by this view, so that it has nothing to do with detailed exegesis.[3]

Understandably, supporters of chiliasm remain unconvinced by this line of thought and firmly deny that this structural question is relevant at all. Why should the church, believing as it does in the resurrection of the body, the new heaven, and the new earth, consider off-limits the idea that the reign of peace will manifest itself in this present temporal dispensation? Against Brunner's objection that sin and its power always remain, chiliasts point to the fact that God's Kingdom is *always* triumphant over sin and death (cf. 1 Cor. 15:26). It seems to me that this rebuttal is telling: one cannot dismiss chiliasm on Brunner's grounds. Such a structure-analysis (in terms of sin, negative forces, mystery) really contributes little of value to the discussion.

Chiliasm cannot, to be sure, escape the aspects of "already" and "not yet" that we have discussed. One might call chiliasm a kind of "realized eschatology," not in the sense of C. H. Dodd's

2. Cf. S. P. de Roos, "Het duizendjarig rijk," *Nederlands theologisch tijdschrift*, VI (1952), 208ff.
3. *Eternal Hope*, p. 76; cf. *Dogmatics*, III (Eng. tr., 1962), 367ff. Charges of utopianism are also brought against those who are not specifically chiliastic in their expectation, e.g., the attempt to realize the Kingdom of God on earth. Cf. W. Pauck, *Das Reich Gottes auf Erde. Utopie und Wirklichkeit* (1928).

realized eschatology, which applies to Christ's present regime, but as a future realization *within this dispensation.*

Let us consider the fundamental motives of this conviction and try to discover why so much opposition has arisen within the church to chiliasm. For one thing, the Reformers considered the notion of a universal kingdom before the parousia as rooted in unbiblical Jewish opinion.[4] But not only the Jewish element was the object of criticism: the whole idea of a reign of peace to be expected in this dispensation was considered to be an unreal fantasy. The church generally thought of chiliasm as something foreign, whose origins and motives were to be sought outside the Christian tradition.

Of late, however, there has been a growing appreciation of chiliasm.[5] It is argued that the excesses of some forms of chiliasm should not serve as an excuse for dismissing it out of hand, that its origins and contents must be analyzed more carefully and objectively. Not only must we examine the possibility of a real millennium at the end of history, but first of all we must honor the unmistakable kernel of truth within it, its motive, that is, the recognition that the gospel of Jesus Christ is meaningful not only for a future, *otherworldly* reality, but also for *our* dispensation, for *current* historical development, for *earthly* reality. Godliness, according to Paul, holds promise for the present as well as for the future (1 Tim. 4:8): chiliasm wants to realize this promise in the present, or at least call attention to its implications for this dispensation.

According to Althaus the most compelling argument for chiliasm is its pointing to the necessary thisworldliness of Christian hope. God's acts include a "yes" to our history, and for

4. Cf. Augsburg Confession, Article XVII: "They condemn others also, who now scatter Jewish opinions, that, before the resurrection of the dead, the godly shall occupy the kingdom of the world, the wicked being every where oppressed." Cf. also Second Helvetic Confession, Chapter XI: "Moreover, we condemn the Jewish dreams, that before the day of judgment there shall be a golden age in the earth...." The qualification of this opinion as Jewish is related to the continuing notion of a realm of salvation to be established in Jerusalem (cf. Justin Martyr, *Dialogue with Trypho,* LXXX). On the opinions of later Lutheran theologians, cf. H. Schmid, *Die Dogmen der evangelischen lutherischen Kirche* (1893), pp. 474ff.

5. Cf. H. Bietenhard, *Das tausendjährige Reich* (1955), pp. 9ff. Bietenhard attributes the unsavory reputation of chiliasm as "Schwärmerei" to the excesses of eschatological speculations by Bengel, the so-called "Catholic Apostolic Church" (the Irvingites), and the Darbyites.

this reason chiliasm has its element of truth. Utopian chiliasm must, of course, be rejected, but chiliasm is symbolically correct as an expression of the connection of concrete historical situations and the new world and of our responsibility to orient everything on earth in the here and now to the coming Kingdom. In its fantastic image of the future, chiliasm intended most of all to remain true to the reality of hope and to the earth over against all mystical and spiritualistic surrender of this world.[6]

What Althaus appreciated in chiliasm was the same element that Bonhoeffer emphasized as essential for true Christian faith, thisworldliness, which manifests itself in the ecstatic expectation of a reign of peace on earth.[7] Heinrich Ott does not hesitate to speak of "the kerygmatic weight of the chiliastic message,"[8] and he believes that he can honor this existential motif on the basis of sanctification.

The renewed attention to the motive of chiliasm warrants our full attention, simply because the traditional critique of chiliasm has often been seen as proof that the church underestimates the value of earthly existence. Berkhof believes that the church has dealt too cavalierly with chiliasm, and that "the tenacity and extent of chiliasm are a reaction to the spiritualism and the lack of historical perspective of the official Church which saw no future for the world, spiritualized the prophecies, and limited her expectation to personal salvation in heaven."[9]

The appreciation of this antispiritualistic motive of chiliasm does not rule out sharp criticism of its utopian aspect. To ap-

---

6. For Althaus's treatment, cf. *Die letzten Dinge*, pp. 299ff., and his article "Eschatologie" in *Die Religion in Geschichte und Gegenwart*.
7. Cf. Bonhoeffer, *Letters and Papers from Prison;* also K. Barth, *Das Problem der Ethik in der Gegenwart* (1924), pp. 134ff. Barth discusses the problems of the meaning of the millennium, the goal of earthly history, and its relation to ethics.
8. *Eschatologie* (1958), p. 65; cf. p. 68. A. Kuenen, *Het duizendjarig rijk* (1875), distilled the following three pure motives of chiliasm: dissatisfaction with the present, firm belief in a better future, and location of this future on earth (pp. 69-72). The recent appreciation for the chiliastic motive is widespread, but not general. Cf., for example, C. Stange, *Das Ende aller Dinge* (1930), pp. 226ff.; R. Prenter, *Schöpfung und Erlösung*, II, 521ff. ("free speculations"); W. Kreck, *Die Zukunft des Gekommenen*, pp. 196ff.; O. Weber, *Grundlagen der Dogmatik*, II (1962), 741, 745; W. Trillhaas, *Dogmatik* (1962), pp. 460ff. Trillhaas sees chiliasm as heretical and utopian, but he does acknowledge that "genuine streams of biblical realism" are expressed in it.
9. *CMH*, pp. 162f.

preciate this motive is to emphasize the human task and responsibility on the earth. But chiliasm cannot be satisfied with mere appreciation of this one element, because there is more at stake here. Chiliasm stands for a sure and concrete earthly expectation. So the point in question is the transition from this one motive to the entire expectation. When Berkhof rejects spiritualism he makes this transition. Chiliasm, he says, will not disappear until its element of truth "has been accepted into the confession and life of the whole church."[10] But Berkhof's element of truth is not the chiliastic motive discussed by Althaus and others, but a real perspective on the earth from the point of view of the crucifixion and resurrection of Jesus Christ. Berkhof complains that "the average Christian does not expect to see any positive signs of Christ's reign in the world. He believes that the world only becomes worse and races in the direction of the antichrist."[11] Nothing essential is expected to take place before the parousia; there is a general "Christian pessimism of culture."[12] Over against this attitude, Berkhof argues that there is justification for talking about a realm of manifest blessings in this present dispensation. To say this is to take over not only the motive but the content of an expectation. The motive, to be sure, is present, but it is filled with an actual and concrete perspective that has not arisen out of humanism, immanentism, heroism, or pacifism, but out of the reality of Christ's triumphant reign, revealing itself in this dispensation.

It is the perspective of the expectation "that after the antichrist a long and happy period will arrive in which the boundaries between heaven and earth begin to disappear, the downtrodden will reign, the suffering church of Christ will be publicly proved right, and the recovered Israel will be the center of the world. A political and social order will rule in which the reign of Christ will be expressed as strong as is possible in a world from which sin, suffering, and death are not yet expelled."[13]

This view is reminiscent of the so-called post-millennialism, which also emphasizes the pervasive power of Christ's rule and

10. *Ibid.*, p. 163. For Nigg this element of truth includes realism over against escapism, responsibility for the earth, the element of hope, active expectation as genuine Christian experience, and finally, the preservation of the concept of the Kingdom; *op. cit.*, pp. 77-79.
11. *CMH*, p. 174.
12. *Ibid.*, p. 173.
13. *Ibid.*, p. 157.

the proclamation of the gospel. This rule will not come via a sudden, transcendent divine intervention, but via a gradual, evolutionary process, culminating in the "interim" of the reign of peace. "Pre-millennialism" objects to this evolutionary chiliasm, evaluating it as superficial optimism about the future of the earth, a kind of social gospel or evolutionism. Pre-millennialism has a very somber view of historical development. It cherishes no expectation of a rule of peace coming along evolutionary lines; rather, it expects a demonic evolution to be interrupted transcendently by Christ coming in His Kingdom of glory.[14]

Berkhof is clearly opposed to this pre-millennial view and its disavowal of any sort of "expansion of the present" in favor of "a new dispensation."[15] Like the post-millennialists, he has in mind an entirely different perspective, something we might call an "intra-historical" perspective, which includes in it traces of evolution, growth, and human activity.[16] As far as their views of historical development are concerned, the pre-millen-

14. There is thus a sharp difference between pre- and post-millennialism. Post-millennialism anticipates the return of Christ after the proclamation of the gospel worldwide, which will lead to the millennium through the conversion of the world. Cf. D. H. Kromminga, *Millennium in the Church* (1945), p. 298: "it expects the millennium to be brought in without any catastrophic events by the mere operation of the Gospel and the Holy Spirit." Elements of this can be found in B. B. Warfield's "The Millennium and the Apocalypse," *Princeton Theological Review*, II (1904), 599-617, which allows for the possibility, via the gospel, of progression to a relatively "golden" age. Pre-millennialism is reminiscent of Joachim of Fiore, who anticipated the Spirit after a process of degeneration in the church. This will be a great turning and human activity will have no part in it. "Dispensationalism" concerns itself with two "pre's" — pre-millennialism and pre-tribulationism, which teaches that the believers will be taken from the earth (the rapture) before the great persecution. The literature on the subject is vast. On premillennialism cf. Kromminga, *op. cit.;* W. H. Rutgers, *Premillennialism in America* (1930); Oswald T. Allis, *Prophecy and the Church* (1945); K. Löwith, *Weltgeschichte und Heilsgeschehen* (2d ed., 1953), pp. 140ff.; Nigg, *op. cit.*, pp. 160ff. For dispensationalism, see also G. C. Aalders, "Het dispensationalisme in Amerika," *Gereformeerde theologisch tijdschrift*, XLVII (1956), 2ff.; and the Scofield Bible.
15. Cf. Rutgers, *op. cit.*, p. 30.
16. It would be unfair to label this kind of post-millennialism "cultural optimism" or humanism, considering its point of departure — for Berkhof — in the gospel and its permeating power. This problem did arise in America, where the social gospel came to the fore in connection with post-millennialism.

nialists and post-millennialists differ completely. The "chiliasm of the church," as Berkhof calls it, resembles the post-millennial view with its expectation of a "still future maximum development of the power of Christ and the Spirit within this dispensation."[17]

Millennium as end-historical event

One thing is clear at this point. Chiliasm — in its sectarian or ecclesiastical form — raises a lot of questions and touches on numerous other problems. We are not dealing here with the incidental exegesis of one passage of Scripture and whether or not it teaches that a millennial reign is to be included in the Christian's expectation. What is at stake is the reality included in Christ's triumph, to which our desire can and must be directed.

Interestingly, the renewed appreciation of chiliasm (both of the motive behind it and of its concrete expectation) that we have mentioned has gone hand in hand with an exegetical shift in connection with the view of the millennium as portrayed in the New Testament as an event at the end of history, an idea we encounter in Cullmann and Bietenhard.[18] Cullmann proceeds from Christ's rule, which began with the crucifixion and resurrection. Already in the present Christ is exercising His lordship over all men and all powers, now that in His ascension

17. *CMH*, p. 166; cf. p. 170, where he discusses how "Christ's order of life forcefully progresses through the world — through aid to the underdeveloped nations — against the old naturalistic patterns of life." Cf. Haitjema, *Dogmatik als apologie* (1948), who not only speaks of an element of truth in chiliasm, but also of a period before the parousia in which Satan will be bound, so that the church may assume its place in cultural life as in a "final *corpus-Christianum*-culture" (p. 338). Cf. also K. H. Miskotte, *Hoofdsom der historie* (1945). Miskotte discusses the important thesis defended by chiliasts that history's fulfilment must be within history, in order to reveal the glory of the Lord as widely as possible (pp. 415, 428f.).

18. Berkhof would include this in his category of "chiliasm of the Church," into which he also places Abraham Kuyper on account of his interpretation of the binding of Satan as end-historical (i.e., not yet having happened). Kuyper indeed thought that the chiliasts were right on this score: the "millennium" must still be awaited (cf. *Van de Voleinding*, IV, 326, 342). However, he viewed Rev. 20:1–21:9 as lying "after the beginning of the parousia," and he does not say anything about an "interim." He does reject the notion of a new historical period in a second parousia (327). Despite his sharp rejection of Augustine's interpretation, Kuyper ought not, it seems to me, to be categorized among the representatives of ecclesiastical chiliasm.

His Kingdom has become an effective, dynamic reality. But this does not mean that "Revelation intends to identify this thousand-year period with the whole period of the Church between Christ's ascension and his return. Revelation thinks rather of a specifically eschatological kingdom to be realized only in the future. It is, so to speak, the very last part of Christ's lordship, which at the same time extends into the new aeon."[19] It is the "final act" of Christ's kingship, in which the church "will appear as part of the coming age." So the millennium is an end-historical category.[20]

Bietenhard interprets the situation similarly. The millennium is "the last period of the dominion of Christ over this age," in which God closes off the history of the world. It still belongs to this era, but bears "from afar" the character of the fulfilment. It comes into being by way of the parousia, which makes the church no longer *ecclesia pressa* but *ecclesia triumphans,* revealing its essence. The new aeon enters mightily into the old world.[21]

Thus, this "end-historical" view rejects the interpretation that the millennium is the rule of Christ during this dispensation. The millennium "is only the final phase and full revelation" of the one messianic kingdom. During this final phase the church will be revealed as the millennial church, and Satan will be bound.[22] In general, those who hold to this point of view disagree with Augustine's conclusion (which was in line with that of Tyconius and influenced by the peace and tranquility of the post-Constantinian church) that the church had entered in upon the millennium.[23] Nigg accuses Augustine of prostituting the expectation of the Kingdom; Scholz speaks in terms of the dissolution of the traditional eschatology; Berkhof says that

19. Cullmann, *The Christology of the NT*, p. 226.
20. Cullmann, "The Kingship of Christ and the Church in the NT," in *The Early Church* (Eng. tr., 1956), p. 119.
21. H. Bietenhard, *Das tausendjährige Reich* (1955), pp. 149, 152.
22. Cf. M. Rissi, *Time and History* (Eng. tr., 1966), pp. 121ff.
23. *De civitate Dei*, XX.ix. E. Kinder believes that Augustine's view expressed here is a slipping away from his actual assessment of the situation and his actual intentions; "Gottesreich und Weltreich bei Augustinus und bei Luther," in *Festgabe für W. Elert* (1955), p. 35. On Augustine's view cf. also H. Scholz' commentary on *De civitate Dei, Glaube und Unglaube in der Weltgeschichte* (1911), pp. 78ff. On Tyconius (whose commentary on Revelation is partially preserved in the compilation of Beatus of Libana), cf. H. A. van Bakel, "Tyconius. Augustinus ante Augustinum," in *Circa Sacra* (1935), pp. 114ff.

Augustine "cast the die against the expectation of a millennial kingdom" for centuries to come.[24]

Indeed, Augustine's view of the millennium did constitute a radical modification of the original chiliasm with its transcendent, intervening reign of peace. One might ask, however, whether Berkhof, on the basis of his own view of the millennium, ought not to have shown more appreciation for Augustine's recognition of the present opportunity of the church, the more so because he does show such appreciation for Eusebius' judgment that signs of Christ's victory were reflected in the conversion and triumph of Constantine.[25] After all, we ought not to judge Augustine on the basis of our own presuppositions centuries later, but on the basis of his own experience and his own time.[26] On Augustine's view, apparently (and this is its similarity to Berkhof's), there were moments that played a decisive role — positive signs. However, it is clear that the arguments for an end-historical millennium strengthen chiliasm in its conviction that any interpretation is erroneous if it sees the millennium as an already realized reality. Chiliasm sees such an interpretation as deafness to the eschatological expectation which fails to hear the music of the future. The millennium can no longer be the object of burning desire. Now, however, Bietenhard says, is the time for unbiased exegesis: "in scientific and ecclesiastical exegesis the correct, end-historical understanding of the millennium is coming more and more into prominence."[27]

It is clear that Cullmann's and Bietenhard's understanding of Revelation 20 cannot be equated with original chiliasm. Cullmann does not hold to the idea of an interim reign of peace

24. Nigg, *op. cit.*, p. 135; Scholz, *op. cit.*, pp. 112, 183f.; Berkhof, *CMH*, p. 161.
25. *CMH*, p. 133.
26. For an account of this experience, cf. H. F. von Campenhausen, "Augustin und der Fall von Rom," in *Tradition und Leben* (1960), pp. 253ff.
27. Bietenhard, *op. cit.*, p. 10. He goes on to say: "The number of adherents of the church-historical interpretation of the thousand-year kingdom today is infinitesimally small." To be sure, he thinks that Augustine's interpretation is still by and large the Roman Catholic interpretation, which is denied by R. Schnackenburg, *God's Rule and Kingdom*, pp. 339ff. Certainly the notion of an intermediate realm is rejected (cf. Chapter V above), but that does not imply the *identity* of millennium and church. Schnackenburg himself rejects the church-historical interpretation as impossible on the ground that Rev. 19:11ff. already describes the parousia. Likewise Schmaus criticizes the Augustinian view, *Katholische Dogmatik*, IV/4/2, 255.

before the parousia in the sequence millennium — release of Satan — parousia. He believes that the millennium begins with the parousia.[28] Cullmann's idea of the millennium as the final act of Christ's lordship is entirely different from the *interim* reign of peace to which original chiliasm looked forward. Schnackenburg's observation against chiliasm — "the Church awaits her Lord *until* the parousia" — does not conflict with the exegeses of Cullmann and Bietenhard. Cullmann's chiliasm does not acknowledge a twofold return of Christ, but makes an immediate connection between the millennium and the parousia.[29]

From what we have said so far, it is evident that, in its exegetical aspect, the entire discussion turns on Revelation 20. Calvin noted that the chiliasts of his day tried to justify their view by appealing to this chapter. There have been suggestions, however, that certain other scriptural passages point in the direction of a millennium.

Berkhof says that Revelation 20 is the only passage in the Bible that discusses the millennium "expressly and in detail."[30] He admits that 1 Corinthians 15:23-28 deals with the reign of Christ, but he considers Paul's words "too brief and too enigmatic" to clarify the issue.[31] Others are much more positive. According to Bietenhard, Paul too was speaking of a twofold resurrection, a resurrection of the dead in a twofold order, when he says "Christ the firstfruits, then (1) at his coming those who belong to Christ, then comes the end" (vv. 23f.), in which is included (2) the resurrection of those who are left.[32] To be sure, Paul says nothing explicit about the resurrection of the

28. Calvin's criticism of chiliasm, that it makes Christ's Kingdom temporary (*Inst.*, III.xxv.5), does not apply to Cullmann. Cf. *Christology of the NT*, p. 231: "This final act only recapitulates what already characterizes the present kingly rule of Christ."

29. According to Berkhof (*CMH*, p. 155), Rev. 20 "describes a phase which follows 13-17, but which immediately precedes the consummation." "John expected that after the antichrist a long and happy period will arrive" during which, among other things, "the recovered Israel will be the centre of the world" (p. 157). It seems to me that Berkhof and Cullmann differ considerably, and that Kuyper is, exegetically, much closer to Cullmann and Bietenhard than to Berkhof; cf., however, his *E Voto Dordraceno*, II, 287.

30. *CMH*, p. 153.

31. *Ibid.*, p. 157; cf. p. 160, where the passage from 1 Cor. seems to play a somewhat more significant role.

32. *Op. cit.*, pp. 55f.

unbelievers,[33] but the resurrection of the believers is "a special act" within the events of the end, so that the consummation of the church is separate from the consummation of the human race. The resurrection of the church is "isolated insofar as the church attains to resurrection in its own peculiar *'tagma.'* " Despite the incongruities between Paul and Revelation (which Bietenhard admits are not easily explained away), the events of the end, he feels, will be consummated in two stages.[34] So, while 1 Corinthians 15 plays practically no part in Berkhof's view, others find in it a reference to that spectacular moment that has always been inherent in chiliasm, the *first* resurrection at the beginning of the millennium.

Exegetically, Berkhof's refusal to commit himself would seem to be on sounder footing.[35] Those who appeal to Paul for a defense of chiliasm must admit that the real motive of chiliasm certainly does not come to the fore in his epistles. The train of thought in 1 Corinthians 15:23f. is not the series: Christ's resurrection, followed by the resurrection of *believers,* and finally by the general resurrection. The emphasis is on being in Christ and the power of His resurrection. The interpretation of the sequence *épeita ... eita* (ASV, RSV — "then ... then"; KJV — "afterwards ... then") as a Pauline reference to a millennium smacks of being too much influenced by Revelation 20.[36] After all, the point of Paul's treatise here is not to establish a definite chronology, but to emphasize the importance of being found in Christ. And since Paul does not mention a third

---

33. *Ibid.*, p. 58.
34. Cf. also K. Aland, "Bemerkungen zum Montanismus und zur frühchrist-lichen Eschatologie," in *Kirchengeschichtliche Entwürfe* (1960), p. 129. K. L. Schmidt also finds the idea of an interim kingdom in 1 Cor. 15; *Die Judenfrage im Lichte der Kapitel 9-11 des Römerbriefes* (1943), p. 64. On the temporal use of *eita*, cf. Rissi, *op. cit.*, pp. 120f. He admits that 1 Cor. 15 certainly does not speak explicitly of this end-phase.
35. Berkhof's reservations about 1 Cor. 15 are probably part and parcel of his preference for the notion of "maximum development" rather than the idea of a spectacular apocalyptic element in the first resurrection. It seems to me that Berkhof's discussion of the exegetical place of this spectacular element in ecclesiastical chiliasm (Bietenhard, for example) lacks precision. To be sure, he thinks of the first resurrection as a return of dead believers to the earth, but this is not decisive for his view so long as it is established that the realm of peace will be established on earth. Cf. Berkhof, *op. cit.*, pp. 166, 156.
36. Schrenk, *Die Weissagung über Israel im NT* (1951), p. 71, claims that the *épeita ... eita* sequence implies that Paul was thinking "chiliastical-ly"; cf. also N. A. Dahl, *Das Volk Gottes* (1941), p. 252.

tagma, it is unwarranted to argue from 1 Corinthians 15 to an interim kingdom, nothing of which is mentioned in the eschatological remarks of the chapter.[37]

Chronology and hermeneutics

It should be clear that the interpretation of the chronology associated with the interim kingdom is crucial for chiliasm. This is true in 1 Corinthians 15 as well as in Revelation 20.[38] A number of scholars have pointed out that in Revelation 19 we read of the Hallelujah Chorus over the fall of Babylon, of the marriage supper of the Lamb, and of the capture of the beast and his prophet. After that, in Revelation 20, the vision of the millennium follows. But whereas the newer exegesis emphasizes the millennium as the *final act* of the *regnum Christi,* original chiliasm placed all the emphasis on the sequence apparent in Revelation 20: *after* Christ's triumph over His enemies, Satan is bound for a thousand years; *thereafter* Satan is loosed to deceive the nations of the earth; *then* this is followed by the creation of the new heaven and the new earth.[39] Consequently, the spectacular and supernatural event of the first bodily resurrection — the resurrection of the believers — is essential to chiliasm. This chiliasm will have nothing to do with the idea of a gradual unfolding of Christ's resurrection power but instead

---

37. Cf. H. Bavinck, *GD,* IV, 661; K. Barth, *The Resurrection of the Dead,* pp. 163ff.; Grosheide, *Comm., ad loc. Télos* (vs. 24) has also been translated "rest"; cf. S. P. de Roos, *op. cit.,* 221. Schnackenburg, Barth, Grosheide and Bietenhard would contest this translation.

38. Bietenhard mentions 1 Thess. 4:15ff. as well because of its chronological element: "the dead in Christ will rise first *(próton);* then *(épeita)* we who are alive, who are left (vv. 16f.). This obviously does not mention a "general" resurrection. The *próton-épeita* refers back to the problem of the Thessalonians (vs. 13). Rigeaux comments that Paul did not concern himself with the resurrection of the others; in an effort to comfort the Thessalonians he points to the resurrection of the dead in Christ as the first terrestrial aspect of the parousia. No interim realm is implied, for those still living will be "caught up together with them *(háma sýn autois)*"; cf. Rigeaux, *op. cit.,* pp. 544f. In the preface to *Hoofdsom der historie,* Miskotte says that one point of view from which to explain Revelation is that the visions bear on the whole of history, adding that there is actually no continuity in the book. The repeated "then I saw" applies only to the order of the visions, not of the events described. Whether Miskotte maintains this principle in his interpretation of chapter 20 is open to question. Cf. also R. Schippers, "Het hoofdsom van Miskotte," *Bezinning,* I (1946), 24.

39. Rissi, *op. cit.,* pp. 13f.; cf. Bavinck, *GD,* IV, 657.

holds to a wondrous "from above," an extrahistorical implantation, a transcendently caused reign of peace as an intermezzo between the times. "This is the first resurrection. Blessed and holy is he who shares in the first resurrection!" (Rev. 20:5f.). The millennium is delimited by the first resurrection and the unshackling of the last conflict. This emphatic proclamation of the first resurrection stands in the light of the spectacular vision that John perceived. He sees those who have been beheaded for their testimony to Jesus Christ and God's Word coming to life (vs. 4).

Some have attempted to dismiss chiliasm — incorrectly — on the ground that verse 4 talks about "souls," which is interpreted as souls without bodies *(animae separatae)*, so that a bodily resurrection is out of the question.[40] Such a critique, however, is not decisive, for there seems to be no soul-body dichotomy in view here. John sees simply that those who had been beheaded come to life again and sit on thrones.[41] The contrast is between life and death, glory and ignominy, justice and unrighteousness. The martyrs rule with Christ and judgment is committed to them (vs. 4).[42] They are made kings and priests. Everything in the vision is suddenly the diametrical opposite of martyrdom. It is a vision of triumph. Naturally, what is decisive, then, is whether this vision should be seen as a proclamation of the future, indicating a historical interim rule, or whether it should be interpreted as a visionary illumination of the life of martyrs.[43]

Now this triumph is portrayed in connection with the bind-

---

40. Greijdanus, *op. cit.*, p. 405, says that John "does not lead us into the sphere of the corporeal. The bodies of these souls remained in their graves. What is being talked about here is souls that lack their bodies and are permitted to go sit on thrones."

41. H. Bietenhard, *op. cit.*, p. 23.

42. *kai krima edóthē autois.* The entirety of 20:4 is closely related to Dan., esp. 7:22, in which the saints of the Most High are given judgment and receive the Kingdom. "Thrones" are mentioned in 7:9. Competence to judge also comes into play eschatologically elsewhere in the NT; cf. the twelve thrones of Matt. 19:28; also 1 Cor. 6:2. Furthermore, the saints are depicted as priests (Rev. 20:6), a combination encountered again in 1:6; 5:10; 1 Pet. 2:9.

43. Greijdanus *(loc. cit.)* sees two groups in 20:4 — the martyrs and all other true believers, but the accent clearly falls on those who did not capitulate in the persecution that arose concerning the mark of the beast. W. Bousset also emphasizes the importance of martyrdom in Revelation; *Die Offenbarung Johannis* (1896), pp. 156ff. Cf. also H. Schlier, "Die Geschichte nach der Offenbarung Johannis," in *Die Zeit der Kirche* (1956), p. 271.

ing of Satan. The language Revelation uses here is forceful and radical: an angel descends with the key to the abyss and a mammoth chain. He seizes *(ekrátēsen)* the dragon, the old serpent, the devil, Satan, binds *(édēsen)* him a thousand years, and throws *(ébalen)* him into the pit, which is shut and sealed *(ékleisen kai esphrágisen)*, so that he may not deceive the nations (20:1f.; cf. Isa. 24:22). Those who interpret the millennium as already realized in the history of the church try to locate this binding in history. Naturally, such an effort is forced to relativize the dimensions of this binding, for it is impossible to find evidence for a radical elimination of Satan's power in that "realized millennium." So the notion of brakes on the devil's power — limitations of it — is substituted for the more radical image of "binding." For example, some have seen this to have taken place in the conversion of Constantine. The decline into the Dark Ages and renewed barbarian attacks on Christianity were then related to the release of Satan.[44] Another interpretation located the millennium between the fourth century and the French Revolution of 1789.[45]

In other words, the millennium was seen as roughly equivalent to the *corpus Christianum*. With such an interpretation of history any age in which the church blossomed was seen as a time when Satan was bound in the pit. The necessary relativizing of John's description of Satan's bondage (remember that Revelation 20 speaks of a *shut* and *sealed* pit) is then explained by the claim that, although Satan is said to deceive the nations no more (vs. 3), this does not exclude satanic activity in Christendom or individual persons.[46] I think it is pertinent to ask whether this sort of interpretation really does justice to the radical proportions of the binding of Satan — that he will not be freed from imprisonment for a thousand years. There is something peculiar about this relativizing of Satan's bondage, as it is described by Berkhof: "the devil does not tempt man . . . to an open and massive revolt against the reign of Christ. But resistance boils under the surface." Furthermore, there is no ideal reign of peace in this view; instead, we hear of the "maximum development" of Christ's dominion, qualified by Berkhof

44. Cf. Greijdanus, *op. cit.*, pp. 403, 410.
45. A. de Bondt, *De Satan*.
46. Greijdanus, *op. cit.*, p. 403.

in these words: "as strong as is possible in a world from which sin, suffering, and death are not yet expelled."[47]

This is a critical point in the discussion of the millennium. Bietenhard recalls a discussion between Gaius of Rome, who taught that Satan is *now* bound, and Hippolytus, who replied that "empirically" this was obviously not so: "the present time in no way justifies the supposition that Satan is bound; rather, everything would seem to indicate that the devil is loose."[48] This is typical of the discussion of this issue. If it proves anything it is that one must be very careful in conjecturing about the binding of Satan. One must take into account not only the passage in Revelation 20, but also the Gospels. Matthew 12:29 refers to a binding in connection with the coming of God's Kingdom. Jesus' analogy here is radical also: evil spirits are driven out by the Spirit of God, just as a "strong man" is first bound, and after that his house is plundered. Then the strong man is truly powerless. Elsewhere, too, Scripture speaks of Christ's triumph in radical words: Satan is thrown out of heaven (Rev. 12:9); he is disarmed (Col. 2:15). This binding simply cannot be understood quantitatively or even geographically (Christian nations *vs.* heathen nations). Christ's triumph is a light that *penetrates through all darkness*. This is the problem that has always confronted the church: on the one side is the triumph, the binding of the strong man; on the other side is the continuing activity of evil, the presence of the devil (the roaring lion of 1 Pet. 5:8), who, after his defeat, has descended to the earth "in great wrath" (Rev. 12:12). The New Testament always seems to present this duality when it talks about Satan's power. Still, Satan's power cannot ultimately compete with the omnipotent one; and according to Revelation, the evil one himself recognizes this limitation of his power: "he knows that his time is short" (Rev. 12:12; cf. 20:3).

The category of "a short time" serves to indicate the already *complete* expulsion of Satan (his disarming) against the background of the profound reality of Christ's triumph. Now what does all this mean in connection with the book as a whole? What does it mean for the believers to rule as kings with Christ? What does John really *see* in his vision of Revelation 20? Are we dealing here with a future Christocracy, different from the

47. Berkhof, *CMH,* pp. 156f.
48. Bietenhard, *op. cit.,* p. 89.

one made real in Christ's resurrection? All forms of chiliasm hold that this is a vision of a future time, a manifest Christocracy on earth, in which the believers will participate.

We may not tamper with the real, graphic nature of the vision of Revelation 20, nor may we spiritualize the first resurrection. But one question is still decisive: does this vision intend to sketch for us a particular phase of *history*? If one does interpret it this way, it seems to me that he must include the first (bodily) resurrection in his concept of a future millennium. And then Berkhof's concept of the millennium is too minimal; it is not sufficiently spectacular and transcendent. A choice is inevitable: either one does not tamper at all with any of the facets of this "end-historical" vision, or one accepts the fact that this vision is not a narrative account of a future earthly reign of peace at all, but is the apocalyptic unveiling of the reality of salvation in Christ as a backdrop to the reality of the suffering and martyrdom that still continue as long as the dominion of Christ remains hidden.[49]

A choice for the latter would not only conform to the nature of the Book of Revelation but would also be consistent with the clarity of the contrast between *cross* and *glory*. Revelation shares in the aspect of triumph that is prominent in all of New Testament eschatology, which is filled — in the present distress and misery — with kerygmatic comfort. That the martyrs will be made alive to occupy thrones is portrayed to the church in visionary terms. Thus, when the vision speaks of the release of Satan, the intent is not to foretell a chronologically long and difficult time, but to show us the victory of Christ, and by contrast the ultimate impotence of the power of Satan. Most people who read this vision come away from it with a sense of awe, terror-stricken by the extent of the deception Satan is able to carry out. But though "their number is as the sand of the sea" (20:8), they will come no further than the walls of the beloved city; once they are there, fire will descend from the heavens to consume them (vv. 8-10). In visionary terms the theme comes again: how powerless Satan really is, how short the time of his freedom (vs. 3), how really minor this war, how ridiculous in the face of Christ and His triumph.

Chronology is what is really at issue in the interpretation of

49. Cf. E. Peterson, "Zeuge der Wahrheit," in *Theologische Traktate* (1951), pp. 167ff.

Revelation 20, and chiliasm has always attached great significance to this chronology. The "literalism" of chiliastic prophecies stands or falls with it. In other words, whether we decide
for or against chiliasm depends on the hermeneutical principles
we apply to the Book of Revelation.[50] Berkhof criticizes chiliasm
for its view of Scripture, according to which the Bible is seen
as a divine book with "very dispersed communications concerning future events." A literal interpretation of prophecy is presupposed; the biblical material is arranged with chronological
precision because of what he calls "a certain intellectualist drive
to localize everything."[51] This critique touches original chiliasm
in an extremely vulnerable spot: its hermeneutics.[52]

Surely Berkhof's point is well taken. But we ought to consider the consequences of it for the so-called ecclesiastical chiliasm as well. If it is incorrect to view the biblical proclamation
as consisting of "dispersed communications concerning future
events" (which we have elsewhere called "reportorial eschatology"), what of the end-historical millennium in Berkhof's
own sense? Berkhof may not be guilty of a "drive to localize
everything" or a search for "chronological precision" but he
does "localize" and "chronologize." The real problem with
chiliasm is not with what Berkhof calls "tables, surveys, and
drawings,"[53] but with "knowledge" of the course of history
under the lordship of Christ in this dispensation. This is the
case for Berkhof as well; he is concerned with "knowledge"
of the decisive transition that is said to be *revealed* to the believer. It is true that Berkhof does not get carried away with
fantasies or in-depth prophecies concerning the future. Every-

50. K. L. Schmidt, "Die Bildersprache in der Apokalypse," *Theologische
Zeitschrift*, III (1947), 174ff., points out the close connection in imagery
between Revelation and Ezekiel, particularly with respect to the word
hōs (like, as); cf. 1:10, 13. "This 'as' extends throughout the entire
book," which indicates the inadequacy and unreality of the rendition
of what was seen and heard.
51. Berkhof, *CMH*, pp. 163-65.
52. Kuyper centers his case on the interpretation of apocalyptic as distinct
from prophecy. He rejects the prophetic interpretation of Revelation,
envisaging instead "apocalyptic" elements in it, thus rejecting the literal
exegesis of the book. Kuyper's prophetic/apocalyptic distinction is
worth noting. Prophecy shows future things as coming forth from what
already exists on earth; apocalyptic shows these future things as coming
down out of heaven without involving itself in the connection that
these future things bear to the present. *E Voto Dordraceno*, II, 281-87.
53. *CMH*, p. 164.

thing is bound up with what has happened, and only in this connection does the reportorial element function. The reportorial element assumes a Christocentric character, but that does not take away the fact that it is a "knowledge" of the future, as is evident from his certainty about the "analogy of the Christ-Event which is being realized throughout the world,"[54] the "maximum development" of Christ's power, and the restoration of Israel.

The extent to which localizing and chronology have their say in Berkhof is readily apparent from his detection of chronological elements in Ezekiel 38-39. God's salvation through the return from Babylon and the rejuvenation of the nation of Israel through the working of the Spirit constitute God's next to the last word only. This restoration of Israel is not the fulfilment: first, Gog-Magog has to appear. Thus, this restoration might be called an "interim rule," a theme to recur in the millennium of Revelation. Despite Berkhof's criticism of fundamentalism and his insistence that chiliasm accords the doctrine of the millennium a central place "which it definitely does not have in the Holy Scripture,"[55] the reportorial element is still just as determinative for his own views about the course of history and *concrete* events. Instead of solving the problem of fundamentalistic chiliasm, Berkhof's view compounds it. Furthermore, it opens him to accusations by chiliasts that he is inconsistent; and it is hard to see how he could satisfactorily answer this criticism, considering that the whole hermeneutics of the Apocalypse is at issue here.

Our purposes here make it impossible to give a detailed account of the compelling history of chiliasm with all its ups and downs.[56] One thing is certain, however. Chiliasm — including ecclesiastical chiliasm — has always strongly opposed spiritualism. Chiliasts have always had a burning, passionate expectation for this earth and earthly existence. In the early church this expectation took the form of imaginative descriptions of the abundant life that would begin with the millennium.[57] This rich expectation was not weakened but reinforced by the conflict between chiliasts and those who spiritualized the expectation and thought of chiliasm as unbiblical. Nigg traces back

54. *Ibid.,* p. 79.
55. *Ibid.,* p. 165.
56. For one such account cf. Norman Cohn, *The Pursuit of the Millennium.*
57. Cf. Nigg, *op. cit., passim.*

to Origen the systematic opposition to chiliasm, an opposition "that did not rest until chiliasm was stamped as heresy."[58] But just because of these very real tensions, it should not be assumed that the real dilemma here was between chiliasm and spiritualism. To be sure, arguments against chiliasm are often expressed in spiritualistic terms, but this does not prove that there is a natural opposition between the two. Origen disputed — on a spiritualistic basis — not only chiliasm, but also the doctrine of the resurrection of the body.[59] Now it is important that the church did confess the resurrection of the body, but it turned its back on chiliasm. So there was apparently a factor other than antispiritualism that led to the church's rejection of chiliasm.

Criticism of chiliasm does not entail a loss of hope for earthly existence or a pessimistic defeatism.[60] The actual point of contention is not a lack of interest in this earth; even less is it disinterest in the new earth in which righteousness dwells (2 Pet. 3:13). Surely no one would seriously try to contend that the passionate expectation of 2 Peter is escapist otherworldliness or a form of spiritualism.[61] Thus the rejection of any spiritualizing of the expectation does not require one to opt for chiliasm. Chiliasm may voice its objections against spiritualism; it can never argue effectively on antispiritualistic grounds against those who do not embrace spiritualism and still question chiliasm. This issue can only be decided on the basis of the understanding of the apocalyptic vision.

Retribution and eschatological revolution

Some interpreters claim that the most prominent theme of Revelation is the idea of retribution, that this book deals extensively with "power," but not with "love."[62] It is said that the book contains an "ill-disguised power struggle," an ethos

58. *Ibid.*, p. 75.
59. Cf. Ned B. Stonehouse, *The Apocalypse in the Ancient Church* (1929), pp. 117ff.; E. Boliek, *The Resurrection of the Flesh. A Study of a Confessional Phrase* (1962), pp. 40ff.
60. Cf. C. H. Lindyer, *Kerk en koninkrijk* (1962), p. 37.
61. The NT message is not just one of the speedy return of the Lord; there is also an admonition to "hasten *(speudō)* the coming of the day of God" (2 Pet. 3:12). Schelkle recalls in this connection the petition "Thy kingdom come"; *Die Petrusbriefe* (1961), p. 229; cf. further Chapter XIV below.
62. Nigg, *op. cit.*, p. 76.

of the resentment and revenge of the loser, the common man against the power of Rome, a desire for self-determination and self-rule that conflicts with the gospel.[63] According to Nigg, Revelation becomes no more sympathetic "just because it is ascribed to the Lamb of God." This is the deepest error of this interpretation. In fact it is the Lamb of God who brings His healing order into the confusion of feelings arising in human hearts. If this is resentment, then Hannah's and Mary's songs of praise (1 Sam. 2:4ff.; Luke 1:51ff.) are also resentment, for both — through visionary illumination — sing of a radical turnabout in all relationships, of disarming and dethroning and exaltation; both reflect an eschatological outlook on the unveiling of reality as it is to the eyes of God. It is, of course, possible for the idea of retribution to arise in a perversion of this religion, but only if it has forgotten the meaning of the Lamb.

The danger of the idea of retribution is not foreign to chiliasm, but there is no reason to disqualify chiliasm with the claim that this notion is inevitably part and parcel of it. One's conviction of this eschatological "turnabout" could produce a radical change in his posture from expectation to activism and "eschatological revolution" supported by appeals to the Book of Revelation, a notion of the realization of God's Kingdom on earth according to which the losers would become winners. W. E. Mühlmann argues that there is a relationship between "adventism" (by which he means expectation) and activism.[64] For genuine chiliasm, he says, the expectation is everything, the expectation of what must come as the gift of God from above — the reign of peace — to the realization of which man cannot contribute. This passivity of expectation can, however, turn into activism with passionate and fatalistic aspects.[65] Mühlmann discovers these tendencies not only in the history of chiliasm, with its activistic and revolutionary aspects, but also in the gospel itself, where he detects traces of the idea of the

---

63. *Ibid.*, p. 74.
64. Mühlmann, *Chiliasmus und Nativismus. Studie zur Psychologie, Soziologie und historische Kasuistik der Umsturzbewegungen* (1961).
65. According to Mühlmann, the tendency to insurrection in the world is due to Judeo-Christian apocalyptic (*op. cit.*, p. 371). By virtue of its immanent structure, chiliasm becomes activist (p. 372). Chiliasm is related to the rise of a new sociological religiosity-type, in Max Weber's words, "plebeian religion" (p. 364). Thus chiliastic aggressiveness diminishes whenever the church appears more "triumphant" (p. 373).

holy war. For this reason, he argues, it has always been difficult
to stem the tide of eschatological activism by appeal to the
gospel.[66] It seems obvious that the gospel knows of no such
activism, even when it calls believers to service. Resentment is
precluded by the new light that illumines both great and small,
both first and last. The key to the critique of this notion of
resentment is found in the proclamation of the great turnabout
brought about by the Kingdom, a message found throughout
the New Testament, but especially in the promises of the Sermon on the Mount, that those who hunger will eat, those who
weep will laugh. To distil a psychology of retribution from this,
on the basis of "the last shall be first," is to mistake grievously
the meaning and source of this turnabout. Eschatological revolution is not a revelation of this biblically decisive aspect, but
of its brutalization and perversion. If there is one place in
the history of eschatological expectations where we can almost
agree with Gamaliel's oversimplified philosophy of history (if
it is merely human it will come to naught; cf. Acts 5:39), it is
in these eschatological revolutions, incarnated in history in blood
and tears only to disappear — too late — from the stage of human
affairs.[67]

66. The line of reasoning here is exceptionally tenuous. Mühlmann sees
    the theme of violence (biázein) in Matt. 11:12 and Luke 16:16 as a
    reflection of Zelotism. Furthermore, he refers to "power- and force-ter-
    minology" in the Gospels and the "Beelzebul pericope" of Luke 11:14-
    23. For a treatment of these passages without the conclusions that
    Mühlmann draws, cf. R. Otto, The Kingdom of God and the Son of
    Man (Eng. tr., 1943), pp. 108ff.; cf. also Stumpff, in TDNT, s.v. zēlóō,
    II, 884ff. Mühlmann does not quote Christ's words in Matt. 26:52 —
    "all who take the sword will perish by the sword" — which surely
    bears on his argument. Not only the "power" of the disciples, but also
    that of Christ — the Lamb — stands in an entirely different context; cf.
    Rev. 13:7 (edóthē autō exousía); Bauernfeind, in TDNT, s.v. nikáō, IV,
    944.
67. A number of worthwhile remarks on this issue are found in M. Scheler,
    "Das Ressentiment im Aufbau der Moralen," in Vom Umsturz der
    Werte, I (1919), 45-236. Scheler, however, seems to contradict himself
    when he says that Luke cannot be absolved of the charge of retribution
    (in connection with Luke 18:25) (pp. 129f.). Prominent in this entire
    discussion is Rev. 6:10 — "how long before thou wilt judge and avenge
    our blood on those who dwell upon the earth?" (cf. 19:2). Behm con-
    trasts the prayer of 6:10 with the "selfish longing to pay back injustice
    with injustice" (cf. Rom. 12:19f.); Komm., p. 41. Nietzsche, in The
    Genealogy of Morals (Eng. tr., 1956), called Revelation the "book of
    hatred . . . the most rabid outburst of vindictiveness in all recorded his-
    tory." It deals, he says, with revenge, especially the revenge of the Jews,

All of this is clarified in Revelation by the place of the all-dominating Lamb. Here is revealed *where* the roots of the first resurrection and the "fulness" of the thousand years are. The visionary perspective, which illumines the dimensions of history in all of its ebb and flow, its rise and fall, already awaits the unveiling that will remove all secrecy forever.

Apocalyptic comfort

There have been countless discussions weighing the relative merits of the church-historical and the end-historical views of the millennium. But as such this is not a pure dilemma. What it boils down to is the question "is the millennium already here or is it still to come?" There seems to be no third alternative. The Book of Revelation, however, confronts us with a totally different problem. The church-historical and end-historical interpretations are much closer to one another than is often thought, for both views are concerned with fixing a phase of history. Over against this we contend that what the Book of Revelation is all about is the illumination of history from the point of view of the as-yet-hidden triumph of the Lord who is coming. The book was written in a time when persecution was today's reality and tomorrow's probability.[68] It was a book for those days already, for that time was near (1:3). It speaks of the hour of trial that is to come over the whole world (3:10). We hear the cries of the souls under the altar, sacrificed for their witness (6:9f.); we see those who have come through the great persecution (7:14). What happens here is described in tremendous perspectives, in apocalyptic proportions: war in heaven (12:7), the anger of the dragon (12:17), the death of the witnesses (11:7f.), the mark of the beast and the great boycott (13:13-17). But the comfort of ultimate victory sounds through all this, now to be proclaimed and some day to be revealed in the eschatological fulfilment. Now is the time for the call to endurance (14:12), for it is the time of the "not yet." But the light does not remain hidden. The last book of the Bible is also the book of singing, the song of Moses and the Lamb, sung by the victors over the beast and his image and the number of his name (15:2ff.). "Blessed is he who reads

"the priestly, rancorous nation *par excellence*" (pp. 185f.). Norman Cohn *(op. cit.)* discusses the reaction-motifs in chiliasm — the dream of making everything over and taking the future into one's own hands.

68. Cf. S. Giet, *L'apocalypse et l'histoire* (1957), pp. 232-34.

aloud the words of the prophecy, and blessed are those who hear, and who keep what is written therein; for the time is near" (1:3).

This is why the Apocalypse is not to be spiritualized; this is why we may not look on the resurrection of chapter 20 as a "spiritual" resurrection (regeneration). It is a radical encouragement on the road to the future in the last days. "The Apocalypse," Haag writes, "is intended to be an unveiling of that which is and will be."[69] It is not a discourse about the future provided to satisfy our curiosity, but something that proclaims and directs us to the incontrovertible salvation of God.[70] Thus, its message is not merely oriented to the present: in reading its message for today, our eyes are directed to the great future. From the point of view of its apocalyptic dimensions things appear different from what we experience in the empirical life of "not yet." Indeed, Revelation is the book of the solution, not of the riddle of history.

All of this may be recapitulated in the question of what is to be understood by the church triumphant. Traditional dogmatics contrasts the church triumphant with the church militant. The New Testament, however, unmistakably indicates that there are aspects of triumph for the church in the time of the "not yet." Paul not only speaks of our being "more than conquerors" (Rom. 8:37); he sees the triumph of Christ made effective when the life of Jesus manifests itself in our bodies (2 Cor. 4:11). All this is not without struggle. It is a triumph whose outcome is hope (Rom. 5:3f.; cf. 2 Cor. 1:4f.). The hiddenness of this triumph can become a temptation for the believers, a temptation to take this eschatological comfort as a facile theodicy instead of as comfort for today. The temptation is especially strong to look at martyrdom in this way. But the whole gospel is at stake here, just as it is when Paul's remark, "I consider that the sufferings of this present time are not worth comparing with the glory that is to be revealed to us" (Rom. 8:18), is taken to be rank escapism. For this insight and perception, this trust, is essential to the passionate anticipation of the great apocalypse that will envelop the entire creation.

No, neither Paul's words of comfort nor the first resurrection of Revelation 20 is a theodicy that misconstrues the cold, hard

---

69. *Die zwei Zeugen* (1957), p. 120.
70. Cf. H. W. Wolff, "Das Geschichtsverständnis der AT Prophetie," in C. Westermann (ed.), *Probleme AT Hermeneutik* (1960), p. 321.

facts of life. Rather, these are consoling promises that suffice in the midst of the irresistibility of the flow of events that presses on us from all sides.[71] The martyrs of Revelation 20, who have sustained the most bitter defeat of all in this life, are now portrayed in a wholly different light. From this the meaning of the disarming of evil, of life, of resurrection, and of the future becomes clear. And when the vision describes the release of Satan in apocalyptic imagery that refers back to Ezekiel,[72] the point is not to cast uncertainty on everything again, but to indicate the extent to which the comfort of the first resurrection is unassailable, even in the face of the ultimate attempt to contradict the incontrovertible triumph of the Lamb (cf. Rev. 17:12 — "for one hour").

So the important choice is not between interpreting the millennium as a feature of church history and interpreting it as something to be awaited at the end of history. Rather, it is the choice between apocalyptic comfort and a strictly chronological narrative account. "Apocalyptic comfort" is not spiritualization; it does not involve some kind of inner light. It is a view of reality seen in eschatological perspective in the last days. The vision of Revelation 20 is too clear and too compelling to allow interpretation of the millennium as a realm of peace "from which sin, suffering and death are not yet expelled."[73]

The millennium is something more than and different from "maximum unfolding" within definite limitations, for the vision of believers ruling with Christ for a thousand years is the precise opposite of *limited* possibilities. Ecclesiastical chiliasm, which awaits the rule of peace, warns against spiritualism and defeatism, and draws attention to the positive signs of Christ's rule, proceeds from an idea of the millennium as *fulfilment* of history.[74] Quite properly, it expects momentous things. But along with the conviction that faith can never expect too much, the question of the certainty of our knowledge arises. For this faith is tied up with a very concrete "knowledge" — about the church's being proved right publicly, about the rule of a political and social order through Christ's power.[75] Here again we are reminded of Mary's Magnificat, with its anticipation of the great

71. Cf. E. Lohmeyer, *Komm.*, p. 196.
72. Cf. M. A. Beek, *op. cit.*, pp. 19ff., 43.
73. Berkhof, *CMH*, p. 157.
74. Miskotte, *op. cit.*, p. 415; cf. p. 429.
75. Berkhof, *CMH*, p. 157.

turnabout — the revolution — in which the mighty are dethroned and those of low degree exalted (Luke 1:52). But this reminder of the Messianic age — the *reality* of what Mary saw — confronts us with the real problem of chiliasm.

The Song of Mary is at once revealing and ominous, admonishing and comforting. Mary *sees* this "reality" in the coming of Christ. Despite Herod, this is no illusion. But the most urgent question is this: Is this reality already manifest, or will it be manifested before Christ's parousia? And if the latter is the case, does Revelation guarantee it? Anyone who believes this is probably inclined to a twofold expectation: of the millennium and of the new Jerusalem; of this earth and of the new earth from which death, tears, and deception will have been banished (Rev. 21:4; 22:15). In this case, there are two fulfilments.[76] Chiliasm, without denying the second fulfilment, focuses all its attention on the first fulfilment as the fulfilment of the promise of God *in* history and not in some kind of "suprahistorical solution."[77] This view of an "intrahistorical" fulfilment is a view of reality with sorrow, tragedy, sin, and grief, and of this Sabbath of God as the final form of Christocracy, distinguishable from the new Jerusalem, which is "the ultimate creative act of God in which all the ages will find their completion."[78]

This view does not faithfully represent the biblical eschatological message, not because we should see this world as a closed system, not because we should — in a fit of deterministic arrogance — throw off belief in miracles, and least of all, not because we ought to be pessimists or defeatists about this earth.

Berkhof sounds an important note of warning against searching more diligently for signs of Christ's cross than of His glory.[79] How often, in looking at this world, we are inclined more to believe in the devil than in Him who through His death destroyed "him who has the power of death" (Heb. 2:14). But, granted all this, the argument for the "first fulfilment" still does not follow. The decision for or against the reduplication of fulfilment finally falls in the area of how we ought to understand the Book of Revelation. It is the question of the meaning of the open door in heaven and of the voice that sounded like a trumpet (Rev. 4:1). All of this took place while John was

76. Miskotte, *op. cit.*, p. 431.
77. *Ibid.*, p. 415.
78. *Ibid.*, pp. 420, 429.
79. Berkhof, *CMH*, p. 133.

"in the spirit" (1:10). Through this open door appear wonderful and unthought-of things. Similarly, Stephen saw the heavens opened and the glory of God, and Jesus standing at God's right hand (Acts 7:55f.). This is no theodicy, missing the gravity and reality of the event, but it is a vision without illusion or disappointment, In these circumstances, "... gazing at him, all ... saw that his face was like the face of an angel" (Acts 6:15).[80]

Chiliasm and Christocracy

Chiliasm really boils down to a special form of Christocracy. Now Christocracy usually talks about the exousia of Christ — His authority over all things since His resurrection and ascension. And it is important to note that in discussions of this Christocracy the same tensions that characterize the Book of Revelation always come up. These are probably illustrated most clearly by the cry of the souls under the altar, "how long?" (Rev. 6:9f.). They are tensions about the certainty of salvation in the midst of this threatening reality. In the context of these tensions of "already" and "not yet," of defeat and victory, the doctrine of the two kingdoms comes up for discussion. The bearing of this doctrine on eschatology is the notion that the fulfilment will bring the dissolution of this duality of kingdoms. Plainly the chiliastic view of God's penultimate mystery is also important in this context. Will this tension, which is sometimes nearly unbearable, always remain on earth, or will it disappear in a realization in Jesus Christ?

This is a critical problem, at least for those who are not ready to abandon earthly existence to meaninglessness. Some contemporary Lutheran theologians have taken the position that the doctrine of the two kingdoms does not limit Christ's universal lordship over all things. Lau says that there can be no doubt that the New Testament teaches a cosmic dominion of Christ, who is proclaimed as the All-powerful.[81] There is no question of an autonomy of the *regnum mundi*.[82] The only tensions are those that arise from the opposition of law and gospel. Objections to this version of the doctrine of the two kingdoms are raised by those who want to consider all of life,

---

80. *hōsei prosopón angélou*. Some commentators think that 6:15 should follow 7:56; cf. E. Haenchen, *Apostelgeschichte*, p. 230.
81. F. Lau, "Die Königsherrschaft Jesu Christi und die lutherische Zweireichelehre," *Kerygma und Dogma*, VI (1960), 312.
82. W. Künneth, *Politik zwischen Dämon und Gott* (1961), pp. 54ff.

society and state included, from a biblical perspective. An example of this is Barth's christological foundation of justice and the state as an attempt to avoid the dangers of dualism. But the disagreement does not stop here: Lau counters Barth with an "irrevocable No to any christological foundation of the state," which he sees as an impossible attempt to bring the norms of the gospel directly to bear in the political realm.[83]

If we look closely at this dispute, we see that the underlying questions apply as well to chiliasm, especially the ecclesiastical type. The interrelatedness of all these questions, we have suggested, stems from the tensions inherent in Christocracy. These are not artificial pseudo-problems.[84] Both Luther and Calvin were very much interested in these questions. What is at issue here is neither an abandonment of the world in favor of a withdrawal into inwardness nor premillennialistic pessimism. This might be the case in a radically dualistic doctrine of the two kingdoms, but neither Luther nor Calvin adhered to such a doctrine. Even life in this world is not without its authority and ordering. It is precisely on this point that Calvin rejects any eschatologically revolutionary sentiment. He criticizes those who recognize no authority above themselves and suppose "that nothing will be safe unless the whole world is reshaped to a new form."[85] So whether or not interest in earthly life is legitimate is not in question. At this point there is no argument between chiliasts and those who dispute chiliasm.

The legitimacy of this interest in earthly life always opens up an outlook on new possibilities.[86] As a result, the decisive

83. *Op. cit.*, pp. 314f. Lau speaks of "the illusionary in Bucer's conception," but directs his argument primarily against Barth. Lau does not see the *regnum mundi* as outside of God's dominion, but it is not "dominion of Christ" in the NT sense of Christ as the "thorn-crowned crucified king" (p. 324).

84. Cf. E. Kinder, "Gottesreich und Weltreich bei Augustin und bei Luther," in *Festschrift W. Elert* (1955), p. 29; J. van den Berg, *Twee regimenten, één Heer* (1961), pp. 23ff.

85. *Inst.*, IV.xx.1.

86. For example, Barth's criticism of Luther becomes exceptionally sharp because he saw in what Luther taught — the isolation of creation and law from gospel — a point of contact for the German development of National Socialism; "Brief an Pfarrer Kooyman," in *Eine Schweizer Stimme* (1948), p. 122. Cf. also Barth's critique of the autonomy of the political realm; "The Christian Community and the Civil Community," in *Against the Stream* (1954), pp. 27ff.; and H. Diem, *K. Barths Kritik am deutschen Luthertum* (1947), pp. 9ff.

question becomes one of the certainty of the chiliastic expectation concerning the future. Chiliasm claims to know of a definite course of history, of a delimited phase of human life into which the reign of peace will come within this dispensation, whether via a spectacular event or via the power of the gospel and of Christ's resurrection.

It is the grounds of this chiliastic certainty, however, that are in question. In other words: has it been revealed to us — as part of the revelation of the cross and resurrection — that the tensions still present in the time of Christocracy will be removed prior to the fulfilment in a great turnabout in all relationships? Two arguments for an affirmative answer to this question have been advanced: (1) the biblical witness of Revelation 20; and (2) the necessity of an "intrahistorical" fulfilment.

The second argument — the necessity of an intrahistorical fulfilment — has often been stressed. Such an intrahistorical fulfilment is not without problems, however, as is apparent from the way the concept of analogy operates in it. Barth uses a concept of analogy, not in a millennialistic sense, but as an indication of the potential of any time when the power of Christ's cross and resurrection are revealed in earthly reality.[87] For Berkhof too this kind of analogy is operative, not restricted to the millennium, but something that is capable of being manifested even now. But in the process of unfolding, this analogical reality takes on special universality. Berkhof speaks of the "tense expectation . . . that this dispensation before the consummation (since and through the advent of Christ) will unveil itself as analogous with his victory."[88] Earlier, he talks of the event of the Kingdom "which is being realized throughout the world by the missionary endeavour, as *an analogy of the Christ-Event which is being realized throughout the world.*"[89] In support of

87. Cf. K. Barth, "Christian Community and Civil Community," p. 32, on the existence of the state "as an allegory, as a correspondence and an analogue to the Kingdom of God which the Church preaches and believes in." Barth typifies this dispensation as "in the midst of this 'world that passeth away,' in the midst of the great, but temporary contrast between Church and State, in the period which the Divine patience has granted us between the resurrection of Jesus Christ and His return"; *Church and State* (Eng. tr., 1939), p. 86. As far as I can see, this concept of analogy bears no traces of millennialism.

88. Berkhof, *CMH*, p. 125.

89. *Ibid.*, p. 79 (italics his).

this, he refers to the parables of the mustard seed and leaven, a reference that gives the notion of growth an important position. Chiliasm cannot accept this idea because it lacks the decisively spectacular elements. The growth-perspective sees, on the basis of Christ and in connection with the believer's responsibility, a new spring sustained by God's gracious sunshine, in which the great transition from the hiddenness to the visibility of Christ's Kingdom has come.

The reaction of chiliasm — ecclesiastical chiliasm included — to this idea is easy to understand in the light of the history of the church. Pessimism is by no means restricted to American pre-millennialism. Indications of captivity to catastrophic evil are so apparent everywhere that one is almost inclined to believe in a determinism of evil. This results in the conviction that evil is an autonomous, unbridled, and omnipotent power, untouched — and untouchable — by the victory obtained through Jesus Christ. What is the origin of this kind of thinking? For one thing, there are a number of scriptural passages, frequently cited in pre-millennial literature. John writes that "the whole world is in the power of the evil one" (1 John 5:19). Paul predicts that "in the last days there will come times of stress. For men will be lovers of self..." (2 Tim. 3:1f.).[90] Peter mentions the "scoffers... following their own passions" (2 Pet. 3:3). Furthermore, the Pauline admonition to "set your minds on the things that are above *(tá ánō)*, not on the things that are on earth *(tá epí tēs gēs)*" (Col. 3:2; cf. vs. 1) seems to concur. After all, will "all these things" not be dissolved (2 Pet. 3:11)? Is not "the form of this world" passing away (1 Cor. 7:31)?

There is no ground for calling these passages expressions of pessimism; but they did play an important role in the early Christian expectation, and post-millennial theories have always had difficulty with them. Still, chiliasts and antichiliasts alike have appealed to these passages in support of pessimism, wrenching them from any context except the perspective of the transcendent realm of peace.[91] On the basis of an unbroken deter-

---

90. C. Bouma, *Komm.,* p. 313, speaks of "generally prevalent evil," referring to the generality of Paul's words *(hoi ánthrōpoi).* In 1 Tim. 4:1 Paul talks about "some" *(tines)* who "will depart from the faith" in later times *(en hystérois kairois).*

91. Schnackenburg calls 1 John 5:19 a "dark, pessimistic saying" *(Komm.,* p. 359), explaining it in terms of the experience of the congregations of Asia Minor in the face of unbelief and hatred. On the use of *kosmos* in John, cf. Sasse, in *TDNT,* s.v., III, 894f. Interestingly, the elements of

minism the world could be written off and earthly life described only in terms of a spreading universal apostasy. Consequently, even less remained of faith and the power of the gospel, which contains the promise of life for the present as well as for the future. Once committed to viewing evil deterministically, one could find daily confirmation in the world around him; in other words, he could boast of having the support of both Scripture and history for his determinism. It is understandable and commendable that opposition arose to this determinism. But one surely must not counter the certainty of this pessimism with the certainty of an intrahistoric fulfilment. Both views ostensibly rely on Scripture, no matter how great the differences between pre- and post-millennialism may be. And if it were in fact Scripture's intention to enrich the believer's "knowledge" of intrahistoric development with a new certainty, there would be every reason to expect a transcendently inbreaking, supernatural millennium along with the first (bodily) resurrection. It would then not be possible — certainly not with an appeal to Revelation 20, which lacks these aspects — to go the route of "maximum development," but only to look for the reign of peace in all its strangeness and wonder.

Now if someone finds it necessary to reject both the certainty of a transcendent millennium and the certainty of an evolutionary penetration into the millennium, it might seem that he must face the future with much less assurance and hope. But does this lesser certainty automatically bring with it a weaker eschatological expectation? After all, certainty is also denied to us in any effort to calculate the date of the parousia; but this does not limit the expectation, it stimulates it. And the same is true with respect to certainty about an intrahistorical fulfilment before the parousia. Faith is always thrown back on the certainty that God's ways are and will remain inscrutable. This excludes any deterministic view of evil, and unless we leave room for what is humanly improbable and surprising, we have never really broken with this determinism. Thus our expectation cannot fail, regardless of what happens. The road to the future can be traveled only one step at a time.

In evil and barren times, times of martyrdom, the trumpets

pessimism suggest themselves to chiliasts (especially premillennialists) in connection with the time prior to the rule of peace, and to anti-chiliasts in an attempt to prove that there can be no such rule of peace before Christ's parousia.

of revelation — of the Book of Revelation — sound, and the proclamation goes out that everything is really different from what men in the depths of bitter experience think it is. The songs of Revelation would sound silly were they not full of the perspective of the history of salvation, and were trust in Him who is the First and the Last not unshaken. Revelation does not presuppose this trust without further ado as something that goes without saying. It is not without reason that the first of the blessings recorded in the Book of Revelation is not for those who die in the Lord (14:13) or for those who are invited to the marriage supper of the Lamb (19:9), but for those who read, hear, and keep what is written, now that "the time is near" (1:3).

This blessedness, which is realized in steadfastness, is not the outcome of a rational theodicy. In times of trial and strife it asserts itself. The way cannot be surveyed; despite that, we do not go blindly into the future. Our eyes are opened wide as we see the day draw near. Still, we "see in a mirror dimly" (1 Cor. 13:12). There are enigmas; there is mystery. No narrative, reporter's account of what the future will be like is provided to alleviate this tension. That is probably the deepest mystery of eschatology: that the joy of this eschatological outlook goes hand in hand with this suspense.

There is a real danger of talking too quickly, too glibly, about this joy, forgetting that it is a gift of God, involving no human initiative whatever. Then Campenhausen's words about joy in the Christian life are to the point: "Perhaps we ought not to talk too much about joy, for that may not be the way to attain it and hold on to it."[92] Still, we are comforted that Paul's reference to our seeing in a mirror, only dimly, is in the context of his great hymn to love, which bears all things and hopes all things (1 Cor. 13:7).

92. H. F. von Campenhausen, "Die Heiterkeit der Christen," in *Tradition und Leben* (1960), p. 431.

CHAPTER ELEVEN

ISRAEL AS SIGN?

THE REASON FOR allotting Israel a separate chapter in a book on eschatology is not difficult to understand. The future of Israel, particularly its conversion and restoration, has always been a prominent topic in discussions of the last things. In recent years there has been renewed attention given to the Jewish people, on the one hand because of the tragic outbursts of antisemitism in our age, which seem to suggest that the tribulations suffered by this people are nearing completion, on the other hand because of the rise of the Jewish state in the land of Palestine. Old and new questions about the function and place of Israel in God's plans in history are coming to the fore again.

Antisemitism and Christianity

An expression one hears often in these discussions is the *riddle* or *mystery* of Israel. The questions that this riddle suggests are primarily exegetical ones, but they are inextricably bound up with the course of Israel's history through the centuries. Is not Israel's history, many have wondered, a clear indication of God's concern for and ultimate objective with Israel as His chosen people? Is it romanticism to trace the finger of God in the history of this people, or is it meaningful? Is Israel's past, in its relation to God, simply past, or is it still relevant in some mysterious way? In the often bitterly emotional discussion of these questions, one detects a general aversion to the idea that Israel, since its "rejection" of the Messiah, has played out its role in the history of God's acts and now goes on in an ordinary, perspectiveless, unmysterious existence with only political importance. Many have argued that we not only may, but must look at Israel differently, and expect its conversion and restoration as fulfilment of divine promises. This is the eschatological relevance of Israel, this expectation of a final, decisive turnabout, in which Israel accepts the Messiah, "the hope of Israel" (Acts 28:20), a turnabout that will serve as one of the most spectacular "signs" of the end-time and of the nearness of the Kingdom. Chiliasm placed this anticipation second only to its expectation of the reign of peace.

In the deepest sense, the question of Israel does not arise from the historical situation of today — the State of Israel in Palestine — but from the specification of Israel as God's chosen people. When this point is brought into the discussion, the debate often becomes very caustic.[1] Those who deny the abiding actuality of Israel's election are often charged with a form of antisemitism. This may sound a bit strange, since we usually think of antisemitism as a theory that takes immediate expression in acts of cruelty and brutality. This denial of the continuing actuality of Israel's election, however, is seen as a definitely negative view of the Jewish people, which provides fertile ground in which antisemitism can grow up, whether or not it leads to persecution of Jews. This negative view, then, is considered to be a highly subjective and prejudicial one, lacking any foundation in historical fact. It is summed up in the popular notion that after the crucifixion of Jesus Israel is nothing more than a "rejected" people, a demonstration of God's judgment. Its history, its entire existence, is seen as overburdened by the shadow of doom. How often we hear, as an explanation of all Jewish history, those words: "His blood be on us and on our children" (Matt. 27:25) ; as if the persecution wrought by man against the Jewish people is somehow "justifiable" in terms of divine judgment, even though those who say these things would dissociate themselves from the more reprehensible aspects of antisemitism. Now as long as there are those who think in these categories, how can there help being a climate that stimulates new acts of antisemitism? Cannot antisemitism itself in a secularized form of Christendom go around representing itself as the executioner of God's judgment? Was this in fact not the

1. E.g., the discussions of Israel at the second assembly of the World Council of Churches in Evanston (1954) were much influenced by the Middle East situation at that time. No positive statement came out of these meetings. Cf. H. Berkhof, "Israel als oecumenisch struikelblok," *In de Waagschaal,* May 28, 1955; articles by J. Sittler, G. Hedenquist, *et al.,* in *The Ecumenical Review* for 1955; and the statement on Israel and antisemitism made at the third assembly of the WCC in New Delhi (1961).

case in the German church, which helped shape the climate so ably suited to Hitler's "final solution" to the Jewish problem?

It is not enough just to recall what antisemitism has done; we must examine the thought-world that allowed these deeds to happen. Even in the Christian church the "causal relationship" between Israel's rejection of the Messiah and its subsequent suffering and despair has often been taken to be self-evident.[2] It is high time to cut ourselves free from this determinism and delve anew into what the Bible says about Israel, with particular attention to the question of whether there is ground for eschatological certainty concerning Israel as a coming "sign" before the Lord's parousia.

We ought first to consider the alleged traces of antisemitism in the New Testament. Paul's supposed "polemic against his persecutors" is said to be a pure example of this. According to Stauffer, Paul considered the wrath over Israel to be irrevocable, to the end; yet he later — in Romans 9-11 — underwent an "astonishing *volte-face*."[3] Others find antisemitism in the New Testament themes of Israel's unbelief, guilt, and rejection of the Messiah. P. Winter elaborates on this — to take only one example — in his arguments that the Gospels are much too easy on Pilate, in order to place the blame for the trial of Jesus on the Jews.[4] T. A. Bürkill finds

2. Probably the most striking example is encountered in H. J. Kraus's article, "Juden und Christen," *Christliches-jüdisches Forum*, No. 26 (1961), 4-6. A. J. Visser discusses the statements of the early church fathers about the Jews, in *Op het spoor van Israël* (1961), pp. 121ff. Cf. Jules Isaac, "Hat der Antisemitismus christliche Ursachen?", *Evangelische Theologie*, XXI (1961), 339ff.; K. H. Kroon, "Ontmoeting met Israël," *Wending*, IV (1949), 406, who speaks of "nineteen centuries of Christianized heathen antisemitism." Although M. A. Beek is more cautious, he nevertheless points out that "the Christian has repeatedly appeared as persecutor," so that he should be considered as "a very critical collaborator"; *Israël. Land, volk, cultuur* (1962), pp. 210ff. In this connection he praises Nes Ammim, the Christian kibbutz in Israel, so highly.

3. Stauffer, *NT Theology* (Eng. tr., 1955), pp. 188-92; and his "Paulus und Israel," in *Juden, Christen, Deutsche* (1961), pp. 307ff. Käsemann speaks of antisemitism in connection with 1 Thess. 2:15; see also his reference to Phil. 3:4-9.

4. Winter, *On the Trial of Jesus* (1961), pp. 51ff. Pilate's star is said to rise in Mark (15:1-15) particularly: Pilate "wondered" (vs. 5), wanted to release Jesus, and found no guilt in Him. Circumstances changed in the fourth century, so that Pilate was no longer necessary as "a witness to Jesus' innocence . . . and Pilate missed canonization" (p. 61). Cf. also J. Blinzler, *The Trial of Jesus* (Eng. tr., 1959).

antisemitism to be particularly prominent in the Gospel of Mark.[5]

Obviously whether or not these remarks are accurate depends on what is meant by antisemitism. Historically, the word has denoted a judgment of Israel out of impure and dishonest motives, according to which Israel is portrayed in the most unfavorable terms, generalized about, and denied any redeeming features. Once one is under the influence of this mode of thought, it is only a short step to interpreting Israel as laboring under the effects of the "inherited guilt" of its past.

It would be possible to debate at great length questions like whether or not the Scriptures are really "soft" on Pilate. But it seems to me that a wholly different question lies behind this one, a question that is much more to the point and comprehends the total picture of Israel. That is the question of Israel's election, a prominent study in nearly all considerations of Israel. For our purposes, we are concerned with more than incidental questions about the exegesis of Romans 11:25; what is at issue is whether or not an outlook on the future follows directly from this election.

The point of departure in the dispute about Israel's election is the *particularity* of this event. Responding to Jean-Paul Sartre's denial of the particularity of the Jewish people, K. H. Miskotte countered that this was the most radical type of antisemitism,[6] for it denies Israel's "unrepeatable election," and it is blind to the depth-dimension of God's guidance of Israel through history. Can a past that has been qualified by election ever come to naught? Can "election of God" as we usually understand it ever be changed into "rejection"? Can the church inherit the place of the chosen people of Israel, so that election passes over to the church?[7] Do we not usually consider God's election as something irrevocable, definitive, and all-powerful; and is it

---

5. Bürkill, "Anti-Semitism in St. Mark's Gospel," *Novum Testamentum*, III (1959), 34-53.

6. In Miskotte's review of Sartre's *Portrait of the Antisemite* (Eng. tr., 1948), in *Grensgebied* (1946).

7. H. J. Schoeps sees this as the primary notion of the church; *Israel und Christenheit* (1961), pp. 43ff.; cf. also R. Pfisterer, "Antisemitismus und Eschatologie," *Evangelische Theologie*, XIX (1959), 269, 274, on the Jews and the "myth of their rejection." T. C. Vriezen points out that F. Delitzsch already rejected talk of Israel's election as a thing of past history as "orthodox antisemitism"; Vriezen, *Die Erwählung Israels nach dem AT*, p. 111.

consequently not meaningless to assume that the election of Israel could be negated by human reaction, even unbelief? Is all this anything more than a dialectic of election and reprobation, making everything depend completely on human decision and reaction? Is the observation "once elected, always elect" not far more to the point?[8] In short, does Israel's election not reflect a groundless preference for this nation above all others, a disposition that manifests divine love and has important consequences for how we think about Israel's future?

We have to take these questions seriously, even as Paul himself returns time and again to the theme of Israel's election in his epistles. "Has God rejected his people?" he asks, and unhesitatingly replies: "By no means!... God has not rejected his people whom he foreknew" (Rom. 11:1f.). Later in the same chapter he tells the Romans that the Jews are "enemies of God for your sake," but are "beloved for the sake of their forefathers" (vs. 28). He explains this all by saying that "the gifts and the call of God are irrevocable" (vs. 29). Paul's emphasis on foreknowledge and irrevocability understandably gives rise to the question whether Israel's history after the rejection of the Messiah can indeed be considered as finished and without further relevance. Is it not obviously self-evident from this irreversibility that there is still a real prospect for the Jewish people? Berkhof does not hesitate to draw this conclusion: that the New Testament answer to the question of Israel's future is obvious — Israel's salvation. "That nation for whom he primarily came, and which before any other is reserved for his glory and service ... will find its way back to its calling.... Here as nowhere else [God's] faithfulness will prove to go beyond and overcome our unfaithfulness."[9] Clearly, Berkhof's choice of the words "obvious" and "must" is founded on the idea of election and its irreversibility, on God's not going back on His promises once given. It is not merely the one isolated text — "and so all Israel will be saved" (Rom. 11:26) — but the whole divine initiative of election that acts as guarantee of the future. What Paul says only confirms this.

In church history and theology the word "election" conjures up the ideas of the prevenient, gracious, and triumphant aspects of the dealings of God with man. Election, it is stressed,

---

8. H. Kraemer, *Het raadsel der geschiedenis* (1941), p. 27.
9. Berkhof, *CMH*, pp. 134f.

does not rest in human effort, faith, or merits. As a matter of divine faithfulness, which cannot be brought to naught by human unfaithfulness, election can never be negated by any human reaction whatever.[10] Can this all be irrelevant for Israel's election? Israel alone was chosen from among the nations (Deut. 14:2; Ps. 147:20; Amos 3:2) to be God's own possession in a very special and unique relationship (Exod. 19:5; Deut. 7:6; 26:18; 1 Sam. 12:22; 1 Chron. 17:21; Ps. 135:4; Isa. 41:8). All this is a manifestation of divine love: "When Israel was a child, I *loved* him" (Hos. 11:1; cf. Deut. 7:8; 33:3). There is no other "reason" for Israel's election than love. This might correctly be characterized as the a priori of divine election. There is no consideration of Israel's "merit" in this divine love.[11] Nor is this divine a priori a formal relationship: it is unmistakably God's act of salvation in leading forth "his people with joy, his chosen ones with singing" (Ps. 105:43). Can this stream be dammed up, this history come to a halt? "How can I give you up, O Ephraim!" (Hos. 11:8).[12]

Election and rejection

All this can hardly be argued about. But differences of opinion do come up when we consider the question of whether there are apparent already in the Old Testament evidences of Israel's rejection. Apart from the problem of harmonizing this with election, the beginnings of this notion must be acknowledged. Did Israel not face the "ominous possibility of rejection?"[13] The same Amos who recognizes the a priori of divine election (3:2) also warns of the possibility that Israel would once again be brought to the level of the nonelect nations like the Philistines and Syrians (9:7).[14] Is there not an explicit reference to Israel's rejection in direct connection with election in 2 Kings 23:27: "I will cast off this city which I have chosen, Jerusalem, and the house of which I said, My name shall be there"?

10. Cf. Canons of Dort, I, 7, 9, 10.
11. Cf. H. Wildberger, *Jahwes Eigentumsvolk* (1960), p. 12. Further evidence of the intimate connection between God's love and His choosing is found in Deut. 4:37; 10:15.
12. Cf. C. van Gelderen-W. H. Gispen, *Komm., ad loc.*, on what is *impossible* for God.
13. Wildberger, *op. cit.*, p. 117.
14. Cf. Berkouwer, *Divine Election* (Eng. tr., 1958), p. 314; G. von Rad, *OT Theology*, II, 136ff.

Time and again, it seems, the two themes go hand in hand: on the one side, rejection; on the other the affirmation that God will not reject. In the time of Jeremiah, when the people were saying that God had rejected those whom He had elected, God promised that He would not reject the descendants of Jacob and David, but would have mercy on them (Jer. 33:23-26).

The multiplicity of Old Testament references to election and rejection can never be understood on the basis of a deterministic doctrine of election, for such a doctrine fails to understand what happens in the relationship between God and His people. That Israel is God's possession rests squarely in divine election, but at the same time there is a further elucidation of what being a possession means, an elucidation that must come as a shock to those who have failed to understand election. "*If you will obey my voice and keep my covenant, you shall be my own possession among all peoples*" (Exod. 19:5; cf. Jer. 7:23). This "conditionalizing of election," as Wildberger calls it, clearly indicates that there is no opposition between election and covenant and that election is more than a *fatum* from which conclusions can be drawn without taking account of one's relationship to God.[15]

It must be acknowledged — if one ever hopes to understand the Old Testament — that there is a correlative connection between election and faith, discipleship, and service of God. Many have recoiled from this explanation, for fear of watering down the doctrine of election with ideas of a deserved reward or belief foreseen by God. But the correlation in election has nothing to do with the worthiness of human acts. Rather it confirms that election is not a *fatum* — a mere divine utterance — either in the bad sense or the good sense of that term. In other words, election does not entail an automatic, safe place of security, an ahistorical positing of salvation not personally related to God. Neither the Old nor the New Testament teaches that kind of doctrine of election. And Romans 9-11 suffices to demonstrate that this was not Paul's concept of election.

Israel's unbelief presented many problems for Paul. Did this unbelief mean that the Word of God had failed (Rom. 9:6)? He radically denies this, since he is convinced that Israel, in its encounter with Yahweh, had not chanced upon a capricious

15. Wildberger, *op. cit.*, pp. 116, 36; W. H. Gispen, *Exodus*, II, 54; H. H. Rowley, *The Biblical Doctrine of Election* (1953), pp. 45, 54.

God, who, having given His word, would then not remain true to it, or be unable to bring it to completion. That would be the case with Israel if election were a point of departure for self-evident conclusions. But this was completely foreign and unacceptable to Paul. Not all descendants of the tribes of Israel are truly Israel, and "not all are children of Abraham because they are his descendants" (vs. 7). Still, this does not make election relative or a hidden, arbitrary "mystery," but it does reject the idea that election is an objective state of affairs beyond relations of faith and unbelief. Paul emphasizes that God's election lacks arbitrariness. After all, He reveals Himself as the compassionate, electing God in such a way that the depth and background of this election cannot be mistaken, because the electing intention has its own structure and style and unassailable fixity: "not because of works but because of his call" (vs. 11). Just because of that one can speak of correlative connections in election (as in the *if* of Exod. 19:5) without relativizing but confirming the a priori of election. Because election is not something arbitrary, to which one must subject himself, and in which one must take heart, it is an indubitable matter, something on which one may always depend but from which no conclusions may be drawn without faith.

Only in this way can the varied election terminology of the Old Testament be understood. It is not something out of the past that we look back on but have nothing to do with. Paul continually concerns himself with the election under the old covenant. Under that covenant the electing God could speak now this way, now that way — now of judgment, now of grace — not because He is unreliable, but because He is faithful. This faithfulness is not a reliable premise from which one can draw conclusions, but a refuge. Paul describes this faithful God who is a refuge correlatively as bestowing His *"riches* on *all who call upon him"* (10:12). Thus when Paul discusses the ways of God and Israel, he can write that human unfaithfulness cannot nullify God's faithfulness (Rom. 3:3). Even when there is an unbelieving reaction in Israel, amounting to a thrusting away *(apōtheisthe)* of the Word of God (Acts 13:46), God apparently did not reciprocate with divine rejection: "God has not rejected his people" (Rom. 11:2). Paul is apparently referring back to Psalm 94:14: "The LORD will not forsake (LXX — *ouk apōsetai*) his people," and to the Old Testament idea of an inheritance that God will not desert, because of the glory of His holy Name: "It has pleased the LORD to make you a people for himself" (1 Sam. 12:22).

For Paul the divine act is so completely and unassailably irrevocable that one can always depend on it. The relationship between God and Israel is not a mutual, chain-reaction type of thing in which evil is repaid with evil. The God of Israel whom Paul knows and witnesses to is completely different. "All day long" He holds out His hands "to a disobedient and contrary people" (Rom. 10:21). Thus Paul's forceful "By no means!" to the question of whether God has rejected His people (11:1) is central to his understanding of this God. H. J. Schoeps sees Paul's belief as grounded in his "Jewish faith in the faithfulness of God, who cannot revoke covenant, law, and election, so surely as He is the God of truth, and cannot make already revealed and realized truth into a lie, not even when Israel has betrayed that truth."[16] Thus Paul sees the rejection of Israel as something impossible and not even worth discussing. The certainty of God's unchanging faithfulness is a matter of His deity. Paul cannot write a single word about Israel without thinking of this unchanging faithfulness. His entire train of thought in Romans 9-11 is determined by this. His reasoning here does not attempt to relativize Israel's election or to make of it something unstable, structured in an entirely different way from what we usually understand by God's election.[17] Paul is as concerned with the reality of God's faithfulness as he is with the riddle of Israel's unbelief. All that he observes in Israel, in all its dark and confused ways, is insufficient to provide a counter-example to God's faithfulness. The "great sorrow and unceasing anguish" (Rom. 9:2) that fills him cannot threaten his certainty that God's word cannot fail.

16. Schoeps, *Paul*, p. 242; cf. *Israel und Christenheit*, p. 45, where he claims that the certainty of Jewish consciousness of faith has always rested in the possession of the Torah. Cf. also E. Peterson, "Die Kirche aus Juden und Heiden," in *Theologische Traktate* (1951), p. 289.

17. Cf. in this connection J. R. Wiskerke, *Volk van Gods keuze* (1955), p. 131, on the so-called "second" election, based on Isa. 14:1 ("the LORD ... will again choose Israel"). Wiskerke says that there was a "lacuna" in the first election and that the second election proclaims a solid peace and an eternal kingdom. Cf. Zech. 2:12 ("the LORD ... will again choose Jerusalem"). The word "lacuna" seems to me unacceptable and unsuitable for conveying the relationship of election and rejection. Cf. the comparison of Israel to the apple of God's eye (Zech. 2:8), which really harks back to God's election of Israel over against its enemies. Cf. also T. C. Vriezen, *Die Erwählung Israels* (1953), pp. 98ff.

Some might claim that the distinction between Romans 11:1, where Paul says that God has not rejected His people, and verse 15 of the same chapter, where he speaks of their rejection (cf. Hos. 9:17), is all too subtle, but apparently this is essential for Paul. This is the only way to understand the most paradoxical expression of these three chapters — Romans 11:28 — where Israel's status is described in a peculiar duality as enemies of God, yet beloved. Spicq comments that there is serious neglect of what the Bible says about the irrevocability of the gifts and call of God (vs. 29).[18] But without this emphasis Romans 9-11 is incomprehensible. What is the concrete meaning of this irrevocability, this nonrejection of Israel, who rejected its Messiah?

The word "irrevocable" means that any capricious or unpredictable changeability is and remains excluded. Spicq refers to Hebrews 7:21: "The Lord has sworn and will not change his mind" (*ou metameléthésetai;* cf. Ps. 110:4). God is not like those two sons in Jesus' parable who were told to go to work in the vineyard (Matt. 21:30). The numerous biblical references to God's "repenting Himself" suffice to show that His unchangeability does not imply fixity or immovability. Rather, it is an unchangeability that brings blessing, an unchangeability to which one can and may unhesitatingly appeal time and again. *Irrevocable:* the word conjures up thoughts of walking a way of no return, a way made decisive because, as Spicq says, "God never retracts His acts of grace and His choices,"[19] a way of divine grace to man, "for godly grief produces a repentance that leads to salvation and brings no regret *(ametaméléton)*" (2 Cor. 7:10). What God does irrevocably constitutes gifts of grace, independent of human achievement, charismata. "He who calls you is faithful" (1 Thess. 5:24). In Romans 9-11 we see Paul using this word "irrevocable" in connection with God's love for Israel, "applying it to the case of Israel, presently unfaithful, but remaining the object of divine favor."[20] If we want to take seriously what the Bible says about the irrevocability of God's grace and calling, understanding it against the backdrop of God's love for Israel as attested in the Old Testament (with a rich-

18. C. Spicq, *"Ametameletos,"* *Revue biblique,* LXVII (1960), 210.
19. *Ibid.,* p. 216.
20. *Ibid.*

ness unsurpassed by the New Testament),[21] we must approach this theological "problem of Israel" in a way that takes full account of this clear testimony.

But given the electing love and faithfulness of God and the irrevocability of His gifts and calling, do the gravity and reality of Israel's guilt and unbelief not automatically diminish? Considering God's unassailable and prevenient grace, does not any human reaction of unfaithfulness become ultimately irrelevant, since it can cast no shadow over God's faithfulness? Unless one reasons deductively from an a priori notion of what election is, it must be admitted that the same light that illumines God's love and steadfastness also brings into bold relief Israel's guilt and unbelief and the tremendous consequences of it. There is no opposition in the acts of God between election and rejection. The latter always appears against the background of the former, which is why it is very serious. It is apparent that Israel could never divorce election from the context in which God framed it, lest the meaning of election be obscured and reduced to determinism, an objectivized election that goes its own way without consideration for faith and unbelief. In the Old Testament guilt stands between election and rejection, and this guilt can be defined as unwillingness to live out of the true election. This explains why the threat of rejection always came to confront a wayward Israel, whereas in the depths of despair election could also be held out as the immovable foundation of comfort and encouragement (cf. Lev. 26:44; Isa. 49:14; 50:1; 54:6; Lam. 5:20).

We must bear all this in mind when reflecting on what Paul says concerning Israel's guilt and unbelief and the consequent break. Historically, this break became evident in the radical change, the cutting off of Israel after its "fall," when salvation forged ahead from the Jews to the Gentiles. In this transition the priority of Israel is still presupposed, in that the gospel must first be preached to them.[22] Not until they reject its message is salvation extended to the Gentiles (Acts 28:28).[23] In Paul's

---

21. Cf. Spicq, "Agape. Prolégomènes à une étude de théologie néotestamentaire," Studia Hellenistica, X (1955), 105-19.

22. The gospel was first preached in synagogues (Acts 13:5, 14; 14:1; cf. 16:13, et al.). Cf. Rom. 1:16 ("to the Jew first"); and above, pp. 129ff.

23. Cf. J. Gnilka, Die Verstockung Israels. Isaias 6,9-10 in der Theologie der Synoptiker (1961), pp. 90ff.

epistle to the Romans, we see neither a mistaking of Israel's priority in the history of salvation, nor an underestimation of Israel's guilt and the consequent break. The former does not relativize the latter, but underscores the meaning of this break as an erroneous conception of the meaning of the priority. So Paul can speak of Israel's prerogatives (Rom. 9:4) and use the metaphor of the olive tree (11:17ff.). The Gentiles who are converted (wild olive shoots) are grafted into Israel (the true olive tree). Thus the mystery of Israel's priority *and* Israel's unbelief can be mentioned in the same breath. An objectivistic doctrine of election would find it impossible to deal with both Israel's rejection and election at the same time. In reality, however, Israel's election does not mean a divine act that lends itself automatically to self-evident conclusions.[24] The seriousness of Israel's failure to accept the Messiah becomes clear only in the light of Israel's election. Similarly, the crucial point in the Parable of the Vineyard (Mark 12:1-12) is that the "owner of the vineyard" will "give the vineyard to others" (vs. 9; cf. Matt. 21:41: ". . . and let out to other tenants who will give him the fruits in their season").[25] In this judgment the house of Israel becomes a fig tree without fruit (Matt. 21:19). This is the meaning of Stephen's words: "You stiff-necked people, uncircumcised in heart and ears, you always resist the Holy Spirit" (Acts 7:51).

This leaves the impression of a *definitive* break with God. Is every tie broken, and God's election frustrated by Israel's unbelief? Is this a separation even more definitive than that portrayed in the words of Hosea: "Call her name Not pitied, for I will no more have pity on the house of Israel, to forgive them at all" (1:6), and the change from the name "My people" to "Not my people?" In Hosea, however, these names later change back to "My people" and "She has obtained pity" (Hos. 2:1). Does not what is said about Israel in the Parable of the Vineyard suggest that another "people" will take Israel's place as

24. E. Dinkler says that "to be elected means, in fact, to be taken away radically from the sphere of claim-making"; "The Historical and the Eschatological Israel in Romans 9-11: A Contribution to the Problem of Predestination and Individual Responsibility," *Journal of Religion*, XXXV (1955), 119.

25. Mark 12 clearly refers back to the Song of the Vineyard (Isa. 5:1-7). Cf. Joachim Jeremias, *The Parables of Jesus*, pp. 55, 124.

God's people?[26] Did not the judgment over the temple jeopardize everything connected with the election, and was not its destruction a "proof of the inner turning away of God from His people"?[27] Does this punishment not prove "that Israel forfeited its calling and its position in the history of salvation?"[28] How much difference is there between this and Paul's denial of Israel's rejection? This is the central, decisive question concerning Israel's role in the outlook for the future.[29]

Paul and Israel

The way of salvation portrayed in Paul's Epistle to the Romans is clear to this extent: via Israel's fall and unbelief it proceeds to the Gentiles, revealing God's acts and intentions as merciful. The real problem does not become obvious until we see that this transition does not exhaust the message of Romans 9-11. The mercy of God is depicted, in that those who had not sought Him have nevertheless found Him (10:20).

26. This "transfer" is a frequent theme in discussions of Israel in connection with the church's self-concept as the new Israel. The point of departure must be the range of the concept *laós* in the NT (cf. Strathmann, in *TDNT*, s.v., IV, 50-57). Strathmann is correct in pointing out that in Rom. 9:23ff. Paul refers the My people of Hosea to the Gentiles who have been converted. Cf. also J. T. Grolle, *Op het spoor van Israël* (1961), p. 158; N. A. Dahl, *Das Volk Gottes* (1941), 210ff.; A. Oepke, *Das neue Gottesvolk* (1950).
27. W. Trilling, *Das wahre Israel* (1959), pp. 66f., cf. R. Hummel, *Die Auseinandersetzung zwischen Kirche und Judentum im Matthäusevangelium* (1963), pp. 136ff.
28. Trilling, *op. cit.*, p. 68. He adds that "all the texts pertinent to this say only this one thing: 'Israel has ceased to be God's chosen people.'" He does not hesitate to use the word "rejection": Jerusalem's desolation is the sign that "God has turned away from His people and rejected them." Gnilka calls the crucifixion the deed that destroyed the election of Israel; *op. cit.*, pp. 138f.
29. Cf. the discussion between A. F. J. Klijn, "Joden en heidenen in Lukas-Handelingen," *Kerk en theologie* (1962), 16-24, and T. C. Vriezen, "Leert Lukas de verwerping van Israël?" *ibid.*, 25-31. Klijn speaks of Israel's ultimate rejection and the playing out of its role as the first in God's order according to Luke. He argues that Luke and Paul differ with respect to the restoration of Israel. Vriezen says that Luke 20:9-18 (the Parable of the Vineyard) is the passage that has always seemed to him to controvert Paul's interpretation of Israel's restoration most clearly, but concludes that this is not the case and that Luke, as historian, does not go as far as Paul. It seems to me that what the Gospels say about the house and temple of Israel does not imply that we should speak of a closed situation in which Israel is irrevocably cut off. Cf. Acts 28:28.

There can be no dispute about that: the light of undeserved mercy is not extinguished, but shines out into the world. But along with this light shining out comes a shadow: Israel as a contrary people (10:21), hardening itself, and "stumbling over the stumbling stone" (9:32).

This does not imply for Paul the failure of the Word of God. The reliable promises of God cannot be pushed to the extreme of asking whether or not Israel will now come to repentance. This reliability of God has now already become evident in the way of both Israel and the Gentiles. The style of election is already evident now that it is apparent that God's elective preference remains: not by works.

But this does not end the discussion of the role of Israel. Paul is not finished when he refers to the pouring out of salvation to the Gentiles. There is a further development of the truth that God's words cannot fail, and Israel assumes a place in this development.

Many have thought that after positing the break Paul has no more to do with Israel as a nation, but cares only for the salvation of individual Jewish people. Supposedly, Paul hinted at this when he said of his own repentance: "an Israelite, a descendant of Abraham, a member of the tribe of Benjamin" (11:1). But if this were a correct interpretation, why would Paul make so much of denying the rejection of Israel? Furthermore, consider his reference to the seven thousand whom God had kept for Himself in the days of Elijah (11:3f.). The point here is a remnant of the election. Paul's intent was not to outline the possibility of individual repentance, but to talk about the nation, of which the remnant was the significant representation. This remnant highlights God's grace (11:5), for the election is not on the basis of works, but by grace (vs. 6). In that remnant is the prospect for the nation, so that "as long as there is a remnant, no one has to doubt the future of the nation."[30] This perspective was the basis of Paul's fervent prayer for their salvation (10:1). As he belonged to the tribe of Benjamin, and as Benjamin represented "the survival of all of Israel and the hope of gaining back the lost tribes,"[31] so all of Israel is subsumed under the perspective of which Paul, in his intense expectation of faith, was speaking. Obviously Paul had not written off Israel in God's salvation plans. The transition from

30. Doekes, *De betekenis van Israëls val* (1915), p. 233.
31. O. Michel, *Der Römerbrief*, p. 235.

Jews to Gentiles did not create a cul-de-sac for the Jewish people. It is not a matter of no longer paying attention to Israel; nor does the attention to be paid them involve a relativizing of their guilt (as if Israel's guilt in rejecting divine election could be relativized!). No, what is involved is the dynamics of the history of salvation. "Their trespass means riches for the world" (11:12), he notes, placing the whole thing in a teleological perspective. "Salvation has come to the Gentiles, so as to make Israel jealous" (11:11).

Israel's fall, their stumbling over the stumbling stone, is not the last word for Paul, nor the definitive, enigmatic end of the matter. The connection between the stone of offense and the fact that those who build their faith on Him are not put to shame proves that the endpoint of this teleological dynamics has not yet been achieved.[32] In the "riches for the world" a new perspective appears to Paul. The one perspective — from the trespass of the Jews to riches for the world — occasions the rise of another: "What will their acceptance mean but life from the dead?" (11:15).

Since Paul saw his apostolate among the Gentiles as related to Israel — via the roundabout way of "riches for the world" — the word "jealous" (11:11) becomes important. Paul had already used this word in Romans 10:19, where he quotes Moses' words in Deuteronomy 32:21: "I will make you jealous of those who are not a nation; with a foolish nation I will make you angry." This Old Testament passage portrays the divine reaction to Israel's guilt. Jealousy, spite, and anger will fill Israel's heart when God offers the privileges He had given them to another people.[33] This jealousy can be interpreted in a bad sense of the term, but when Paul refers back to this Old Testament passage in Romans 11:11, it is no longer to jealousy as anger or spite, but to jealousy for receiving oneself what has become the portion of others, the Gentiles.[34] In Deuteronomy, what God does is depicted as calling forth only anger because of Israel's pretentious, exclusivistic notion of election. One is reminded of the reaction of the Jews in Antioch (Acts 13:45). But now

---

32. Cf. Isa. 8:14; 28:16; I Pet. 2:7f. On the connections between the OT and NT cf. G. Stählin, *Skandalon. Untersuchungen zur Geschichte eines biblischen Begriffs* (1930), 187-200.
33. Cf. H. N. Ridderbos' commentary *ad* Rom. 10:19.
34. Cf. J. Ridderbos, *KV* on Romans, p. 253; N. A. Dahl, *Das Volk Gottes*, pp. 245ff.

there is room for something new — an insight on the part of Israel into the mercy of what God does, according to His own nature, revealing Himself to the Gentiles who had not sought Him and showing Himself to those who had not asked for Him (10:20). This is the way that Israel can learn the meaning of electing grace and thus — in the reflection of the Gentiles — learn to understand its own election.

This is why, after talking about jealousy, Paul can go back to the words of Isaiah 65:2: "All day long I have held out my hands to a disobedient and contrary people" (10:21). This applies to an Israel who "did not ask for" God (vs. 20). "Israel is to recognise in the Saviour of the world the Messiah who had as such been concealed from it. It is to perceive in God's mercy to the ignorant and lost outside who its own God is and what He is also and primarily for Israel."[35] Thus, this jealousy is a matter of realizing and rediscovering divine mercy.

This raises the striking possibility of a reversal of Zechariah's prophecy of Gentiles taking hold of the robe of a Jew, saying, "Let us go with you, for we have heard that God is with you" (8:23). Now God's mercy becomes completely evident in the great light that comes on and strikes the eyes of Israel. It is a light for those who were outside, lost, estranged from God's glory, far from His house, "Not my people." Now they are admitted to God's house as friends and children. The electing grace of God is revealed as an indubitable reality, a new testimony to the Israel that had failed to understand the meaning of its elective privileges.

What did this new attention for Israel — new in the sense of the history of salvation — include, concretely, for Paul? What is the relation between this new perspective and Israel's rejection (apobolé — Rom. 11:15). If "their rejection" in this verse is to be understood as a divine act of rejecting them, and not merely as Israel's rejection of the Messiah, that is, if rejection and reprobation are not synonymous, then Paul's understanding of Israel's new perspective becomes all the more significant. Paul struggles with these questions. He is familiar with Israel's history and does not take Israel's guilt lightly. He draws no facile conclusions, but writes with deep sorrow. "I could wish that I myself were accursed (anáthema)," he says, "for the sake of my brethren, my kinsmen by race" (Rom. 9:3). And in his view of

35. K. Barth, *CD*, II/2, 279.

the future, Paul distinguishes rejection and reprobation. Thus he thinks about more than what once was Israel's portion and now has come to an end. That "past" did indeed play a role in his thinking, but in a distinctive way. Consider his typification of Israel as an olive tree. The Gentiles' participation in the divine plan of salvation is described in terms of the grafting of a wild olive shoot into the tree so that it may partake in the richness of the tree. There is no warrant for the wild branches (the Gentile Christians) to elevate themselves above the natural ones that were broken off. Should they pretend to be superior, they would be committing the same error as Israel did: misunderstanding salvation and election by grace. They must avoid this danger by "continuing in God's kindness" (11:22).[36] Here we see the central thought of Romans 9-11: the style, norm, and principle of God's election: *not by works*.[37] Both Jews and Gentiles must abide by this principle. But Paul does not restrict his warning to the Gentile Christians: he addresses the Jews again as well.[38] The current dismal condition of Israel can well serve as a warning, but in addition there comes the promise that "if they do not persist in their unbelief, they will be grafted in" (11:23).

By raising the matter of this regrafting Paul demonstrates a definite progression in his thought. Unmistakably this is an open door: over against all talk of irrevocability and closed situations, Paul refers to God's "power to graft them in again" (vs. 23). Paul describes this regrafting in some detail: the grafting of the Gentiles, the wild branches, was "contrary to

36. Significantly, Paul does not say that they should continue in the faith, but in God's kindness *(chrēstótēs)*. Both are essentially identical, but the reference to "kindness" brings out more sharply the unmerited, correlative character of the faith. Cf. E. Kühl, *Zur paulinischen Theodicee* (1897), p. 42.

37. Kühl calls this a "law of faith," a "norm of the achievement of salvation," which excludes all self-aggrandizement; *ibid.*, pp. 38, 42.

38. Dinkler *(loc. cit.)* sees a "decisive contradiction" between Rom. 9:6-13 and Rom. 11:1-32. Chapter 9, he says, deals with "the eschatological selection" *(ekloge)*; in Chapter 11, the promise is still very much the possession of the historical people." Such a contrast between the two chapters seems to me incorrect: both chapters are dominated by this *ekloge*. Furthermore, by Dinkler's own admission, the "discrepancy may be somewhat softened" because the status of historical Israel as such was no guarantee of salvation. The "Israel ... Israel" of 9:6 is not a view of two Israels, but a critical clarification on the basis of the prevalent *ekloge*.

nature," a foreign, new event. Israel, on the other hand, he speaks of as "natural branches." This does not mean that Israel's return to faith is a simple and "natural" occurrence. But, should Israel not persist in its unbelief, the grafting process will re-unite the branches with the richness of *their own* root. In other words, Israel will learn to understand election, and recognize God's purpose. And if the miraculous grafting of wild branches can take place, "how much more will these natural branches be grafted back into their own olive tree" (vs. 24).

The mystery of Israel

"Will be grafted back. . . ." Is this a more positive statement than is verse 23, where the condition, "if they do not persist in their unbelief," is added? Is verse 23 not a statement of a *possibility;* verse 24 of an *actuality?* Zahn argues that there is a progression here from possibility and conceivability to an actual prediction of the future. Doekes agrees. Michel feels that Paul's concrete "knowledge" (in verse 24) was founded in a divine revelation that had unveiled for him this future turn of events. Nygren speaks in terms of Paul as an "apocalyptic," one who has a special insight into the historical process of di-vine salvation and the purposes of God in history. In other words a *special revelation* had been entrusted to Paul. On this view, one might say that Romans 11:24 is a sudden, incidental, fragmentary narrative prediction of the future of Israel.[39]

This raises an important question. Was Paul given a special revelation by God concerning the future of Israel — a mystery of which only Paul knew — or could this future have been ex-pected on the grounds of God's promises and His election, which ultimately cannot be negated by unbelief? Note that after Paul talks about the mystery (vv. 25-27), he returns to the uniqueness of Israel: "as regards the gospel they are enemies of God, for your sake; but as regards election, they are beloved for the sake of their forefathers" (vs. 28). Then he goes on to mention the irrevocable gifts and call of God (vs. 29). One gets the impression from verse 29 that this irrevocability is in the forefront of Paul's thinking, rather than any contingent

---

39. Cf. Doekes, *op. cit.*, p. 244; commentaries *ad loc.* by Michel, Nygren, Zahn; *KV* on Romans, pp. 246f.: what Paul had posited as a possibility might have been dismissed by his readers as highly improbable, but in vs. 24 he can go further because of what God had revealed to him. See also J. Munck, *Christus und Israel* (1956), p. 99.

revelation of the future, which would have struck him as surprising.

It seems to me that neither of these two alternatives — special revelation or obvious conclusion — does full justice to Paul's words. Paul has been talking about the roundabout way in which the meaning of election has been clarified in the history of salvation, that is, by God's compassion on the Gentiles. In discussing this, his thoughts naturally return to Israel. The obvious evidence of the meaning of election — that it is not by works — leads him to consider the regrafting of Israel. Rather than reflecting speculatively about a "possibility" in the future, he faces that future with expectation grounded in the clearly revealed salvation. In a concrete historical situation he is, as it were, standing at the window to watch what Israel is going to do. That he has not suddenly shifted into the sphere of prediction regarding the regrafting of Israel as "mystery" is evidenced by his admonition to both Gentile Christians and Jews, which can be summed up for both of them in an "if." This "if" is not a simple possibility, but an indication of what goes out to all on the basis of what we have called the "style" of God's election. On the other hand, the Word of divine promise does not lend itself to static, "logical" conclusions. Even when Israel turned away, this Word was not discredited, but *confirmed.* For this reason, one can also not say that in Romans 11 Paul suddenly switches to the notion that there is a divine self-evidence involved in the conversion of Israel, as though God's faithfulness could and would appear only after Israel had been converted. When Berkhof says that "here as nowhere else his faithfulness will prove to go beyond and overcome our unfaithfulness,"[40] the reply might well be that already in Romans 9 Paul had pointed out that "proof" on the basis of the nature and structure of divine election.

It seems to me that much of the confusion over these three chapters of Romans stems from an interpretation that makes God's promise analogous to human promises. In other words, God's promise is looked on as a kind of "prediction" of what is going to happen some day, independent of human reaction. If God's promise were of that sort, it would logically follow that the Word of God had failed in Israel's unbelief. From Paul's denial that the Word had failed, it follows that he had a much

40. Berkhof, *CMH,* p. 135.

different estimate of it. In the Word the promise of God is always present and appealing in the personal sphere, in the voice and witness of God to man, in the dynamics of the divine acts. That is what never fails. So it was from the beginning, circumscribed by the conditional "if" of Exodus 18:5. In the course of the history of Christian dogma, the emphasis on this "if" among the Arminian Remonstrants led some theologians to shy away from any notion of conditionality at all. Such fears are justifiable if the condition is understood *meritorially* (election on the ground of . . .) rather than *correlatively*. But both the Old Testament and Paul are very unambiguous in stating that for one who has faith there is room for only one dictum: *not by works*.

Election can never be understood by reflecting on an "idea of election" that entails objective conclusions, but only before the face of the merciful and electing God and in connection with the clear and unarbitrary nature of His election. Hence, already in Romans 9 Paul portrays the transcendence and indubitability of God's faithfulness and calling over against the dark shadows of Israel's unbelief. It is incorrect to claim that not until Romans 11 does this idea appear. And when Berkhof speaks about a "proof" that God's faithfulness overcomes human unfaithfulness, it is clear that this proof is already evident in Romans 9, because the meaning of election *(ekloge)* is the one and only meaning. The notion that God's faithfulness does not really come into play until Paul's "prediction" of Israel's repentance in Romans 11:24 is the source of much confusion here. But this notion in turn presupposes that the irrevocability of God's gifts and call are problematical until Israel's salvation proves their reliability. This, however, ignores what Paul said already in Romans 3:3-4: "what if some were unfaithful? Does their faithlessness nullify the faithfulness of God? By no means! Let God be true, though every man be false." One cannot ignore this decisive remark when discussing chapter 11.

There is a warning, implicit in Paul's words, to the reader of Romans 11 not to wish to be "wiser than God" or to go beyond what is written, particularly in the direction of playing down what is sometimes called the "apocalyptic mystery" of the chapter. Paul introduces this mystery with cautionary words: "Lest you be wise in your own conceits" (vs. 25). The major question, deserving of very serious attention, is what Paul means by this "mystery" that he wants the believers to understand. There is no argument that by calling this a "mystery" Paul does not mean that it is something mysterious in the sense of occult. Paul's general use of the word *mystērion* indicates a hiddenness that is to be revealed at an appointed time. Examples of this Pauline usage are found in Romans 16:25-26 and Colossians 1:26: a mystery hidden for ages and now revealed. Again, in Ephesians 3:4-6 he writes of the mystery of Christ, not made known in other generations, but now revealed to His apostles and prophets, that the "Gentiles are fellow heirs, members of the same body, and partakers of the promise in Christ Jesus through the gospel." These three passages are certainly not occult apocalyptic predictions concerning the future, but rather refer to things that were hidden but are now revealed in the course of the history of salvation.[41]

The point of these examples is clear: the mysteries Paul is talking about are realities that have already been unveiled. But the mystery of Romans 11:25 is different: here the reality is still confronted with the problem of Israel. The veil *(kálymma)* has not yet been lifted. There might be said to be a perspective on this unveiling in the conditional "if they do not persist in their unbelief" (vs. 23), but it is still only an "if." Some individuals have repented, thus removing one evil (2 Cor. 3:16), but Israel continues in its own ways.

Paul, however, goes on to elucidate the mystery thus: "a hardening has come upon part of Israel, until the full number of the Gentiles come in; and so all Israel will be saved" (Rom. 11:25f.). These are surely not three separate, independent themes.[42] The coming in of the Gentiles cannot be isolated from Israel's unbelief; the "and so" of verse 26 clearly emphasizes their relationship. Paul's attention was directed to the works of God, which contain a tremendous dynamic and teleology as regards the relationship between Israel and the Gentiles and *vice versa*. His point of departure for this is the hardening

41. The term "mystery" is used in a completely different sense in the phrase "the mystery of Israel." O. J. R. Schwarz points out that this coinage gained currency through the writings of Maritain and Péguy to indicate the mysterious continuity of Israel through the centuries. In the same sense, it is prevalent in Jewish literature. In J. Cools, *et al., Het mysterie van Israël* (1957), p. 137. On "mystery" in the New Testament see also Herricus Schillebeeckx, *De sacramentele heilsoeconomie* (1952), pp. 35ff. For examples of Pauline "mysteries" related to the future, cf. 1 Cor. 15:51; 2 Thess. 2:7.
42. Cf. commentaries *ad loc.,* by O. Michel and H. N. Ridderbos.

(pórōsis) of part of Israel. This is not an entirely new idea: already in verse 7 he mentions that the elect obtained what they sought, but the rest were hardened *(epōróthēsan)*. This partial nature of the hardening is the presupposition for what follows. The hardening is not an obduracy of all the combined family of Israel without exceptions.[43] Because it is a hardening of *part* of Israel, the situation is open, not closed. But what follows, "until the full number of the Gentiles come in," is truly surprising. Evidently this "until" refers to a limit or end of Israel's unfaithfulness.

In opposition to the chiliastic interpretation of Romans 11:25, it has often been emphasized that Paul did not say "thereafter" (in other words, Israel would be saved *after* the full number of the Gentiles have come in), but "and so" *(hoútōs)*, indicating the manner in which Israel would return. Thus, it is contended, all Israel would be saved *in the same way* as the Gentiles. What Paul meant by "Israel," many have concluded, was not the nation of Israel, but the totality of those to be saved, both Jews and Gentiles, the believers, the true, spiritual Israel. A further reference is often made in this context to Galatians 6:16 — "Peace and mercy be upon all who walk by this rule, upon the Israel of God" — which is also said to refer to the spiritual Israel, the church as the new Israel. On this view Romans 11:25 has no peculiar reference to Israel.

But it is indeed open to question whether Paul, in writing to the Galatians, had in mind the church as the new Israel. The meaning may well be: peace and mercy to those who orient themselves to the rule of the new creation in Christ, and also peace and mercy be upon the Israel of God, that is, upon those Jews who have turned to Christ. In any case, Galatians 6:16 cannot be used to prove that Romans 11:25 is talking about the spiritual Israel. Doekes raises another serious objection to this spiritualizing interpretation: he points out that Romans 9-11 mentions Israel eleven times, of which ten are obvious references to Israel as a nation, so that there is no reason suddenly to interpret 11:26 as referring to the spiritual community. Thus Ridderbos, in opposition to Calvin, maintains the specific meaning of Israel; and H. M. Matter correctly observes that the "spiritual Israel" interpretation cannot be harmonized with Paul's train of thought. A final support for the literal

43. Zahn, *Komm.*, p. 523.

interpretation is the argument that in verse 28 — after talking about the salvation of all Israel — Paul speaks of the people of Israel again as "beloved for the sake of their forefathers." The discussion of Israel is not interrupted in verse 26, so that the question remains: what does Paul mean by "the salvation of all Israel?"[44]

"Israel" remained a compelling issue for Paul because of the irrevocable gifts and call of God. He sees the mercy that the Gentiles have received after their disobedience, and concludes that "so they [the Jews] have now been disobedient in order that by the mercy shown to you [the Gentiles] *they also may receive mercy*" (vs. 31).[45]

Thus the point here is surely mercy for a disobedient *Israel*. From this many have concluded that undoubtedly the real content of the mystery of Romans 11:25 is that *in the end of time* all Israel will be saved — an eschatological mystery following the coming in of the Gentiles. In this case, it is something that still must take place, in the last generation, when this will become reality. Thus K. L. Schmidt talks about Israel's being saved "in the last hour." "God will accomplish one more special deed, as it is portrayed in Christ's story: the lost son hastening toward the Father." On this view, "all Israel" means "Judaism at the last day." The plans of the God of Abraham, Isaac, and Jacob are not destroyed by the Jewish rejection of the Messiah. History *ends* with the people of Abraham. "Why did Paul rejoice so?" At the *spiritual* Israel? No. It was at the prospect of *Israel's* salvation.[46]

Understood in this sense, Israel's repentance is clearly taken as a *sign*. There is a protest against minimizing Paul's words.

44. On Rom. 11:25f. and Gal. 6:16 cf. K. L. Schmidt, *Die Judenfrage im Lichte der Kapitel 9-11 des Römerbriefes* (1943), pp. 10ff.; H. Schlier, *Der Brief an die Galater* (1949), p. 209; P. A. van Stempvoort, *De brief van Paulus aan de Galaten* (2d ed., 1961), p. 193; N. A. Dahl, "Zur Auslegung von Gal. 6:16," *Judaica*, VI (1950); Doekes, *op. cit.*, p. 233; H. N. Ridderbos, *Comm.*, *ad loc.*; Calvin, *Comm. ad* Rom. 11:26 ("I extend the word *Israel* to include all the people of God"; Calvin also refers to Gal. 6:16); H. M. Matter, "Waarheid en Verdichting rondom Rom. 11:26a," *Arcana Revelata* (1951), p. 67; and *De toekomst van Israël in het licht van het NT* (1953).

45. J. Munck suggests that Paul speaks about the disobedience of the Gentiles (cf. Eph. 2:2 *et al.*) in order to be able to place the conduct of the Gentiles on a par with that of the Jews; *Christus und Israel*, p. 104.

46. K. L. Schmidt, *op. cit.*, pp. 31-34.

Moreover, the "maximum interpretation" is related to repentance in the last generation. But it is precisely this viewpoint that is the object of considerable confusion. Can this really be Paul's meaning? Is that the source of Paul's joy — a "maximum interpretation" that allows for the conversion only of that fraction of the nation which will exist at the end of time? Is that the realization of God's irrevocable gifts and call?[47] These questions are all the more important because they cannot be dismissed as proceeding from a "spiritualization" of Romans 11:26.

H. N. Ridderbos admits to having changed his opinion on this subject. At first, he interpreted Romans 11 as dealing with a great religious conversion of Israel in its entirety in the last days; later he concluded that Paul was talking about "those in Israel who, through the proclamation of the gospel, repented and turned to the Lord during the course of history," in other words, a "pleroma" that represents the whole nation.[48] He no longer discusses the pleroma in his commentary, but emphasizes "the apostle's expectation of a much more comprehensive and adequate representation of Israel than can be expressed by the qualification 'remnant.' "[49] That is, Paul expected a restoration that, irrespective of numbers, far exceeded the impression left by the term "remainder." Berkhof and Ridderbos would seem to agree that what is in view here is a more comprehensive representation.

Does this solve the problem of the maximum interpretation of "all Israel?" And can what stimulated Paul also be applied to our contemporary understanding of the "end-time" and the last days? To answer these questions involves the use of the concepts "sign" and "representation." Is there not good reason to suppose that Paul was not referring to what we think of as the future (the last generation), but was thinking of his own time as the last days? Thus, Ridderbos sees Paul as unconcerned with any "post-historic" dimension, but interested in the contemporaneous situation. On this interpretation Romans 11:26 does not predict "a sudden revelation of a chiliastic mystery," but addresses itself to the expectation of God's works in history

47. Cf. H. N. Ridderbos, *Comm.*, pp. 70f.; Bavinck, *GD*, IV, 651.
48. Ridderbos, *Israël in het NT in het bijzonder volgens Rom. 9-11* (1955), pp. 59, 64.
49. Ridderbos, *Comm.*, p. 265; cf. also his discussion of Berkhof's *Christ the Meaning of History* in *Gereformeerde Weekblad*, September 26, 1958.

in the form of the *ekloge*. This seems to me to be the real focal point of the exegesis. The real question is not the more or less "comprehensive representation of Israel" that will be saved, but Paul's concern for the future of all Israel. Paul was not preoccupied with Israel's distant future, but with what he could see — God's mercy being poured out on the Gentiles, who in their new status as God's people disclosed the meaning of election. He does not deduce any logical conclusions for Israel from this, but he is reminded by this faithfulness of God of what is now the direction of God's works. Thus he can retain both the "if," the condition (11:23), *and* the possibility of his provoking his fellow Jews to jealousy "and thus save some of them" (11:14).[50] This is not the kind of abstract possibility about which we often say "Well, everything is possible!"; rather, it demonstrates Paul's engagement in prayer and action on behalf of Israel and with how it might be regrafted into the olive tree. Paul meditates and writes in prayerful expectation, not calculating, but placing an attentive ear to the movement of God's work through history. When he sees the mercy shown to the Gentiles, his eyes turn once again to Israel. He does not think in chronological categories, nor does he speculate about hidden mysteries, nor does he attempt a narrative account of future events. He is simply concerned with the Israel of his day. Of course, we approach Paul after a time span of twenty centuries, but we may not project these centuries back into the expectation of the apostle.

There are good grounds for believing that Paul constantly lived in strong, intense expectation of the immediate coming of the Lord. He tells the Romans, "it is full time now for you to wake from sleep. For salvation is nearer to us now than when we first believed" (13:11). In this eschatological tension, with eyes fixed on the ways of God, Paul faces history. The prospect for Israel — understanding the meaning of election and consequently being stirred to jealousy — arises out of the fulness of the Gentiles. In Romans 11:26 Paul does not suddenly become an apocalyptic or a soothsayer: he is writing about the evidence of the mercy that had historically come to be. In this

50. *ei pōs parazēlōsō mou tēn sárka*; cf. KJV: "*if by any means* I may provoke to emulation them which are my flesh"; RSV: "*in order to* make my fellow Jews jealous"; NEB: "*when* I try to stir emulation in the men of my own race."

348   THE RETURN OF CHRIST

way "all Israel will be saved." If this "will" is understood as
a foretelling of a future event, the verse not only becomes isolated as a "mystery," but must also be admitted as a novelty in
Pauline thinking. But "will" can also be understood as a
praying, serving, active orientation toward Israel's return to
the way that is now open to it.

We mentioned several pages back the important consideration that Paul did not use the word "thereafter" but "and so"
to introduce verse 26. Now we do not mean to set these two
words up as opposites, but it is a fact that "and so" connotes
more of an indissoluble relationship than a temporal connection. Once this relationship is understood, there should be no
inclination to minimize what Paul has to say about Israel. Paul
was not talking about a remnant, but about the fulness of
Israel, and from the beginning of these three chapters, where
he talks about his "great sorrow and unceasing anguish" (9:2),
to his concluding doxology (11:33-36), he is filled with a radical missionary spirit. He begins with the historical situation
of Israel's unbelief, an unbelief so disastrous that he could
wish himself accursed for the sake of the Jews (9:3). Nowhere
does he relativize or rationalize Israel's guilt. But he constantly
sees the light of God's mercy over Israel's way, as God extends
His hands to that errant nation (10:21). Now a new way has
been revealed, not by some mysterious revelation, but through
the work of God. Bornkamm writes: "In respect of this proclamation Paul does not appeal to a revelation imparted to him.
His interpretation is based on the fact that he sets the promise
implied in the divine election of Israel in relation to what
is on a human view the contradictory present ... and he is thus
able to see the eschatological meaning of what takes place here
and now."[51] Paul continues in an expectation for all Israel,
which now will find its way back to the Father's house.[52] Misunderstanding disappears, now that God's mercy has been shed
on those who as Gentiles had been no people. Those who had
once been afar off have been brought near (Eph. 2:13, 17),[53]
and God's elective purpose has become apparent. The bad sense
of jealousy in Deuteronomy 32:21 has been transformed into
something good, and the end of the matter is not speculative

51. In *TDNT*, s.v. *mystērion*, IV, 822f.
52. Cools, *op. cit.*, p. 69.
53. Cf. J. J. Meuzelaar, *Der Leib des Messias* (1961), pp. 61ff.

predictions or self-evident conclusions, but a doxology to the acts of God.[54]

From our perspective, centuries after Paul, there is a danger of looking at his concern for Israel as the unveiling of a chiliastic secret, and seeing it as some kind of apocalyptic schema or narrative. Such an interpretation raises a peculiar dilemma: either the "last" generation (as "all Israel") shall return, or Paul was mistaken. This position, however, ignores the extent to which Paul, convinced by the evidence of salvation among the Gentiles, concentrated his attention on the *maximum* possibilities *in his own time*. This expectation is not that of apocalyptic, but something that generates tremendous apostolic activity.

The faithfulness of God

On the ground that Israel represented a "particularistic" phase in God's plans, some scholars have accused chiliasm of reverting back from universalism to particularism, especially in its view of the return and restoration of Israel, which, it is alleged, reduces the universal dimension to nothing more than an intermezzo, since the goal of God's plans is directed to the future of Israel. Insofar as this criticism aims at the strongly particularistic tendencies that are undoubtedly found in some versions of chiliasm, it is to the point. But it is well to realize that the universal perspective that dominated Pauline thinking too did not diminish his expectation for Israel. Contrary to chiliasm, the coming in of the full number of the Gentiles is not an intermezzo, but neither is Israel's history an intermezzo for Paul, because the new status of the Gentiles, brought about by God's merciful election of them, opened new vistas for the people of Israel.

The crucial point about Israel seems to me to be whether it is justifiable to draw a relation of *entailment* between God's faithfulness and Israel's return to grace. Earlier we saw that Berkhof emphasizes the self-evidence of this relationship and in fact takes it as the basic motif of what he says about Israel. He applies this not only to Romans 11, but also to Matthew 23:38-39, "Behold, your house is forsaken and desolate. For I tell you,

54. Cf. Berkouwer, *Divine Election*, pp. 65f.

you will not see me again, until you say, 'Blessed is he who comes in the name of the Lord' " (cf. Luke 13:35). "These are expressions of what was for Israel, on the basis of Old Testament promises, a divine matter-of-fact."[55] There are radical differences of belief as to how these passages of Scripture are to be interpreted. Does this sharp proclamation of judgment indicate a repentant acceptance of Israel's Messiah or a forced admission of Christ's lordship at the parousia?[56]

The reason why many have been reluctant to refer this passage to Israel's repentance is that the words appear in the context of a proclamation of judgment — the last call, an ominous warning.[57] But what we are interested in here is the allegedly *self-evident nature* of these words. Now Berkhof does not have in mind a superficial or simplistic self-evidence, but a self-evidence closely related to the love and the faithfulness of God. Even so, it does not seem legitimate to speak of divine self-evidence. Berkhof's "divine matter-of-fact" is rooted in the promise of God. But this matter-of-fact attitude towards the permanence of their election was Israel's dominant problem, and the prophets had spoken against it as an unjust conclusion drawn from an incorrect understanding of God's faithfulness (cf. Amos 9:7). Israel's erroneous notion is not what Paul has in mind when he talks about God's faithfulness. It is essential for an understanding of God's faithfulness to realize that one cannot deduce conclusions from this faithfulness as one might deduce conclusions from a premise. God's faithfulness can be comprehended, not through a strictly logical process, but only through faith and repentance. Self-evidence — "matter-of-factness" — is a concept foreign to the genius of God's faithfulness,

55. Berkhof, *CMH,* p. 140; cf. pp. 134f.

56. Grosheide *(Comm., ad loc.)* and H. N. Ridderbos *(KV* on Matthew, II, 139) point out that the same words of blessing were addressed to Jesus on His triumphal entry (Matt. 21:9; cf. also Phil. 2:9ff.).

57. Berkhof mentions in this connection Luke 21:24, which says that the Gentiles will have dominion over Jerusalem "until the times of the Gentiles are fulfilled." Munck *(op. cit.,* p. 101) wonders whether Luke was influenced by Paul. Schrenk rejects this suggestion, *Die Weissagung über Israel im NT* (1951), p. 15. Luke 21 refers specifically to the end of foreign domination over Jerusalem, which is not what Paul has in mind in Rom. 11.

and it may not be incorporated into the kerygma as though it were a general truth.[58]

For Paul, God's faithfulness is not a matter of divine self-evidence; instead, Paul points out the correlation between God's mercy and the believer's faith. What is unchangeable is what we have called the "style" of divine election — "not by works." This is the basis of certainty of faith and understanding God's faithfulness. Faith can build on this faithfulness as on a sure foundation, but not because the latter is a general truth enabling us systematically to judge where we and our neighbors stand. Berkhof is entirely correct in saying that man's unfaithfulness cannot nullify God's trustworthiness; indeed, Paul says that in so many words: "What if some were unfaithful? Does their faithlessness nullify the faithfulness of God? By no means!" (Rom. 3:3f.; cf. 1 Cor. 10:13; 2 Thess. 3:3). But this does not support the conclusion that man's unfaithfulness has no destructive effect at all. For Paul reminds Timothy that "if we deny him, he will also deny us" (2 Tim. 2:12; cf. Matt. 10:33). This is the meaning of God's faithfulness: "He cannot deny himself" (2 Tim. 2:13). Even when He denies, He remains true. The offer of the gospel is meant seriously: it requires a responsible decision. For that reason there is nothing "automatic" or "self-evident" about man's relation to God. In repentance one can always fall back on God's faithfulness,[59] recognizing how much one can rely on Him. This is Paul's concern, even when he is talking about God's promise and irrevocable call.

The charge has sometimes been made that rejection of the chiliastic exegesis of Romans 11:26 is a step towards anti-semitism and ignores the warning against opinionation with which Paul introduces this verse. To be sure, the admonition not to be "wise in your own conceits" ought never to be forgotten, considering how often antisemitism has indeed penetrated into the church. There is indeed a danger that, on the basis of a

58. To what extent this self-evidence played a role in Judaism is amply demonstrated by H. J. Schoeps in *Israel and Christenheit*. We noted above (fn. 16) that Jewish faith found its certainty in its election and possession of the Torah. This confidence allowed for the possibility of punishment by God, but never rejection. Thus many Jews faced martyrdom with equanimity.

59. Cf. Canons of Dort, V, 5: "until, when they change their course by serious repentance, the light of God's fatherly countenance again shines upon them."

traditional view of the history of post-crucifixion Israel, one would be inclined to minimize Paul's concern for the nation of Israel and interpret the "Israel" of Romans 11:26 as a "spiritual Israel." Whether or not this tends toward "antisemitism," it may well stem from a view of Israel as a closed book as far as God's plan is concerned. Consequently, Israel is seen as no longer fitting into God's pattern except perhaps in the case of individual conversions of Jewish people. This is a far cry from Romans 11.[60] Just because Paul's comments are not to be construed as a sudden revelation of a chiliastic mystery, the intensity and dynamic of his thoughts are not to be underestimated. It is clear that Paul was wrapped up, not in some remote future, but in what already was becoming history, God's *present* mercy being poured out over *all*. In Paul's concentrated expectation of the coming of the Lord, he focused his attention on all Israel in an outlook of prayer, expectation, and service. In the centuries since Paul wrote these words, however, many have succumbed to the temptation of postponing his mystery into an "end-time" not yet begun. But Paul thought of Israel in terms of God's promise, His irrevocable gifts and calling. He could ponder the conditionality of Israel's salvation — "if they do not persist in their unbelief" — and be concerned at the same time with *all* Israel, now that the way to their salvation was obvious. He still saw Israel standing in the light of the election and promise; and he understood well the intrinsically merciful structure of God's elective acts. Thus he could recall Isaiah's prophecy of the banishment of ungodliness from Jacob (Rom. 11:26f.; cf. Isa. 59:20f.; 27:9), a clear reference to God's covenant and the forgiveness of sins, a lasting perspective that cannot be abrogated by human guilt and unbelief.

Christians and Jews

That Israel should be forever lost, permanently and irretrievably damned because of its rejection of the Messiah, was the furthest thing from Paul's mind. His apostolic activity makes that clear. Paul did not think of Israel as the "wandering Jew" of medieval legend, who was said to have taunted Christ on the way to Calvary and was thus consigned to drift aimlessly and hopelessly across the face of the earth until the last day. Paul

60. Cf. F. Kuiper, "Paulus tussen Joden en niet-Joden," *Wending*, IV (1949), p. 384.

was gripped by the prospect for all Israel, and the coming in of the Gentiles spurred this hope in him.

How different from what the Christian church has often held, when it has seen the key to the history of Israel as contained in the angry denunciation "His blood be on us and on our children" (Matt. 27:25)! How often it is forgotten that this statement does not govern the works of God, and that Israel's history cannot thus be subjected to such determinism.[61] More and more Christians are coming to see another direction in the biblical witness. This does not mean that Israel's historical situation or the crucifixion is ignored. On Good Friday 1959, Pope John XXIII deleted the reference to the *perfidia* of the Jews from the liturgical prayer.[62] This was not meant to depreciate or ignore history, but to admit that the church may not judge this history without the clear awareness that what happened led, through an act of God, to the proclamation of the gospel "to the Jew first, and also to the Greek" (Rom. 1:16).[63]

This raises the question of whether the basis of mission work among the Jews differs from that of the proclamation of the Word to all people. In other words, is the preaching of the gospel to the Jews included in the preaching to all the nations, or is there a particular ground for directing the gospel to the Jews?[64] I take this to be a false dilemma. Certainly there is no "more" or "less" involved: any quantitative difference between preaching the gospel to Jews and to Gentiles is excluded by Paul's words in Romans 11:32: "For God has consigned all men to disobedience, that he may have mercy upon all." When chiliasm makes Israel the particularistic center of its scheme, it does not thereby really show a greater appreciation for Israel but a lesser evaluation. Schrenk is to the point: "Paul is not at all concerned with giving eschatological preference to Israel in the sense of its spiritual centrality, and he is even less concerned with its national political restoration."[65] Paul's con-

---

61. Cf. Berkouwer, *Het licht der wereld* (1960), ch. XXXII.
62. F. Heer mentions other charges against the Jews that were set aside later that year; *Juden, Christen, Deutsche*, p. 189.
63. J. Isaac, "Hat der Antisemitismus christliche Wurzeln?", *Evangelische Theologie*, XXI (1961), 351, expresses his appreciation for Pope John XXIII.
64. Cf. the study by the Nederlandse Hervormde Kerk, *Israël en de Kerk* (2d ed., 1960), p. 24.
65. Schrenk, *op. cit.*, p. 37.

cern was for Israel — all Israel — to discover the meaning of its existence, its election, and so to live, along with the Gentiles, under God's mercy. This concern does away with any problematics of who is central and who is peripheral. The emphasis is upon God's "mercy upon all" — and this thought leads Paul directly into his doxology (11:33-36). "I tell you," Jesus says, "many will come from east and west and sit at table with Abraham, Isaac, and Jacob in the kingdom of heaven" (Matt. 8:11). In the reality of this eschaton there can no longer be any trace of doubt about the true midpoint.[66]

Finally, we return to the question whether a future restoration of Israel may and must be reckoned among signs of the end. An affirmative reply to this question suggests a kind of objective knowledge, which soon leads even to conclusions about the duration of the world. But there is a complication with respect to the way in which the concept "sign" is employed in this context. For example, some have already seen a "sign" in the continued existence of the Jewish people, particularly with the rise of the Jewish state. It is suggested that there is something very important about the rise of this state during the generation when the very existence of the Jewish people was threatened. Zimmerli asks whether this does not show "that the surprising new embodiment of Israel should be proclaimed by us as God's public Yes to the promise He made to the people He elected from among all peoples."[67] Even Berkhof, who explicitly wants to avoid romanticizing or speculating about the State of Israel, says that "this nation . . . is at least a presage of God's future dealings with His people."[68]

---

66. It is unclear what exactly Berkhof means by saying that in the millennial kingdom "the recovered Israel will be the centre of the world" *(CMH,* p. 157). Not that Berkhof is alone in this ambiguity: Calvin, commenting on Rom. 11:26, applies the word "Israel" to *all* the people of God (fn. 44 above), and yet goes on to say that in the completion of the "salvation of the whole Israel of God . . . the Jews, as the first born in the family of God, [will] obtain the first place."

67. W. Zimmerli, "Das neue Israel," *Evangelische Theologie,* XVII (1957), 494.

68. *Op. cit.,* p. 152. Cf. *Israël en de Kerk,* p. 41: "a sign of God." The immediate derivation of knowledge about God from the events of history is rejected as "natural theology," but reference is made, nevertheless, to "God's footprints in today's history." The concept of "sign" is circumscribed in a threefold sense: as a sign of our impotence, as a sign of God's faithfulness, and as a sign of Israel's being led on a new way (pp. 42f.).

Notice that the concept of sign is changed here, a shift that is expressed in the distinction between *sign* and *presage*. The "presage" (the State of Israel) does not yet imply the "sign" (Israel's restoration), but it does function on this historical plane as indication of the eschatological sign. And this raises an important problem. The eschatological "sign," after all, is not an arbitrary sign, but a sign of the signifying thing which already begins to be outlined as eschaton. A *presage* is a less weighty matter. Consequently, where it involves an *interpretation* of history, especially a political event, it is filled with uncertainties. Thus Berkhof reckons with the possibility that this "presage ... will disappear like a *fata morgana* with a change in the political atmosphere."[69] An eschatological sign cannot, by its very nature, be such a mirage. This also raises the question of how far we can interpret history on the way to the future. This question is significant for eschatological expectation, because this expectation is directed to the future in an historical situation full of uncertainties. Is it possible by means of historical analysis to assume history into the eschatological expectation?

There is a parallel here to the question of the continued existence of Israel. Karl Barth deals with this in his discussion of "The Divine Ruling." While this is admittedly a hidden regime, it does display certain "constant elements." Although the divine rule cannot be deduced from these constants, they nevertheless can become "signs and witnesses."[70] According to Barth, the history of the Jews is "the most astonishing and provocative" of these constants.[71] History shows that the saying of

69. *Op. cit.*, p. 152. According to Berkhof, "so far as religion is concerned, the matter is from all angles still ambiguous." Cf. also Berkhof's, "De staat Israël en de theologie," *In de Waagschaal*, June 4, 1955. The problems are condensed in numerous questions, for example, whether a particular military victory of Israel over her Arab neighbors ought to be seen as a divine miracle. K. H. Kroon protests that this interpretation is a kind of "Zionist natural theology" (quoted by J. M. Hasselaar, "Israël blijft aktueel," *In de Waagschaal*, August 10, 1957). Cf. also the foreword to M. A. Beek, *Israël. Land, volk, cultuur.* Beek does not look at the State of Israel "in a romantic religious light," nor does he see it as a "sign" of the imminent end of days.
70. *CD*, III/3, 199.
71. *Ibid.*, p. 210. The other constants are the history of the Holy Scripture and of the church.

356   THE RETURN OF CHRIST

Zechariah 2:8 — "for he who touches you touches the apple of his eye" — is still applicable to this people.[72]

What is noteworthy in Barth's appraisal of the Jews is that the eschatological sign is not of an "end-time" nature. Instead, it is a sign that goes along with all of history. Antisemitic sentiment, according to Barth, is not generated by the personal traits of the Jews, but by what the Jew is: "the Jew ... belongs to the elected people, but he also belongs to the people which is unfaithful to its election."[73] This is how Israel is a sign and seal, and thus it must continue. Instead of in an eschatological perspective, Israel is a sign in its *habitual unfaithfulness*. "In the Jew there is revealed the primal revolt, the unbelief, the disobedience, in which we all are engaged."[74]

Israel as *eschatological* sign is entirely different. This involves a "knowledge," the fixing of a historical national event that will some day appear. With regard to the certainty about the eschatological sign, it is sometimes suggested that the exegesis of what the Bible says about Israel has often been influenced by antipathy to the Jewish people. Now it is no simple matter to identify with certainty the motives behind any exegesis. But what is determinative here is that the apostolic concern with Israel centers on the faithfulness, love, and election of God. For Paul this was a matter of intense actuality. In view of the centuries that separate us from Paul, we sometimes have a hard time grasping the relevance of what Paul says for our own eschatological expectation. We are inclined to think of the future as something yet before us; thus we transpose what Paul wrote and all the corresponding questions concerning the salvation of the last generation, God's faithfulness over the entire nation, and the like, to an "end-time" that has not yet dawned. By doing that we tend to miss completely the *actual, present* reality of the New Testament expectation, the note of "when you see these things taking place, you know" (Mark 13:29).[75]

We should not look at Paul's expectation that the parousia

72. *Ibid.*, p. 218.
73. *Ibid.*, p. 219.
74. *Ibid.*, p. 222.
75. Cf. also Rom. 11:31. H. N. Ridderbos *(Comm., ad loc.)* and H. M. Matter, "Aldus zal geheel Israël behouden worden," in *Arcana Revelata* (1951), p. 68, correctly call attention to Paul's *Naherwartung* in their exegeses of Rom. 11.

was near as we look at something that later turned out to be an error. "The Christian faith," Strobel notes, "clings to the right to expect everything from God at all times."[76] Paul operated with this type of expectation. He does not appear as an apocalyptic prophet with an esoteric mystery to impart, but as someone with a watchful eye on the dealings of God. He was not in a position to solve riddles, certainly not the enigma of Israel's unbelief. What he does know is that in the way now opened up the expectation for all Israel lives again. This is something entirely different from the twentieth-century confusion of the New Testament concept of the "last days" as meaning an "end-time" which is thought to be the time when all the signs — including that of Israel — will take on meaning. On the other hand, this does not mean that Paul's teachings can be reduced to a subjective expectation that has no relevance for us. For everything that we read here is concentrated in the continuing actuality of "jealousy" as a link in the chain of God's salvation-history.

We cannot overestimate the extent to which contempt for the Jews in the course of the centuries — even in the church — has broken down and hindered this "jealousy," and closed off the way that Paul saw opened. The church is a hindrance for the Jewish people on their way back to the "hope of Israel" not because it wishes to be the people of God, but because it falls into the abyss of not really being the people of God in the deepest and fullest sense of the word, without pride (Rom. 11:20) and without being wise in its conceits (Rom. 11:25) because no human being may boast in the presence of God (1 Cor. 1:28f.). When the church no longer merely believes in election, but confesses it and lives according to it, then the light to which Paul looked beams forth. When that light does not shine, when election is no more than a topic of endless debates and a bone of limitless contention, all perspective disintegrates. All that remains then is a discussion of Israel, laden with sentimentality, hardly productive of what Paul calls "jealousy."

The depth, and above all, the meaning of God's gracious election is the critical point in any "dialogue" between church and synagogue. If there is to be room for an actual expectation it must stem from the image that the church portrays on the

76. Strobel, *op. cit.,* p. 305.

basis of gracious election, the justification of the ungodly, the sinners, the enemies (Rom. 5:6, 8, 10). Then it will be clear that election never was nor is now a *fatum*, but is the source of the highest pardon and the deepest humility.

Thus we are not confronted with an apocalyptic mystery of the "end-time," but are compelled to a living expectation in our own lifetime. The only way to be a light in the world is through Him who was found by those who did not seek Him (Rom. 10:20). Scripture is full of familiar references to the correlation between seeking and finding (cf. Ps. 27:8; Amos 5:4; Matt. 7:7). But the gospel goes beyond this correlation. The cornerstone of the expectation is this: that the blood of Jesus cleanses Jew and Gentile, Gentile and Jew, beyond what Jew or Gentile could ever have expected. In this outlook on the church as a living sign lies the actuality of Paul's expectation for *all* Israel in the last days — and the failure of the church to live up to it.

CHAPTER TWELVE

VISIO DEI

HAVING CONSIDERED several questions pertaining to the signs of the times, we shall now turn our attention to a subject that often receives only token appraisal in dogmatics, the *visio Dei* — the vision of God or beatific vision. In Chapters VI and VII above, we discussed the expectation of the resurrection of the body and the eschatological perspective on the new earth, concluding that there is no disharmony or competition between expecting the vision of God and expecting the new earth; between interest in the earth, where — at long last — righteousness will dwell, and interest in "God as all in all." Because of the intrinsic harmony between these two, let us turn back to what the Bible says about the eschaton, a testimony that clearly and explicitly includes the *visio Dei*.

It would be unfair to approach this subject with an a priori suspicion of it because of its misuse in certain mystical circles, or because it seems entirely speculative, or because it is thought to erase the boundaries between God and man. Not that such aberrations do not happen: there are those who recoil from faulty notions of a vision of God in earthly life only to indulge in speculation about the eschatological vision of God. Furthermore, many are influenced by the notion that invisibility — mentioned in Article I of the Belgic Confession along with eternity, immutability, infinity, omnipotence, and the like — is one of God's essential and eternal attributes.

Seeing in the Bible

The undeniable fact, however, is that the vision of God *is* included in the scriptural witness, and we may not ignore this subject. Reaction against, or fear of, speculation does not justify avoiding the issue. After all, the purpose of this study is not to penetrate recklessly into the inscrutability of God or to transgress the unapproachable light in which He dwells (1

Tim. 6:10). Scripture itself takes the initiative in speaking about the vision of God. To be sure, its references to the vision of God are relatively uncommon by comparison to the frequency of other images and concepts used to describe salvation. But even if it is true that this relative infrequency is explicable as a reaction to the Greek mentality, which placed a great deal of stock in "beholding,"[1] it is nevertheless true that the beatific vision is mentioned expressly as a matter of joy in the Bible. Furthermore, it radiates a message of comfort and admonition: "Blessed are the pure in heart," Jesus says, "for they shall *see God*" (Matt. 5:8). "Strive for peace with all men, and for the holiness without which no one will *see the Lord*" (Heb. 12:14). There is an eschatological outlook as well: "His servants shall worship him; they shall *see his face*" (Rev. 22:4). The biblical witness on this score is a proclamation that comes to us with unmistakable connections with life on earth: purity, righteousness, and service (1 John 3:6; 3 John 11).

The first thing we notice, however, about the biblical references to seeing God is their variety; and it is no simple matter to detect a harmony in them. On the one hand, we read of seeing God; on the other, we get the impression that He is invisible. As we noted, it is particularly the latter idea that deeply impressed itself on the historical church. The belief is that it is radically and totally impossible to see God, an impression confessed in the doctrine of the *invisibilitas Dei*. The Old Testament tells us that no one can see God and live (Exod. 33:20); John goes further: "no one has ever *(pópōte)* seen God" (John 1:18; cf. 1 John 4:12); and Paul takes it to the ultimate: "no man has ever seen or can see" God (1 Tim. 6:16). It is as if invisibility is an indubitable attribute of God (cf. 1 Tim. 1:17). This would seem to leave a treatise on the beatific vision out of the question entirely. Now God's invisibility does not, of course, imply that He is unknowable, as if man had no choice but to be agnostic. The invisible God is revealed, and man is enabled to encounter Him and commune with Him. But this revelation of friendship with God (Ps. 25:14; James 2:23) and even walking with Him (Gen. 5:24)

---

1. Cf. E. Baert, "Het thema van de zalige Godsanschouwing in de Griekse patristiek tot Origenes," *Tijdschrift voor Theologie*, I (1961), 289. Baert argues that because of the influence of Hellenistic mysticism and Greek appreciation for contemplation, later theology placed greater emphasis on seeing God than did the NT.

docs not cancel out God's invisibility.[2] So it is easy to see why the invisibility of God has, for many, come to stand on the same level as His other eternal properties. Does this not suggest that all talk of "seeing God" is metaphorical, and is this not confirmed by Hebrews 11:27, which says that Moses "endured *as* seeing him who is invisible?"

Such questions are perfectly understandable. In answer to them we should note that the Bible speaks of seeing in yet another way. There are passages in the Bible where seeing God is spoken of as a deadly danger. Obviously, it is not at all a dogmatized "invisibility" that accounts for this, but the very possibility of seeing Him.

Gideon feared for his life when he saw the angel of the Lord, but the Lord consoled him and told him he would not die (Judg. 6:22). Manoah and his wife both feared themselves doomed: "We shall surely die, for we have seen God" (Judg. 13:22). The *possibility* of seeing God is the background of the fear of the consequences. Thus Moses "hid his face, for he was afraid to look at God" (Exod. 3:6). Isaiah, seeing the Lord sitting on His throne, lamented "Woe is me! For I am lost ... for my eyes have seen the King, the LORD of Hosts" (Isa. 6:5). However, there are also passages in the Old Testament that do not include this fear for the consequences of seeing God. In particular Moses, in his unique position among Israel, spoke "mouth to mouth, clearly, and not in dark sayings" and he saw "the form of the LORD" (Num. 12:8).[3] Moses, Aaron, Abihu, and seventy elders "saw the God of Israel" and He "did not lay his hand on [them]" (Exod. 24:9-11). There are numerous other texts that might be cited,[4] but these should suffice to show that the idea of seeing God cannot simply be dismissed out of hand because of a dogmatic abstraction about the "invisibility" of God. All these encounters reflect the goodness of God in His gracious nearness, His condescending love and mercy. We may well ask — in fact, we must ask — what these passages concerning "seeing" and "not-seeing" mean.

2. Cf. Michaelis, in *TDNT*, s.v. *horatós, aóratos*, V, 369f.
3. Hebrew — *temûnâh;* LXX — *tén dóxan kyríou eiden;* Dutch — *gelijkenis* (Nieuwe Vertaling — *gestalte); French — forme;* KJV — "similitude"; NEB — "the very form."
4. Among them: Gen. 32:30; Num. 6:24-26; Deut. 32:20; 34:10; 1 Kings 22:19; Job 33:26; 42:5; Pss. 11:7; 13:1; 24:6; 30:7; 34:6; 42:2; 44:24; 63:2; 84:7; 95:2; 100:2; 105:4; 123:2; Isa. 38:11; Amos 9:1; Micah 3:4; 1 Pet. 3:12.

Do we have here two opposing thought-complexes — visibility and invisibility? The answer to this must be negative. Even the expressly attested cases of "seeing" do not indicate a human ability or organ that as such enables us to see God, as if the Lord were "before our eyes." In each of the instances seeing God is a matter of His gracious presence, not something neutral. Even Moses, despite his unique position, experienced that limitation. When he asked Yahweh to see His glory, the reply was: "You cannot see my face; for man shall not see me and live" (Exod. 33:18, 20). Only if God's hand covers Moses while He passes by can Moses see Him, and then only His back, not His face (vs. 23). W. H. Gispen has compared this "seeing" to looking at the afterglow that remains after the setting of the sun.[5]

Man cannot visually grasp God. God can never be the *object* of his vision. Seeing issues out of God's nearness; and when this seeing of God becomes reality, it becomes apparent how it transcends the neutrality of human seeing. Invariably, God's being seen, His "appearance" is portrayed as something beyond human grasp. "The Old Testament never says *what* the people saw concretely; the description is always indirect."[6] A typical description of His appearance reads: "and there was under his feet as it were a pavement of sapphire stone, like the very heaven for clearness" (Exod. 24:10). The form of Yahweh is such that we are left with the impression of indescribability. When His glory appeared, "it was like a devouring fire on the top of the mountain in the sight of the people of Israel" (Exod. 24:17).

There is a divine condescension, which, though it does not take place outside of the seeing of opened eyes, does happen under cover of a cloud (Exod. 34:5). The majestic is always in plain sight, as, for example, at the dedication of the temple, when the priests could not stand to minister because of the cloud (1 Kings 8:11). "The LORD has said that he will dwell in thick darkness" (vs. 12), but precisely in this way the house is filled with His glory. His appearance takes place in various manifestations that make His presence noticeable while making it *visually* clear that God is not the *self-evident object* of seeing.

5. *KV* on Exodus, *ad loc.*
6. E. Fascher, *Deus invisibilis* (1931), p. 55. Cf. Wolf W. Graf-Baudissin, "'Gott schauen' in der AT Religion," *Archiv für Religionswissenschaft*, XVIII (1915), esp. pp. 202ff.

This comes impressively to the fore in Ezekiel 1, in a variety of images and comparisons that portray God's unapproachable elusiveness and elevation above human grasp: the prophet describes, in numerous similes, "the appearance of the likeness of the glory of the Lord" (vv. 26-28). It is never possible to speak of a direct, detached, inclusive perception on the analogy of our seeing what is before our eyes. When the Lord appeared on Mount Sinai, the forbidding voice warned the Israelites not to attempt to penetrate the mystery of God "lest they break through to the Lord to gaze and many of them perish" (Exod. 19:21).

It is clear that when the Bible talks about God, it does not suggest abstract, metaphysical properties imparted to us in isolation from His relationship to man and from the mode of His revelation. Clearly, man does not and cannot approach God as he does the many objects that "catch his eye," which he perceives without difficulty. In other words, when the Bible talks about "seeing God" it is not talking about a mere physical technique; it is not suggesting a visibility that automatically — if the eyes are but open — leads to perception. This is why some have spoken of the divine "ineffability"[7] and suggested the principle that "man is always the recipient and never the author of revelation."[8] This is demonstrated clearly in the Old Testament: even the unique "face to face" relation of Moses to God does not have to do with a simple, static correlation between eyes and seeing. Yahweh *speaks* to Moses face to face, as one speaks with a friend. Michaelis notes a later "material preponderance of hearing over seeing"[9] in descriptions of these encounters. This is not intended as an anthropological division between hearing and seeing (as if man did have direct access to God via hearing), but indicates what is prevalent in the relationship — the divine initiative: His voice, His word, which makes known His will (cf. Num. 7:89; Deut. 4:12, 15).

What is important is not the perceivable presence but the revelation in the word, which calls for response and reaction. The relation between God and man is a matter of an en-

7. Michaelis, in *TDNT*, s.v. *horáō*, V, 365.
8. *Ibid.*, 329.
9. *Ibid.*, 330; cf. Kittel, *ibid.*, s.v. *akoúō*, I, 217f.; Lohse, *ibid.*, s.v. *prósōpon*, VI, 772ff. Note also the connection between "appeared" and "said" (Gen. 12:7; cf. 2 Chron. 18:18).

counter, an event, a revelation, in which man does not approach God on the basis of his own capabilities, but is called to Him and experiences this calling as a gift. Thus, hearing is in no sense a devaluation of seeing. Though it may be appropriate, with Rudberg, to call the Greeks "a people of the eye,"[10] it will not do to describe the Hebrews as a people of the ear alone, as if their eyes did not need to be opened to all the works of God's hands and to God Himself in the appearance of His glory. But what Israel did have to learn was that it did not live in the sphere of self-evidence or by perceiving "phenomena," but lived before the face of the speaking God (cf. Ps. 78:3, 12, 43).

Only if we see what the Bible says about not seeing God against this background of the ineffability of God can we understand how the Bible attaches such importance to seeing God.[11] Seeing is also emphasized in the New Testament, in connection with the time of salvation. As the way was prepared for the coming of God's Kingdom, things were seen that could not have been seen by the kings and prophets of days gone by, and, as Jesus tells the disciples, "Blessed are the eyes which see what you see!" (Luke 10:23; cf. Matt. 13:16f.).[12] It is a seeing on the basis of the reality of the salvation that has come as a light to the world. The eyes are opened in a new morning and discover the mystery. There is reality taking shape that can be *heard* and *seen* (cf. Matt. 11:4). The eyes are drawn to the Lamb of God (cf. John 1:29, 36, 46). This is certainly not a neutral, objective, self-evident relationship, or simple "perception," but a discovery that can be made only because the eyes have been enlightened by seeing Christ incarnate (John 1:14) and the signs of His Kingdom (John 9:35-37; 11:40; 12:37; Matt. 11:21f.). It is written, for example, that the Father can be *seen* through

10. Quoted by Michaelis, *loc. cit.*, 319.
11. On the ineffability of God, see also R. Bultmann, "Untersuchungen zum Johannesevangelium," *Zeitschrift für die NT Wissenschaft*, XXIX (1930), 169-92; Bultmann discusses the difference between the invisibility of the deity in Greek religion and Israelite-Jewish religion. In the latter there is no notion of invisibility as a necessary attribute of God. "In the OT the notion throughout is this: that one *can* see God with human eyes, but that one *may not* see Him" (178). Cf. also Lohse, in *TDNT*, *loc. cit.*; H. M. Kuitert, *De mensvormigheid Gods* (1962), pp. 245ff.
12. Cf. Michaelis, *loc. cit.*, 347.

the revelation of His Son (John 14:9; cf. 12:45).[13] This is said in the same Gospel that claims that no one has ever seen the Father. That not-seeing of God stands over against the revelation of His only Son, who is in His bosom and makes Him known (John 1:18).

It is clear that seeing and perceiving cannot be dissociated from faith. A genuine encounter is involved, which can be described as *seeing* and *believing*, just as "the other disciple," approaching the tomb on Easter morning, "saw and believed" (John 20:8). The eyes are undoubtedly important, but their importance depends completely upon the condition of the heart. "Seeing is also a kind of hearing; that is to say, it, too, is a receiving of revelation."[14] Decision-making with respect to the manifestation of Christ's Kingdom is a matter of the heart — the eye may be either sound or unsound (Matt. 6:22f.; cf. Mark 4:12; Isa. 6:9f.). The gravity of seeing becomes apparent when the blindness of the eyes and the hardening of the heart are done away with. This involves something qualitatively different from "mere ocular awareness"[15] that has nothing to do with faith. In the gospel, then, it is a matter of actually seeing (which is why Nathanael — with all his reservations — had to "come and see" — John 1:48), but at the same time insight or discovery is involved.

In this connection we note a great variety of seeing in the New Testament in connection with the continuity of the Kingdom in salvation-history. Jesus tells His disciples that a time will come when they will no longer see (John 16:16), a time of hiddenness. Yet this time is placed in the context of Christ's return (vs. 22), and in that context the fact of not seeing does not disrupt communion with the Lord. If there is blessing for those who, living in the time of salvation, saw (cf. Luke 10:23), there is also blessing for those who do not see but nevertheless believe (John 20:29). These two phases in the history of salvation are united in the *eyewitnesses,* who, as ministers, go out into the world to proclaim salvation (cf. Luke 1:2). Consider

13. Kittel, in *TDNT*, s.v. *akouō*, I, 220, refers to the Johannine "strong emphasis on seeing"; cf. also W. Stählin, *Das Johannëische Denken* (1954); G. L. Philips, "Faith and Vision in the Fourth Gospel," in *Studies in the Fourth Gospel* (1957), pp. 83ff.; C. H. Dodd, *The Interpretation of the Fourth Gospel* (1953), pp. 165ff.
14. Michaelis, *loc. cit.,* 348.
15. Philips, *op. cit.,* p. 84.

the transfiguration (Matt. 17:1-13). In addition to the reality of "seeing" in this event, we detect its temporality and transitoriness (cf. the cloud in vs. 3; and Jesus' remark in vs. 9). And throughout the account there is reference to words (vv. 3, 5, 7, 9), and an obvious orientation to the subsequent proclamation, when the community becomes one of believers who follow Him though they have not seen (ouk idóntes) Him (1 Pet. 1:8). The time of walking by faith, rather than by sight (2 Cor. 5:7), when the Lord has not yet appeared in all His glory (Col. 3:4), has begun. No longer is there the directness of the voice of "Majestic Glory" nor the "eyewitnesses of his majesty" (2 Pet. 1:16f.). Now the church is led by the much surer word of prophecy (vs. 19). But even now it is not just a matter of decisions of the heart alone, without any seeing, for the author of Hebrews talks about a reality that stands before the eyes so inevitably that Moses' steadfastness can be referred to in terms of "seeing him who is invisible" (11:27). Paul, too, talks about the certainty of the believers, who have the eyes of their hearts enlightened (Eph. 1:18).[16]

In other words, contact has not disappeared into estrangement or secrecy. Perception and discovery remain, and although there is a difference between this seeing and the eschatological vision of God, the reality of "the eyes of the heart" on this earth is not something unreal with no practical value. Rather, it is a matter of the silence of the attention, the opened eyes, prayer. Some have spoken in this connection of contemplation, often in this way anticipating the vision of God and neglecting the difference between contemplation in the here and now and the eschatological visio Dei. But the idea of contemplation should not lead to a neglect of what the eyes of faith actually see.[17]

16. Cf. Ps. 19:8: "the commandment of the Lord is pure, enlightening the eyes." On the extrabiblical use of the expression, cf. H. Schlier, Der Brief an die Epheser (2d ed., 1958), p. 80; Hans Urs von Balthasar, Herrlichkeit, I, 168f., on Pierre Rousselot's doctrine of the "eyes of faith" and its relation to Newman's "illative sense."

17. An excellent Roman Catholic study of contemplation is Hans Urs von Balthasar, Prayer (Eng. tr., 1961). Balthasar places strong emphasis on the hearing of the Word: "The Catholic tradition of contemplation must recapture the element adopted by Protestantism as its watchword and standard, and which has become somewhat alien to Catholics: hearing the word of Scripture..." (pp. 23f.). "Contemplation must always be a renewed 'hearing' of what 'the Spirit speaks to the Church' (Apoc. II.7; etc.)" (p. 59). Note also his valuable biblical perspectives on activism (p. 115) and mysticism (pp. 117ff.). Cf. Herrlichkeit, I, 123ff.

For here there is no longer a distinction between seeing and believing. Faith, which Hebrews tells us is "the conviction (élenchos) of things not seen" (11:1), sees with these "eyes of the heart." This conviction of faith itself stands in an eschatological perspective: it is "the assurance (hypóstasis) of things hoped for." There is a seeing, an outlook, an insight into the things that cannot be seen, a certainty of the eyes of the heart, which cannot be affected by any reality "before the eyes" (cf. Heb. 2:9; 12:2; Rom. 4:19f.). Against the background of this tension, which is even reflected in the choice of words, sounds the promise of the future — the prospect of a new, surprising visio Dei.

Vision and Fruition

Because the Scripture emphatically speaks about seeing God as an eschatological gift, it is apparent that the "invisibility" of God is not an "attribute" of the divine nature. Rather, in its references to God's invisibility, the Bible points to the unapproachable light, the highness and majesty of God, and impresses upon man the miracle of God's revealing of Himself, of man's ability to encounter Him, of God's making His face to shine upon man. The New Testament as well as the Old portrays God's ineffability; and the beatific vision does not break through this ineffability, but is an eschatological gift. There is no talk of making God the object of our eyes; instead we hear of the gracious revelation of God's countenance.[18] On the basis of the gospel, it may be concluded that in the revelation of Jesus Christ His intermediacy to the Father is unlocked already as salvation's true possession in the present dispensation. "Through him we both have access (prosagōgén) in one Spirit to the Father" (Eph. 2:18), Paul writes; and Peter tells us that the purpose of Christ's death was to "bring us to God" (1 Pet. 3:18).

Consequently, there is no discontinuity between the present dispensation and the eschaton. However, saying this does not take away from the fact that our full attention is drawn to a perspective on the eschatological mystery of God's countenance, a perspective whose explication is never theoretical.

18. Bultmann sees in the NT, particularly in the aóratos theós (cf. Col. 1:15; 1 Tim. 1:17; Heb. 11:27), a terminology that arose "in connection with other Hellenistic divine predications"; "Untersuchungen zum Johannesevangelium," loc. cit., p. 187. He does not consider this to be a violation of the biblical view of God's invisibility.

The beatific vision, we notice on closer examination, is correlatively joined to sanctification. It is not a neutral prediction; it is not a metaphysical concept. It is a matter of "access" to God, which is intimately related to earthly life and its relation to God. Not only are we told that the pure in heart shall see God (Matt. 5:8), we are warned that no one who has not been sanctified shall ever see the Lord (Heb. 12:14). John depicts the future as seeing God as He is, immediately adding the admonition: "every one who thus hopes in him purifies himself as he is pure" (1 John 3:3). The relationship between sanctification in life and the vision of God is apparently decisive. "No one who sins has either seen him or known him" (1 John 3:6). One does not theorize about this from the sidelines: the beatific vision affects our life in the here and now every day.

In addition, the New Testament describes the vision of God as the terminal on the way from the "already" to the "presently." Paul was especially concerned with this way. The continuity of this pilgrimage is variously illustrated: the "imperfect" and "perfect" (1 Cor. 13:10); knowing in part and understanding fully (vs. 12); "seeing in a mirror dimly" and seeing "face to face." Both knowing and seeing are included. In the "now" there is a degree of knowing and even of seeing, but it is imperfect and incomplete: "in a mirror dimly."[19] 1 Corinthians 13:12 defines the structure of the present dispensation. We see in a mirror "in a riddle" (ASV margin).

In the Old Testament Yahweh's mode of appearance to the prophets was different from the way He approached Moses. He made Himself known to the prophets in visions and spoke with them in dreams, whereas He addressed Moses "face to face,

19. Grosheide emphasizes the imperfections of early metal mirrors, with their vague images that did not enable one to see things as they really were; *Comm.*, p. 348. Kittel disagrees, on the ground that this is an archaeologically unsound view. He emphasizes instead the aspect of "enigma" or "riddle," which played a role in prophetic revelation. Neither James 1:23 nor 2 Cor. 3:18 says anything about lack of clarity in the picture reflected in a mirror. In *TDNT*, s.v. *aínigma*, I, 178ff. It seems to me that the intention of the author is not entirely clear in Kittel's article; at any rate, for our purposes here the choice between one interpretation and the other is not decisive: the reference to "riddle" *(en ainígmati)* is sufficient to establish the contrast between "now" and "presently." Cf. also Zahn: "mediated, reflected, and, on that account, less fresh, certain, and living, therefore, in any case incomplete" *(Komm.*, p. 402); Wendland: "to see indirectly through a mirror, therefore not the thing itself" *(Komm., ad loc.)*.

clearly, and not in dark speech" (Num. 12:8). The contrast implies that the former required explanation, whereas the latter was self-sufficient and needed no interpretation (cf. Judg. 14: 12-14; Prov. 1:6). Paul, then, indicates that the riddle is the structural form of human seeing and knowing in this dispensation. The enigmatic character has not yet been taken away; and therein lies the difference between now and then. In other words, Paul apparently sees the relationship between "now" and "then" as similar to that between God's appearance to Moses and the prophets. The designation "face to face" is reserved for the eschaton.

Moses' unique status is used to describe Paul's "then," when things will no longer be surrounded by the shroud of secrecy but directness and intimacy will prevail.[20] The transition from "now" to "then" is also compared to the transition from "child" to "man" (1 Cor. 13:11), and Paul specifically refers to giving up something — childish ways. Human maturity is the analogy of the eschaton. In all of this the eschaton is not explained, yet one becomes aware of a definite continuity from the "now" to the "then." Furthermore, according to verse 12 — "Now I know in part; then I shall understand fully, even as I have been fully understood" — eschatological "knowledge" is on the same level as our being known by God. We are far removed here from all speculation. This "face to face" relationship is filled with a mysterious reciprocity. This is not an identification of human knowledge and divine knowledge, but knowing does stand in connection with being known, just as loving God is related to being known by Him (1 Cor. 8:3). To the Galatians Paul writes: "now . . . you have come to know God, or rather (mállon dé) to be known by God" (4:9).

The eschaton is not grounded in human activity, but in the love and knowledge of God, which is why there is no breach between the "now" and the "then," despite the continuity and transition to the eschaton. The continuity between "now" and "then" is evidenced in love. But this continuity cannot jeopardize our perspective on the vision of God or extinguish our expecta-

20. Cf. Num. 12:8 (peh 'el-peh; LXX stóma katá stóma); Exod. 33:11 ("face to face, as a man speaks to his friend"); Deut. 34:10 (pānîm 'el-pānîm; LXX prósōpon katá prósōpon); Deut. 5:4 (where the words refer to Yahweh's speaking with the people). See also J. Ridderbos, Deuteronomie, I, 102.

tion. The certainty of faith is not the end of the road; rather, faith is the certainty of things hoped for (Heb. 11:1).

What is the relationship between the eschatological vision of God and the notion of "seeing" employed by the New Testament to designate communion with God in this earthly life? In other words, what is the relationship between this present age and the age to come, a relationship the church has always maintained without diminishing the fulness of the eschaton?[21] This harks back to the biblical teaching of the first fruits of the Spirit (Rom. 8:23) and the reference of the author of Hebrews to tasting the powers of the age to come (6:5). But despite this pledge or prelude or gift already present, the awareness of incompleteness remains, stimulating the church to anticipate the new reality of what was promised, the eschatological vision — face to face. A correlation has sometimes been drawn between *visio* and *fruitio*. It would be unfair to represent this *fruitio* as false mysticism. It was a concept maintained primarily to do justice to the depth and riches of the experience of the grace of God. It points to what Psalm 25:14 calls "the friendship of the LORD." Fruition, therefore, is not limited strictly to the eschaton. Eschatological fruition contains the idea of fulfilment, but a fulfilment connected with what is presently experienced in this dispensation: tasting the powers of the age to come and the heavenly gift (Heb. 6:4f.).[22] In metaphorical language of human sense organs, reference is made to salvation, and just as salvation is not an exclusively eschatological term in the Bible, neither is fruition. Fruition is not something wholly other than faith and compliance with God's will, but it does indicate that the whole man, heart and experience included, is involved in faith, and that the object of this faith is not something that remains foreign to him, to be apprehended by intellect alone. Salvation penetrates into every corner of the heart and brings about there an "assimilation" of truth.[23] It includes something of enthusiasm, a condition of being seized totally and irrevocably, as is often reflected in the apostolic witness as delight in salva-

---

21. Cf. Heidelberg Catechism, Q. 58, on the beginning of eternal joy, in distinction from the perfect blessedness after this life. Cf. also Q. 103 (the eternal Sabbath).

22. *geusaménous tês dōreás tês epouraniou.* . . . The word *geúomai* is found in 1 Pet. 2:3 as well, in relation to the Lord's being *chrēstós,* a quotation from Ps. 34:8.

23. Cf. Balthasar, *Herrlichkeit,* I, 129.

tion and the abundance of the response to it (cf. for example John 21:25; Eph. 3:8, 20; Col. 3:16; Rev. 5:12; 7:12).

This is neither "ecstasy" (meaningless withdrawal from actualities of ordinary existence) nor contemplation (as over against activity), but diligent attention to keeping the Word in one's heart, lest it be suffocated and disappear.[24] The idea of going into one's room and shutting the door before praying (Matt. 6:6) is not to flee from reality, but a concentration, a seeing, that guards against confusion. This explains too what James wrote about "the implanted word, which is able to save your souls" (1:21). To remain in His love (John 15:9f.), to abide in Him (vv. 4, 5, 6, 7) in this wonderful continuity is the point of contact between this age and the one to come. In the coming age this fruition will be stripped of its tensions, freed from all assaults, its riddles solved.

This fruition played an important part in the theologies of both Augustine and Calvin. In the *Institutes* Calvin describes the eschaton in terms of enjoyment of the presence of God as "the acme of happiness" (III.xxv.11). He speaks of the pleasantness of the very sight of heaven, and of satisfaction through the full fruition of happiness.[25] The witness of Scripture to this fruition apparently triumphs over all hesitations about talking about this out of a fear of hedonistic reaction.[26] Fruition, after all, is not the fulfilment of a self-centered longing in the Christian church, but the reflection of the abundant glory, grace, and love of God, which exclude any self-centeredness.[27]

24. On Paul's ecstasy (2 Cor. 5:13), cf. Oepke, in *TDNT*, s.v. *ékstasis, exístēmi*, II, 457f., 460. On the "contemplative" versus the "active" cf. Luke 10:38-42 (Mary and Martha). Balthasar refers to Isaiah's vision and the prophet's response, "Send me" (Isa. 6:8): "Our mission, our assent to God's personal will in the concrete, springs from the contemplation of God's eternal truth and our assent to it"; *Prayer*, p. 228.

25. *Inst.*, III.xxv.2 *(donec plena fruitio nos satiet)*. On Augustine cf. R. Lorenz, "Fruitio Dei bei Augustin," *Zeitschrift für die Kirchengeschichte*, LXI (1950), 75-132; E. B. J. Postma, *Augustinus' de beata vita* (1946), pp. 202ff.; Anders Nygren, *Agape and Eros* (Eng. tr., 1953), pp. 503ff.

26. On the profound critique of *hēdonē* in the NT cf. Stählin, in *TDNT*, s.v., II, 918ff., particularly his comments on "NT joy" (p. 926).

27. Bavinck writes *(GD, IV, 704)*: "*Visio, comprehensio, fruitio Dei* constitute the essence of future blessedness" (cf., however, II, 157). See also K. Schilder, *Wat is de hemel?* (Dutch ed.), p. 179.

The visio Dei *in church history*

Historically, the church has been much interested in the ideas of fruition and the beatific vision. Medieval Christianity is sometimes alleged to have had an idea of the church and of the presence of the Lord that excluded or slighted an eschatological outlook. But it cannot be denied that pronouncements concerning the beatific vision were in the forefront of theological discussions in that era. The joyous aspect of the vision of God received particular attention when it was united with fruition and rest *(requies)*.[28] The intent was clear: not mysticism, but proper justice to the biblical perspective of "face to face." That means that the idea of seeing God did not disappear behind a vague concept of fruition. On the contrary, serious reflection arose about seeing God. This reflection ties in very closely with the emphasis of the Bible on the new and surprising after all the vicissitudes of seeing and not-seeing during the history of salvation. Eschatologically it is a matter of unequivocal usage: *visio Dei* means seeing God. Some day — they meant to confess — He will be seen, no longer in confusing incompleteness, no longer within the structure of riddles, no longer with the limitations of "Lord, I believe, help my unbelief," but in a way that approximates the experiences of Moses — face to face.

This interpretation of an undisturbed, problem-free *visio beata* calls to mind a teaching of Roman Catholicism concerning a beatific vision in this present dispensation, namely, during the lifetime of Jesus Christ on earth. This view attributed a "beatifying vision" to Him during His earthly life, including His passion. In the course of time this vision, which was accepted on the ground of the hypostatic union of the two natures, came to be questioned in terms of how it related to the shadows and sorrows that surrounded His life much of the time. A kenotic element came to be included in the vision, and the question was raised whether it was possible to reconcile this beatific vision with the rest of what we know about Jesus' earthly life.

28. Cf. the following sections in Denzinger: the Council of Vienna in 1311 — *lumen gloriae* and *fruitio* (475); Benedict XII in 1336 (530); the Council of Trent (984). Secondary sources on the medieval doctrine of the *visio beata* include Nikolaus Wicki, "Die Lehre von der himmlischen Seligkeit in der mittelalterliche Scholastik von Petrus Lombardus bis Thomas von Aquin," *Studia Freiburgensia* (1954), pp. 95ff.; J. Oswald, *Eschatologie* (1869), pp. 38ff.; Scheeben-Atzberger, *Dogmatik,* IV (1898), 862ff.

No such problems occur with respect to the eschatological vision of God, of course, since sorrow, suffering, tears, and death will have been eliminated in the eschaton. Understandably, Roman Catholic dogma at this point, proceeding from the idea of Christ's uninterrupted vision of God, had greater difficulty with its Christology than with its eschatology.

In this connection another question came up: can believers share in the beatific vision while here on earth? The apostle Paul comes readily to mind — his "visions and revelations" of being "caught up to the third heaven" and into Paradise (1 Cor. 12: 1-4). How is this Pauline "rapture" related to the beatific vision? All kinds of ambiguities arise in connection with these questions, because Paul does not say what he saw, but merely that he "heard things that cannot be told" (árrēta rhḗmata), which man may not utter.[29] This "unspeakableness" of Paul's experience meant that it could contribute little to reflection on the beatific vision. And so the central issue remained that of the *eschatological* vision of God. In the course of the history of the church, the eschatological vision of God came to be known as the "essential vision of God," the *visio Dei per essentium*.[30]

29. On this passage cf. K. Schilder, *Wat is de hemel?*, p. 187 (Dutch ed., 1935). Schilder erroneously substitutes "saw" for "heard" in describing Paul's experience, as does Balthasar, *Herrlichkeit*, I, 346. For the rest, Schilder does distinguish between Paul's "ecstatic" state and the eschatological vision of God. Balthasar points out a contrast with John, who in heaven rediscovers the reality of the earth from the perspective of heaven (cf. Rev. 1:10). Obviously Paul's experience must remain obscure for us, which accords with Paul's purpose in telling it in the first place.

30. On Christ's *visio* see also Berkouwer, *Conflict with Rome* (Eng. tr., 1957), pp. 203ff.; P. Schoonenberg, *Het geloof van ons doopsel*, III (1958), 144ff.; E. Schillebeeckx, "Het bewustzijnsleven van Christus," *Tijdschrift voor Theologie* (1961), 231ff., which discusses E. Gutwenger's *Bewusstsein und Wissen Christi*, with its view of a *kenosis* in the *visio Christi*; K. Rahner, "Dogmatic Reflections on the Knowledge and Self-Consciousness of Christ," *Theological Investigations,* V, 193-215. Rahner wants to attribute "a direct union of [Jesus'] consciousness with God, a visio immediata, during his earthly life, but this without qualifying or having to qualify it as 'beatific.' " It would be heretical, he argues, to deny "the fact that Jesus was not simply as blessed on earth as the Saints in heaven" (p. 203). Rahner feels that traditional Roman Catholic theology does not exclude further reflection on this point. It seems to me that this further interpretation is something new in the tradition to meet the Reformation's references to the reality of the humiliated Lord. See also the various Roman Catholic doctrinal handbooks, which differ very little on this score; also A. Theodoros, "Die Lehre von der Vergottung des Menschen bei den griechischen

The crucial question is whether — and if so how — such an "essential" vision of God is possible for man. The question is crucial because what is at stake is the eschatological beholding of God's *being*. The extraordinary nature of this vision has led to all sorts of divergent opinions about it with respect to its completeness. We should remember, however, that there are ecclesiastical pronouncements that relate the vision to 1 John 3:2: "we shall see him as he is." Now Bavinck describes the "essential" vision of God as the vision of God "as He is in Himself" *(ut in se est)*. He goes on to mention — without commenting on the differences between the two — the decision of the Council of Florence concerning the vision of God "as He is" *(sicuti est)*. But this is precisely where the trouble lies. The Florentine "as He is" is a biblical expression; *"sicuti est"* is taken right from the Vulgate. The "essential" vision was seen as the dynamic, eschatologically new vision of the depth, the reality, the *being* of God. In analyzing the latter vision, Bavinck detects in it the influences of neo-Platonic mysticism. He points out that the majority of Reformation theologians either refused to consider the "obscure questions" of Scholasticism, among which he includes this vision, or rejected the beatific vision *per essentiam* altogether. Such reluctance, he says, is entirely in harmony with Scripture, since God in His essence cannot be known.[31] Actually, Bavinck takes "essential vision" to be identical to "comprehension," and argues that every vision of God requires a divine revelation, a condescension by God.

But why start with the *essence* of God and argue about whether it can be seen (as the Scholastics claimed) or not (as Bavinck claimed)? It is more profitable to begin by noticing that the Middle Ages talked in terms of both the biblical "as He is" and the *visio per essentiam*. It is incorrect to identify these two. The *visio per essentiam* undoubtedly involves much more, and is far more complicated, than the biblical "as He is." The difficulties arose when some in ecclesiastical circles were no longer satisfied with the words "as He is" and began to use the term "essence." As early as Benedict XII (1336) there was talk of the saints "who saw the essence of God." There was no mediating element in this vision: the saints were thought in-

Kirchenvätern," *Kerygma und Dogma*, VII (1961), 283ff.; and, from an earlier era, H. Lennerz, "Ist die Anschauung Gottes ein Geheimnis?", *Scholastik*, VII (1932), 208ff.
31. *GD*, II, 154, 157, Eng. tr., *The Doctrine of God*, pp. 180-83.

tuitively to see God "face to face." The church seems not to have intended by this to say that man can "grasp" the vision through an innate capacity without revelation. The seeing is explicitly placed against the background of the divine essence manifesting itself, revealing itself. Man cannot attain this height out of his own capacities. God is not an "object" of his seeing.[32]

But Florence in 1439 went further. It spoke of clearly seeing the triune God, *as He is*.[33] It is apparently this expression that has come to be seen as identical to the *visio per essentiam*. But clearly the two cannot be so easily identified. Identifying these two involves a jump from the scriptural "as He is" *(sicuti est)* to "as He is *in Himself" (ut in se est)*, which then is taken to be the essence of God. This then becomes the central feature of the reflection concerning the beatific vision, and here is where the difficulties and complications arise. The upshot is that the vision *per essentiam* becomes "one of the most prominent and absorbing, but also most difficult problems of dogmatics."[34]

One of the perplexing problems is whether created human nature can cope with such an "essential vision of God." Scholasticism tended more and more to answer this question negatively. The essential vision of God was in no way denied,[35] but it could not be explained very well given man's creatureliness. (Here of course we confront the old anthropological problem of the possibilities and limitations of human nature.)[36] Accord-

32. For the Latin text cf. Denz. 530. Like Bavinck, Schilder *(Heaven — What Is It?*, pp. 62ff.) oversimplifies by contrasting *visio per essentiam* and revelation. Cf. also Aquinas on Chrysostom, *Summa Theologica*, I, q. 12, a. 1; V. Lossky, *Vision de Dieu* (1962), pp. 13f.
33. ... *intueri clare ipsum Deum trinum et unum, sicuti est* ... ; Denz. 693. Both Benedict XII and Florence were concerned with the *visio* in the intermediate state, but this is fulfilled in the eschatological *visio*. Cf. Denz. 547a, 1647.
34. Scheeben-Atzberger, *Handbuch der katholischen Dogmatik*, IV (1903), 863.
35. At this point the Roman Catholic Western church differed from the Eastern Orthodox tradition, which admitted a *visio Dei*, but not *per essentiam*. The essence of God, the Eastern councils of the 14th century taught, is absolutely invisible; and one may only speak of a *visio Dei* in terms of the energy that proceeds from God. Prominent in this connection is the teaching of Gregory Palamas (1296-1359). Cf. Lossky, *op. cit.*, chapter 18, on the Palamite synthesis; also *Theologische Woordenboek*, s.v. *Hesychasten*. The Hesychasts taught that a vision of God was possible in this life through asceticism.
36. Cf. Aquinas, *Summa Theologica*, I, q. 12, a. 1, beginning with the question whether any created intellect is able to see God *per essentiam;* cf. a. 2; *Summa Contra Gentiles*, III.53f.

ingly, the *visio Dei per essentiam* came to be seen as possible only through a special gift that qualified man for the vision, known as the light of glory *(lumen gloriae)*. Because of man's creatureliness, the essential vision was an ontic impossibility; the light of glory, therefore, took on a strictly supernatural character. It enabled man to see God in His essence, the triune and one God.[37]

Thus the familiar distinction between natural and supernatural also affects the vision. It is worth noting that much later it came to be accepted that the two cannot be separated, resulting once again in knotty problems with the vision. These questions were raised by Henri de Lubac, who argued in his *Surnaturel — Études historiques* (1946) that man cannot be considered as a "pure creature," existing purely in the natural order. The latter position had been prominent in post-Tridentine theology, but originally created man had been seen as *inclined* to the ultimate vision of God. On the earlier view of a created inclination to the vision, the *visio Dei* is not so far removed from nature as it is on the view that the vision is a debt to nature *(debitum naturae)*. De Lubac was not arguing that man has a *right* to the beatific vision, but merely that his nature includes a "natural desire" *(desiderium naturale)* for it. De Lubac's view became the object of sharp criticism on the ground that it relativized the distinctly supernatural nature of the vision. The vision, it was argued, could in no way be explained in terms of created nature.[38]

37. This was not simply a theological matter; there was also an ecclesiastical dimension insofar as the Council of Vienna (1311) addressed itself to the problem in terms of the teachings of the Béguines and Béghards, who denied that such a *lumen gloriae* was necessary; cf. Denz. 471, 475; Bartmann, *Dogmatik*, II, 477. Scholasticism did differ on the supernatural character of the ability to see God, some defending the claim that it was a matter of restoring an ability lost through sin. Cf. Wicki, *op. cit.*, pp. 148ff., on Hugh of St. Victor.

38. One of the "erroneous opinions" against which the encyclical *Humani Generis* (1950) was apparently directed was De Lubac's. "Others destroy the gratuity of the supernatural order since God, they say, cannot create intellectual beings without ordering and calling them to the beatific vision" (par. 26; tr. Joseph C. Fenton, quoted in Leith, ed., *Creeds of the Churches*, p. 475). De Lubac claims that this is a misunderstanding of him. Cf. also James M. Connolly, *Voices of France* (1961), p. 87; and also *contra* De Lubac, P. Kreling, "Notities bij de Lubac's *Surnaturel*," *Werkgenootschap voor Katholieke Theologie in Nederland*, 1950, p. 18.

It is not our purpose to judge for one side or the other in this dispute, but it is evident where the problem lies.[39] Is there a structural incongruity between created nature and the vision of God? The doctrine of the essential vision of God requires that something be added to man's nature, an enrichment enabling him to behold true being. In reaction to Protestant criticism, it was emphasized that the boundary between Creator and creature is not abolished, but that the ultimacy of the vision, which needs to be maintained, requires this supernatural gift. Thus the notion of the "light of glory" raises an ontic, anthropological problem, a structural problem with respect to the limitations of created nature.[40]

Obviously, this is entirely different from the existential faith-problem raised by the biblical testimony that the pure of heart shall see God (Matt. 5:8) and that none shall see the Lord except with holiness (Heb. 12:14). We do not mean to imply that the theological tradition we have been discussing ignores or repudiates this "conditionality," but it does make the first order of business concerning the vision of God the ontic problem, the problem of the necessity of the "light of glory."

What is meant by this "supernaturally added enrichment?" First of all, it does not mean that the "light of glory" enables man to comprehend God exhaustively: the identification of *visio* and *comprehensio* is vigorously disavowed, contrary to the identification of the two by Bavinck and Schilder (cf. footnote 32 above). Canon I of the Fourth Lateran Council (1215) sets forth God's incomprehensibility as an eternal property.[41] But it is something so great, so profound, that a specific qualification through the "light of glory" is necessary. This supernatural light is a "mysterious reality," a total mystery, "a supernatural, created power of recognition infused into the soul," through

---

39. The problem comes into even sharper focus when we consider that the notion of *debitum naturae* was already rejected by the bull *Ex omnibus afflictionibus* (1567), over against the teachings of Michel Baius (1513-1589); Denz. 1001-1080, esp. 1021; cf. also 1385, *contra* the French Jansenist Pasquier Quesnel (1634-1719). To be sure, De Lubac criticizes Baius in Chapter I of *Surnaturel*, but essentially the same problematics comes to the fore in De Lubac as in Baius. J. P. van Dooren argues that De Lubac misrepresents Baius; *Michael Baius. Zijn leer over de mens* (1958), pp. 18ff.
40. Cf. Thomas Aquinas, *Summa contra Gentiles*, III.53.
41. Quoted in Leith, *op. cit.*, p. 57.

which the vision is made possible without any intermediate vehicle.[42]

Clearly, seeing God *per essentiam* is much more complicated than the biblical "as He is." After all, John did not intend his statement as a subject of profound reflection, but as a word of comfort to the community. However, as we have noted, the idea of God's essence requires that the "as He is" be expanded into "as He is *in Himself*," that is to say, as He is apart from the relations He has established. That this is the meaning of the *visio Dei per essentiam* is demonstrated vividly by the denunciation of Antonio Rosmini-Serbati in the nineteenth century. Rosmini associated the vision with God's relation to creation and to the salvation granted by Him. Against this, Pope Leo XIII posited that the vision did not have to do with God the creator, provider, redeemer, and sanctifier, but with God *in His essence*. On earth, such a vision is out of the question, because all knowledge is mediate. Thus ontologism, with its idea of an immediate vision of God, is to be repudiated.[43] In the eschaton, however, man will find himself in a different order, the order of supernatural intuition and vision. Whereas in the earthly dispensation the organ applicable to the vision is lacking, in the eschaton the "light of glory" provides the necessary qualification.[44] It is ontically necessary for created human nature to aspire to the mystery of the essential vision of God.

Of course, this is not the only aspect of Roman Catholic thought on the beatific vision. There are other treatments that are on a more biblical plane. Schmaus, for example, writes that we cannot "seize upon God from within ourselves in immediate recognition, rather that we can penetrate into His mystery only to the extent that He discloses Himself to us."[45] Clearly, however, this ineffability of God is not only applicable to the

---

42. Bartmann, *Dogmatik*, I, 95. Cf. H. Lennerz, "Ist die Anschauung Gottes ein Geheimnis?", *Scholastik*, VI (1932), 208ff.; Oswald, *op. cit.*, p. 46: "in what this *lumen* consists we do not know."

43. On Rosmini cf. Denz. 1928, 1930. Atzberger (*op. cit.*, p. 862) notes a correspondence between Rosmini's doctrine and that of the Palamites (cf. fn. 35 above). The ontologism of Rosmini and Gioberti was condemned by the Inquisition in 1861 (Denz. 1659ff.). One might conclude that Roman Catholic dogma considers ontologism an anticipation of the eschaton.

44. Schmaus, *Katholische Dogmatik*, IV/2, 598.

45. *Ibid.*

eschaton. It applies to the present no less (cf. Matt. 16:17), and forms the basic thought of both Old and New Testaments, which deny that God can ever be the object of the autonomous "grasp" of man's eyes. More important, therefore, in connection with the essential vision is Schmaus's conclusion that *sin* prevents man from seeing God. This is a strongly biblical motif, reminiscent of Augustine, who consistently referred to this limitation. It would be astonishing indeed if this obviously biblical motif were not reflected in a discussion of the beatific vision *per essentiam*. But the singular thing is that in addition to this *central* biblical motif, there is another limitation, that is, that "man is incapable in his own strength of seeing God immediately, not merely on account of his situation in the history of salvation, but on the ground of his nature, that is, ontologically." On the basis of our created human nature, we are in a position to know God only in "His creations, people, things, experiences." Consequently, between the possibilities of our creaturely existence and the essential vision of God there exists an *ontic* incongruity.[46]

What this all boils down to is a synthesis between the biblical motif and the epistemological motif of the natural and supernatural. In this synthesis there is a dual limitation on the *visio Dei per essentiam*. But when the Bible talks about seeing God, the beatific vision is correlatively joined to purity of heart; and precisely on the basis of this correlation, which is the heart of the kerygma, it is impossible to introduce the other limitation of ontic incongruity. A review of the history of dogma shows that the latter soon begins to dominate the reflection, and the actual biblical understanding of the vision begins to fade.[47] And the doctrine of "light of glory" is the chief reason for this fading away.[48]

46. *Ibid.;* cf. Aquinas, *Summa Theologica,* I, q. 12, a. 2.
47. It seems to me that this is especially clear in the dogmatics of J. Pohle; cf. his *Dogmatik,* III (1922), 589ff.
48. The alleged scriptural support for the doctrine of a supernatural "light of glory" inevitably includes Ps. 36:9 ("in thy light do we see light"); cf. Aquinas, *Summa Theologica,* I, q. 12, a. 12. Ps. 36 indeed deals with illumination, but not with a supernatural elevation. Cf. vs. 11: this light provides courage and insight in the face of the arrogance of the wicked. Nor is 1 Cor. 2:9 ("what no eye has seen...") proof for the "light of glory" as some have suggested, for Paul is referring to what God has prepared in the revelation of Jesus Christ (cf. vs. 8; Isa. 64:4).

Seeing God "as He is"

One may not, of course, go so far in repudiating the supernatural light of glory as to deny the light and illumination and contrasting blindness of which both Old and New Testament speak. Paul talks about the blinding of the eyes of unbelievers, which keeps them from seeing the gospel of the glory of Christ, who is the likeness of God (2 Cor. 4:4). The kind of illumination required here plays a part on nearly every page of Scripture. It is an act of the God who called light into being (vs. 6). This light illumines the hearts of believers, who are "sons of light and sons of the day" (1 Thess. 5:5), called to "walk in the light" (1 John 1:7). This light cannot be separated into categories of internal and external illumination.[49] It is also mentioned with reference to the future glory, the city whose light is the glory of God, whose lamp is the Lamb, a light for all the nations (Rev. 21:23f.; 22:5). But this illumination is on an entirely different plane from that of the supernatural "light of glory," the ontic necessity, which issues from an epistemological, anthropological problematic. The real and repeated scriptural "problem" is not that of natural/supernatural, but confronts us in the context of admonitions about the eschatological revelation of God's glory.[50] Nowhere in the Bible is an isolated problem of knowledge involved, simply admonition and promise. Apparently, any preoccupation with the "anthropological" possibility of a vision of God is wholly superfluous.

This is already clear from the fact that the biblical notion of the vision of God, though it implies a difference from earthly existence, nowhere speaks of a *break* with it. Yet the perspective on the vision arises in connection with the transition from the "now" to the "then." This difference is not an anthropological or epistemological problem, and if one argues that it is, he must divest Christ's words in John 14:7 — *"henceforth* you know him [the Father] and have seen him" — of their significance, encouragement, and comfort. When the disciples took this "mode" of seeing to be insufficient, as typified by Philip's request, "Lord, show us the Father, and we shall be satisfied" (vs. 8), this question could only be answered by a question of radical astonishment: "Have I been with you so long, and yet you do not know

49. For a summary of uses of light in the OT and NT, cf. Oepke, in *TDNT*, s.v. *lámpō*, IV, 22ff.
50. Cf. K. Stückert, "Vom Schauen Gottes," *Zeitschrift für Theologie und Kirche,* VI (1896), 492ff.

me?" (vs. 9). However, should this "seeing" indeed be sufficient, their understanding of the relationship between "already" and the future would be secure, and no theoretical difficulties could then arise.[51] The promise of the vision of God becomes a proclamation in the midst of earthly life. Just as the powers of the age to come are already being tasted in this present world (Heb. 6:4), so too there is a light out of the future, a light that has everything to do with our eyes and our seeing, penetrating into this earthly existence. This nexus is so unmistakably clear that it cannot escape anyone. Thus Schmaus writes of the possibility of an "earthly presentiment" of the beatific vision, and of a "dawn of the heavenly vision."[52] It is difficult to understand this glow of dawn on the basis of an epistemological notion of a "light of glory," but it is incontrovertibly biblical.

Thus biblical "seeing" is never "unreal" — neither the seeking of God's face (Ps. 24:6; 27:8f.), nor coming into His presence (Ps. 95:2), nor the fear that He will hide His face (Ps. 27:9). There is only one problem that always arises here, and it is not a theoretical problem of whether or not we can see God, but a problem of the heart. And the "mystery" involved is not that centering around the words "as He is in Himself," but centering around purity of heart and holiness: *we shall see him as he is* (1 John 3:2).[53]

The connection between earthly seeing and the beatific vision should not lead to the conclusion that the eschatological vision is a comprehensive reality. We do well to heed Calvin's warning that the knowledge we now possess from the Word of God, though true, is yet a far cry from the manifestation that we await in seeing "face to face."[54] John prefaces his perspective on the future glory of the vision with the awareness that "it does not yet appear what we shall be" (1 John 3:2). This is not agnosticism, but a realization that the veil has not yet been removed. Our being children of God is still a matter of breathless, intense expectation. Part of the reality of the vision of God is that it can only be known and understood in the vision itself. That is why all our talk of it is inadequate. What are

---

51. Cf. Schmaus, *op. cit.*, p. 598.
52. *Ibid.*, p. 606.
53. It is profitable to consider the context of this saying: God's love, our being His children, future revelation, self-purification against sin (vv. 1-3). Cf. R. Schnackenburg, *Die Johannesbriefe*, pp. 152ff.
54. Cf. his commentary *ad* 1 Cor. 13:12; *Inst.*, III.xxv.2, 10, 11.

we to make of Schmaus's explanation: "The vision of God does not happen, by its nature, with the bodily eye, but with the spirit"? It would be better to be satisfied with what he says elsewhere, that the vision of God is "a loving look at the unveiled countenance of God."[55] To say more than that is, in effect, to say less. The vision of God is not something that is explained to us, but something that is promised to us in a time when we see only through a mirror in riddles (1 Cor. 13:12).

The word "unveiling," of course, is a translation of the Greek *apokálypsis,* and not a specific word for the reality of the eschaton. But what word would better express the mystery that has already begun to be manifested before illumined eyes? This unveiling is no epistemological problem related to the essence of God. God's "essence" cannot be abstracted or isolated from His relation to man in the revelation of His love, mercy, wrath, judgment, and all the measures He has taken and still takes in history. Nor does the eschatological perspective lend itself to such abstractions, as if God could ever be known — in His essence — apart from His concern for our salvation, as if He did not reveal Himself as the living, intimate, merciful and sustaining God precisely in this concern for man's salvation (cf. Luke 1:78f.). This should be sufficient to restrain us from longing to see Him "as He is in Himself." This is not to say that one may not talk about God's essence. Whether or not that is legitimate depends entirely on why one reflects on it. But to strive for a relationless "as He is in Himself" even while defending a so-called "ontological" doctrine of the trinity, does not rise much above a form of mere modalism.[56] When the Book of Revelation depicts the future, we see the basic lines of God's concern for

---

55. Schmaus, *op. cit.,* p. 601. H. Ott *(Eschatologie,* p. 45) asks, "Is the concept of *visio Dei* further able to be concretized?" His answer: "Probably there is room for a more profound existential interpretation." However, what he then adds to this — that it is clear "that we do not have to do with a problem of optics" — holds little promise as far as such an existential interpretation is concerned.

56. This, however, is not the basic idea of modalism. The church did not reject modalism on the grounds of its strong emphasis on God's revelation and on the economy of His acts in the history of salvation, but because it saw in these "only" a revelation, thus assailing the reality of the revelation. Thus the answer to Q. 25, Heidelberg Catechism, that we speak of three, Father, Son, and Holy Spirit, because God has so revealed Himself in His Word, is not modalism, because the revelation is taken seriously. Thus there is no question of playing off a "salvation-economical" aspect against an "ontological" aspect.

salvation very clearly in the central position of the Lamb who illuminates the city (21:22f.). The names on the foundation of the city are those of the twelve apostles (21:14). And when it is announced that God's servants will see His face, we are given at the same time a view of "the throne of God and of the Lamb" (22:1; cf. 3:21; 3:12). "The glory of God is never — not for one moment — divorced from the Lamb; the trinitarian light is never separated from the light of Christ the incarnated one."[57]

If there is anywhere that the Bible talks about the "being" of God or describes His reality it is in the Book of Revelation. There is no doubt about the glory of God, but an abstract *ut in se est* — "as He is in Himself" — dies away on our lips when we confront the vision of the Bride, the wife of the Lamb and the new Jerusalem, "having the glory of God" (21:9f.). When this city descends from the heavens, adorned as a bride, the dwelling of God is with men, and He Himself dries every tear from the eyes of His people (21:3; cf. Exod. 33:14f.).

So the isolated intricacies of a *visio Dei per essentiam* are completely foreign to the Word of God, something quite different from the Johannine "as He is." In the divergence between the Greek and Latin theologies of the vision of God both sides occupied themselves with the "essence" of God, Aquinas and the West alleging that in the *visio beata* this essence could be seen, Gregory Palamas and the East alleging that it could not. Both operated with a notion of the essence of God that could better be described by "as He is in Himself" than by the biblical "as He is." A choice for one or the other is therefore impossible (although we would concede that with Aquinas' view there is a better chance of retaining the perspective of the "as He is" than there is with Palamas, who divided what was indivisible). But the transition — in the West as well as the East — from the biblical expression of the Council of Florence, "as He is," to the theoretical "as He is in Himself" tends to threaten the message of comfort and extinguish the true light.[58]

Although John's "as He is" as a description of the eschatological vision of God has frequently been misunderstood and

57. Balthasar, *Herrlichkeit*, I, 421.
58. When one thinks of the Johannine "as He is" the predications of 1 John 4:8 and 16 also suggest themselves: "God is love." That there is no distinction here is made evident by the entire context of vv. 7-21. Cf. Nygren, *Agape and Eros*, pp. 146ff.; Stauffer, in *TDNT*, s.v. *agapáō*, I, 49-53 (on Paul and John).

distorted and subjected to all kinds of speculation, it nevertheless presents a clear and unmistakable perspective. It is an outlook — and at the same time an insight — that tells us that, in
the *visio Dei,* we shall know how much we need to repent in
dust and ashes with Job (42:6) ; we shall recognize how often
our own eyes have been shrouded here on earth by our questions
— some of them legitimate, most of them not; we shall realize
how true and reliable and authentic is the earthly *visio,* the
earthly seeking of God's face (cf. Ps. 67:1f.) ; and we shall understand how profound was the Lord's encouragement to His disciples that "henceforth" they would see the Father (John 14:7).

Visio Dei *and* visio mundi

Something remains to be said in this connection about the
relation of all this to the problem of theodicy.[59] Every attempt
to formulate a theodicy is really an effort to grasp the beatific
vision now, in this life, to solve life's enigmas with this "insight,"
to replace the walk of faith with the walk of sight. Such unjustifiable anticipations reflect the impotence and poverty of
theodicies, no matter how much scholarly effort is spent on them.
No theodicy can ever give satisfactory answers or hope to a dis-
quieted and doubting heart. Despite its good intentions, its
solutions always ring hollow and are often irritating and even
contemptible. Not until the vision of God in the city that is
lighted by the Lamb will these enigmas be explained. Only then
will we comprehend "the breadth and length and height and
depth" (Eph. 3:18). Thus the revelation of the "essence" of
God, considered apart from His relationship to His creation, will
not do as an explanation of the beatific vision. We need the
vision of the true God, in contrast to what we see in Him now
with the restricted vision of God through our error-prone hearts
and blinded eyes. When we stumble (Ps. 73:2) in this life, when
God wearies us (Mic. 6:3), when we are terrified (Mark 6:50),
we are like the disciples when they *saw* Jesus walking on the
sea and "thought it was a ghost *(phántasma)"* (Mark 6:49), "for
they did not understand about the loaves, but their hearts were
hardened" (vs. 52). The cure for this hardness of heart is the
eschatological outlook on the solution to these enigmas, the
stilling of our doubts before the face of God "as He is." The

59. Cf. Berkouwer, *The Providence of God* (Eng. tr., 1952), chapter VIII,
"The Problem of Theodicy."

solution comes when He dwells with us and reveals Himself in
the answer to our prayer: "Let thy work be manifest to thy
servants, and thy glorious power to their children" (Ps. 90:16).

The clarity of this blessed, blessing vision sets aside all our
theological misconceptions about God's perfections, His righteousness and wrath, Israel and the Gentiles, faith and unbelief,
history and the harvest, election and human responsibility, the
meaning of life, Adam and Christ, the substitutionary atonement,
theopaschitism ... so much the lamp of the Lamb will shine.

There is no need for a detailed proof that no tension exists
between this vision of God and the vision of this world. To
discover tensions here would be a serious misunderstanding of
the eschatological mystery. That is obvious, as we saw in our
discussion of the new earth (Chapter VII), from the centrality
of the new heaven and the new earth in the Revelation of John.
This is certainly not something that draws our attention only
peripherally. Nor does it allow any room for a spiritualistic or
personalistic eschatology. We read of God's dwelling with men
and of all things being made new (Rev. 21:5). Without tension,
all the facets of the eschaton are harmoniously integrated. So
one need not hesitate to speak of the vision of the earth. Because God wipes away all tears and renews all things, there is
no longer any competition between attention to God and attention to "things." The *visio Dei* does not exclude the *visio
mundi*: it gives it meaning and fulfils it. The *visio mundi* does
not endanger the *visio Dei*. Around the throne of God and the
Lamb His servants worship Him; "they shall see his face, and
his name shall be on their foreheads" (Rev. 22:4). We are confronted here with remote things, but they are no longer *strange*
things. The secret of the future is this: "Blessed is he who keeps
the words of the prophecy of this book" (Rev. 22:7).

One very significant question, which may seem to jeopardize
everything, remains. When Scripture sets the vision of God in
such a clear and strong correlative relation to purity and holiness, so that without holiness no one will see God (Heb. 12:14),
is the eschatological comfort not thereby seriously imperiled?
We should never underestimate the gravity of this question.
Is not this an exceptionally difficult qualification, which threatens
to overshadow all else? Why such strong emphasis on purity
of heart (Matt. 5:8; Ps. 73:1), sanctification (1 John 3:3, 6, 9),
and service (Rev. 22:3f.)? Is it only a saintly elite who can
confidently and unashamedly enter the gate to the beatific vision?

First of all, this correlation may not be denied or done away with: it retains its relevance and strength throughout (cf. Rev. 21:8, 27; 22:11, 15). But one would be missing the point to construe these passages as a sort of last-minute moralism closing out the biblical message. These verses do not mean to go back on the gospel of the Lord, the good news that the tax collectors and harlots go into the Kingdom of God first (Matt. 21:31). Christ's words remain: "I came not to call the righteous but sinners" (Mark 2:17). There is no room for a revival of Pharisaism in the city lighted by the Lamb. The last word is still "the grace of the Lord Jesus" (Rev. 22:21).

Yet the gospel's message to the sinner is not without obligation, any more than is the call from darkness to the service of the Lord. There is a connection between earthly existence and the beatific vision, not a moralistic one, but one inherent in discipleship as the lived reality of faith, without which faith cannot be faith. When our eyes are enlightened through faith in an authentic seeing, the surprise of the vision of God appears. The way to this vision is the way of sanctification. This outlook cannot arise through morbid, self-defeating introspection, but only through "abiding in the vine," as Christ says. "You are already made clean," Christ assures us, "by the word which I have spoken to you" (John 15:3). This is followed by the admonition: "Abide in me, and I in you" (vs. 4). The promise of the vision inspires the believer to "strive for" holiness (Heb. 12:14),[60] to "press on toward the goal, the prize of the upward call of God in Christ Jesus" (Phil. 3:14). All of this can be recapitulated in the words of Revelation 21:7: "He who conquers shall have this heritage, and I will be his God and he shall be my son." In the pilgrimage come both the promise and the admonition. "Every one who thus hopes in him purifies himself as he is pure" (1 John 3:3). What John says here makes explicit the structure of the eschatological proclamation in its entirety. It is not a narrative of remote events irrelevant to life today, but a concrete *knock on the door.*

Our understanding and realizing the blessed, blessing vision of God depends ultimately on this trilogy of purity, sanctification, and service. And seven times the Word repeats the warning: "He who has an ear, let him hear what the Spirit says to the churches" (Rev. 2:7, 11, 17, 29; 3:6, 13, 22).

60. Cf. Berkouwer, *Faith and Sanctification* (Eng. tr., 1952), pp. 101ff.

CHAPTER THIRTEEN

APOCATASTASIS?

WE HAVE SEEN how closely the eschatological condition of salvation is related to present earthly existence and the decisions of the heart made in this life. We noted this particularly in the preceding chapter with respect to the vision of God. All of this introduces a topic in eschatology that has been the subject of a great deal of discussion — "universal" reconciliation, sometimes technically known as apocatastasis. Does the expectation of faith include an expectation of a universal reconciliation, the return of all men to the Father's house with its many mansions, the restoration of everything broken down by human pride, and the ultimate, universal, and infinite triumph of divine mercy over all obstacles to it? The question of the legitimacy of this doctrine has always been prominent in Christian theology, and has had repercussions outside the church as well, in connection with the church's doctrines of heaven and hell. Sometimes the doctrine of apocatastasis is expressed as a cautious conjecture, other times it is posited as a sure confidence that, in the end, when sin will have run its course, we shall see the restoration of all things and beatitude, not for some, but for all.

The grounds of universalism

In the history of dogmatics, the word "universalism" has often been used to indicate the width and breadth of the reconciling act of God in Christ Jesus.[1] This word has been the subject of a great deal of controversy, which has not been limited to theoretical, or even exegetical, disputes. It has become an

---

1. A distinction is usually made between absolute universalism and relative universalism. The latter is derived from the universality of Christ's sacrifice — *Christus pro omnibus mortuus est* — but does not conclude the salvation of all, since not all accept the reconciliation in faith. For further explication cf. Bavinck, *GD,* III, 450ff.

emotional issue, reflecting an intensity of feeling that could not make peace with the reality of lostness, the thought that some of one's fellow men will be eternally damned. Is there not an irresoluble incongruity, it was asked, between accepting the idea of damnation and thinking of one's neighbor, a fellow human being to whom one must relate in love even if he is an unbeliever? How can one — as a human being and as a Christian — deny the doctrine of universal reconciliation and still maintain a feeling of solidarity, of living together with the other people in this world?[2]

There is a danger here of adopting a condescending attitude toward such emotion-laden arguments, especially when they concern a strong awareness of human solidarity. There has always existed a wide difference of opinion about Moses' plea that God, if He should not forgive the people their sins, would blot him out of "thy book which thou hast written" (Exod. 32:32f.), and Paul's wish that he himself be "accursed and cut off from Christ" for the sake of his fellow Jews (Rom. 9:3).[3] These examples should suffice to restrain us from dismissing a conscious awareness of solidarity with all human beings as mere rebellion or denial of guilt.[4] Nonetheless, the idea persists that such human feelings cannot be determinative for making conclusions about

2. Cf. the reflections of Teilhard de Chardin, *The Divine Milieu* (Eng. tr., 1960), pp. 128ff.; and C. Journet, *Le mal. Essai théologique* (1960), pp. 207ff.
3. On Moses, cf. K. Schilder, *Heidelbergse Catechismus*, II, 47; and W. H. Gispen, *KV* on Exodus, II, 194ff. Gispen sees Moses here as a "type of the Mediator Christ Jesus." On Paul, cf. Luther, *Lectures on Romans* (ed. W. Pauck, 1961), pp. 260ff. Luther sees this statement of Paul as an indication of "the strongest and utmost kind of love." Cf. also Calvin's commentary *ad loc.*, where he asserts that Paul's "perfect love" is of the kind that overcomes *eternal* death.
4. The motif of solidarity is prominent in the writings of Hans Urs von Balthasar, especially in his reflections on Charles Péguy (1873-1914). Péguy left the Catholic Church (though he returned to it later) "on account of the 'intolerableness' of what was taught about hell." Cf. Balthasar, "Some Points of Eschatology," in *Word and Redemption*, p. 163; *Science, Religion, and Christianity* (Eng. tr., 1958), pp. 137f.; *Herrlichkeit*, II (1962), pp. 803ff. Balthasar refers chiefly to Péguy's *Le mystère de la charité de Jeanne d'Arc* (1909). To read Péguy is to be impressed by the extent to which the passionate feeling of solidarity can arise. In this emotional response the concept of one's own lostness plays a role, as does the thought of the one sheep that is lost and, when found, brings joy to heaven.

the future, and that this plea, found in Schleiermacher,[5] among others, cannot play a decisive role in theological reflection on the subject. There must be a firmer foundation than human feeling for a norm.[6] It is at this point that universalism makes its appeal to the irresistible love of God, which is sufficient to overcome all obstacles in the eschaton. The question is, how can this divine love — for God is Love — ever run aground on human apostasy or intransigence? If the omnipotent God is Love, and if this love is revealed in grace against human resistance, are not this love and its last word *irresistible grace*? Saying this is not meant to deny the reality of sin and guilt, but to base the prospect for the future on divine love and divine omnipotence. Is there not good reason to believe that in the final revelation of all things it will be different from what has been traditionally taught about hell and damnation?[7] Why minimize God's mercy? Is it not limitless and inexhaustible (cf. Exod. 34:6; Ps. 86:13)?

Obviously, this defense of universalism on the basis of God's love[8] may not be rejected out of hand without further biblical

5. Cf. Schleiermacher, *The Christian Faith* (Eng. tr., 1928), pp. 721f. on "sympathy." Schleiermacher expands on this motif: "Hence we ought at least to admit the equal rights of the milder view, of which likewise there are traces in Scripture; the view, namely, that through the power of redemption there will one day be a universal restoration of all souls." Cf. also *Die Religion in Geschichte und Gegenwart*, s.v. *Wiederbringung aller;* Buchberger, ed., *Lexikon für Theologie und Kirche*, I (1930), s.v. *Apokatastasis.*

6. Augustine discusses this in his *Enchiridion*, CXII, CXIII. He considers the appeal of "some, indeed very many" to Ps. 77:9: "'Hath God,' they say, 'forgotten to be gracious? hath he in anger shut up his tender mercies?'" Interestingly enough, Augustine is willing to "let them suppose, if the thought gives them pleasure, that the pains of the damned are, at certain intervals, in some degree assuaged." Even so, he argues, the death of the wicked "shall abide for ever . . . whatever men, prompted by their human affections, may conjecture. . . ."

7. Cf. O. Riemann, *Die Lehre von der Apokatastasis, das heisst der Wiederbringung aller* (1889). There is a great deal of variety in the arguments for general reconciliation. For example, the appeal to Matt. 12:32 (". . . forgiven, either in this age or in the age to come") and 1 Pet. 3:18f. (Christ's preaching to "the spirits in prison"), as indicating the possibility of repentance after death, differs from the doctrine of conditional immortality (annihilationism), which makes immortality the possession of only the regenerate.

8. J. A. T. Robinson defends such an appeal; "Universalism — Is It Heretical?", *Scottish Journal of Theology*, II (1949), 139-55. Robinson's emphasis is on the "omnipotence" of God's love, grounded in "a necessity of the divine nature." To be sure, man is given a choice, but the principle of divine love still applies: "its will to lordship is inexhaustible and

investigation, especially because it is proposed with such strongly doxological overtones. Universalism does not wish to deny the guilt of sin or weaken the wrath of God. But it sees sin and wrath as *temporary,* on the ground that God's wrath and punishment are aimed at the salvation of all men. In any case there is no intention of making human feelings the basis of this doctrine. Deeper grounds are sought for the universal eschatological expectation.[9]

The establishment of this doctrine on the basis of divine love and grace can be traced back to the early church in the figure of Origen, who did not exclude even the demons from eventual restoration. Origen founded his doctrine on the reconciling power of the resurrected Christ, through whom the love of God reduces all resistance to nothing. Later, this particular theme of Origen surfaced again and again, although sometimes in a limited form.[10] In our own time, C. S. Duthie has referred to a distinct "movement in Christian thought towards universal

ultimately unendurable: the sinner *must* yield." For if this were not so, it would be "the final mockery of His nature," which God would not tolerate. Similarly, H. Schumacher, *Das biblische Zeugnis von der Versöhnung des Alls* (1959), pp. 126ff., speaks of apocatastasis as an "exigency of God's being."

9. We shall not consider the appeal to a separate divine revelation, found, for example, in the English mystic Jane Leade (1623-1704). Mrs. Leade claimed to have received numerous divine revelations from 1670 to the end of her life. Mrs. Leade's defense of apocatastasis influenced the German Lutheran mystic Johann Wilhelm Petersen (1649-1727) and his wife. The Petersens had at first disputed Mrs. Leade's teaching, but during the course of the dispute became themselves convinced of the biblical character of apocatastasis. Cf. K. Lüthi, "Die Erörterung der Allversöhnungslehre durch das pietistische Ehepaar Johannes Wilhelm und Johanna Eleanora Petersen," *Theologische Zeitschrift,* XII (1956), 362.

10. For Origen's doctrine, cf. G. Müller, "Origenes und die Apokatastasis," *Theologische Zeitschrift,* XIV (1958), 174ff.; R. P. C. Hanson, *Allegory and Event. A Study of the Sources and Significance of Origen's Interpretation of Scripture* (1959), p. 335. Hanson argues that "universalism in Origen's thought is a necessary conclusion from his basic premises, and not, as it is in most modern thought, a 'larger hope' grounded on a strong belief in God's love and a kindly feeling toward all humanity, however degraded. In Origen's view for God to fail in reconciling . . . any beings at all, even only one or two, would be for God . . . to compromise himself with change and becoming and corruption." It seems to me that the contrast between Origen and the "larger hope" of modern thought is not very clearly defined. Among consistently Origenistic modern works is Giovanni Papini, *De duivel. Problematiek ener toekomstige diabologie* (1954), p. 296; cf. also Schumacher, *op. cit.,* pp. 168ff.

salvation."[11] H. G. Jones speaks of "the immense dominance and aggressiveness of universalism during the last fifty years."[12] For one this betokens a profounder understanding of the all-encompassing love of God; for another it is a regrettable recession, if not *the* heresy of modern time.

How much does this universalism reflect a concern for solidarity in the common dangers that confront humanity and how much of it reflects a minimizing of the gravity of sin? It is certainly no simple matter to develop a "phenomenology" of universalism. In any case, universalism is coming increasingly to rely on the omnipotent love of God. E. F. Ströter, for example, states that the ground for universal reconciliation is the cross of Golgotha: "how great, how overwhelming His triumph, His power, His glory!"[13] It is this triumphant, doxological note that W. Michaelis also expresses, when he says that universal reconciliation is no longer a matter of supposition, but of certainty. "Christ will be joyfully and hopefully certified as propitiator for all in an unimagined way. The world awaits the word of reconciliation. It is up to us to bring it."[14]

The extent of the influence of the idea of the ultimate triumph of the love of God is especially obvious in those thinkers who originally reject apocatastasis, but then go back on their rejection because of this notion of triumph.[15] Berdyaev is a

---

11. "Ultimate Triumph," *Scottish Journal of Theology*, XIV (1961), 169. Otto Weber comments that in the present-day ecumenical situation of the church we encounter a latent doctrine of universal reconciliation; *Grundlagen der Dogmatik*, II (1962), 504. At the time Bavinck wrote *GD* (4th ed., 1930), he detected more sympathy for conditionalism (i.e., conditional immortality) among theologians than for apocatastasis, which, he says, has always been "taught by only a few persons" (IV, 693).

12. "Universalism and Morals," *Scottish Journal of Theology*, III (1950), 27. Jones refers to the teachings of Robinson's article (see fn. 8 above) as "*the* heresy," and recalls the dire words of Jer. 23:17 against the false prophets who assure the people that no evil will befall them.

13. Ströter, *Die Allversöhnung in Christus* (2d ed., 1920), p. 159. Ströter takes 2 Cor. 5:19 as the motto for his book: "God was in Christ reconciling the world to himself."

14. Michaelis, *Die Versöhnung des Alls. Die freie Botschaft von der Gnade Gottes* (1950), p. 157. In the same line is Ethelbert Stauffer, *NT Theology* (Eng. tr., 1955), pp. 222ff. Stauffer writes that "God's irresistible grace and will is destined to overcome the most obdurate opposition."

15. One cannot dismiss the doctrine of apocatastasis out of hand by arguing that it has a "philosophical" character and that pantheism is at the root of it because it makes all things return successively to God,

case in point. He rejected apocatastasis on the basis of human freedom. "Origen's doctrine of apocatastasis contradicts his own doctrine of freedom. The salvation of the whole world . . . is conceived as the result of an externally determined process independent of human liberty. All creatures will be compelled in the end to enter the Kingdom of God." Berdyaev considers this to be a rationalistic doctrine. Yet in the end he is back in the camp of Origen: "We can and must believe that the power of hell has been vanquished by Christ, and that the final word belongs to God and to the Divine meaning. The conception of hell deals not with the ultimate but with the penultimate realities. . . . Hell disappears in the fathomless and inexpressible depth of the Godhead."[16] The strong accent on freedom so important to Berdyaev's thought is ultimately incapable of withstanding the triumph of grace.

Simply because the doctrine of universalism continues to be advocated in strongly Christological and doxological terms, it cannot be summarily dismissed. It would be inadequate, for example, to challenge universalism on the ground that eternal punishment is a self-evident consequence of the idea of retribution. This is the notion behind the argument that there is such an appalling breadth of evil in the world that it is impossible for all of it to be absorbed in a final divine remission that would cover all guilt. This "impossibility," as a counterargument to apocatastasis, follows from the acceptance of the notion of vindicative justice. Pohle contends that there is and indeed must be divine justice as retributive justice because it "avenges and restores the disturbed moral order through a serious sanction." He adds, by way of analogy, that even a human judge cannot operate without this vindicative and retributive element. According to him, the glory of God is no less exalted in the mode of retributive justice than it is "in His

just as they proceeded from Him; Bavinck, *GD*, IV, 693. It is true that for some the *Urzeit-Endzeit*-motif plays a role; Papini finds Origen to be inspired by the Stoic doctrine of cosmic cycles *(op. cit.*, p. 297). But overall, especially today, the Christological redemption-motif plays the dominant role.

16. Cf. Berdyaev, *The Destiny of Man* (Eng. tr., 1937), pp. 273-83. According to Berdyaev, one can only believe in hell if he does not fully accept the power of Christ. He accuses the church of thus having taken over elements of Manicheism. "Not infrequently [Christians] believed in the power of the devil more than in the power of God and of Christ" (p. 280).

benevolent love to His saints."[17] This is indeed a peculiar protest against universal reconciliation. Apparently one is to think
of two parallel lines, divine mercy and divine justice, two divine properties, juxtaposed and sometimes even opposed to one
another, each in its own right. Not only love, but also justice
must run its course. This notion is reminiscent of Kant's moral
argument for the existence of God, in which justice also plays
an important role with respect to the future life.[18] This argument
against universalism can be rejected out of hand as a form of
mere moralism rooted in an unbiblical concept of God. The
Bible gives no warrant for isolating God's love and justice in
this fashion.

Such a duality breaks down because God's justice is revealed
precisely in the cross. Because of this, any argument against
apocatastasis that requires the justice of God to be satisfied
in an eternal punishment is invalid and unbiblical. Such a
moralistic critique diminishes the perspective on the simplicity
and harmony of God's virtues. It assumes that, if the justice of
God is a reality, it must also be manifest, so that it must be
impossible for *all* guilt to be "swept away like a cloud" (Isa.
44:22). An appeal is often made, then, to examples of guilt
that are so horrifying as to make it unthinkable that they would
some day — in the eschaton — be thought of no more. In other
words, only in punishment can the reality of divine justice and
God's wrath against sin become manifest. Obviously, in this
criticism of universal reconciliation everything comes about very
simply. The final judgment is seen as corresponding to the guilt
and rebellion of human evil, which will receive due retribution in eternal punishment. Vindicative justice requires this
punishment.

What is biblically illegitimate about this line of reasoning
is that it looks on reconciliation for our own sins as a real

17. Pohle, *Dogmatik*, III (7th ed., 1922), 609.
18. I wonder whether it is justifiable to speak of heaven and hell as if they
were "postulates" of our thought; cf. H. Bavinck, *Wijsbegeerte der
openbaring* (1908), p. 271. Bavinck refers to Kant's idea of a balance
between virtue and happiness in the hereafter (p. 294n.). See also
Haitjema, *Dogmatiek als Apologie*, p. 347, where he argues that "the
final judgment as a moral crisis automatically postulates a twofold
'outcome' of history." It seems to me that in this "postulate" — just as
in the doctrine of apocatastasis — there is an element of presumed self-
evidence that, as an a priori conclusion, falls outside the realm of
proclamation.

possibility, in distinction from reconciliation for the sins of certain other people, whose guilt necessarily requires final judgment. How different from Paul, who lived in complete surprise over the grace that overflowed for him: "I am the foremost of sinners; but I received mercy *(makrothymia)* for this reason, that in me, as the foremost, Jesus Christ might display his perfect patience for an example *(hypotýposis)* to those who were to believe in him for eternal life" (1 Tim. 1:15f.). The mercy shown to Paul is not an exclusive but an inclusive reality. The surprising and undeserved fact that the door of salvation has been opened to him serves as the proclamation of comfort to others. Here one can see how great God's compassion is toward the worst of all sinners, once a blasphemer and a persecutor of the Christian community, and later only the "very least of all the saints" (Eph. 3:8).

On such a person God's grace was poured out in an unexpected and undeserved abundance, on the basis of which His mercy to others becomes for Paul, though not self-explanatory, something much more comprehensible. Reflecting on his own acceptance Paul sees it as *exemplary* and *inclusive,* illustrating through what depths of darkness the Son of righteousness can penetrate with its brilliant light (cf. Acts 9:4; 22:7; 26:13).

Therefore, the theory of vindicative justice, illustrated by the punishment to be meted out to others, cannot serve as repudiation of the doctrine of apocatastasis. When Scripture deals with the seriousness of sin, the constant affront to God, it indeed reflects the utter depravity and lostness of man, but its good news of reconciliation is nevertheless directed straight at this condition. If the logic of vindicative and distributive justice did indeed have validity over against apocatastasis, not only would universal reconciliation have to be rejected, but any reconciliation at all would be impossible in principle. In criticizing universal reconciliation one must be careful not to mount an attack that assails reconciliation itself and eclipses the view of the totally surprising, unexpected aspect of the divine reaction to guilt, rebellion, estrangement, lawlessness, and fall. "For the Son of man came to seek and save the lost" (Luke 19:10).

Those who try to disprove universalism on the basis of vindicative justice forget that the forgiveness they eagerly attribute to themselves and deny to others is not merely a matter of cancelling a debt of a few denarii but one of many talents (Matt. 18:23ff.); that Christ died for the ungodly and the enemies of God (Rom. 5:6, 10); that this is how God justifies the ungodly (Rom. 4:5). No, the problems that the doctrine of apocatastasis raises are too profound to be explained away by simple reference to God's justice. The deeper questions deserve very conscientious attention. The doctrine of universal rconciliation pleads, on the basis of the evident love of God, for extreme humility and for the belief that *our* justification serves as example and provides perspective for others. The attitude is summed up by H. Vogel: "If there is hope from God even for me, how much more so for others!"[19]

The rejoinder may be made that such considerations are irrelevant, since Scripture speaks very clearly about a "twofold destination" of mankind in the eschaton. But disputes have arisen about a number of passages of Scripture, particularly a number of so-called "universal" texts. When the Bible talks about salvation, it does so in a way that calls up the idea of a truly overflowing abundance. Time and again this abundance leads to doxology, to exclamations of praise. Thus we are confronted with the intensity and boundlessness of the acts of God. In the time of salvation that has dawned, the irrepressible power of grace breaks through abundantly against the ever-increasing power of sin (cf. Rom. 5:15ff.).[20] The church has always looked on this grace in line with the testimony of the New Testament as an abundance, in all its inconceivable unlimitedness, as something surprising, as a reality not to be explained on the basis of anything in us. It does not pertain to only some: we read that God loved the *world* (John 3:16); that the Lamb of God takes away the sin of the *world* (John 1:29); that God was in Christ reconciling the *world* to Himself (2 Cor. 5:19); that Christ is the expiation *(hilasmós)* for our sins, and not for ours only but also for the sins of the whole *world* (1 John 2:2); that Christ is the Savior *(sōtér)* of the *world* (John 4:42), the Savior of *all men* (1 Tim. 4:10); that God desires *all men* to be saved

19. *Gott in Christo* (1952), p. 1018.
20. On this abundance in Paul, cf. Hauck, in *TDNT*, s.v. *perisseúō*, VI, 60ff. Note also the translations of *hyperperisseúein* in the various English versions of Rom. 5:20 (e.g., RSV "grace abounded all the more"; NEB "grace immeasurably exceeded it"; Phillips "grace is wider and deeper still"); 2 Cor. 7:4 (KJV "I am exceeding joyful"; ASV "I overflow with joy"; RSV "I am overjoyed"); Eph. 3:20 (RSV "to do far more abundantly"; NEB "to do immeasurably more"). Cf. also the connection Paul makes in Rom. 3:7 — "through my falsehood God's truthfulness abounds...."

(*sōthḗnai*) and brought to the knowledge of truth (1 Tim. 2:4), not wishing that any should perish (2 Pet. 3:9); that the grace of God has appeared for the salvation of *all men* (Titus 2:11).

Such passages have understandably had an important bearing on universalism, both relative and absolute. In the exchange between universalists and those who oppose it, the former consistently draw their conclusions from passages like these, while the latter appeal to other passages of Scripture that oppose the idea of universal reconciliation. Surely, this subject demands close attention, because what is at issue is the eternal lot of mankind, and its repercussions are important for the proclamation of the gospel and for the salvation-concern of every believer. It is a topic laden with the serious urgency of the grace and the judgment of God.

Recent discussions of universalism

In modern times, the problem of apocatastasis has once again come to the fore in connection with the so-called universal and particular texts of Scripture. The protagonists of apocatastasis try to prove that the entire biblical account is universalistically oriented, and to refute "objections on the basis of scriptural texts."[21] Over against these are others who are reluctant to accept such a "synthesis," pleading instead that all passages be left as they are and treated accordingly. So Althaus writes that the message of the gospel demands a radical decision, but that at the same time there are universal passages that seem to include "*all*."[22] He detects in this two main lines that are theoretically incompatible. The one line proceeds via the urgency of a personal choice and decision to a "twofold destination"; the other leads to apocatastasis. Something paradoxical enters the expectation, but man cannot choose between the two lines. Althaus wants to dissociate the problem from an objectivized concept (*either* there is a "twofold destination" *or* there is an apocatastasis); and thus he concludes there is only room for the dynamics of faith and preaching, in which man, in biblical fear and trembling, concerns himself with his own and with others' future.

It is apparent, then, that Althaus is not primarily concerned

---

21. H. Schumacher, *op. cit.*, p. 133.
22. P. Althaus, *Die Christliche Wahrheit*, II, 487ff.; cf. H. Ott, *Eschatologie*, p. 71: "Both notions seem to be attested to in the NT."

with the contradiction — the two irreconcilable lines — but with
an understanding of the intensity of faith according to which
one can only be concerned with the salvation proclaimed to us.
It is worth noting that contemporary theology is quite concerned with this approach to the future. The question is, how
does one deal with the perspective? Do we have to do with
an "objective" knowledge concerning apocatastasis or the "twofold destination"? Or is faith's approach toward the eschaton
something different, something wrapped up in proclamation,
prayer, and man's struggle on his way to the future? Here, of
course, a strong argument against apocatastasis suggests itself,
that is, that this doctrine minimizes the urgency of the proclamation of salvation and the personal responsibility of man's own
decisions. At the same time, the alleged *factuality* of the "twofold destination" theory is also rejected, on the ground that one
may not speak of "knowledge" about it outside the context of
faith and unbelief.

The effort behind all of this is to relate the gravity of
the eschaton once again with the kerygma. This is not to say
that the kerygma is the source of immediate and thorough
answers to the numerous questions that arise about the lot of
mankind. But it is an acknowledgment that Scripture deals with
the future only in the context of preaching, appeal, and demand
for response.[23]

A similar approach is to be found in contemporary Roman
Catholic theology: the protest against a neutral "knowledge" of
eschatological "facts" that some day will be. Again, it is a protest arising from a close connection made between dogmatics
and preaching, on the ground that dogmatics may not go beyond
eschatological preaching. Hans Urs von Balthasar typifies this
approach. He sees something of a paradox in the variety of
biblical testimony on this point: "Scripture lets the possible,
indeed the actual twofold outcome of the judgment remain
'unreconciled' alongside the prospect of universal reconciliation;
nor is there any possibility of subordinating one to the other."
Which is not to say that the church in history has not tried —
Origen, for example, opting for apocatastasis, Augustine defend-

---

23. Prenter writes that faith does not know the question of whether or
not there is an apocatastasis: "faith only knows the judgment with the
twofold destination" in connection with the "endless torments" of losing
Jesus Christ, a reference to the Augsburg Confession, Art. XVII.
Schöpfung und Erlösung, II, 538ff.

ing eschatological duality. Balthasar rejects both, charging that Augustine's point of view "enfeebles faith in eschatological doctrine."[24] His concern is with the tension in which the future is presented in the biblical message. The gospel does not talk of judgment in order to orient us to unchangeable facts that some day will be and we must accept as true. He agrees with the sarcastic comment of Charles Péguy "that Dante had passed through hell as a tourist," for one cannot talk about the future neutrally and objectively without the stakes of one's own life, which is confronted with the eschaton. One cannot "look at hell as one looks at an objective painting."[25] In the understanding of the gospel something else comes into play: hope. That does not imply that one may argue from this through a gnostic system to an apocatastasis. Judgment lies exclusively in the hand of Jesus Christ. The gospel leaves this an open question, and it may not be closed by an a priori. On the basis of the concept of grace in one's own lostness, he must always remain open to the ever greater light of divine love.[26]

It would be unfair to discover a doctrine of apocatastasis in this. Balthasar's rejection of "gnosis" in Origen and the consequent notion of "self-evidence" is too clear to mistake. But Balthasar does plead for an eschatology that takes into account at all points the tension of faith, the call, and human responsibility. One might say that the point is not to weaken the seriousness of all this through apocatastasis, but to accent the serious through the thought of a pilgrimage to the future.

So the gospel confronts us with two possibilities, both of them to be taken completely seriously, not like an "as if." Karl Rahner joins the protest against a theoretical and neutral approach to the eschatological judgment. "True eschatological discourse must exclude the presumptuous knowledge of a universal apocatastasis and of the certainty of the salvation of the individual *before* his death, as well as a certain knowledge of a damnation which has actually ensued."[27] One may only sketch the broad outlines

24. Balthasar, "Some Points of Eschatology," *loc. cit.*, p. 163.
25. Balthasar, *Science, Religion, and Christianity*, p. 136.
26. Cf. *ibid.*, p. 142: "Faith is offered no other solution of the torturing question of the loss of the brethren than that it should lose itself in the abyss of God. This is the only gesture by which man can be assimilated to the rhythm of these abysses and, through grace, learn to abandon himself completely to love."
27. *Theological Investigations*, IV, 339; "hence on principle only *one* predestination will be spoken of in Christian eschatology" (p. 340).

that can be detected on the basis of the gospel in the present-day pilgrim situation. That means — over against apocatastasis — that one must read the eschatological assertions of the church and Scripture "as affirming that damnation is a genuine and inevitable possibility for the pilgrim."[28]

One might wonder whether this mode of approach to the last things is in complete harmony with Roman Catholic tradition,[29] but our concern here is with the fact that an attempt is being made to do justice to the pilgrim situation in which the gospel exclusively sets the eschaton. Schoonenberg depicts Rahner's view as making the warning-character the key to interpretation;[30] in other words, the last things are always to be dealt with in an unbreakable connection with the preaching of God's salvation.

Finally, in this connection, let us consider Karl Barth's position. Barth is often accused of accepting the doctrine of universal reconciliation, but he in fact emphatically rejected it on numerous occasions. Emil Brunner grants that "Barth's doctrine is not that of Origen and his followers." But he adds that Barth went much further than Origen and his followers. Brunner contends that "Barth is in absolute opposition, not only to the whole ecclesiastical tradition, but — and this alone is the final objection to it — to the clear teaching of the New Testament."[31]

When we turn from Brunner's critique to Barth himself, it becomes clear that he, like Balthasar, is concerned with the open

28. *Ibid.*, p. 339n.
29. Numerous pronouncements of the Roman Catholic Church throughout history establish the "fact that hell lasts eternally ... a Catholic dogma in the strongest sense" (Scheeben-Atzberger, *op. cit.*, IV, 828).
30. In *De Bazuin*, December 10, 1960. Cf. also J. Loosen, *Lexikon für Theologie und Kirche*, s.v. *Apokatastasis*, I, 711f.
31. Brunner, *Dogmatics*, I (Eng. tr., 1950), 346ff. An examination of Brunner's own view of the judgment shows that he, who is so opposed to Barth's view, accents the existential aspects of the gospel in connection with the eschaton as well. Thus he mentions the "two doctrines of damnation and universal salvation. They are not logically compatible. ... They are true only when taken together, and this togetherness is understood only if we are participants, if we cease to be spectators who ask 'Is there this, or is there that?' I can only really hear the apostolic *kerygma* of justification and the word of universal salvation that belongs to it when I hear along with it the Word of judgment" (*ibid.*, III, 423). Here Brunner's view is similar to that of Althaus. Cf. also *Eternal Hope*, p. 203. On Barth, see also Michaelis, *op. cit.*, p. 10.

situation of the proclamation. Dealing with the final reprobation of man, he sets up the following twofold defense: "The
Church will not then preach an *apokatastasis,* nor will it preach
a powerless grace of Jesus Christ or a wickedness of men which
is too powerful for it."[32] The thesis of apocatastasis is an idea
that one cannot venture if he wishes to respect the freedom of
divine grace. But it is equally wrong to think that this universal
perspective is impossible a priori.[33] Both these statements are
abstractions that cannot be any part of the message of Christ.
One must say "no" to apocatastasis, "for a grace which automatically would ultimately have to embrace each and every one
would certainly not be free grace. It surely would not be God's
grace."[34] But the hope that God's freedom will manifest itself
in universal salvation is not forbidden: "Strange Christianity,
whose most pressing anxiety seems to be that God's grace might
prove to be all too free on this side, that hell, instead of being
populated with so many people, might some day prove to
be empty."[35]

Barth follows this line through to the end of his dogmatics.
When he considers the doctrine of reconciliation, he anticipates
and deals with an eschatological question: "Can we count upon
it or not that this threat will not finally be executed, that the
sword will not fall . . . ?" His answer is twofold: first of all, one
may not *count on* this unexpected aspect of grace; one may
only *hope* for it "as an undeserved and inconceivable overflowing
of the significance, operation and outreach of the reality of God
and man in Jesus Christ." God does not owe rebellious man
this grace, and thus the postulate of apocatastasis is unjustifiable,
even by references to the cross and resurrection. Second, however,
"there is no good reason why we should forbid ourselves, or
be forbidden, openness to the possibility that in the reality
of God and man in Jesus Christ there is contained much more
than we might expect and therefore the supremely unexpected
withdrawal of that final threat. . . ." We may not reckon with
this possibility as though we had a claim to it, but "we are

32. *CD,* II/2, 477.
33. *Ibid.,* 417f.
34. Barth, "The Proclamation of God's Free Grace," in *God Here and Now*
    (Eng. tr., 1964), p. 34. Cf. *The Heidelberg Catechism for Today* (Eng.
    tr., 1964), p. 82: "He is the Judge! there can be no doctrine of uni-
    versal salvation."
35. "The Proclamation of God's Free Grace," *loc. cit.*

surely commanded ... to hope and pray cautiously and yet distinctly that, in spite of everything which may seem quite conclusively to proclaim the opposite, His compassion should not fail, and that in accordance with His mercy which is 'new every morning' He 'will not cast off for ever' (Lam. 3:22f., 31)."[36]

Obviously Althaus, Balthasar, Rahner, and Barth all reject the doctrine of apocatastasis. What they are saying is not a rehashing of Origen, but a new way of looking at the last things. The preaching of the last things, they argue, must be related to the sphere of faith and responsibility, and is not a matter of objective, theoretical, neutral postulates. One might ask whether the emphasis on hope in this new approach (particularly in Barth) does not also affect the nature of the kerygma.[37] But the big difference between these contemporary theologians and Origen is that Origen started with a conclusion from the love of God as an essential divine attribute and then made that conclusion dominant in his doctrine of apocatastasis. To be sure, all of this has a Christological ring to it,[38] but even on that basis it remains a conclusion, a consequence, that remains outside the dynamics of preaching and faith. And the point of the radical critique of apocatastasis by contemporary Protestant and Catholic authors is precisely that any conclusions outside of the realm of preaching and responsibility are to be rejected, and all discussion of the judgment is to be related to the proclamation of reconciliation.[39]

The church has, implicitly or explicitly, repudiated the doctrine of apocatastasis time and again in the course of history. Very early Origen's views, including his eschatology, were condemned by the church. It has sometimes been contended, however, that the church did not actually reject the doctrine of apocatastasis as such, but a particular form of it. According to Jean Daniélou, Origen was condemned because he taught

36. *CD*, IV/3/1, 477f. Compare Thurneysen's comment, quoted by Michaelis, *op. cit.*, p. 152: "It is certainly not biblical to set up a doctrine of eternal punishment in hell. Jesus Himself set up no such doctrine. One should speak of hell in order to point to Him who subdued it. This is not meant to establish a doctrine of universal reconciliation."
37. Cf. Berkouwer, *The Triumph of Grace*, pp. 111ff.
38. Cf. G. Müller, "Origenes und die Apokatastasis," *Theologische Zeitschrift*, XIV (1958), 187.
39. Cf. K. Schilder, *Wat is de hel?* (1920), p. 91: "The proclamation of hell in the Bible itself is *never separated from the preaching of reconciliation*" (italics his).

that in the future "the soul will return to the purely spiritual state it was in before it came down into the body." It was particularly this last point, Daniélou argues, for which the Second Council of Constantinople (553) condemned Origen, under the name of apocatastasis.[40] The church disputed the Platonic distortion of the doctrine of restoration in Christ, in which Origen short-changed the decisive character of the history of salvation. Müller agrees that this was the reason for the anathema against Origen. This is confirmed, he says, by the fact that Gregory of Nyssa also taught apocatastasis, but without Origen's cyclical interpretation, and he escaped condemnation by the church.[41]

Admittedly, Origen's doctrine of apocatastasis was closely related to his doctrine of metempsychosis, but the church unquestionably condemned his doctrine of universal reconciliation as well. The anathema is expressed against the Origenists, who taught that the punishment of evil spirits and the ungodly was only temporary, and after a certain time would come to an end, and there would be a complete apocatastasis.[42]

The rejection of the temporal aspect did not play a prominent role in the course of the history of this doctrine. In fact, there is scarcely any more of the real problematics of apocatastasis after this. Numerous ecclesiastical pronouncements concern "hell," not in connection with universal reconciliation, but in connection with other doctrines. For example, the *visio Dei* is said to be the immediate experience of the true saints in contrast to those who die in sin, who "immediately after death descend to the depths, where they will be tortured with infernal punishment."[43] Furthermore, an examination of the numerous ecclesiastical pronouncements on original sin shows that what is determinative is not the doctrine of apocatastasis, but the relation between sin and God's judgment. These dogmatic utterances are colored by the problems with the doctrine of hell, not with the question of whether it exists or not. Hell is spoken of as an established fact, about which man has knowledge. It would be no exaggeration to say that this is the real

---

40. Daniélou, *Origen* (Eng. tr., 1955), pp. 288f.
41. G. Müller, *loc. cit.*, p. 189.
42. Cf. the *Canones adversus Origenem* (543), Denz. 203-211. These canons were confirmed by the Second Council of Constantinople ten years later. Canon 1 rejects the pre-existence of souls as well.
43. Denz. 531.

irritant to the proponents of the doctrine of apocatastasis: that people speak about hell so calmly and assuredly as about an eschatological "circumstance" about which Scripture enlightens us. And the question arises again and again whether there is , not good reason for further reflection on this score in the light of the gospel of grace for godless men.

The biblical evidence: love and judgment

If we consider the scriptural evidence for apocatastasis, we note that the Greek word *apokatástasis* appears once in the Bible, in Acts 3:21. Peter is addressing the Jews who had crucified Jesus. "What God foretold by the mouth of all the prophets," he tells them, "was that his Christ should suffer" (Acts 3:18). In this connection he calls for their repentance, "that your sins may be blotted out, that times of refreshing may come from the presence of the Lord, and that he may send the Christ appointed for you, Jesus, whom heaven must receive until the time for establishing all *(áchri chrónōn apokatastáseōs pántōn)* that God spoke by the mouth of his holy prophets from of old" (vv. 19-21). There is good reason to believe that this involves an eschatological perspective,[44] similar to that of the restoration *(apokathistáneis)* of the kingdom of Israel discussed in Acts 1:6. But it is a restoration already spoken of in the Old Testament in terms of repentance and a return to God, and in the New Testament with reference to Elijah as the one who will restore all things (cf. Matt. 17:11; Mark 9:12f.; Mal. 4:5).[45] This restoration is not to be confused with what later came to be known as apocatastasis. Acts 3:21 appears in the context of warning: Peter follows immediately with a quotation from Moses in verse 23, which says that "every soul that does not listen to that prophet shall be destroyed from the people" (cf. Deut. 18:15-19; 30:1-5).[46] From this point of view, then, what is said

44. Cf., however, Grosheide, *Komm., ad loc.*
45. Cf. F. Mussner, "Die Idee des Apokatastasis in der Apostelgeschichte," in *Lex tua veritas. Festschrift für H. Junker* (1961), pp. 293ff.; M. de Jonge, "De apokatastasis pantoon in Hand. 3:21," *Vox Theologica,* XIX (1948), 68ff.; J. W. Doeve, "Apokatastasis in Act 3,21 een voorbereiding?", *ibid.,* 165ff.
46. Noteworthy also in this connection is James's speech at the Council of Jerusalem; Acts 15:13-21. James quotes Amos 9:11f. (the rebuilding of the fallen dwelling of David) in connection with God's intent of gathering a people from the Gentiles. Cf. Mussner, *op. cit.,* pp. 299f., 305. C.

by Peter is not an announcement about the eschaton that transcends faith and unbelief but something that demands a religious decision in the time before the parousia. Understandably, then, the proponents of the doctrine of apocatastasis are
hesitant to base their doctrine on Acts 3:21.[47]

Ephesians 1:10, though it does not use the word *apokatástasis*,
has often been resorted to in defense of the doctrine of universal
reconciliation. Paul does speak here of a restoration, the uniting *(anakephalaiósasthai)* of all things in Christ. The verse undoubtedly refers to a universality, as does Colossians 1:20, where
Paul says that God was pleased to reconcile *(apokatalláxai)* to
Himself "all things, whether on earth or in heaven." This is
the source of the title of Michaelis' book, *Die Versöhnung des
Alls*. Peace comes through the blood of the cross; the object
of the reconciliation here and of the "uniting" in Ephesians
1:10 is "all things" *(tá pánta)*. Michaelis denies that "all things"
refers only to the unconscious segment of creation. The conscious part of creation — man — is not excluded. Michaelis sees
Colossians 1:20 as an enriched version of Ephesians 1:10; the
peace of Christ extends over all.

The important question is whether this indeed confirms
the idea of universal reconciliation, for everywhere the universal
and triumphant perspective is inseparable from the message
of salvation which calls for faith and repentance. Paul points
to the central meaning of Jesus Christ as it shall be manifest
some day and to the comforting thought that through Christ
death is deprived of its threatening power. Christ is the one
in whom "all things hold together" (Col. 1:17) and who has
received all authority (Matt. 28:18). Universality is certainly
not lacking in the New Testament; nowhere does Scripture
leave the impression that the works of God are deficient or

　　van Gelderen, *Amos* (1933), *ad loc.*, calls Acts 15:14ff. "one of the most
　　noteworthy cases of Scripture quotation in the NT" in connection with
　　vs. 12, the possession of the remnant of Edom and of all the nations.
47. Cf. Michaelis, *op. cit.*, pp. 18-21; O. Riemann, *op. cit.*, pp. 23ff. Cf. also
　　Oepke, in *TDNT*, s.v. *apokatástasis*, I, 389: "On rather dubious grounds
　　... [Acts 3:20f.] has been the basis of the theological use of the word
　　from the time of Origen." Oepke sees the text as reflecting "the concept
　　of the new Messianic creation which was current in Judaism"; whether
　　or not the NT teaches a final restoration of all fallen sinners is, he
　　says, a "very different question" (p. 392). H. Schumacher, *Das biblische
　　Zeugnis von der Versöhnung des Alls*, p. 94, is very reluctant on this
　　score: "a passage ambiguous with respect to grammar and contents."

incomplete. But the conclusion that some draw from this — that everyone will partake in this salvation — is rejected by most exegetes on the ground that such a conclusion is not inherent in the line of thought here.[48] A conclusion of universal salvation is even less defensible in connection with a third example of a future perspective — the eschatological regeneration *(palingenesia;* RSV "the new world") "when the Son of man shall sit on his glorious throne" (Matt. 19:28). The emphasis here falls explicitly and emphatically on following Jesus and receiving eternal life.[49]

Clearly the doctrine of apocatastasis cannot be based on the several passages of Scripture dealing expressly with the eschatological perspective of the restoration of all things. Even those who attempt such an appeal want to find a deeper reason, which is the triumphant love of God, which includes and will include *all.* Apocatastasis is then seen as the direct consequence of this love. Nothing can serve as a counterexample to this argument. Even punishment is only a pedagogical means to this end. This is similar to Origen's concept of God's wrath, which sees punishment as having an "educative" character. "God's love intends the good to triumph in the end."[50]

We noted earlier the decisive importance of the idea that apocatastasis is a self-evident conclusion from the essence of the love of God. Understandably, the counter-argument to this emphasizes that wherever the New Testament speaks of the love of God in Jesus Christ, it also mentions the judgment. Let us consider some of these passages.

John 3:16, for example, follows the statement about God's love for the world with these words: "that whoever believes in

48. Note the connection in both Eph. 1 and Col. 1 between Christ as Head and the church as body, and the relation of this to Eph. 1:10 and Col. 1:20.

49. This does not have to do with what later dogmatics has called "regeneration," but with the eschaton, even though some have tried to link this (spiritual) regeneration with following Jesus; cf. P. Gennrich, *Die Lehre von der Wiedergeburt* (1907), pp. 4ff.; Büchsel, in *TDNT,* s.v. *palingenesia,* I, 688.

50. Cf. Daniélou, *Origen,* p. 285. Judgment is not denied, only its permanence. In this connection the attempt is made to interpret the "eternal" of "eternal punishment" as meaning something other than unlimited time. Cf. Michaelis, *op. cit.,* pp. 41ff., on the radical words of judgment found, e.g., in Matt. 18:8; 25:46; Mark 9:48; 2 Thess. 1:9; Jude 7.

him should not perish but have eternal life." Later in the chapter, John says that "he who does not obey the Son shall not see life, but the wrath of God rests upon him" (vs. 36). Paul's testimony of God's reconciling acts in Christ is followed by the challenge "be reconciled to God" (2 Cor. 5:19f.). The entire New Testament makes an important point of human reaction to salvation. This appears in the moments of Messianic suffering, when Christ wept, "Would that even today you knew the things that make for peace!" (Luke 19:42; cf. Paul's reaction in Rom. 9:2ff.; Phil. 3:18). The gravity of the situation is revealed on the emotional plane of Christ's life when He discovers that Israel does not know the time of God's visitation (Luke 19:44). "How often," He laments, "would I have gathered your children together as a hen gathers her brood under her wings, and you would not" (Matt. 23:37). Christ wanted to gather them together *(ēthélēsa episynagagein)*, but they did not want to be gathered together *(ouk ēthelḗsate)*. Obviously the doctrine of apocatastasis cannot ignore the way this intransigence rises up as a dark power over against the compelling, appealing, disquieting strength of Christ's call.

In fact, the advocates of the doctrine of apocatastasis have repeatedly tried to show that they are not ignoring this call, the disturbing urgency of the human response, by deducing universal reconciliation from the triumphant love of God. This raises a crucial problem for the discussion of universal reconciliation. The problem comes into especially sharp focus in Bengel, for example, who is said to have accepted the doctrine of apocatastasis, but to have thought it dangerous and therefore to have objected to its being taught.[51] It is not clear how it is possible or justifiable not to teach what is so immediately included in the (proclaimed!) love of God, especially since triumphant grace, according to the doctrine, belongs to the very

51. Pauly, *Realenzyklopädie der klassischen Altertumswissenschaft*, s.v. *Apokatastasis*, I, 619. Schumacher (*op. cit.*, p. 250) quotes Bengel as saying that whoever preaches apocatastasis "is telling tales out of school." C. S. Duthie ("Ultimate Triumph," *loc. cit.*, p. 170), writes that it "cannot become the subject of preaching in the form of dogma." The problem is apparent already in Origen, who explains Paul's use of "many" rather than "all" in Rom. 5:19 as an effort to "leave the simpler and slacker an incentive for striving for salvation" (R. P. C. Hanson, *op. cit.*, p. 334).

essence of God's love.[52] This raises the question whether the a prioris and self-evidence of apocatastasis do not do violence to the seriousness of the proclamation. Most proponents of the doctrine deny this. They refer to Paul's response to the question "Are we to continue in sin that grace may abound?" — "By no means!" (Rom. 6:1f.) — as a parallel. In other words, the evident scriptural testimony to salvation and judgment, warning and call may not be devaluated. But, they continue, these words of judgment constitute the means of the ultimate triumph of grace.

The warnings must be taken seriously, it is argued, particularly because Scripture expressly mentions real punishment and real judgment, which are therefore the objects of human fear.[53] But in the *final* analysis, the irresistible power of grace will force the capitulation of all rebellion against it.[54] But then is the seriousness of it all — which the defenders of apocatastasis agree must be maintained — still a biblical seriousness? The question is all the more valid because the context of the New Testament words about judgment never suggests that the ultimate extinction of resistance is self-evident. The appeals to Scripture made by proponents of apocatastasis always emphasize the love of God and the universal structure, but almost never mention the admonitions and the ominous warnings themselves. The reason for this is that the element of "ultimate extinction of resistance" is completely absent in these admonitions. Yet, had Bengel been right, this would be precisely where it might have been expected,

52. It is understandable that consistent advocates of apocatastasis completely oppose this notion of "you may believe it but not preach it." E.g., Schumacher (*op. cit.*, p. 177): "God's messages do not exist, in principle, to be suppressed"; Ströter asks whether this perspective of apocatastasis is thus meant only for "initiates" (cf. Schumacher, *op. cit.*, p. 250).

53. According to Schumacher, "a doctrine of universal reconciliation without the full proclamation of God's judgment in this time and in the new age is a serious heresy" (*ibid.*, p. 245).

54. Judgment is, according to Schumacher, "a component of God's plan of salvation" (*ibid.*). Similarly, Ströter sees hell as proof of God's love, because it is a means to an end that will surely be attained (*op. cit.*, p. 246). Robinson called this warning "an utterly necessary part of the preaching," while "God's summing up of all men in Christ ... [is] the ultimate fact and outcome of the universe"; "Universalism — A Reply," *Scottish Journal of Theology*, II (1949), 379ff., a response to T. F. Torrance, "Universalism or Election?", *ibid.*, 310ff., itself a response to Robinson, "Universalism — Is It Heretical?", *ibid.*, 139ff.

on the basis of the love of God. So we must conclude that the doctrine of apocatastasis has not succeeded in proving that it does not relativize or jeopardize the decisive gravity of the proclamation.

The doctrine of apocatastasis, it must be admitted, has often flourished in reaction against the frequent failure of the church throughout history to take seriously the "universal" passages of Scripture. The depreciation of these passages has sometimes followed from a particular doctrine of election that leaves no room for the universal invitation to salvation, on the ground that salvation could honestly and truly be offered only to the elect. The set-up is clear on this view: there is no universality at all, only strict particularity. And if one encounters a text in the Bible with a general offer of salvation, he explains it away by arguing that the speaker had no way of knowing who were included in the closed number of the elect and thus had to use the word "all." But there was no real offer of salvation to all. Obviously this extreme does as much violence to the seriousness of the proclamation as apocatastasis does.

To see the general preaching to all as a call to faith and repentance is surely correct. But the question immediately arises: What is the (preached) *content* of this faith? What is the *content* of this concrete message that calls to faith? In short, what is the meaning and intention of this knock on the door? The message of salvation is never just the announcement of a conditional maxim of the form "if anyone believes he shall be saved." The Canons of Dort speak of a promise that "ought to be declared and published to all nations, and to all persons promiscuously and without distinction, to whom God out of His good pleasure sends the gospel" (II,5). What is meant is thus a very seriously intended call to the proclaimed salvation, which is brought within the horizon of *all* in one way or another *in* the call. The Canons make explicit what salvation is: it is Christ offered in the gospel (III-IV,9). If one does not take seriously what is acceptable to God, "namely, that those who are called should come unto Him" (III-IV,8), one must conclude that faith has a *creative* character, creating a situation that did not exist. This total misunderstanding of faith cannot possibly refute the claims of apocatastasis based on the "universal" texts of Scripture. If one weakens the proclamation of salvation through a concept of faith as meritorial or creative, he assails the penetrating seriousness of the proclamation.[55]

The aim of the universal preaching is the same as of the universal words of Scripture: both deal with the world and God's will. Often people have tried to counter the claims of universalism by taking these universal words as in fact particular, interpreting them on the basis of the contrast between the elect and the reprobate as applying only to the elect.[56] Such an argument, however, can never convince universalism, because the application to the elect alone cannot be exegeted from the texts. The profound meaning of the fact that the gospel *must* be published to all (Canons of Dort, II,5) cannot be denied; and this gospel is and remains the glad tidings, the good news. The urgent call of the gospel goes out to everyone indiscriminately, because God's work in Jesus Christ is directed to the world (cf. Matt. 24:14; 28:19).

To deny universalism is not necessarily to fall into a form of particularism. The direction of the gospel to the world has nothing to do with an a priori apocatastasis, but testifies to the fact that God has no pleasure in the death of the wicked, but would "rather that he should turn from his way and live" (Ezek. 18:23). It is no accident that so many of the universal texts in the Bible underscore this correlative connection between salvation and faith (e.g., John 3:16; 1 Tim. 2:4; 2 Pet. 3:9), but make no announcements about a present or future state of affairs. It is impossible that the proclamation of salvation should go out to all, but be "actually" intended not for all but only for the elect, and that the rest would be called to acts of repentance and faith that had no real and present object anyway. This would certainly be a devaluation of the word "gospel." The passionate defense of the universal offer of salvation is deeply rooted in the message itself, which must be published, and in which God presents Himself as the God who in Christ was reconciling the world to Himself. It is impossible to sum the whole thing up by telling everyone, "Honestly, whoever comes to Christ will be saved,"[57] as if the whole gospel were defined by this kind of maxim. The true preaching of the gospel does use very nearly the same words. Confronted by the

---

55. Cf. Berkouwer, *Divine Election* (Eng. tr., 1960), pp. 220ff., on the emphasis on preaching the gospel in the Canons of Dort.
56. *Ibid.*
57. Cf. C. Bouma, *Geen algemene verzoening* (1928), p. 163.

suicidal intentions of the Philippian jailer, Paul first clears the way ("Do not harm yourself") in order to present a call to faith in Jesus, an appeal that this Lord Jesus is really and immediately present in the hour of deepest distress (Acts 16: 28-31). This is something more than the announcement of a general maxim. It is preaching in earnest, with promise and comfort and encouragement. The believing to which the Philippian jailer is called is not meritorial, not creative. And he who proclaims the gospel — in whatever situation — as Paul did in the jail in Philippi has a message to bring that goes out to the whole world.

The church has always wrestled with this matter of the universality of the preaching of salvation, and in the Canons of Dort it has maintained the gravity that urges a solemn decision. It confesses in the same Canons that Christ's perfect sacrifice and satisfaction for sin "is of infinite worth and value, abundantly sufficient to expiate the sins of the world world" (II,3; cf. Heid. Cat., Q. 37).

Already in the twelfth century Peter Lombard distinguished between "sufficiently" and "efficaciously," a distinction that did not solve the problem; and theologians continued to be concerned with both the seriousness of God's call and the misjudgment of God's love.[58] But even though no one should attempt a rational synthesis of these that goes beyond the experience of faith to establish a logical conclusion, that does not mean that this seriousness can be divorced from its context and made into formal proclamation without a truly admonishing, necessitating power. At this point we encounter Bavinck's profound analysis: that the authors of the Canons of Dort did not proceed in response to an "all or not all" dilemma.

The objection to the Arminian Remonstrants was directed against their idea that the sense of "Christ's sacrifice for all"

---

58. On Lombard, cf. Bavinck, *GD*, III, 453. Cf. also Calvin's Commentary *ad* 1 John 2:2 ("he is the expiation for our sins, and not for ours only but for the sins of the whole world"). Calvin is strong in his rejection of general reconciliation: the idea that the reprobates are included in this "all" is the "dream of the fanatics," "a monstrous idea ... not worth refuting," "an absurdity." He agrees with the statement that "Christ suffered sufficiently for the whole world but effectively only for the elect," but denies that it is an appropriate exegesis of this text. The real question focuses on the word "sufficiently," chiefly because — according to Bavinck, *ibid.*, IV, 7 — this "sufficiency" is not discussed as a matter of theoretical possibility, but is assumed into the preaching.

was that the *possibility* of salvation was obtained for all through Him. The objection of the Canons of Dort was to the doctrine of *potential reconciliation,* according to which human decision must lead to the realization of this possibility. And when Bavinck discusses the call to salvation he argues that this call retains its meaning even for those who reject it, because it is "the proof of God's unending love for all sinners without distinction and seals the word that He has no pleasure in the death of a sinner, but in his turning away and living." Furthermore, this call "proclaims that the sacrifice of Christ is sufficient for the reconciliation of all sinners."[59] The proclamation of the gospel is serious because the cross must be preached to all "without distinction," to tax-collectors and sinners, as a preaching of what is truly more than an objective "rule." It is the call to understand the seriousness of "the things that make for peace" (*tá prós eirénēn* — Luke 19:42). If one fails to understand the depth of Christ's weeping over Jerusalem, if one fails to see God's hands held out "all day long to a disobedient and contrary people" (Isa. 65:2; Rom. 10:21), he isolates God's disposition towards man from the cross. And when that happens, the "universal" texts of the Bible lose their meaning, and the gravity of the preaching, even if it is not denied, is no longer taken seriously.[60]

In sharp reaction to the particularizing of the "universal" texts of the Bible, with its disregard for a number of biblical motifs, universalism follows a different course, concluding that the love of God implies apocatastasis. In spite of recognition of guilt and judgment, the kerygma fades away into the positive announcement of an unassailable end, upon which the human decision of faith or unbelief has no bearing. The a priori of

59. *GD,* IV, 6f. According to Bavinck, the protest was not first of all against reconciliation for all, but arose because the Arminians, "speaking this way, conceived of salvation in a totally different way and detracted from the name of Jesus" (*ibid.,* III, 463). Cf. his comments on preaching the gospel not to men as elect or reprobate, but as sinners, *ibid.,* IV, 5. On 1 John 2:2, see also Kuyper, *Uit het Woord,* II/1 (1894), 29-43; on 2 Pet. 3:9, *ibid.,* 59ff.

60. See further in this connection the discussion of the controversy within the Christian Reformed Church in America, which led to the establishment of the Protestant Reformed Church under Herman Hoeksema. Cf. K. Schilder, *Heidelbergse Catechismus,* II, 237ff., 259ff.; A. C. De Jong, *The Well-Meant Gospel Offer. The Views of H. Hoeksema and K. Schilder* (1954), chapters III and V. For general background see also Berkouwer, *Divine Election,* chapter VII.

love creates the possibility of speculation. The actuality of judgment as portrayed in John's Gospel is seen on this view as only a pedagogical device, which thus presents no problems. Along such lines the dispute has continued between a universalism with a priori certainty and a particularism that allows the seriousness of the preaching to become obscured. The two seem to be irreconcilable opposites, but they do meet at one decisive point: both formally maintain the seriousness of the preaching, but for neither can the preaching any longer genuinely function in a way that is worthy of faith.

Essentially universalism looks at salvation as eschaton outside the realm of proclamation. Apocatastasis — in spite of the doxological context in which it is set — becomes a conclusion that precedes the dynamics and the appeal of the proclamation and is established by it. The love of God becomes the point of departure for this reasoning; any connection with the preaching of salvation and judgment is lost.

Now, in order to strengthen this conclusion from the love of God (that *the* decision takes place already in the essence of God), the faith-experience of irresistible grace is brought into the discussion. By this grace the believer knows and realizes that he did not come to faith through his own initiative, but that grace triumphed over all obstacles. One confesses that God showed Himself in His omnipotence, the omnipotence of His seeking love, in one's own life. All of this is then adduced as evidence, as it were, in a formal proof of apocatastasis. But even this doctrinal support is outside of the realm of proclamation: it is an a priori, theoretical notion, first of the love of God, then of its consequences. An eschatological doctrine of perseverance automatically follows, and the answer to unbelief is an emotional and rational "nevertheless. . . ." In this way it becomes obvious that the doctrine of apocatastasis is a static, timeless, unkerygmatic doctrine, a form of gnostic thought over against God and His love.

In contrast, the biblical witness to the love of God always treats it in a kerygmatic context and never announces it as a "fact" that goes over the heads of those to whom it is addressed and refers to a static eschatological fact. The message, the call does not demand a *quid pro quo* or "participation" in salvation, but trust and faith. Outside of this correlative application of the seriousness of the gospel, nothing can be said about the future that would make one any the wiser. If one tries to concern himself with it objectively, he finds himself ending up in a certain coldness, able to draw conclusions, but conclusions that have lost their comforting and admonishing character. Neither deeper theological reflection nor emotionality will take away this chill. Remember the question of one of those following Jesus: "Lord, will those who are saved be few?" And Jesus' reply is: *"Strive* to enter by the narrow gate" (Luke 13:23f.). En route to the eschaton, no objective information is given but that of faith: "Strive...." When the disciples, after Jesus' encounter with the rich young man, asked in consternation who then could be saved, their attitude was certainly not one of theological inquisitiveness. Jesus' answer, therefore, was highly encouraging: "With men this is impossible, but with God all things are possible" (Matt. 19:27).

The structure of all questions about the eschaton is decisive for the answers that are given during this pilgrimage. The voices of the heralds who point the way sound in reply to the good question. To their voice we must listen.[61]

The seriousness of the gospel proclamation

The proclamation of salvation is a witness of profound seriousness. The New Testament constantly presents an apparent ultimatum that is inextricably connected with this proclamation.

It would be a mistake to underestimate this seriousness. The Word speaks of being cast away and rejected, of curse and judgment. The proclamation of the gospel contains a warning against unbelief, and the way of unbelief is portrayed as the way of outermost darkness and lostness and the severance of all relationships. In a variety of images and concepts, the Gospels warn against the possibility of a "definitive destruction."[62] Such warnings are not meant to orient us to the eschaton, but continually to confront us with an admonition to open our eyes to the light and see the salvation, not to harden our hearts (cf. Heb. 3).

The momentousness of the decision is set in the middle of life. It has to do with everyday things like insulting one's brother

---

61. Friedrich, in *TDNT*, s.v. *kērýssō*, III, 706f., likens Jesus' preaching, "itself event," to the "blast of the trumpet" of the heralds who proclaimed the year of jubilee in Israel. Cf. also T. L. Haitjema, *Dogmatiek als apologie,* pp. 357ff.; J. T. Bakker, *Kerygma en Prediking* (1957), pp. 13ff.
62. Oepke, in *TDNT,* s.v. *apóllymi,* I, 396.

(Matt. 5:22), succumbing to temptation (vs. 29; 18:9), failing to show compassion (25:41-46). All of these things are related to the eschaton in a complete seriousness that concerns life, and has nothing to do with moralism (cf. Matt. 18:35). Eschatological admonition is so close to everyday existence that any intricate theoretical reflection and search for information or gnosis is excluded and every individual — with responsibility for his neighbors — is set anew on the right way to the future.[63]

On what is this great seriousness founded? It is not based on human legalism or moralism, which can often assume such radical and serious airs. Rather, it is rooted in the *reality of the gospel*. It is in the context of that gospel that the subject of the outer darkness arises. Paul speaks of evil and shame as the works of those who are enemies of the cross (Phil. 3:19). Elsewhere, he equates not knowing God with failure to obey the gospel of the Lord Jesus (2 Thess. 1:8). The darkness is portrayed in spatial categories: it is being removed from the presence of the Lord and from the glory of His power (2 Thess. 1:9; cf. Isa. 2:20f.), as distinct from being in His presence forever (1 Thess. 4:17). The presence of the Lord can give rest, kindness, and light, "but the face of the Lord is against those who do evil" (1 Pet. 3:12; Ps. 34:15f.).

All such threats are not arranged symmetrically beside the gospel, but proceed from it and can be understood only in its light. The outer darkness is contrasted to the brilliant light; the gospel's saving disturbance penetrates the religious terrain where everyone presumes to be safe and secure. This false safety and security are broken down by the meaning of the Kingdom. There is not merely a simple correlation between sin and judgment, but a contrast between those who come from east and west to sit at table with Abraham, Isaac, and Jacob in the Kingdom of heaven and those who will be cast into outer darkness (Matt. 8:12). The gospel speaks of a wedding feast and of the man who is found without a wedding garment and is doomed to a similar fate (Matt. 22:13; cf. 25:30). On the one side the gospel proclaims the Kingdom, the wedding feast, the light, the opened door; on the opposite side darkness, desertion, the

---

63. In this connection see also the comments of R. Schippers on the connection between the sheep and goats of Matt. 25:33 and Ezek. 34; *Gelijkenissen van Jezus* (1962), pp. 76ff. On the eschatological perspective of "those who have done good" (John 5:29), cf. P. A. van Stempvoort, "Het oordeel in het NT," *Vox theologica*, XXIV (1953), 157ff.

flames of the unquenchable fire (Mark 9:43, 48) .[64] The relationship of this to the gospel accentuates and illuminates the
seriousness of these warnings.

Perhaps no single New Testament word has stimulated the
imagination more or drawn quite so many conflicting reactions
as the term "Gehenna," which is often taken to be a recapitula-
tion of all other messages of gravity and threat.[65] The word
itself refers back to the horrible idolatrous cultic rites practiced
in the Valley of Hinnom, south of Jerusalem, during the time
of the prophet Jeremiah. The curse of Yahweh rested upon
this cult, and long thereafter the word "Gehenna" continued to
express how far the ultimate outer darkness contrasted with the
light in which it is good to live. This primeval note reflecting
decayed Israelite life in its misrepresentation of God's love
serves in the New Testament to proclaim the gospel that calls
men back from the terror of this darkness to the salvation and
light of God.[66] The New Testament speaks of the outer darkness in a warning to the people of the covenant in connection
with the exclusion from the Kingdom of heaven of the "sons
of the kingdom" (Matt. 8:11f.) . Gehenna is the shadow outlined
by the great light; nothing can be said about it without also
dealing expressly with the light, just as nothing can be said
of the Valley of Hinnom without mentioning Jerusalem as
well.[67] We are not given any description of Gehenna; only a
warning to avoid it. Moreover, it is a warning that speaks to
the present, as we see in James's warning against the sins of the
tongue, "an unrighteous world . . . set on fire by hell" (James
3:6) ; and in Jesus' description of the Pharisees as children of

64. On Mark 9:49 (*pás gár pyrí alisthésetai*), cf. G. Sevenster, *Christologie*,
p. 53.
65. The word *géenna* is found in Matt. 5:22, 29, 30; 10:28; 18:9; 23:15, 33;
Mark 9:43, 45, 47; Luke 12:5; James 3:6.
66. The background of this is the provoking or vexing (*kā'as*) of Yahweh;
cf. Jer. 32:29f., 32. The depth of this irritation is manifested in
Yahweh's remark: "*though* I have taught them persistently they have
not listened to receive instruction" (vs. 33). The Israelites "set up their
abominations in the house which is called by my name" (vs. 34). In
ch. 19, where Jeremiah is told to proclaim his message in the Valley of
Hinnom, Yahweh refers to Himself specifically as "the God of Israel"
(vs. 3). Cf. also 2 Chron. 28:3; 33:6 ("provoking him to anger"). The
theme of offended, misunderstood love and Yahweh's faithfulness is
prominent in Hosea's prophecy; cf. 11:12; 13:4-6; 14:8. Ephraim, according to 12:14, "has given bitter provocation."
67. On this relation cf. Schilder, *Wat is de hel?*, p. 15.

hell because their mission had nothing to do with the proclamation of salvation (Matt. 23:15).

In the course of time the word "hell," as translation of the Greek *géenna*, was divorced from the relationships in which it is invariably found in Scripture, and came to be treated by many as a ruthless threat, an expression of extreme harshness, in which all feelings of compassion had perished. When this happened, the critical relationship in the New Testament between "Gehenna" and the invitation, love, and covenant of God was lost. This did not happen only to the word "hell"; there are many theological terms — among them "sin," "guilt," "grace," and "judgment" — whose meanings are not transparently obvious. But it is the unmistakable duty of the church always to place these concepts in their proper biblical context. Has this always happened? Has the church's preaching always warned, in a responsible way, against *provoking* the love of God? Has its message not been plagued again and again by moralism, making it well-nigh impossible to free the word "hell" from totally false associations? Unfortunately, the latter is too often true. People speak of "heaven" and "hell" as if they were objective magnitudes like any other thing, situation, or place. Who knows how much damage is done, for example, in the life of a young child who is subjected to moralistic preaching of "hell" as the final outcome of "sin" without the light of the joy of the gospel? "Hell" can easily assume a magical, terrifying dimension that speaks only of the incalculable, all-consuming wrath of God, and says nothing of His love. And when, in times of catastrophe, "hell" comes to be associated with the abyss of human distress ("the *hell* of Stalingrad") or the pinnacle of human cruelty ("the *hell* of Dachau"), it is inevitable that the variety of meaning in the word comes to be confused.

History reveals the almost limitless capabilities of man for atrocities against his fellow man. Jesus forewarns His disciples about that. They will be put out of the synagogue; whoever kills them will think himself to be offering service to God (John 16:2). Why will all this take place? "Because they have not known the Father, nor me" (John 16:3). It is not difficult to understand why the word "hell" has come to be associated only with cruelty and hatred if it is proclaimed without regard for the preaching of the only way out.

Protests are constantly heard against preaching about the judgment of God. Even outside of the Christian faith it is often said that "judgment" is not in harmony with "the love of God." Such reasoning basically displays only a contrasting of "concepts." If instead of these "concepts," the reality of the living God is taken into consideration, the picture is drastically altered. Then it becomes plain why David, placed before a choice in an inevitable divine judgment, casts himself rather at the mercy of God than at that of men (2 Sam. 24:14). It is possible and meaningful to choose for God's hand and against man's because God is a God of compassion. For the most part the protest against "hell" arises in a merciless world that is well aware of how its own judgment — of others — runs its course to the bitter end. Thus we speak without hesitation of "hell," of demons, of deprivation. But how can we guard against false associations if we look at God's judgments as roughly the divine equivalent of human judgments? For what man does to his fellow man is without gospel. It is like Jonah, who wants to die in his merciless anger against Nineveh (4:3, 9) at the same time as God in His mercy is making a new opportunity for the thousands and thousands of sinners there (vs. 11).

If God's judgment is discussed responsibly all these false associations are removed by the understanding that "God sent the Son into the world, not to condemn the world, but that the world might be saved through him" (John 3:17).

The preaching of hell

There is probably no more outspoken critique of the proclamation of judgment than that of Berdyaev, who saw the preaching of hell as an effort at spiritual and moral subjugation. This tradition elevates the primitive, sadistic human instincts to the level of dogma. "The idea of hell has been turned into an instrument of intimidation, of religious and moral terrorism." This terrorizing reality came to play a dominant role in the preaching and discipline of the church. At first, he argues, it served successfully as a check on heresy, but today it merely estranges millions from the church. The human spirit has experienced so many ordeals and has descended to such depths that man is now impervious to hell-fire preaching. He faces it with contempt or resignation, certainly not with terror.[68]

68. Cf. Berdyaev, *Truth and Revelation* (Eng. tr., 1953), chapter VIII; *The Destiny of Man*, p. 278; *Freedom and the Spirit* (Eng. tr., 1935), pp. 324ff.

Anyone familiar with the history of church and theology will recognize that Berdyaev's pathos- and revolt-laden criticism cannot be rejected out of hand. The warnings of the gospel have often been superficially objectified and moralized, deprived of the context of comfort in which the Lord Himself brought them. A pessimistic preoccupation with the number of the saved came to dominate the discussion of the issue. Then, later, hell was demythologized after the judgment — divorced from the gospel — had assumed the form of an irritant and a terror. But all of this offensive proclamation has nothing to do with the scandal of the cross. Is it so surprising then that most people hear in the word "hell" only the sounds of cruelty and hatred, a weapon maintained by "the church" to keep "the world" in line?

How much a caricature this is becomes evident when we read what Peter says — that judgment will begin with the house of God (1 Pet. 4:17). One can only understand God's judgment if he realizes that "many that are first will be last, and the last first" (Matt. 19:30) ; that the tax collectors and harlots will enter the Kingdom first (Matt. 21:31) ; that not everyone who says "Lord, Lord" will enter in, but only those who do the will of God (Matt. 7:21). This critical aspect of the judgment dominates. Unless we are aware of what Peter says about where judgment will begin — the New Testament counterpart to the searching of *Jerusalem* with the lamps of Yahweh (Zeph. 1:12) — whatever we say about judgment will be rigidified and out of tune and lacking in the seriousness of the gospel that that the Spirit will bring, convincing men of sin because they do not believe in Christ (John 16:9).

All the threatening words of the gospel stand in this light. The biblical presentation of judgment is not meant as an orientation to an event, but as something to disturb man on the basis of the wealth of the gospel. An earnest admonition is involved, such as that given by Abraham to the rich man in connection with his five brothers on earth (Luke 16:27-31).[69] This seriousness must be subjected to critical scrutiny: genuine earnestness is not a speculation about fear or egoism, but has deeper roots. The proclamation of God's full salvation and the earnest admonition do not limit one another, but are indissolubly related.

69. Cf. Schippers, *Gelijkenissen van Jezus*, p. 161.

Again and again, the discussion of apocatastasis raises the question: why is the preaching of good tidings intertwined with such an earnest and threatening warning? Does this not relativize the radical character of the gospel and make everything finally depend on man's own decision? These questions have always been very significant in reflections on the relationship between the salvation and grace of God and man's free will. The doctrine of apocatastasis leaves the impression that human decision is of little, if any, consequence in the face of triumphant irresistible grace. This seems to pose a dilemma: apocatastasis or complete human freedom.

Biblically this apparently unavoidable dilemma does not exist. First of all, the believer is surely conscious of his own choice, his own decision, but he knows at the same time that this decision is, in fact, a capitulation. *In faith,* he knows that faith is not a matter of his own contribution or participation in salvation. Accordingly, the manifestation of the fulness of salvation as God's gift lies precisely in the decision of faith.

But there is another reaction to the proclamation of salvation, the reaction of unbelief. And this is the locus of the deepest difficulties in the doctrine of apocatastasis. It is apparent that Scripture does not take this unbelief to be irrelevant, but warns against it with the utmost seriousness. This warning assumes the form of a threat.[70] Some have seen this notion of a threat as irreconcilable with the gospel.

It is true that man may use threats perversely in his interpersonal relations. Paul, writing to masters who were abusing their slaves, admonishes them to "forbear threatening" (Eph. 6:9). Presumably, this refers to harsh and hardhanded treatment of these slaves, coercing them to obey. It was similar to the intimidation by which the scribes attempted to forbid the apostles from speaking in the name of the Lord (Acts 4:17, 21, 29).

This kind of threatening does not characterize the gospel. Undeniably, the tone of the gospel is entirely different, and the tone of the threat reveals its background or cause. The background of the gospel's threat is its intent to call men back from the paths of darkness lest they prefer it to the light. This is the *exclusive* content of all biblical warning and threatening.

---

70. Cf. Canons of Dort, V, 14: "He preserves ... [this work of grace in us] by the exhortations, threatenings, and promises [of His Word] ... and by the use of the sacraments."

Mention of judgment always engenders mention of mercy, patience, and compassion. The seriousness of the joyful news of the gospel becomes manifest when man does not take the proclamation of salvation in earnest (Heb. 2:3). This is the radical difference between the gospel's "threatening" and un-evangelical terror. The latter is horrifying but not really serious, for it lacks any real character of appeal. The evangelical reference to judgment — that the Lord is to be feared (2 Cor. 5:11) — is a qualified threat, because it is the other side of the invitation, of the abundant riches to which the kerygma attests. So Paul goes on to say that "the love of Christ controls us, because we are convinced that one has died for all" (5:14). The seriousness of the warning is lost if the judgment is portrayed as a terrifying reality; it can only be seen from one criterion: its connection with the gospel.

We have to admit that "hell" is often spoken of more for its psychological effect than out of truly evangelical concern. Surveying the minimal results of such preaching, theologians and preachers have sometimes been shocked. What they fail to realize is that this preaching is as ineffectual as terrifying sermons about death, which are even less successful in creating more receptivity to the gospel. The gospel does not sound in that kind of preaching, and hell becomes a terror for the soul, but still only an irrelevant abstraction. This is one of the worst ways in which preaching can go astray, for it falls short of the standards of clarity and seriousness of the gospel of the cross that is proclaimed to all.

In this connection let us consider a confession of the church that relates hell and salvation very closely: the confession of Christ's descent into hell, which is clearly and inextricably connected with the proclamation of judgment, so that the one can be understood only if the meaning of the other is clear. The historic interpretation of the *descensus ad inferos* is a complex matter, and we shall not go into detail about it in this volume.[71] But according to all the interpretations of it, what is said in this article of the Creed about "hell" is related to the life and death of Jesus Christ. Apart from questions about the correct interpretation of this part of the Apostles' Creed, let us look here at what the Heidelberg Catechism says about it. The Cate-

---

71. For a more detailed account see Berkouwer, *The Work of Christ* (Eng. tr., 1965), pp. 174-79.

chism (Q. 44) relates this descent to the depth and darkness of Christ's passion, so deep and so dark that, confessionally, it seemed justifiable to speak of it as hell.[72] It is particularly Christ's abandonment that comes for the Catechism to be the central point of His indescribable suffering and anguish. Furthermore, it may be said that there is really a great degree of unanimity between the idea that Christ's descent was part of His humiliation and the idea that it was part of His exaltation. For the church the victory over all powers is rooted precisely in the cross, and in the New Testament as well both themes — humiliation and exaltation — are present. Accordingly, it is possible in either case to consider the descent into hell according to the explanation of the Catechism in terms of abandonment and comfort. Therefore, Christ's descent into hell makes it impossible to treat "hell" in isolation. Because of this descent the call to faith sounds, and we are no longer able to talk in terms of self-evident conclusions. Whatever Christ's descent into hell meant to the early church, His saving work in this descent was placed in relation to the ultimate threat, and it is that — whether as humiliation or exaltation — which is confessed as the gracious triumph over the power of hell. The gospel calls us to believe in this triumph, to be comforted by it. This is not demythologizing of hell; it is more an exorcism of it — *in faith*.[73]

As a result, every treatment of "hell" as an independent topic lacks genuine seriousness. It may assume the appearance of earnestness, but such seriousness is not of the biblical kind, which talks about the beauty "of the feet of those who preach good news" (Rom. 10:15). This seriousness is not something that can be analyzed on psychological or anthropological grounds, but only on the basis of the salvation proclaimed (cf. Heb. 2:3). If this is ignored, salvation and judgment become far removed from each other, and the preaching of the judgment becomes an isolated, intimidating prophecy of doom, which ultimately will fall on deaf ears. The call to faith and the warning can only go out in the light of Christ's abandonment and His encounter with the outer darkness. Thus the preaching of judgment does not relativize the depth and universality of the gospel,

---

72. Cf. J. N. D. Kelly, *Early Christian Creeds* (2d ed., 1960), pp. 378-83; W. Bieder, *Die Vorstellung von der Höllenfahrt Jesu Christi* (1949); H. Diem, *Dogmatik*, II (1955), 275-87; Bo Reicke, *The Disobedient Spirits and Christian Baptism* (1946).
73. Diem, *op. cit.*, 287.

but confirms it according to the incontrovertible witness of the whole New Testament. On the basis of the gospel the serious-ness of this preaching becomes manifest and real. We may not trifle with this seriousness; we may not come to "self-evident" conclusions, not even on the basis of God's love, as if God's love were revealed to us more highly and more deeply than it is there in the midst of our earthly existence where the grace *(cháris)*, goodness *(chrēstótēs)*, and loving kindness *(philanthrō-pía)* of God have appeared (Titus 2:11; 3:4).

The person who waters down or denies this seriousness on the basis of an a priori conclusion like the doctrine of apoca-tastasis throws his own life into a bewildering confusion. Faith knows that self-evidence can have no place in life. The a priori conclusion of apocatastasis caricatures the confession of the per-severance of the saints. On the way of this perseverance, the Belgic Confession says (Art. 23), we must pray with David: "Enter not into judgment with thy servant; for no man living is righteous before thee" (Ps. 143:2); and on this way Paul's warning sounds as well: "Let any one who thinks that he stands take heed lest he fall" (1 Cor. 10:12).

So the warning of the gospel, if its seriousness is properly preached, does not have the characteristics of terror: it is the compelling voice of a guide, of the gospel itself. Without this unity, every word of warning becomes meaningless. And only the community that goes its way in fear and trembling (Phil. 2:12), but committed to preaching the Word and letting the light shine forth in the world, can admonish and warn. Ad-mittedly, these irreversible, essential relationships have frequent-ly been lost in the historic church. Along with this loss has come a devaluation or dismissal of this seriousness, explained away in terms of a changing world-view, psychology, existential-ism, demythologizing, and the like. As a result many are skeptical that the preaching of judgment can ever be listened to again after all the misconceptions and perversions of it that have been rampant. In any case, it will only be possible if Christ's descent into hell is rightly understood, and if the depths out of which the message arises are appreciated, if the truth that this message serves to reveal "the things that make for peace" (Luke 19:42) is grasped.

In summary, it is extremely dangerous to think and talk about "the love of God" and what "follows" from it outside of the gospel. This has happened time and again in the history of the church: God's love is talked about in terms of a prioris, necessary conclusions, and self-evidence. Apocatastasis then becomes the crowning keystone of the structure of human thought. This doctrine and its conclusion can appeal to our sense of charity — in our thought and expectation as well. So it is easy to see why so many are captivated by apocatastasis in times of great human distress. How difficult it is to allow all our thoughts and meditations to be limited by what the gospel reveals to us of the tender mercy of God, which is not the point of departure for logical conclusions on our part, but is proclaimed to us "to guide our feet into the way of peace" (Luke 1:79). On this way of peace that has been opened up to us there is room for only one "conclusion," only one "necessity" — the necessity that confronted Paul as he faced the future: "Necessity *(anángkē)* is laid upon me. Woe to me if I do not preach the gospel!" (1 Cor. 9:16).

The history of the doctrine of apocatastasis reveals a persistent and almost irresistible inclination to go outside the proclamation of the gospel to find a deeper gnosis, whether in the form of certain knowledge or only as surmise. Over and over the question addressed to Jesus arises in the history of the church: "Lord, will those who are saved be few?" Jesus' answer seems so noncommittal, so evasive: "Strive to enter by the narrow door" (Luke 13:23f.). But this evasiveness is only apparent. This *is* the answer to *this* question. As long as we see only in a mirror, in riddles, many questions will remain unanswered. But *this* question has been answered, once for all time.

CHAPTER FOURTEEN

THE COMING OF THE KINGDOM

THE CHURCH'S EXPECTATION of the return of Jesus Christ has always been closely associated with the second petition of the Lord's Prayer — "Thy Kingdom come." Even when it saw the Kingdom in terms of what was already accomplished by Christ, and thus did not interpret it exclusively as something of the future, the church recognized an eschatological tone and content to this petition. The Heidelberg Catechism concludes its explanation of this petition with these words: "until the perfection of Thy kingdom arrive wherein Thou shalt be all in all" (Q. 123; cf. 1 Cor. 15:28). This "perfection" reflects what the New Testament says about the fulfilment of the world, the ultimate goal of all events, and the universal lordship of God over all things.

Obviously, the expectations of the "perfection" of the Kingdom and of the return of Christ are not two separable expectations. When we expect Christ's return, our eyes are directed to Him who has come as Ruler of a realm that is the antithesis of all the powers of this world. And then when we pray "Thy Kingdom come" — for the full and unchallenged revelation of the perfection of the Kingdom — we are uttering a prayer peculiar to the time of waiting, the time of the unmistakable "not yet," a dispensation of tension and imperfection. Accordingly, it is understandable that the Catechism also brings into consideration in its discussion of this petition "the works of the devil" and "every power that exalts itself" against God. Furthermore, it is easy to see why reflections on the Kingdom have always involved the relation between what has come, what has been granted us through Christ, and the salvation still to be expected in the perfection of the Kingdom. So the church's concept of the Kingdom also includes the doxology of the Lord's Prayer: "for thine is the kingdom" (Matt.

6:3).[1] Here too is the tension between what is already reality and what is still to come. This tension has led to different ideas as to what one's relation to the future is. In other words, does the Lord's Prayer concern itself primarily with an *expectation,* or with a *mandate,* seeing that the Kingdom of God has already come in one way or another?

We must begin with the realization that this is a *prayer.* Even so, some have primarily seen in this petition the element of mandate, of working for God's Kingdom. Too often its seriousness, its expectation, are distorted into different forms of activism. Others, in reaction to this, interpret the coming of the Kingdom in purely futuristic terms. We cannot forget, as we try to deal with the tensions between these two approaches, that the New Testament never portrays the eschaton as a futuristic concern unrelated to today. So it is in no sense de-eschatologizing for the Catechism to explain this petition in the following terms: "so rule us by Thy Word and Spirit that we may submit ourselves more and more to Thee." The authors of the Catechism guarded themselves against objectivizing the Kingdom in the future and letting it be irrelevant to the present affairs of man. On the other hand, they did not want the expectation to be obscured by an exaggerated emphasis on activity. Everything is subjected to the twofold tension of increased submission to God's will and continued expectation of the fulness of the Kingdom.

"Thy Kingdom come" is a petition for an act of God and a reminder that the coming of the Kingdom is not the automatic result of the development of immanent forces. The coming of God's Kingdom is no less a matter of prayer than are daily bread and forgiveness of sin. The coming of God's Kingdom in perfection will reveal Him as the Hearer of every prayer; yet it is clear at the same time that our praying for this is not a matter of passivity. It must be accompanied by a definite, future-oriented activity: "what sort of persons ought you to be in lives of holiness and godliness, waiting for *(prosdokóntas)* and hastening *(speúdontas)* the coming of the day

---

1. This conclusion to the Lord's Prayer is lacking entirely in Luke (11:2-4), and the textual critical evidence for it is weak in Matthew. See further on this matter F. W. Grosheide, *Comm.,* ad loc.; H. N. Ridderbos, *KV* on Matthew, *ad loc.* It is surprising, however, how little this textual critical uncertainty has influenced the church in its use of Scripture. This applies as well to the story of the woman taken in adultery (John 7:53—8:11) and the longer ending of Mark (16:9-20).

of God" (2 Pet. 3:11f.) .[2] That does not mean fleeing from the reality of present life, but moving toward and seeking the Kingdom (Matt. 6:33), looking forward to the city that has foundations (Heb. 11:10).

Regnum Dei *and* regnum Christi

In this context of present reality and the expectation of fulfilment, some have not only distinguished between an "already" and a "not yet," but also between the nature of the Kingdom now and that of the perfection of the Kingdom. In particular, the distinction is drawn in terms of the present Kingdom as the Kingdom of Christ, and the coming Kingdom as the Kingdom of God. Although a contrast or opposition is not made between the two, a definite boundary between them is envisaged. One day, in the eschaton, the Kingdom of Christ will pass over into the Kingdom of God, and God will be all in all. Among contemporary theologians Oscar Cullmann in particular has made this sharp distinction between *regnum Dei* and *regnum Christi*. Although he recognizes that the two coincide as far as content is concerned, he maintains that a chronological distinction has to be made, since the Kingdom of God is a "future quantity."[3] "From the point of view of time" the Kingdom of Christ "represents a power of its own" until the parousia; then it will come to an end.[4]

Cullmann's distinction has been subjected to criticism on several points. The New Testament, it is argued, does not treat the Kingdom of God as only a "future quantity." Furthermore, Paul speaks of God as "the King of ages" (1 Tim. 1:17). Nor do the parables of the Kingdom favor such a distinction. One might ask whether the Kingdom of God is not present in the Kingdom of Christ.[5] But Cullmann insists that Paul

---

2. The believers are called to "be zealous to be found by him without spot or blemish" (vs. 14). It is to this end that "the whole moral seriousness of Christians is to be directed"; Harder, in *TDNT*, s.v. *spoudázō*, VII, 565. On the "hastening" of the day, see K. H. Schelkle, *Die Petrusbriefe* (1961), p. 229; Maurer, in *TDNT*, s.v. *prosdokáō*, VI, 726.

3. Cullmann, "The Kingship of Christ and the Church in the NT," in *The Early Church*, p. 109.

4. *Ibid.*, p. 116.

5. Cf. A. A. van Ruler, *De vervulling der wet*, p. 89; Schmidt, in *TDNT*, s.v. *basileia*, I, 581: "This *basileia* of Jesus Christ is also the *basileia* of God.... There is no reference to the *basileia* of Christ apart from that of God" (cf. Eph. 5:5); Berkouwer, *The Work of Christ*, pp. 217ff., 229ff.

definitely teaches the end of the Kingdom of Christ in 1 Corinthians 15:24 and 28, where he writes that in the end, after
destroying every rule and authority and power, Christ will deliver the Kingdom to God the Father. Then Paul adds that
"when all things are subjected to him, then the Son himself
will also be subjected to him who put all things under him,
that God may be everything to everyone."[6] Clearly, even if we
do not find the *regnum Christi / regnum Dei* distinction elsewhere in the New Testament we must deal with what Paul says
here. Is this perhaps a hint that our thoughts of the future
must end, not with Christ, but with God? Is Christ's return
merely the next-to-last event, to be followed by the eschaton?
Does this indicate that there is an interim that will culminate
in the Kingdom of God? Is eschatology rather of a strictly
theocentric nature, and not at all Christocentric?

Cullmann sees Paul's words here about the "delivery" of
the Kingdom to God and the subjection of Christ as not only
indicating the fulfilment of Christ's role as Messiah; 1 Corinthians 15:28 is "a very important passage for Christology," indeed,
it is "the key to all New Testament Christology."[7] "Paul leads
us in 1 Corinthians 15:28 to the very threshold of a complete
eschatological absorption of the Son in the Father."[8] What Paul
means to say, Cullmann maintains, is that in this "end" it is
no longer necessary "to distinguish between the Father and
his Word of Revelation."[9] When the New Testament mentions
the Son, it is always directly related to the revelation of God.[10]
Cullmann concludes from this that Father and Son are one
in their activity and that the Son of God is God insofar as
God reveals Himself in salvation-event.[11] So it is easy to see
why 1 Corinthians 15:28 provides a key to understanding New
Testament Christology for Cullmann, for he rejects all speculation about the two natures of Christ and focuses his attention
on the activity of God.[12] For this reason, Paul's outlook on

6. Cf. J. Héring, *Le royaume de Dieu et sa venue* (1937), p. 175.
7. On the fulfilment of Christ's mediatorial work, cf. Cullmann, *Christ and Time*, pp. 109, 199; on 1 Cor. 15:28, *The Christology of the NT*, p. 293.
8. *Ibid.*, p. 248.
9. *Ibid.*, p. 268.
10. *Ibid.*, p. 248.
11. *Ibid.*, pp. 293, 326f.
12. "It is possible to speak of the Son only in connection with the revelation of God"; *ibid.*, p. 248. "The NT neither is able nor intends to give

Christ's subjection to the Father is of especial importance. Our purposes here do not allow us to delve into Cullmann's view of Christology,[13] but it should be clear that in our search for the eschatological perspective of God's Kingdom we cannot ignore 1 Corinthians 15. What Paul says there has played a significant role in eschatology as well as Christology.

In any case, Paul does not say anything about an absorption or disappearance of the Son into the Father,[14] but speaks of the delivering of the Kingdom and Christ's "subjection" to the Father. This subjection of Christ was at issue in the trinitarian and Christological disputes of the early church. At that time the church countered the so-called doctrine of subordinationism with the confession that the Son is "homo-ousios" with the Father — of the same essence. But there was another interpretation of the situation that did not dispute the confession of "homo-ousios," but in fact based everything squarely on this belief. The center of the dispute was the teaching of Marcellus of Ancyra, who appealed to Paul's reference to "subjection" in 1 Corinthians 15:28. For this appeal he was accused by some

information about how we are to conceive the being of God beyond the history of revelation, about whether it really is a being only in the philosophical sense"; *ibid.*, p. 327. Already in *Christ and Time* Cullmann rejected all speculation concerning Christ's natures as unbiblical because "all speech concerning Christ ceases at the point where his redemptive work has concluded"; p. 128.

13. This would be possible only in connection with the entire confession of the Trinity. We should point out, though, that the problem of "functional Christology" (the activity of God in distinction from the ontological aspect) has come more and more to the fore. P. Gaechter criticizes Cullmann's "functional" or "dynamic" Christology in connection with Cullmann's rejection of speculation about Christ's natures and his view of the Logos in the NT; *Zeitschrift für katholische Theologie,* LXXXII (1960), 88-100. Gaechter accuses Cullmann of mere modalism on account of the disappearance "without a trace" of the Son after the Revelation. For Cullmann's own view, his reply to his Roman Catholic critics (G. Bavaud in *Choisir,* 1960, as well as Gaechter), in *Scottish Journal of Theology,* XV (1962), 36-43, is important. Cullmann claims to see no difference between the NT and Chalcedon on this score. For the whole question of "functional Christology" see Ingo Hermann, *Kyrios und Pneuma. Studien zur Christologie der paulinischen Hauptbriefe* (1961).

14. Replying to his critics, Cullmann does not use the word *Aufgehen* ("absorption") any more. "He will not disappear after the establishment of the Kingdom"; *Scottish Journal of Theology, loc. cit.,* p. 40.

of modalism.[15] Marcellus sided with Athanasius against the subordinationism of Arius, who had taught that the Son was a creature. Against this doctrine the church had pronounced that the Son had not creationally proceeded from the will of the Father. Marcellus' approach to the problem of subjection was entirely different from that of Arius. He saw in the Son a revelational mode and power of God Himself, who had appeared already in creation and manifested Himself in the divine salvation-economy, which realized itself and took form in Christ. Marcellus' chief concern was to maintain the unity of God. He taught that the rule of the Logos would some day end in the eschatological fulfilment. That is, everything the Logos does is directed at a particular goal; once this goal has been attained, the Logos will return into God and surrender His special mode of being, in order to participate in the divine lordship with the Father as complete monad. Accordingly, the Logos has no post-existence, since after the purpose of salvation has been achieved, He will be absorbed into the Father; consequently, there will be no distinction between Father and Son.[16] Marcellus felt that what the church confessed about the Son jeopardized the "monarchy" of God, an obvious indication that he misunderstood the dogma of the church, which is in fact a confirmation of this monarchy. But Marcellus thought that the return of the Son into the Father was demanded by a consistent application of the doctrine of "homo-ousios."[17] Further-

15. Hilary of Poitiers accused Marcellus of writing a book "about the subjection of the Lord." The charge of modalism is reminiscent of Gaechter's evaluation of Cullmann; cf. fn. 13 above.

16. On Marcellus, see further, T. Zahn, *Marcellus von Ancyra* (1867); W. Gericke, *Die Entwicklungsgeschichte der Marcellus-forschung von Rettberg bis zur Gegenwart* (1939); J. A. Heyns, *Die grondstruktuur van die modalistische triniteitsbeschouwing* (1953), pp. 70ff.; G. Kretschmar, *Studien zur frühchristlichen Trinitätstheologie* (1956), p. 19.

17. Gericke comments *(op. cit.,* p. 2): "The thought of the monarchy of God — the idea of monotheism and the struggle against pluralism — is indeed the most burning concern that Marcellus advocated in his book. All other ideas, even that of 'subjection,' are subordinated to and classified under this great controlling thought." For this monotheistic motif Marcellus appealed to texts like Isa. 43:10f.; 45:21; Hos. 13:4. See also C. Andresen, "Zur Entstehung und Geschichte des trinitarischen Personbegriffes," *Zeitschrift für die NT Wissenschaft,* LII (1961), 32ff.; E. Schwarz, "Zur Geschichte des Athanasius," in *Gesammelte Schriften,* III (1959), 230ff. On the unity of God and the confession of Christ in general, cf. R. Bring, "Christologie und Monarchie Gottes," in *Die Leibhaftigkeit des Wortes. Festschrift für A. Köberle* (1958), pp. 199ff.

more, he thought that Paul's comments confirmed his position: the Son represents a temporal, revelational interim.

Marcellus' views of the Logos and the eschatological "end" have had little influence on the church. His modalism was re-pudiated, his contention that it followed necessarily from the confession of "homo-ousios" denied, and his appeal to 1 Corin-thians 15:28 rejected. Yet the "interim" theory and the mean-ing of Paul's words continue to be a matter of great interest. What is meant by Christ's delivering the Kingdom? What does His "subjection" mean? What are the consequences of all this? These are the decisive questions. What is at issue is always a strong concept of the historical, goal-oriented acts of God.

In recent years, this eschatological perspective has again come up for discussion as a result of the explicitness with which A. A. van Ruler speaks of a Messianic intermezzo in connection with 1 Corinthians 15, and the far-reaching conclusions he draws from this, for example Christ's eventual resignation of His human nature. "He ceases to be the Messiah; He only causes things to be saved, in order that in the joy of their existence they may praise God and the Lamb."[18] This end, according to Van Ruler, does not in any way play down the uniqueness and decisiveness of Christ's mediatorial work. On the contrary, this is precisely its uniqueness and decisiveness: because once the goal aimed for is achieved, the present turns out to have been nothing more than interim. Once this great goal is attained, the union between the Son and His human nature can come to an end. Van Ruler speaks of a "being undone" of the humanity of God in Jesus Christ, when all mediation will come to an end, and there will remain nothing between God and the existence of things.[19] The idea of an intermezzo is most clearly illustrated when Van Ruler refers to Christ as an "emer-gency measure" of God with regard to human sin and guilt, a measure that is by its very nature temporary.[20] Ultimately it is

---

18. *De vervulling der wet* (1947), p. 149. Cf. also his article, "De verhouding van het kosmologische en het eschatologische element in de Chris-tologie," *Nederlands theologisch tijdschrift,* XVI (1962). We shall not concern ourselves here with the fact that there is also a pneumatic intermezzo; cf. *De vervulling der wet,* pp. 142ff.

19. *De vervulling der wet,* pp. 92f.; cf. p. 215. Van Ruler refers in this connection to Zech. 14:20.

20. Van Ruler adds: "The thesis that Jesus Christ was an emergency meas-ure relates to the incarnate Son rather than the eternal Son. Thus the doctrine of the Trinity is not affected by it, and it has nothing whatever

a matter not so much of the grace of God as of His glory.[21] Thus Van Ruler has little difficulty with 1 Corinthians 15: "It seems to me," he says, "that it is completely self-explanatory."[22]

Without equating Van Ruler's ideas with those of Marcellus, I think it is quite obvious that the problem of an intermezzo occupies a crucial place in both views. The church traditionally has proceeded in another direction. One might say of Van Ruler's point of view that it addresses a question to that tradition: has ecclesiastical tradition been fully aware of the meaning and implications of the Messianic intermezzo? To be sure, it has concerned itself from time to time with the intermezzo — not only out of Christological but also out of eschatological interest — but without drawing Van Ruler's conclusions from it.

In connection with this dissenting tradition it is interesting to note that Van Ruler thinks to discover the idea of the Son's laying aside of His flesh in Calvin. Earlier F. W. Korff had written that Calvin believed and explicitly maintained that the humanity of Christ was not imperishable, but that Calvin's followers disagreed with him on that score.[23] Calvin, it must be said, was intensely concerned about the eschatological perspective of 1 Corinthians 15. He writes that Christ, "having discharged the office of Mediator, will cease to be the ambassador of His Father and will be satisfied with that glory which He enjoyed before the creation of the world. . . . Then, also, God shall cease

to do with Subordinationism"; *The Christian Church and the OT*, p. 69. Even if one gives this intention its due, it seems to me one can still ask whether one can distinguish so easily here, and whether "emergency measure" can really capture the sense of what the New Testament calls the great "mystery of our religion" (1 Tim. 3:16). On this score, cf. H. Berkhof, *Schepping en voleinding* (1961), p. 234.

21. *De vervulling der wet*, p. 90.

22. It does not follow that he thinks it to be an unimportant passage; he speaks of "the forceful passage in 1 Corinthians 15 (verses 24 and 28)", *Nederlands theologisch tijdschrift, loc. cit.*

23. Servetus appealed to 1 Cor. 15:24-28 in connection with his antitrinitarian views; cf. Heyns, *op. cit.*, p. 117. For Korff's interpretation cf. his *Christologie*, I (1940), 251. Among those who did not follow Calvin in this area Korff mentions Bavinck and Kuyper. Bavinck claims that there is no evidence at all in the Bible for this position *(GD*, III, 481). Kuyper writes: "Christ became man and shall eternally remain man. He will not lay aside his humanity, but lives in our flesh and shall eternally prevail in our flesh"; *De vleeswording des Woords*, p. 31. Kuyper is talking in this context primarily about the critique of Hieronymus Zanchius in his *De incarnatione Filii Dei* (1601).

to be the Head of Christ, for Christ's own deity will shine of itself, although as yet it is covered by a veil."[24] Commenting on 1 Corinthians 15:27-28, Calvin writes that "Christ is now the intermediary between us and the Father, so that He may bring us to Him in the end." But this will change some day. "When the veil has been removed, we will see God plainly, reigning in His majesty, and the humanity of Christ will *no longer* be in between us to hold us back from a nearer vision of God." For Calvin the issue is not one of Christ's abdicating His lordship, but that He will transfer it in some way or other (*quodam modo traducet*) from His humanity to His glorious divinity.

But 1 Peter 1:11 talks about "the eternal Kingdom of our Lord and Savior Jesus Christ." Does this conflict with 1 Corinthians 15? Calvin says no, and thus arrives at the above-mentioned formulation, about which Van Ruler concludes: "The veil of flesh is removed; the humanity of Christ no longer mediates; the entire role of Mediator has had its day."[25] Now Calvin's thoughts admittedly seem to be directed at this end. When Christ's work will have come to its completion after the destruction of death, there will be an unobstructed vision of God in which Christ's human nature will no longer be in between. But did Calvin construe this to mean the *abolition* of Christ's human nature? In the first place, there is no explicit evidence for this in Calvin's words. According to Calvin, we know God in the person of Jesus Christ. Christ is the way to the Father; and when the role of Mediator is fulfilled and the way to the Father indeed opened, Christ's humanity will no longer remain in between. The mediating is fulfilled; the journey has run its course. Calvin is talking about the perspective of God Himself at the end of this journey; he is thus occupied with the intermezzo, the economy of salvation. And Calvin states that this goal will be reached. But he says nothing about Christ's laying aside of His human nature. And nothing in the tradition of Reformed theology supports the idea of the perishability of Christ's human nature.

Although there is no biblical ground for speaking of an undoing of the *assumptio carnis,* the words "deliver" and "subject" found in 1 Corinthians 15 must still be dealt with. At the very least, they indicate that an impressive change will take

24. *Inst.,* II.xiv.3.
25. *De vervulling der wet,* p. 92.

place, a phase will have run its course, a goal will have been
achieved, once the last enemy has been dethroned and all is
subjected to Christ. The Bible, of course, also speaks of a
definite goal to which Christ's work on earth was directed. On
the cross He called out "It is finished *(tetélestai)*" (John 19:30;
cf. vs. 28). Earlier, in His high priestly prayer, He says: "I
glorified thee on earth, having accomplished *(teleiôsas)* the work
which thou gavest me to do" (John 17:4; cf. 13:1 — "to the
end"). Christ's purpose was to accomplish God's work (4:34;
5:36), to fulfil His charge, which was to lay down His life and
to take it up again (10:18). This mandate ended when this
work had been completed. The letter to the Hebrews particularly gives one the impression of work completed, accomplished
by Him at the end of the age, when He appeared to "put away
sin by the sacrifice of himself" (9:26).

The fact that Christ referred to this deed as complete even
before His death indicates how certain and irreversible His
passion really was. He saw the completed work on the basis
of what became unalterable reality in the cross. It is the fulfilment, the culmination, full of the glory for which Christ
prayed in the high priestly prayer (John 17:1; cf. 12:23f.). This
is the Christ, the one sent by the Father, fulfilling His mandate.
Everything in that work is directed to God. It is in this light
that we see His glorification, the exousia given to Him in heaven
and on earth (Matt. 28:18), the name above every name be-
stowed on Him (Phil. 2:9), the Kingdom appointed for Him
(Luke 22:29).

We usually think of Christ's life as consisting of two phases:
humiliation and later exaltation. Dependence, subjection, and
obedience are the signs of His humiliation (cf. John 4:34; 5:19,
30; Phil. 2:8; Heb. 5:8). God's glorification of His Son then
constitutes the answer to this humiliation (Phil. 2:9). On this
view, the "end" is thought to be Christ's exaltation after suffering (Luke 24:26; 1 Pet. 1:11). Having come into His glorious
Kingdom, He will be Lord over the living and the dead (Rom.
14:9). In other words, any trace of subjection and dependence
seems to be eliminated by the coming of Christ's Kingdom.

But now Paul suddenly upsets this neat scheme by referring
to an ultimate eschatological subjection, which evidently indicates a final transition on the way of salvation and the Kingdom.
At that time, according to Paul, Christ will deliver the Kingdom
to God the Father. There is a dominion of Christ that will

last "until he has put all enemies under his feet" (1 Cor. 15:25). All powers, rules, and authority will be deposed, even death, the last enemy, "for God has put all things in subjection under his feet" (vs. 27). This is Paul's train of thought: until this point Christ must prevail as king, then the great eschatological transition will come and the delivering of the Kingdom to the Father. Paul supports his argument here by quoting Psalm 110:1. Similarly, Marcellus of Ancyra used this verse in support of his eschatology.

But let us look at Psalm 110 more closely. Here there is no thought of temporal limitation ("Christ must reign until . . ."). No, the psalmist has in mind the ascendancy of the priest-king at God's right hand with a view to what is to come, that is, the total victory over all foes.[26] Hebrews interprets this passage: "But he, when he had offered one sacrifice for sins, for ever sat down at the right hand of God; henceforth expecting till his enemies be made the footstool of his feet" (10:12f.).[27] This "till" is no limitation on Christ's kingship, but a perspective, an outlook, on the total victory. Christ is portrayed as at the right hand of God "for ever." For Christ Himself there is still room for "expecting" (ekdechómenos), for waiting, until His glory will be total and manifest (a surprising thought in itself, as Michel notes).[28]

Paul's use of Psalm 110, however, gives importance to the *end* of Christ's rule in connection with His "delivering" of the Kingdom. Bachmann writes that Paul "placed a special meaning on the 'until' of Psalm 110, insofar as he, without regard for the tendency of the Psalm itself, connects it with an allusion to the end-point of the reality of the messianic dominion."[29] So Paul does not pick up this idea of "awaiting," but instead

---

26. N. H. Ridderbos writes, "Het lied van den Priester-Koning," *Vox theologica*, XV (1944), 103: "The time after the subjection of the enemies does not come into view." A. H. Edelkoort, "Psalm 110," *ibid.*, 87, states that the "till" of Ps. 110:1 does not imply that the sitting at the right hand will cease when the enemies have been made a footstool.
27. Translation as given in ASV margin. There is difference of opinion as to whether the "for ever" (eis tó diēnekés) should be construed with what precedes ("when he had offered") or with what follows ("sat down"). In favor of the former are KJV, ASV, RSV, NEB; in favor of the latter the Vulgate, ASV margin, Moffatt, Jerusalem Bible, Luther. For a summary of arguments pro and con cf. F. F. Bruce, *New International Commentary* on Hebrews (1964), ad loc. (p. 237n.) (tr. note).
28. *Der Hebräerbrief*, p. 226.
29. Bachmann, *Komm., ad loc.*

focuses his attention on the *end* of Christ's rule, the "delivering" of the Kingdom to God. "Until" is not so much an indication of the eschatological fulness of Christ's regime as a significant view of that end in which Christ will subject Himself to the Father.

Our purposes here do not allow us to delve into Paul's seemingly peculiar hermeneutics and the implications this has for our understanding of the authority of God's word. Our concern is rather with the great emphasis Paul put on the "delivering" and "subjection." Strangely enough, the church has never felt a sense of tension or contradiction about this seeming antinomy of the delivery of the Kingdom and the eternal rule of Jesus Christ. It always has assumed that His kingship would last, not only on the basis of the "for ever" of Hebrews 10:12, but also because other scriptural references seem to depict the permanency of the Messianic kingship (cf. Ps. 89:4). Luke's Gospel records Gabriel's promise to Mary that the Messiah will reign as king over the house of Jacob forever, "and of his kingdom there will be no end *(ouk éstai télos)"* (1:33; cf. 2 Pet. 1:11). This is the universal dimension of Christ's rule, fulfilling the Old Testament prophecy of the Prince of Peace: "Of the increase of his government and of peace there will be no end, upon the throne of David, and over his kingdom" (Isa. 9:7; cf. 2 Sam. 7:24). From passages like these the early church derived its confession that the Kingdom of Christ would have no end.[30]

Nevertheless, it must not be concluded that a contradiction exists between this and 1 Corinthians 15.[31] When the New Testament talks about the eternal realm of Christ, it indicates its inviolable glory. It cannot be overpowered and subjugated by other powers. It is the Kingdom portrayed in eschatological preaching as the eschaton, when "you may eat and drink at my table in my kingdom" (Luke 22:29). Paul's eschatology is not in conflict with this for the simple reason that he was dealing with another aspect that is related to the total fulfilment of the Messianic mandate. The "delivering" of the Kingdom to

30. Cf. the Nicene Creed: "whose Kingdom shall have no end," words, according to J. N. D. Kelly, "taken bodily from St. Luke." Kelly argues that they were directed against Marcellus; *Early Christian Creeds* (2d ed., 1960), p. 338.
31. See E. Lövestam, "Son and Saviour. A Study of Acts 13:32-37," *Coniectanea Neotestamentica,* XVIII (1961), 79, 112.

the Father takes place after everything has been subjected to the Son, after every rule and authority and power has been dethroned, in other words, in the ultimate revelation of the immeasurable and irresistible power and glory. Once Christ's lordship is total and universal, the Kingdom will be delivered to the Father. Countless attempts have been made to render Paul's exceptional language here intelligible. Bavinck, for instance, distinguishes between the mediation of reconciliation and that of union.[32] Kuyper distinguished between a *regnum essentiale*, grounded in creation, and a *regnum oeconomicum*, which enters into this world as a *speciale quid* for the purpose of restoring the *regnum essentiale*.[33]

But Paul, apparently not anticipating misunderstanding on this score, makes no such distinctions. For he goes on to speak of the "subjection" of the Son (His subjecting Himself). This is a familiar New Testament word, and it implies submission and dependence. The term *hypotagē* is used in the New Testament in connection with man's subjection to authority (Rom. 13:1), the subjection of the young to their elders (1 Pet. 5:5; cf. Eph. 5:21), of woman to man (1 Cor. 14:34), of believers to God (James 4:7), and of all things to Jesus Christ (1 Cor. 15:27). It is this word, then, that Paul uses to describe the eschatological event. Christ's subjection to the Father conforms to a particular *order*.[34] It is not a matter of force or coercion, but a willing submission, because the intrinsic meaning of this order is seen and respected. In this way the Son subjects Himself to the Father.

The emphasis and directness with which Paul says all this has raised a number of questions about the implications of this for the doctrine of the trinity. Bachmann writes that "harmonizing what Paul says with the doctrine of the trinity is not a

32. *GD*, III, 480f.
33. Kuyper, *Dictaten Dogmatiek*, V (*Locus de Magistratu*), 186ff. It seems to me that there is a point of contact here between Kuyper and Van Ruler, although they draw differing conclusions.
34. The use of this idea in the New Testament is discussed at length in Else Kähler, *Die Frau in den paulinischen Briefen* (1960), esp. pp. 172ff., 187ff. On the subjection of women to men, compare 1 Tim. 2:11 — "Let a woman learn in silence with all submissiveness" (*en pásē hypotagē*). The submissiveness is contrasted in vs. 12 to having authority over men (*authentein andrós*). 1 Pet. 3:5f. confirms this exhortation with a reference to Sarah's exemplary obedience to Abraham, "calling him lord."

matter of exegesis,"[35] which presupposes that such an harmonization is necessary. This is a consequence of the fact that the questions raised are primarily eschatological. From the point of view of the history of salvation, these questions do not seem to be all that relevant, because at that level the subjection of the Son to the Father involves fewer difficulties. Yet in principle, the same relationship is at issue.

Already in the economy of Christ's saving work on earth, we encounter the idea of the subjection and dependence of the Son. He is portrayed as under orders from above. He has *been sent*. Arian Christology naturally had no problems with this situation, because it considered the Son to be a creature, come forth from the Father's will, and therefore inherently subservient to Him. But the problem becomes a bit more involved when we consider that this Christ, who is indeed subject to the Father and obedient to Him, is also said to be the one in whom all the fulness of God dwells (Col. 1:19), in whom the whole fulness of deity dwells bodily (Col. 2:19).

Arianism is generally classified among the most dangerous heresies in the history of dogma. Yet what a mystery we involve ourselves in when we — correctly — reject Arius! A whole new manner of thinking about God is implied: speaking of Christ's subjection without denying His true divinity. This mystery is not original in 1 Corinthians 15; it is already found in the Gospels. Paul then follows this line of thought to indicate that Christ's work and His Kingdom are oriented entirely to the eschatological fulfilment. Paul is certainly in agreement with the rest of Scripture on the matter of Christ's exaltation after His humiliation, but evidently there is still room to speak of an *hypotagé*, a subjection. Paul relates this to the fact that God Himself has subjected all things to Christ (1 Cor. 15:27). Thus what is determinative for Paul's way of thinking here is the aspect of the economy of salvation. He zeroes in on the eschaton, the fulfilment.

Far from being a devaluation of Christ and His Kingdom, this in fact accents their glory and majesty at the point when Christ delivers the Kingdom to God the Father. No dilemma of Christocentrism versus theocentrism or *regnum Christi* versus *regnum Dei* arises. Everything centers on the fulfilment of what becomes salvation-laden reality. Now it becomes fully — escha-

35. *Komm.,* p. 444.

tologically — clear that this work has been completed, the mandate accomplished to the fullest. Obviously the intricacies of trinitarian theology are not Paul's interest here. He is concerned with the reality and depth of the fulfilment. What Paul says about Christ's delivering the Kingdom and subjecting Himself to the Father does not conflict with the eschatological perspective of the rest of the New Testament,[36] where there is no suggestion of a transition from the Christocentric to the theocentric, where the eschatological perspective is described on the basis of the reality of Christ's kingship,[37] where the figure of Christ is predominant, the throne of God and of the Lamb (Rev. 22:1, 3; cf. 7:10; 14:4), and where the doxology sounds to Him who is seated on the throne and the Lamb that was slain (5:13; 13:8), the lamp lighting the city of God (21:23).[38] The entire structure of the eschaton that is described is Christocentrically *and* theocentrically determined, and the language of apocalyptic resorts to a manifold of imagery to portray what is *one* glory. Because the Christocentric does not stand opposed to the theocentric (cf. 22:5 — *"the Lord God* will be their light"; 21:22 — "the temple is the Lord God almighty *and* the Lamb"),

36. Lindyer (*op. cit.,* p. 3) suggests that it would not be impossible for Paul still to refer to a "kingdom of Christ" even after the Kingdom has been delivered to the Father.

37. In this connection we are reminded as well of Paul's own expression of the eschatological perspective in 2 Tim. 4:1, where he charges Timothy "in the presence of God and Christ Jesus who is to judge the living and the dead, and by his appearing and his kingdom *(kaí tén epipháneian autoú kai tén basileían autoú)."* For the most part, however, the specific form that is given to 1 Cor. 15:24 and 28 is not in accord with the NT witness to the conquering of the powers, a witness that is determined by the "already" and "not yet." Cullmann himself emphasizes this tension *(Christology of the NT,* p. 225), referring to 1 Pet. 3:22 (the subjection of angels, authorities and powers in connection with the session of Christ) and the use of the word *katargeín* ("to subject" or "to destroy") in the NT. Cf. Chapter IV above, p. 112. On the basis of this duality of meaning, Christ's "delivering" of the Kingdom to the Father (after the total victory) is indeed salient (as completion), but it cannot serve as an *exclusive* aspect of the eschatological fulfilment. Cf. Cullmann's treatment of Heb. 10:13 and 1 Cor. 15:25 as exceptional in not presupposing the ascension of Jesus as the chronological beginning point of His lordship *(ibid.,* pp. 224f.).

38. For a fuller appreciation of the prominence of this imagery note also the references to the blood of the Lamb (12:11), the book of life of the Lamb (13:8; 21:27), the Lamb on Mount Zion (14:1), the song of the Lamb (15:3), the marriage supper of the Lamb (19:9), the names of the twelve apostles of the Lamb (21:14).

we can see how incorrect it is to pose such a dilemma. We hear Christ describe Himself in the same words that we hear in the Old Testament to describe Yahweh: "I am the first and the last" (Rev. 22:13; cf. 1:8; 2:8; 21:6; in the Old Testament, Isa. 44:6; 48:12).

The only way this centrality of God and the Lamb could be seen as conflicting with Paul's statements in 1 Corinthians 15:24-28 would be to interpret the latter as positing an absorption of the Son into the Father. But Paul's point is that on the basis of the glory of the completed work of Christ and the totality of His triumph the perspective of God as all in all becomes manifest. And precisely this is what shows that, however exceptional Paul's expression of the eschatological event may be in comparison with what the rest of the New Testament says, it does capture the fulfilment of the work of Jesus Christ, the fulfilment that the whole New Testament portrays in terms of the predominance in the entire eschaton of the theocentric figure of the Lamb.[39]

The analogy of earthly kingship

So an eschatological Kingdom is the goal of the ways of God. What does it mean that the eschaton is thus described (to be sure not exclusively, but nonetheless emphatically) by analogy to earthly kingship? We cannot understand this eschatological Kingdom unless we look into this analogy. The biblical use and meaning of the Greek word *basileia* forms the point of contact here for explicating the Kingdom of God in connection with the idea of an earthly kingdom.

39. Contra the idea of the "dissolution" of the Son in the Father see H. Berkhof, *Schepping en voleinding*, p. 230. Cf. also K. Dijk, "Over de laatste dingen," in *Het einde der eeuwen* (1953), pp. 205ff. On the dominance of the Lamb in the eschaton see W. Koester, "Lamm und Kirche in der Apokalypse," in *Festschrift für M. Meinertss* (1951), pp. 152ff. Illustrative for this structure is the connection with the historical aspect of Christ's revelation, work, and Kingdom, and the references to Jerusalem. Heb. 12:22 speaks of "the heavenly Jerusalem"; Rev. of "the new Jerusalem" (3:12; 21:2) and "the holy city Jerusalem" (21:10). The whole problematics of Jerusalem comes into play here, but at the same time the portrayal of the eschaton in these historical terms — the city with "twelve foundations, and on them the twelve names of the twelve apostles of the Lamb" (21:14). In this connection cf. 11:8 (Sodom and Egypt); Gal. 4:25; Heb. 13:12-14; J. C. DeYoung, *Jerusalem in the NT* (1960), pp. 103ff., 118ff.; W. Bieder, *Ekklesia und Polis im NT und in der alten Kirche* (1941), pp. 5ff.

The functioning of an earthly kingdom in salvation-history can be seen in the history of Israel, where this concept was used to portray the coming Messiah and the messianic kingdom. But this immediately raises the problem of the rise and development of kingship in Israel. The Old Testament makes it clear that Israel's desire for a king stemmed from their failure to appreciate fully God's complete dominion over His people. Delivered from the Midianites, the men of Israel said to Gideon: "Rule over us," to which Gideon replied, "I will not rule over you, and my son will not rule over you; the LORD will rule over you" (Judg. 9:22f.).[40] This is not meant to deny the possibility of the charismatic functions of particular persons or to set such charisma in opposition to the theocracy, but to reject the desire for security in an hereditary system of government, as if God's leading and control in themselves were not security enough but needed supplementation and strengthening.[41] Such an attitude came to the fore when Israel later asked for a king (1 Sam. 8:6-8). Yahweh even refers to it as a rejection of Him from being king over them.[42] Later the Israelites themselves recognized that "we have added to all our sins this evil, to ask for ourselves a king" (12:19). So the real problem in kingship is not that any idea of representative and centralized government is impossible, but the motivation behind the request for a king. In Israel's case the motivation had perverted the essence of this representation. The amazing thing in Israel's history is that its wish was fulfilled by Yahweh. And thus a new problem arises: does the Israelite monarchy in fact bring to expression the true meaning of theocracy and is it thus a suitable analogy of the ultimate messianic kingdom? Or does the Israelite monarchy contradict everything the messianic kingdom stands for and thus form a contrast rather than an analogy?

Historically it was both contrast and analogy. The possibility

40. Note that the Israelites are not asking for a king specifically, but asking Gideon, "rule over us." Cf. C. J. Goslinga, *KV* on Judges, I, 147ff.; A. A. Koolhaas, *Theocratie en Monarchie in Israël* (1957), pp. 48ff.
41. Compare the drama of the rule of Abimelech in Judg. 9 with Deborah's words to Barak: "Does not the LORD go out before you?" (Judg. 4:14).
42. Israel's wish is seen as being of one piece with their history of forsaking Yahweh and serving other gods (8:8). Furthermore there is in it an element of wanting to be like other nations (8:20). Yahweh is mentioned as Israel's king often in the OT, e.g., Num. 23:21; 1 Sam. 12:12; Isa. 6:5; and in numerous psalms. Cf. O. Eissfeldt, "Jahwe als König," *Zeitschrift für die AT Wissenschaft,* XLVI (1928), 89ff.

for the earthly kingship to be a real, if relative, analogy to the messianic kingship is already indicated in the limitations on the king outlined in Deuteronomy 17:14-20. The analogy could only be maintained if the king acted in conformity with his anointing, realizing his dependence on God and resisting the temptation to set himself up as an absolute ruler.[43] But the other possibility was realized even more often, not only in Saul's reign,[44] but in the many succeeding kings who renounced the theocracy. In response to these kings came the prophetic grievance: "They made kings, but not through me. They set up princes, but without my knowledge" (Hos. 8:4).[45]

The Israelite monarchy, then, is not a consistent analogy of God's future lordship. It may represent God's rule (cf. Prov. 8:15); it may even reflect the true theocracy.[46] But on the other hand, it may also exceed its limitations and finally perish. "Where now is your king, to save you; where are all your princes to defend you — those of whom you said, 'Give me a king and princes'? I have given you kings in my anger, and I have taken them away in my wrath" (Hos. 13:10f.). A monarchy that has lost its sense of purpose is meaningless: "We fear not the LORD, and a king, what could he do for us?" (Hos. 10:3).[47] Only if the royal majesty truly reflects God's gracious and just acts can it be considered an analogy of the kingship of the Messiah and

43. Cf. K. J. Popma, *Eerst de Jood, maar ook de Griek* (1950), pp. 43ff. Those kings who remembered this basic limitation, pointing to rather than impeding the view of Yahweh as king in concrete deeds of justice and righteousness, are praised by Yahweh. Jeremiah asks Jehoiakim, "Do you think you are a king because you compete in cedar?", contrasting him with his father, who did justice and righteousness, and judged the case of the poor and needy: "Is not this to know me? says the LORD" (22:15f.). On Josiah's reign cf. 2 Kings 23:25, which portrays him as unique among the kings. Cf. also Ps. 72:1-4, 7, 12-14.

44. The account of Saul as king is repeatedly placed in the setting of his anointing (1 Sam. 10:1; 15:1; 24:6; 26:9f.).

45. Cf. C. van Gelderen and W. H. Gispen, *Komm.*, ad loc., on the non-theocratic and non-Davidic elements in Israelite politics. On whether or not there is a "Hoseanic" theory of monarchy (cf. Hos. 13:10), cf. P. A. H. de Boer, *Het koningschap in Oud-Israël* (1938), p. 8.

46. Cf. T. C. Vriezen, *An Outline of OT Theology*, pp. 212ff.; N. H. Ridderbos, *KV* on Psalm 2.

47. The ambivalence of monarchy comes out clearly in Hos. 3:4f.: Israel without king or prince "shall return and seek the LORD their God, and David their king; and they shall come in fear to the LORD and to his goodness in the latter days." Cf. Jer. 30:9; Ezek. 37:22-24.

be included in the eschatological perspective of the coming messianic kingdom.[48]

The New Testament indicates and proclaims the reality of the messianic kingdom of Christ, thus showing the true meaning of the Old Testament analogy. The tensions between the rule of God and man's revolt, between the boundaries set by God and man's urge to exceed them, have disappeared in the unrestricted rule of Christ.[49] This new kingship needs no longer to be limited horizontally by the offices of prophet and priest, because all of these are included in the single messianic office. It is a Kingdom that bears no resemblance to the sinister background of Israel's demands for a king to fill the vacuum of leadership and deliver them from external threats and aggression. It is a Kingdom in which God's dominion is consummated in the form of a King who is Prophet and Priest as well, in which the meaning and goal of God's acts of salvation and redemption are revealed.[50] Hence, it is portrayed in the gospel as a Kingdom of joy, peace, and righteousness. All the tensions that attended Israel's monarchy and ultimately contributed to its downfall have disappeared. This Kingdom will have no end (Luke 1:33).

An exhaustive and precise definition of this Kingdom is impossible. It is described in many of Jesus' parables, but these remain parables — images and analogies — which can never serve as complete definitions. We do get a sense of the multiformity, inaccessibility, and universality of this coming Kingdom. All these images and analogies must be maintained, however, in

48. On the meaning and problematics of monarchy in Israel, cf. H. J. Kraus, *Die Königsherrschaft Gottes im AT. Untersuchungen zu den Liedern von Jahwés Thronbesteigung* (1951), pp. 90ff. Kraus emphasizes that the monarchy — properly understood and limited — did not compete with the dominion of Yahweh. For the boundaries Kraus points to the independence of the prophets and to the psalms. Cf. also S. Mowinckel, *He That Cometh* (1956), pp. 68ff.

49. Consider the account of Christ's temptation in the wilderness. The devil showed him all the kingdoms (*basileia*) of the world, their authority (*exousía*) and glory (*dóxa*) (Luke 4:5f.). The decisive element in Christ's response to him is His outlook on this glory: "You shall worship the Lord your God, and him only shall you serve" (4:8). Christ's way was, to be sure, a way to *exousía* (Matt. 28:19) and *dóxa* (Luke 24:26), but it was a way without tension with respect to the Kingdom of God. Cf. the discussion of this pericope by R. Morgenthaler, "Roma — Sedes Satanae," *Theologische Zeitschrift*, XII (1956), 289ff.

50. On Christ's kingly office during His suffering, cf. Berkouwer, *The Work of Christ* (Eng. tr., 1965), pp. 72ff.

order that our outlook on this coming Kingdom not be obscured.

Such an obscuring could take place, for example, if we were to approach the Kingdom exclusively on the basis of its *power*. The connotations of the word Kingdom could easily lead to an overemphasis on this aspect. The Kingdom, of course, cannot be understood without doing full justice to this aspect of its power, which is certainly essential to the notion of it. Any reference to the Kingdom automatically conveys the idea of a sovereign power of disposition, of incontrovertible dominion. Often the kingship of God is portrayed in direct connection with His power, for example, when Revelation 11:15 says that "the kingdom of the world has become the kingdom of our Lord and of his Christ." Old and New Testament alike see God as the Mighty One (cf. 1 Chron. 29:11f.; Pss. 93:1f.; 96:10; 97:1f.), the *pantokrátōr*, the Almighty (Rev. 11:17; 21:22), the King of kings (1 Tim. 6:15; Rev. 17:14), the King of the ages (Rev. 15:3; cf. Jer. 7:10, "King of the nations").

In the face of all this, however, we may not isolate the aspect of power, which is related inextricably to God's glory and the fulness of His virtues. We who know from history of countless perversions of power tend to accent the contrast between power and glory. "Power" calls to our minds despotism, the "mighty" who deserve fully to be put down from their thrones (Luke 1:52), arbitrarily exercised power, megalomania, established injustice. Power on this view is something to recoil from, something that threatens. But the New Testament picture of God's power has nothing to do with this kind of brute force, this perverted power without glory. We must rid our idea of power of such unsavory associations if we are to understand what the Bible means by the power of God. A striking example is the application of the Greek word *despótēs* to God by Simeon (*"Lord,* now lettest thou thy servant depart" — Luke 2:29) and by the saints under the altar (*"O Sovereign Lord,* holy and true" — Rev. 6:10), and to Jesus by Peter ("the *Master* who bought them" — 2 Pet. 2:1) and Jude ("our only *Master* and Lord [*kýrios*]" — vs. 4). Obviously, the word has none of the connotations of cruelty and tyranny that we associate with "despotism." Similarly, it is instructive to note how Paul links the idea of "the Lord Almighty" with God's being among His people, His being a father and their being sons and daughters (2 Cor. 6:16-18).

So we may not reckon God's power as an isolated *potentia* in the face of which man, powerless, can only respond in submissive resignation. Certainly it is not the so-called *potentia absoluta,* a familiar nemesis in the history of dogma. Calvin agrees that nothing is higher than God's will, yet "we do not advocate the fiction of 'absolute might'; because this is profane, it ought rightly to be hateful to us."[51] Now Psalm 93 paints a clear picture of the boundless power of God. Thus, the flaw in the doctrine of *potentia absoluta* is not that it overrates or overemphasizes God's power, but that it sees this power, this omnipotence, as a formal, essential property of divinity and thus abstracts from the fulness of revelation and the acts of God. "God can do everything" becomes the slogan; and no matter how stable this *potentia* of God is considered to be, the result is inevitably a speculative metaphysics of divine possibilities that overshadows the certainty of salvation.[52]

So one may confess the omnipotence of God and yet not be true to the biblical witness, if he formalizes the omnipotence into a slogan like "God can do everything" and uses this slogan as the background of what He in fact has done and continues to do. The only possible human correlate of *potentia absoluta* is submissive resignation, in Miskotte's words, "a cool respect."[53] The Bible always portrays God's Kingdom in the context of His glory (cf. 1 Thess. 2:12). It is never revealed as an isolated "God can do everything," but as something that cannot be seen apart from what He has done and is doing and will do — His help, His salvation, His deliverance. Jesus indicated the close relationship here when He said, "Seek first his kingdom and his righteousness" (Matt. 6:33; cf. Pss. 45:6f.; 72:1, 19).

51. *Inst.,* III.xxiii.2.
52. On omnipotence and *potentia absoluta* see further K. Rahner, *Schriften zur Theologie,* I (1954), p. 129; W. Pannenberg, *Die Prädestinationslehre des Duns Scotus* (1954), pp. 133ff.; K. Barth, *CD,* II/1, 539ff.; Bavinck, *GD,* II, 205f.
53. *Als de goden zwijgen* (1956), p. 174. Miskotte points out the frequency of the expression "the Almighty" in the dialogues of Job. Cf. J. de Groot and A. R. Hulst, *Macht en wil* (1952), p. 111. It is not a question of revising the creed — "I believe in God the Father Almighty" — but of the stance of the Book of Job with respect to the "theology" of Job's friends. Is Kroeze's comment correct that the Book of Job is "the book of the sovereignty of God"; *KV* on Job (1960), p. 17? In any case it is mandatory to distinguish the sovereignty of God from *potentia absoluta.* This is only possible by not isolating God's sovereignty from His other perfections. Cf. DeGroot-Hulst, *op. cit.,* p. 113; and Rahner, *Schriften zur Theologie,* I, 106ff., on the "decisive point of the OT concept of God." One should also consider in this connection the "weakness of God" which "is stronger than men" (1 Cor. 1:25).

No, the Kingdom of God evokes human reactions other than resignation. It is something for which believers are thankful, a glorious reality about which they sing songs of praise (Rev. 11:17f.). And besides this gratitude as a subjective correlate of the divine Kingdom, there are all sorts of other relations with human life that give an insight into the structure of the Kingdom. In the power of the Kingdom that has come and is coming we do not encounter a property of God external to us but a gripping reality that strikes us in the midst of our own life. And so that which would be impossible on the basis of an abstract approach to the Kingdom becomes in the New Testament the very heart of the proclamation. Let us look more closely at this manifold biblical proclamation.

One may be called to the Kingdom (1 Thess. 2:12), become an heir of it (James 2:5; Matt. 25:34). One may enter it (John 3:5) or be excluded from it (Matt. 8:12; Mark 10:15). The Kingdom is proclaimed as gospel (Matt. 9:35); it is identified with the poor in spirit (Matt. 5:3; cf. Luke 6:20) and with those persecuted for righteousness' sake (Matt. 5:10). Its King is Yahweh, of whom Israel had confessed: "Who is like thee, O LORD, among the gods? Who is like thee, majestic in holiness, terrible in glorious deeds, doing wonders?" (Exod. 15:11; cf. vv. 13, 18; Deut. 33:5). To this Almighty One Israel prayed: "Be our arm every morning, our salvation in the time of trouble" (Isa. 33:2), confident that He would be the scourge of those who do not hear His voice (vs. 3; cf. 37:14-20).

It is clear, then, why God's power can be spoken of so rapturously. His acts are acts of "exercised power,"[54] leadership, care and patient concern. Yahweh is King, but He is also Shepherd; and it is in that form that He is revealed to His people (cf. Mic. 2:12f.; Isa. 40:11; Ezek. 34:20-24). The same context can be found in the New Testament as well as in the Old. The immense wealth and variety of the Kingdom cannot be qualified by one specific function; it is always described in terms of a multiformity of themes: "Now the *salvation* and the *power* and the *kingdom* of our God and the authority of his Christ have come" (Rev. 12:10).

God's dominion can be spoken of in exalted warnings to the proud (Luke 1:51), but also in the comforting salvation-laden words of redemption. And when we speak of God's power

54. Schnackenburg, *op. cit.*, p. 7.

in the superlative degree — He is all-powerful — we do well to remember that what is referred to is "the working of his great might which he accomplished in Christ when he raised him from the dead" (Eph. 1:19f.; cf. 3:20; 6:10; Col. 1:11).

All of these correlations do not detract from the completeness and dominance of the Kingdom, but should lead us to avoid abstractions that only confuse our outlook on the totality and glory of the Kingdom. A variety of biblical concepts is used to depict this glory of the Kingdom. When Jesus was asked by one of the convicts executed with Him to remember him, His reply opens up "Paradise" to the criminal (Luke 23:42f.). Furthermore, this Kingdom is said to consist in power, not in talk (1 Cor. 4:20); it means righteousness and peace and joy in the Holy Spirit (Rom. 14:17). It is as if what little of righteousness, beauty, and glory still remain in this broken and tarnished world is all caught up in the proclamation of the coming Kingdom. Thus the future has been described as the creation of a new earth and new heaven where righteousness dwells (2 Pet. 3:13), the marriage supper of the Lamb (Rev. 19:9), a city without a temple (21:22), a city with foundations (Heb. 11:10), a new Jerusalem (Rev. 3:12), a homeland to be sought (Heb. 11:14ff.).

Just as the Old Testament perspectives on the future borrow from earthly images (cf. Isa. 11:6-9; 65:19f.; Zech. 8:4f.), so too the New Testament presents visions of the future in terms of abundance (Rev. 22:2), relief (21:6; 22:17), life (22:1), and light (21:23; 22:5). Furthermore, this glory is portrayed in terms of what will be missing in this coming Kingdom, this homeland, this city with foundations: death, sorrow (Rev. 21:4), falsehood (21:27; 22:15), anything accursed (22:3), tears (21:4; cf. Isa. 33:24; 35:10).

All of these illustrations of the eschaton are close to the central proclamation of God's Kingdom. None of this glory and beauty that is portrayed as eschatological reality is ever isolated or independent, as if the call to this future appealed hedonistically to man's self-centeredness.[55] There can be no doubt

---

55. Over against Jeremias' contention that "the term 'paradise' is so rare in the NT ... [because] it could so easily divert attention to the external aspects" (in *TDNT*, s.v. *parádeisos*, V, 772), Berkhof notes, correctly, that these external aspects do play an important role in the Revelation of John (*Schepping en Voleinding*, p. 225). Cf. also Luke 23:43; 2 Cor. 12:3; Rev. 2:7; 22:2, 14.

about it: *this* glory is completely qualified by the gracious, glorious and royal presence of God. The source of this glory is completely clear in the New Testament.[56] Understandably, then, the New Testament and the Christian church have placed such a strong emphasis on the term "Kingdom" without thereby neglecting the other aspects of the eschaton. This is not a result of an isolation of the "power"-dimension of the Kingdom, but a result of the personal, royal presence in which all this glory finds its source and center and through which "God himself will be with them" (Rev. 21:3).

The images in which the glory and beauty of the eschaton are described[57] do not depersonalize the salvation of the future, but derive their meaning and riches from the blessed nearness of God. The New Testament is undeniably less apprehensive in talking about the reality of earthly joy in the eschaton than were those who later feared the excesses of hedonism and egocentrism. The eschatological promise of salvation is really directed straight at man. It speaks of eating of the tree of life; of the crown of life, the hidden manna, the white stone, the new name (Rev. 2:7, 10, 17); of the new song (14:3). Eschatological prophecy is directed *at man*. From the biblical point of view this does not in any way jeopardize the eschatological perspective of "God all in all" or His unapproachable glory. The problematics of "anthropocentric" versus "theocentric," which has created such havoc in traditional theological circles, is a false dilemma on the basis of this eschaton.[58]

The "tensions" that arise here can only stem from a misunderstanding of the relationship between God and man. To ward off such a misunderstanding the gospel continually warns against

56. Rev. 21:2 — "the holy city, the new Jerusalem, coming down out of heaven from God" (*ek toú ouranoú apó toú theoú*); cf. vs. 10; 3:12. See also J. C. DeYoung, *Jerusalem in the NT*, pp. 145ff.

57. Among them, the white garments with golden crowns (Rev. 4:4), the sea of glass (15:2), the harps of God (15:2), the bride adorned (21:2), the heritage (21:7), the crystal-clear jasper (21:11), the city, pure gold and clear as glass (21:18), the pearl gates (21:21), the absence of night (21:25), the twelve fruits of the tree of life (22:2), the leaves of the tree "for the healing of nations" (22:2), and the worship of God (22:9).

58. Against this dilemma cf. H. Berkhof, *Schepping en Voleinding*, p. 231. To reject this dilemma does not mean, however, that a "theocentric" protest to a *particular* anthropocentric theology has no relevance or validity. Against the misunderstanding that the "theocentric" excludes the element of "for us," cf. E. Schaeder, *Theozentrische Theologie*, II (2d ed., 1928), pp. 6ff.

an egoistical religion, in which God merely becomes a means to a desired end — salvation. Such a religion soon results in pseudo-Christianity, which no longer has anything to do with the two basic ingredients of love to God and to fellow man. It is a religion that talks about salvation, joy, life, paradise, and heaven, without understanding what these words really mean. Once these ideas are uprooted from their context, one no longer has anything really to do with the new name (Rev. 2:17), with being a pillar in God's temple (3:12), or with sitting with Christ on His throne (3:21). Such a religious abstraction is the exact opposite of the biblical eschatological perspective. Some critics of religion have suggested that the whole concept of religion, Christianity included, is merely man's self-centered drive toward wish-fulfilment, and that the imagery of wedding feast, inheritance, and Paradise is clear proof of this. Such an interpretation is understandable: the way many people live seems to afford daily confirmation of this theory. But the eschatological perspective of the Bible makes it clear that the old has passed away and all things have been made new. Right at this point is the wonder of the eschaton. The question is, can we already understand this eschatological harmony? We may be tempted to contrast God's glory with man's, God's rule with ours (cf. Rev. 22:5), God as the focal point with the eschatological importance of man. But all such contrasts fade out in the light of the eschatological perspective, not because the "God all in all" is disregarded, not because the glory of God disappears, not because Christ is no longer the bright morning star (Rev. 22:16), the first and the last (vs. 13). No, the key to it is that the glory of God does not exclude but includes the glory of man. This human glory, so prominent in the pages of Scripture, is not in competition with God's glory; and it has nothing to do with the exchange of "the glory of the immortal God for images resembling mortal man" (Rom. 1:23). Rather, the glory of God is revealed in the glory of man, in the "glory that is to be revealed to us" (Rom. 8:18).[59]

59. The gospel itself reveals it as a deep mystery that all such tension and competition is done away with in the eschaton. But this mystery is not totally foreign to earthly life, for even in this life Christ's disciples are told to let their light shine before men (Matt. 5:16). They are the light of the world (vs. 14), but this does not conflict with Christ as the Light of the world (John 8:12). Paul urges the Philippians to "shine as lights in the world" (2:15); according to Daniel, "those who are wise shall shine like the brightness of the firmament" (12:3; cf. Matt. 13:43

We should be careful to distinguish sharply at this point between biblical meekness and that false humility which even has difficulty mentioning aloud the participation of man in the eschatological fulfilment. Such a false humility[60] is ultimately the product of hidden pride, which balks at accepting God's grace and for which the eschatological gift becomes a stumbling block. (One might even call this an eschatological Pelagianism.) The true gospel message liberates man from this narrowness, graciously and majestically creating room for true humility and gratitude.

This eschaton also, then, will lay to rest the familiar discussions of natural versus supernatural and the eschatological "elevation" of human nature. The problem of creatureliness has always been central to these discussions; and many have tried to define and do full justice to this "elevation" while consciously avoiding the pitfalls of pantheism. Terms like "apotheosis" or "deification" have been introduced into the eschatological vocabulary by some, and at once hotly disputed by others.[61] The meaning and extent of redemption are the heart of the issue. Is God's Kingdom something more than just a restoration of what has been lost? Is not the deepest meaning of the eschatological mystery this, that it will supersede and transcend the original created nature of man? The peculiar thing about this line of thought is that those who want to attribute so much to redemption are driven to describe it with mundane analogies that remind one anew of renewal and restoration. It is as if according to God's intention the glory of creatureliness sets up certain boundaries that cannot be transgressed, and any effort to attribute something more to man in the eschaton runs against these boundaries. Those who defy these boundaries need to be reminded that "it does not yet appear what we shall be" (1 John 3:2). This remark by John sets the limit to our penetration of the eschatological mystery. When we speak of that mystery, then, we cannot, in the very nature of the case, make

— "like the sun in the kingdom of their Father"). To miss this biblical perspective is to flee from this new responsibility in a false — and facile — humility.

60. This is not to be confused with the "self-abasement" of some of the Colossians, against which Paul warns them (2:18, 23). The Colossian error was linked with the worship of angels. Cf. H. N. Ridderbos, *Comm., ad loc.*

61. Cf. E. Hendrikx, "De leer van de vergoddelijking in het oud-Christelijk geloofsbewustzijn," in *Genade en Kerk* (1953), p. 101.

a simple identification of end-time and original-time. The fact that the eschaton is filled with the mystery of history — the *Lamb* in the Book of Revelation — warns us against both over-simplification and speculation.[62] Yet it is equally clear that a legitimate reaction to the doctrine of the deification of man and to all threats to man's creatureliness may never lead us to mistake the gift of glory that is essential to the eschatological promise.[63] This glory is the background of the joy that prevails throughout the entire gospel and that structures every doxology.[64] In no way does this joy in the *pro nobis* conflict with God's glory, but it is completely included in it.

The seriousness of the prayer

A sharp, dualistic separation between the present and future, as if the eschaton were a reality presently strange and completely unknowable, is definitely unbiblical. Just as the Catechism relates the second petition of the Lord's Prayer to our continuous submission "more and more" to Word and Spirit (Q. 123), so also the eschatological preaching and promise always continue to function in the present as comfort and admonition. Naturally,

62. Berkhof points out the dangers of both oversimplifying and speculating (e.g. Schleiermacher and Scholten in the 19th century); *Schepping en Voleinding*, p. 235. Some exegetes and theologians have tried to explicate the "difference" here by reference to the angels, who long to look into the things of the gospel (1 Pet. 1:10-12). Those who argue thus point out the difference between these angels and the insight into the mystery of reconciliation and redemption out of lostness. Clearly the aspect of experience meant here — the *pro nobis* — does not remove the veil from the eschatological mystery, nor does it intend to. In this connection cf. Eph. 3:10: "that through the church the manifold wisdom of God might now be made known to the principalities and powers in the heavenly places." Cf. also K. H. Schelkle, *Die Petrusbriefe* (1961), p. 43.

63. Cf. Hendrikx, *op. cit.*, pp. 101f. Hendrikx discusses the difficulty that Catholic mystics have with avoiding the appearance of pantheism (p. 114). Also, A. Theodoros, "Die Lehre von der Vergottung des Menschen bei den griechischen Kirchenvätern," *Kerygma und Dogma*, VII (1961).

64. Cf. Hans Urs von Balthasar, *Herrlichkeit*, I (1961), 115. Consider the expressions of praise in Eph. 3:18, 20f. ("within us" and "to him be the glory"); Rom. 8:21 ("the glorious liberty of the children of God"); 2 Cor. 7:4 ("I am overjoyed"). On the incomparability of salvation, see 1 Cor. 2:9 (cf. Isa. 64:4). For the difference between this enthusiasm and the various forms of enthusiastic spiritualism that lack the Pauline realism and sobriety, see O. Kuss, "Enthousiasmus und Realismus bei Paulus," in *Festgabe für T. Kaufmann* (1959), pp. 23ff.

this doxology is related to the eschaton, but it is by no means foreign to life in the present. The doxological is essentially linked with true faith and love. This song of praise is not a powerless recognition of and subjection to the power of Christ like the confession of the man with an unclean spirit: "I know who you are, the Holy One of God" (Mark 1:24; cf. 3:11). No, it is a doxology in countless forms, replete with worship, gratitude, meekness, and praise. In our present earthly life, with its "not yet," this doxology comes when the word of Christ dwells in us richly as we sing "psalms and hymns and spiritual songs" with thankfulness in our hearts to God (Col. 3:16).

The doxology, as long as it is sung on the earth, continues to be overshadowed by the deficiencies that characterize this life, including religious egocentrism. But unless the powers of the age to come operate in this life (Heb. 6:5), our perspective on the eschaton will fade, and the harmony of prayer, thankfulness and watchfulness will be disrupted (Col. 4:2f.).[65] Eschatology then simply degenerates into a last chapter of dogmatics, an irrelevant futurism lacking any appeal, a future age with no word for the present. The doxology is silenced; and when that happens a great crisis in perseverance results, for only the doxology offers resistance against the pitfalls, temptations, and darkness that still lurk in the present dispensation of "not yet."

So the whole of the eschatological expectation can finally be recapitulated in the well-known petition "Thy Kingdom come." If we understand it anywhere, we understand here that our prayers too are tested, tested for the seriousness with which they take their place in the Christian life. On this point the gospel is clear: the prayer "Thy Kingdom come" is unreal and worthless unless its meaning and its consequences are understood. Numerous questions in the area of eschatology remain to remind us that we still see only in a mirror, dimly (1 Cor. 13:12). But none of these riddles threatens the clarity of the eschatological call, a challenge that can be heard and understood in this time of the "not yet." The way to that which is to be revealed has its beginnings in what is already revealed. This is the full meaning of the earthly pilgrimage to the future. This is the pilgrimage Paul describes to the Philippians: "Brethren, I not consider that I have made it my own; but one thing

65. Cf. Chapter I above, pp. 20ff.; E. Lövestam, "Über die NT Aufforderung zur Nüchternheit," Studia Theologica, XI (1958), 80ff.

I do, forgetting what lies behind and straining forward to what lies ahead, I press on toward the goal for the prize of the upward call of God in Christ Jesus" (3:13f.). This expectation is profoundly affected by the "not yet," but it also recognizes itself to be on the way on which no one goes astray. It spells intensity, desire, humility, and certainty.

Thy Kingdom come! It is all summed up in this petition: the outlook on the consummation, the calling in the present, and no less the surety that quiets our hearts within us. This quietness is a familiar theme in the Bible. In the prophetic appeal it can be proclaimed on the basis of the reality of God's judgment (Isa. 23:2; 41:1), but there is also a stillness full of expectation: "Be still before the LORD and wait patiently for him" (Ps. 37:7). Here is relief from strife: "The LORD will fight for you, and you have only to be still" (Exod. 14:14). Now this quiet expectation is surely not passivity; it is rather a silence that awaits the coming acts of God, a silence that is essential for the eschatological expectation. And it is at this point that the prayer "Thy Kingdom come" finds its strength.

It is not for nothing that the gospel message links this silence, oriented by faith to the coming Kingdom, to the omnipotence of God, not as in an identification with the infinite power of God, but as faith directed to the mighty acts of God. Jesus' question to the panicking disciples on the sea hits the nail on the head: "Where is your faith?" (Luke 8:25). Again, we hear the man with the epileptic child ask Christ for help "if you can do anything." Jesus' reply is: "If you can! All things are possible to him who believes" (Mark 9:22f.). Beyond what, according to human criteria, seems possible and impossible, there is the expectation of faith with its unbounded possibilities. I think it is incorrect to speak here of the "creative" function of faith, because all the power of this faith is made clear only on account of its orientation to God's power. But we are confronted in these "possibilities" of faith with a profundity in the prayer for the coming of the Kingdom that we seldom plumb.

It is no exaggeration to say that this prayer releases powers and that we are often unconscious of what we are doing when we pray for the coming of the Kingdom. The temptation to say with the scoffers of 2 Peter 3 that nothing has changed since the beginning of creation is probably greater than we superficially realize it to be. But just as the prayer of the saints in Revelation 8 immediately released visible and audible power on earth — "peals of thunder, loud noises, flashes of lightning, and an earthquake" (vs. 5) — so the prayer "Thy Kingdom come" is no stammering monologue, but a prayer that expects an answer. And every time we pray the Lord's Prayer there is reason for us to go and stand at the window of expectation.

How often in the congregation of the Lord the glow of this expectation is extinguished. On the basis of the apocalyptic structurization of the eschatological promise, the church has — even within the bounds of traditional eschatology — distanced itself inwardly from the future, and set its eye on what might happen *on the way to the future*. In this obscuring of the expectation, a crisis arises for life itself, and "de-eschatologizing" sets in, more and more overshadowing the meaning of the present.

The church must dare to assume responsibility for the prayer "Thy Kingdom come," without reservations. This courage before the face of Him who hears prayer is essential to the doxology that begins already in this life, and will some day change into the new song. It is a hymn to the acts of God, made manifest in history, celebrated and proclaimed, which call time and again — in hiddenness — to a new confidence that does not disappoint.

Thy Kingdom come....

INDEX OF PRINCIPAL SUBJECTS

INDEX OF PERSONS

INDEX OF SCRIPTURES